The Concise St. Martin's Guide to Writing

EIGHTH EDITION

The Concise St. Martin's Guide to Writing

Rise B. Axelrod
University of California, Riverside

Charles R. Cooper
University of California, San Diego

bedford/st.martin's
Macmillan Learning
Boston | New York

For Bedford/St. Martin's

Vice President, Editorial, Macmillan Learning Humanities: Edwin Hill
Senior Program Director for English: Leasa Burton
Program Manager: Molly Parke
Marketing Manager: Vivian Garcia
Director of Content Development: Jane Knetzger
Executive Development Manager: Jane Carter
Developmental Editor: Leah Rang
Senior Content Project Manager: Peter Jacoby
Content Workflow Supervisor: Joe Ford
Production Supervisor: Robin Besofsky
Media Project Manager: Melissa Skepko-Massi
Editorial Services: Lumina Datamatics, Inc.
Composition: Cenveo Publisher Services.
Photo Editor: Angela Boehler
Permissions Editor: Jen Roach
Senior Art Director: Anna Palchik
Text Design: Jerilyn Bockorick
Cover Design: John Callahan
Printing and Binding: LSC Communications

Manufactured in the United States of America.
2 1 0 9 8 7
f e d c b a

For *information, write:* Bedford/St. Martin's, 75 Arlington Street,
Boston, MA 02116

ISBN 978-1-319-05854-8

Acknowledgments

Text acknowledgments and copyrights appear at the back of the book on page A–1, which constitute an extension of the copyright page. Art acknowledgments and copyrights appear on the same page as the art selections they cover.

Preface

When we first wrote *The Concise St. Martin's Guide to Writing*, our goal was to provide the clear guidance and practical strategies students need to harness their potential as writers, both in college and in the wider world. We also wanted to provide both experienced and novice instructors with the time-tested tools they need to coach their students as they develop skills for writing successfully in college and beyond. These goals have guided our development of the core features of the *Concise Guide* as well as the many exciting features that keep the eighth edition fresh and useful.

Core Features of the *Concise Guide*

The Concise St. Martin's Guide retains its emphasis on active learning by providing practical guides to writing and integrating reading and writing through hands-on activities for critical thinking, reading, analysis, and synthesis.

Practical Guides to Writing

Each chapter in Part One offers practical, flexible guides that help students draft and revise a variety of analytical and persuasive essays. Honed by experience, the acclaimed writing guides offer surefire invention strategies to get students started, sentence strategies to get students writing, and thoughtful peer review and troubleshooting strategies to help students make their writing effective for any rhetorical situation.

Commonsensical and easy to follow, the Guides to Writing teach students how to

- assess the rhetorical situation, focusing on purpose and audience, with special attention to the basic features of each assignment type;
- ask probing analytical questions about what they're reading, which can help make them more reflective writers;
- practice finding answers through various kinds of research, including memory search, field research, and traditional source-based research.

Each Guide to Writing begins with a **Starting Points** chart, offering students multiple ways of finding the help they need when they need it. Each also includes a **Peer Review Guide** to help students assess their own writing and the writing of their classmates and a **Troubleshooting Guide** to help students find ways to improve their drafts. The charts and guides are organized and color-coded to emphasize the basic features of the particular assignment. In short, the Guides to Writing help students make their writing thoughtful, clear, organized, compelling—and effective for the rhetorical situation.

Purpose-Driven Assignment Chapters

Each chapter in Part One introduces a commonly assigned reason for writing. By working through several assignment types, students learn to identify and use relevant and effective strategies to achieve their purpose with their readers. "Remembering an Event," a memoir assignment, challenges students to reflect on the autobiographical and cultural significance of their experience. "Explaining a Concept," an analysis assignment, asks students to make a new subject interesting and informative for their readers. A cluster of argument chapters—from "Arguing a Position" and "Proposing a Solution" to "Justifying an Evaluation"—requires students to develop an argument that not only is well reasoned and well supported but also responds constructively to readers' likely questions and concerns.

Systematic Integration of Critical Reading and Reflective Writing

Students are asked to read and analyze a range of contemporary selections, attending both to the writer's ideas and to the strategies the writer uses to present those ideas to readers. Each Guide to Reading provides

- an annotated student essay that prompts readers to answer questions about how it is composed;
- a pair of compelling professional selections to demonstrate the basic features of writing to achieve a particular purpose;
- activities following each professional selection that prompt students to read actively by asking them to reflect on the essay and relate it to their own experience, and also to read like writers by focusing their attention on the writer's strategies. (Chapter 10 also provides an array of strategies students can use to read critically.)

What's New

Although the eighth edition of *The Concise St. Martin's Guide to Writing* builds on the success of previous editions, many of the strategies the *Concise Guide* employs have changed in order to connect more effectively with today's students, who are used to visual rhetoric online and are increasingly challenged by demands on their time, attention, and energy.

New Literacy Narrative Chapter

A new introductory chapter, **"Composing Literacy,"** offers a quick and engaging way to start off a course. Students first learn about the **rhetorical situation**, a basic literacy concept. They are then invited to read three brief, engaging literacy narratives that demonstrate an array of literacies. Novelist Amy Tan reflects on the differences in the way she uses language with her mother and the way she communicates with academic audiences, science-fiction writer William Gibson remembers the shared cultural experience of watching TV, and cartoonist Lynda Barry looks back on her imaginative interaction with the classifieds. Finally, students are invited to reflect on their own literacy experiences and to compose a literacy narrative.

New Analyzing and Synthesizing Opposing Arguments Project

A new Chapter 5 provides a bridge to help move students from personal and expository to argumentative writing by modeling how to review and critique a variety of positions in preparation for adopting and defending a position of their own. The Guide to Reading shows student Maya Gomez as she works through the stages of analyzing an academic conversation—from summarizing a source to creating an annotated bibliography to reporting on an array of positions to analyzing conflicting positions, all on the same issue. The Guide to Writing provides a host of activities to help students develop their own summary, annotated bibliography, report, or analysis. The argument chapters that follow show students how to apply what they've learned by analyzing a variety of claims and then thoughtfully defending their own.

A New Chapter on Analyzing and Composing Multimodal Texts

A new Chapter 13, **"Analyzing and Composing Multimodal Texts,"** explains *multimodality* and walks students through the process of analyzing and designing a multimodal text, remixing text-based compositions in new modalities and genres, and creating presentations that take advantage of modalities from the linguistic and visual to the aural, spatial, and gestural.

New Student Models and Professional Readings

The Part One chapters provide three new professional selections by well-known authors Malcolm Gladwell, John Tierney, and Emily Nussbaum, as well as five new selections by student writers.

Now with LaunchPad

LaunchPad, Macmillan's customizable online course space, includes an e-book version of the text and offers an array of new materials, such as additional student essays; adaptive quizzing; multimedia tutorials; and other resources that you can adapt, assign, and mix with your own.

Council of Writing Program Administrators Outcomes Statement

The Concise St. Martin's Guide to Writing, Eighth Edition, helps students build proficiency in the four categories of learning that writing programs across the country use to assess their students' work: rhetorical knowledge; critical thinking, reading, and writing; writing processes; and knowledge of conventions. The following chart shows in detail how *The Concise St. Martin's Guide* helps students develop these proficiencies. (Note: This chart aligns with the latest WPA Outcomes Statement, ratified in July 2014.)

DESIRED OUTCOMES	RELEVANT FEATURES OF *THE CONCISE ST. MARTIN'S GUIDE TO WRITING*, EIGHTH EDITION
Rhetorical Knowledge	
Learn and use key rhetorical concepts through analyzing and composing a variety of texts.	• Chapter 1, **"Composing Literacy,"** provides students with a clear, workable definition of the rhetorical situation and asks students to apply that knowledge as they read literacy narratives and compose one of their own. • In each of the chapters in Part One, **"Writing Activities"** (Chapters 2–8), students **read**, **analyze**, and **compose a variety of texts**. A Guide to Reading asks students to analyze texts (including student writing and professional selections) in terms of **purpose**, **audience**, and **genre**. Each Guide to Writing supports students with detailed help for composing in a variety of genres, including memoir, profile, concept analysis, position argument, and evaluation. • Chapter 10, **"A Catalog of Reading Strategies,"** provides tools for analyzing texts. • The new Chapter 13, **"Analyzing and Composing Multimodal Texts,"** encourages students to consider how genre expectations and discipline requirements affect compositions.
Gain experience reading and composing in several genres to understand how genre conventions shape and are shaped by readers' and writers' practices and purposes.	• Chapter 1 and the Part One chapters emphasize the connection between **reading and composing**: Each introduces students to the basic features of writing with that purpose; provides a group of engaging reading selections, along with apparatus that asks students to think about how the reading demonstrates the basic features; then, through a Guide to Writing, leads them through the process of composing their own text. • The new graphic memoir by Lynda Barry (Chapter 1) challenges students' understanding of what an academic reading selection is or can be. • The **readings** in Part One, which represent a range of texts and genres, are annotated and framed with comments and questions that **focus students on key features of the assignment** and help spark ideas for their own compositions. • A new Chapter 5, **"Analyzing and Synthesizing Opposing Arguments,"** invites students to build an essay step by step, from **summary** to **annotated bibliography** to **report** to **analysis**. By adapting their writing, students come to understand how academic writers build deep understanding. • The new Chapter 13, **"Analyzing and Composing Multimodal Texts,"** challenges students to analyze and compose selections in a variety of modalities and to reimagine writing primarily in the linguistic mode to take advantage of other modalities and genres.

DESIRED OUTCOMES	RELEVANT FEATURES OF *THE CONCISE ST. MARTIN'S GUIDE TO WRITING*, EIGHTH EDITION
Rhetorical Knowledge (continued)	
Develop facility in responding to a variety of situations and contexts, calling for purposeful shifts in voice, tone, level of formality, design, medium, and/or structure.	• In Part One, students practice **responding to a variety of rhetorical situations and contexts**. These chapters also point out what makes a text structurally sound, while the Guides to Writing help students systematically develop their own processes and structures. Sentence strategies in these chapters help composers deal with issues of **voice**, **tone**, and **formality**. • Chapter 13, **"Analyzing and Composing Multimodal Texts,"** invites students to consider how changes to the rhetorical situation, especially genre and medium, shape decisions about tone, level of formality, design, medium, and structure. It also walks students through the **rhetorical choices** involved in the **design** of any text.
Understand and use a variety of technologies to address a range of audiences.	• One of the book's assumptions is that most students compose in digital spaces for varied audiences and use different media for doing so. This is woven throughout the text. • Online tutorials in LaunchPad for *The Concise St. Martin's Guide* include **how-tos for using technology**: e.g., digital writing for specific **audiences** and purposes, creating presentations, integrating photos, and appealing to a prospective employer. • Chapter 13, **"Analyzing and Composing Multimodal Texts,"** helps students understand the needs and requirements involved in design both in print and online. It also offers instruction on how to prepare and deliver multimodal presentations.
Match the capacities of different environments (e.g., print and electronic) to varying rhetorical situations.	• Chapter 13, **"Analyzing and Composing Multimodal Texts,"** invites students to remix a textual composition into one that makes use of a variety of modalities. It also provides guidance on how to make effective design choices for electronic documents, from decisions about formatting and font sizes to those involving visuals and screen shots. • See also the section above: "Understand and use a variety of technologies to address a range of audiences."

(continued)

DESIRED OUTCOMES	RELEVANT FEATURES OF *THE CONCISE ST. MARTIN'S GUIDE TO WRITING*, EIGHTH EDITION
Critical Thinking, Reading, and Composing	
Use composing and reading for inquiry, learning, critical thinking, and communicating in various rhetorical contexts.	• Chapter 1, **"Composing Literacy,"** asks students to reflect on their own literacy experiences and to extrapolate from the literacy narratives they are reading. • **Analyze & Write** activities in Part One (Chapters 2–8) ask students to **read like a writer**, identifying ideas, techniques, and strategies that they can apply in their own compositions. **Make Connections** activities encourage students to put what they've read in the context of the world they live in. These preliminary reflections come into play in the Guides to Writing, in which students are asked to draw on their thoughts and experiences to write meaningfully. **Reflecting on What You Have Learned** sections, which conclude Chapters 2–8, ask students to think critically about the genre in which they have been reading and composing. • A new Chapter 5, **"Analyzing and Synthesizing Opposing Arguments,"** challenges students to think critically about texts representing a range of positions, to analyze and synthesize information from an array of texts, and to compare and contrast positions on a controversial issue. • Chapter 9, **"A Catalog of Invention and Inquiry Strategies,"** and Chapter 10, **"A Catalog of Reading Strategies,"** provide strategies students can use to read critically and apply what they've learned.
Read a diverse range of texts, attending especially to relationships between assertion and evidence, to patterns of organization, to the interplay between verbal and nonverbal elements, and to how these features function for different audiences and situations.	• Chapters 1–8 include a **range of professional selections** and **student essays**. The Guides to Reading and Writing in Chapters 2–8 include advice on **effective strategies for supporting claims and using evidence (both textual and visual)**; the Guides to Writing include **assignment-specific suggestions for organization**, some tailored to specific types of audiences. • The Guides to Writing in the argument chapters (Chapters 6–8) offer advice on **framing** topics to appeal to the audience and recommend techniques and strategies for **responding to alternative views** readers may hold. • The section **"Reimagine your writing in a new genre or medium"** (Chapter 13) invites students to consider how a change of audience will affect aspects of the composition. • Part Three, **"Research Strategies"** (Chapters 14–17), especially Chapter 15, **"Evaluating and Using Sources,"** emphasizes the importance of **using evidence** effectively to support one's views.

DESIRED OUTCOMES	RELEVANT FEATURES OF *THE CONCISE ST. MARTIN'S GUIDE TO WRITING*, EIGHTH EDITION
Critical Thinking, Reading, and Composing (continued)	
Locate and evaluate (for credibility, sufficiency, accuracy, timeliness, bias, and so on) primary and secondary research materials, including journal articles and essays, books, scholarly and professionally established and maintained databases or archives, and informal electronic networks and Internet sources.	• The chapters in Part Three, **"Research Strategies"** (Chapters 14–17), provide extensive coverage of **finding**, **evaluating**, and **using** print and electronic resources, with guidance for responsibly using the Internet, e-mail, and online communities for research. • Chapter 14, **"Planning a Research Project and Selecting Sources,"** addresses finding sources using **catalogs** and **databases** and developing sources through **field research**. • Chapter 15, **"Evaluating and Using Sources,"** emphasizes strategies for **evaluating print** and **digital sources** and distinguishing between **scholarly** and **popular** sources.
Use strategies—such as interpretation, synthesis, response, critique, and design/redesign—to compose texts that integrate the writer's ideas with those from appropriate sources.	• A new Chapter 5, **"Analyzing and Synthesizing Opposing Arguments,"** challenges students to synthesize, analyze, and compare sources from a range of positions on a controversial topic. It provides a bridge to help move students from personal and expository genres to argumentative ones by modeling how to review and critique a variety of informative and persuasive documents in preparation for adopting and defending a position of their own. • Chapters 6–8 ask students to argue for a position, a solution, and an evaluation and to **anticipate** and **respond to opposing positions** and **readers' objections** to the writer's thesis. • Chapters 6–8 are complemented by Chapter 12, **"Arguing,"** which provides strategies for **making assertions**, **offering support**, and **avoiding logical fallacies.** • Chapter 15, **"Evaluating and Using Sources,"** offers detailed **strategies** for synthesizing information and ideas from sources and **integrating research** into an academic research project. Specifically, there is advice on how to integrate and introduce quotations, how to cite paraphrases and summaries so as to distinguish them from the writer's own ideas, and how to avoid plagiarism. Sentence strategies and research coverage in several Part One chapters offer additional support.
Processes	
Develop a writing project through multiple drafts.	• In Chapters 2–8, Guides to Writing prompt students to **compose** and **revise**. These chapters include activities for **inventing**, **researching**, **planning**, **composing**, **evaluating**, and **revising** their writing over the course of **multiple drafts**.

(continued)

DESIRED OUTCOMES	RELEVANT FEATURES OF *THE CONCISE ST. MARTIN'S GUIDE TO WRITING*, EIGHTH EDITION
Processes (continued)	
Develop flexible strategies for reading, drafting, reviewing, collaborating, revising, rewriting, rereading, and editing.	• The Guides to Writing in Chapters 2–8 offer extensive, assignment-specific advice on **reading**, **drafting**, **rethinking**, and **revising** at multiple stages. The **Ways In** activities and **Starting Points** and **Troubleshooting Guide** charts encourage students to discover, review, and revise. The activities urge students to start from their strengths, and the charts offer specific, targeted advice for students facing different challenges. • Chapter 9, **"A Catalog of Invention and Inquiry Strategies,"** offers numerous helpful suggestions for idea generation. • Chapter 10, **"A Catalog of Reading Strategies,"** provides a variety of strategies for reading analytically and critically. • See also the section below: "Experience the collaborative and social aspects of writing processes."
Use composing processes and tools as a means to discover and reconsider ideas.	• Central to Chapters 2–8 is the idea of using **composing to discover ideas**, especially through the **Ways In** activities in each Guide to Writing. Strategies for **evaluating**, **revising**, and **editing** help students reconsider their ideas over the course of multiple drafts. • See also Chapter 9, **"A Catalog of Invention and Inquiry Strategies,"** and Chapter 14, **"Planning a Research Project and Selecting Sources."**
Experience the collaborative and social aspects of writing processes.	• This goal is implicit in several **collaborative activities** in Part One: **Practicing the Genre** activities at the beginning of the chapter; **Make Connections** activities after the readings; and, in the Guides to Writing, **Test Your Choice** activities and **Peer Review Guides** all provide opportunities to work collaboratively.
Learn to give and to act on productive feedback to works in progress.	• The **Evaluating the Draft, Peer Review Guide, Improving the Draft,** and **Troubleshooting Guide** sections in the Guides to Writing in each Part One chapter offer students **specific advice on constructively criticizing**—and **praising**—their own work and the work of their classmates, then reflecting and acting on the comments they've received.

DESIRED OUTCOMES	RELEVANT FEATURES OF *THE CONCISE ST. MARTIN'S GUIDE TO WRITING*, EIGHTH EDITION
Processes (continued)	
Adapt composing processes for a variety of technologies and modalities.	• As noted in the rhetorical knowledge section on p. ix, one of the book's assumptions is that most students compose in digital spaces for varied audiences and use different media for doing so. This is woven throughout, especially in Chapters 2–8. • Chapter 13, **"Analyzing and Composing Multimodal Texts,"** challenges students to analyze and compose in multiple modalities: linguistic, visual, aural, spatial, and gestural. It invites students to reimagine a primarily linguistic text in another medium or genre, addresses design differences related to medium of delivery (print versus digital), and invites students to pull together what they've learned throughout the chapter to create a multimodal presentation. • The **LaunchPad** version of *The Concise St. Martin's Guide to Writing* offers a digital course space and an interactive e-book. It also offers integrated digital tutorials, such as online **how-tos for using technology**: e.g., digital writing, creating presentations, integrating photos, and appealing to a prospective employer.
Reflect on the development of composing practices and how those practices influence their work.	• See the section above: "Use composing processes and tools as a means to discover and reconsider ideas." • In addition, a **Reflecting on What You Have Learned** section concludes each chapter in Part One (Chapters 2–8) and asks students to think critically about the type of writing they've read and written, and to consider their own composing experiences.
Knowledge of Conventions	
Develop knowledge of linguistic structures, including grammar, punctuation, and spelling, through practice in composing and revising.	• Assignment-specific **editing** and **proofreading** advice appears in the **Edit and Proofread Your Draft** sections in each Part One chapter (Chapters 2–8).
Understand why genre conventions for structure, paragraphing, tone, and mechanics vary.	• Chapters 2–8 emphasize the importance of audience and how expectations differ. For example, several readings emphasize differences in expectations for documenting sources, depending on whether the audience is academic or popular. • Chapter 13, **"Analyzing and Composing Multimodal Texts,"** invites students to consider how changes to the rhetorical situation, especially genre and medium, shape decisions about tone, level of formality, design, medium, and structure. • **Assignment-specific issues of structure, paragraphing, tone,** and **mechanics** are also addressed in the sentence strategies and **Edit and Proofread Your Draft** sections of each Guide to Writing in the Part One chapters.

(continued)

DESIRED OUTCOMES	RELEVANT FEATURES OF *THE CONCISE ST. MARTIN'S GUIDE TO WRITING*, EIGHTH EDITION
Knowledge of Conventions (continued)	
Gain experience negotiating variations in genre conventions.	• Students **read**, **analyze**, and **compose a variety of texts** in Part One, **"Writing Activities"** (Chapters 2–8). In each of these chapters, a Guide to Reading asks students to analyze texts in terms of **purpose**, **audience**, and the **basic features** of the genre. • Part Three, **"Research Strategies,"** allows students to gain experience as they compose an **academic research project**. • Chapter 13, **"Analyzing and Composing Multimodal Texts,"** provides students with opportunities to gain experience negotiating genre conventions.
Learn common formats and/or design features for different kinds of texts.	• **"Design a Multimodal Text"** and **"Criteria for Analyzing Document Design"** are covered in Chapter 13. • Examples of **specific formats for a range of texts** appear on pp. 449–59 (research project in MLA style); pp. 469–70 (research project in APA style); and p. 399 (multimodal presentation).
Explore the concepts of intellectual property (such as fair use and copyright) that motivate documentation conventions.	• Chapter 5, **"Analyzing and Synthesizing Opposing Arguments,"** covers creating an annotated bibliography and invites students to consider the ways in which it is acceptable (and unacceptable) to reuse one's own writing. • Chapter 10, **"A Catalog of Reading Strategies,"** covers various strategies useful when working with sources, including annotating, summarizing, and synthesizing. • The book's research coverage (mainly in Chapters 14–17) teaches specific strategies for **integrating** and **citing** source material. A dedicated section on Acknowledging Sources and Avoiding Plagiarism appears on pp. 419–21. Chapter 15, **"Evaluating and Using Sources,"** offers detailed coverage of using sources fairly.
Practice applying citation conventions systematically in their own work.	• Several of the activities following reading selections in Chapters 2–8 challenge students to **recognize differences in citation conventions** in popular and academic writing. A number of reading selections include **citations** or **lists of links** to sources. • **Research sections** in each Guide to Writing help students with the details of using and documenting sources by providing genre-specific examples of what (and what not) to do. • Student essays in Chapters 3–8 offer models for documenting sources in a list of works cited or references.

DESIRED OUTCOMES	RELEVANT FEATURES OF *THE CONCISE ST. MARTIN'S GUIDE TO WRITING*, EIGHTH EDITION
Knowledge of Conventions (continued)	
	• Coverage of applying citation conventions is covered in Part Three, **"Research Strategies."** Chapter 15, **"Evaluating and Using Sources,"** offers detailed advice on how to integrate and introduce quotations, how to cite paraphrases and summaries so as to distinguish them from the writer's own ideas, and how to avoid plagiarism. Chapters 16 and 17 offer instruction and documentation models in **MLA and APA style** in addition to an annotated sample student research project (MLA style) and a sample reference list (APA style).

Acknowledgments

We owe an enormous debt to all the rhetoricians and composition specialists whose theory, research, and pedagogy have informed *The Concise St. Martin's Guide to Writing*. We would be adding many pages to an already long book if we were to name everyone to whom we are indebted; suffice it to say that we have been eclectic in our borrowing.

We must also acknowledge immeasurable lessons learned from all the writers—professionals and students alike—whose work we analyzed and whose writing we used in this and earlier editions.

Many instructors and students have contributed ideas and criticism over the years. For responding to detailed questionnaires about the seventh edition, we thank Jaclyn Allen, Bismarck State College; Diane K. Bates, Delaware Technical Community College; Suzanne Biedenbach, Georgia Gwinnett College; Emily Cosper, Delgado Community College; Susan Cruea, Bowling Green State University; Christine Peters Cucciarre, University of Delaware; Cynthia Hamlett, Chaffey College; Joann Heck-Meiter, Rock Valley College; Nina B. Keery, Massachusetts Bay Community College; Carrie Krantz, Washtenaw Community College; Julia Laffoon-Jackson, Hopkinsville Community College; Kody Lightfoot, College of Southern Nevada; Monica Mankin, Delgado Community College; Axel Montepeque, California State University, Northridge; Matthew Oakes, Rock Valley College; Jonathan Randle, Mississippi College; Lester Stowers, University of Missouri; Julie Thompson, Gateway Community College; Jennifer Roloff Welch, Rock Valley College; Jeana West, Murray State College; and Andrew Wright, University of Michigan–Dearborn.

In addition, we'd like to thank reviewers who provided invaluable feedback on a draft of the new Chapter 5 (originally composed for *The St. Martin's Guide to Writing*, Eleventh Edition): Kara Alexander, Baylor University; Gretchen Bartels, California Baptist University; Mary Brantley, Holmes Community College; Julie Kratt, Cowley County Community College; Dana Prodoehl, University of Wisconsin–Whitewater; Sayanti Ganguly Puckett,

Johnson County Community College; Matthew Schmeer, Johnson County Community College; Marcia Seabury, University of Hartford; David Taylor, St. Louis Community College–Meramec; and Jeana West, Murray State College.

For this edition of *The Concise St. Martin's Guide,* we gratefully acknowledge the contributions of Jason Dockter, Lincoln Land Community College, who wrote new content on multimodal composing and suggested cuts and other changes to chapters on analyzing visuals, designing for page and screen, and composing a multimodal presentation to create the new Chapter 13, **"Analyzing and Composing Multimodal Texts."**

For the eleventh edition of *The St. Martin's Guide,* from which *The Concise St. Martin's Guide* is derived, we are particularly grateful to Alison Warriner, who helped revise several of the Part One chapters, and to Gray Scott and Wallace Cleaves, who made recommendations for reading selections, helped draft some of the reading apparatus, and were generally available as a sounding board and a font of good advice, especially in rethinking Chapter 5. Wallace Cleaves we also thank for his astute revisions and updates to the instructor's manual, including writing entirely new content on teaching Chapters 1 and 5 and composing reading comprehension and summary quizzes (with model summaries as feedback) for all the new reading selections in the text. (The reading comprehension quizzes are auto-graded in the LaunchPad version of *The Concise St. Martin's Guide,* and model summaries are provided as feedback for the summary quizzes. Both are also available in the online instructor's manual.) Danise Hoover, Hunter College, provided expert advice as we updated the research coverage. Finally, we are especially grateful to the student authors for allowing us to use their work in *Sticks and Stones* and the *Concise Guide.*

We want to thank many people at Bedford/St. Martin's, especially the *Concise Guide's* editor, Leah Rang, whose invaluable expertise and indomitable good humor made this book possible; Jane Carter, Executive Development Editor, without whom this book would not have been written; Suzanne Chouljian and Stephanie Cohen, Assistant Editors, for their help wrangling permissions and making valuable editorial suggestions; Senior Content Project Manager Peter Jacoby, who worked miracles keeping all the details straight and keeping the book on schedule; and Associate Media Editor Will Stonefield, who helped us envision and create our customizable course space and interactive e-book, LaunchPad for *The Concise St. Martin's Guide to Writing.*

Jamie Thaman made many valuable contributions to this revision with her careful copyediting, as did Umadevi Soundararajan and Lori Lewis with their meticulous proofreading, and Christine Hoskin with her indexing of the text. Joe Ford kept the whole process running smoothly. Thanks also to the immensely talented design team—book designer Jerilyn Bockorick as well as Bedford/St. Martin's art director Anna Palchik. Our gratitude also goes to Hilary Newman, Rosemary Spano, Linda Winters, Kalina Ingham, and Martha Friedman for their thoughtful and conscientious work on the permissions program for text and visuals.

We also thank Karen Henry, former Editorial Director for English and Music; Leasa Burton, Senior Program Director, English; and Molly Parke, Program Manager for Rhetorics—all of whom offered valued advice at many critical stages in the process. Thanks as well to Edwin Hill, Vice President–Editorial (Humanities), for his adroit leadership of Bedford/St. Martin's, and Marketing Manager Vivian Garcia for her tireless efforts on behalf of the *Concise Guide.*

Rise dedicates this book to her husband, Steven, and their son, Jeremiah, who are both distinguished teachers and scholars, and to Sophie and Amalia, two young women whose writing she very much looks forward to reading.

We're all in. As always.

Bedford/St. Martin's is as passionately committed to the discipline of English as ever, working hard to provide support and services that make it easier for you to teach your course your way.

Find **community support** at the Bedford/St. Martin's English Community (community.macmillan.com), where you can follow our *Bits* blog for new teaching ideas, download titles from our professional resource series, and review projects in the pipeline.

Choose **curriculum solutions** that offer flexible custom options, combining our carefully developed print and digital resources, acclaimed works from Macmillan's trade imprints, and your own course or program materials to provide the exact resources your students need.

Rely on **outstanding service** from your Bedford/St. Martin's sales representative and editorial team. Contact us or visit macmillanlearning.com to learn more about any of the options below.

LaunchPad for *The Concise St. Martin's Guide to Writing:* Where Students Learn

LaunchPad provides engaging content and new ways to get the most out of your book. Get an interactive e-book combined with assessment tools in a fully customizable course space, and then assign and mix our resources with yours.

- **Autoscored reading quizzes**—a five-question multiple-choice comprehension quiz and a summary quiz with a model summary as feedback—are available for every professional selection in the text.
- **Additional student essays** from *Sticks and Stones and Other Student Essays* are available for six of the assignment chapters in Part One.
- **Diagnostics** provide opportunities to assess areas for improvement and assign additional exercises based on students' needs. Visual reports show performance by topic, class, and student as well as improvement over time.
- **Prebuilt units**—including readings, videos, quizzes, and discussion groups—are easy to adapt and assign by adding your own materials and mixing them with our high-quality multimedia content and ready-made assessment options, such as **LearningCurve** adaptive quizzing and Exercise Central.
- Use LaunchPad on its own or **integrate it** with your school's learning management system so that your class is always on the same page.

LaunchPad for *The Concise St. Martin's Guide to Writing* can be purchased on its own or packaged with the print book at a significant discount. An activation code is required. To order LaunchPad for *The Concise St. Martin's Guide to Writing* with the print book, use ISBN 978-1-319-13846-2. For more information, go to **launchpadworks.com**.

Choose from Alternative Formats of *The Concise St. Martin's Guide to Writing*

Bedford/St. Martin's offers a range of formats. Choose what works best for you and your students:

- *Paperback* To order the paperback edition, use ISBN 978-1-319-05854-8.
- *Popular e-book formats* For details on our e-book partners, visit **macmillanlearning .com/ebooks**.

Instructor Resources

You have a lot to do in your course. We want to make it easy for you to find the support you need—and to get it quickly.

The Instructor's Resource Manual for The Concise St. Martin's Guide is available as a PDF that can be downloaded from macmillanlearning.com. Visit the instructor resources tab for *The Concise St. Martin's Guide*. In addition to chapter overviews and teaching tips, the instructor's manual includes sample course plans and syllabi, learning objectives, tips for addressing special challenges, and specific classroom activities.

Contents

4 Explaining a Concept 95

6 Arguing a Position 183

PART 2 Critical Thinking and Writing Strategies

PART 3 Research Strategies

1

Composing Literacy

More people are writing today than ever before, and many are switching comfortably from one genre or medium to another—from tweeting to blogging to creating multimedia Web pages. Learning to be effective as a writer is a continuous process as you find yourself in new writing situations using new technologies and trying to anticipate the concerns of different audiences. "The illiterate of the twenty-first century will not be those who cannot read and write," futurist Alvin Toffler predicted, "but those who cannot learn, unlearn, and relearn."

Understanding the Rhetorical Situation

Central to success in writing across the spectrum of possibilities today is understanding your **rhetorical situation**, any situation in which you produce or receive a text. Ask yourself these questions whenever you encounter a new rhetorical situation:

1. *Who* is the **audience**? How does the audience's prior knowledge, values, and beliefs influence the production and reception of the text?
2. *What* **genre** or type of text is it? How do genre conventions (what we call the text's *basic features*) influence the production and reception of the text?
3. *When*—at what time or for what **occasion**—is the text produced? Is it timely?
4. *Where*—in what social or cultural **context**—will the communication take place? How does the situation influence the production and reception of the text?
5. *How*—in what **medium**—is the text experienced? How does the medium influence the production and reception of the text?
6. *Why* communicate? What is the **purpose** or goal driving the author's choices and affecting the audience's perceptions of the text?

Composing with an awareness of the rhetorical situation means writing not only to express yourself but also to engage your readers and respond to their concerns. You write to influence how your readers think and feel about a subject and, depending on the genre, perhaps also to inspire them to act.

Genres are simply ways of categorizing texts—for example, we can distinguish between fiction and nonfiction; subdivide fiction into romance, mystery, and science-fiction genres; or break down mystery even further into hard-boiled detective, police procedural, true crime, and classic whodunit genres. Composing with genre awareness affects your choices—what you write about (topic), the claims you make (thesis), how you support those claims (reasons and evidence), and how you organize it all.

Each genre has a set of conventions, or basic features, that readers expect texts in that genre to use. Although individual texts within the same genre vary a great deal—for example, no two *proposals*, even those arguing for the same solution, will be identical—they nonetheless include the same basic features. For example, everyone expects a proposal to identify the problem (usually establishing that it is serious enough to require solving) and to offer a solution (usually arguing that it is preferable to alternative solutions because it is less expensive or easier to implement).

Still, these conventions are not recipes but rather broad frameworks within which writers are free to be creative. Most writers, in fact, find that frameworks make creativity possible. Depending on the formality of the rhetorical situation and the audience's openness to innovation, writers may also remix features of different genres or media, which you can learn more about in Chapter 13, "Analyzing and Composing Multimodal Texts."

Like genre, the medium in which you are working also affects many of your design and content choices. For example, written texts can use color, type fonts, charts, diagrams, and still images to heighten the visual impact of the text, delivering information vividly and persuasively. If you are composing Web pages or apps, you have many more options to make your text truly multimedia—for example, by adding hyperlinks, animation, audio, video, and interactivity to your written text.

Reflecting on Your Own Literacy

Learning—especially learning to communicate with new audiences and in new genres benefits from what we call **reflection** (or metacognition)—thinking critically about *how* as well as *what* you are learning. Extensive research confirms that reflection makes learning easier and faster. In fact, recent studies show that writing even a few sentences about your thoughts and feelings before a high-stress paper or exam can help you reduce stress and boost performance.

Spend a few minutes thinking about your own literacy experiences: *What memories stand out as formative?* You may define *literacy* narrowly as the ability to read and write—as it has been traditionally defined—or you may think of it more broadly as the ability to make meaning in the multiplicity of languages and genres, media, and communication practices, we are increasingly called on to use. Here are several questions and examples that may help you remember and reflect on your own literacy experiences:

- *When did you realize that you use language differently for different audiences and purposes?*

> Recently, I was made keenly aware of the different Englishes I do use. I was giving a talk . . . about my writing, my life, and my book, *The Joy Luck Club*. The talk was going along well enough, until I remembered one major difference that made the whole talk sound wrong. My mother was in the room. And it was perhaps the first time she had heard me give a lengthy speech, using the kind of English I have never used with her. I was saying things like, "The intersection of memory upon imagination" and "There is an aspect of my fiction that relates to thus-and-thus"—a speech filled with carefully wrought grammatical phrases, burdened, it suddenly seemed to me, with nominalized forms, past perfect tenses, conditional phrases, all the forms of standard English that I had learned in school and through books, the forms of English I did not use at home with my mother.
>
> —Novelist Amy Tan, from "Mother Tongue"

- *What do you think are the personal and cultural effects of acquiring new literacies (such as learning another language, using social media, playing sports or video games)?*

> I can remember my father bringing home our first [television] set—this ornate wooden cabinet that was the size of a small refrigerator, with a round cathode-ray picture tube and wooden speaker grilles over elaborate fabric. Like a piece of archaic furniture, even then. Everybody would gather around at a particular time for a broadcast—a baseball game or a variety show or something. . . . We know that something happened then. We know that broadcast television did something—did everything—to us, and that now we aren't the same, though broadcast television, in that sense, is already almost over. I can remember seeing the emergence of broadcast television, but I can't tell what it did to us because I became that which watched broadcast television.
>
> —Science-fiction author William Gibson, from "The Art of Fiction No. 211," the *Paris Review*

- *How did reading stimulate your imagination?*

—Cartoonist and author Lynda Barry, an excerpt from "Lost and Found"

Composing Your Own Literacy Narrative

This chapter invites you to compose a **literacy narrative**. Your instructor may add specific requirements to this assignment, but in general you are to write about a memorable literacy experience—learning, unlearning, or relearning, as Toffler would say, to communicate with others. Some ideas are offered at the end of this chapter to help you choose a subject. But first let's consider the assignment's rhetorical situation.

Apply the rhetorical framework: who? what? when? where? how? and why?

Since this is the beginning of a new course, you could view this assignment as an opportunity to introduce yourself to your instructor and classmates by choosing a literacy experience, genre, or medium (assuming your instructor gives you leeway to choose) that would enable you to make a particular impression on your readers. For example, if you want to emphasize the importance of reading graphic novels or playing video games in your literacy development, you might consider composing your literacy narrative as a graphic memoir (like the Lynda Barry selection on pp. 4–5) or video game.

Like the remembered event narrative in Chapter 2, a literacy narrative tells a story about a person or an event from your own life. To be effective, it must do the following:

- Tell a compelling story.
- Vividly describe the people and places.
- Convey the event's or person's significance in your life, and how the event or person affected your literacy practices or your understanding of the power and complexity of the ways we try—and sometimes fail—to communicate with one another.

These are the basic features of the genre.

The first part of the Guide to Reading in Chapter 2 (pp. 10–28) provides a more detailed introduction to the basic features of remembered event narratives, and the Guide to Writing in that chapter (pp. 29–45) supports the drafting and revising of such narratives. Use those sections to help you invent as you draft and revise your literacy narrative.

Devise a topic.

You may already have an idea about what you'd like to write about. But if not, the following ideas may give you a jumping-off point:

- An influential person who played a role—for good or ill—in your literacy education
- A challenging project that required using a literacy you had not yet mastered
- An occasion when you had to display literacy in a particular academic discipline
- A new literacy you had to learn at a workplace
- An experience learning how to communicate better with classmates, team members, siblings, or people in your community

Your instructor may ask you to post your thoughts to a class discussion board or compose a fully developed literacy narrative. If your instructor approves, you might also consider using multimedia—for example, creating a Web page with visuals, audio, and video.

PART ONE

Writing Activities

2

Remembering an Event

Were you arrested—when you were thirteen? Why would a child remember being chased by an adult stranger as glorious? Did you have a celebrity idol that helped you define yourself? These are just a few of the exhilarating, disquieting, provocative subjects remembered in this chapter. The kind of autobiography you will be reading and writing in this chapter is public, intended to be read by others. Writing for others not only enables us to revisit our past but also gives us an opportunity to represent ourselves to others. Our own and other people's life stories can help us see ourselves differently. They can give us insight into the cultural influences that helped shape who we are and what we value. They can show us what we have in common with others as well as what makes each of us unique.

People write memoirs for various purposes and audiences and publish them as narratives or graphics in a variety of media (print, digital, audiovisual). In college courses, you may be invited to use your own experience as an example or as a kind of case study to apply, analyze, or evaluate ideas you are studying. A student in a linguistics course, for example, might analyze a conversation she had with her brother through the lens of Deborah Tannen's theory that women tend to view problems as opportunities to share their feelings, whereas men typically treat problems as occasions for practical solutions. In the community, writers may reveal personal stories to educate and inspire. For example, a blogger might reveal her own history of domestic violence to help readers understand how some victims become trapped by their own hope and denial. Even in professional and business settings, personal stories can play a role. At a conference, a manager might use the story of his encounter with a disgruntled employee to open a discussion of ways to defuse confrontations in the workplace.

In this chapter, we ask you to write about an event you remember. Choose one that will engage your instructor and classmates, that has significance for you, and that you feel comfortable sharing. From reading and analyzing the selections in the Guide to Reading that follows, you will learn how to make your own story interesting, even exciting, to read. The Guide to Writing (pp. 29–45) will show you ways to use the basic features of the genre to tell a vivid and dramatic story and to entertain readers while giving them insight into the event's significance—its meaning and importance.

PRACTICING THE GENRE

Telling a Story

The success of remembered event writing depends on how well you tell your story. The challenge is to make the story compelling and meaningful for readers—that is, to make readers care about the storyteller and curious to know what happened. To practice creating an intriguing story about an event in your life, get together with two or three other students and follow these guidelines:

Part 1. Choose an event that you feel comfortable describing, and think about what makes it memorable (for example, a conflict with someone else or within yourself, the strong or mixed feelings it evokes, the cultural attitudes it reflects). What will be the turning point, or *climax*, and how will you build up to it? Then take turns telling your stories.

Part 2. After telling your stories, discuss what you learned:

- **What did you learn about the genre from listening to others' stories?** Describe what struck you most upon hearing each other's stories. For example, identify something in each story that was engaging (perhaps by being suspenseful, edgy, or funny) or that helped you identify with the storyteller. What do you think the point or significance of each story is—in other words, what makes the event so memorable?
- **Think of a storytelling strategy someone else used that you could try in your own story.** For example, could you use dialogue to show how someone talks and acts, vivid details to describe how the scene looked and felt, action verbs to make the story exciting, and reflection to clarify why the story was significant to you?

Analyzing Remembered Event Essays

As you read the selections in this chapter, you will see how different authors craft stories about an important event in their lives.

- Jean Brandt looks back on getting caught shoplifting (pp. 14–18).
- Annie Dillard recalls the consequences of a childhood prank (pp. 18–20).
- Jenée Desmond-Harris reflects on the death of her idol, rapper Tupac Shakur (pp. 23–26).

Analyzing how these writers tell a dramatic, well-focused story; use vivid, specific description to enliven their writing; and choose details and words that help readers understand why the event was so memorable will help you see how you can employ these same techniques when writing your autobiographical story.

Determine the writer's purpose and audience.

Many people write about important events in their lives to archive their memories and to learn something about themselves. Choosing events that are important to them personally, writers strive to imbue their stories with meaning and feeling that will resonate with readers. That is, they seek to help readers appreciate what we call the event's autobiographical **significance**—why the event is so memorable for the writer and what it might mean for readers. Often writers use autobiographical stories to reflect on a conflict that remains unresolved or one they still do not fully understand. Autobiographical stories may not only prompt readers to reflect on the writer's complicated and ambivalent emotions, puzzling motivations, and strained relationships but also help readers see larger cultural themes in these stories or understand implications the writer may not have even considered.

When reading the selections about remembered events that follow, ask yourself questions like these:

What seems to be the writer's purpose (or multiple, perhaps even conflicting, purposes)?

- To understand what happened and why, perhaps to confront unconscious and possibly uncomplimentary motives?
- To relive an intense experience that might resonate with readers and lead them to reflect on similar experiences of their own?
- To win over readers, perhaps to justify or rationalize choices made, actions taken, or words used?
- To use personal experience as an example that readers are likely to understand?
- To reflect on cultural attitudes at the time the event occurred, perhaps in contrast to current ways of thinking?

How does the writer want readers to react?

- To understand or empathize with the writer?
- To think anew about a similar experience of their own?
- To see the writer's experience as symptomatic of a broader social phenomenon?
- To assess how well the story applies to other people and situations?

Assess the genre's basic features.

Basic Features
A Well-Told Story
Vivid Description
Significance

As you read about the remembered events in this chapter, analyze and evaluate how different authors use the basic features of the genre. The examples that follow are drawn from the reading selections that appear later in this Guide to Reading.

A WELL-TOLD STORY

Read first to see how the story attempts to engage readers:

- By letting readers into the storyteller's (or narrator's) point of view (for example, by using the first-person pronoun *I* to narrate the story)
- By arousing curiosity and suspense
- By clarifying or resolving the underlying *conflict* through a change or discovery of some kind

Many of these basic narrative elements can be visualized in the form of a **dramatic arc** (see Figure 2.1), which you can analyze to see how a story creates and resolves dramatic tension.

Notice the narrating strategies used to create **action sequences**. Narrating action sequences relies on such strategies as using action verbs (such as *walked*) in different tenses or in conjunction with prepositional phrases or other cues of time or location to depict movement and show the relation among actions in time. In the following example, notice that *I walked* occurred in the past—after *I had found* and before *I was about to drop it*:

Action verbs

> I walked back to the basket where I had found the button and was about to drop it when suddenly, instead, I took a quick glance around, assured myself no one could see, and slipped the button into the pocket of my sweatshirt. (Brandt, par. 3)

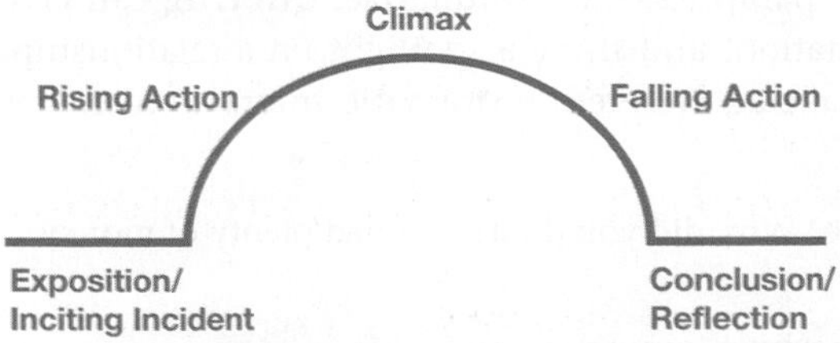

FIGURE 2.1 Dramatic Arc
The shape of the arc varies from story to story: Not all stories devote the same amount of space to each element, and some may omit an element or include more than one.

- **Exposition/Inciting Incident:** Background information and scene setting, introducing the characters and the initial conflict or problem that sets off the action, arousing curiosity and suspense
- **Rising Action:** The developing crisis, possibly leading to other conflicts and complications
- **Climax:** The emotional high point, often a turning point marking a change for good or ill
- **Falling Action:** Resolution of tension and unraveling of conflicts; may include a final surprise
- **Conclusion/Reflection:** Conflicts come to an end but may not be fully resolved, and writer may reflect on the event's meaning and importance—its significance

In addition to moving the narrative along, action sequences may also contribute to the overall feeling—or *dominant impression*—and help readers understand the event's significance. In this example, Brandt's actions show her ambivalence or inner conflict. While her actions seem impulsive ("suddenly"), they are also self-conscious, evidenced by her stopping midway to see if anyone is watching.

VIVID DESCRIPTION OF PEOPLE AND PLACES

Look for the describing strategies of **naming**, **detailing**, *and* **comparing**. In this example, Annie Dillard uses all three strategies to create a vivid description of a Pittsburgh street on one memorable winter morning:

Naming
Detailing
Comparing

> The cars' tires laid behind them on the snowy street a complex trail of beige chunks like crenellated castle walls. I had stepped on some earlier; they squeaked. (Dillard, par. 5)

Notice the senses the description evokes. In the example above, Dillard relies mainly on visual details to identify the color, texture, and shape of the snowy tire tracks. But she also tells us what the chunks of snow sounded like when stepped on.

Think about the impression made by the descriptions, particularly by the comparisons (similes and metaphors). For example, Dillard's comparison of tire tracks to crenellated castle walls suggests a kind of starry-eyed romanticism, an impression that is echoed by her reflections at the end of the story. As you will see, descriptions like this contribute to the *dominant impression*, which helps readers grasp the event's significance.

Finally, notice how **dialogue** *is used to portray people and their relationships.* Autobiographers use dialogue to characterize the people involved in the event, showing what they're like by depicting how they talk and interact. Speaker tags identify who is speaking and indicate the speaker's tone or attitude. Here's a brief example that comes at the climax of Dillard's story, when the man finally catches the kids he's been chasing:

Speaker tag

> "You stupid kids," he began perfunctorily. (Dillard, par. 18)

Consider why the writer chose to quote, paraphrase, or summarize. **Quoting** can give dialogue immediacy, intensify a confrontation, and shine a spotlight on a relationship. For example, Brandt uses quoting to make an inherently dramatic interaction that is much more intense.

> "I don't understand. What did you take? Why did you do it? You had plenty of money with you."
>
> "I know but I just did it. I can't explain why. Mom, I'm sorry."
>
> "I'm afraid sorry isn't enough. I'm horribly disappointed in you." (pars. 33–35)

Paraphrasing enables the writer to choose words for their impact or contribution to the dominant impression:

Paraphrase cue

> Next thing I knew, he was talking about calling the police and having me arrested and thrown in jail, as if he had just nabbed a professional thief instead of a terrified kid. (Brandt, par. 7)

The clichés (*thrown in jail* and *nabbed*) mock the security guard, aligning Brandt with her father's criticism of the police at the story's end.

Summarizing gives the gist. Sometimes writers use summary because what was said or how it was said isn't as important as the mere fact that something was said:

Summary cue — The chewing out was redundant, a mere formality, and beside the point. (Dillard, par. 19)

AUTOBIOGRAPHICAL SIGNIFICANCE

Look for remembered feelings and thoughts from the time the event occurred. Notice that in the first example Brandt announces her thoughts and feelings before describing them, but in the second example she simply shows her feelings by her actions:

Emotional response — The *thought* of going to jail terrified me. . . . I *felt* alone and scared. (par. 17)

Long after we got off the phone, . . . I could still distinctly hear the disappointment and hurt in my mother's voice. I cried. (36)

Look also for present perspective reflections about the past. In this example, Desmond-Harris uses rhetorical questions (questions she poses and then answers) to set up her present-day adult perspective on her past:

Rhetorical questions — Did we take ourselves seriously? Did we feel a real stake in the life of this "hard-core" gangsta rapper, and a real loss in his death? We did, even though we were two mixed-race girls raised by our white moms in a privileged community. (par. 8)

Notice that writers sometimes express both their past and their present feelings, either to contrast them or to show that they have not changed. Observe the time cues Desmond-Harris uses to distinguish between past and present feelings:

Time cues — I mourned Tupac's death then, and continue to mourn him now, because his music represents the years when I was both forced and privileged to confront what it meant to be black. (Desmond-Harris, par. 9)

Mark word choices in descriptive and narrative passages that contribute to the dominant impression and help to show why the event or person was significant. For example, Brandt depicts her feeling of shame vividly in this passage:

As the officers led me through the mall, I sensed a hundred pairs of eyes staring at me. My face flushed and I broke out in a sweat. (par. 18)

Consider whether the story's **significance** *encompasses mixed or ambivalent feelings and still-unresolved conflicts.* For example, notice the seesawing of feelings Brandt reports:

- Right after shoplifting, Brandt tells us, "I thought about how sly I had been" and "I felt proud of my accomplishment" (par. 5).
- After she is arrested, she acknowledges mixed feelings: "Being searched, although embarrassing, somehow seemed to be exciting. . . . I was having fun" (19).

- It is only when she has to face her mother that Brandt lets her intense feelings show: "For the first time that night, I was close to tears" (26).
- At the end, however, by transferring the blame from Brandt to the police, her father seems to leave the conflict essentially unresolved and repressed: "Although it would never be forgotten, the incident was not mentioned again" (39).

Readings

Jean Brandt | *Calling Home*

As a first-year college student, Jean Brandt wrote about a memorable event that occurred when she was thirteen: She shoplifted and was caught. As you read about Brandt's experience, you might want to think about these shoplifting factoids (unreliable because they show who is getting caught but not necessarily who is shoplifting): According to the National Association for Shoplifting Prevention (NASP), shoplifting is pretty equal among genders, socioeconomic classes, and ethnicities, and contrary to expectation, only about 25 percent of shoplifters are kids, including teenagers (shopliftingprevention.org); Christmas season is a peak shoplifting period; some shoplifters report a "high" after getting away with it; shoplifting is seldom premeditated and is possibly related to peer pressure and what is often called "consumer culture," the ideology that buying things brings intangibles like happiness, status, identity, and belonging.

As you read,

- consider which, if any, of this information about shoplifting affects your view of Brandt or your understanding of her story;
- think about Brandt's primary purpose in choosing this event and in presenting it as she does, given that she was writing for her instructor and classmates;
- answer the questions in the margins; your instructor may ask you to post your answers to a class blog or discussion board or to bring them to class.

Basic Features
A Well-Told Story
Vivid Description
Significance

1 As we all piled into the car, I knew it was going to be a fabulous day. My grandmother was visiting for the holidays; and she and I, along with my older brother and sister, Louis and Susan, were setting off for a day of last-minute Christmas shopping. On the way to the mall, we sang Christmas carols, chattered, and laughed. With Christmas only two days away, we were caught up with holiday spirit. I felt light-headed and full of joy. I loved shopping—especially at Christmas.

How well do these descriptive details help you visualize the scene?

2 The shopping center was swarming with frantic last-minute shoppers like ourselves. We went first to the General Store, my favorite. It carried mostly knickknacks and other useless items which nobody needs but buys anyway. I was thirteen years old at the time, and things like buttons and calendars and posters

would catch my fancy. This day was no different. The object of my desire was a 75-cent Snoopy button. Snoopy was the latest. If you owned anything with the Peanuts on it, you were "in." But since I was supposed to be shopping for gifts for other people and not myself, I couldn't decide what to do. I went in search of my sister for her opinion. I pushed my way through throngs of people to the back of the store where I found Susan. I asked her if she thought I should buy the button. She said it was cute and if I wanted it to go ahead and buy it.

What is your first impression of Brandt?

3 When I got back to the Snoopy section, I took one look at the lines at the cashiers and knew I didn't want to wait thirty minutes to buy an item worth less than one dollar. I walked back to the basket where I had found the button and was about to drop it when suddenly, instead, I took a quick glance around, assured myself no one could see, and slipped the button into the pocket of my sweatshirt.

4 I hesitated for a moment, but once the item was in my pocket, there was no turning back. I had never before stolen anything; but what was done was done. A few seconds later, my sister appeared and asked, "So, did you decide to buy the button?"

How do these action verbs (highlighted) and dialogue contribute to the drama?

5 "No, I guess not." I hoped my voice didn't quaver. As we headed for the entrance, my heart began to race. I just had to get out of that store. Only a few more yards to go and I'd be safe. As we crossed the threshold, I heaved a sigh of relief. I was home free. I thought about how sly I had been and I felt proud of my accomplishment.

6 An unexpected tap on my shoulder startled me. I whirled around to find a middle-aged man, dressed in street clothes, flashing some type of badge and politely asking me to empty my pockets. Where did this man come from? How did he know? I was so sure that no one had seen me! On the verge of panicking, I told myself that all I had to do was give this man his button back, say I was sorry, and go on my way. After all, it was only a 75-cent item.

7 Next thing I knew, he was talking about calling the police and having me arrested and thrown in jail, as if he had just nabbed a professional thief instead of a terrified kid. I couldn't believe what he was saying.

8 "Jean, what's going on?"

9 The sound of my sister's voice eased the pressure a bit. She always managed to get me out of trouble. She would come through this time too.

10 "Excuse me. Are you a relative of this young girl?"

11 "Yes, I'm her sister. What's the problem?"

12 "Well, I just caught her shoplifting and I'm afraid I'll have to call the police."

13 "What did she take?"

14 "This button."

15 "A button? You are having a thirteen-year-old arrested for stealing a button?"

16 "I'm sorry, but she broke the law."

17 The man led us through the store and into an office, where we waited for the police officers to arrive. Susan had found my grandmother and brother, who, still shocked, didn't say a word. The thought of going to jail terrified me, not because of jail itself, but because of the encounter with my parents afterward. Not more than ten minutes later, two officers arrived and placed me under arrest. They said that I was to be taken to the station alone. Then, they handcuffed me and led me out of the store. I felt alone and scared. I had counted on my sister being with me, but now I had to muster up the courage to face this ordeal all by myself.

How does your understanding of Brandt deepen or change through what she reveals about her feelings and thoughts?

18 As the officers led me through the mall, I sensed a hundred pairs of eyes staring at me. My face flushed and I broke out in a sweat. Now everyone knew I was a criminal. In their eyes I was a juvenile delinquent, and thank God the cops were getting me off the streets. The worst part was thinking my grandmother might be having the same thoughts. The humiliation at that moment was overwhelming. I felt like Hester Prynne being put on public display for everyone to ridicule.

19 That short walk through the mall seemed to take hours. But once we reached the squad car, time raced by. I was read my rights and questioned. We were at the police station within minutes. Everything happened so fast I didn't have a chance to feel remorse for my crime. Instead, I viewed what was happening to me as if it were a movie. Being searched, although embarrassing, somehow seemed to be exciting. All the movies and television programs I had seen were actually coming to life. This is what it was really like. But why were criminals always portrayed as frightened and regretful? I was having fun. I thought I had nothing to fear—until I was allowed my one phone call. I was trembling as I dialed home. I didn't know what I was going to say to my parents, especially my mother.

20 "Hi, Dad, this is Jean."

21 "We've been waiting for you to call."

22 "Did Susie tell you what happened?"

23 "Yeah, but we haven't told your mother. I think you should tell her what you did and where you are."

How does this dialogue add to the drama?

24 "You mean she doesn't even know where I am?"

25 "No, I want you to explain it to her."

26 There was a pause as he called my mother to the phone. For the first time that night, I was close to tears. I wished I had never stolen that stupid pin. I wanted to give the phone to one of the officers because I was too ashamed to tell my mother the truth, but I had no choice.

27 "Jean, where are you?"

28 "I'm, umm, in jail."

29 "Why? What for?"

30 "Shoplifting."

31 "Oh no, Jean. Why? Why did you do it?"

32 "I don't know. No reason. I just did it."

33 "I don't understand. What did you take? Why did you do it? You had plenty of money with you."

34 "I know but I just did it. I can't explain why. Mom, I'm sorry."

35 "I'm afraid sorry isn't enough. I'm horribly disappointed in you."

36 Long after we got off the phone, while I sat in an empty jail cell, waiting for my parents to pick me up, I could still distinctly hear the disappointment and hurt in my mother's voice. I cried. The tears weren't for me but for her and the pain I had put her through. I felt like a terrible human being. I would rather have stayed in jail than confront my mom right then. I dreaded each passing minute that brought our encounter closer. When the officer came to release me, I hesitated, actually not wanting to leave. We went to the front desk, where I had to sign a form to retrieve my belongings. I saw my parents a few yards away and my heart raced. A large knot formed in my stomach. I fought back the tears.

What is the effect of interweaving storytelling and describing with remembering thoughts and feelings in this paragraph?

37 Not a word was spoken as we walked to the car. Slowly, I sank into the back seat anticipating the scolding. Expecting harsh tones, I was relieved to hear almost the opposite from my father.

What do you learn from Brandt's account of her father's reaction?

38 "I'm not going to punish you and I'll tell you why. Although I think what you did was wrong, I think what the police did was more wrong. There's no

excuse for locking a thirteen-year-old behind bars. That doesn't mean I condone what you did, but I think you've been punished enough already."

How well does this final paragraph help you understand the event's significance?

39 As I looked from my father's eyes to my mother's, I knew this ordeal was over. Although it would never be forgotten, the incident was not mentioned again.

Annie Dillard | From *An American Childhood*

Courtesy of Michele Strub

ANNIE DILLARD, professor emeritus at Wesleyan University, won the Pulitzer Prize for nonfiction writing with her first book, *Pilgrim at Tinker Creek* (1974). Since then, she has written eleven books in a variety of genres. These include *Teaching a Stone to Talk* (1988), *The Writing Life* (1990), *The Living* (1993), *Mornings Like This* (1996), and *The Maytrees (2007)*. Dillard also wrote an autobiography of her early years, *An American Childhood* (1987), from which the following selection comes.

As you read, consider the following questions:

- How do the first two paragraphs in the selection prepare readers to understand the story's significance?
- Why do you think Dillard sets the scene by describing the time and place with so much specificity?

1 Some boys taught me to play football. This was fine sport. You thought up a new strategy for every play and whispered it to the others. You went out for a pass, fooling everyone. Best, you got to throw yourself mightily at someone's running legs. Either you brought him down or you hit the ground flat out on your chin, with your arms empty before you. It was all or nothing. If you hesitated in fear, you would miss and get hurt: you would take a hard fall while the kid got away, or you would get kicked in the face while the kid got away. But if you flung yourself wholeheartedly at the back of his knees—if you gathered and joined body and soul and pointed them diving fearlessly—then you likely wouldn't get hurt, and you'd stop the ball. Your fate, and your team's score, depended on your concentration and courage. Nothing girls did could compare with it.

2 Boys welcomed me at baseball, too, for I had, through enthusiastic practice, what was weirdly known as a boy's arm. In winter, in the snow, there was neither baseball nor football, so the boys and I threw snowballs at passing cars. I got in trouble throwing snowballs, and have seldom been happier since.

3 On one weekday morning after Christmas, six inches of new snow had just fallen. We were standing up to our boot

tops in snow on a front yard on trafficked Reynolds Street, waiting for cars. The cars traveled Reynolds Street slowly and evenly; they were targets all but wrapped in red ribbons, cream puffs. We couldn't miss.

4 I was seven; the boys were eight, nine, and ten. The oldest two Fahey boys were there—Mikey and Peter—polite blond boys who lived near me on Lloyd Street, and who already had four brothers and sisters. My parents approved Mikey and Peter Fahey. Chickie McBride was there, a tough kid, and Billy Paul and Mackie Kean too, from across Reynolds, where the boys grew up dark and furious, grew up skinny, knowing, and skilled. We had all drifted from our houses that morning looking for action, and had found it here on Reynolds Street.

5 It was cloudy but cold. The cars' tires laid behind them on the snowy street a complex trail of beige chunks like crenellated castle walls. I had stepped on some earlier; they squeaked. We could not have wished for more traffic. When a car came, we all popped it one. In the intervals between cars we reverted to the natural solitude of children.

6 I started making an iceball—a perfect iceball, from perfectly white snow, perfectly spherical, and squeezed perfectly translucent so no snow remained all the way through. (The Fahey boys and I considered it unfair actually to throw an iceball at somebody, but it had been known to happen.)

7 I had just embarked on the iceball project when we heard tire chains come clanking from afar. A black Buick was moving toward us down the street. We all spread out, banged together some regular snowballs, took aim, and, when the Buick drew nigh, fired.

8 A soft snowball hit the driver's windshield right before the driver's face. It made a smashed star with a hump in the middle.

9 Often, of course, we hit our target, but this time, the only time in all of life, the car pulled over and stopped. Its wide black door opened; a man got out of it, running. He didn't even close the car door.

10 He ran after us, and we ran away from him, up the snowy Reynolds sidewalk. At the corner, I looked back; incredibly, he was still after us. He was in city clothes: a suit and tie, street shoes. Any normal adult would have quit, having sprung us into flight and made his point. This man was gaining on us. He was a thin man, all action. All of a sudden, we were running for our lives.

11 Wordless, we split up. We were on our turf; we could lose ourselves in the neighborhood backyards, everyone for himself. I paused and considered. Everyone had vanished except Mikey Fahey, who was just rounding the corner of a yellow brick house. Poor Mikey, I trailed him. The driver of the Buick sensibly picked the two of us to follow. The man apparently had all day.

12 He chased Mikey and me around the yellow house and up a backyard path we knew by heart: under a low tree, up a bank, through a hedge, down some snowy steps, and across the grocery store's delivery driveway. We smashed through a gap in another hedge, entered a scruffy backyard and ran around its back porch and tight between houses to Edgerton Avenue; we ran across Edgerton to an alley and up our own sliding woodpile to the Halls' front yard; he kept coming. We ran up Lloyd Street and wound through mazy backyards toward the steep hilltop at Willard and Lang.

13 He chased us silently, block after block. He chased us silently over picket fences, through thorny hedges, between houses, around garbage cans, and across streets. Every time I glanced back, choking for breath, I expected he would have quit. He must have been as breathless as we were. His jacket strained over his body. It was an immense discovery, pounding into my hot head with every sliding, joyous step, that this ordinary adult evidently knew what I thought only children who trained at football knew: that you have to fling yourself at what you're doing, you have to point yourself, forget yourself, aim, dive.

14 Mikey and I had nowhere to go, in our own neighborhood or out of it, but away from this man who was chasing us. He impelled us forward; we compelled him to follow our route. The air was cold; every breath tore my throat. We kept running, block after block; we kept improvising, backyard after backyard, running a frantic course and choosing it simultaneously, failing always to find small places or hard places to slow him down, and discovering always, exhilarated, dismayed, that only bare speed could save us—for he would never give up, this man—and we were losing speed.

15 He chased us through the backyard labyrinths of ten blocks before he caught us by our jackets. He caught us and we all stopped.

16 We three stood staggering, half blinded, coughing, in an obscure hilltop backyard: a man in his twenties, a boy, a girl. He had released our jackets, our pursuer, our captor, our hero: he knew we weren't going anywhere. We all played by the rules. Mikey and I unzipped our jackets. I pulled off my sopping mittens. Our tracks multiplied in the backyard's new snow. We had been breaking new snow all morning. We didn't look at each other. I was cherishing my excitement. The man's lower pants legs were wet; his cuffs were full of snow, and there was a prow of snow beneath them on his shoes and socks. Some trees bordered the little flat backyard, some messy winter trees. There was no one around: a clearing in a grove, and we the only players.

17 It was a long time before he could speak. I had some difficulty at first recalling why we were there. My lips felt swollen; I couldn't see out of the sides of my eyes; I kept coughing.

18 "You stupid kids," he began perfunctorily.

19 We listened perfunctorily indeed, if we listened at all, for the chewing out was redundant, a mere formality, and beside the point. The point was that he had chased us passionately without giving up, and so he had caught us. Now he came down to earth. I wanted the glory to last forever.

20 But how could the glory have lasted forever? We could have run through every backyard in North America until we got to Panama. But when he trapped us at the lip of the Panama Canal, what precisely could he have done to prolong the drama of the chase and cap its glory? I brooded about this for the next few years. He could only have fried Mikey Fahey and me in boiling oil, say, or dismembered us piecemeal, or staked us to anthills. None of which I really wanted, and none of which any adult was likely to do, even in the spirit of fun. He could only chew us out there in the Panamanian jungle, after months or years of exalting pursuit. He could only begin, "You stupid kids," and continue in his ordinary Pittsburgh accent with his normal righteous anger and the usual common sense.

21 If in that snowy backyard the driver of the black Buick had cut off our heads, Mikey's and mine, I would have died happy, for nothing has required so much of me since as being chased all over Pittsburgh in the middle of winter—running terrified, exhausted—by this sainted, skinny, furious redheaded man who wished to have a word with us. I don't know how he found his way back to his car.

[REFLECT] Make connections: Acting fearlessly.

At the beginning of the essay, Dillard tells about being taught by the neighborhood boys the joy of playing football, particularly the "all or nothing" of diving "fearlessly" (par. 1). Recall an occasion when you had an opportunity to dive fearlessly into an activity that posed some challenge or risk or required special effort. For example, you may have been challenged, like Dillard, by your teammates at a football game or by a group of volunteers helping during a natural disaster. Or you may have felt pressured by friends to do something that went against your better judgment, was illegal, or was dangerous. Your instructor may ask you to post your thoughts to a class discussion board or to discuss them with other students in class. Use these questions to get started:

- What made you embrace the challenge or resist it? What do you think your choice reveals about you at the time of the event?
- Dillard uses the value term *courage* to describe the fearless behavior she learned playing football. What value term would you use to describe your experience? For example, were you being *selfless* or *self-serving; responsible* or *irresponsible;* a *follower, a leader,* or *a self-reliant individual*?

[ANALYZE] Use the basic features.

A WELL-TOLD STORY: CONSTRUCTING AN ACTION SEQUENCE

Throughout this story, Dillard creates compelling *action sequences* by using a variety of strategies. In this first example, she combines action verbs with prepositional phrases to help readers visualize what it was like to move rapidly from place to place:

Action verbs Prepositional phrases	He chased Mikey and me around the yellow house and up a backward path we knew by heart: under a low tree, up a bank, through a hedge, down some snowy steps, and across the grocery store's delivery driveway. We smashed through a gap in another hedge. (par. 12)

Here's an example in which she uses short phrases, often with similar sounding words and parallel sentence structures, to convey a sense of repeated action:

Similar sounds Parallel structures	He impelled us forward; we compelled him to follow our route. . . . We kept running, block after block; we kept improvising, backyard after backyard. (par. 14)

ANALYZE & WRITE

Write a paragraph analyzing one of Dillard's action sequences:

1. Skim paragraphs 11–14, marking similar words and parallel sentence structures, action verbs, and prepositional phrases. (Don't feel you have to mark every instance, but get a sense of how often Dillard uses these strategies.)
2. How well do these narrative strategies work to represent action? How does using the same strategies over and over contribute to the effect?
3. Try writing an action sequence of your own, using parallel sentence structure, prepositional phrases, and words that echo one another, as Dillard does.

VIVID DESCRIPTION OF PEOPLE AND PLACES: CREATING A DOMINANT IMPRESSION

The describing strategies of naming, detailing, and comparing portray people and places vividly:

Naming Detailing Comparing	The shopping center was swarming with frantic last-minute shoppers like ourselves. (Brandt, par. 2)

Brandt *names* a familiar location for readers. She selects *details* carefully to conjure a specific image of that shopping center before Christmas. Perhaps most evocatively, she uses a metaphor to *compare* the shopping mall to a "swarming" beehive, a comparison that reinforces the image of "frantic" shoppers in a place teeming with hurried, excited people.

Describing strategies like Brandt's not only help readers imagine the scene and people at a particular place and time but also contribute to the dominant impression. The description evokes Brandt's youthful excitement, suggests the crowds and chaos that motivated Brandt to pocket the button, and foreshadows the swarm of intense and conflicted feelings Brandt experiences as the story unfolds.

ANALYZE & WRITE

Write a paragraph analyzing Dillard's use of naming, detailing, and comparing to help readers visualize the man who chased her and to create a dominant impression:

1. Skim paragraphs 9–10 and 16–21, highlighting Dillard's use of naming, detailing, and comparing to describe the man.
2. Dillard's description of the man is spare, with only a few carefully chosen details. What kinds of details does Dillard focus on, and what do they suggest about the man? Who is he? Where does he come from? Why would he bother to chase the kids?
3. Notice the repetition of the word *normal* in paragraphs 10 and 20. What about the man makes him seem like a "normal adult," and what makes him seem anything but normal? How does Dillard help the reader reconcile these contrasting images to form a dominant impression?

AUTOBIOGRAPHICAL SIGNIFICANCE: SHOWING AND TELLING

Writers use both *showing* and *telling* to convey the autobiographical significance of an event, what it meant at the time, and why it continues to be memorable. As you've seen, **showing**—in narrating the story and in describing people and places—not only helps make the writing vivid but also creates a dominant impression. However, showing alone cannot help readers fully grasp an event's significance. Readers also need **telling**, the writer's explicit comments and reflections. In this example, Brandt uses showing and telling to give readers a clear understanding of how she felt at the time:

Telling
Showing

> As the officers led me through the mall, I sensed a hundred pairs of eyes staring at me. My face flushed and I broke out in a sweat. Now everyone knew I was a criminal. . . . The humiliation at that moment was overwhelming. I felt like Hester Prynne being put on public display for everyone to ridicule. (par. 18)

Narrators may use telling to articulate remembered feelings and thoughts from the time the event occurred and to present perspective on the event—what the writer feels and thinks now, looking back on it after time has passed.

To alert readers that they are telling, writers sometimes announce their reflections with words like *felt* and *thought*. But they may also choose words that name or imply a particular emotion or thought (for example, "The humiliation at that moment was overwhelming" [Brandt, 18]).

Similarly, to signal a shift from the past to the present perspective, writers sometimes announce the transition with words such as *then* and *now*. But a more subtle strategy is to use sophisticated word choices that show a deeper, more mature understanding of the experience (for example, when Brandt compares herself to Hester Prynne, from Nathaniel Hawthorne's novel *The Scarlet Letter*, "being put on public display for everyone to ridicule" [par. 18]).

ANALYZE & WRITE

Write a paragraph analyzing Dillard's use of telling to convey the event's significance:

1. Skim paragraphs 11–21, noting where Dillard *tells* readers her thoughts and feelings. (Don't feel you have to mark every instance, but try to get a sense of how much she tells as well as what she tells readers.)
2. Review what you have highlighted to determine which of the passages indicate Dillard's remembered thoughts and feelings from the time the incident occurred and which indicate what she thinks and feels now, looking back on the event from her present adult perspective. How can you tell the difference between her past and present perspectives?

RESPOND Consider possible topics: Remembering unexpected adult actions and reactions.

Like Dillard, you could write about a time when an adult did something entirely unexpected during your childhood—an action that seemed dangerous or threatening to you, or something humorous, kind, or generous. Consider unpredictable actions of adults in your immediate or extended family, adults you came to know outside your family, and strangers. As you consider these possible topics, think about your purpose and audience: What would you want your instructor and classmates to learn from reading about this event?

Jenée Desmond-Harris | *Tupac and My Non-thug Life*

Courtesy of Jenée Desmond-Harris

JENÉE DESMOND-HARRIS is the race, law, and politics reporter at Vox.com. Before that, she was White House correspondent and associate editor at the *Root*, an online magazine dedicated to African American news, social justice, and culture. A graduate of Howard University and Harvard Law School, Desmond-Harris has been a contributor to such news outlets as *Time* magazine, CNN, MSNBC, and the *Huffington Post*. The following selection was published in the *Root* in 2011. It chronicles Desmond-Harris's reaction to the murder of gangsta rap icon Tupac Shakur in a Las Vegas drive-by shooting in 1996. Desmond-Harris mentions Tupac's mother, Afeni, as well as the "East Coast–West Coast war"—the rivalry between Tupac and the Notorious B.I.G. (Biggie Smalls), who was suspected of being involved in Tupac's murder.

As you read, consider the photograph that appeared in the article:

- What does the photograph capture about the fifteen-year-old Desmond-Harris?
- What does its inclusion say about Desmond-Harris's perspective on her adolescent self and the event she recollects?

1 I learned about Tupac's death when I got home from cheerleading practice that Friday afternoon in September 1996. I was a sophomore in high school in Mill Valley, Calif. I remember trotting up my apartment building's stairs, physically tired but buzzing with the frenetic energy and possibilities for change that accompany fall and a new school year. I'd been cautiously allowing myself to think during the walk home about a topic that felt frighteningly taboo (at least in my world, where discussion of race was avoided as delicately as obesity or mental illness): what it meant to be biracial and on the school's mostly white cheerleading team instead of the mostly black dance team. I remember acknowledging, to the sound of an 8-count that still pounded in my head as I walked through the door, that I didn't really have a choice: I could memorize a series of stiff and precise motions but couldn't actually dance.

2 My private musings on identity and belonging—not original in the least, but novel to me—were interrupted when my mom heard me slam the front door and drop my bags: "*Your friend died!*" she called out from another room. Confused silence. "*You know, that rapper you and Thea love so much!*"

Mourning a Death in Vegas

3 The news was turned on, with coverage of the deadly Vegas shooting. Phone calls were made. Ultimately my best friend, Thea, and I were left to our own 15-year-old devices to mourn that weekend. Her mother and stepfather were out of town. Their expansive, million-dollar home was perched on a hillside less than an hour from Tupac's former stomping grounds in Oakland and Marin City. Of course, her home was also worlds away from both places.

4 We couldn't "pour out" much alcohol undetected for a libation, so we limited ourselves to doing somber shots of liqueur from a well-stocked cabinet. One each. Tipsy, in a high-ceilinged kitchen surrounded by hardwood floors and Zen flower arrangements, we baked cookies for his mother. We packed them up to ship to Afeni with a handmade card. ("Did we really do that?" I asked Thea this week. I wanted to ensure that this story, which people who know me now find hilarious, hadn't morphed into some sort of personal urban legend over the past 15 years. "Yes," she said. "We put them in a lovely tin.")

5 On a sound system that echoed through speakers perched discreetly throughout the airy house, we played "Life Goes On" on a loop and sobbed. We analyzed lyrics for premonitions of the tragedy. We, of course, cursed Biggie. Who knew that the East Coast–West Coast war had two earnest soldiers in flannel pajamas, lying on a king-size bed decorated with pink toe shoes that dangled from one of its posts? There, we studied our pictures of Tupac and re-created his tattoos on each other's body with a Sharpie. I got "Thug Life" on my stomach. I gave Thea "Exodus 1811" inside a giant cross. Both are flanked by "West Side."

6 A snapshot taken that Monday on our high school's front lawn (seen here) shows

The author (left) with her friend Thea

Courtesy of Jenée Desmond-Harris

the two of us lying side by side, shirts lifted to display the tributes in black marker. Despite our best efforts, it's the innocent, bubbly lettering of notes passed in class and of poster boards made for social studies presentations. My hair has recently been straightened with my first (and last) relaxer and a Gold 'N Hot flatiron on too high a setting. Hers is slicked back with the mixture of Herbal Essences and Blue Magic that we formulated in a bathroom laboratory.

7 My rainbow-striped tee and her white wifebeater capture a transition between our skater-inspired Salvation Army shopping phase and the next one, during which we'd wear the same jeans slung from our hip bones, revealing peeks of flat stomach, but transforming ourselves from Alternative Nation to MTV Jams imitators. We would get bubble coats in primary colors that Christmas and start using silver eyeliner, trying—and failing—to look something like Aaliyah.[1]

Mixed Identities: Tupac and Me

8 Did we take ourselves seriously? Did we feel a real stake in the life of this "hard-core" gangsta rapper, and a real loss in his death? We did, even though we were two mixed-race girls raised by our white moms in a privileged community where we could easily rattle off the names of the small handful of other kids in town who also had one black parent: Sienna. Rashea. Brandon. Aaron. Sudan. Akio. Lauren. Alicia. Even though the most subversive thing we did was make prank calls. Even though we hadn't yet met our first boyfriends, and Shock G's proclamations about putting satin on people's panties sent us into absolute giggling fits. And even though we'd been so delicately cared for, nurtured and protected from any of life's hard edges—with special efforts made to shield us from those involving race—that we sometimes felt ready to explode with boredom. Or maybe because of all that.

9 I mourned Tupac's death then, and continue to mourn him now, because his music represents the years when I was both forced and privileged to confront what it meant to be black. That time, like his music, was about exploring the contradictory textures of this identity: The ambience and indulgence of the fun side, as in "California Love" and "Picture Me Rollin'." But also the burdensome anxiety and outright anger—"Brenda's Got a Baby," "Changes" and "Hit 'Em Up."

10 For Thea and me, his songs were the musical score to our transition to high school, where there emerged a vague, lunchtime geography to race: White kids perched on a sloping green lawn and the benches above it. Below, black kids sat on a wall outside the gym. The bottom of the hill beckoned. Thea, more outgoing, with more admirers among the boys, stepped down boldly, and I followed timidly. Our formal invitations came in the form of unsolicited hall passes to go to Black Student Union meetings during free periods. We were assigned to recite Maya Angelou's "Phenomenal Woman" at the Black History Month assembly.

11 Tupac was the literal sound track when our school's basketball team would come charging onto the court, and our ragtag group of cheerleaders kicked furiously to "Toss It Up" in a humid gymnasium. Those were the games when we might breathlessly join the dance team after our cheer during time-outs if they did the single "African step" we'd mastered for BSU performances.

Everything Black—and Cool

12 . . . Blackness became something cool, something to which we had brand-new access. We flaunted it, buying Kwanzaa candles and

[1] A hit rhythm-and-blues and hip-hop recording artist. Aaliyah Dana Haughton died in a plane crash at age twenty-two. [Editor's note]

insisting on celebrating privately (really, just lighting the candles and excluding our friends) at a sleepover. We memorized "I Get Around"[2] and took turns singing verses to each other as we drove through Marin County suburbs in Thea's green Toyota station wagon. Because he was with us through all of this, we were in love with Tupac and wanted to embody him. On Halloween, Thea donned a bald cap and a do-rag, penciled in her already-full eyebrows and was a dead ringer.

13 Tupac's music, while full of social commentary (and now even on the Vatican's playlist), probably wasn't made to be a treatise on racial identity. Surely it wasn't created to accompany two girls (*little* girls, really) as they embarked on a coming-of-age journey. But it was there for us when we desperately needed it.

[2] Tupac Shakur's first top-twenty single, released in 1993 on *Strictly 4 My N.I.G.G.A.Z.*, Shakur's second studio album. [Editor's note]

[REFLECT] Make connections: Searching for identity.

Remembering high school, Desmond-Harris describes the emergence of "a vague, lunchtime geography to race: White kids perched on a sloping green lawn and the benches above it. Below, black kids sat on a wall outside the gym" (par. 10).

School, particularly high school, is notorious for students' forming peer groups or cliques of various kinds—by ethnicity, gender, popularity, and so on. Recall the cliques in your own school and think about the roles they played, both positive and negative, in your search for identity. Your instructor may ask you to post your thoughts to a class discussion board or blog, or to discuss them with other students in class. Use these questions to get started:

- Did you associate with any particular groups, and if so, why did you choose those groups?
- How did being in a particular group or not being in that group affect your sense of yourself?
- Why do you think it is important for her "coming-of-age journey" that Desmond-Harris felt that the group at the "bottom of the hill beckoned" (par. 10)? The word *beckoned* here can be read in two ways: that she felt the need to be a part of the group, or that members of the group invited her to join them. Consider how these possible interpretations affect your understanding of her remembered event.

[ANALYZE] Use the basic features.

A WELL-TOLD STORY: FINDING THE ARC OF THE STORY

We have seen that the dramatic arc (Figure 2.1, p. 11) is often used to organize a remembered event narrative around a central conflict, arousing curiosity and suspense as it builds toward a climax or emotional high point before resolving the conflict or at least bringing it to a conclusion. This is basically the structure Brandt and Dillard use to tell their stories. Writers, however, do not always follow this straightforward pattern; they may emphasize certain elements of the arc and downplay or even skip others.

ANALYZE & WRITE

Write a paragraph analyzing the structure of Desmond-Harris's story:

1. Desmond-Harris could have built up to the surprising news of Tupac's death, using it as the dramatic climax of her story. Why do you think she chose to use his death as the "inciting incident" with which to begin her story?
2. How does the opening paragraph shed light on the conflict at the heart of Desmond-Harris's story?
3. What do the girls' actions as they mourn Tupac's death (pars. 3–7) as well as their later actions (pars. 10–12) suggest about how the inciting incident of Tupac's death led them to deal with the underlying conflict?

VIVID DESCRIPTION OF PEOPLE AND PLACES: USING VISUALS AND BRAND NAMES

Desmond-Harris provides lots of concrete details to enliven her narrative. She also uses a photo and refers to brand names to convey to readers an exact sense of what the girls were like. Notice that she recounts the Sharpie tattooing and then actually shows us a photo of her and her friend Thea displaying their tattoos. But Desmond-Harris does not let the photo speak for itself; instead, she describes the picture, pointing out features, such as their hairstyles and outfits, that mark the girls' identity. Consider the references to particular styles and brand names (such as "our skater-inspired Salvation Army shopping phase") that tag the various roles they were trying on at that time of their lives (par. 7).

ANALYZE & WRITE

Write a paragraph or two analyzing Desmond-Harris's use of a photograph and brand names to enhance her descriptions:

1. Skim paragraphs 5–7, highlighting the specific details in the photo that Desmond-Harris points out as well as the brand names (usually capitalized) and the modifiers (like *skater-inspired*) that make them more specific.
2. Look closely at the photograph itself, and consider its purpose.
   - Why do you think Desmond-Harris included it?
   - What does the photograph contribute or show us that the text alone does not convey?
3. Consider the effect that the photo and the brand names have on you as a reader (or might have on readers close to Desmond-Harris's age). How do they help readers envision the girls? What is the dominant impression you get of the young Desmond- Harris from these descriptive details?

For more about analyzing visuals, see Chapter 13.

AUTOBIOGRAPHICAL SIGNIFICANCE: HANDLING COMPLEX EMOTIONS

Remembered events that have lasting significance nearly always involve mixed or ambivalent feelings. Therefore, readers expect and appreciate some degree of complexity. Multiple layers of meaning make autobiographical stories more, not less, interesting. Significance that seems simplistic or predictable makes stories less successful. For example, if Brandt's story had ended with her arrest and left out the conversations with her parents, readers would have less insight into Brandt's still intense and unresolved feelings.

ANALYZE & WRITE

Write a paragraph or two analyzing Desmond-Harris's handling of the complex personal and cultural significance of her remembered event:

1. Skim the last two sections (pars. 8–13), noting passages where Desmond-Harris shares her remembered feelings and thoughts at the time, and passages where she gives readers her present perspective as an adult reflecting on the experience. How does Desmond-Harris use her dual perspective—that of the fifteen-year-old experiencing the event and the thirty-year-old writing about it—to help readers understand the event's significance?
2. Look closely at paragraph 8, and consider how Desmond-Harris helps her readers grasp the significance of the event by using sentence strategies like these:
   - Rhetorical questions (questions writers ask and answer themselves)
   - Repeated words and phrases
   - Intentional sentence fragments (incomplete sentences used for special effect)

Note that in academic writing, sentence fragments—even those that are used purposely for rhetorical effect—may be frowned on. One of the instructor's purposes in assigning a writing project is to teach students to use formal academic writing conventions, a process that includes distinguishing between complete sentences and sentence fragments, and knowing how to identify and correct sentence fragments.

[RESPOND] Consider possible topics: Recognizing a public event as a turning point.

Like Desmond-Harris, you could write about how a public event—such as a celebrity death or marriage, an act of heroism or charity, or even the passage of a law—helped (or forced) you to confront an aspect of your identity. Consider the complexities of your reaction—the significance the event had for you at the time, and the significance the event has for you now. You might make a list of physical traits, as well as beliefs about or aspects of your sense of identity, that changed as a result of the event.

The Writing Assignment

Write about an event in your life that will engage readers and that will, at the same time, help them understand the significance of the event. Tell your story dramatically and vividly.

This Guide to Writing is designed to help you depict your own remembered event and apply what you have learned from reading other selections in the same genre. The Starting Points chart will help you find the guidance you need, when you need it.

STARTING POINTS: REMEMBERING AN EVENT

A Well-Told Story

How can I come up with an event to write about?

- Consider possible topics. (pp. 23, 28)
- Choose an event to write about. (p. 31)
- Test Your Topic: Considering Your Purpose and Audience (pp. 31–32)

How can I interest my audience and hold its attention?

- Shape your story. (p. 32)
- Test Your Story: Facing an Audience (p. 34)
- Write the opening sentences. (p. 38)

How can I make my story dramatic?

- Assess the genre's basic features: A well-told story. (pp. 11–12)
- A Well-Told Story: Constructing an Action Sequence (p. 21)
- A Troubleshooting Guide: A Well-Told Story (p. 40)

How should I organize my story?

- Shape your story. (p. 32)
- Assess the genre's basic features: A well-told story. (pp. 11–12)
- A Well-Told Story: Finding the Arc of the Story (p. 26)
- Clarify the sequence of actions. (p. 34)

(continued)

Vivid Description of People and Places

How can I describe the place where the event occurred vividly and specifically?

- Assess the genre's basic features: Vivid description of people and places. (pp. 12–13)
- Describe key people and places vividly, and show their significance. (p. 35)

How can I make the people in my story come alive?

- Assess the genre's basic features: Vivid description of people and places. (pp. 12–13)
- Describe key people and places vividly, and show their significance. (p. 35)
- Vivid Description of People and Places: Using Visuals and Brand Names (p. 27)
- Use dialogue to portray people and dramatize relationships. (p. 36)
- A Troubleshooting Guide: Vivid Description of People and Places (p. 41)

Autobiographical Significance

How can I help readers grasp the significance of my remembered event?

- Assess the genre's basic features: Autobiographical significance. (pp. 13–14)
- Autobiographical Significance: Showing and Telling (pp. 22–23)
- Autobiographical Significance: Handling Complex Emotions (pp. 27–28)
- Clarify your story's significance. (pp. 36–37)
- A Troubleshooting Guide: Autobiographical Significance (pp. 41–42)

How can I create a dominant impression?

- Assess the genre's basic features: Autobiographical significance. (pp. 13–14)
- Autobiographical Significance: Showing and Telling (pp. 22–23)
- Clarify your story's significance. (pp. 36–37)

Writing a Draft: Invention, Research, Planning, and Composing

The activities in this section will help you choose an event to write about and develop it into a story that is well-told, vivid, and meaningful. Do the activities in any order that makes sense to you (and your instructor), and return to them as needed as you revise.

Choose an event to write about.

To make a compelling story, the event you choose to write about should

- take place over a short period of time (preferably just a few hours);
- center on a conflict (an internal struggle or an external confrontation);
- disclose something significant about your life;
- reveal strong and possibly complex or ambivalent feelings (rather than superficial or sentimental ones).

Make a list of possible events in your life that you would feel comfortable writing about. If you are having trouble coming up with promising events to write about, try the following:

- Review the Consider Possible Topics sections on pp. 23 and 28, and reread any notes you made in response to those suggestions.
- Consult Web sites where people post stories about their lives, such as the *Moth, Story Preservation Initiative, the Sixties Project,* or *StoryCorps*. Try also typing *memory project, survivor stories,* or a similar word string into the search box of your browser.

If you need more ideas, the following may give you a jumping-off point:

- A difficult situation (for example, when you had to make a tough choice and face the consequences, or when you let someone down or someone you admired let you down)
- An occasion when things did not turn out as expected (for example, when you expected to be criticized but were praised or ignored instead, or when you were convinced you would succeed but failed)
- An incident that changed you or that revealed an aspect of your personality (such as initiative, insecurity, ambition, jealousy, or heroism)
- An incident in which a conflict or a serious misunderstanding with someone made you feel unjustly treated or caused you to mistreat someone else
- An experience that made you reexamine a basic value or belief (such as a time when you were expected to do something that went against your values, or a time when you had to make a decision about which you were deeply conflicted)
- An encounter with another person that led you to seriously consider someone else's point of view, changed the way you viewed yourself, or altered your ideas about how you fit into a group or community
- An event that revealed other people's surprising assumptions about you (as a student, friend, colleague, or worker)

TEST YOUR TOPIC

Considering Your Purpose and Audience

After you have made a tentative topic choice, ask yourself the following questions:

- Will I be able to reconstruct the story, place, and people in enough detail to help my readers imagine what it was like? (As you probe your memory, you may remember more details, but you may also need to fill in or re-create some details.)

- Do I feel comfortable sharing this experience with my instructor and classmates—revealing what I did, thought, and felt at the time? What concerns or anxieties do I have about the impression they will have of me?
- Will I be able to help my readers understand the personal and social dimensions of the underlying conflict? Will my own understanding of its significance deepen as I write about it?

If you lose confidence in your choice after answering these questions, return to your list and choose another event.

Shape your story.

Once you have selected an event, begin by making a simple sketch of your story. Here is a sample *outline* you can modify to fit your needs. (Remember that each section need not be the same length; the exposition and conclusion/reflection may be very brief—a sentence or two—while the rising action and climax may run for several paragraphs.)

I. **Exposition/Inciting Incident:** Set the scene and show how the conflict or problem started.

II. **Rising Action:** Build tension and suspense, showing how the crisis developed or worsened.

III. **Climax:** End the suspense by dramatizing the most critical moment or turning point.

IV. **Falling Action:** Show how the tension diminished as the conflict moved toward resolution.

V. **Conclusion/Reflection:** Bring closure to the story, and reflect on the event's overall significance.

Then you can use the following Ways In suggestions to anticipate your readers' likely questions and flesh out your chronology.

WAYS IN

HOW DO I DEVELOP A DRAMATIC ARC?

Ask yourself the following questions:

What is the underlying conflict, the dilemma facing my narrator?

To answer, provide some EXPOSITION, *the background information that will help your readers understand the situation:*

▶ I wanted ________ but didn't want to ________. So I ________.

EXAMPLE The object of my desire was a 75-cent Snoopy button. . . . I took one look at the lines at the cashiers and knew I didn't want to wait thirty minutes. (Brandt, pars. 2, 3)

What started it?

To answer, dramatize the INCITING INCIDENT, *the crisis that set off the conflict or triggered the event.*

Use an action sequence:

▸ I did ________. But then ________.

EXAMPLE A black Buick was moving toward us down the street. We all spread out, banged together some regular snowballs, took aim, and, when the Buick drew nigh, fired. (Dillard, par. 7)

Use dialogue:

▸ " ________," ________ announced excitedly.

EXAMPLE *"Your friend died!"* she called out from another room. (Desmond-Harris, par. 2)

What will happen?

To answer, intensify the story's **RISING ACTION** *to arouse curiosity and build suspense and excitement.*

▸ He ________ us. We ________.

EXAMPLE He ran after us, and we ran away from him, up the snowy Reynolds sidewalk. At the corner, I looked back; incredibly, he was still after us. . . . This man was gaining on us. He was a thin man, all action. All of a sudden, we were running for our lives. (Dillard, par. 10)

What did it lead to?

To answer, dramatize the **CLIMAX**. It may be the only climax or one of several, as in Brandt's story.

▸ I thought I had ________, but then ________.

EXAMPLE I was home free. I thought about how sly I had been. . . . An unexpected tap on my shoulder startled me. (Brandt, pars. 5–6)

▸ When she told me, " ________," I knew I had ________.

EXAMPLE "I'm afraid sorry isn't enough. I'm horribly disappointed in you." Long after we got off the phone, while I sat in an empty jail cell, waiting for my parents to pick me up, . . . I cried. (Brandt, pars. 35–36)

How did it turn out?

To answer, summarize the **FALLING ACTION**, *showing how the conflict subsides and complications unravel.*

▸ Afterward, I ________.

EXAMPLE When the officer came to release me, I hesitated, actually not wanting to leave. We went to the front desk, where I had to sign a form to retrieve my belongings. (Brandt, par. 36)

Why does my story matter?

To answer, conclude with **REFLECTIONS** *on the event's significance:*

▸ I realized then that ________.

EXAMPLE As I looked from my father's eyes to my mother's, I knew this ordeal was over. Although it would never be forgotten, the incident was not mentioned again. (Brandt, par. 39)

TEST YOUR STORY

Facing an Audience
Get together with two or three other students to try out your story. Your classmates' reactions will help you determine whether you are telling it in an interesting or exciting way.

Storytellers: Take turns telling your stories briefly. Try to pique your listeners' curiosity and build suspense, and watch your audience to see if your story is having the desired reaction.

Listeners: Briefly tell each storyteller what you found most intriguing about the story. For example, consider these questions:

- Were you eager to know how the story would turn out?
- What was the inciting incident? Did it seem sufficient to motivate the climax?
- Was there a clear conflict that seemed important enough to write about?

Clarify the sequence of actions.

Excerpts from the reading selections in this chapter demonstrate how writers clarify when different actions occur in relation to each other. Try using some of these strategies to help your readers keep track of what happened when.

Manage **tenses** *to show the sequence of actions occurring over time.* You can use the simple past tense (*was, felt*) to depict an action and use other tenses (*remember, accompany, had been*) to show what occurred before or after—or what is currently happening as the author writes.

Past tense Present tense Earlier past (past perfect)	I was a sophomore in high school in Mill Valley, Calif. I remember trotting up my apartment building's stairs, physically tired but buzzing with the frenetic energy and possibilities for change that accompany fall and a new school year. I'd been cautiously allowing myself to think during the walk home about a topic that felt frighteningly taboo. (Desmond-Harris, par. 1)

Use **time cues** *(such as* when, now, then, *and* as*) to help readers understand how one action relates to another in the time sequence:*

Both actions occur at the same time	As we all piled into the car, I knew. (Brandt, par. 1)
One action follows another	When I got back to the Snoopy section, I took one look at the lines . . . and knew I didn't want to wait. (Brandt, par. 3)

Refer to **calendar** *or* **clock time** *to establish when the event took place.*

On one weekday morning after Christmas (Dillard, par. 3)

For more on transitions of time, see Chapter 11.

Describe key people and places vividly, and show their significance.

The following excerpts show how the writers whose stories appear in this chapter use strategies like naming, detailing, comparing, selecting sensory details, and providing an overview of the setting to bring key people and places to life. Try using some of these strategies in your own writing to make people and places come alive.

- *Use* **naming** *and* **detailing** *to help readers visualize people and understand the roles they play in your story*. For example, identify people by name, occupation, or relationship to you; specify how they act, talk, look, and gesture:

  Mikey and Peter—polite blond boys who lived near me on Lloyd Street (Dillard, par. 4)

  My rainbow-striped tee and her white wifebeater capture a transition between our skater-inspired Salvation Army shopping phase and the next one. (Desmond-Harris, par. 7)

- *Add* **comparisons** *to convey what's distinctive about the person and to help create a dominant impression:*

  This sainted, skinny, furious redheaded man (Dillard, par. 21)

  Who knew that the East Coast–West Coast war had two earnest soldiers in flannel pajamas, lying on a king-size bed decorated with pink toe shoes that dangled from one of its posts? (Desmond-Harris, par. 5)

- *Specify* **sensory details**—*size, shape, color, sounds, textures, smells, tastes—of key features of the scene that contribute to the dominant impression you want to create:*

  Tupac was the literal sound track when our school's basketball team would come charging onto the court, and our ragtag group of cheerleaders kicked furiously to "Toss It Up" in a humid gymnasium. (Desmond-Harris, par. 11)

- *Give readers an* **overview** *of the place, or take them on a* **tour** *of it:*

  We ran across Edgerton to an alley and up our own sliding woodpile to the Halls' front yard; he kept coming. We ran up Lloyd Street and wound through mazy backyards toward the steep hilltop at Willard and Lang. (Dillard, par. 12)

- *Weave* **active, specific verbs** *and* **vivid descriptive details** *into your action sequences:*

  I whirled around to find a middle-aged man, dressed in street clothes, flashing some type of badge. (Brandt, par. 6)

  I had just embarked on the iceball project when we heard tire chains come clanking from afar. (Dillard, par. 7)

- *Consider scanning, uploading, or attaching a* **photograph** *or* **video** *to help readers picture people and places*. Make sure you introduce it or use a caption to demonstrate its relevance.

  A snapshot taken that Monday on our high school's front lawn (seen here) shows the two of us lying side by side. (Desmond-Harris, par. 6)

Use dialogue to portray people and dramatize relationships.

Dialogue—in the form of quotation, paraphrase, or summary—can give readers a vivid impression of the people and their relationships while also enhancing the drama. The following excerpts may give you ideas about how you might use dialogue in your own story.

- *Insert a* **quotation** *to dramatize a key moment or characterize a relationship:*

  I was too ashamed to tell my mother the truth, but I had no choice.

  "Jean, where are you?"

  "I'm, umm, in jail." (Brandt, pars. 26–28)

- *Use* **summary** *to emphasize thoughts, feelings, or actions or simply to move the story along:*

  As we crossed the threshold, I heaved a sigh of relief. I was home free. I thought about how sly I had been and I felt proud of my accomplishment.

  An unexpected tap on my shoulder startled me. I whirled around to find a middle-aged man . . . politely asking me to empty my pockets. (Brandt, pars. 5–6)

- *Use* **speaker tags** *to identify each speaker and intersperse remembered thoughts:*

  "Did we really do that?" I asked Thea this week. I wanted to ensure that this story, which people who know me now find hilarious, hadn't morphed into some sort of personal urban legend over the past 15 years. "Yes," she said. "We put them in a lovely tin." (Desmond-Harris, par. 4)

To learn more about quoting, paraphrasing, and summarizing, see Chapter 15.

Clarify your story's significance.

Try using some of these strategies to refine your understanding and presentation of the event's significance. Some of these sentences may make their way into your story; others may simply help you understand your reactions, so you can depict the event's significance more clearly.

WAYS IN

HOW CAN I HELP MY READERS UNDERSTAND THE SIGNIFICANCE OF MY STORY?

Reexamine the UNDERLYING CONFLICT *to determine what your story is really about.*

▸ I was confused, torn between ________ and ________.

EXAMPLE Did we feel a real stake in the life of this "hard-core" gangsta rapper, and a real loss in his death? We did, even though we were . . . in a privileged community. Even though . . . we'd been so delicately cared for, nurtured and protected from any of life's hard edges—with special efforts made to shield us from those involving race—that we sometimes felt ready to explode with boredom. Or maybe because of all that. (Desmond-Harris, par. 8)

Consider whether you now have INSIGHT *into your motivation that you did not have at the time or whether you feel just as bewildered today as you did then.*

▸ I still don't understand why I ________.

EXAMPLE "I just did it. I can't explain why." (Brandt, par. 34)

- How could ________? I now think ________.

EXAMPLE What precisely could he have done to prolong the drama of the chase and cap its glory? I brooded about this for the next few years. . . . He could only chew us out there . . . , after months or years of exalting pursuit. (Dillard, par. 20)

Examine any **INCONSISTENCIES** *or* **AMBIVALENCE** *in the language you used to tell the story or to describe people and places.* These apparent contradictions may lead you to a deeper understanding of why the event continues to be so fraught for you.

- Why did ________?

EXAMPLE But how could the glory have lasted forever? We could have run through every backyard in North America until we got to Panama. But when he trapped us at the lip of the Panama Canal, what precisely could he have done to prolong the drama of the chase and cap its glory? I brooded about this for the next few years. He could only have fried Mikey Fahey and me in boiling oil, say, or dismembered us piecemeal, or staked us to anthills. (Dillard, par. 20)

Recall your **REMEMBERED FEELINGS** and **THOUGHTS** *from when the event occurred.*

- Before / during / after the event, I felt ________. I showed or expressed these feelings by ________.

EXAMPLE I could still distinctly hear the disappointment and hurt in my mother's voice. I cried. . . . I felt like a terrible human being. (Brandt, par. 36)

Explore your **PRESENT PERSPECTIVE**, *what you think and feel now as you look back.*

- I realize now that my feelings have not changed. I still ________.
- Looking back at the event, I realize I was probably trying to ________, though I didn't appreciate that fact at the time.

EXAMPLE Did we take ourselves seriously? . . . We did . . . even though we'd been so delicately cared for, nurtured and protected from any of life's hard edges—with special efforts made to shield us from those involving race—that we sometimes felt ready to explode with boredom. Or maybe because of all that. (Desmond-Harris, par. 8)

Reconsider your **PURPOSE** *and* **AUDIENCE** *in light of your developing understanding of the event's significance.* Determine what you want your readers to think and feel after reading your story.

- When my readers finish the story, I want them to better appreciate ________.
- The point was that ________.

EXAMPLE The point was that he had chased us passionately without giving up, and so he had caught us. Now he came down to earth. I wanted the glory to last forever. (Dillard, par. 19)

Write the opening sentences.

Review what you have already written to see if you have something that would work to launch your story, or try out some of these opening strategies:

Begin with a **surprising statement**:

> I learned about Tupac's death when I got home from cheerleading practice that Friday afternoon in September 1996. (Desmond-Harris, par. 1)

Set the **scene**—*a specific time and place*—*and* **mood**:

> I knew it was going to be a fabulous day. . . . [We] were setting off for a day of last-minute Christmas shopping. (Brandt, par. 1)

Reflect on something from your past that provides **context** *for the event:*

> I got in trouble throwing snowballs, and have seldom been happier since. (Dillard, par. 2)

But don't agonize over the first sentences because you are likely to discover the best way to begin only after you have written a rough draft.

Draft your story.

By this point, you have done a lot of writing to

- develop a plan for a well-told story;
- come up with vivid details to help your readers imagine what happened;
- think of strategies for showing or telling the autobiographical significance of your event;
- try out a way to launch your story.

Now stitch that material together to create a draft. The next two parts of this Guide to Writing will help you evaluate and improve your draft.

Evaluating the Draft: Using Peer Review

Your instructor may arrange a peer review session in class or online, where you can exchange drafts with your classmates and give one another a thoughtful critical reading, pointing out what works well and suggesting ways to improve the draft. A good critical reading does three things:

1. It lets the writer know how clear, vivid, and meaningful the story seems to readers.
2. It praises what works best.
3. It indicates where the draft could be improved and makes suggestions on how to improve it.

One strategy for evaluating a draft is to use the basic features of remembered event essays as a guide.

A PEER REVIEW GUIDE

A Well-Told Story	How effectively does the writer tell the story? **Summarize:** Highlight the inciting incident and the climax of the story. **Praise:** Cite a passage where the storytelling is especially effective—for example, a place where the story seems to flow smoothly and maintain the reader's interest, or where narrative action is compelling or exciting. **Critique:** Tell the writer where the storytelling could be improved—for example, where the suspense slackens, the story lacks tension or conflict, or the chronology is confusing.
Vivid Description of People and Places	Do the descriptions help you imagine what happened? **Summarize:** Choose a passage of description and analyze how—and how well—it uses the describing strategies of naming, detailing, and comparing. **Praise:** Identify a description that is particularly vivid—for example, a graphic sensory description or an apt comparison that makes a person or place come alive. **Critique:** Tell the writer where the description could be improved—for example, where objects in the scene are not named or described with enough specific detail (colors, sounds, smells, textures), or where the description is sparse. Note any description that contradicts the dominant impression; this may suggest how the significance can be made more complex and interesting.
Autobiographical Significance	Is it clear why the event was important to the writer? **Summarize:** Briefly describe the story's dominant impression, and tell the writer why you think the event was significant. **Praise:** Give an example of where the significance comes across effectively—for example, where remembered feelings are expressed poignantly, where the present perspective seems insightful, or where the description creates a strong dominant impression that clarifies the significance. **Critique:** Tell the writer where the significance could be strengthened—for example, if the conflict is too easily resolved, if a moral seems tacked on at the end, or if more interesting meanings could be drawn out of the experience.

Before concluding your review, be sure to address any of the writer's concerns that have not already been addressed.

Improving the Draft: Revising, Editing, and Proofreading

Start improving your draft by reflecting on what you have written thus far:

- Review comments from your classmates, instructor, or writing center tutor. What are your readers getting at?
- Take another look at your notes and ideas. What else should you consider?
- Review your draft. What else can you do to make your story compelling?

Revise your draft.

If your readers are having difficulty with your draft, try some of the strategies listed in the Troubleshooting Guide that follows. They can help you fine-tune your presentation of the genre's basic features.

A TROUBLESHOOTING GUIDE

A Well-Told Story

My readers tell me that the story starts too slowly.

- Shorten the exposition, spread it out more within the story, or move it to a later part of the story.
- Move a bit of dialogue or narrative action up front.
- Start with something surprising but critical to the story.

My readers find the chronology confusing.

- Add or change time transitions.
- Look for inadvertent tense shifts and fix them.

My readers feel that the suspense slackens or that the story lacks drama.

- Add remembered feelings and thoughts to heighten anticipation.
- Add an action sequence to build to a climax or high point.
- Cut or shorten background exposition and unnecessary description.
- Build rising action in stages, with multiple high points.

My readers find the conflict vague or unconnected to the autobiographical significance.

- Think about the conflict's multiple and possibly contradictory meanings.
- Add remembered feelings or thoughts to suggest multiple meanings, and cut those that don't clarify the significance.
- Add your present perspective to make the significance clearer and to bring out the implications.
- Add dialogue or narrative action to clarify the conflict.

Vivid Description of People and Places

My readers feel that the people in the story don't come alive.

- Add details about distinctive physical features or mannerisms.
- Add speaker tags to the dialogue to characterize people and relationships.
- Read your dialogue aloud, and revise to make the language more natural and appropriate to the person.

My readers have trouble visualizing the places I describe.

- Name objects in the scene.
- Add sensory details (colors, sounds, smells, textures).
- Use a comparison—metaphor or simile—to evoke a particular mood or attitude.
- Add a visual—a photograph or other memorabilia.

My readers feel that some descriptions weaken the dominant impression.

- Omit unnecessary details.
- Add adjectives, similes, or metaphors to strengthen the dominant impression.
- Rethink the impression you want your writing to convey and the significance it suggests.

Autobiographical Significance

My readers do not identify or sympathize with me.

- Add background details or explain the context.
- Reveal the cultural influences acting on you, or emphasize the historical period in which the event occurred.
- Show readers how you have changed or were affected by the experience.

My readers don't understand the significance of the story.

- Use irony or humor to contrast your present perspective with your past behavior, feelings, or attitudes.
- Show that the event ended but that the conflict was not resolved.
- Use dialogue to show how your relationships with people in your story changed.
- Indicate how the event continues to influence your thoughts or actions.

(continued)

Autobiographical Significance

My readers think the significance seems too pat or simplistic.

- Develop contradictions or show ambivalence to enrich the implications.
- Use humor to comment ironically on your past behavior or current contradictory feelings.
- Stress the social or cultural dimensions of the event.
- Revise Hollywood-movie clichés, simple resolutions, or tagged-on morals.

Edit and proofread your draft.

Four problems commonly appear in essays about remembered events: misused words and expressions, dull word choices and flabby sentences, incorrectly punctuated or formatted dialogue, and misused past-perfect verbs. The following guidelines will help you check your essay for these common errors.

Using the Right Word or Expression

The Problem Many familiar sayings and expressions are frequently heard but not often seen in writing, so writers often mistake these expressions. Consider the following sentences:

> Chock it up to my upbringing, but having several children play butt naked around my feet certainly curved my appetite for parenthood.
>
> The deer was still jerking in its death throws, but for all intensive purposes it was dead.

Within those two sentences are five commonly mangled expressions. To the ear, they may sound right, but in each case the author has heard the expression incorrectly and written down the wrong words.

Note: The expressions should be *chalk it up, buck naked, curbed my appetite, death throes,* and *for all intents and purposes.*

The Correction You can find and debug these kinds of errors by following these steps:

1. Highlight or circle common expressions of two or more words in your writing project (especially those you've heard before but haven't seen in writing).
2. Check each expression in a dictionary or in a list of frequently misused words.
3. Consider revising the expression: If you have heard the expression so often that it "sounds right," it may be a cliché. A fresh expression will be more powerful.

Choosing Vivid Language and Cutting Flab

The Problem Early drafts often include vague or overly general word choices and flabby sentences. Cutting words that add little, making verbs active, and replacing weak word choices with stronger ones can greatly increase the power of a remembered event essay.

The Correction Taking the following three steps can help you tighten your language and make it more powerful:

1. Circle empty intensifiers, such as *just, very, certain,* and *really*. Now reread each sentence, omitting the circled word. If the sentence still makes sense without the word, delete it.
2. Circle all forms of the verb *to be* (such as *am, is, are, was,* and *were*). Now reread each sentence that includes a circled word, and ask yourself, could I revise the sentence or combine it with another sentence to create an active construction?

   ▶ The ^barking^ dog ~~was barking. He~~ took off after Jasper as he raced toward Third Avenue.

   ▶ ^Sarah double-knotted the rope^ ~~The rope was tied~~ around the oak in the front yard.

3. Review your descriptions, highlighting or underlining adjectives, adverbs, and prepositional phrases. Now reread them, imagining a more specific noun or verb that could convey the same idea in fewer words.

   ▶ ^A Humvee sped^ ~~A large, black truck moved quickly~~ across the parking lot.

Resolving Dialogue Issues

The Problem Remembered event essays often include dialogue, but writers sometimes have trouble using the conventions of dialogue correctly. One common problem occurs with punctuation marks:

- In American English, the opening quotation mark hugs the first word of the quotation. Periods and commas belong inside the closing quotation mark, but other end punctuation can go inside or outside the closing quotation mark, depending on whether the punctuation belongs to the quotation or to the end of the sentence.
- Speaker tags reflect what the speaker was thinking, feeling, or doing.
- A new paragraph is typically used to indicate a change in speaker.

The Correction Revise the punctuation, add speaker tags, or start a new paragraph as needed:

▶ "Jean, what's going on^?^"~~?~~ my sister ^asked^ ~~questioned~~.

▶ A few seconds later, my sister appeared and asked, "So^,^ did you decide to buy the button?"^¶^"No, I guess not."

Using the Past Perfect

The Problem Remembered event essays often mention events that occurred before the main action. To convey this sequence of events, writers use the past-perfect tense rather than the simple past tense:

Past Perfect	**Simple Past**
had traveled	traveled
had been	was
had begun	began

Failing to use the past perfect when it is needed can make your meaning unclear. (What happened when, exactly?)

The Correction Check places where you recount events to verify that you are using the past perfect to indicate actions that had already been completed at the time of another past action (she *had finished* her work when we saw her).

▸ I had three people in the car, something my father ^*had* told me not to do that very morning.

▸ Coach Kernow told me I ~~ran~~ ^*had run* faster than ever before.

Note for Multilingual Writers It is important to remember that the past perfect is formed with *had* followed by a past participle. Past participles usually end in *-ed, -d, -en, -n,* or *-t*—*worked, hoped*—although some are irregular (*eaten, taken, bent, begun, chosen*).

▸ Before Tania went to Moscow last year, she had not really ~~speak~~ ^*spoken* Russian.

Reflecting on What You Have Learned

You have learned a great deal about this genre from reading several autobiographical stories and writing one of your own. To consolidate your learning, reflect not only on what you learned but also on how you learned it.

ANALYZE & WRITE

Write a blog post, a letter to your instructor or a classmate, or an e-mail message to a student who will take this course next term, using the writing prompt that seems most productive for you:

- Explain how what you wanted your readers to learn about you from reading your story influenced one of your decisions as a writer, such as how you used the dramatic arc to shape your story around a conflict, how you used dialogue to intensify the drama and convey the significance, or how you integrated your remembered thoughts and feelings into your storytelling.
- Discuss what you learned about yourself as a writer in the process of writing this essay. For example, what part of the process did you find most challenging? Did you try anything new, like getting a critical reading of your draft or outlining your draft in order to revise it? If so, how well did it work?
- If you were to give advice to a fellow student who was about to write a remembered event essay, what would you say?

- Which of the readings (in this chapter or elsewhere) influenced either your choice of an event to write about or how you told the story? Explain the influence, citing specific examples comparing the two.
- If you got good advice from a critical reader, explain exactly how the person helped you—perhaps by questioning the conflict in a way that enabled you to develop your story's significance, or by pointing out passages that needed clearer time markers to better orient readers.

3

Writing Profiles

What happens behind the scenes at a mortuary? What happens when kids visit their moms in prison? These questions are explored in the entertaining and thought-provoking profiles in this chapter. Profiles are mini-documentaries, like the podcasts and shows created by the producers of *Radiolab* and *This American Life*. They take us behind the scenes through slice-of-life portraits. As cultural ethnography, profiles range from a day-in-the-life to a longer immersion study of people at work or at play. Intensively researched, they rely primarily on *field research* techniques of observation and interview to provide what is sometimes called *thick description,* because the information is interwoven with the profiler's analysis and interpretation—what we call **perspective**—to capture and convey a full experience.

People compose profiles for various purposes and audiences and publish them in a variety of media (print, digital, audiovisual). For example, a college student studying management might observe and interview a work group's collaborators, then post her profile on the class Web site. A participant in the restoration of a Depression-era mural might construct a multimedia profile of the community effort for the city's Web site to celebrate the project. A security officer might develop a Prezi presentation profiling a number of shoplifters apprehended over the last year to educate sales staff about shoplifting.

In this chapter, we ask you to compose a profile based primarily on your firsthand field research—observational visits and interviews. Whether you choose something you know well or something you want to learn about, you will need to focus on it as if for the first time and choose details that will not only make it come alive for your readers but also show them why your subject is intriguing and important. From reading and analyzing the selections in the Guide to Reading that follows, you will learn how to weave information and insight to construct a rich tapestry that entertains as it informs. The Guide to Writing (pp. 72–94) will show you ways to use the basic features of the genre to depict your subject clearly and compellingly from a perspective that will allow you to inform and entertain your readers while also conveying your subject's cultural, social, or personal significance.

PRACTICING THE GENRE

Conducting an Interview

Part 1. Get together in a small group to practice interviewing, a crucial skill for composing profiles. First, ask for a volunteer from the group to act as the interviewee. It should be someone knowledgeable about a subject that is relatively unfamiliar to the other group members, such as a sport, hobby, type of music, video game, profession, or academic subject. The rest of the group should take a couple of minutes to make a list of questions about the subject. Then have one person serve as the interviewer (or take turns asking questions). Listen to what is being said, and respond with follow-up questions as needed. Take notes not only on what is said (quoting or summarizing) but also on the way it is said. For example, does the interviewee appear to be bored or animated, authoritative or uncertain?

Part 2. Discuss what you learned about profiles and about conducting an interview:

- **What did you learn about how profiles can make information interesting?** For a profile to be effective, it must depict the subject vividly and be thought-provoking. Take turns identifying one thing the interviewee said—for example, an illuminating fact, an amusing anecdote, or a surprising judgment—that would be likely to engage the interest of an audience.
- **What did you learn about conducting an interview?** With the other members of your group, compare your thoughts about what was easiest and hardest—for example, preparing questions, listening and following up, taking notes, or considering what might be interesting to an audience.

Analyzing Profiles

As you read the selections in this chapter, you will see how different authors create a compelling profile.

- Brian Cable anxiously visits a mortuary and ends up in the embalming room (pp. 51–57).
- Amanda Coyne captures Mother's Day in a women's prison (pp. 58–62).
- Gabriel Thompson goes undercover to learn about harvesting lettuce firsthand (pp. 65–68).

Analyzing how these writers organize and present the information they gathered from firsthand observations, interviews, and background research; adopting a role as spectator or participant-observer; and conveying a thought-provoking perspective on the subject will help you see how you can employ these same techniques when composing your own observational profile.

Determine the writer's purpose and audience.

Researching a profile gives writers a great deal of information about their subject, enabling them to impart their special perspective or insight into its cultural significance. Profilers seek to enlighten and entertain their audience, creating a fascinating—and occasionally disconcerting—portrait of other people at work or at play. When reading the profiles that follow, ask yourself questions like these:

What seems to be the writer's main purpose?

- To inform readers about some aspect of everyday life that they rarely get to experience intimately?
- To give readers a behind-the-scenes look at an intriguing or unusual activity?
- To surprise readers by presenting familiar subjects in unexpected ways?
- To bridge the distance between outsiders' preconceptions and others' experience?

What does the writer assume about the audience?

- That readers know nothing or very little about the subject?
- That their expectations will be challenged?
- That their interest will be piqued?
- That they will be intrigued by the writer's ideas or what people do or say?

Basic Features

Specific Information

A Clear, Logical Organization

Writer's Role

A Perspective on the Subject

Assess the genre's basic features.

As you read the profiles in this chapter, analyze and evaluate how profile writers employ the genre's basic features. The examples that follow are drawn from the reading selections that appear later in this Guide to Reading.

SPECIFIC INFORMATION ABOUT THE SUBJECT

Read first to learn about the subject. Much of the pleasure of reading a profile comes from the way the profile interweaves bits of information and insight into a rich tapestry of lively narrative, arresting quotations, and vivid descriptions.

Notice the describing strategies of **naming**, **detailing**, *and* **comparing**. These strategies help readers visualize places and people and create a dominant impression:

Naming Detailing Comparing	We passed into a bright, fluorescent-lit "display room." Inside were thirty coffins. . . . Like new cars on the showroom floor, they gleamed. (Cable, par. 18)

In this example, using the detail *fluorescent-lit* helps clarify what Cable means by *bright* and also reinforces the simile comparing the coffins on display to cars in a showroom.

Think about the different kinds *of information, or* **topics**, *the writer touches on.* In profiling a mortuary, for example, Cable identifies different jobs (funeral director and mortician), explaining the training people undergo and the tasks they perform, and also presents facts about the cost of funerals and ideas about cultural attitudes toward death.

Consider the sources of the information and how the information is presented. Some of the information comes from the writer's firsthand observation, but much of it comes from interviews and background research. To present this information, profile writers rely on three basic strategies—quotation, paraphrase, and summary:

QUOTATION	"We're in *Ripley's Believe It or Not,* along with another funeral home whose owners' names are Baggit and Sackit," Howard told me, without cracking a smile. (Cable, par. 14)
PARAPHRASE	We ask one another where we are from, how long a drive we had. (Coyne, par. 3)
SUMMARY	I came across several articles describing the causes of a farmworker shortage. The stories cited an aging workforce, immigration crackdowns, and long delays at the border that discourage workers with green cards. (Thompson, par. 5)

Profiles in academic contexts—for class and scholarly publication—are expected to cite their sources formally (see, for example, Cable's use of parenthetical citation and a works-cited list), but general-interest publications seldom include documentation beyond links to other Web pages. Ask your instructor whether you should cite your sources and, if so, what academic style you should follow.

See Chapters 16 and 17 to learn about the conventions for citing and documenting sources in two popular academic styles.

A CLEAR, LOGICAL ORGANIZATION

Determine whether the profile's basic organizational plan is **narrative**, *as a story occurring over time;* **spatial**, *as a guided tour of a place; or* **topical**, *as bits of information organized into categories.* Look for cues like these that help orient readers.

Narrative Cues

CALENDAR AND CLOCK TIME	On my first day (Thompson, par. 6) It's now 3:00. Visiting ends at 3:30. (Coyne, par. 19)
ACTION VERBS	I bend over, noticing that most of the crew has turned to watch. (Thompson, par. 8) She grabs the hand and he swats with the other. Eventually, she pulls him toward her and smells the top of his head, and she picks up the cards or the toy herself. (Coyne, par. 13)
TRANSITIONS OF TIME	While the other adults (Coyne, par. 2) First, I'm handed . . . Next comes the *gancho.* (Thompson, par. 6)

Spatial Cues

PREPOSITIONAL PHRASES	The main lobby, adjacent to the reception room (Cable, par. 5) We are standing in front of the double glass doors that lead to the outside world. (Coyne, par. 20)
DIRECTIONS	Here in the visiting room (Coyne, par. 1) To my left, in the distance . . . To my right (Thompson, par. 1)
LOCATIONS	Visiting his mother in prisons in Kentucky, Texas, Connecticut (the Pit of Fire) (Coyne, par. 12)

Topical Cues or Logical Transitions

SEQUENCE	In addition, the burial site (Cable, par. 24) Once, after being given this weak explanation . . . (Coyne, par. 18)
EMPHASIS	Even, or especially, if that world is a female federal prison camp. (Coyne, par. 4)
CONTRADICTION	But thinking about the next seven weeks doesn't benefit anyone. (Thompson, par. 2) On the contrary, his bitterness (Coyne, par. 13)
CAUSE	Because of their difference (Coyne, par. 11)
CONCLUSION	So I am to be very careful and precise (Thompson, par. 12)
SPECULATION	Perhaps such an air of comfort makes it easier for the family to give up their loved one. (Cable, par. 24)

Also notice whether the writer uses a different organizational pattern in particular passages. For example, Cable's profile of a mortuary follows a spatial plan overall, beginning with him outside the building and moving first into the reception room and lobby, then into a chapel, followed by the display room, and finally the embalming room. But much of the information within this general structure is presented topically; for example, he uses his position in the display room to relate information about caskets—what they are made of, their price range, the increasing cost of funerals, and so on.

To learn more about cueing the reader, see Chapter 11.

THE WRITER'S ROLE

Think about the role the writer assumes in relation to the subject:

- As a **spectator**, the writer takes a position, like that of the reader, looking in on the people and their activities. Although profile writers sometimes refer to themselves using the first-person pronoun "I" to place themselves in the scene and tell us what they are thinking, they often maintain the role of a detached observer:

  I found the funeral director in the main lobby, adjacent to the reception room. Like most people, I had preconceptions about what an undertaker looked like. Mr. Deaver fulfilled my expectations entirely. Tall and thin, he even had beady eyes and a bony face. . . . Indeed, he looked like death on two legs. (Cable, par. 5)

- As a **participant-observer**, the writer participates in the activity being profiled in order to acquire insider knowledge. Participant-observers rely on the first-person pronoun "I" to place themselves in the scene and tell us what they are doing there, as this example from Thompson's investigative profile of his work as a lettuce picker illustrates:

  I stand up gingerly. It's only my third day in the fields, but already my 30-year-old body is failing me. (par. 2)

A PERSPECTIVE ON THE SUBJECT

Think about the writer's **perspective** *on the subject.* What is the main idea or cultural significance of the profile? To understand the writer's perspective, it might help to also consider the writer's main purpose; the audience to whom the profile was originally addressed; as well as where, when, and how (in what medium) it was published. *Identify any passages where the perspective is communicated to readers*

- by **telling**—saying explicitly what the writer thinks about the subject:

  Death may be the great leveler, but one's coffin quickly reestablishes one's status. (Cable, par. 17)

- by **showing**—creating a dominant impression through description and narration:

  The mothers take deep whiffs from the backs of their children's necks. . . . They hold them tight and take in their own second scent—the scent assuring them that these are still their children and that they still belong to them. (Coyne, par. 2)

Readings

Brian Cable | *The Last Stop*

This profile of a neighborhood mortuary was originally written when Brian Cable was a first-year college student. "Death," as he explains in the opening sentence, "is a subject largely ignored by the living," so it is not surprising that he notices people averting their eyes as they walk past the mortuary on a busy commercial street. Cable, however, walks in and takes readers on a guided tour of the premises. As he presents information he learned from observing how the mortuary works—from the reception room up front to the embalming room in back—and from interviewing the people who work there, Cable invites us to reflect on our own feelings and cultural attitudes toward death.

As you read,

- notice how Cable uses humor to defuse the inherent seriousness of his subject;
- consider the significance of the quotation from Mark Twain with which Cable opens his profile;
- answer the questions in the margin; your instructor may ask you to post your answers to a class blog or discussion board or to bring them to class.

Basic Features
Specific Information
A Clear, Logical Organization
Writer's Role
A Perspective on the Subject

Let us endeavor so to live that when we come to die even the undertaker will be sorry.

— Mark Twain, *Pudd'nhead Wilson*

1 Death is a subject largely ignored by the living. We don't discuss it much, not as children (when Grandpa dies, he is said to be "going away"), not as adults, not even as senior citizens. Throughout our lives, death remains intensely private. The death of a loved one can be very painful, partly because of the sense of loss, but also because someone else's mortality reminds us all too vividly of our own.

2 More than a few people avert their eyes as they walk past the dusty-tan building that houses the Goodbody Mortuary. It looks a bit like a church—tall, with gothic arches and stained glass. In the back, it looked somewhat like an apartment complex—low, with many windows stamped out of red brick. (See fig. 1.)

Cable tells us what he expected. How does the opening — including the title and epigraph (introductory quote) — influence what you expect from his profile?

3 It wasn't at all what I had expected. I thought it would be more like Forest Lawn, serene with lush green lawns and meticulously groomed gardens, a place set apart from the hustle of day-to-day life. Here instead was an odd tan structure set in the middle of a business district.

What organizational plan for the profile emerges in pars. 4 and 5?

4 I was apprehensive as I climbed the stone steps to the entrance. I feared rejection or, worse, an invitation to come and stay. The door was massive, yet it swung open easily on well-oiled hinges. "Come in," said the sign. "We're always open." Inside was a cool and quiet reception room. Curtains were drawn against the outside glare, cutting the light down to a soft glow.

Justin Cressy

Fig. 1. The Goodbody Mortuary

5 I found the funeral director in the main lobby, adjacent to the reception room. Like most people, I had preconceptions about what an undertaker looked like. Mr. Deaver fulfilled my expectations entirely. Tall and thin, he even had beady eyes and a bony face. A low, slanted forehead gave way to a beaked nose. His skin, scrubbed of all color, contrasted sharply with his jet black hair. He was wearing a starched white shirt, gray pants, and black shoes. Indeed, he looked like death on two legs.

What does the detailed description of Deaver in pars. 5 and 6 contribute to Cable's profile of the mortuary?

6 He proved an amiable sort, however, and was easy to talk to. As funeral director, Mr. Deaver ("Call me Howard") was responsible for a wide range of services. Goodbody Mortuary, upon notification of someone's death, will remove the remains from the hospital or home. They then prepare the body for viewing, whereupon features distorted by illness or accident are restored to their natural condition. The body is embalmed and then placed in a casket selected by the family of the deceased. Services are held in one of three chapels at the mortuary, and afterward the casket is placed in a "visitation room," where family and friends can pay their last respects. Goodbody also makes

What role has Cable adopted in writing the profile? When does it become clear?

Why do you think Cable summarizes the information in par. 6 instead of quoting Howard?

arrangements for the purchase of a burial site and transports the body there for burial.

7 All this information Howard related in a well-practiced, professional manner. It was obvious he was used to explaining the specifics of his profession. We sat alone in the lobby. His desk was bone clean, no pencils or paper, nothing—just a telephone. He did all his paperwork at home; as it turned out, he and his wife lived right upstairs. The phone rang. As he listened, he bit his lips and squeezed his Adam's apple somewhat nervously.

8 "I think we'll be able to get him in by Friday. No, no, the family wants him cremated."

What does this observation reveal about Cable's perspective?

9 His tone was that of a broker conferring on the Dow Jones. Directly behind him was a sign announcing "Visa and MasterCard Welcome Here." It was tacked to the wall, right next to a crucifix.

Why do you think Cable quotes Howard in par. 10 instead of paraphrasing or summarizing?

10 "Some people have the idea that we are bereavement specialists, that we can handle emotional problems which follow a death: Only a trained therapist can do that. We provide services for the dead, not counseling for the living."

What does this observation contribute to the dominant impression?

11 Physical comfort was the one thing they did provide for the living. The lobby was modestly but comfortably furnished. There were several couches, in colors ranging from earth brown to pastel blue, and a coffee table in front of each one. On one table lay some magazines and a vase of flowers. Another supported an aquarium. Paintings of pastoral scenes hung on every wall. The lobby looked more or less like that of an old hotel. Nothing seemed to match, but it had a homey, lived-in look.

12 "The last time the Goodbodys decorated was in '99, I believe. It still makes people feel welcome."

13 And so "Goodbody" was not a name made up to attract customers but the owner's family name. The Goodbody family started the business way back in 1915. Today, they do over five hundred services a year.

14 "We're in *Ripley's Believe It or Not*, along with another funeral home whose owners' names are Baggit and Sackit," Howard told me, without cracking a smile.

How does Cable make the transition from topic to topic in pars. 15–18?

15 I followed him through an arched doorway into a chapel that smelled musty and old. The only illumination came from sunlight filtered through a stained glass ceiling. Ahead of us lay a casket. I could see that it contained a man dressed in a black suit. Wooden benches ran on either side of an aisle

that led to the body. I got no closer. From the red roses across the dead man's chest, it was apparent that services had already been held.

16 "It was a large service," remarked Howard. "Look at that casket—a beautiful work of craftsmanship."

17 I guess it was. Death may be the great leveler, but one's coffin quickly reestablishes one's status.

18 We passed into a bright, fluorescent-lit "display room." Inside were thirty coffins, lids open, patiently awaiting inspection. Like new cars on the showroom floor, they gleamed with high-gloss finishes.

What does the comparison to a new-car showroom in pars. 18–21 reveal about Cable's perspective?

19 "We have models for every price range."

20 Indeed, there was a wide variety. They came in all colors and various materials. Some were little more than cloth-covered cardboard boxes, others were made of wood, and a few were made of steel, copper, or bronze. Howard told me prices started at $500 and averaged about $2,400. He motioned toward the center of the room: "The top of the line."

21 This was a solid bronze casket, its seams electronically welded to resist corrosion. Moisture-proof and air-tight, it could be hermetically sealed off from all outside elements. Its handles were plated with 14-karat gold. The Promethean casket made by the Batesville Casket Company is the choice of celebrities and the very wealthy. (See fig. 2.) The price: a cool $25,000–$30,000 (Russell).

22 A proper funeral remains a measure of respect for the deceased. But it is expensive. In the United States, the amount spent annually on funerals

Where does the information in pars. 22–23 come from? How can you tell?

REUTERS/Mario Anzuoni/Landov

Fig. 2. "The top of the line." The Promethean casket that Michael Jackson was buried in

is around $12 billion (Grassley), with the average price about $7,000 ("NFDA Releases")—not counting the burial plot. Among ceremonial expenditures, funerals are second only to weddings. As a result, practices are changing. Howard has been in this business for forty years. He remembers a time when everyone was buried. Nowadays, with burials costing more than $7,000 a shot (Grassley), people often opt instead for cremation—as Howard put it, "a cheap, quick, and easy means of disposal." In some areas of the country, according to Howard, the cremation rate is now over 60 percent. Observing this trend, one might wonder whether burials are becoming obsolete. Do burials serve an important role in society?

Why do you think Cable uses a rhetorical question here?

23 For Tim, Goodbody's licensed mortician, the answer is very definitely yes. Burials will remain in common practice, according to the slender embalmer with the disarming smile, because they allow family and friends to view the deceased. Painful as it may be, such an experience brings home the finality of death. "Something deep within us demands a confrontation with death," Tim explained. "A last look assures us that the person we loved is, indeed, gone forever."

Whose perspective does this statement reflect? How do you know?

24 Apparently, we also need to be assured that the body will be laid to rest in comfort and peace. The average casket, with its innerspring mattress and pleated satin lining, is surprisingly roomy and luxurious. Perhaps such an air of comfort makes it easier for the family to give up their loved one. In addition, the burial site fixes the deceased in the survivors' memory, like a new address. Cremation provides none of these comforts.

Is Tim's definition of mortuary science helpful? Why or why not?

25 Tim started out as a clerk in a funeral home but then studied to become a mortician. "It was a profession I could live with," he told me with a sly grin. Mortuary science might be described as a cross between pre-med and cosmetology, with courses in anatomy and embalming as well as in restorative art.

Which information in par. 26 comes from observation and which comes from interviewing Tim? How do you know?

26 Tim let me see the preparation, or embalming, room, a white-walled chamber about the size of an operating room. Against the wall was a large sink with elbow taps and a draining board. In the center of the room stood a table with equipment for preparing the arterial embalming fluid, which consists primarily of formaldehyde, a preservative, and phenol, a disinfectant. This mixture sanitizes and also gives better color to the

skin. Facial features can then be "set" to achieve a restful expression. Missing eyes, ears, and even noses can be replaced.

27 I asked Tim if his job ever depressed him. He bridled at the question: "No, it doesn't depress me at all. I do what I can for people and take satisfaction in enabling relatives to see their loved ones as they were in life." He said that he felt people were becoming more aware of the public service his profession provides. Grade-school classes now visit funeral homes as often as they do police stations and museums. The mortician is no longer regarded as a minister of death.

28 Before leaving, I wanted to see a body up close. I thought I could be indifferent after all I had seen and heard, but I wasn't sure. Cautiously, I reached out and touched the skin. It felt cold and firm, not unlike clay. As I walked out, I felt glad to have satisfied my curiosity about dead bodies, but all too happy to let someone else handle them.

How effective is this ending?

Works Cited

Grassley, Chuck. Opening remarks. *Joint Hearing on Pension Tension: Does the Pension Benefit Guaranty Corporation Deliver for Retirees,* United States, Senate, Special Committee on Aging and the Committee on Small Business, Government Printing Office, 21 Sept. 2000, www.aging.senate.gov/imo/media/doc/publications/9212000.pdf. 106th Congress, 2nd session, Senate Hearing 106-38.

"NFDA Releases Results of Member General Price List Survey." *National Funeral Directors Association,* 1 Aug. 2013, nfda.org/news-a-events/all-press-releases/3719-nfda-releases-results-of-member-general-price-list-survey.html.

Russell, John. "Batesville Casket Is Coy about Starring Role in Jackson Funeral." *ABC News,* 9 July 2009, abcnews.go.com/Business/story?id=8042342.

Twain, Mark. *Pudd'nhead Wilson.* Pocket Books, 2004, p. 45.

Amanda Coyne

The Long Good-Bye: Mother's Day in Federal Prison

Courtesy of Amanda Coyne

AMANDA COYNE earned a master of fine arts degree in creative writing at the University of Iowa, where she was the recipient of an Iowa Arts Fellowship. She was the cofounder of and a writer for the *Alaska Dispatch*, an award-winning online news site. Her work has appeared in publications such as *Harper's*, the *New York Times Magazine*, *Bust*, *Newsweek*, and the *Guardian*. Coyne coauthored a book about oil and politics in Alaska entitled *Crude Awakening: Money, Mavericks, and Mayhem in Alaska* (2011). She also started a blog about Alaska politics in 2013.

"The Long Good-Bye," her first piece of published writing, originally appeared in *Harper's*. Coyne uses direct observation and interview to study the behavior of a particular community. In this profile, Coyne examines women who have been incarcerated and separated from their children to see how the mothers and children negotiate their difficult relationships.

As you read, consider the following questions:

- What stresses seem to affect the family relationships described in this profile?
- What do you think is the author's attitude toward these stresses? How can you tell what she thinks and feels?

1 You can spot the convict-moms here in the visiting room by the way they hold and touch their children and by the single flower that is perched in front of them—a rose, a tulip, a daffodil. Many of these mothers have untied the bow that attaches the flower to its silver-and-red cellophane wrapper and are using one of the many empty soda cans at hand as a vase. They sit proudly before their flower-in-a-Coke-can, amid Hershey bar wrappers, half-eaten Ding Dongs, and empty paper coffee cups. Occasionally, a mother will pick up her present and bring it to her nose when one of the bearers of the single flower—her child—asks if she likes it. And the mother will respond the way that mothers always have and always will respond when presented with a gift on this day. "Oh, I just love it. It's perfect. I'll put it in the middle of my Bible." Or, "I'll put it on my desk, right next to your school picture." And always: "It's the best one here."

2 But most of what is being smelled today is the children themselves. While the other adults are plunking coins into the vending machines, the mothers take deep whiffs from the backs of their children's necks, or kiss and smell the backs of their knees, or take off their shoes and tickle their feet and then pull them close to their noses. They hold them tight and take in their own second scent—the scent assuring them that these are still their children and that they still belong to them.

3 The visitors are allowed to bring in pockets full of coins, and today that Mother's Day flower, and I know from previous visits to my older sister here at the Federal Prison Camp for women in Pekin, Illinois, that there is always an aberrant urge to gather immediately around the vending machines. The sandwiches are stale, the coffee weak, the candy bars the ones we always pass up in a convenience store. But after we hand the children over to their mothers,

we gravitate toward those machines. Like milling in the kitchen at a party. We all do it, and nobody knows why. Polite conversation ensues around the microwave while the popcorn is popping and the processed-chicken sandwiches are being heated. We ask one another where we are from, how long a drive we had. An occasional whistle through the teeth, a shake of the head. "My, my, long way from home, huh?" "Staying at the Super 8 right up the road. Not a bad place." "Stayed at the Econo Lodge last time. Wasn't a good place at all." Never asking the questions we really want to ask: "What's she in for?" "How much time's she got left?" You never ask in the waiting room of a doctor's office either. Eventually, all of us—fathers, mothers, sisters, brothers, a few boyfriends, and very few husbands—return to the queen of the day, sitting at a fold-out table loaded with snacks, prepared for five or so hours of attempted normal conversation.

4 Most of the inmates are elaborately dressed, many in prison-crafted dresses and sweaters in bright blues and pinks. They wear meticulously applied makeup in corresponding hues, and their hair is replete with loops and curls—hair that only women with the time have the time for. Some of the better seamstresses have crocheted vests and purses to match their outfits. Although the world outside would never accuse these women of making haute-couture fashion statements, the fathers and the sons and the boyfriends and the very few husbands think they look beautiful, and they tell them so repeatedly. And I can imagine the hours spent preparing for this visit—hours of needles and hooks clicking over brightly colored yards of yarn. The hours of discussing, dissecting, and bragging about these visitors—especially the men. Hours spent in the other world behind the door where we're not allowed, sharing lipsticks and mascaras, and unraveling the occasional hair-tangled hot roller, and the brushing out and lifting and teasing . . . and the giggles that abruptly change into tears without warning—things that define any female-only world. Even, or especially, if that world is a female federal prison camp.

5 While my sister Jennifer is with her son in the playroom, an inmate's mother comes over to introduce herself to my younger sister, Charity, my brother, John, and me. She tells us about visiting her daughter in a higher-security prison before she was transferred here. The woman looks old and tired, and her shoulders sag under the weight of her recently acquired bitterness.

6 "Pit of fire," she says, shaking her head. "Like a pit of fire straight from hell. Never seen anything like it. Like something out of an old movie about prisons." Her voice is getting louder and she looks at each of us with pleading eyes. "My *daughter* was there. Don't even get me started on that place. Women die there."

7 John and Charity and I silently exchange glances.

8 "My daughter would come to the visiting room with a black eye and I'd think, 'All she did was sit in the car while her boyfriend ran into the house.' She didn't even touch the stuff. Never even handled it."

9 She continues to stare at us, each in turn. "Ten years. That boyfriend talked and he got three years. She didn't know anything. Had nothing to tell them. They gave her ten years. They called it conspiracy. Conspiracy? Aren't there real criminals out there?" She asks this with hands outstretched, waiting for an answer that none of us can give her.

10 The woman's daughter, the conspirator, is chasing her son through the maze of chairs and tables and through the other children. She's a twenty-four-year-old blonde, whom I'll call Stephanie, with Dorothy Hamill hair and matching dimples. She looks like any girl you might see in any shopping mall in middle America. She catches her

chocolate-brown son and tickles him, and they laugh and trip and fall together onto the floor and laugh harder.

11 Had it not been for that wait in the car, this scene would be taking place at home, in a duplex Stephanie would rent while trying to finish her two-year degree in dental hygiene or respiratory therapy at the local community college. The duplex would be spotless, with a blown-up picture of her and her son over the couch and ceramic unicorns and horses occupying the shelves of the entertainment center. She would make sure that her son went to school every day with stylishly floppy pants, scrubbed teeth, and a good breakfast in his belly. Because of their difference in skin color, there would be occasional tension—caused by the strange looks from strangers, teachers, other mothers, and the bullies on the playground, who would chant after they knocked him down, "Your Momma's white, your Momma's white." But if she were home, their weekends and evenings would be spent together transcending those looks and healing those bruises. Now, however, their time is spent eating visiting-room junk food and his school days are spent fighting the boys in the playground who chant, "Your Momma's in prison, your Momma's in prison."

12 He will be ten when his mother is released, the same age my nephew will be when his mother is let out. But Jennifer, my sister, was able to spend the first five years of Toby's life with him. Stephanie had Ellie after she was incarcerated. They let her hold him for eighteen hours, then sent her back to prison. She has done the "tour," and her son is a well-traveled six-year-old. He has spent weekends visiting his mother in prisons in Kentucky, Texas, Connecticut (the Pit of Fire), and now at last here, the camp—minimum security, Pekin, Illinois.

13 Ellie looks older than his age. But his shoulders do not droop like his grandmother's. On the contrary, his bitterness lifts them and his chin higher than a child's should be, and the childlike, wide-eyed curiosity has been replaced by defiance. You can see his emerging hostility as he and his mother play together. She tells him to pick up the toy that he threw, say, or to put the deck of cards away. His face turns sullen, but she persists. She takes him by the shoulders and looks him in the eye, and he uses one of his hands to swat at her. She grabs the hand and he swats with the other. Eventually, she pulls him toward her and smells the top of his head, and she picks up the cards or the toy herself. After all, it is Mother's Day and she sees him so rarely. But her acquiescence makes him angrier, and he stalks out of the playroom with his shoulders thrown back.

14 Toby, my brother and sister and I assure one another, will not have these resentments. He is better taken care of than most. He is living with relatives in Wisconsin. Good, solid, middle-class, churchgoing relatives. And when he visits us, his aunts and his uncle, we take him out for adventures where we walk down the alley of a city and pretend that we are being chased by the "bad guys." We buy him fast food, and his uncle, John, keeps him up well past his bedtime enthralling him with stories of the monkeys he met in India. A perfect mix, we try to convince one another. Until we take him to see his mother and on the drive back he asks the question that most confuses him, and no doubt all the other children who spend much of their lives in prison visiting rooms: "Is my Mommy a bad guy?" It is the question that most seriously disorders his five-year-old need to clearly separate right from wrong. And because our own need is perhaps just as great, it is the question that haunts us as well.

15 Now, however, the answer is relatively simple. In a few years, it won't be. In a few years we will have to explain mandatory minimums, and the war on drugs, and the murky conspiracy laws, and the enormous

amount of money and time that federal agents pump into imprisoning low-level drug dealers and those who happen to be their friends and their lovers. In a few years he might have the reasoning skills to ask why so many armed robbers and rapists and child-molesters and, indeed, murderers are punished less severely than his mother. When he is older, we will somehow have to explain to him the difference between federal crimes, which don't allow for parole, and state crimes, which do. We will have to explain that his mother was taken from him for five years not because she was a drug dealer but because she made four phone calls for someone she loved.

16 But we also know it is vitally important that we explain all this without betraying our bitterness. We understand the danger of abstract anger, of being disillusioned with your country, and, most of all, we do not want him to inherit that legacy. We would still like him to be raised as we were, with the idea that we live in the best country in the world with the best legal system in the world—a legal system carefully designed to be immune to political mood swings and public hysteria; a system that promises to fit the punishment to the crime. We want him to be a good citizen. We want him to have absolute faith that he lives in a fair country, a country that watches over and protects its most vulnerable citizens: its women and children.

17 So for now we simply say, "Toby, your mother isn't bad, she just did a bad thing. Like when you put rocks in the lawn mower's gas tank. You weren't bad then, you just did a bad thing."

18 Once, after being given this weak explanation, he said, "I wish I could have done something really bad, like my Mommy. So I could go to prison too and be with her."

19 It's now 3:00. Visiting ends at 3:30. The kids are getting cranky, and the adults are both exhausted and wired from too many hours of conversation, too much coffee and candy. The fathers, mothers, sisters, brothers, and the few boyfriends, and the very few husbands are beginning to show signs of gathering the trash. The mothers of the infants are giving their heads one last whiff before tucking them and their paraphernalia into their respective carrying cases. The visitors meander toward the door, leaving the older children with their mothers for one last word. But the mothers never say what they want to say to their children. They say things like, "Do well in school," "Be nice to your sister," "Be good for Aunt Berry, or Grandma." They don't say, "I'm sorry I'm sorry I'm sorry. I love you more than anything else in the world and I think about you every minute and I worry about you with a pain that shoots straight to my heart, a pain so great I think I will just burst when I think of you alone, without me. I'm sorry."

20 We are standing in front of the double glass doors that lead to the outside world. My older sister holds her son, rocking him gently. They are both crying. We give her a look and she puts him down. Charity and I grasp each of his small hands, and the four of us walk through the doors. As we're walking out, my brother sings one of his banana songs to Toby.

21 "Take me out to the—" and Toby yells out, "Banana store!"

22 "Buy me some —"

23 "Bananas!!"

24 "I don't care if I ever come back. For it's root, root, root for the—"

25 "Monkey team!"

26 I turn back and see a line of women standing behind the glass wall. Some of them are crying, but many simply stare with dazed eyes. Stephanie is holding both of her son's hands in hers and speaking urgently to him. He is struggling, and his head is twisting violently back and forth. He frees one of his hands from her grasp, balls up his fist, and punches her in the face. Then he walks with purpose through

the glass doors and out the exit. I look back at her. She is still in a crouched position. She stares, unblinking, through those doors. Her hands have left her face and are hanging on either side of her. I look away, but before I do, I see drops of blood drip from her nose, down her chin, and onto the shiny marble floor.

[REFLECT] Make connections: Unfair punishment.

Coyne reflects near the end of the essay that she wishes her nephew Toby would "have absolute faith that he lives in a fair country" (par. 16). Yet she expects that, like Stephanie's son, Ellie, Toby will become bitter and angry when he understands that "his mother was taken from him for five years not because she was a drug dealer but because she made four phone calls for someone she loved" (par. 15).

Think about an occasion when you were punished unfairly—for breaking a school rule, perhaps, or neglecting to fulfill an expectation of your parents. Although you willingly admit having done it, you may still feel that the punishment was unjustified. Consider what you did and why you think the punishment was unfair. Your instructor may ask you to post your thoughts on a class discussion board or to discuss them with other students in class. Use these questions to get started:

- Why do you think the punishment was unfair? For example, were the rules or expectations that you broke unclear or unreasonable? Were they applied to everyone or applied selectively or at the whim of those in power?
- Coyne uses the value term *unfair* to describe what's wrong with the punishment her sister and some of the other women received. Why do you think Coyne believes her sister's punishment is unfair? Why does Stephanie's mother think Stephanie's punishment was unfair? Do you agree or disagree?

[ANALYZE] Use the basic features.

SPECIFIC INFORMATION ABOUT THE SUBJECT: USING ANECDOTES

Including **anecdotes**—brief narratives about one-time events—can be a powerful way to convey detailed information about a subject. Coyne, for example, exposes the effects of separation on mothers and children through powerful anecdotes portraying what happened between Stephanie and her son, Ellie, during their visit.

ANALYZE & WRITE

Write a few paragraphs analyzing Coyne's use of anecdotes to present information:

1. Reread paragraphs 13 and 26, underlining the words that Coyne uses to present Ellie's actions and putting brackets around the words Coyne uses to present his mother's reactions.
2. What do you learn from these anecdotes about the effects on Stephanie and Ellie of enforced separation?

A CLEAR, LOGICAL ORGANIZATION: NARRATING A DAY IN THE LIFE

Coyne uses narrative as a kind of exoskeleton, a shell within which to hold the information and ideas she wants to present to her readers. The occasion is specific: visiting hours at the federal prison on Mother's Day. The opening paragraphs situate the profile in time and space, and the concluding paragraphs—signaled with the time marker "It's now 3:00. Visiting ends at 3:30" (par. 19)—recount what happened at the end of the visit. Within this narrative framework, however, Coyne does not follow a strict chronological order. Some events occur at the same time as other events. For example, paragraphs 1 to 3 present actions that occur at the same time: While mothers are getting reacquainted with their children (pars. 1 and 2), family members are using the vending machines and chatting with one another (par. 3).

ANALYZE & WRITE

Write a couple of paragraphs analyzing Coyne's use of narrative organization:

1. Reread the essay, noting in the margin when the events are happening in relation to the events in earlier paragraphs and highlighting any time markers, such as prepositional phrases locating actions in time, clock time, or verb tenses (past, present, future, and so on).
2. Coyne could have organized her essay topically, presenting a series of insights and impressions from the many visits she has made instead of focusing on one Mother's Day. How does her choice help you understand the situation of the women and their families?

THE WRITER'S ROLE: ACTING AS A PARTICIPANT-OBSERVER

As a participant-observer, Coyne is in a unique situation. Indeed, she was probably only able to gain access to the prison because her sister was an inmate. Having a personal relationship with the subject she is profiling, then, gives Coyne access. It also gives her familiarity, as this is not her first visit to the prison. In addition, it may also give her special insight into the personal and cultural aspects of the situation she is profiling. Writing about her own family, however, could lead Coyne to blur the distinction between the genres of observational profile and autobiography. This activity invites you to think about these two genres—both how they differ and how they may intersect or overlap.

ANALYZE & WRITE

Write a paragraph analyzing the genre mixing in "The Long Good-Bye":

1. Reread to find passages in which Coyne refers to her family and reflects on the significance of this Mother's Day visit. One of the distinguishing features of autobiography is that it attempts to shed light on complex, often ambivalent or conflicted feelings and relationships. How does "The Long Good-Bye" explore the writer's relationship with her sister and nephew?
2. Now think about "The Long Good-Bye" as an observational study, a kind of ethnography examining the culture of a community. What do you learn about the community of "convict-moms" (par. 1), as she calls them, and the challenges they face? How does Coyne shift readers' attention from her family to the broader community?

A PERSPECTIVE ON THE SUBJECT: USING CONTRAST

Unlike arguments supporting positions or justifying evaluations, which tell readers directly what the writer thinks and why, profiles often lead readers to draw a particular conclusion on their own, using strategies like comparing and contrasting. For example, Cable quotes the funeral director drawing a distinction between his job and that of a psychologist to clarify what a mortuary does and does not offer clients:

Contrast cue

> "We provide services for the dead, not counseling for the living." (par. 10)

Notice that he juxtaposes, or places side by side, the different professions.

Contrasts can also be used to foreground particular aspects of the subject. In this example, Cable uses contrast to call attention to the appearance and location of the mortuary, highlighting the difference between his expectations and the reality he finds:

Contrast cue

> I thought it would be more like Forest Lawn, serene with lush green lawns and meticulously groomed gardens, a place set apart from the hustle of day-to-day life. Here instead was an odd tan structure set in the middle of a business district. (par. 3)

ANALYZE & WRITE

Write a couple of paragraphs analyzing how Coyne uses contrast to convey her perspective:

1. Skim Coyne's profile, highlighting the cues or transitional words and phrases that indicate contrast. Analyze at least one of the contrasts you find. What is being contrasted? How does the contrast help you understand the writer's perspective?
2. Note in the margin which paragraphs focus on Coyne's sister Jennifer and her son, Toby, and which focus on Stephanie and her son, Ellie. Does Coyne juxtapose the two families or use cues to highlight the contrasts—or does she use both strategies? What differences between the two families does Coyne emphasize? Since contrasts tend to be worth pointing out when there are also important similarities, consider what similarities Coyne wants readers to think about.
3. Consider how Coyne uses contrast—between people, between the world of the prison and the world outside, and between what is and what could have been—to help convey her perspective on the plight of women like her sister and children like her nephew.

To learn more about transitions, see Chapter 11; transitions indicating a contrasting or opposing view are listed on p. 363.

[RESPOND] Consider possible topics: Profiling one instance of a recurring event.

Like Coyne, you could profile an activity occurring over a short period of time, in a relatively small space, involving only a few people. Consider, for example, profiling a team practicing, a musical group rehearsing, or researchers working together in a lab. Try to make more than one observational visit to see the group in action, and arrange to talk with people on every visit, perhaps capturing a few digital images to help you understand the group and possibly also to illustrate it.

Gabriel Thompson | *A Gringo in the Lettuce Fields*

Courtesy of Gabriel Thompson

GABRIEL THOMPSON has worked as a community organizer and written extensively about the lives of undocumented immigrants in the United States. His books include *There's No José Here: Following the Hidden Lives of Mexican Immigrants* (2006), *Calling All Radicals: How Grassroots Organizers Can Help Save Our Democracy* (2007), and *Working in the Shadows: A Year of Doing the Jobs (Most) Americans Won't Do* (2010), from which the following selection is taken. The photograph showing lettuce cutters at work (p. 66) is from Thompson's blog, *Working in the Shadows*.

"A Gringo in the Lettuce Fields" falls into the category of immersion journalism, a cultural ethnography that uses undercover participant observation over an extended period of time to get an insider's view of a particular community.

As you read, consider the ethical implications of this kind of profile:

- What does Thompson's outsider status enable him to understand—or prevent him from understanding—about the community?
- How does Thompson avoid—or fail to avoid—stereotyping or exploiting the group being profiled?
- Toward the end, Thompson tells us that one of the workers "guesses" that he "joined the crew . . . to write about it" (par. 17). Not all participant-observers go undercover; why do you think Thompson chose to do so? What concerns would you have if you were the writer? If you were a member of the group being profiled?

1 I wake up staring into the bluest blue I've ever seen. I must have fallen into a deep sleep because I need several seconds to realize that I'm looking at the Arizona sky, that the pillow beneath my head is a large clump of dirt, and that a near-stranger named Manuel is standing over me, smiling. I pull myself to a sitting position. To my left, in the distance, a Border Patrol helicopter is hovering. To my right is Mexico, separated by only a few fields of lettuce. "*Buenos días,*" Manuel says.

2 I stand up gingerly. It's only my third day in the fields, but already my 30-year-old body is failing me. I feel like someone has dropped a log on my back. And then piled that log onto a truck with many other logs, and driven that truck over my thighs. "Let's go," I say, trying to sound energetic as I fall in line behind Manuel, stumbling across rows of lettuce and thinking about "the five-day rule." The five-day rule, according to Manuel, is simple: Survive the first five days and you'll be fine. He's been a farmworker for almost two decades, so he should know. I'm on day three of five—the goal is within sight. Of course, another way to look at my situation is that I'm on day three of what I promised myself would be a two-month immersion in the work life of the people who do a job that most Americans won't do. But thinking about the next seven weeks doesn't benefit anyone. *Day three of five.*

3 "Manuel! Gabriel! Let's go! *¡Vámonos!*" yells Pedro, our foreman. Our short break is over. Two dozen crew members standing near the lettuce machine are already putting on gloves and sharpening knives. Manuel and I hustle toward the machine, grab our own knives from a box of chlorinated water, and set up in neighboring rows, just as the machine starts moving slowly down another endless field.

4 Since the early 1980s, Yuma, Ariz., has been the "winter lettuce capital" of America. Each winter, when the weather turns cold in Salinas, California—the heart of the nation's lettuce industry—temperatures in sunny Yuma are still in the 70s and 80s. At the height of Yuma's growing season, the fields surrounding the city produce virtually all of the iceberg lettuce and 90 percent of the leafy green vegetables consumed in the United States and Canada.

Courtesy of Gabriel Thompson

5 America's lettuce industry actually needs people like me. Before applying for fieldwork at the local Dole headquarters, I came across several articles describing the causes of a farmworker shortage. The stories cited an aging workforce, immigration crackdowns, and long delays at the border that discourage workers with green cards who would otherwise commute to the fields from their Mexican homes.[1] Wages have been rising somewhat in response to the demand for laborers (one prominent member of the local growers association tells me average pay is now between $10 and $12 an hour), but it's widely assumed that most U.S. citizens wouldn't do the work at any price. Arizona's own Senator John McCain created a stir in 2006 when he issued a challenge to a group of union members in Washington, D.C. "I'll offer anybody here $50 an hour if you'll go pick lettuce in Yuma this season, and pick for the whole season," he said. Amid jeers, he didn't back down, telling the audience, "You can't do it, my friends."

6 On my first day I discover that even putting on a lettuce cutter's uniform is challenging (no fieldworkers, I learn, "pick" lettuce). First, I'm handed a pair of black galoshes to go over my shoes. Next comes the *gancho*, an S-shaped hook that slips over my belt to hold packets of plastic bags. A white glove goes on my right hand, a gray glove, supposedly designed to offer protection from cuts, goes on my left. Over the cloth gloves I pull on a pair of latex gloves. I put on a black hairnet, my baseball cap, and a pair of protective sunglasses. Adding to my belt a long leather sheath, I'm good to go. I feel ridiculous.

7 The crew is already working in the field when Pedro walks me out to them and introduces me to Manuel. Manuel is holding an 18-inch knife in his hand. "Manuel has been cutting for many years, so watch him to see how it's done," Pedro says. Then he walks away. Manuel resumes cutting, following a machine that rolls along just ahead of the crew. Every several seconds Manuel bends down, grabs a head of iceberg lettuce with his left hand, and makes a quick cut with the knife in his right hand, separating the lettuce from its roots. Next, he lifts the lettuce to his stomach and makes a second cut, trimming the trunk.

[1] A green card is an immigration document that allows noncitizens to work legally in the United States, whether they live here or commute across the border. Undocumented workers (or illegal immigrants, depending on your position) lack green cards. [Editor's note]

He shakes the lettuce, letting the outer leaves fall to the ground. With the blade still in his hand, he then brings the lettuce toward the gancho at his waist, and with a flick of the wrist the head is bagged and dropped onto one of the machine's extensions. Manuel does this over and over again, explaining each movement. "It's not so hard," he says. Five minutes later, Pedro reappears and tells me to grab a knife. Manuel points to a head of lettuce. "Try this one," he says.

8 I bend over, noticing that most of the crew has turned to watch. I take my knife and make a tentative sawing motion where I assume the trunk to be, though I'm really just guessing. Grabbing the head with my left hand, I straighten up, doing my best to imitate Manuel. Only my lettuce head doesn't move; it's still securely connected to the soil. Pedro steps in. "When you make the first cut, it is like you are stabbing the lettuce." He makes a quick jabbing action. "You want to aim for the center of the lettuce, where the trunk is," he says.

9 Ten minutes later, after a couple of other discouraging moments, I've cut maybe 20 heads of lettuce and am already feeling pretty accomplished. I'm not perfect: If I don't stoop far enough, my stab—instead of landing an inch above the ground—goes right through the head of lettuce, ruining it entirely. The greatest difficulty, though, is in the trimming. I had no idea that a head of lettuce was so humongous. In order to get it into a shape that can be bagged, I trim and trim and trim, but it's taking me upward of a minute to do what Manuel does in several seconds.

10 Pedro offers me a suggestion. "Act like the lettuce is a bomb," he says. "Imagine you've only got five seconds to get rid of it."

11 Surprisingly, that thought seems to work, and I'm able to greatly increase my speed. For a minute or two I feel euphoric. "Look at me!" I want to shout at Pedro; I'm in the zone. But the woman who is packing the lettuce into boxes soon swivels around to face me. "Look, this lettuce is no good." She's right: I've cut the trunk too high, breaking off dozens of good leaves, which will quickly turn brown because they're attached to nothing. With her left hand she holds the bag up, and with her right she smashes it violently, making a loud pop. She turns the bag over and the massacred lettuce falls to the ground. She does the same for the three other bags I've placed on the extension. "It's okay," Manuel tells me. "You shouldn't try to go too fast when you're beginning." Pedro seconds him. "That's right. Make sure the cuts are precise and that you don't rush."

12 So I am to be very careful and precise, while also treating the lettuce like a bomb that must be tossed aside after five seconds.

13 That first week on the job was one thing. By midway into week two, it isn't clear to me what more I can do to keep up with the rest of the crew. I know the techniques by this time and am moving as fast as my body will permit. Yet I need to somehow *double* my current output to hold my own. I'm able to cut only one row at a time while Manuel is cutting two. Our fastest cutter, Julio, meanwhile can handle three. But how someone could cut two rows for an hour—much less an entire day—is beyond me. "Oh, you will get it," Pedro tells me one day. "You will most definitely get it." Maybe he's trying to be hopeful or inspiring, but it comes across as a threat.

14 That feeling aside, what strikes me about our 31-member crew is how quickly they have welcomed me as one of their own. I encountered some suspicion at first, but it didn't last. Simply showing up on the second day seemed to be proof enough that I was there to work. When I faltered in the field and fell behind, hands would come across from adjacent rows to grab a head or two of my lettuce so I could catch up. People whose names I didn't yet know would ask me how I was holding up, reminding

me that it would get easier as time went by. If I took a seat alone during a break, someone would call me into their group and offer a homemade taco or two.

15 Two months in, I make the mistake of calling in sick one Thursday. The day before, I put my left hand too low on a head of lettuce. When I punched my blade through the stem, the knife struck my middle finger. Thanks to the gloves, my skin wasn't even broken, but the finger instantly turned purple. I took two painkillers to get through the afternoon, but when I wake the next morning it is still throbbing. With one call to an answering machine that morning, and another the next day, I create my own four-day weekend.

16 The surprise is that when I return on Monday, feeling recuperated, I wind up having the hardest day of my brief career in lettuce. Within hours, my hands feel weaker than ever. By quitting time—some 10 hours after our day started—I feel like I'm going to vomit from exhaustion. A theory forms in my mind. Early in the season—say, after the first week—a farmworker's body gets thoroughly broken down. Back, legs, and arms grow sore, hands and feet swell up. A tolerance for the pain is developed, though, and two-day weekends provide just enough time for the body to recover from the trauma. My four-day break had been too long; my body actually began to recuperate, and it wanted more time to continue. Instead, it was thrown right back into the mix and rebelled. Only on my second day back did my body recover that middle ground. "I don't think the soreness goes away," I say to Manuel and two other co-workers one day. "You just forget what it's like not to be sore." Manuel, who's 37, considers this. "That's true, that's true," he says. "It always takes a few weeks at the end of the year to get back to normal, to recover."

17 An older co-worker, Mateo, is the one who eventually guesses that I have joined the crew because I want to write about it. "That is good," he says over coffee at his home one Sunday. "Americans should know the hard work that Mexicans do in this country."

18 Mateo is an unusual case. There aren't many other farmworkers who are still in the fields when they reach their 50s. It's simply not possible to do this work for decades and not suffer a permanently hunched back, or crooked fingers, or hands so swollen that they look as if someone has attached a valve to a finger and pumped vigorously. The punishing nature of the work helps explain why farmworkers don't live very long; the National Migrant Resources Program puts their life expectancy at 49 years.

19 "Are you cutting two rows yet?" Mateo asks me. "Yes, more or less," I say. "I thought I'd be better by now." Mateo shakes his head. "It takes a long time to learn how to really cut lettuce. It's not something that you learn after only one season. Three, maybe four seasons—then you start understanding how to really work with lettuce."

[REFLECT] Make connections: Switching perspectives.

Thompson temporarily joined a community of lettuce cutters to get an insider's perspective on their work. Think about your own experience as a member of a group that was visited and observed, even for a short period of time. Perhaps an administrator visited one of your classes or a potential coach or recruit observed your team. Consider what it was like being studied by a stranger. Your instructor may ask you to post your thoughts about the experience on a discussion board or to discuss them with other students in class. Use these questions to get started:

- As an insider, how did you and the other group members feel about being the subject of someone else's gaze?
- What were you told about why your group was being visited and what assumptions or concerns did you have about the visitor? Were you concerned about the visitor's motives—for example, wondering if the person was really there to evaluate the group or its members?
- Suppose Thompson wanted to write a piece of immersion journalism about a community (such as a religious group, sports team, fraternity, or sorority) of which you are a member. What elements of Thompson's profile, if any, would cause you to trust or distrust his reporting? What ethical challenges might immersion journalists like Thompson face by going undercover?

[ANALYZE] Use the basic features.

SPECIFIC INFORMATION ABOUT THE SUBJECT: USING QUOTATION, PARAPHRASE, AND SUMMARY

Profile writers—like all writers—depend on the three basic strategies for presenting source material: quoting, paraphrasing, and summarizing. Each strategy has advantages and disadvantages. It's obvious why Cable chose this quotation: "We're in *Ripley's Believe It or Not*, along with another funeral home whose owners' names are Baggit and Sackit" (par. 14). But making decisions about what to quote and what to paraphrase or summarize is not always that easy.

ANALYZE & WRITE

Write a few paragraphs analyzing Thompson's decisions about how to present information from different sources:

1. Skim the essay to find at least one example of a quotation and one paraphrase or summary of information gleaned from an interview or from background research.
2. Why do you think Thompson chooses to quote certain things and paraphrase or summarize other things? What could be a good rule of thumb for you to apply when deciding whether to quote, paraphrase, or summarize? (Note that when writing for an academic audience, in a paper for a class or in a scholarly publication, all source material—whether it is quoted, paraphrased, or summarized—should be cited.)

To learn more about quoting, paraphrasing, and summarizing, see Chapter 15.

A CLEAR, LOGICAL ORGANIZATION: NARRATING AN EXTENDED PERIOD

Some profile writers do field research, observing and interviewing over an extended period of time. As an immersive journalist, Thompson spent more than two months as a member of one crew. To give readers a sense of the chronology of events, he uses time cues (such as calendar and clock time, transitions like *next*, and prepositional phrases such as *on my first day*). These cues are especially useful because Thompson's narrative does not always follow a straightforward chronology. He also describes the process of cutting lettuce in detail.

ANALYZE & WRITE

Write a paragraph analyzing Thompson's use of time cues and process narration:

1. Skim the profile, highlighting the time cues. Why do you imagine Thompson decided not to follow a linear chronology? How well does he use time cues to keep readers from becoming confused?
2. Why do you think Thompson devotes so much space (pars. 6–12) to narrating the process of cutting lettuce? What does this detailed narrative offer to readers?

For more about time markers, see pp. 49–50.

THE WRITER'S ROLE: GOING UNDERCOVER

Like Coyne, Thompson acts as a participant-observer. But unlike Coyne, his role is covert. He does not watch lettuce cutters from the sidelines or announce himself as a journalist but instead works among them. His informal interviews take place during work and on breaks (even at the homes of his coworkers over the weekend). Nevertheless, there is a significant difference between a two-month experiment and a personal account written by a lettuce cutter like Mateo after a lifetime on the job. A profile writer may participate but is always an outsider looking in.

ANALYZE & WRITE

Write a paragraph or two analyzing Thompson's use of the participant-observer role:

1. Skim the text, noting at least one place where Thompson
   - reminds readers of his status as an outsider (for example, when he refers to a coworker as a "near-stranger" [par. 1]);
   - tells readers about something he thinks will be unfamiliar to them (for example, when he explains that people do not "'pick' lettuce" [par. 6]);
   - calls attention to his own incompetence or failings (for example, when he describes his first attempt to cut lettuce [par. 8]).
2. Why do you think Thompson tells us about his errors and reminds us that he is an outsider? What effect are these moves likely to have on his audience?
3. How do the writers whose profiles appear in this chapter use their outsider status to connect with readers?

A PERSPECTIVE ON THE SUBJECT: PROFILING A CONTROVERSIAL ISSUE

Two other profiles in this chapter also touch on a controversial subject about which people have strong opinions. Cable addresses the commercialization of death, and Coyne, the unfairness of the legal system. Although profiles do not usually make an explicit argument the way essays arguing a position do, they convey the writer's perspective on the issue and try to influence readers' thinking about it.

ANALYZE & WRITE

Write a few paragraphs analyzing Thompson's perspective:

1. Skim the profile looking for a passage or two where you get a clear understanding of the issue and what Thompson thinks about it.
2. Consider also what you learn about the issue and Thompson's perspective on it from the title of the profile, "A Gringo in the Lettuce Fields," and the title of the book from which it is excerpted, *Working in the Shadows: A Year of Doing the Jobs (Most) Americans Won't Do.*
3. If Thompson were to make an explicit argument supporting his view of this issue, how do you think his argument would likely differ from this profile? How effectively does Thompson use the genre of the investigative profile to achieve his purpose? How well suited do you think the profile genre is for arguing a position on a controversial issue as well as informing readers about it?

RESPOND Consider possible topics: Immersing yourself.

Thompson's experience suggests two possible avenues for research: You could embed yourself in a group, participating alongside group members, and then write about that experience—for example, you might join a club on campus or try an unusual sport. Alternatively, you could observe life in an unfamiliar group, watching how a meeting or event unfolds, interviewing members to learn about their practices, and conducting additional research to learn about the group.

The Writing Assignment

Profile an intriguing person, group, place, or activity in your community. Observe your subject closely, and then present what you have learned in a way that both informs and engages readers.

This Guide to Writing is designed to help you compose your own profile and apply what you have learned from reading other profiles. This Starting Points chart will help you find the guidance you need, when you need it.

STARTING POINTS: WRITING A PROFILE

Specific Information about the Subject

How do I come up with an appropriate subject to profile?

- Consider possible topics. (pp. 64, 71)
- Choose a subject to profile. (p. 74)
- Test Your Choice: Considering Your Purpose and Audience (pp. 74–75)

How can I gather information on my subject?

- Conduct your field research. (pp. 75–80)
- Chapter 14, Finding Sources and Conducting Field Research

How can I make my subject come to life?

- Assess the genre's basic features: Specific information about the subject. (p. 49)
- Specific Information about the Subject: Using Anecdotes (p. 62)
- Specific Information about the Subject: Using Quotation, Paraphrase, and Summary (p. 69)
- Use quotations that provide information and reveal character. (p. 80)
- Consider adding visual or audio elements. (p. 81)
- A Troubleshooting Guide: Specific Information about the Subject (p. 89)

A Clear, Logical Organization	How should I organize my profile? • Assess the genre's basic features: A clear, logical organization. (pp. 49–50) • A Clear, Logical Organization: Narrating a Day in the Life (p. 63) • A Clear, Logical Organization: Narrating an Extended Period (pp. 69–70) • Create an outline that will organize your profile effectively for your readers. (pp. 81–82) • A Troubleshooting Guide: A Clear, Logical Organization (pp. 90–91)
The Writer's Role	What role should I adopt in researching and presenting my subject? • Assess the genre's basic features: The writer's role. (p. 51) • The Writer's Role: Acting as a Participant-Observer (p. 63) • The Writer's Role: Going Undercover (p. 70) • Determine your role in the profile. (pp. 82–83) • A Troubleshooting Guide: The Writer's Role (p. 91)
A Perspective on the Subject	How do I develop and express a clear perspective on the subject? • Determine the writer's purpose and audience. (p. 48) • Assess the genre's basic features: A perspective on the subject. (p. 51) • A Perspective on the Subject: Using Contrast (p. 64) • A Perspective on the Subject: Profiling a Controversial Issue (pp. 70–71) • Develop your perspective on the subject. (pp. 83–85) • Clarify the dominant impression. (p. 85) • A Troubleshooting Guide: A Perspective on the Subject (p. 91)

Writing a Draft: Invention, Research, Planning, and Composing

The activities in this section will help you choose a subject to profile and develop your perspective on the subject. Do the activities in any order that makes sense to you (and your instructor), and return to them as needed as you revise.

Although some of the activities will take only a few minutes to complete, the essential field research—making detailed observations and conducting interviews—will take a good deal of time to plan and carry out. Your writing in response to many of these activities can be used as part of your rough draft, which you will be able to improve after receiving feedback from your classmates and instructor.

Choose a subject to profile.

To create an informative and engaging profile, your subject—whether it's a person, a group of people, a place, or an activity—should be one

- that sparks your interest or curiosity;
- your readers will find interesting and informative;
- you can gain access to and observe in detail in the time allowed;
- about which (or with whom) you can conduct in-depth interviews.

Note: Whenever you write a profile, consider carefully the ethics involved in such research: You will want to be careful to treat participants fairly and with respect in the way you both approach and depict them. Discuss the ethical implications of your research with your instructor, and think carefully about the goals of your research and the effect it will have on others. You may also need to obtain permission from your school's ethics review board.

Make a list of appropriate subjects. Review the Consider Possible Topics sections on pp. 64 and 71, and consult your school's Web site to find intriguing places, activities, or people on campus. The following ideas may suggest additional possibilities to consider:

- A place where people come together because they are of the same age, gender, sexual orientation, or ethnic group (for example, a foreign language–speaking dorm or fraternity or sorority), or a place where people of different ages, genders, sexual orientations, or ethnic groups have formed a community (for example, a Sunday morning pickup basketball game in the park, LGBT club, or barbershop)
- A place where people are trained for a certain kind of work (for example, a police academy, cosmetology program, truck driving school, or boxing ring)
- A group of people working together for a particular purpose (for example, students and their teacher preparing for the academic decathlon, employees working together to produce something, law students and their professor working to help prisoners on death row, or scientists collaborating on a research project)

TEST YOUR CHOICE

Considering Your Purpose and Audience

After you have made a tentative choice, ask yourself the following questions:

- Do I feel curious about the subject?
- Am I confident that I will be able to make the subject interesting for my readers?
- Do I believe that I can research this subject sufficiently in the time I have?

Then get together with two or three other students:

Presenters. Take turns identifying your subjects. Explain your interest in your subject, and speculate about why you think it will interest readers.

Listeners. Briefly tell each presenter what you already know about his or her subject, if anything, and what might make it interesting to readers.

Conduct your field research.

To write an effective profile, conduct **field research**—*interviews and observations—to collect detailed, firsthand information about your subject.* Many writers begin with observations to get the lay of the land and identify people to interview, but you can start with interviews. You may even be able to make observations and conduct interviews during the same visit. If you are thinking of adopting the role of participant-observer, turn first to "Determine Your Role in the Profile" (pp. 82–83), and consider whether you need to request permission before conducting your research. Before your interview or observation, draft preliminary questions; when you appear for your interview or observation, dress appropriately and bring equipment for taking notes, recording, or filming. (Be sure to ask permission before recording or filming.) The following activities will help you plan and carry out your field research.

To learn more about conducting observations and interviews, see Chapter 14.

WAYS IN

HOW CAN I MANAGE MY TIME?

Try this BACKWARD PLANNING *strategy:*

1. Construct a calendar marking the date the project is due and any other intermediate due dates (such as the date the first draft, thesis, or topic is due).
2. Work backward, adding dates by which key stages or milestones should be reached to make your due dates. For example, mark the following:
   - The date by which final revisions to text and images are needed
   - The date on which peer review is scheduled
   - The date by which the first draft should be completed
   - The date by which initial interviews and observations should be conducted (leave at least a week for this process)
   - The date by which interviews and observations must be scheduled (leave at least several days for this process)

(continued)

A SAMPLE SCHEDULE

Sunday	Monday	Tuesday	Wednesday	Thursday	Friday	Saturday
	1 Arrange interviews & observations →	2	3	4	5 Research interview subject, locations	6
7	8 Conduct interviews & observations →	9	10	11	12	13
14	15	16 Write-ups completed	17	18	19 First draft due	20 Conduct any extra research
21	22 Call/E-mail with follow-up questions	23 Revise draft →	24	25	26 Revised draft due	27
28	29	30	31			

WAYS IN

HOW DO I SET UP AND PREPARE FOR INTERVIEWS AND OBSERVATIONS?

1. *List the people you would like to interview or places you would like to observe.* Include a number of possibilities in case your first choice doesn't work out.
2. *Write out your intentions and goals, so you can explain them clearly to others.*
3. *Call or e-mail for an appointment with your interview subject, or make arrangements to visit the site.* Explain who you are and what you are doing. Student research projects are often embraced, but be prepared for your request to be rejected.

Note: Be sure to arrange your interview or site visit as soon as possible. The most common error students report making on this assignment is waiting too long to make that first call. Be aware, too, that the people and places you contact may not respond immediately (or at all); be sure to follow up if you have not gotten an answer to your request within a few days.

4. *Make notes about what you expect to learn before you write interview questions, interview your subject, or visit your site.* Ask yourself questions like these:

Interview

- How would I define or describe the subject?
- What is the subject's purpose or function?
- Who or what is associated with it?
- What about it will interest me and my readers?
- What do I hope to learn about it?

Observation

- How would I define or describe my subject?
- What typically takes place at this location? Who or what will I likely observe?
- What will interest me and my readers?
- What do I expect to learn about my subject?
- How will my presence affect those I am observing?

5. *Write some interview questions in advance, or ask yourself some observation questions to help you determine how best to conduct your site visit.*

Interview

Ask for stories:

▸ Tell me how you got into ________.

▸ Tell me about something that surprised/pleased/frustrated you.

Let subjects correct misconceptions:

▸ What myths about ________ would you most like to bust?

Ask about the subject's past and future:

▸ How has ________ changed over the years, and where do you think it's going?

Observation

Consider your **PERSPECTIVE:**

- Should I observe from different vantage points or from the same location?
- Should I visit the location at different times of day or days of the week, or would it be better to visit at the same time every day?
- Should I focus on specific people, or should I identify roles and focus on people as they adopt those roles?

6. *Conduct some preliminary research on your subject or related subjects if possible, and revise your questions or plans accordingly.*

WAYS IN

HOW DO I CONDUCT INTERVIEWS?

Take notes:

- Clearly distinguish **QUOTATIONS** from **PARAPHRASES** or **SUMMARIES** by inserting quotation marks where needed.
- Record the interview, if allowed, but also take notes. Politely ask interviewees to speak slowly, repeat themselves, or confirm your quotations if necessary. (Interviewees often fear being misquoted and will usually appreciate that you're being careful.)
- In addition to writing down what your subject says, use **NAMING**, **DETAILING**, and **COMPARING** to capture the interviewee's tone, gestures, and mannerisms.
- To generate **ANECDOTES**, ask how the interviewee first got involved with the place or activity; if there was a key event worth noting; and what most concerns the interviewee; and what has been the biggest influence on his or her experience, for good or ill.
- To elicit **PROCESS NARRATIVES**, ask how something works, what happens if it breaks, whether it has always been done the same way, how it has changed, and how it could be improved.
- To **CLASSIFY**, **COMPARE**, or **CONTRAST**, ask what kind of thing it is, how it's like and unlike others of its kind, and how it compares to what it was like in the past.
- To help you with your **PERSPECTIVE**, ask why the subject is important, how it contributes to the community, or how it could be improved. Ask who would disagree with these perspectives.
- Finally, ask for the interviewee's preferences (e-mail or phone) for handling your follow-up questions, if any.

HOW DO I CONDUCT OBSERVATIONS?

Take notes:

- Note your surroundings, using all of your senses: sight, hearing, smell, taste, touch.
- Describe the place from multiple vantage points, noting furnishings, decor, and so on, and sketch the layout.
- Describe people's appearance, dress, gestures, and actions.
- Make a record of interesting overheard conversation.
- Note your reactions and ideas, especially in relation to your preconceptions. What surprises you?
- If you can get permission, observe how people interact with one another.

Consider your **ROLE**:

- If you are new to the subject and would like to have a **PARTICIPANT-OBSERVER** role, ask permission to take part in a small way for a limited time.
- If you are an insider, adopt the position of a **SPECTATOR** to help you find a new angle and learn something new. (For example, if you're on the football team, focus on the cheerleaders or the people who maintain the field.)

Collect artifacts, or take videos or photos:

- Collect any brochures or other written material you might be able to use, either to prepare for interviews or to include in your essay.
- Consider taking photographs or videos, if allowed. Try a pan shot scanning the scene from side to side or a tracking shot indicating what you see as you enter or tour the place.

Reflect on the interview. Review your notes right after the interview, adding any impressions and marking promising material, such as

- anything that calls into question your or your readers' likely preconceptions;
- details that could paint a vivid portrait of the person;
- quotable phrases that could help you capture the tone or mood of the subject;
- questions you still need answered.

Write up your interview. Write a few paragraphs reporting what you learned from the interview:

- Choose notable quotes, and summarize or paraphrase other bits of information.
- Try to add speaker tags to describe the person's tone of voice, gestures, and appearance while speaking.
- Consider whether something important was left unsaid or was misrepresented—and, if so, how that might extend or complicate your understanding of the subject.

Do follow-up interviews, or interview another person:

- Follow up to check facts or get clarification, but be careful not to waste your interviewee's time.
- Arrange to talk to another person who has different kinds of information to share.

Reflect on your observations. Take five minutes right after your visit to think about what you observed, and write a few sentences about your impressions of the subject:

▶ The most interesting aspect of the subject is ______ because ______.

▶ Although my visit confirmed that ______, I was surprised to learn that ______.

▶ My dominant impression of the subject is ______.

Write up your observations:

- Write a few paragraphs reporting what you observed during your visit.
- Include as many sensory details as you can.
- Think of comparisons that might capture what's special or intriguing about the subject.
- Consider the dominant impression you want to make and what impression your word choices actually make. Explore contradictions between your intentions and your words to develop a more nuanced description.

Consider whether you need a follow-up observation:

- Consider a follow-up visit to observe from a new angle.
- Consider a follow-up observation to visit the site at another time.

WAYS IN

HOW SHOULD I PRESENT THE INFORMATION I'VE GLEANED FROM INTERVIEWS AND OBSERVATIONS?

Review the notes from your interviews and observations, selecting the information to include in your draft and how you might present it. Consider including the following:

- **DEFINITIONS** of key terms readers will find unfamiliar
- **COMPARISONS** or **CONTRASTS** that make information clearer or more memorable
- **LISTS** or **CATEGORIES** that organize information logically
- **PROCESSES** that readers will find interesting or surprising

Use quotations that provide information and reveal character.

Good profiles quote sources so that readers can hear what people have to say in their own voices. The most useful quotations are those that reveal the style and character of the people you interviewed. **Speaker tags** (like *she said, he asked*) help readers determine the source of a quotation. You may rely on an all-purpose verb or a more descriptive verb to help readers imagine speakers' attitudes and personal styles:

> "Try this one," he says. (Thompson, par. 7)

> "Take me out to the"—and Toby yells out, "Banana store!" (Coyne, par. 21)

Adding a word or phrase to a speaker tag can reveal something relevant about the speaker's manner or provide context:

> "We're in *Ripley's Believe It or Not,* along with another funeral home whose owners' names are Baggit and Sackit," Howard told me, without cracking a smile. (Cable, par. 14)

> Once, after being given this weak explanation, he said, "I wish I could have done something really bad, like my Mommy. So I could go to prison too and be with her." (Coyne, par. 18)

> "Let's go," I say, trying to sound energetic as I fall in line behind Manuel, stumbling across rows of lettuce and thinking about "the five-day rule." (Thompson, par. 2)

In addition to being carefully introduced, quotations must be precisely punctuated. Fortunately, there are only two general rules:

1. Enclose all quotations in a pair of quotation marks, one at the beginning and one at the end of the quotation.
2. Separate the quotation from its speaker tag with appropriate punctuation, usually a comma. (Commas and periods usually go inside the closing quotation mark, but question marks go inside or outside, depending on whether the question is the speaker's or the writer's.) If you are quoting more than one sentence, be careful to punctuate the separate sentences properly.

For more about integrating quotations, see Chapter 15.

Consider adding visual or audio elements.

Think about whether visual or audio elements—photographs; postcards; menus; or snippets from films, television programs, or songs—would strengthen your profile. If you can recall profiles you've seen in magazines, on Web pages, or on television shows, what visual or audio elements were used to create a strong sense of the subject? Profiles don't require such elements to be effective, but they can be helpful.

Note: Be sure to cite the source of visual or audio elements you didn't create, and get permission from the source if your profile is going to be published on a Web site that is not password protected.

Create an outline that will organize your profile effectively for your readers.

Here are two sample outlines you can modify to fit your needs, depending on whether you prefer a **narrative** plan (to give a tour of a place, for example) or a **topical** plan (to cluster related information). Even if you wish to blend features of both outlines, seeing how each basic plan works can help you combine them. Remember that each section need not be the same length; some sections may require greater detail than others.

For more on clustering and outlining, see Chapter 9.

Narrative Plan

I. **Begin by describing the place from the outside.**

II. **Present background information.**

III. **Describe what you see as you enter.**

IV. **Introduce the people and their activities.** (This may require several paragraphs.)

V. **Tour the place.** Describe what you see as you move from one space to the next. Integrate information wherever you can, and comment about the place or the people as you go. (This may require several paragraphs.)

VI. **Conclude with reflections on what you have learned about the place.**

Topical Plan

I. **Begin with a vivid image of the person in action.**

II. **Present the first topic** (for example, a trait of the person or of his or her work). Use dialogue, description, narration, process description, evaluation, or interpretation to illustrate this topic. (Presentation of each topic may require several paragraphs.)

III. **Present the second topic** (and continue as above until you have presented all topics).

IV. **Conclude with a bit of action or dialogue.**

The tentative plan you choose should reflect the possibilities in your material as well as your purpose and your understanding of your audience. When using a narrative plan, use verb tenses and transitions of space and time to make the succession of events clear; when using a topical plan, use logical transitions to help readers move from topic to topic. As you draft, you will almost certainly discover new ways of organizing parts of your material.

Determine your role in the profile.

Consider the advantages and disadvantages of the spectator and participant-observer roles, noting the examples and sentence strategies illustrating them. Then choose the role that best allows you to achieve your purpose with your readers.

WAYS IN

WHICH ROLE WILL BEST HELP ME CONVEY THE EXPERIENCE OF MY PROFILE SUBJECT?

Choose the **SPECTATOR** *role to:*

- provide readers with a detailed description or guided tour of the scene.

  ▶ X was dressed in ________ with ________ and ________, doing ________ as s/he ________-ed.

  ▶ Inside, you could see ________. The room was ________ and ________.

  EXAMPLE The door was massive, yet it swung open easily on well-oiled hinges. “Come in,” said the sign. “We’re always open.” Inside was a cool and quiet reception room. Curtains were drawn against the outside glare, cutting the light down to a soft glow. (Cable, par. 4)

- create an aura of objectivity, making it appear as though you’re just reporting what you see and hear without revealing that you have actually made choices about what to include in order to create a **DOMINANT IMPRESSION**.

  ▶ The shiny new/rusty old tools were laid out neatly/piled helter-skelter on the workbench, like ________.

  EXAMPLE Many of these mothers have untied the bow that attaches the flower to its silver-and-red cellophane wrapper and are using one of the many empty soda cans at hand as a vase. They sit proudly before their flower-in-a-Coke-can, amid Hershey bar wrappers, half-eaten Ding Dongs, and empty paper coffee cups. (Coyne, par. 1)

Caution: The **SPECTATOR** role may cause readers to:

- feel detached, which can lead to a lack of interest in the subject profiled;
- suspect a hidden bias behind the appearance of objectivity, undermining the writer’s credibility.

Choose the PARTICIPANT-OBSERVER *role to:*

- profile physical activities through the eyes of a novice, so readers can imagine doing the activity themselves.
  - ▶ I picked up the ________. It felt like ________ and smelled/tasted/sounded like ________.

  EXAMPLE The greatest difficulty, though, is in the trimming. I had no idea that a head of lettuce was so humongous. In order to get it into a shape that can be bagged, I trim and trim and trim. (Thompson, par. 9)

- reveal how others react to you.
  - ▶ X interrupted me as I ________-ed.
  - ▶ As I struggled with ________, Y noticed and ________-ed.

  EXAMPLE People whose names I didn't yet know would ask me how I was holding up, reminding me that it would get easier as time went by. (Thompson, par. 14)

Caution: The PARTICIPANT-OBSERVER role may cause readers to:

- wonder whether your experience was unique to you, not something they would have experienced;
- think that the person, place, group, or activity being profiled seemed secondary in relation to the writer's experience.

Develop your perspective on the subject.

Try some of these activities to deepen your analysis and enhance your readers' understanding of your subject's cultural significance.

WAYS IN

HOW CAN I DEVELOP A PERSPECTIVE FOR MY PROFILE?

Explore the CULTURAL SIGNIFICANCE *of your subject:*

If you are focusing on a **place** (like a mortuary or a prison visiting room), consider what intrigues you about its culture by asking yourself questions like these:

- Who are the insiders at this place, and why are they there?
- How does the place affect how insiders talk, act, think, feel?
- What function does the place serve in the wider community?
- What tensions are there between insiders and outsiders or between newcomers and veterans?

▶ X and Y say ________ and ________ because they want to ________, but they seem to feel ________ because of the way they do ________.

(continued)

EXAMPLE And I can imagine the hours spent preparing for this visit. . . . The hours of discussing, dissecting, and bragging about these visitors—especially the men. . . . And the giggles that abruptly change into tears without warning—things that define any female-only world. Even, or especially, if that world is a female federal prison camp. (Coyne, par. 4)

If you are focusing on an **activity** (like cutting lettuce), ask yourself questions like these:

- Who benefits from it?
- What value does it have for the insider community and for the wider community?
- How has the activity or process changed over time, for good or ill?
- How are outsiders initiated into the activity?

▶ It's important to recognize ________ because ________.

▶ ________ [date or event] marked a turning point because ________.

EXAMPLE The five-day rule, according to Manuel, is simple: Survive the first five days and you'll be fine. He's been a farmworker for almost two decades, so he should know. I'm on day three of five—the goal is within sight. (Thompson, par. 2)

If you are focusing on a **person** or **group of people**, ask yourself questions like these:

- What sense of identity do they have?
- What customs and ways of communicating do they have?
- What are their values and attitudes?
- What are their social hierarchies, and what do they think about them?
- How do they see their role in the community?

▶ X values/believes ________, as you can see from the way s/he ________.

▶ Members of group X are more likely to ________ than are people in the general population because ________.

EXAMPLES He said that he felt people were becoming more aware of the public service his profession provides. (Cable, par. 27)

That feeling aside, what strikes me about our 31-member crew is how quickly they have welcomed me as one of their own. I encountered some suspicion at first, but it didn't last. Simply showing up on the second day seemed to be proof enough that I was there to work. (Thompson, par. 14)

Define your **PURPOSE** *and* **AUDIENCE**. Write for five minutes exploring what you want your readers to learn about the subject and why. Use sentence strategies like these to help clarify your thinking:

▶ In addition to my teacher and classmates, I envision my ideal readers as ________.

▶ They probably know ________ about my subject and believe ________.

- ▶ They would be most surprised to learn ________ and most interested in ________.
- ▶ I can help change their opinions of X by ________ and get them to think about X's social and cultural significance by ________.

State your main point. Review what you have written, and summarize in a sentence or two the main idea you want readers to take away from your profile. Readers don't expect a profile to have an explicit thesis statement, but the descriptive details and other information need to work together to convey the main idea.

Clarify the dominant impression.

The descriptive details, comparisons, and word choices you use and the information you supply should reinforce the dominant impression you are trying to create. For example, the dominant impression of Cable's profile is his—and our—anxiety about death, beginning with his apprehension upon entering the mortuary and ending with his daring to touch a dead body. But, as Cable shows, the dominant impression need not be simplistic. Readers appreciate profiles that reveal the richness and complexity of the subject, as Cable does by describing the Goodbody Mortuary looking "a bit like a church—tall, with gothic arches and stained glass" and "somewhat like an apartment complex" (par. 2). Although he makes fun of the crass commercialism of Howard's side of the business, Cable lets Tim make the joke instead of being the joke: Becoming a mortician "'was a profession I could live with,' he told me with a sly grin" (par. 25).

WAYS IN

HOW DO I FINE-TUNE MY DOMINANT IMPRESSION?

Identify your intended **DOMINANT IMPRESSION.** Write for five minutes sketching out the overall impression you want readers to take away from your profile. What do you want readers to think and feel about your subject?

Reread your notes and write-ups, looking for words and phrases that help convey your overall impression. In Brian Cable's profile, phrases like "His desk was bone clean" (par. 7) help reinforce the sense of death Cable associated with the funeral director. A later sentence—"His tone was that of a broker conferring on the Dow Jones" (par. 9)—complicates his initial assessment and helps create the overall impression of the funeral home and its employees as being in the business of death.

If your initial dominant impression seems too simplistic, look for any contradictions or gaps in your notes and write-ups that you can use to develop the subject's complexity. You might start with one of the following sentence strategies and elaborate from there:

- ▶ Although X clearly seemed ________, I couldn't shake the feeling that ________.
- ▶ Although Y tries to/pretends to ________, overall/primarily he/she/it ________.

Write the opening sentences.

Review your invention writing to see if you have something that would work to launch your essay, or try some of these opening strategies:

Begin with an **arresting scene:**

> You can spot the convict-moms here in the visiting room by the way they hold and touch their children and by the single flower that is perched in front of them—a rose, a tulip, a daffodil. (Coyne, par. 1)

Offer a **remarkable thought** *or* **occasion** *that triggered your observational visit:*

> Death is a subject largely ignored by the living. (Cable, par. 1)

Start with a **vivid description:**

> I wake up staring into the bluest blue I've ever seen. (Thompson, par. 1)

But don't agonize over the first sentences because you are likely to discover the best way to begin only after you have written a rough draft.

Draft your profile.

By this point, you have done a lot of research and writing to

- develop something interesting to say about a subject;
- devise a plan for presenting that information;
- identify a role for yourself in the essay;
- explore your perspective on the subject.

Now stitch that material together to create a draft. The next two parts of this Guide to Writing will help you evaluate and improve your draft.

Evaluating the Draft: Using Peer Review

Your instructor may arrange a peer review session in class or online, where you can exchange drafts with your classmates and give one another a thoughtful critical reading, pointing out what works well and suggesting ways to improve the draft. A good critical reading does three things:

1. It lets the writer know how well the reader understands the cultural significance of the subject.
2. It praises what works best.
3. It indicates where the draft could be improved and makes suggestions on how to improve it.

One strategy for evaluating a draft is to use the basic features of profiles as a guide.

A PEER REVIEW GUIDE

Specific Information about the Subject

Does the writer portray the subject in enough well-chosen detail to show us why it's interesting?

Summarize: Tell the writer one thing you learned about the subject from reading the essay.

Praise: Point out one passage where the description seems especially vivid, a quotation stands out, or another writing strategy works particularly well to present information.

Critique: Point out one passage where description could be added or where the description could be made more vivid, where a quotation that falls flat should be paraphrased or summarized, or where another writing strategy could be used.

A Clear, Logical Organization

Is the profile easy to follow?

Summarize: Identify the kind of organization—narrative, topical, or a blend of the two—that the writer uses.

Praise: Comment on the cues the writer gives that make the profile easy to follow. For example, point to a place where one topic leads logically to the next or where transitions help you follow the tour or narrative. Also, indicate what in the opening paragraphs grabs your attention or why you think the ending works well.

Critique: Point to information that seems out of place or instances where the chronology is confusing. If you think the opening or ending could be improved, suggest an alternative passage in the essay that could work as an opening or an ending.

The Writer's Role

Is the author's role clear, whether it is spectator, participant-observer, or both?

Summarize: Identify the role the writer adopts.

Praise: Point to a passage where the spectator or participant-observer role enables you to identify with the writer, enhancing the essay's immediacy or interest.

Critique: Point out any problems with the role—for example, if the participant-observer role becomes distracting or if the spectator role seems too distant.

(continued)

A Perspective on the Subject	Does the author have a clear point of view on the subject? **Summarize:** State briefly what you believe to be the writer's perspective on the subject and the dominant impression you get from the essay. **Praise:** Give an example of where you have a strong sense of the writer's perspective through a comment, description, quotation, or bit of information. **Critique:** Tell the writer if the essay does not have a clear perspective or convey a dominant impression. To help him or her find one, explain what interests you about the subject and what you think is important. If you see contradictions in the draft that could be developed to make the profile more complex and illuminating, briefly explain.

Before concluding your review, be sure to address any of the writer's concerns that have not already been addressed.

Improving the Draft: Revising, Editing, and Proofreading

Start improving your draft by reflecting on what you have written thus far:

- Review critical reading comments from your classmates, instructor, or writing center tutor. What are your readers getting at?
- Take another look at the notes from your interviews, observations, and earlier writing activities. What else should you consider?
- Review your draft. What else can you do to make your profile fascinating?

Revise your draft.

If your readers are having difficulty with your draft, try some of the strategies listed in the Troubleshooting Guide. They can help you fine-tune your presentation of the genre's basic features.

A TROUBLESHOOTING GUIDE

Specific Information about the Subject

My readers tell me that the people do not come alive.

- Describe a physical feature, a mannerism, or an emotional reaction that will help readers imagine or identify with each person.
- Include speaker tags that characterize how people talk.
- Paraphrase long, dry quotations that convey basic information.
- Use short quotations that reveal character or the way someone speaks.
- Make comparisons.
- Use anecdotes or action sequences to show people in action.

My readers say the place is hard to visualize.

- Name objects in the scene.
- Add sensory detail—sight, sound, smell, taste, touch, temperature.
- Make comparisons.
- Consider adding a visual—a photograph or sketch, for example.

My readers say that there is too much information, and it is not clear what is important.

- Prioritize based on the perspective and dominant impression you want to convey, cutting information that does not reinforce the perspective.
- Break up long blocks of informational text with quotations, narration of events, or examples.
- Vary the writing strategies used to present the information: Switch from raw factual reporting to comparisons, examples, or process descriptions.
- Consider which parts of the profile would be more engaging if presented through dialogue or summarized more succinctly.

My readers say visuals could be added or improved.

- Use a photo, a map, a drawing, a cartoon, or any other visual that might make the place or people easier to imagine or the information more understandable.
- Consider adding textual references to any images in your essay or positioning images more effectively.

(continued)

A Clear, Logical Organization

My readers say the narrative plan drags or rambles.

- Try adding drama through dialogue or action sequences.
- Summarize or paraphrase any dialogue that seems dry or uninteresting.
- Give the narrative shape: Establish a conflict, build tension toward a climax, and resolve it.
- Make sure the narrative develops and has a clear direction.

My readers say my topically arranged essay seems disorganized or out of balance.

- Rearrange topics into new patterns, choosing the structure that makes the most sense for your subject. (Describe a place from outside to inside or from biggest to smallest; describe a process from start to finish or from cause to effect.)
- Add clearer, more explicit transitions or topic sentences.
- Move, remove, or condense information to restore balance.

My readers say the opening fails to engage their attention.

- Consider alternatives: Think of a question, an engaging image, or a dialogue you could open with.
- Go back to your notes for other ideas.
- Recall how the writers in this chapter open their profiles: Cable stands outside, in front of the mortuary; Thompson awakens in the lettuce fields, his break over.

My readers say that transitions are missing or are confusing.

- Look for connections between ideas, and try to use those connections to help readers move from point to point.
- Add appropriate transitional words or phrases.

My readers say the ending seems weak.

- Consider ending earlier or moving a striking insight to the end. (Often first drafts hit a great ending point and then keep going. Deleting the last few sentences often improves essays.)
- Consider ending by reminding readers of something from the beginning.
- Recall how the writers in this chapter end their profiles: Cable touches the cold flesh of a cadaver; Coyne watches a mother bleed after being punched by her son.

A Clear, Logical Organization	My readers say the visual features are not effective. • Consider adding textual references to any images in your essay or positioning images more effectively. • Think of other design features—drawings, lists, tables, graphs, cartoons, headings—that might make the place and people easier to imagine or the information more understandable.
The Writer's Role	My readers say the spectator role is too distant. • Consider placing yourself in the scene as you describe it. • Add your thoughts and reactions to one of the interviews. My readers say my approach to participation is distracting. • Bring other people forward by adding material about them. • Reduce the material about yourself.
A Perspective on the Subject	My readers say the perspective or dominant impression is unclear. • Try stating your perspective by adding your thoughts or someone else's. • Make sure the descriptive and narrative details reinforce the dominant impression you want to convey. • If your perspective is complex, you may need to discuss more directly the contradictions or complications you see in the subject. My readers don't find my perspective interesting. • An "uninteresting" perspective is sometimes an unclear one. Check with your readers to see whether they understood it. If they didn't, follow the tips above. • Readers sometimes say a perspective is "uninteresting" if it's too simple or obvious. Go back through your notes, looking for contradictions, other perspectives, surprises, or anything else that might help you complicate the perspective you are presenting.

Edit and proofread your draft.

Several errors often occur in profiles, including problems with the punctuation of quotations and the integration of *participial phrases*. The following guidelines will help you check your essay for these common errors.

Checking the Punctuation of Quotations

Because most profiles are based in part on interviews, you have probably quoted one or more people in your essay. When you proofread your writing, check to make sure you have observed the strict conventions for punctuating quotations:

What to Check For

- All quotations should have quotation marks at the beginning and the end.
  - ▶ "What exactly is civil litigation? ” I asked.
- Commas and periods go *inside* quotation marks.
  - ▶ "I'm here to see Anna Post, ",/ I replied nervously.
  - ▶ Tony explained, "Fraternity boys just wouldn't feel comfortable at the Chez Moi Café. ".
- Question marks and exclamation points go *inside* closing quotation marks if they are part of the quotation, *outside* if they are not.
  - ▶ After a pause, the patient asked, "Where do I sign?"?
  - ▶ Willie insisted, "You can *too* learn to play Super Mario!"!
  - ▶ When was the last time someone you just ticketed said to you, "Thank you, Officer, for doing a great job?"?
- Use commas with speaker tags (*he said, she asked*) that accompany direct quotations.
  - ▶ "This sound system costs only four thousand dollars," Jorge said.
  - ▶ I asked, "So where were these clothes from originally?"

Integrating Participial Phrases

The Problem Consider the following sentence:

▶ Snoring blissfully, Bob reclined in his chair.

You know that "Snoring blissfully" applies to Bob, because in English, modifying phrases or clauses like *snoring blissfully* are understood to apply to the nouns they precede or follow. That's why when you read the following sentence,

▶ Exhausted after 28 hours of studying, Regina sighed loudly.

you know that Regina studied for twenty-eight hours. So what does the following sentence, taken from a 2003 government press release, mean?

▶ Suspected to have been started by an arsonist, the fire investigation team

. . . continues its search for the person(s) responsible.

As written, it means that the fire investigation team may have been started by an arsonist. That may not be what the author of this sentence meant, but that's what the sentence says. This kind of error—called a *dangling modifier*—can confuse readers (or make them chuckle).

The Correction When editing or proofreading your writing, look for modifying clauses or phrases. In each case, ask yourself whether the person or thing performing the action in the modifier is named immediately before or after the modifier. If it isn't, you have several options for fixing the error:

Change the subject of the sentence.

▶ Suspected to have been started by an arsonist, the fire burned nearly 60,000 acres before being brought under control.

Change the modifier.

▶ Suspecting that an arsonist started the fire, the fire investigation team . . . continues its search for the person(s) responsible.

Move the modifying phrase or clause.

▶ The fire investigation team continues its investigation into the fire, suspected to have been started by an arsonist.

A Common Problem for Multilingual Writers: Adjective Order

The Problem In trying to present the subject of your profile vividly and in detail, you have probably included many descriptive adjectives. When you include more than one adjective in front of a noun, you may have difficulty sequencing them. For example, do you write *a large old ceramic pot* or *an old large ceramic pot*?

The Correction The following list shows the order in which adjectives are ordinarily arranged in front of a noun:

1. *Amount* (a/an, the, six)
2. *Evaluation* (good, beautiful, ugly, serious)
3. *Size* (large, small, tremendous)
4. *Shape, length* (round, long, short)
5. *Age* (young, new, old)
6. *Color* (red, black, green)
7. *Origin* (Asian, Brazilian, German)
8. *Material* (wood, cotton, gold)
9. Noun used as an adjective (computer [as in *computer program*], cake [as in *cake pan*])

Seventeen (1.) small (3.) green (6.) buds appeared on my birch sapling.

He tossed his daughter a (1.) nice (2.) new (5.) yellow (6.) tennis (9.) ball.

The (1.) slender (4.) German-made (7.) gold (8.) watch cost a great deal of money.

Reflecting on What You Have Learned

You have learned a great deal about this genre by reading several profiles and writing one of your own. To consolidate your learning, reflect not only on what you learned but also on how you learned it.

ANALYZE & WRITE

Write a blog post, a letter to your instructor or a classmate, or an e-mail message to a student who will take this course next term, using the writing prompt that seems most productive for you:

- Explain how your purpose and audience—what you wanted your readers to learn about your subject from reading your profile—influenced *one* of your decisions as a writer, such as what kinds of descriptive details you included, what method of organization you used, or the role you adopted in writing about your subject.
- Discuss what you learned about yourself as a writer in the process of writing this profile. For example, what part of the process did you find most challenging? Did you try anything new, like getting a critical reading of your draft or outlining your draft in order to revise it? If so, how well did it work?
- If you were to give advice to a fellow student who was about to write a profile, what would you say?
- Which of the readings in this chapter influenced your essay? Explain the influence, citing specific examples from your profile and the reading.
- If you got good advice from a critical reader, explain exactly how the person helped you—perhaps by questioning your perspective in a way that enabled you to refocus your profile's dominant impression, or by pointing out passages that needed more information or clearer chronology to better orient readers.

4

Explaining a Concept

Is the greatest threat to humanity a natural phenomenon we haven't really considered? Are the complex feelings of love rooted in simple biology? What happens to our judgment when we make too many decisions in one day? These are a few of the questions that are answered in the intriguing concept explanations in this chapter. Much of your reading and writing as a college student involves learning the concepts that are the building blocks of academic subjects. These concepts may include principles (such as *equal justice*), theories (such as *evolution*), ideas (such as *commodification*), conditions (such as *state of flow*), phenomena (such as *inflation*), or processes (such as *socialization*). To communicate effectively and efficiently about a subject—whether you are writing to your instructor, your boss, or your friends, or writing an essay exam, a blog post, or a presentation—you need to be able to use and explain concepts clearly and compellingly.

People analyze and explain concepts for various purposes and audiences and publish them in a variety of media. For example, a student in a cultural studies course might use the concept of cultural framing theory as a lens through which to analyze the politics of sexuality in advertising, then publish her essay in a student journal at her school. A parent might use Prezi software to explain the concept of surveying in advertising to her child's fifth-grade class. A business consultant might create a video to define and demonstrate 3-D imaging and to explain its role to potential buyers of driverless cars.

In this chapter, we ask you to analyze and explain a concept that you think will be unfamiliar to your readers. Whether you tackle a concept you've studied in college or choose one from your job or your favorite pastime, you need to answer your readers' inevitable "So what?" question: Why should they want to understand the concept? Analyzing the selections in the Guide to Reading that follows will help you learn how to make your concept explanation interesting and informative. The Guide to Writing later in the chapter will show you ways to use the basic features of the genre—including how to use visuals and multimedia—to make an unfamiliar concept not only understandable but also compelling to your readers.

PRACTICING THE GENRE

Explaining an Academic Concept

Part 1. First, think of a concept you recently learned in one of your courses. Next, take a few minutes to plan how you will explain it to classmates who may not know anything about the subject. Consider whether it would be helpful to do any of the following:

- Identify the course and the context in which you learned it
- Give your listeners a dictionary definition
- Tell them what kind of concept it is
- Compare it to something they may already know
- Give them an example
- Explain why the concept is important or useful

Part 2. In small groups, take two or three minutes each to explain your concept. Then discuss what you learned:

- **What did you learn about the genre from listening to others' explanations?** To think about purpose and audience in explaining a concept, tell one another whether you thought the "So what?" question was adequately answered: What, if anything, piqued your interest or made you feel as though the concept might be worth learning about? What strategies used by group members did you find were particularly effective?
- **What did you learn about explaining?** With the other members of your group, compare your thoughts about what was easiest and hardest about explaining a concept—for example, choosing a concept you understood well enough to explain to others; making it interesting, important, or useful to group members; or deciding what would best help your audience understand the concept in the time you had.

Analyzing Concept Explanations

As you read the selections in this chapter, you will see how different authors explain concepts:

- Jonathan Potthast explains the devastating consequences that would follow the eruption of a supervolcano (pp. 100–106).
- Anastasia Toufexis analyzes the biological basis of love (pp. 106–9).
- John Tierney explains the hidden danger of decision fatigue (pp. 112–15).

Analyzing how these writers develop a surprising or interesting focus for their explanation, organize the explanation to draw readers in and keep them reading, use examples and other writing strategies to make the topic compelling, and integrate sources to make their claims convincing will help you see how you can employ these same techniques to make your own concept explanations successful.

Determine the writer's purpose and audience.

How well a writer analyzes and explains a concept can demonstrate how well he or she understands it. That is why this kind of writing is so frequently assigned in college courses. But it is also a popular genre outside the classroom, where effective writers manage to make the most esoteric topics interesting and important. These authors understand that a concept explanation risks being dry and uninteresting to those not already intrigued by the topic, so they make an effort to zero in on a focus that will excite the curiosity of their readers. When reading the concept explanations that follow, ask yourself questions like these:

What seems to be the writer's main purpose?

- To inform readers about an important idea or theory?
- To show how a concept has promoted original thinking and research in an area of study?
- To better understand the concept by explaining it to others?
- To demonstrate knowledge of the concept and the ability to apply it?

What does the writer assume about the audience?

- That readers will be unfamiliar with the concept and need an introduction that will capture their interest?
- That readers will know something about the concept but want to learn more about it?
- That the primary reader will be an instructor who knows more about the concept than the writer does and who is evaluating the writer's knowledge?

Assess the genre's basic features.

Basic Features
A Focused Explanation
A Clear, Logical Organization
Appropriate Explanatory Strategies
Smooth Integration of Sources

As you read the concept explanations in this chapter, evaluate how effectively different authors employ the genre's basic features. The examples that follow are drawn from the reading selections that appear later in this Guide to Reading.

A FOCUSED EXPLANATION

Read first to identify the concept. Ask yourself:

- "What is the focus or main point?" This point is the *thesis* of a concept explanation, comparable to what we call autobiographical significance in remembered event essays and perspective in profiles. The point answers the "So what?" question: Why are you telling me about this concept? Why is it interesting or important?
- "What should I include and what should I leave out?" These decisions are often dictated by readers—how much they already know about the topic and how interested in the topic they are. For college writing and some other contexts, the focus may be dictated by a specific question or prompt. For example, Jonathan Potthast's instructor asked students to analyze a concept they had learned about in another course, conducting additional research as needed to explain the concept to a reader with little or no background in the subject.

A CLEAR, LOGICAL ORGANIZATION

Consider whether the concept explanation is clearly and logically organized. Notice how each writer develops a plan that does the following:

- States the thesis or main point early on

Concept	Let's put love under a microscope.
Main point	When rigorous people with Ph.D.s after their names do that, what they see is not some silly, senseless thing. No, their probe reveals that love rests firmly on the foundations of evolution, biology and chemistry. (Toufexis, pars. 1–2)

- Divides the information into clearly distinguishable topics and forecasts them in the order in which they will be discussed

Topic Forecast	Decision fatigue helps explain why ordinarily sensible people get angry at colleagues and families, splurge on clothes, buy junk food at the supermarket and can't resist the dealer's offer to rustproof their new car. (Tierney, par. 5)

- Guides readers by providing cues or road signs

Transition	Even more astounding, ash in the air after a volcano can temporarily cause dramatic changes to the climate. (Potthast, par. 7)
	Afterward, all the participants were given one of the classic tests of self-control: holding your hand in ice water for as long as you can. (Tierney, par. 9)
	If, in nature's design, romantic love is not eternal, neither is it exclusive. (Toufexis, par. 8)

APPROPRIATE EXPLANATORY STRATEGIES

Look for explanatory strategies—such as definition, classification, comparison-contrast, example, illustration, and cause-effect—that help readers understand the topic:

DEFINITION Defining characteristic Term being defined	Each person carries in his or her mind a unique subliminal guide to the ideal partner, a "love map." (Toufexis, par. 17)
COMPARISON-CONTRAST Cue Term being contrasted	While Western culture holds fast to the idea that true love flames forever (the movie *Bram Stoker's Dracula* has the Count carrying the torch beyond the grave), nature apparently meant passions to sputter out in something like four years. (Toufexis, par. 6)
EXAMPLE Cue Examples	When they forced themselves to remain stoic during a tearjerker movie, afterward they gave up more quickly on lab tasks requiring self-discipline, like working on a geometry puzzle or squeezing a hand-grip exerciser. (Tierney, par. 6)
ILLUSTRATION (WITH VISUAL) Reference to a visual in the text	Like hurricanes, the power of volcanoes is measured using an exponential scale, the Volcanic Explosivity Index, or VEI, (fig. 1). (Potthast, par. 1)
CAUSE-EFFECT Cause Effect	To a fatigued judge, denying parole seems like the easier call not only because it preserves the status quo . . . but also because it leaves more options open. (Tierney, par. 11)

For more on strategies for cueing readers, see Chapter 11.

SMOOTH INTEGRATION OF SOURCES

Notice how writers draw on research, as well as their own experiences and observations, to explain the concept. How do writers establish their authority by smoothly integrating information from sources into the explanation? Does the writer quote, paraphrase, or summarize the source material? How does the writer establish the source's expertise and credibility? The following examples demonstrate some strategies:

QUOTE Signal phrase plus credentials	According to Joel Achenbach, a reporter on science and politics for magazines and newspapers such as *National Geographic*, *Slate*, and the *Washington Post*, . . . a super-eruption 2.1 million years ago . . . "[left] a hole in the ground the size of Rhode Island" (Achenbach 1). (Potthast, par. 9)
Parenthetical citation	In the wake of the . . . eruption, a pyroclastic flow "swept down the mountain, flattening forests, overtaking escaping vehicles and killing several people who stood absolutely no chance of moving out of its path" ("Lahars"). (Potthast, par. 2)
PARAPHRASE Signal phrase plus credentials	It is the difference between passionate and compassionate love, observes Walsh, a psychobiologist at Boise State University in Idaho. (Toufexis, par. 14)

SUMMARY
Signal phrase plus credentials

Decision fatigue is the newest discovery involving . . . ego depletion, a term coined by the social psychologist Roy F. Baumeister . . . [who] began studying mental discipline in a series of experiments . . . [that] demonstrated that there is a finite store of mental energy for exerting self-control. (Tierney, par. 6)

How writers treat sources depends on the writing situation. Certain formal situations, such as college assignments or scholarly publications, require writers to cite sources in the text and document them in a bibliography (called a list of **works cited** in many humanities disciplines and a list of **references** in the sciences and social sciences). Students and scholars are expected to cite their sources formally because readers will judge the work in part by what the writers have read and how they have used it. They may also be interested in locating the sources and reading more about the topic for themselves. (Jonathan Potthast's essay, below, provides an example of academic citation.) For writing that appears in popular sources, such as magazine and newspaper articles, readers do not expect references or publication information to appear in the text, but they do expect sources to be identified and their expertise established in some way. (The articles by Toufexis and Tierney, on pp. 106–9 and 112–15, provide examples of informal citation.)

Readings

Jonathan Potthast | *Supervolcanoes: A Catastrophe of Ice and Fire*

ORIGINALLY, Jonathan Potthast wrote this essay analyzing and explaining supervolcanoes for his composition course. Following his instructor's recommendation, Potthast chose a concept he had learned about in another course. He used a number of sources, including articles and books, some of which he accessed through his library's Web site. His instructor required his citation format to be the one used for the humanities, from the Modern Language Association (MLA).

As you read, consider the following:

- How does Potthast interest readers in his subject?
- Why do you think he compares supervolcanoes to asteroid impacts and hurricanes?
- Answer the questions in the margin. Your instructor may ask you to post your answers to a class blog or discussion board or to bring them to class.

1 Possibly the most destructive natural disaster, short of a large asteroid impact, would be the eruption of a supervolcano. Supervolcanoes are volcanoes that produce eruptions thousands of times the size of ordinary volcanoes. Like hurricanes, the power of volcanoes is measured using an exponential scale, the Volcanic Explosivity Index, or VEI (fig. 1).

2 A brief synopsis of the effects of regular volcanoes can provide clues as to how destructive the eruption of a supervolcano would be. Volcanic eruptions

Basic Features

A Focused Explanation

A Clear, Logical Organization

Appropriate Explanatory Strategies

Smooth Integration of Sources

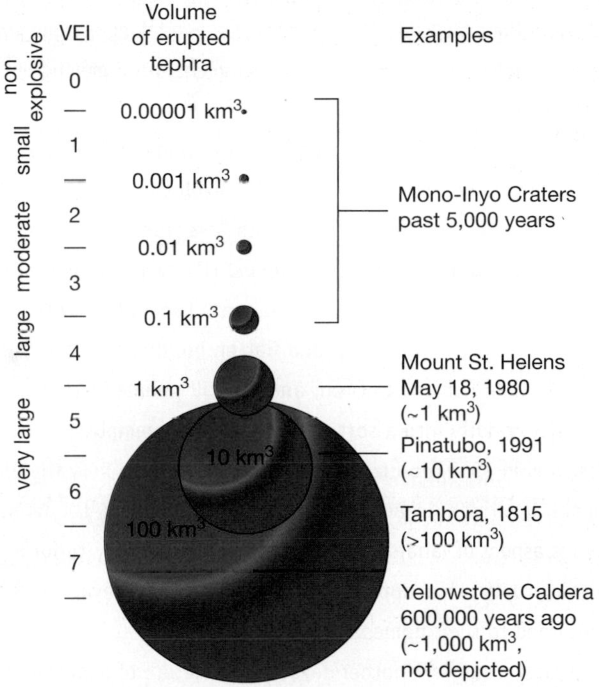

Fig. 1. "Volcanic Explosivity Index (VEI)." *Volcano World*, Department of Geosciences, Oregon State U and Oregon Space Grant Consortium, volcano.oregonstate.edu/eruption-styles. Accessed 22 Dec. 2014.

How does the VEI help the reader follow Potthast's explanation?

How does Potthast use categories to organize his explanation?

feature several dangerous physical effects, including pyroclastic flows, pyroclastic surges, lahars, tephra falls, and massive amounts of fine ash particles in the air. Pyroclastic flows, which are dense superheated mixtures of ash, rock, and gas, are the most deadly feature of volcanoes. They are often as hot as 1,400 degrees Fahrenheit and flow at rates of hundreds of miles per hour, making prior evacuation the only possible means of escape. Driven by gravity, pyroclastic flows destroy everything in their path, and "they pose lethal hazard from incineration, asphyxiation, burial, and impact" (United States, "Pyroclastic"). In the wake of the May 18, 1980, Mt. St. Helens eruption, a pyroclastic flow "swept down the mountain, flattening forests, overtaking escaping vehicles and killing several people who stood absolutely no chance of moving out of its path" ("Lahars").

3 In addition, by rapidly heating phreatic (underground) water, volcanic eruptions can trigger violent steam-driven explosions. The water from these phreatic eruptions can then combine with lava from pyroclastic flows to create devastating mudslides called *lahars*. (Rainwater or melting snow can also combine with lava flows to form lahars.) Lahars flow with enough force to uproot trees, carry away cars, and flatten buildings ("Lahars"). They flow much faster than humans can run, and can kill people instantly. When cooled, they solidify into a sort of concrete. For example, the eruption of Mt. Vesuvius in 79 CE produced lahars large enough to bury the entire city of Pompeii in what quickly became solid volcanic rock ("Lahars"). The most dangerous aspect of lahars, however, lies in their ability to form long after a volcanic eruption has apparently ceased, even after evacuated inhabitants have returned to their homes.

4 Pyroclastic surges, another devastating feature of many volcanoes, are composed of gas and particles of volcanic ash which move as quickly as pyroclastic flows but are less dense. P. J. Baxter, a physician specializing in occupational and environmental medicine at Cambridge University and a consultant to the World Health Organization on volcanoes, notes that humans exposed even briefly to pyroclastic surges face serious burns as well as risks of asphyxia (suffocation) and hypoxia (oxygen deprivation to body tissue). The extreme heat of the surges, if not hot enough to kill a person instantly, can kill a person by burning their lungs, throat, and windpipes so severely that those organs swell to the point of preventing any air from getting in.

5 Tephra falls, or showers of pieces of volcanic rock ejected from a volcano, can also be deadly to those nearby. The sheer force of a tephra "rain" can cause roofs to collapse and people without shelter to be battered to death (Horwell and Baxter). While tephra presents an immediate and short-lived danger, however, fine ash particles in the air cause more lasting damage. Heavy ash deposits can destroy vegetation, causing widespread famine and suffering to animals that depend on those plants for food. Inhaling fine volcanic ash can cause silicosis, an irreversible lung disease (Horwell and Baxter). Ash particles also cause damage to moving parts in machinery and vehicles.

6 Aside from the obvious immediate destruction of these physical effects, a volcanic eruption can also have a surprising aftermath. For example, following the 1996 Soufreire Hills volcano, hydrogen sulfide and sulfur dioxide (gases produced in the eruption) combined to form sulfuric acid; this, mixed with the rainwater, destroyed acres of cloud forest (Brosnan). Coral reefs could be destroyed in a similar manner.

How effectively does Potthast make the transition from the damaging physical features of volcanoes to their unexpected consequences?

7 Even more astounding, ash in the air after a volcano can temporarily cause dramatic changes to the climate. For instance, in the years following the eruption of Tambora in Indonesia on April 5, 1815, fine particles of volcanic ash and aerosols created a fog-like layer in the atmosphere that blocked some of the sun's rays and led to temporary global cooling of about five and a half degrees Fahrenheit ("Mount Tambora"). In Europe and North America, 1816 became known as "the year without a summer"; the New England states, for example, experienced a "killing frost through June, July, and August" ("Mount Tambora"). Although "enough grains, wheat, and potatoes were harvested to prevent a famine," crops such as corn, beans, and squash were destroyed before they could be harvested, hay crops were meager, and "there were reports of people eating raccoons, pigeons, and mackerel" (Foster). Other recent major volcanoes, such as Krakatoa in 1883, have produced similar cooling effects: "On the average, temperature dropped by as much as 1.2°C in the succeeding year. In the years that followed, global climates were very erratic, stabilizing only 4 years after" (Villanueva).

How effectively does Potthast weave information together from several sources in this paragraph?

8 Luckily, no supervolcano has erupted in recorded history. Several supervolcanoes exist today, but most are under the ocean, and all are considered dormant or extinct. According to National Parks Service geologists, a catastrophic eruption would probably provide a good deal—maybe even years—of advance

What is the effect on the reader of this transitional paragraph?

warning, and other geologic events ("a serious increase in earthquakes, ground deformation, and geyser basin temperature") would occur within days or weeks of the eruption (United States, "Yellowstone's" 00:02:27-52).

9 A dormant supervolcano close to home is in Yellowstone National Park. According to Joel Achenbach, a reporter on science and politics for magazines and newspapers such as *National Geographic, Slate,* and the *Washington Post,* three super-eruptions have occurred there, with one just 640,000 years ago (a blink of an eye in geologic terms). Even more powerful was a super-eruption 2.1 million years ago that "[left] a hole in the ground the size of Rhode Island" (Achenbach 1). The caldera, or crater, of the Yellowstone supervolcano is about 45 miles across and, over time, has been eroded and covered by glaciers and forests; part of the caldera's rim is invisible, hidden beneath the surface of Lake Butte.

10 It was thought that the volcano was extinct, but activity is making scientists rethink that view (Achenbach 2). A huge magma chamber lies deep under the volcano's caldera. When shifted by earthquakes and pressed by hot rock, the land above it rises and falls. An earthquake swarm in the mid-1980s made Yellowstone drop, so that it was about eight inches lower ten years later (Achenbach 2). More recently, "portions of the caldera have surged upward at a rate of nearly three inches a year, much faster than any uplift since close observations began in the 1970's" (Achenbach 3). Such activity indicates a live volcano.

What does Potthast achieve in these concluding paragraphs? How does it work for you?

11 Although a catastrophic eruption is far from imminent, one is possible. If a super-eruption were to occur here, the results would be devastating: A Yellowstone eruption, for example, could deposit a 10-foot layer of ash that would destroy vegetation 1,000 miles away. Toxic gases would sweep across much of the nation, making "two-thirds of the U.S. . . . uninhabitable . . . forcing millions to leave their homes" (Bates). Burning plants would generate vast amounts of carbon dioxide that would increase the greenhouse effect and ultimately contribute to global warming, but the immediate effect of a supervolcanic eruption would be dramatic global cooling. While Tambora created a "year without summer," a supervolcanic eruption would "potentially plunge the Earth into years of 'volcanic winter'" (Achenbach 2). According to science writer Charles Choi, a supervolcanic eruption would have an impact comparable to that of a mile-wide asteroid, killing many millions of people and changing the entire global landscape.

What makes Potthast's sources seem authoritative?

Works Cited

Achenbach, Joel. "When Yellowstone Explodes." *National Geographic Magazine,* Aug. 2009, pp. 1-3.

Bates, Daniel. "Is the World's Largest Super-Volcano Set to Erupt for the First Time in 600,000 Years, Wiping Out Two-Thirds of the U.S.?" *Daily Mail,* Associated Newspapers, 25 Jan. 2011, www.dailymail.co.uk/sciencetech/article-1350123/Worlds-largest-volcano-Yellowstone-National-Park-wipe-thirds-US.html.

Baxter, P. J. "Blast, Burns, Asphyxia and Hypoxia: How Do Pyroclastic Surges Damage Humans?" *Montserrat Volcano Observatory,* Michigan Technical University, Department of Geology, www.montserratvolcano.org/humans.htm. Accessed 6 May 2014.

Brosnan, Deborah M. "Ecological Impacts of the Montserrat Volcano: A Pictorial Account of Its Effects on Land and Sea Life." *Sustainable Ecosystems Institute,* 21 Oct. 2005, www.mona.uwi.edu/cardin/virtual_library/docs/1007/1007.pdf.

Choi, Charles Q. "Supervolcano Not to Blame for Humanity's Near-Extinction." *LiveScience,* Purch, 29 Apr. 2013, www.livescience.com/29130-toba-supervolcano-effects.html.

Foster, Lee. "1816—The Year Without Summer." *Climate Corner,* United States, Department of Commerce, National Oceanic and Atmospheric Administration, www.erh.noaa.gov/car/Newsletter/htm_format_articles/climate_corner/yearwithoutsummer_lf.htm. Accessed 21 Mar. 2015.

Horwell, Claire J., and Peter J. Baxter. "The Respiratory Health Hazards of Volcanic Ash: A Review for Volcanic Risk Mitigation." *Bulletin of Volcanology,* vol. 69, no. 1, 2006, pp. 1-24. *Springer Link,* doi:10.1007/s00445-006-0052-y.

"Lahars and Pyroclastic Flows." *The Geography Site,* 16 May 2006, www.geography-site.co.uk/pages/physical/earth/volcanoes/pyroclastic%20flows.html.

"Mount Tambora." *Encyclopaedia Britannica,* 2016, www.britannica.com/place/Mount-Tambora.

United States, Department of the Interior, Geological Survey. "Pyroclastic Flow Hazards at Mount St. Helens." *Volcano Hazards Program,* 22 Jan. 2013, volcanoes.usgs.gov/volcanoes/st_helens/st_helens_hazard_77.html.

---, ---, National Parks Service. "Yellowstone's Restless Giant." *Yellowstone National Park,* 27 Apr. 2007, www.nps.gov/media/video/view.htm?id =FEF54BF6-155D-451F-6725EBD604F1CD16.

Villanueva, John Carl. "Mount Krakatoa." *Universe Today,* 18 Sept. 2009, www.universetoday.com/40601/mount-krakatoa/.

Anastasia Toufexis | *Love: The Right Chemistry*

ANASTASIA TOUFEXIS has been an associate editor of *Time*, senior editor of *Discover*, and editor in chief of *Psychology Today*. She has written on subjects as diverse as medicine, health and fitness, law, the environment, education, science, and national and world news. Toufexis has won a number of awards for her writing, including a Knight-Wallace Fellowship at the University of Michigan and an Ocean Science Journalism Fellowship at Woods Hole Oceanographic Institution. She has also lectured on science writing at Columbia University, the University of North Carolina, and the School of Visual Arts in New York. The essay below was originally published in *Time* magazine.

As you read, consider the following questions:

- How would you describe the tone Toufexis adopts in this essay, at least in the beginning? How effective do you think this tone was for her original readers? How appropriate would it be for a college paper?
- Given her purpose and audience, how effective is the visual in helping readers understand her rather technical explanation?

Love is a romantic designation for a most ordinary biological—or, shall we say, chemical?—process. A lot of nonsense is talked and written about it.

—Greta Garbo to Melvyn Douglas in *Ninotchka*

1 O.K., let's cut out all this nonsense about romantic love. Let's bring some scientific precision to the party. Let's put love under a microscope.

2 When rigorous people with Ph.D.s after their names do that, what they see is not some silly, senseless thing. No, their probe reveals that love rests firmly on the foundations of evolution, biology and chemistry. What seems on the surface to be irrational, intoxicated behavior is in fact part of nature's master strategy—a vital force that has helped humans survive, thrive and multiply through thousands of years. Says Michael Mills, a psychology professor at Loyola Marymount University in Los Angeles: "Love is our ancestors whispering in our ears."

3 It was on the plains of Africa about 4 million years ago, in the early days of the human species, that the notion of romantic love probably first began to blossom or at least that the first cascades of neurochemicals began flowing from the brain to the bloodstream to produce goofy grins and sweaty palms as men and women

gazed deeply into each other's eyes. When mankind graduated from scuttling around on all fours to walking on two legs, this change made the whole person visible to fellow human beings for the first time. Sexual organs were in full display, as were other characteristics, from the color of eyes to the span of shoulders. As never before, each individual had a unique allure.

4 When the sparks flew, new ways of making love enabled sex to become a romantic encounter, not just a reproductive act. Although mounting mates from the rear was, and still is, the method favored among most animals, humans began to enjoy face-to-face couplings; both looks and personal attraction became a much greater part of the equation.

5 Romance served the evolutionary purpose of pulling males and females into long-term partnership, which was essential to child rearing. On open grasslands, one parent would have a hard—and dangerous—time handling a child while foraging for food. "If a woman was carrying the equivalent of a 20-lb. bowling ball in one arm and a pile of sticks in the other, it was ecologically critical to pair up with a mate to rear the young," explains anthropologist Helen Fisher, author of *Anatomy of Love*.

6 While Western culture holds fast to the idea that true love flames forever (the movie *Bram Stoker's Dracula* has the Count carrying the torch beyond the grave), nature apparently meant passions to sputter out in something like four years. Primitive pairs stayed together just "long enough to rear one child through infancy," says Fisher. Then each would find a new partner and start all over again.

7 What Fisher calls the "four-year itch" shows up unmistakably in today's divorce statistics. In most of the 62 cultures she has studied, divorce rates peak around the fourth year of marriage. Additional youngsters help keep pairs together longer. If, say, a couple have another child three years after the first, as often occurs, then their union can be expected to last about four more years. That makes them ripe for the more familiar phenomenon portrayed in the Marilyn Monroe classic *The Seven-Year Itch*.

8 If, in nature's design, romantic love is not eternal, neither is it exclusive. Less than 5% of mammals form rigorously faithful pairs. From the earliest days, contends Fisher, the human pattern has been "monogamy with clandestine adultery." Occasional flings upped the chances that new combinations of genes would be passed on to the next generation. Men who sought new partners had more children. Contrary to common assumptions, women were just as likely to stray. "As long as prehistoric females were secretive about their extramarital affairs," argues Fisher, "they could garner extra resources, life insurance, better genes and more varied DNA for their biological futures. . . ."

9 Lovers often claim that they feel as if they are being swept away. They're not mistaken; they are literally flooded by chemicals, research suggests. A meeting of eyes, a touch of hands or a whiff of scent sets off a flood that starts in the brain and races along the nerves and through the blood. The results are familiar: flushed skin, sweaty palms, heavy breathing. If love looks suspiciously like stress, the reason is simple: the chemical pathways are identical.

10 Above all, there is the sheer euphoria of falling in love—a not-so-surprising reaction, considering that many of the substances swamping the newly smitten are chemical cousins of amphetamines. They include dopamine, norepinephrine and especially phenylethylamine (PEA). Cole Porter knew what he was talking about when he wrote, "I get a kick out of you." "Love is a natural high," observes Anthony Walsh, author of *The Science of Love: Understanding Love and Its Effects on Mind and Body*. "PEA gives you that silly smile that you flash at strangers. When we meet someone who is attractive to us, the whistle blows at the PEA factory."

11 But phenylethylamine highs don't last forever, a fact that lends support to arguments that passionate romantic love is short-lived. As with any amphetamine, the body builds up a tolerance to PEA; thus it takes more and more of the substance to produce love's special kick. After two to three years, the body simply can't crank up the needed amount of PEA. And chewing on chocolate doesn't help, despite popular belief. The candy is high in PEA, but it fails to boost the body's supply.

12 Fizzling chemicals spell the end of delirious passion; for many people that marks the end of the liaison as well. It is particularly true for those whom Dr. Michael Liebowitz of the New York State Psychiatric Institute terms "attraction junkies." They crave the intoxication of falling in love so much that they move frantically from affair to affair just as soon as the first rush of infatuation fades.

13 Still, many romances clearly endure beyond the first years. What accounts for that? Another set of chemicals, of course. The continued presence of a partner gradually steps up production in the brain of endorphins. Unlike the fizzy amphetamines, these are soothing substances. Natural pain-killers, they give lovers a sense of security, peace and calm. "That is one reason why it feels so horrible when we're abandoned or a lover dies," notes Fisher. "We don't have our daily hit of narcotics."

14 Researchers see a contrast between the heated infatuation induced by PEA, along with other amphetamine-like chemicals, and the more intimate attachment fostered and prolonged by endorphins. "Early love is when you love the way the other person makes you feel," explains psychiatrist Mark Goulston of the University of California, Los Angeles. "Mature love is when you love the person as he or she is." It is the difference between passionate and compassionate love, observes Walsh, a psychobiologist at Boise State University in Idaho. "It's Bon Jovi vs. Beethoven."

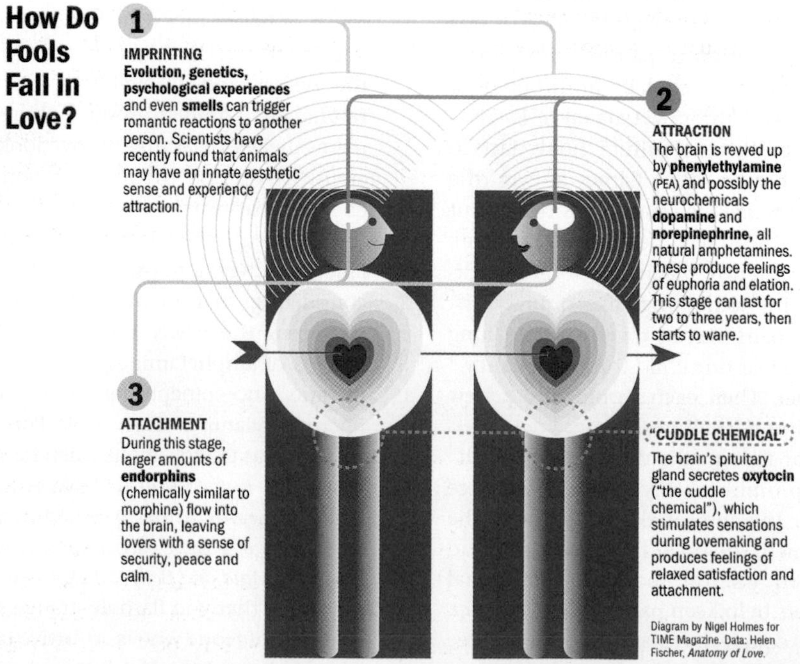

15 Oxytocin is another chemical that has recently been implicated in love. Produced by the brain, it sensitizes nerves and stimulates muscle contraction. In women it helps uterine contractions during childbirth as well as production of breast milk, and seems to inspire mothers to nuzzle their infants. Scientists speculate that oxytocin might encourage similar cuddling between adult women and men. The versatile chemical may also enhance orgasms. In one study of men, oxytocin increased to three to five times its normal level during climax, and it may soar even higher in women.

16 Chemicals may help explain (at least to scientists) the feelings of passion and compassion, but why do people tend to fall in love with one partner rather than a myriad of others? Once again, it's partly a function of evolution and biology. "Men are looking for maximal fertility in a mate," says Loyola Marymount's Mills. "That is in large part why females in the prime childbearing ages of 17 to 28 are so desirable." Men can size up youth and vitality in a glance, and studies indeed show that men fall in love quite rapidly. Women tumble more slowly, to a large degree because their requirements are more complex; they need more time to check the guy out. "Age is not vital," notes Mills, "but the ability to provide security, father children, share resources and hold a high status in society are all key factors."

17 Still, that does not explain why the way Mary walks and laughs makes Bill dizzy with desire while Marcia's gait and giggle leave him cold. "Nature has wired us for one special person," suggests Walsh, romantically. He rejects the idea that a woman or a man can be in love with two people at the same time. Each person carries in his or her mind a unique subliminal guide to the ideal partner, a "love map," to borrow a term coined by sexologist John Money of Johns Hopkins University.

18 Drawn from the people and experiences of childhood, the map is a record of whatever we found enticing and exciting—or disturbing and disgusting. Small feet, curly hair. The way our mothers patted our head or how our fathers told a joke. A fireman's uniform, a doctor's stethoscope. All the information gathered while growing up is imprinted in the brain's circuitry by adolescence. Partners never meet each and every requirement, but a sufficient number of matches can light up the wires and signal, "It's love." Not every partner will be like the last one, since lovers may have different combinations of the characteristics favored by the map.

19 O.K., that's the scientific point of view. Satisfied? Probably not. To most people—with or without Ph.D.s—love will always be more than the sum of its natural parts. It's a commingling of body and soul, reality and imagination, poetry and phenylethylamine. In our deepest hearts, most of us harbor the hope that love will never fully yield up its secrets, that it will always elude our grasp.

[REFLECT] Make connections: How love works.

The chemistry of love is easily summarized: Amphetamines fuel romance; endorphins and oxytocin sustain lasting relationships. As Toufexis makes clear, however, these chemical reactions do not explain why people are attracted to each other in the first place. Rather, she claims that an attraction occurs because each of us carries a "unique subliminal guide," or "love map" (par. 17), that leads us unerringly to a partner. Make a short list of the qualities in a partner that would appear on your "love map," and then consider Toufexis's explanation. Your instructor may ask you to post your thoughts on a class discussion board or to discuss them with other students in class. Use these questions to get started:

- What role do factors such as family, friends, community, the media, and advertising play in constructing your love map?
- Why do you think Toufexis ignores the topic of sexual orientation?
- According to Toufexis, men typically look for "maximal fertility," whereas women look for security, resources, status, and a willingness to father children (par. 16). Does this explanation seem convincing to you? Why or why not?

[ANALYZE] Use the basic features.

A FOCUSED EXPLANATION: EXCLUDING OTHER TOPICS

In writing about a concept as broad as love, Toufexis had to find a way to narrow her focus. Writers choose a focus in part by considering the **rhetorical situation**—the purpose, audience, medium, and genre—in which they are writing. Student Jonathan Potthast was limited by the fact that he was writing in response to his instructor's assignment. As a science writer for *Time* magazine, Toufexis probably also had an assignment—to report on current scientific research. How does Toufexis make the science interesting and understandable to her nonscientist readers?

ANALYZE & WRITE

Write a paragraph analyzing how Toufexis focuses her explanation:

1. What is the focus or main point of Toufexis's essay? How do you think she answers readers' potential "So what?" question?
2. How do the title, epigraph, and opening paragraphs help you identify this focus or main point?
3. How do you think Toufexis's purpose, audience, and genre (an article for a popular newsmagazine) affected her focus?

A CLEAR, LOGICAL ORGANIZATION: CUEING THE READER

Experienced writers know that readers often have trouble making their way through new and difficult material. To avoid having them give up in frustration, writers strive to construct a reader-friendly organization: They include a thesis statement that asserts the focus or main point—the answer to the "So what?" question. In addition, writers sometimes include a *forecasting statement,* which alerts readers to the main topics to be discussed, and *transitional words and phrases* to guide readers from topic to topic.

ANALYZE & WRITE

Write a paragraph or two analyzing the strategies Toufexis uses to organize her essay for readers:

1. Skim the essay, and note in the margin where she announces her concept and forecasts the topics she uses to organize her explanation. Then highlight the passage where she discusses each topic. How well does her forecast work to make her essay readable?

2 Study how Toufexis connects the topic of "love maps" (pars. 17–18) to the topics she discussed earlier in the essay. Identify any sentences that connect the two parts of the article, and assess how well they work.

APPROPRIATE EXPLANATORY STRATEGIES: USING VISUALS

Both Potthast and Toufexis use a visual to help explain their concept. In Potthast's case, the visual comes from one of his sources. In contrast, Toufexis's visual was most likely created after her article was written, by the magazine's art editor, Nigel Holmes. Notice also that whereas Potthast, following a convention of academic writing, refers in the text of his essay to the visual he includes, labeling it "Fig. 1" and providing a title and source, Toufexis does not refer to the visual in her text or provide a caption.

ANALYZE & WRITE

Write a paragraph analyzing Toufexis's use of the visual:

1 Consider the visual apart from the rest of the article. What can you learn from the visual itself? What makes it easy or hard to read?

2 Skim Toufexis's essay to mark where she discusses each of the stages in the process described in the flowchart. Considering her original audience, how well does the flowchart work as a map to help readers navigate through the somewhat technical content of her explanation? Would it have been helpful for Toufexis to have referred to and labeled the visual?

SMOOTH INTEGRATION OF SOURCES: ESTABLISHING CREDIBILITY

To establish their credibility on the subject, writers need to convince readers that the information they are using is authoritative. They can do this in a number of ways, but giving the professional credentials of their sources is a conventional strategy.

ANALYZE & WRITE

Write a paragraph or two analyzing how Toufexis establishes the credentials of her sources:

1 Skim the essay, underlining the name of each source she mentions. Then go back through the essay to highlight each source's credentials. When Toufexis provides credentials, what kinds of information does she include?

2 Consider the effectiveness of Toufexis's strategies for letting readers know the qualifications of her sources. Given her original audience (*Time* magazine readers), how well do you think she establishes her sources' credentials? If she were writing for an academic audience (for example, for your instructor), what would she have to add?

[RESPOND] Consider possible topics: Examining other aspects of love.

Like Toufexis, you could write an essay about love or romance, but you could choose a different focus—for example, the history of romantic love (how did the concept of romantic love develop in the West, and when did it become the basis of marriage?), love's cultural characteristics (how is love regarded by different American ethnic groups or in world cultures?), its excesses or extremes (what is sex addiction?), or the phases of falling in and out of love (what is infatuation?). You could also consider writing about other concepts involving personal relationships, such as jealousy, codependency, stereotyping, or homophobia.

John Tierney | *Do You Suffer from Decision Fatigue?*

© Fred R. Conrad/The New York Times/Redux

JOHN TIERNEY has been a columnist for the *New York Times* since 1990, where he has worked as a general assignment reporter and a regular columnist, writing for the *New York Times Magazine* and for the Metro section in a column called The Big City. Currently he writes a column, Findings, for the Science Times section. He has worked for several other magazines and newspapers, among them the *Atlantic, Discover, Esquire, Newsweek, Outside,* and the *Wall Street Journal.* In collaboration with novelist Christopher Buckley, Tierney co-wrote the comic novel *God Is My Broker* (2012), a parody of financial and spiritual self-help books. The following essay (originally published in 2011 in the *New York Times Magazine*) was adapted from a book he wrote with Roy F. Baumeister, *Willpower: Rediscovering the Greatest Human Strength* (2011).

As you read, consider the following:

- Think about the effectiveness of the opening scenario that describes the decisions made by the parole board; what is Tierney's purpose in starting with this anecdote?
- Ponder the relationship you see between decision fatigue and willpower.

1 Three men doing time in Israeli prisons recently appeared before a parole board consisting of a judge, a criminologist and a social worker. The three prisoners had completed at least two-thirds of their sentences, but the parole board granted freedom to only one of them. Guess which one:

> Case 1 (heard at 8:50 a.m.): An Arab Israeli serving a 30-month sentence for fraud.
> Case 2 (heard at 3:10 p.m.): A Jewish Israeli serving a 16-month sentence for assault.
> Case 3 (heard at 4:25 p.m.): An Arab Israeli serving a 30-month sentence for fraud.

2 There was a pattern to the parole board's decisions, but it wasn't related to the men's ethnic backgrounds, crimes or sentences. It was all about timing, as researchers discovered by analyzing more than 1,100 decisions over the course of a year. Judges, who would hear the prisoners' appeals and then get advice from the other members of the board, approved parole in about a third of the cases, but the probability of being paroled fluctuated wildly throughout the day. Prisoners who appeared early in the morning received parole about 70 percent of the time, while those who appeared late in the day were paroled less than 10 percent of the time.

3 The odds favored the prisoner who appeared at 8:50 a.m.—and he did in fact receive parole. But even though the other Arab Israeli prisoner was serving the same sentence for the same crime—fraud—the odds were against him when he appeared (on a different day) at 4:25 in the afternoon. He was denied parole, as was the

Jewish Israeli prisoner at 3:10 p.m, whose sentence was shorter than that of the man who was released. They were just asking for parole at the wrong time of day.

4 There was nothing malicious or even unusual about the judges' behavior, which was reported . . . by Jonathan Levav of Stanford and Shai Danziger of Ben-Gurion University.[1] The judges' erratic judgment was due to the occupational hazard of being, as George W. Bush once put it, "the decider." The mental work of ruling on case after case, whatever the individual merits, wore them down. This sort of decision fatigue can make quarterbacks prone to dubious choices late in the game and C.F.O.'s prone to disastrous dalliances late in the evening. It routinely warps the judgment of everyone, executive and nonexecutive, rich and poor—in fact, it can take a special toll on the poor. Yet few people are even aware of it, and researchers are only beginning to understand why it happens and how to counteract it.

5 Decision fatigue helps explain why ordinarily sensible people get angry at colleagues and families, splurge on clothes, buy junk food at the supermarket and can't resist the dealer's offer to rustproof their new car. No matter how rational and high-minded you try to be, you can't make decision after decision without paying a biological price. It's different from ordinary physical fatigue—you're not consciously aware of being tired—but you're low on mental energy. The more choices you make throughout the day, the harder each one becomes for your brain, and eventually it looks for shortcuts, usually in either of two very different ways. One shortcut is to become reckless: to act impulsively instead of expending the energy to first think through the consequences. (Sure, tweet that photo! What could go wrong?) The other shortcut is the ultimate energy saver: do nothing. Instead of agonizing over decisions, avoid any choice. Ducking a decision often creates bigger problems in the long run, but for the moment, it eases the mental strain. You start to resist any change, any potentially risky move—like releasing a prisoner who might commit a crime. So the fatigued judge on a parole board takes the easy way out, and the prisoner keeps doing time.

6 Decision fatigue is the newest discovery involving a phenomenon called ego depletion, a term coined by the social psychologist Roy F. Baumeister[2] . . . [who] began studying mental discipline in a series of experiments, first at Case Western and then at Florida State University. These experiments demonstrated that there is a finite store of mental energy for exerting self-control. When people fended off the temptation to scarf down M&M's or freshly baked chocolate-chip cookies, they were then less able to resist other temptations. When they forced themselves to remain stoic during a tearjerker movie, afterward they gave up more quickly on lab tasks requiring self-discipline, like working on a geometry puzzle or squeezing a hand-grip exerciser. Willpower turned out to be more than a folk concept or a metaphor. It really was a form of mental energy that could be exhausted. The experiments confirmed the 19th-century notion of willpower being like a muscle that was fatigued with use, a force that could be conserved by avoiding temptation. To study the process of ego depletion, researchers concentrated initially on acts involving self-control—the kind of self-discipline popularly associated with willpower, like resisting a bowl of ice cream. They weren't concerned with routine decision-making, like choosing between chocolate and vanilla, a mental process that they assumed was quite distinct and much less strenuous. Intuitively, the chocolate-vanilla choice didn't appear to require willpower.

But then a postdoctoral fellow, Jean Twenge, started working at Baumeister's laboratory right after planning her wedding. 7
As Twenge studied the results of the lab's

ego-depletion experiments, she remembered how exhausted she felt the evening she and her fiancé went through the ritual of registering for gifts. Did they want plain white china or something with a pattern? Which brand of knives? How many towels? What kind of sheets? Precisely how many threads per square inch?

8 "By the end, you could have talked me into anything," Twenge told her new colleagues. The symptoms sounded familiar to them too, and gave them an idea. A nearby department store was holding a going-out-of-business sale, so researchers from the lab went off to fill their car trunks with simple products—not exactly wedding-quality gifts, but sufficiently appealing to interest college students. When they came to the lab, the students were told they would get to keep one item at the end of the experiment, but first they had to make a series of choices. Would they prefer a pen or a candle? A vanilla-scented candle or an almond-scented one? A candle or a T-shirt? A black T-shirt or a red T-shirt? A control group, meanwhile—let's call them the nondeciders—spent an equally long period contemplating all these same products without having to make any choices. They were asked just to give their opinion of each product and report how often they had used such a product in the last six months.

9 Afterward, all the participants were given one of the classic tests of self-control: holding your hand in ice water for as long as you can. The impulse is to pull your hand out, so self-discipline is needed to keep the hand underwater. The deciders gave up much faster; they lasted 28 seconds, less than half the 67-second average of the nondeciders. Making all those choices had apparently sapped their willpower. . . .

10 Any decision, whether it's what pants to buy or whether to start a war, can be broken down into what psychologists call the Rubicon model of action phases, in honor of the river that separated Italy from the Roman province of Gaul. When Caesar reached it in 49 BC, on his way home after conquering the Gauls, he knew that a general returning to Rome was forbidden to take his legions across the river with him, lest it be considered an invasion of Rome. Waiting on the Gaul side of the river, he was in the "predecisional phase" as he contemplated the risks and benefits of starting a civil war. Then he stopped calculating and crossed the Rubicon, reaching the "postdecisional phase," which Caesar defined much more felicitously: "The die is cast."

11 The whole process could deplete anyone's willpower, but which phase of the decision-making process was most fatiguing? To find out, Kathleen Vohs, a former colleague of Baumeister's now at the University of Minnesota, performed an experiment [that] showed that crossing the Rubicon is more tiring than anything that happens on either bank—more mentally fatiguing than sitting on the Gaul side contemplating your options or marching on Rome once you've crossed. As a result, someone without Caesar's willpower is liable to stay put. To a fatigued judge, denying parole seems like the easier call not only because it preserves the status quo and eliminates the risk of a parolee going on a crime spree but also because it leaves more options open: the judge retains the option of paroling the prisoner at a future date without sacrificing the option of keeping him securely in prison right now.

12 Once you're mentally depleted, you become reluctant to make trade-offs, which involve a particularly advanced and taxing form of decision making. In the rest of the animal kingdom, there aren't a lot of protracted negotiations between predators and prey. To compromise is a complex human ability and therefore one of the first to decline when willpower is depleted. You become what researchers call a cognitive miser, hoarding your energy. If you're shopping, you're liable to look at only one dimension, like price: just give me the cheapest. Or you

indulge yourself by looking at quality: I want the very best (an especially easy strategy if someone else is paying).

13 Decision fatigue leaves you vulnerable to marketers who know how to time their sales, as Jonathan Levav, the Stanford professor, demonstrated in experiments involving . . . new cars. . . . The car buyers . . . had to choose, for instance, among 4 styles of gearshift knobs, 13 kinds of wheel rims, 25 configurations of the engine and gearbox and a palette of 56 colors for the interior. As they started picking features, customers would carefully weigh the choices, but as decision fatigue set in, they would start settling for whatever the default option was. And the more tough choices they encountered early in the process—like going through those 56 colors to choose the precise shade of gray or brown—the quicker people became fatigued and settled for the path of least resistance by taking the default option. By manipulating the order of the car buyers' choices, the researchers found that the customers would end up settling for different kinds of options. . . . Whether the customers paid a little extra for fancy wheel rims or a lot extra for a more powerful engine depended on when the choice was offered and how much willpower was left in the customer. . . .

14 It's simple enough to imagine reforms for the parole board in Israel—like, say, restricting each judge's shift to half a day, preferably in the morning, interspersed with frequent breaks for food and rest. But it's not so obvious what to do with the decision fatigue affecting the rest of society. . . . Today we feel overwhelmed because there are so many choices. . . . Choosing what to have for breakfast, where to go on vacation, whom to hire, how much to spend—these all deplete willpower, and there's no telltale symptom of when that willpower is low. It's not like getting winded or hitting the wall during a marathon. Ego depletion manifests itself not as one feeling but rather as a propensity to experience everything more intensely. When the brain's regulatory powers weaken, frustrations seem more irritating than usual. Impulses to eat, drink, spend and say stupid things feel more powerful (and alcohol causes self-control to decline further). . . . Like the depleted parole judges, [ego-depleted humans] become inclined to take the safer, easier option even when that option hurts someone else.

Links

1. Danziger, Shai, et al. "Extraneous Factors in Judicial Decisions." *Proceedings of the National Academy of Sciences for the United States of America*, vol. 108, no. 17, 2011, pp. 6889–92.
2. "Dr. Roy Baumeister." *Faculty Directory, Psychology Department,* Florida State U, 2013.

[REFLECT] Make connections: Your own experience with decision fatigue.

Tierney writes about a judge whose fairness is undermined by decision fatigue. Think about your own experience making decisions. Have you ever made a decision that you regretted, or avoided making a decision when decisiveness was important? Your instructor may ask you to post your thoughts on a class discussion board or to discuss them with other students in class. Use these questions to get started:

- Think about a decision that you regretted making (or not making). How may decision fatigue have influenced you? What else might have influenced your decision (for example, peer pressure or fear of disappointing a loved one)?

- Tierney points out that it would be easy to reform the schedule of the parole board to take the decision fatigue out of their day, but that "it's not so obvious what to do with the decision fatigue affecting the rest of society" (par. 14). What steps could you take to ease decision fatigue? How would society change if we all had fewer decisions to make? What would we gain, and what would we be giving up?

[ANALYZE] Use the basic features.

A FOCUSED EXPLANATION: USING AN EXAMPLE

Examples often play a central role in writing about concepts because concepts are general and abstract, and examples help make them specific and concrete. Examples can also be very useful tools for focusing an explanation. Toufexis, for example, uses examples of popular films (*Bram Stoker's Dracula, The Seven-Year Itch*) to illustrate different conceptions of love norms. John Tierney uses Jean Twenge's experience of registering for wedding gifts to illustrate how decision fatigue can erode shoppers' willpower.

ANALYZE & WRITE

Write a paragraph analyzing how Tierney uses the example of one judge deciding the fate of three prisoners to illustrate the concept of decision fatigue:

1. Skim paragraphs 1–4. How do these paragraphs help readers understand the concept of decision fatigue?
2. Now look back at paragraph 4. How does this paragraph answer the "So what?" question readers of concept explanations inevitably ask? In other words, how does it provide a focus for Tierney's explanation of the concept and help readers grasp why the concept is important?
3. Finally, reread paragraph 13, in which Tierney explains how marketers use decision fatigue. Why do you suppose Tierney includes this information in his explanation of the concept?

A CLEAR, LOGICAL ORGANIZATION: CREATING COHESION

Cohesive devices help readers move from paragraph to paragraph and section to section without losing the thread. The most familiar cohesive device is probably the transitional word or phrase (*however, next*), which alerts readers to the relationship among ideas. A less familiar but equally effective strategy is to repeat key terms and their synonyms or to use pronouns (*it, they*) to refer to the key term. A third strategy is to provide cohesion by referring to earlier examples, often bringing a selection full circle by referring to an opening example at the end of the essay.

ANALYZE & WRITE

Write a paragraph or two analyzing how Tierney creates cohesion in "Do You Suffer from Decision Fatigue?":

1. Skim paragraphs 1–4, marking every word (or number) related to time. How does Tierney use time to lend cohesion to his essay? How effectively does this strategy help readers navigate this essay and understand its main point?

2 Select a series of three or four paragraphs, and analyze how Tierney knits the paragraphs together. Can you identify any repeated words or concepts, or any pronouns that refer to terms in the preceding paragraph? Does Tierney use transitional words or phrases to link one paragraph to the next?

3 Finally, reread the last paragraph. How does Tierney lend closure to his essay? How effective is his strategy?

APPROPRIATE EXPLANATORY STRATEGIES: USING A VARIETY OF STRATEGIES

Writers typically use a variety of strategies to explain a concept. Potthast, for example, *defines* the concept of *supervolcano*, *classifies* the historic eruptions, *illustrates* their consequences, and explores *causes* and "dangerous physical *effects*" (par. 2, emphasis added) of supervolcanoes. Here are a few examples of sentence patterns Potthast uses to present some of these explanatory strategies:

Definition

EXAMPLE Supervolcanoes are volcanoes that produce eruptions thousands of times the size of ordinary volcanoes. (par. 1)

- X is a member of class Y with ________, ________, and ________ [distinguishing traits].

Classification

EXAMPLE Volcanic eruptions feature several dangerous physical effects, including pyroclastic flows, pyroclastic surges, lahars, tephra falls, and massive amounts of fine ash particles in the air. (par. 2)

- X is made up of three basic parts: ________, ________, and ________.

Cause-Effect Reasoning

EXAMPLE If a super-eruption were to occur here, the results would be devastating. . . . Toxic gases would sweep across much of the nation, making "two-thirds of the U.S. . . . uninhabitable . . . forcing millions to leave their homes" (Bates). (Potthast, par. 11)

- The causes of X are varied, but the most notable are ________ and ________.
- The effects of X may include ________, ________, and ________.

ANALYZE & WRITE

Write a paragraph analyzing how Tierney uses definition, classification, cause-effect reasoning, and other strategies (such as example, comparison-contrast, or process analysis) to explain decision fatigue:

1 Skim Tierney's essay, looking for and highlighting examples of two or three different types of explanatory strategies.

2 Now select one strategy that you think is particularly effective, and explain why you think it works so well. What does the strategy contribute to the explanation of decision fatigue? How does it help answer the "So what?" question?

SMOOTH INTEGRATION OF SOURCES: DECIDING WHEN AND HOW TO CITE SOURCES

Writers of concept explanations nearly always conduct research; incorporate information from sources into their writing using summary, paraphrase, and quotation; and identify their sources so that readers can identify them as experts. But how they acknowledge their sources depends on the conventions of their writing situation. Toufexis, writing for *Time* magazine's general audience, makes clear that her sources are experts by mentioning their credentials in signal phrases:

> Says Michael Mills, a psychology professor at Loyola Marymount University in Los Angeles: "Love is our ancestors whispering in our ears." (par. 2)

But she does not include a formal citation or a list of works cited at the end of the article. Sometimes Potthast uses a signal phrase to make his source's expertise clear; sometimes he merely includes a citation in his text. But in all cases, he includes a full citation in his list of works cited because this is required when writing for an academic audience.

ANALYZE & WRITE

Write a paragraph or two analyzing the kinds of materials Tierney incorporates from sources and how he identifies his sources so that his readers know they can be trusted:

1. Skim the essay, highlighting places where Tierney quotes, paraphrases, or summarizes information from sources. What information does he provide to identify his sources, and how does this information help readers know the sources are trustworthy? Try to determine which information comes from published sources, which from interviews, and which from Tierney's own general knowledge of the topic.
2. Again skim the essay, this time looking for places where Tierney uses an exact quotation from a source. Why do you think he decided to use an exact quotation rather than merely summarizing or paraphrasing the idea?
3. Finally, think about the purpose of citing sources. Why is simply identifying sources with a word or two in the text generally sufficient for nonacademic situations, while academic writing situations require in-text citations and a list of sources? Given your experience reading online, do you think hyperlinks should replace formal citations? Why or why not?

[RESPOND] Consider possible topics: Examining how emotions influence behavior.

Because behavioral research can help us understand ourselves in new ways, essays that shed light on psychological phenomena can be fascinating to readers. A writer could explore cognitive dissonance, the foot-in-the-door phenomenon, or social loafing, for example. Recent research explores the concept of ego depletion in relation to dieting and depression. Like ego depletion, post-traumatic stress disorder was named only in the last few decades, and scientists are only now discovering new ways to treat it. Consider entering the concept you are seeking to explain into the search field of a database in the social sciences, like *PsycArticles* or *Social Sciences Full Text*, to find an interesting topic you might never have thought of on your own.

The Writing Assignment

Explain an important and interesting concept, one you already know well or are just learning about. Consider what your readers are likely to know and think about the concept, what they are likely to find interesting about the topic, what you might want them to learn about it, and whether you can research it sufficiently in the time you have.

This Guide to Writing is designed to help you compose your own concept explanation and apply what you have learned from analyzing other concept explanations. Use the Starting Points chart to help you find answers to questions you might have about explaining a concept.

STARTING POINTS: EXPLAINING A CONCEPT

A Focused Explanation

How do I come up with a concept to write about?

- Consider possible topics. (pp. 111, 118)
- Choose a concept to write about. (p. 121)
- Test Your Choice: Considering Your Purpose and Audience (p. 122)

How can I decide on a focus for my concept?

- Assess the genre's basic features: A focused explanation. (p. 98)
- Conduct initial research on the concept. (pp. 122–23)
- Focus your explanation of the concept. (p. 123)
- Test Your Choice: Evaluating Your Focus (p. 124)
- Conduct further research on your focused concept. (p. 124)

How can I make my concept clear and interesting to my readers?

- A Focused Explanation: Excluding Other Topics (p. 110)
- A Focused Explanation: Using an Example (p. 116)
- Focus your explanation of the concept. (p. 123)
- Test Your Choice: Evaluating Your Focus (p. 124)
- Write the opening sentences. (pp. 129–30)
- A Troubleshooting Guide: A Focused Explanation (p. 133)

(continued)

A Clear, Logical Organization

How should I organize my explanation so that it's logical and easy to read?

- Assess the genre's basic features: A clear, logical organization. (p. 98)
- Draft your working thesis. (pp. 124–25)
- Create an outline that will organize your concept explanation effectively for your readers. (p. 125)
- A Troubleshooting Guide: A Clear, Logical Organization (pp. 133–34)

What kinds of cues should I provide?

- Assess the genre's basic features: A clear, logical organization. (p. 98)
- A Clear, Logical Organization: Cueing the Reader (pp. 110-11)
- A Clear, Logical Organization: Creating Cohesion (pp. 116-17)
- Draft your working thesis. (pp. 124-25)
- Design your writing project. (p. 125)

Appropriate Explanatory Strategies

What's the best way to explain my concept? What writing strategies should I use?

- Assess the genre's basic features: Appropriate explanatory strategies. (p. 99)
- Appropriate Explanatory Strategies: Using Visuals (p. 111)
- Appropriate Explanatory Strategies: Using a Variety of Strategies (p. 117)
- Consider the explanatory strategies you should use. (pp. 125–26)
- Use summaries, paraphrases, and quotations from sources to support your points. (p. 127)
- Use visuals or multimedia illustrations. (pp. 127–28)
- A Troubleshooting Guide: Appropriate Explanatory Strategies (pp. 134–35)

Smooth Integration of Sources

How should I integrate sources so that they support my argument?

- Assess the genre's basic features: Smooth integration of sources. (pp. 99–100)
- Smooth Integration of Sources: Establishing Credibility (p. 111)
- Smooth Integration of Sources: Deciding When and How to Cite Sources (p. 118)
- Use appositives to integrate sources. (p. 128)
- Use descriptive verbs in signal phrases to introduce information from sources. (p. 129)
- A Troubleshooting Guide: Smooth Integration of Sources (p. 135)

Writing a Draft: Invention, Research, Planning, and Composing

The activities in this section will help you choose a concept and develop an explanation that will appeal to your readers, using appropriate explanatory strategies as well as photographs, tables, charts, and other illustrations. Do the activities in any order that makes sense to you (and your instructor), and return to them as needed as you revise.

Choose a concept to write about.

List possible concepts you might write about. For the best results, your concept should be one that you

- understand well or are eager to learn more about;
- think is important and will interest your readers;
- can research sufficiently in the allotted time;
- can explain clearly in the length prescribed by your instructor.

Review the Consider Possible Topics activities on pp. 111 and 118, and reread notes you made in response to those suggestions. The following list suggests some good concepts:

- **Biology, nursing, and the physical sciences:** morphogenesis, electron transport, phagocytosis, homozygosity, diffusion, mass, energy, gravity, entropy, communicable diseases, epidemiology, toxicology, holistic medicine, pathogen
- **Business and economics:** opportunity cost, elasticity of demand, negative externalities, minimum wage, affirmative action, collective bargaining, robotics, flex time, family leave
- **Environment:** fracking, toxic waste, endangered species, sustainability, climate change
- **Identity and community:** multiculturalism, racism, sexism, social contract, community policing, social Darwinism, identity politics, public space
- **Literature and cultural studies:** irony, semiotics, dystopia, canon, postmodernism, realism, genre, connotation
- **Psychology and sociology:** assimilation/accommodation, social cognition, emotional intelligence, the Stroop effect, trauma, theory of mind, deviance, ethnocentrism, social stratification, acculturation, cultural relativism, patriarchy
- **Management and finance:** risk management, leveraged buyout, deregulation, branding, economy of scale, monopoly capitalism, socially conscious investing

TEST YOUR CHOICE

Considering Your Purpose and Audience

To decide whether to proceed with this concept, ask yourself the following questions:

- Can I answer my readers' inevitable "So what?" question and make the concept seem interesting and worth knowing about?
- Am I interested in the concept, and can I focus my explanation?
- Do I know enough about the concept now, or can I research it in the time I have?

Conduct initial research on the concept.

Start by surveying what you already know about the topic, so you can better determine what gaps you need to fill. The following activity will help you begin putting your ideas into words, which you may be able to use as you draft.

WAYS IN

WHAT DO I ALREADY KNOW ABOUT THE CONCEPT?

To determine what you already know, ask yourself questions like these, using the sentence strategies as jumping-off points to answer them:

Why is my concept worth writing about?

- ▶ My concept is important/useful for the study of ______ because ______ [list reasons].

What writing strategies can I use to explain the concept?

- ▶ My concept can be divided into the following categories: ______, ______, and ______. (Classification)
- ▶ Examples of my concept include ______, ______, and ______. (Examples)
- ▶ My concept is a ______ [member of a larger category] that is/does/has these defining characteristics: ______, ______, and ______. (Definition)

Research your concept in three stages:

1. Gain an overview of the concept.
2. Identify an aspect of the concept to focus on.
3. Conduct enough research to learn about this aspect of the concept.

A reference database, such as the *Gale Virtual Reference Library* or *Web of Science*, can provide you with an overview of your concept as well as

- names of experts on your subject;
- terms, phrases, or synonyms that you might use as search terms later;
- interesting aspects of the concept that you might want to focus on.

You may need to read several articles covering your topic to get the information you need. A search engine can also help you get an overview: Enter the word *overview* or *definition* with the name of your concept, and skim the top ten search results to get a general sense of your topic. You can then bookmark useful links or save them in a separate file. Limiting your results to those from *.edu, .gov,* or *.org* domains is more likely to generate reliable results.

To learn more about conducting research, see Chapter 14.

Focus your explanation of the concept.

What interests you most about your topic? What do you think will most interest your readers? The following activity will help you find a way to focus your explanation.

WAYS IN

WHAT MAKES THE CONCEPT INTERESTING TO ME AND MY READERS?

List two or three aspects of your concept that interest you, and then answer the following questions:

- Why does this aspect interest you?
- How is it relevant to your life, family, community, work, or studies?
- What do you already know about this aspect of the concept? What would you like to learn about it?

Analyze your **AUDIENCE** *by brainstorming answers to the following questions:*

- Who are your readers, and in what context will they be reading your explanation?
- What are they likely to know about the concept, about related concepts, or about the subject in general? How can you build on what they already know?
- How would you answer your readers' "So what?" question? Think of at least one aspect of the concept that is relevant to their life, family, community, work, or studies.
- If you suspect that your readers are likely to have faulty assumptions, misunderstandings, or outdated ideas about the concept (or about the subject in general), how can you clarify the concept for them?

Consider **WRITING STRATEGIES** *that will help you explain your concept and why it matters.* Write for a few minutes in response to one or more of the following questions:

- What is my concept similar to?
- What parts or features distinguish it from other concepts?
- What are its cultural or historical contexts?

If you find that you don't have enough to write about, return to the previous section to conduct additional research, broaden your concept by adding cultural or historical contexts, or check sources or class readings to look for broader concepts of which your concept is a part.

TEST YOUR CHOICE

Evaluating Your Focus

Get together with two or three other students to test the way you've focused your explanation.

Presenters. Briefly describe your intended audience, identify the aspect of the concept that you will focus on, and explain both what you find interesting or relevant about it and what you think your readers will find interesting or relevant. (If your listeners do not find your focus appropriate or interesting, consider returning to your list of possible concepts and repeating the activities above.)

Listeners. Briefly tell the presenter whether the focus sounds appropriate and interesting for the intended audience. Share what you think readers are likely to know about the concept and what information might be especially interesting to them.

Conduct further research on your focused concept.

Your instructor may expect you to do in-depth research or may limit the number and types of sources you can use. Readers will want to be shown that your sources are reliable, and they may even want to read the original source documents for themselves.

To learn more about finding sources, see Chapter 14; evaluating your sources, see Chapter 15; citing sources, see Chapter 16 (MLA style) or Chapter 17 (APA style).

Draft your working thesis.

An essay explaining a concept is made up of three basic parts:

- an opening that will engage readers' interest
- a thesis statement that announces the concept and its focus, and possibly forecasts the main topics
- information about the concept, organized by topic

You may draft a working thesis statement and other parts of your explanation before deciding on an opening your readers will find engaging. If you prefer to sketch out an opening first, however, turn to the section "Write the Opening Sentences" (p. 129), and return to this section later.

The **thesis statement** in a concept explanation announces the concept to be explained and identifies the writer's focus on the concept. It may also forecast the topics to be explored. Here's an example of a thesis statement (from "Love: The Right Chemistry") that successfully announces the concept and the writer's focus. It also forecasts the topics the writer will cover:

Concept
Focus

O.K., let's cut out all this nonsense about romantic love. Let's bring some scientific precision to the party. Let's put love under a microscope.

When rigorous people with Ph.D.s after their names do that, what they see is not some silly, senseless thing. No, their probe reveals that love rests firmly on the foundations of evolution, biology and chemistry. (Toufexis, pars. 1–2)

Forecast topics

To draft your thesis statement, consider using some of your writing from the Ways In activities in the section "Focus Your Explanation of the Concept" (p. 123). You may also want to forecast the topics you will cover.

Create an outline that will organize your concept explanation effectively for your readers.

Once you have drafted a working thesis, you may want to devise a tentative outline, drawing on your invention and research notes. An effective outline for a concept explanation should be divided into separate topics that are conceptually parallel. Toufexis, for example, focuses on the scientific foundations of love, and so she divides the topics she will cover into evolution, biology, and chemistry. Once you have decided on your topics, present them in a logical order (for example, from most familiar to least familiar).

Below is a simple outline for an essay explaining a concept, which you may use as a starting point:

I. **Introduction:** Attempts to gain readers' interest in the concept, but may not name the concept immediately.

II. **Thesis:** Identifies the concept in a sentence or two; may include a brief definition, an example, or another strategy to clarify the focus, and may forecast topics that will be addressed later.

III. **Background:** Provides the social, cultural, historical, or scientific background readers will need to understand the concept.

IV. **Topic 1:** Contains appropriate examples, evidence, and explanatory strategies.

V. **Topic 2:**

VI. **Topic 3 (etc.):**

VII. **Conclusion:** Might summarize information, give advice about how to use or apply the information, or speculate about the future of the concept.

Use your outline to guide your drafting, but do not feel tied to it. You may figure out a better way to sequence your topics as you write.

Design your writing project.

Consider whether you want to use headings to indicate the topics to be discussed; bullets or numbers to highlight lists; and tables, graphics, or other visuals to make your explanation clearer.

To learn more about design, see Chapter 13.

Consider the explanatory strategies you should use.

To explain your concept, consider which strategies would be most useful. Ask questions like these:

- How would you define it?
- What examples would help your readers understand it?

- How is it similar to or different from other related concepts?
- How does it happen or get done?
- What are its causes or effects?

Keep in mind that your goal is not only to inform your readers but also to engage their interest. The following activity provides sentence strategies you can use to explore the best ways to explain your concept; these strategies may also help you start drafting your essay.

WAYS IN

WHAT WRITING STRATEGIES CAN I USE TO EXPLAIN MY FOCUSED CONCEPT?

How is the concept **DEFINED?** What broader class does it belong to, and how does it differ from other members of its class?

- ▶ X is a/an ________ [principle/theory/idea/condition/phenomenon/process] distinguished by ________ [defining characteristics].

What **EXAMPLES** *or* **ANECDOTES** *can make the concept less abstract and more understandable?*

- ▶ Experts/Scientists/The public first became aware of X in [year], when ________ (citation).
- ▶ Interest in X has been rising/declining because of ________, ________, and ________.

How does this concept **COMPARE** *or* **CONTRAST** *with related concepts with which your readers may be more familiar?*

- ▶ Many people think X means ________, but it might be more accurate to say it means ________.
- ▶ X is similar in some ways to Y. However, unlike Y, X is/has/does ________, ________, and ________.

How can aspects of the concept be **CLASSIFIED** *to make it easier for readers to understand?*

- ▶ Professor A says there are several categories/subtypes/versions of X, including ________, ________, and ________ (citation).

What **PROCESS** *must occur?* How does this concept happen, or how does one go about doing it?

- ▶ To perform X, a person/performer/participant starts by ________. Then he/she/it does ________, ________, and ________. The process ends when ________.

What are this concept's **CAUSES** *or* **EFFECTS?**

- ▶ X occurs when ________.
- ▶ Before X can occur, the following condition(s) must be met: ________.
- ▶ Experts disagree over the causes of X. Professor Smith, for example, believes ________ (citation). Professor Jones, in contrast, argues ________ (citation).

Use summaries, paraphrases, and quotations from sources to support your points.

Summaries, paraphrases, and quotations from sources are frequently used to explain concepts or reinforce an explanation. The Ways In activity below can help you decide when to summarize, paraphrase, or quote.

For more about using information from sources to support your ideas and integrating supporting information into your writing, see Chapter 15.

WAYS IN

WHEN SHOULD I SUMMARIZE, PARAPHRASE, AND QUOTE?

Use **SUMMARY** *to give the gist of a research report or other information.*

- Recent research suggests that ________ (citation).

Use **PARAPHRASE** *to provide specific details or examples when the language of the source is not especially memorable.*

- According to Dr. Smith, the most important element to keep in mind is ________ (citation).

Use **QUOTATION** *to capture language that is particularly vivid, clear, or technical; to convey an expert's voice; or to discuss the source's choice of words.*

- Professor Y recently noted that "________" (citation).

Remember that in academic writing projects, you will need to cite the sources of all summaries, paraphrases, and quotations. In most cases, use signal phrases (*Professor Y explained*) to provide context for source information and in-text citations (page references in MLA style, year of publication in APA style) so that readers can locate the source in your works-cited or reference list. A list of works cited or references should be provided at the end of your concept explanation.

Your readers will want you to explain how the ideas from the sources you cite reinforce the points you are making; therefore, comment on sources, making the relationship between your ideas and the supporting information from sources absolutely clear.

Use visuals or multimedia illustrations.

Concept explanation essays do not require illustrations, but they can be an effective tool. The medium in which your concept explanation appears will determine the types of illustrations you can use. For example, papers can include visual images such as photographs and flowcharts. Web pages can include music, film clips, and animated graphs. Oral presentations can use the Web or presentation slides (such as PowerPoint), with still or moving images and sound files embedded in the slides.

When deciding whether to include illustrations, consider the following:

- Can you create your own graphics (for example, by using spreadsheet software to create bar graphs or pie charts)?

- Will you need to borrow materials that others have created (for example, by downloading materials from the Internet, taking screenshots from Web sites or DVDs, or scanning visuals from books or magazines)? Remember that borrowed material must be cited, including the sources of data you use to create graphs and tables.
- Will your writing be published on a Web site that is not password protected? If so, you may need to obtain permission from the source.

Use appositives to integrate sources.

When you write your essay, you'll have to tell readers about the credentials of experts you quote, paraphrase, and summarize. Instead of providing this information in separate sentences, you can use an *appositive* to embed this information smoothly and clearly into another sentence.

An **appositive** is a noun or pronoun that, along with modifiers, gives more information about another noun or pronoun. Here is an example from one of the reading selections earlier in the chapter:

Noun Appositive	"Love is a natural high," observes Anthony Walsh, author of *The Science of Love: Understanding Love and Its Effects on Mind and Body.* (Toufexis, par. 10)

By placing the credentials right after the expert's name, this sentence provides readers with the information they need, exactly where they need it.

Appositives can be used for many different purposes, as these examples suggest:

Appositive Noun	DEFINE A KEY TERM	Each person carries in his or her mind a unique subliminal guide to the ideal partner, a "love map." (Toufexis, par. 17)
	IDENTIFY PEOPLE AND THINGS	Decision fatigue is the newest discovery involving a phenomenon called ego depletion, a term coined by the social psychologist Roy F. Baumeister. (Tierney, par. 6)
	GIVE EXAMPLES	For example, following the 1996 Soufreire Hills volcano, hydrogen sulfide and sulfur dioxide (gases produced in the eruption) combined to form sulfuric acid. (Potthast, par. 6)

Notice that the last example uses parentheses instead of commas to set off the appositive from the rest of the sentence. Although commas are more common, parentheses or dashes are often used if the writer wants to give the appositive a different emphasis or if the appositive itself contains commas.

Use descriptive verbs in signal phrases to introduce information from sources.

When introducing quotations, paraphrases, or summaries, writers often use a **signal phrase**—the source author's name plus a verb—to alert readers to the fact that they are borrowing someone else's words or ideas. Often the verb (italicized in the examples below) is neutral:

> "That is one reason why it feels so horrible when we're abandoned or a lover dies," *notes* Fisher. (Toufexis, par. 13)

> "By the end, you could have talked me into anything," Twenge *told* her new colleagues. (Tierney, par. 8)

Sometimes, however, the verb may be more descriptive—even evaluative:

> "As long as prehistoric females were secretive about their extramarital affairs," *argues* Fisher, "they could garner extra resources, life insurance, better genes and more varied DNA for their biological futures." (Toufexis, par. 8)

The verb *argues* emphasizes the fact that what is being reported is an interpretation that others may disagree with.

As you refer to sources in your concept explanation, choose carefully among a wide variety of precise verbs to introduce your sources. Here are a number of possibilities: *suggests, reveals, questions, brings into focus, finds, notices, observes, underscores.*

In academic writing, merely mentioning the author's name in a signal phrase is not sufficient. In most cases, you must also include in-text citations that provide the page number from which the borrowed material is taken and include full bibliographic information in a list of works cited or references, so readers can trace the source for themselves.

For more about integrating sources into your sentences and constructing signal phrases, see Chapter 15.

Write the opening sentences.

Review what you have written to see if you have something that would work to launch your concept explanation, or try out some of these opening strategies:

Begin with a **surprising** *or* **provocative quotation** *or* **aspect** *of the concept:*

> O.K., let's cut out all this nonsense about romantic love. Let's bring some scientific precision to the party. Let's put love under a microscope. (Toufexis, par. 1)

Offer an **anecdote** *or* **example** *illustrating the concept:*

> Three men doing time in Israeli prisons recently appeared before a parole board consisting of a judge, a criminologist and a social worker. The three prisoners had completed at least two-thirds of their sentences, but the parole board granted freedom to only one of them. Guess which one:
>
> > Case 1 (heard at 8:50 a.m.): An Arab Israeli serving a 30-month sentence for fraud.
> >
> > Case 2 (heard at 3:10 p.m.): A Jewish Israeli serving a 16-month sentence for assault.
> >
> > Case 3 (heard at 4:25 p.m.): An Arab Israeli serving a 30-month sentence for fraud. (Tierney, par. 1)

Make a **comparison** *or* **contrast** *that relates the concept to something readers are likely to know:*

> Possibly the most destructive natural disaster, short of a large asteroid impact, would be the eruption of a supervolcano. Supervolcanoes are volcanoes that produce eruptions thousands of times the size of ordinary volcanoes. Like hurricanes, the power of volcanoes is measured using an exponential scale, the Volcanic Explosivity Index, or VEI (fig. 1). (Potthast, par. 1)

But don't agonize over the first sentences because you are likely to discover the best way to begin only after you have written a rough draft.

Draft your explanation.

By this point, you have done a lot of research and writing to

- find an interesting focus and develop a working thesis statement;
- try out writing strategies that can help you explain your concept;
- create an outline for presenting that information;
- come up with ways to integrate your sources smoothly;
- try out a way to launch your explanation.

Now stitch that material together to create a draft. The next two parts of this Guide to Writing will help you evaluate and improve your draft.

Evaluating the Draft: Using Peer Review

Your instructor may arrange a peer review session in class or online, where you can exchange drafts with your classmates and give one another a thoughtful critical reading, pointing out what works well and suggesting ways to improve the draft. A good critical reading does three things:

1. It lets the writer know how well the reader understands the concept.
2. It praises what works best.
3. It indicates where the draft could be improved and makes suggestions on how to improve it.

One strategy for evaluating a draft is to use the basic features of concept essays as a guide.

A PEER REVIEW GUIDE

A Focused Explanation

Is the explanation focused?

Summarize: Tell the writer, in one sentence, what you understand the concept to mean and why it is important or useful.

Praise: Identify something in the draft that will especially interest readers.

Critique: Tell the writer about any confusion or uncertainty you have about the concept's meaning, importance, or usefulness. Indicate if the focus could be clearer or more appropriate or if the explanation could have a more interesting focus.

A Clear, Logical Organization

Is the concept explanation clear and easy to follow?

Summarize: Look at the way the essay is organized by making a scratch outline.

Praise: Give an example of where the essay succeeds in being readable—for instance, in its overall organization, forecast of topics, or use of transitions.

Critique: Identify places where readability could be improved—for example, the beginning made more appealing, a topic sentence made clearer, or transitions or headings added.

Appropriate Explanatory Strategies

Are writing strategies used effectively to analyze and explain the concept?

Summarize: Note which explanatory strategies the writer uses, such as definition, comparison-contrast, example, cause–effect, classification, or process analysis.

Praise: Point to an explanatory strategy that is especially effective, and highlight research that is particularly helpful in explaining the concept.

Critique: Point to any places where a definition is needed, where more (or better) examples might help, or where another explanatory strategy could be improved or added. Note where a visual (such as a flowchart or graph) would make the explanation clearer.

(continued)

Smooth Integration of Sources	Are sources incorporated into the essay effectively? **Summarize:** Note each source mentioned in the text, and check to make sure it appears in the list of works cited, if there is one. Highlight signal phrases and in-text citations, and identify appositives used to provide experts' credentials. **Praise:** Give an example of the effective use of sources—a particularly well-integrated quotation, paraphrase, or summary that supports and illustrates the point. Note any especially descriptive verbs used to introduce information. **Critique:** Point out where experts' credentials are needed. Indicate quotations, paraphrases, or summaries that could be more smoothly integrated or more fully interpreted or explained. Suggest verbs in signal phrases that may be more appropriate.

Before concluding your review, be sure to address any of the writer's concerns that have not already been addressed.

Improving the Draft: Revising, Editing, and Proofreading

Start improving your draft by reflecting on what you have written thus far:

- Review critical reading comments from your classmates, instructor, or writing center tutor. What are your readers getting at?
- Take another look at the notes from your earlier research and writing activities. What else should you consider?
- Review your draft. What else can you do to make your explanation effective?

Revise your draft.

If your readers are having difficulty with your draft, or if you think there is room for improvement, try some of the strategies listed in the Troubleshooting Guide. They can help you fine-tune your presentation of the genre's basic features.

A TROUBLESHOOTING GUIDE

A Focused Explanation

My readers think that my topic seems thin, that I don't have enough to write about. (The focus is too narrow.)

- Broaden your concept by adding scientific, cultural, or historical comparisons and contrasts.
- Look up your concept using reference sources to find additional subject terms for larger concepts that include it.
- Conduct a Web search using the name of your concept and *overview* or *definition*. Use the Advanced Search feature to focus on sites with a *.edu*, *.gov*, or *.org* domain.
- If your concept comes from another course you are taking, check your textbook or lecture notes for broader, related topics.

My readers don't find my focus interesting.

- Conduct additional research, focusing on finding information likely to be of value and interest to your readers.
- Consider ways to answer your readers' "So what?" question — perhaps by showing them how they could use the concept; building on their interests or what they already know; or clarifying their mistaken, faulty, or outdated assumptions or ideas.
- Consider using humor, anecdotes, or visuals to engage readers' interest.
- Ask yourself whether the focus is interesting to you. If it isn't, choose a different focus. If it is, ask yourself how you can communicate your enthusiasm to your readers—perhaps with anecdotes, examples, or illustrations.

A Clear, Logical Organization

My readers don't find my organization clear and logical.

- Reread your thesis statement to be sure that it clearly announces the concept and perhaps forecasts the topics.
- Outline your material to be sure that it is divided into separate topics that are presented in a logical order.

My readers say that the beginning doesn't capture their interest.

- Review your opening paragraphs to be sure that you clearly introduce your concept and your focus.
- Try starting with an anecdote, an interesting quotation, a surprising aspect of the concept, a concrete example, or a similar lead-in.
- Consider stating explicitly what makes the concept worth thinking about and how it relates to your readers' interests.

(continued)

A Clear, Logical Organization

My readers feel that the essay doesn't flow smoothly from one part to the next.

- Outline your essay, dividing it into major parts—introduction, main topics, and conclusion. Reread the end of each major part and the beginning of the next to make sure you have provided transitional cues (for example, the strategic repetition of words or phrases, use of synonyms, rhetorical questions). If there are none, add some.
- Consider adding headings to make the topical sections easier to identify.

My readers feel that the ending falls flat.

- Consider ending by speculating on what the future will bring—how the concept might be redefined, for example.
- Consider relating the ending to the beginning—for example, by recalling an example or a comparison.

Appropriate Explanatory Strategies

My readers don't understand my explanation.

- Consider whether you have used the most appropriate writing strategies for your topic—defining, classifying, comparing and contrasting, narrating, illustrating, describing, or explaining cause and effect.
- Recheck your definitions for clarity. Be sure that you have explicitly defined any key terms your readers might not know.
- Add transitional cues (transitional words and phrases, strategic repetition, and so on).
- Add headings and bulleted or numbered lists to help readers follow the discussion.

My readers want more information about certain aspects of the concept.

- Expand or clarify definitions by adding examples or using appositives.
- Add examples or comparisons and contrasts to relate the concept to something readers already know.
- Conduct additional research on your topic, and cite it in your essay.

My readers think visuals would help them better understand the concept.

- Check whether your sources use visuals (tables, graphs, drawings, photographs, and the like) that might be appropriate for your explanation. If you are publishing your concept explanation online, consider video clips, audio files, and animated graphics as well.
- Consider drafting your own charts, tables, or graphs, or adding your own photographs or illustrations.

Appropriate Explanatory Strategies

My readers think my summaries are vague, my paraphrases are too complicated, or my quotations are too long or uninteresting.

- Revise the summaries to emphasize a single key idea.
- Restate the paraphrases more succinctly, omitting irrelevant details. Consider quoting important words.
- Quote only a few memorable words or phrases from a source.

My readers aren't sure how source information supports my explanation of the concept.

- Check to be sure that you have appropriately commented on all cited material, making its relation to your ideas absolutely clear.
- Expand or clarify accounts of research that your readers find unconvincing on grounds apart from the credibility of the source.

Smooth Integration of Sources

My readers think that the quotations, summaries, and paraphrases don't flow smoothly with the rest of the essay.

- Reread all passages where you quote sources. Ask yourself whether you provide enough context or clearly establish the author's credentials.
- Use signal phrases to place sources in context. Consider using descriptive verbs in signal phrases to give your readers more information about what your source is saying and why you are referring to it.
- Use appositives to integrate information about your sources smoothly and clearly.

My readers are concerned that my list of sources is too limited.

- Do additional research to balance your list, taking particular care that you have an adequate number of credible sources.
- If you have difficulty finding sources, ask your instructor or a librarian for help.

My readers wonder whether my sources are credible.

- Clearly identify all sources, and fully state the credentials of all cited authorities, using appositives where appropriate.
- Eliminate sources that are clearly identified and well integrated but that are not relevant, credible, or otherwise appropriate.

Edit and proofread your draft.

Two kinds of errors occur often in concept explanations: mixed constructions and missing or unnecessary commas around adjective clauses. The following guidelines will help you check your essay for these common errors.

Avoiding Mixed Constructions

What Is a Mixed Construction? A **mixed construction** in a sentence is a combination of structures that don't work together properly according to the rules of logic or English grammar. Mixed constructions often occur when a writer attributes information to a source, defines a term, or provides an explanation. In particular, watch out for definitions that include *is when* or *is where* and explanations that include *the reason . . . is because,* which are likely to be both illogical and ungrammatical.

The Problem Sentences are logically or grammatically incoherent.

The Correction Replace *when* or *where* with a noun that renames the subject or with an adjective that describes the subject.

▶ Depression is ~~where~~ *a disorder in which* people feel sad, guilty, or worthless, and lack energy or focus.

Delete either *the reason . . . is* or *because.*

▶ ~~The reason~~ *P* ponds become meadows ~~is~~ because plant life collects in the bottom.

Check subjects and predicates to make sure they are logically and grammatically matched, and delete any redundant expressions.

▶ ~~According to~~ Eleanor Smith/ ~~she~~ said that the best movie of the year was *Fury Road.*

▶ According to Eleanor Smith, ~~she said that~~ the best movie of the year was *Fury Road.*

Using Punctuation with Adjective Clauses

What Is an Adjective Clause? An **adjective clause** includes both a subject and a verb, gives information about a noun or a pronoun, and often begins with *who, which,* or *that*:

▶ It is common for schizophrenics to have delusions *that they are being persecuted.* [adjective clause: *that they are being persecuted*; subj.: *they*; verb: *are*]

Because adjective clauses add information about the nouns they follow—defining, illustrating, or explaining—they can be useful in writing that explains a concept.

The Problem Adjective clauses may or may not need to be set off with a comma or commas. To decide, determine whether the clause is essential to the meaning of the sentence. Essential clauses should *not* be set off with commas; nonessential clauses *must* be set off with commas.

The Correction Mentally delete the clause. If taking out the clause does not change the basic meaning of the sentence or make it unclear, add a comma or commas.

▶ Postpartum neurosis, which can last for two weeks or longer, can adversely affect a mother's ability to care for her infant.

If the clause follows a proper noun, add a comma or commas.

▶ Nanotechnologists defer to K. Eric Drexler, who speculates imaginatively about the use of nonmachines.

If taking out the clause changes the basic meaning of the sentence or makes it unclear, do *not* add a comma or commas.

▶ Seasonal affective disorders are mood disturbances/ that occur in fall/winter.

Reflecting on What You Have Learned

You learned a great deal about this genre from reading several explanations of a concept and writing a concept explanation of your own. To consolidate your learning, reflect not only on what you learned but also on how you learned it.

ANALYZE & WRITE

Write a blog post, a letter to your instructor or a classmate, or an e-mail message to a student who will take this course next term, using the writing prompt that seems most productive for you:

- Explain how your purpose and audience—what you wanted your readers to learn from reading your concept explanation—influenced *one* of your decisions as a writer, such as how you focused the concept, how you organized your explanation, how you used writing strategies to convey information, or how you integrated sources into your essay.
- Discuss what you learned about yourself as a writer in the process of writing this essay. For example, what part of the process did you find most challenging? Did you try anything new like getting a critical reading of your draft or outlining your draft in order to revise it?
- If you were to give advice to a fellow student who was about to write a concept explanation, what would you say?
- Which of the readings in this chapter influenced your essay? Explain the influence, citing specific examples from your essay and the reading.
- If you got good advice from a critical reader, explain exactly how the person helped you—perhaps by questioning your definitions, your use of visuals, the way you began or ended your essay, or the kinds of sources you used.

5

Analyzing and Synthesizing Opposing Arguments

Should people with kidney disease be allowed to buy someone else's extra kidney? Should Americans be required to show a special ID to vote? Should college athletes be paid to play? Should candy-flavored e-cigarettes be banned? Debates on issues like these are rampant in online chat rooms, workplaces, and college classrooms. Whether you want to participate in the debate or simply educate yourself, a good place to start is by researching and analyzing the opposing arguments. This kind of intellectual work is done by individuals at their home computers, by community and business leaders in public forums, by professors in academic journals and at conferences, and by students for class in reports, research projects, and oral presentations.

Unlike other *Concise St. Martin's Guide* chapters, this one does not focus on a single genre but instead presents four interrelated genres on a single controversial topic:

1. **Summary:** A concise recap of one source's main ideas
2. **Annotated Bibliography:** A list of sources with summaries and commentaries exploring how each source could be used
3. **Report:** An informative introduction, explaining the topic's importance and the controversy surrounding it
4. **Analysis of Opposing Arguments (or Comparative Analysis):** A perceptive examination of the values underlying two (or more) opposing points of view on the topic

These genres give you the opportunity to practice the fundamental thinking and composing processes of *analysis* and *synthesis* that are required throughout the college curriculum and in most kinds of workplace writing.

Analysis and synthesis are processes that go hand in hand. When you *analyze* what people have said and written about a controversial issue, you take it apart, focusing on important elements—for example, why the topic is significant, what makes it controversial, and what the different points of view on the topic are. When you *synthesize*, you forge connections, showing how different points of view relate to one another, perhaps demonstrating where they agree and disagree or where they fit into a broader framework.

In this chapter, the main purpose of your analysis and synthesis is *explanatory*: to help your audience understand a controversial topic as well as the different points of view and the values on which they are based. In Chapters 6–8, you enter the debate to argue for

- your own point of view on a topic (Chapter 6)
- an alternative solution to a problem (Chapter 7)
- your evaluation of some aspect of the topic (Chapter 8)

The processes you will engage in for the writing projects in this chapter will be good preparation for writing a thoughtful argument, whether for a college course, for the wider community, or for an employer.

Each of the genres in this chapter—summary, annotated bibliography, report, and comparative analysis—can be used as an end in itself or as a stepping stone in a larger composing process. For example, consider the various purposes and audiences for a summary:

- You can use a summary to help you recall sources you've read and determine what's important, help your audience decide if a text is worth reading, or demonstrate to an instructor that you have read and understood a source.
- You can combine a summary with additional summaries of other sources on a topic, notes about how each of the sources will be used, and bibliographic citations to create an annotated bibliography.

- You can adapt or remix the summary, using it, perhaps, in a research report that succinctly describes what various sources have said on a topic, or in an analysis to provide readers with an overview of the topic before delving into what drives a controversy.

Because this chapter covers four genres, the Guides to Reading and Writing look different from those in other chapters. Whereas other chapters typically include three reading selections illustrating variations on a single genre, the selections in this chapter illustrate the four different genres. Furthermore, whereas the selections in other chapters are written by different authors, all of the examples in this chapter were composed by the same writer, student Maya Gomez. As you read Gomez's writing, you will see how each genre serves as part of a multistage project. Later in the chapter, the Guide to Writing offers suggestions for composing each genre independently or as part of your own multistage project.

PRACTICING A GENRE

Analyzing Opposing Arguments

To get a sense of what's involved in analyzing and synthesizing opposing arguments, get together with two or three students to explore how people typically argue about a topic.

Part 1. As a group, choose a controversial issue with which you are all familiar, such as whether there should be a community service requirement for graduation, whether college athletes should be paid, or whether a college education—like kindergarten through twelfth grade—should be free to everyone who qualifies.

Then make a list of several pro and con arguments people use to support their opposing views of the issue you've chosen. For example, a common pro argument is that student athletes should be paid because colleges gain financially from their hard work and expertise. A con argument against paying student athletes is that colleges already pay them indirectly through expensive coaching programs. (You do not need to have an opinion on this issue yourself; you simply need to recall or guess what others have said or would say.)

Part 2. Discuss what you learned about analyzing and synthesizing opposing arguments:

- Was it easier to think of the pro or the con arguments? How did considering who benefits or whose interests are being served help you think of the opposing arguments?
- Look back at the opposing arguments, and try to identify the values driving them. How did you go about identifying an argument's underlying values?

Analyzing Four Genres

As you read the selections in this chapter, you will see how one student, Maya Gomez, moves from summarizing a proposal to solve the shortage of kidneys for transplant, to creating an annotated bibliography of sources on the topic of the kidney shortage, to reporting on the topic, and finally to analyzing the basic values underlying the disagreement between the proponents of two opposing arguments.

- In the summary of "A Moral Market" (p. 146), Gomez recaps the main argument of Eric Posner's proposal.
- In the annotated bibliography "Compensating Kidney Donors" (pp. 147–49), Gomez compiles a list of the sources she consulted, annotating each entry with a summary and a commentary on how she plans to use the source in her report or analysis essay.
- In the report "Possible Solutions to the Kidney Shortage" (pp. 149–55), Gomez introduces the broad topic of kidney transplantation, focusing on the kidney shortage and some of the controversial ideas for encouraging more people to donate their kidneys.
- In the analysis "Satel vs. the National Kidney Foundation: Should Kidney Donors Be Compensated?" (pp. 155–59), Gomez exposes to critical examination the basic values underlying the opposing positions taken by Sally Satel and the National Kidney Foundation.

Examining how Maya Gomez summarizes, analyzes, and synthesizes diverse sources—and presents an array of information and different points of view clearly and impartially—will help you see how you can employ the same techniques when composing your own summary, annotated bibliography, report, or comparative analysis on a controversial topic.

Determine the writer's purpose and audience.

The purposes a writer may have will differ, of course, depending on the genre in which he or she is composing and who the intended audience is:

Genre	If the intended audience is . . .	then the purpose is likely to be . . .
Summary	• a reader interested in the topic	• to get a sense of what the source says
	• a writer who has read the source him- or herself	• to identify and record the source's main ideas
	• an instructor who will evaluate the writer's work	• to demonstrate understanding by presenting a clear, concise, and accurate description of the source's main ideas

(continued)

Genre	If the intended audience is . . .	then the purpose is likely to be . . .
Annotated Bibliography	• a writer who is doing research	• to make a record of sources and explore their usefulness
	• other researchers looking for sources for their own project	• to inform others about sources on the topic
	• an instructor who has assigned and will evaluate the bibliography	• to indicate which sources have been consulted and present a clear, accurate summary of the sources' main ideas along with an analysis of how they may be used in a later writing project
Report Explaining a Controversial Topic	• readers who want to learn about the topic	• to inform readers about the topic, explaining its significance and different points of view
	• an instructor who has assigned and will evaluate the report	• to demonstrate understanding by explaining the topic and the different points of view clearly, accurately, and impartially
Analysis of Opposing Arguments	• readers familiar with the topic but not likely to have read the sources	• to identify the crux of the disagreement and clarify the values driving the different points of view
	• an instructor who has assigned and will evaluate the analysis	• to demonstrate understanding by presenting a clear, perceptive, impartial analysis of the values underlying the opposing arguments

Assess the genres' basic features.

As you read the summary, annotated bibliography, report, and analysis in this chapter, consider how the author, Maya Gomez, incorporates the basic features of each genre. You will find that the different genres share some basic features, but may not demonstrate the features in the same way.

AN INFORMATIVE EXPLANATION

To be effective, writing in all four of the genres needs to provide an informative explanation, although each goes about doing so in a slightly different way. A **summary** need only capture the main idea of a source concisely and accurately, answering the question, *What does the source say about the topic?*

An **annotated bibliography** expands on that summary to analyze how useful potential sources might be, given the writer's purpose and audience. An annotated bibliography not only answers the question *What does the source say about the topic?* but also *How might each source be useful to the writer? How might sources be related?* and *What bibliographical information will be needed to cite the source for an academic writing project?*

<table>
<tr><th></th><th>Summary</th><th>Annotated Bibliography</th><th>Report</th><th>Comparative Analysis</th></tr>
<tr><td rowspan="2">An Informative Explanation</td><td rowspan="2">Analyzes the source's main ideas</td><td>Analyzes sources' main ideas and usefulness</td><td>Analyzes the topic, its significance, and disagreements</td><td>Analyzes the opposing arguments to identify the underlying values at the crux of their disagreement</td></tr>
<tr><td>Synthesizes sources' relationships</td><td>Synthesizes information and points of view</td><td>Synthesizes by comparing opposing arguments on the topic</td></tr>
<tr><td rowspan="3">A Clear, Logical Organization</td><td>Includes a thesis statement to identify the source's main idea</td><td>Includes topic sentences identifying each source's main idea and how it might be used</td><td colspan="2">Includes a thesis statement and topic sentences</td></tr>
<tr><td colspan="4">Includes transitions to signal logical connections</td></tr>
<tr><td colspan="4">May use other types of cues, such as repetition of key terms and synonyms, headings, and a forecast of subtopics</td></tr>
<tr><td rowspan="2">Smooth Integration of Sources</td><td></td><td>Includes a formal citation for each source</td><td colspan="2">Includes a formal citation for each source in a works-cited list</td></tr>
<tr><td>Uses a signal phrase to identify author's credentials, title, and source information</td><td>Identifies author and provides credentials in summary of each source</td><td colspan="2">Identifies author of each source, providing credentials in text in a signal phrase or identifying source in a parenthetical citation</td></tr>
<tr><td rowspan="4">Appropriate Explanatory Strategies</td><td colspan="4">Describes source's main ideas</td></tr>
<tr><td colspan="4">Narrates source's "moves" (for example: whether the source argues, describes, or contrasts)</td></tr>
<tr><td colspan="2"></td><td colspan="2">May use a number of writing strategies, such as example, classification, and cause-effect, to help readers understand the topic</td></tr>
<tr><td colspan="2"></td><td colspan="2">May present facts or statistics visually</td></tr>
</table>

A **report** analyzes sources further to determine where they stand on the topic. It synthesizes sources to determine where they overlap and diverge, and to categorize information or ideas, so that readers can readily identify the main issues and conflicts. A report answers the questions *What is the topic? Why is it controversial?* and *What are the main opinions on the topic?*

A **comparative analysis** focuses on two (or more) sources to identify the positions the different writers hold and probe below the surface to determine what drives their positions apart. It answers the questions *What is the crux of the disagreement? What values, priorities, interests, or fears drive the disagreement on the topic?*

A CLEAR, LOGICAL ORGANIZATION

Similarly, all four genres must be clearly and logically organized. Summaries rely on transitional words and phrases (such as *because* or *therefore*) to make the relationships among sentences clear for readers. Since each summary is only a paragraph long, more cueing devices are unnecessary. The annotations in an annotated bibliography also rely mainly on transitional words and phrases to link sentences, but they may also repeat key terms (or their synonyms) to make clear how sources relate to one another.

Longer writing projects, like reports and analyses, use a full array of strategies. For example, in addition to transitional words and phrases and repetition of key terms and synonyms, Gomez's report includes a thesis statement with a forecast of the subtopics, headings to introduce each subsection, and a topic sentence to state each section's main idea:

THESIS Forecast of subtopics	This report will survey an array of ideas that have been proposed to encourage people to donate their kidneys, including changing to an opt-out system of organ donation after death, facilitating paired kidney exchanges, reducing financial disincentives, and offering incentives. (par. 3)
HEADING Headings keyed to forecast	Change from Opt-In to Opt-Out Donation after Death
TOPIC SENTENCE	There has been some discussion about changing from an opt-in system that requires a signed pledge to donate organs after death to an opt-out system that presumes consent. (par. 4)

To learn more about thesis statements, topic sentences, and headings, see Chapter 11.

SMOOTH INTEGRATION OF SOURCES

Summaries, annotated bibliographies, reports, and comparative analyses all smoothly integrate sources. A summary is very brief, so it makes sense that it would identify the source in the opening sentence, incorporating the author's name and the title of the selection (and perhaps the author's credentials and publication information) in a signal phrase: "In his article 'A Moral Market,' published by *Slate* in 2014, law professor Eric Posner proposes" (Gomez, p. 146).

Because each entry in an annotated bibliography begins with a formal citation, its summary section need not repeat the title and publication information, although it typically begins with the author's name and credentials: "In this article, law professor Eric Posner proposes" (Gomez, p. 146).

Reports and analyses—both longer writing projects for an academic audience—include a formal citation in a works-cited list and also identify the source of quotations, paraphrases, or summaries as well as visual material in in-text citations—a combination of signal phrases and parenthetical citations corresponding to the works-cited list. Consider these examples:

QUOTATION
Signal phrase
Parenthetical citation

The key passage of NOTA prohibiting compensation states that "it shall be unlawful for any person to knowingly acquire, receive, or otherwise transfer any human organ for valuable consideration for use in human transplantation" (Sec. 301a). (Report, par. 7; Analysis, par. 2)

PARAPHRASE
Parenthetical citation

For example, in 2013, a little more than 11,000 of the nearly 17,000 kidney transplants in the U.S. were from deceased donors (National Kidney Foundation, "Organ Donation"). (Report, par. 4)

SUMMARY
Parenthetical citation

A number of states have already passed legislation to reduce the burden on living donors ("Financing"). (Report, par. 10)

APPROPRIATE EXPLANATORY STRATEGIES

Both summaries and annotated bibliographies briefly describe the source's main idea. They also narrate the source's moves: Does the source *argue* a position? *State* a claim? *Concede* or *refute* opposing views?

Reports and analyses go further, using a variety of writing strategies. For example, Maya Gomez employs

- *definition* to provide an explanation for a concept:

  "Valuable consideration" is a term used in law to refer to in-kind exchange or monetary value. (Report, par. 7)

- *classification* to group ideas or information into categories:

  Forecast of topics

  An array of ideas . . . have been proposed to encourage people to donate their kidneys, including changing to an opt-out system . . . , facilitating paired kidney exchanges, reducing financial disincentives, and offering incentives. (Report, par. 3)

- *comparison and contrast* to point out similarities and differences:

  Contrast cue
  Position 1
  Position 2

  Satel's disagreement with the NKF is essentially about morality. Or rather, it is about what she sees as the NKF's moral absolutism in what she assumes is "a morally pluralistic society" (par. 21). (Analysis, par. 6)

- *cause-effect* to explain what motivates a writer (in this instance, the NKF) to hold one position rather than another:

  Cause-effect cue

  If the act of giving is tainted, for example by self-interest rather than selflessness, then the gift itself becomes unacceptable. (Analysis, par. 5)

Readings

Maya Gomez | *Summary: "A Moral Market"*

AS A FIRST-YEAR college student, Maya Gomez began a multistage project by writing a summary of one of her sources, "A Moral Market" by Eric Posner. Your instructor may ask you to read "A Moral Market" (p. 146) so you can judge how effectively Gomez summarizes the article.

Gomez's instructor gave the class four directives:

1. Summarize the source's main ideas and arguments, leaving out the details
2. Present the source accurately and impartially
3. Keep the summary brief (four to six sentences)
4. Avoid quoting the source (except for occasional key words)

(Other instructors may have different requirements.)

To compose the summary, Gomez used the Ways In activity "How Do I Write a Summary?" (pp. 164–65), in the Guide to Writing later in this chapter.

Basic Features

An Informative Explanation

A Clear, Logical Organization

Smooth Integration of Sources

Appropriate Explanatory Strategies

As you read, consider the following:

- Consider why Gomez begins with information about the source's publication and its author
- Whether you get a clear picture of the source's argument from reading the summary.

For more about writing a summary, see Chapter 10, pp. 341-42, and Chapter 15, p. 428.

Why do you think Gomez includes a quotation in the summary?

Why does Gomez give a play-by-play description of the source's explanatory strategies?

In his article "A Moral Market," published by *Slate* in 2014, law professor Eric Posner proposes a solution to the kidney shortage. He argues that, unlike the unpopular proposal to sell kidneys, his proposal for an "altruism exchange" would be politically acceptable because it is based on altruism, not the profit motive. He supports this argument by analyzing the public enthusiasm for the Norwood Act, which shows that people do not object to a kidney being exchanged for something of value; rather, they object to the donor profiting from such an exchange. Therefore, Posner proposes that a donor should be rewarded with an organ transplant (for someone other than the donor) or with a monetary donation to the donor's preferred charity.

Maya Gomez | *Annotated Bibliography: Compensating Kidney Donors*

MAYA GOMEZ compiled an annotated bibliography to keep track of the research she was doing for her kidney donor compensation project. Following is a brief excerpt from her bibliography, showing entries for three of her sources. (Use Gomez's citation notes to find the sources, then compare Gomez's summaries to the sources themselves.) Note that Gomez titled her bibliography, but did not add an introduction indicating its purpose and scope because she did not intend for it to be read by anyone other than her instructor and herself. (See Chapter 14, pp. 405–6, to see what an introduction to an annotated bibliography might look like.) As she read each source, Gomez used the Ways In activities "How Do I Write a Summary?" (pp. 164–65) and "How Do I Draft a Commentary for an Annotated Bibliography?" (p. 166).

Notice that each entry in the annotated bibliography has three parts:

1. the MLA style citation (later used in the works-cited lists for the Report and Analysis essays)
2. a *summary* of the source's main ideas and argument
3. a *commentary* reflecting on how the source might be used in a report or an analysis

As you read, consider the following:

Basic Features
An Informative Explanation
A Clear, Logical Organization
Smooth Integration of Sources
Appropriate Explanatory Strategies

- Gomez clearly indicates which part of her annotation is the summary and which is the commentary. Why is distinguishing between these two parts important for an annotated bibliography?
- Following her professor's instructions, Gomez reused her summary of Eric Posner's "A Moral Market," which she had turned in for a grade (see p. 146). Why do you think her professor judged that recycling her work in this context would be acceptable and not be considered self-plagiarism? (If you are not sure whether reusing or remixing your own writing will be acceptable for a particular assignment, be sure to ask your instructor.)

For more about writing an annotated bibliography, see Chapter 14, pp. 405–6.

Becker, Gary S., and Julio J. Elías. "Cash for Kidneys: The Case for a Market in Organs." *The Wall Street Journal*, Dow Jones, 18 Jan. 2014, www.wsj.com/articles/SB10001424052702304149404579322560004817176.

Why do you think citations begin with the last name of the first author?

Economists Becker and Elías argue for a straightforward but highly controversial proposal to solve the kidney shortage by paying people to donate their extra kidney for transplantation. To demonstrate the dire need for kidneys to transplant, they cite statistics, illustrated by a graph showing the difference between the numbers on the waiting list and the low, flat rate of transplant surgeries. They use their own research to refute the alternative solution that changing from informed to implied consent for deceased donors would reduce

How well does this thesis statement explain the main idea, or *gist*, of the article?

How helpful is it to identify the authors' explanatory strategies?

the shortage. They also refute objections that payment would not solve the problem, that it is immoral, that it would exploit the poor, and that it would reduce altruistic donations. On the issue of morality (the main criticism made by opponents of compensation), Becker and Elías compare the immorality of paying for kidneys to the immorality of dooming "thousands" on the waiting list to death.

Why compare this proposal to Posner's? What does this commentary lead you to expect about Gomez's report?

I could use this proposal as an example of a radical or extreme solution but one offered by Becker, a Nobel Prize–winning economist at the University of Chicago, and Elías, a professor of economics at a university in Argentina. Becker and Elías have the authority to carry off a proposal this bold. Their proposal also stands in sharp contrast to the NKF's opposition to financial compensation and Eric Posner's compromise. I'll certainly use it in my report.

"Financial Incentives for Organ Donation." *National Kidney Foundation,* 1 Feb. 2003, www.kidney.org/news/newsroom/positionpaper03.

How clear is this analysis of the source's main argument?

This NKF position statement claims that the prohibition against financial incentives in the National Organ Transplant Act (NOTA) should not be removed. It presents a concise summary of the main arguments against payment: paying for body parts devalues human life, paying would be coercive and exploitative, and paying wouldn't be effective in eliminating the shortage and might discourage altruistic donors. After acknowledging that other organizations support pilot studies to see whether payment would help, the NKF asserts its opposition to pilot studies, arguing that, once done, paying for kidneys cannot be undone. The statement concludes by repeating the NKF's commitment to working to solve the problem through improved public relations and professional practices, but not by paying for kidneys.

How fair and impartial is this annotation?

How important is the date and author in choosing sources?

I think I will use the NKF position statement as the voice of the status quo. Note that it was written in 2003 and hasn't been changed since, even though NOTA has been amended several times to allow paired kidney exchanges and to limit disincentives. I could compare the NKF statement to Becker and Elías's recent proposal, "Cash for Kidneys." Or I could compare it to Satel's op-ed, "When Altruism Isn't Moral." Using Satel's critique of the current altruism-only policy would enable me to contrast the NKF's moral values argument.

Compare to Gomez's report and analysis.

Posner, Eric. "A Moral Market." *Slate*, 17 Oct. 2014, www.slate.com/articles/news_and_politics/view_from_chicago/2014/10/kidney_donation_exchange_to_increase_donated_organs_ethically_and_altruistically.html. In this article, law professor Eric Posner proposes a solution to the kidney shortage. He argues that, unlike the unpopular proposal to sell kidneys, his proposal for an "altruism exchange" would be politically acceptable because it is based on altruism, not the profit motive. He supports this argument by analyzing the public enthusiasm for the Norwood Act, which shows that people do not object to a kidney being exchanged for something of value; rather, they object to the donor profiting from such an exchange. Therefore, Posner proposes that a donor should be rewarded with an organ transplant (for someone other than the donor) or with a monetary donation to the donor's preferred charity.

How do transitions like *unlike*, *because*, and *therefore* help readers?

If I focus my comparative analysis on the morality of altruism, I could use Satel as a critique of Posner. Is Posner's altruism-exchange proposal really different from the NKF-supported altruism-only transplant policy? Satel critiques an altruism-only transplant policy because it forces everyone to follow the same view of morality. (What's the opposite of moral pluralism?)

How does Gomez explore ways of synthesizing her sources?

Maya Gomez | *Report: Possible Solutions to the Kidney Shortage*

FOR THIS REPORT—the third writing project in the sequence—Maya Gomez builds on the research she did on kidney transplantation, exploring the problem of the kidney shortage and solutions that have been tried or proposed. She synthesized information and ideas from sources, categorizing them into three topics. As she composed her report, Gomez relied on her annotated bibliography together with quotations she had included in her notes and annotations she had made on copies of her sources.

As you read,

- consider why Gomez begins her report with an anecdote about the Herrick brothers.
- notice that Gomez includes two graphs and headings; what do you think they contribute to the report?
- answer the questions in the margins; your instructor may ask you to post your answers to a class blog or discussion board or to bring them to class.

If your instructor has asked you to compose a report, turn to the Guide to Writing for help choosing a topic, finding sources, synthesizing information from those sources, and composing a report. Use the Starting Points chart (pp. 160–62) to locate the sections you need.

Basic Features
A Informative Explanation
A Clear, Logical Organization
Smooth Integration of Sources
Appropriate Explanatory Strategies

How does knowing this history help readers understand the topic?

Why do you think Gomez explains what Figure 1 shows?

1 The "first successful kidney transplant" took place in 1954 when Ronald Herrick donated one of his kidneys to his identical twin Richard, who was dying of kidney disease ("Milestones"). Richard and Ronald's successful tandem surgery was a historic event ushering in the era of kidney transplantation. Today, kidney transplantation has become routine. Because of improvements in blood and tissue typing, together with the development of powerful immunosuppressant drugs, it is no longer necessary for an identical twin or even a relative to make the donation. As long as the donor and recipient are compatible, kidneys can be transplanted from strangers as well as relatives, from living as well as deceased donors.

2 Nevertheless, the shortage of kidneys has gotten worse, not better. According to the National Kidney Foundation (NKF), more than 120,000 people with End Stage Renal Disease (ESRD) are on the U.S. transplant waiting list, with "nearly 3,000 new patients" joining the list every month and an estimated 12 patients dying every day while waiting for a kidney ("Organ Donation"). As fig. 1 below shows, the number of people with kidney disease has risen dramatically during recent decades.

3 Even though the number of donated kidneys has doubled, the gap between the number of people on the waiting list and the number of transplantations

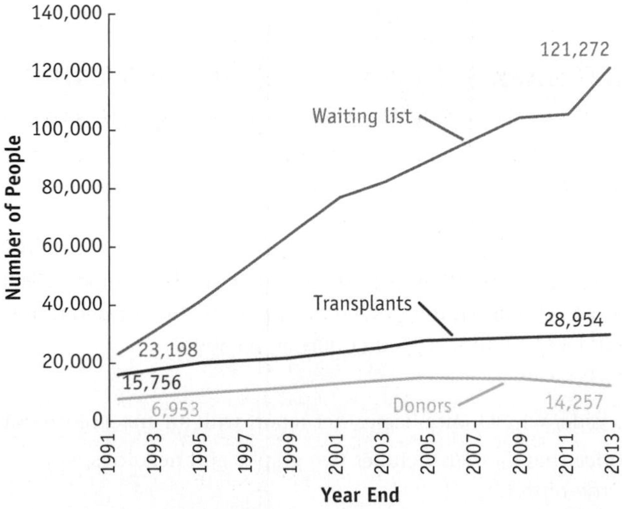

Fig. 1. The Gap Continues to Widen. Data from United States, Department of Health and Human Services, Health Resources and Services Administration. *Organ Procurement and Transplantation Network*, 1 May 2015, optn.transplant.hrsa.gov/.

performed has widened because of the scarcity of available kidneys. Clearly, the number of donated kidneys falls far short of the number needed. This report will survey an array of ideas that have been proposed to encourage people to donate their kidneys, including changing to an opt-out system of organ donation after death, facilitating paired kidney exchanges, reducing financial disincentives, and offering incentives.

How useful is this forecast?

Change from Opt-In to Opt-Out Donation after Death

4 There has been some discussion about changing from an opt-in system that requires a signed pledge to donate organs after death to an opt-out system that presumes consent. But no action has been taken. Currently, two-thirds of the kidneys used for transplant typically come from someone who has recently died. For example, in 2013, a little more than 11,000 of the nearly 17,000 kidney transplants in the U.S. were from deceased donors ("Organ Donation").

How do the transitions help readers?

5 Those who oppose changing to an opt-out system object either because they don't trust the state not to abuse its power (for example, they fear that the state would order organs to be taken from patients who would not otherwise die), or because they fear medical personnel would make a mistake (for example, that organs would be taken from those who were wrongly considered dead). In contrast, advocates of changing to an opt-out system favor it because they think it would help close the gap between supply and demand. A recent international study "found that countries using opt-out systems had higher total numbers of kidneys donated" than countries with opt-in systems (McIntosh). Nonetheless, economists Becker and Elías argue that the increase in donated kidneys would not be "large enough to eliminate the sizable shortfall in the supply of organs in the U.S." (par. 10). So, although changing to an opt-out system would help, it would not be enough, by itself, to solve the kidney shortage.

How clear are these causal explanations?

Facilitate Paired Kidney Exchanges

6 Unlike the question of whether to change to an opt-out donation system, the question of whether the law should be changed to permit paired kidney exchanges was met with quick action. In 2007, the Charlie W. Norwood Living Organ Donation Act was passed unanimously to amend the 1984 National Organ Transplant Act (NOTA) that established U.S. transplant policy and outlawed any form of compensation for organ donors.

How effective are this subheading and topic sentence?

How clear are these definitions?

7 The key passage of NOTA prohibiting compensation states that "it shall be unlawful for any person to knowingly acquire, receive, or otherwise transfer any human organ for valuable consideration for use in human transplantation" (sec. 301a). "Valuable consideration" is a term used in law to refer to in-kind exchange or monetary value. A paired kidney exchange essentially trades a biologically incompatible kidney, usually donated by a family member, for a compatible one donated by a stranger. Legalizing paired exchanges enables relatives to save the life of a loved one even when their kidneys are not compatible. As fig. 2 shows, most living donor kidneys come from direct donations or paired exchanges from relatives.

8 Advances in computer matching have also made possible long chains of paired kidney exchanges. Unfortunately, however, the total number of living donor transplants, including those from paired kidney exchanges, is relatively low and has been declining in recent years. Research suggests that the decline may be due largely to the financial crisis of 2007 that led to housing foreclosures and high unemployment, making the financial disincentives to donating an even greater hardship for many people (Rodriguez et al.).

Remove Disincentives

9 Most stakeholders agree that it's a good idea to remove at least some of the disincentives to donation, such as travel expenses to the transplant center.

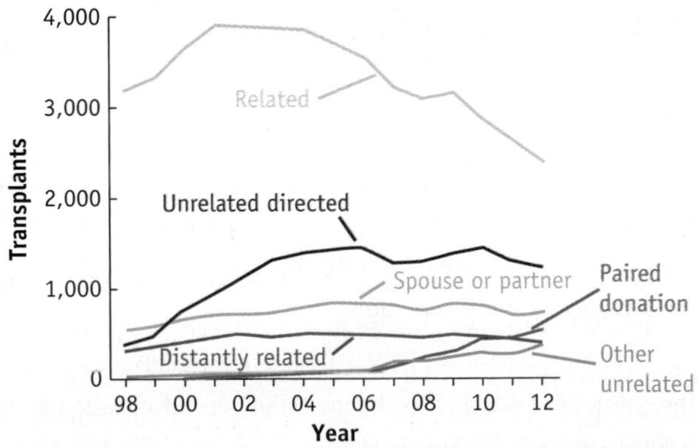

Fig. 2. Kidney transplants from living donors. Data from United States, Department of Health and Human Services, Health Resources and Services Administration. *OPTN/SRTR Annual Data Report: Kidney*, Scientific Registry of Transplant Recipients, 2012, srtr.transplant .hrsa.gov/annual_reports/2012/pdf/01_kidney_13.pdf.

The National Kidney Foundation, one of the most conservative advocacy groups, had been adamantly opposed to financial compensation of any kind since 2002 ("Financial"). But in 2009, when the waiting list reached 100,000, the NKF announced that it planned to work with Congress to craft legislation that will address all the barriers to donation ("Organ Shortage"). The NKF's "End the Wait!" campaign supports reimbursing living donors "for all expenses involved in the donation, including lost wages" and also subsidizing donors' "state-of-the-art medical care" and "life insurance coverage" ("Organ Shortage").

10 According to Transplant Living, a service of the nonprofit organization UNOS, a number of states have already passed legislation to reduce the burden on living donors ("Financing"). Congress has also passed two laws: the Organ Donor Leave Act (1999), which gives federal employees who donate kidneys paid leave, and the Organ Donation and Recovery Improvement Act (2004), which reimburses travel and living expenses for low-income organ donors who qualify for a grant (United States, "Selected"). However, most potential donors do not benefit from these laws.

Offer Incentives

11 The idea that money should be offered, not just to counter the financial costs associated with donating but also as an incentive to encourage donors, is the most controversial of all the proposals that have been considered. In 2014, the thirtieth anniversary of NOTA, debate heated up on financial incentives. A radical proposal, aptly titled "Cash for Kidneys," was published in *The Wall Street Journal* by two respected economists, Julio Elías and Nobel Laureate Gary Becker, who argue that the only way to "close the gap between the demand and supply of kidneys" is to pay people for their kidneys.

12 For the NKF and other opponents of financial compensation, the Becker and Elías proposal to pay for kidneys recalls the 1983 proposal by Dr. Barry Jacobs to buy kidneys from healthy poor people in Third World countries and sell them to Americans (Sullivan). It was Jacobs's plan that led to NOTA's strict prohibition against compensation in the first place. And, as we have seen, although Congress has been willing to modify NOTA to permit paired kidney exchanges and reimburse some donor expenses, it has staunchly resisted any substantial change to the valuable consideration clause.

13 The main arguments against financial compensation—the immorality of treating body parts as commodities and using poor people's kidneys as spare parts for the rich—have not changed since NOTA was passed (Gomez). What has changed in the last thirty years, however, is that the kidney shortage has grown to crisis proportions and that desperate people have found ways around the law by means of transplant tourism and the illegal organ trade. But as Sally Satel, herself a kidney transplant recipient, acknowledges in "The Case for Compensating Kidney Donors": "It is easy to condemn the black market and the patients who patronize it. But you can't fault people for trying to save their own lives" (par. 9).

Note the sources' dates, publication venues, and authors. How appropriate do the sources appear to be? Does the selection seem fair and balanced?

Works Cited

Becker, Gary S., and Julio J. Elías. "Cash for Kidneys: The Case for a Market in Organs." *The Wall Street Journal,* Dow Jones, 18 Jan. 2014, www.wsj.com/articles/SB10001424052702304149404579322560004817176.

"Financial Incentives for Organ Donation." *National Kidney Foundation,* 1 Feb. 2003, www.kidney.org/news/newsroom/positionpaper03.

"Financing Living Donation." *Transplant Living,* United Network for Organ Sharing, www.transplantliving.org/living-donation/financing-living-donation/. Accessed 1 May 2015.

Gomez, Maya. "Satel vs. the National Kidney Foundation: Should Kidney Donors Be Compensated?" Paper, Huntly College, Writing 1101, 2015.

McIntosh, James. "Organ Donation: Is an Opt-In or Opt-Out System Better?" *Medical News Today,* Medi-Lexicon International, 24 Sept. 2014, www.medicalnewstoday.com/articles/282905.php.

"Milestones in Organ Transplantation." *National Kidney Foundation,* www.kidney.org/transplantation/transaction/Milestones-Organ-Transplantation. Accessed 2 May 2015.

"Organ Donation and Transplantation Statistics." *National Kidney Foundation,* 8 Sept. 2014, www.kidney.org/news/newsroom/factsheets/Organ-Donation-and-Transplantation-Stats.

"Organ Shortage Needs Multi-Faceted Approach." *National Kidney Foundation,* 29 Jan. 2009, www.kidney.org/news/newsroom/nr/89.

Rodriguez, James R., et al. "The Decline in Living Kidney Donation in the United States: Random Variation or Cause for Concern?" *Transplantation,* vol. 96, no. 9, Nov. 2013, doi:10.1053/j.ajkd.2013.10.034.

Satel, Sally. "The Case for Compensating Kidney Donors." *Pacific Standard,* Miller-McCune Center for Research, Media and Public Policy, 12 Mar. 2015, www.psmag.com/health-and-behavior/the-case-for-compensating-kidney-donors.

Sullivan, Walter. "Buying of Kidneys of Poor Attacked." *The New York Times,* 24 Sept. 1983, www.nytimes.com/1983/09/24/us/buying-of-kidneys-of-poor-attacked.html.

United States, Congress, House. *Charlie W. Norwood Living Donation Act.* Government Printing Office, 7 Dec. 2007. 110th Congress, House Report 710.

---, ---, ---. *National Organ Transplant Act.* Government Printing Office, 19 Oct. 1984. 98th Congress, House Report 98-1127.

United States, Department of Health and Human Services, Health Resources and Services Administration. "Selected Statutory and Regulatory History of Organ Transplantation." *Organdonor.gov: Donate the Gift of Life,* www.organdonor.gov/legislation/legislationhistory.html. Accessed 2 May 2015.

Maya Gomez

Analysis: Satel vs. the National Kidney Foundation: Should Kidney Donors Be Compensated?

FOR THIS ANALYSIS, Maya Gomez compares two reading selections: the National Kidney Foundation's policy statement "Financial Incentives for Organ Donation" and Sally Satel's op-ed "When Altruism Isn't Moral." From her earlier research, Gomez learned that the National Kidney Foundation (NKF) plays a central role as defender of the status quo, resisting proposals to compensate donors and even opposing a pilot study to see whether financial compensation would encourage donors. To contrast with this position, she selected an article by Sally Satel, an outspoken opponent of the NKF's altruism-only policy.

As you will see, Gomez's comparative analysis builds on her report. Whereas her report gives a brief history of kidney transplantation and introduces the main arguments in the debate, her analysis zeroes in on the pivotal disagreement between the NKF and Satel about moral values—in particular, the virtue of altruism.

Because this was the fourth part of an assignment sequence, Gomez's instructor told the class that remixing their own words and ideas without citation (which could be seen as self-plagiarism) would be acceptable in this context. You will see that Gomez recycles whole sentences from her report, especially in the opening paragraphs. If you write a comparative analysis of your own, you will want to clarify your instructor's expectations regarding the recycling of your own language and ideas from your other projects.

Basic Features

An Informative Explanation

A Clear, Logical Organization

Smooth Integration of Sources

Appropriate Explanatory Strategies

As you read,

- notice how Gomez introduces the two documents and sets up the analysis comparing their underlying values;
- answer the questions in the margins; your instructor may ask you to post your answers to a class blog or discussion board or to bring them to class.

If your instructor has asked you to compose an analysis, turn to the Guide to Writing for help choosing a topic, finding sources, analyzing and comparing sources, and composing an analysis. Use the Starting Points chart (pp. 160–62) to locate the sections you need.

Why do you think Gomez opens with a sentence adapted from her report?

1 According to the National Kidney Foundation (NKF), more than 120,000 people are on the U.S. transplant waiting list, with "nearly 3,000 new patients" joining the list every month and an estimated 12 patients dying every day while waiting for a kidney ("Organ Donation"). The NKF, the nation's foremost nonprofit advocacy group for kidney disease patients, bemoans the worsening kidney shortage and "advocates for ways to increase the supply of organs for transplantation" ("Policy"). However, the NKF Web site also claims responsibility for the current U.S. transplant policy that outlaws financial compensation for organ donors—a ban seen by many as the major obstacle to reducing the kidney shortage.

2 In fact, the NKF claims it played a central leadership role not only in drafting the National Organ Transplant Act (NOTA) but also in getting the law passed through its impressive lobbying power ("History"). The key passage of NOTA prohibiting compensation states that "it shall be unlawful for any person to knowingly acquire, receive, or otherwise transfer any human organ for valuable consideration for use in human transplantation" (Sec. 301a). Although the law has been modified to permit kidney exchanges and remove several disincentives to donation (Gomez), the "valuable consideration" clause has been defended by the NKF. At the same time, it has been criticized by proponents of alternative solutions to the kidney shortage.

Why do you think she refers to her own report?

3 One of the most vocal critics of NOTA's prohibition against compensating donors, and of the NKF's advocacy in particular, is Sally Satel, M.D. A prolific author, Satel has written extensively about transplant policy for distinguished

venues such as *The New York Times*, *The Washington Post*, and *The Wall Street Journal*. She edited the book *When Altruism Isn't Enough: The Case for Compensating Organ Donors*. She is also a lecturer in psychiatry at the Yale University Medical School and a resident scholar at the American Enterprise Institute, a conservative think tank "committed to expanding liberty, increasing individual opportunity and strengthening free enterprise" ("About"). And she is a kidney transplant recipient. In a 2009 op-ed, Satel gave vent to her disappointment in the NKF, accusing the group of trying "to sabotage any attempt to explore the possibility of rewarding organ donors," and even misrepresenting a study of donor motivation ("National").

Why give so much information about Satel?

4 This essay compares the underlying values driving the arguments in the NKF position statement "Financial Incentives for Organ Donation" and Satel's article "When Altruism Isn't Moral." Their views are diametrically opposed. Whereas the NKF defends the status quo and urges retention of the valuable consideration clause, Satel deplores the "woeful inadequacy of our nation's transplant policy" and proposes "rewards" to "encourage more living and posthumous donation" (pars. 5, 6). The basis of their disagreement is the proper role of altruism. The NKF emphatically endorses the current "altruistic system" (par. 5). Satel, in contrast, argues that current policy is failing precisely because it is an "altruism-only system" (par. 13).

Why wait so long to name the texts being analyzed?

5 Altruism, according to Satel, is "the guiding narrative of the transplant establishment," its underlying ideology or value system (par 5.). The NKF would agree with Satel's description of current policy requiring that "organs should be a 'gift of life'" and donating should be "an act of selfless generosity" (Satel, par. 5). In using the phrase "altruistic gift of life," the NKF statement makes explicit the connection between the act of giving and what is being given (par. 2). If the act of giving is tainted, for example by self-interest rather than selflessness, then the gift itself becomes unacceptable. That is why, in the anecdote that Satel uses to begin her article, the transplant surgeons need to be convinced that Matt Thompson, the potential donor, "was donating his kidney for the right reasons"—namely, for purely altruistic reasons (pars. 1–2).

6 Satel's disagreement with the NKF is essentially about morality. Or rather, it is about what she sees as the NKF's moral absolutism in what she assumes is "a morally pluralistic society" (par. 21). The NKF statement represents a

Why do you think Gomez corrects herself here?

worldview in which there are certain moral truths about which it is assumed everyone agrees. Examples of moral certainty in the NKF policy statement include the claims that "payment for organs is wrong" and "inconsistent with our values as a society" (pars. 6, 2).

How effective is this topic sentence?

7 We can see the NKF's and Satel's opposing views of morality played out in their arguments about the commodification of human organs. The NKF statement explains what is wrong with treating the human body as a commodity: "Any attempt to assign a monetary value to the human body, or body parts, either arbitrarily, or through market forces, diminishes human dignity" (par. 2). This argument is based on the belief that the human body is not something to be treated as "property" to be bought and sold (par. 2). Rather, it is sacred, made in God's image.

What does this paragraph do?

8 Satel refutes the commodification argument in a number of ways. For example, she points out that commodifying body parts has a long legal tradition from Hammurabi to current personal injury law (par. 19). She also questions the cause-effect reasoning that commodifying body parts is necessarily dehumanizing: "There is little reason to believe—nor tangible evidence to suggest—that these practices depreciate human worth or undermine human dignity in any way" (par. 19). But her main argument is about how we evaluate "the goodness of an act" (par. 18), in other words, our moral reasoning.

9 Satel critiques the NKF's way of assessing moral value by arguing that its moral logic relies on "false choice" reasoning. She summarizes the NKF's thinking this way: "Giving a kidney 'for free' is noble but accepting compensation is illegitimate" (par. 11). This distinction between altruistic gift giving and receiving a reward hinges on the idea that inserting a reward into the exchange commercializes it and damages the act's moral purity. Satel quotes Kieran Healy, a professor at Duke University studying economic sociology, to describe the either/or dilemma that framing the debate around altruism creates: "the debate is cast as one in which existing relations of selfless, altruistic exchange are threatened with replacement by market-based, for-profit alternatives" (par. 11).

How does Gomez use classification here?

10 In other words, Satel thinks the NKF sets up a false choice between selflessness and self-interest. In contrast to the NKF, Satel believes that mixed motives probably drive most gift giving. For example, she suggests

several self-interested motives that may be involved in giving the "gift of life"—such as offering "an organ as an act of redemption," "a way to elicit praise and social acceptance," or "a way to avoid the shame and guilt of allowing a relative to suffer needlessly and perhaps even die" (par. 13).

11 Purity of motivation plays a key role for the NKF in evaluating "the goodness of an act." But for Satel, what appears to matter most is that the act has the potential to save a human life. For her, it doesn't matter if the donor gains materially, earns enhanced social status, or just gets a "'warm glow'" of self-satisfaction "from performing acts of charity" (par. 16). Instead of "remuneration" crowding out "generosity" (par. 15), as critics of financial compensation like the National Kidney Foundation claim, Satel argues that the opposite is true: the combination of payment with the opportunity to do good could offer a real solution to "increase the pool of transplantable organs" (par. 18).

How effective are Gomez's examples?

How effective is this way of concluding the comparative analysis?

Works Cited

"About." *American Enterprise Institute,* 2015, www.aei.org/about/.

"Financial Incentives for Organ Donation." *National Kidney Foundation,* 1 Feb. 2003, www.kidney.org/news/newsroom/positionpaper03.

Gomez, Maya. "Possible Solutions to the Kidney Shortage" Paper, Writing 1101, Huntly College, 2015.

"History." *National Kidney Foundation,* www.kidney.org/about/history. Accessed 30 Apr. 2015.

"Organ Donation and Transplantation Statistics." *National Kidney Foundation,* 8 Sept. 2014, www.kidney.org/news/newsroom/factsheets/Organ-Donation-and-Transplantation-Stats.

"Policy and Legislation." *National Kidney Foundation,* 2015, www.kidney.org/advocacy/issues.

Satel, Sally. "The National Kidney Foundation's Bizarre Logic." *American Enterprise Institute,* 11 June 2009, www.aei.org/publication/the-national-kidney-foundations-bizarre-logic/.

---. "When Altruism Isn't Moral." *American Enterprise Institute,* 30 Jan. 2009, www.aei.org/publication/when-altruism-isnt-moral/.

United States, Congress, House. *National Organ Transplant Act.* Government Printing Office, 19 Oct. 1984. 98th Congress, House Report 98-1127.

The Writing Assignment

Your instructor may ask you to compose all or part of the following multistage project:

1. Summarize one or more sources on a controversial topic.
2. Compile an annotated bibliography on the topic.
3. Synthesize information from the articles you have read to write an informative report introducing the topic to your audience.
4. Analyze two (or more) articles that take conflicting positions on the topic, comparing and contrasting the values underlying the opposing positions.

This Guide to Writing is designed to help you compose your own summary, annotated bibliography, report, and analysis, applying what you have learned from reading an example of each of these genres. This Starting Points chart will help you find answers to any questions you might have. Use the chart to find the guidance you need, when you need it.

STARTING POINTS: COMPOSING A SUMMARY, AN ANNOTATED BIBLIOGRAPHY, A REPORT, OR AN ANALYSIS

An Informative Explanation

How do I find a topic to write about?

- Practicing a Genre: Analyzing Opposing Arguments (p. 140)
- Choose a controversial topic to write about. (pp. 162–63)
- Test Your Choice: Choosing a Topic (p. 163)
- Conduct research to find sources. (p. 163)

How can I summarize my sources?

- Assess the genre's basic features: An informative explanation. (pp. 142–44)
- Summary: "A Moral Market" (Maya Gomez) (p. 146)
- Summarize sources and annotate your working bibliography. (pp. 164–66)

How do I annotate sources for an annotated bibliography?

- Annotated Bibliography: Compensating Kidney Donors (Maya Gomez) (pp. 147–49)
- Summarize sources and annotate your working bibliography. (pp. 164–66)

An Informative Explanation	How can I cite my sources properly? • Chapter 16, Citing and Documenting Sources in MLA Style • Chapter 17, Citing and Documenting Sources in APA Style
	How do I interest my audience? • Determine the writer's purpose and audience. (pp. 141–42) • Test Your Choice: Choosing a Topic (p. 163) • Analyze your audience. (pp. 166–67)
	How can I focus my explanation? • Brainstorm subtopics for a report. (p. 167) • Choose opposing argument essays to analyze. (pp. 167–68) • Synthesize sources for a report or an analysis. (pp. 168–69) • Analyze and compare the opposing argument essays. (pp. 169–70) • Draft a working thesis for your report or analysis. (pp. 170–71) • Test Your Choice: Evaluating Your Analysis (p. 170) • A Troubleshooting Guide: An Informative Explanation (pp. 178–79)
A Clear, Logical Organization	How do I organize a report or analysis? • Assess the genre's basic features: A clear, logical organization. (p. 144) • Brainstorm subtopics for a report. (p. 167) • Synthesize sources for a report or an analysis. (pp. 168–69) • Analyze and compare the opposing argument essays. (pp. 169–70) • Test Your Choice: Evaluating Your Analysis (p. 170) • Draft a working thesis for your report or analysis. (pp. 170–71) • Create an outline to organize your report or analysis effectively for your readers. (p. 171) • A Troubleshooting Guide: A Clear, Logical Organization (p. 179)
Smooth Integration of Sources	How do I integrate sources? • Assess the genre's basic features: Smooth integration of sources. (pp. 144–45) • Summarize sources and annotate your working bibliography. (pp. 164–66) • Develop your report or analysis. (p. 176) • A Troubleshooting Guide: Smooth Integration of Sources (pp. 179–80)

(continued)

Appropriate Explanatory Strategies

What kinds of explanatory strategies are appropriate in a report or an analysis?

- Assess the genre's basic features: Appropriate explanatory strategies. (p. 145)
- Use visuals or multimedia illustrations to enhance your explanation. (p. 175)
- Draft your report or analysis. (p. 176)
- A Troubleshooting Guide: Appropriate Explanatory Strategies (pp. 179–80)

Writing a Draft: Invention, Research, Planning, and Composing

The activities in this section will help you choose a topic and find sources, compose summaries and commentaries for an annotated bibliography, analyze and synthesize your sources, report on the topic, and write an analysis comparing two opposing argument essays. Your writing in response to many of these activities can be used in rough drafts, which you will be able to improve after receiving feedback from your classmates and instructor. Do the activities in any order that makes sense to you (and your instructor), and return to them as needed as you revise.

Choose a controversial topic to write about.

When choosing a topic to write about, keep in mind that it must be

- a controversial issue (one that people disagree about);
- a topic about which you can report impartially—you may already be interested in the topic and have a strong opinion about it, but you must be able to represent other views on the topic fairly;
- a topic that you can research in the time you have and on which you are likely to find a range of opinions;
- a topic that is likely to interest you and your readers.

You may already have a controversial topic in mind. (Or perhaps your instructor has already assigned you a topic.) If so, complete the Test Your Choice: Choosing a Topic activity that follows. If you do not, you could

- search for op-ed articles in newspapers and blogs, using LexisNexis Academic or other databases accessible through your college library;
- survey such Web sites as procon.org or controversialissues.org, or the Room for Debate page on the *New York Times*'s Web site (nytimes.com);
- revisit the topic you discussed in the Practicing a Genre activity (p. 140);
- glance at the reading selections in Chapters 6–8 to see whether any of the readings or topics mentioned there pique your interest.

Here are a few controversial topics to get you thinking:

- Voter ID laws: Are they needed to stop voter fraud, or are they a way to suppress voting among poor and ethnic minorities?
- E-cigarettes: Are they safe, or do they perpetuate nicotine addiction?
- School uniforms: Do school uniforms level the socioeconomic playing field or worsen socioeconomic divisions?

TEST YOUR CHOICE

Choosing a Topic

After you have made a provisional choice, ask yourself the following questions:

- What do I already know and think about the topic? Do I find it important and interesting enough to justify spending the time necessary to do the research and writing required?
- What are my readers likely to know about it? Will they have strong opinions, or will I need to show them why they should care about it? Will they be open to learning about different points of view on the topic?

Then get together with two or three other students to take turns trying out your topics with potential readers. Ask group members questions like the following:

- What, if anything, do you already know about the topic? What do you think are the main opposing points of view on it? Do you have an opinion about it?
- What basic values (such as freedom, equality, honesty, and justice) seem to be involved in discussions of this topic?
- What questions about the topic would you like answered? For example, would you like to know how it started or changed over time, who has been involved in discussions of the topic, and what interests they represent?

Conduct research to find sources.

Now that you have a tentative topic and a sense of your readers' knowledge of it, along with their questions about it, use the following research tips to locate relevant sources:

- Search a database, such as *Academic OneFile* (InfoTrac) or *Academic Search Complete* (EBSCOhost).
- For topics likely to have been dealt with by a government agency, explore USA .gov—the U.S. government's official Web portal—or conduct an Advanced Google search, limiting results to those with a .gov domain.
- Follow up on sources cited in the texts and Web sites you have looked at.

For each potential source you find,

1. add a citation to your working bibliography;
2. save a copy of the source or a line for further reference;
3. take notes or draft a summary as you read.

For more about developing key terms and searching for sources, see Chapter 14; for more about evaluating sources, see Chapter 15; for help adding a commentary to a summary in an annotated bibliography, complete the Ways In activity "How Do I Draft a Commentary?" (p. 166). For citation models and detailed instructions on creating an entry for a works-cited or reference list, see Chapter 16 (MLA style) or Chapter 17 (APA style).

Summarize sources and annotate your working bibliography.

The following activities will be useful if you are writing a summary of a single source or compiling an annotated bibliography of several sources.

The length of the summary will depend on the length of your source, the reason you are writing the summary, and your readers' expectations. Typically, one paragraph is sufficient to summarize a brief source for a stand-alone summary or an annotated bibliography, but consult your instructor if you are not sure.

WAYS IN

HOW DO I WRITE A SUMMARY?

1. *Highlight the* **THESIS** *and* **MAIN SUPPORTING IDEAS (REASONS)** *as you read the source. (You may have to reread it several times to distinguish the main points from the details.)*
2. *Compose an* **OUTLINE** *of the main ideas—using your own words.*
3. *Put the source away and draft the summary from your outline. (This can help you avoid inadvertent plagiarism and retain the order of your source's ideas.)*

- Introduce the source in a **SIGNAL PHRASE** (author's name plus a verb that captures the move the author is making, such as *argues, supports, describes,* and so on). For a summary, include publication information, like the title and date of publication, in the opening sentence.

  ▶ In his book/article/op-ed ________ [title] (date), X, a professor of ________ at School A, asserts/reports ________.

  EXAMPLE In his article "A Moral Market," published by *Slate* in 2014, law professor Eric Posner proposes . . . (Gomez, "Summary")

- In a summary for an annotated bibliography, just include the author's name and credentials; publication information will be included in the bibliographic citation.

  ▶ In this book/article/op-ed, X, professor of ________ at School A, asserts/reports ________.

  EXAMPLE In this article, law professor Eric Posner proposes a solution to the kidney shortage. (Gomez, "Annotated Bibliography")

- State the **THESIS** in your own words.

  ▶ X argues that the best way to solve the problem is to ________.

  ▶ Professor X contradicts Dr. Y, explaining that ________.

EXAMPLE Economists Becker and Elías argue for a straightforward but highly controversial proposal to solve the kidney shortage problem by paying people to donate their extra kidney for transplantation. (Gomez, "Annotated Bibliography")

- List the main supporting ideas (or reasons) in the same order in which they appear in the source.

▶ X responds to such criticisms as ________, ________, and ________.

▶ X claims that ________. He also argues that ________.

EXAMPLE [Becker and Elías] also refute objections that payment would not solve the problem, that it is immoral, that it would exploit the poor, and that it would reduce altruistic donations. (Gomez, "Annotated Bibliography")

- Use **TRANSITIONS** (such as *and, also, but,* and *therefore*) and other cues (such as repeating key terms or using synonyms to refer to key terms) to show readers how the ideas relate to one another.

▶ Although/Whereas/Unlike Dr. A's position, Dr. B's contention is that ________.

EXAMPLE [Posner] argues that, unlike the unpopular proposal to sell kidneys, his proposal for an "altruism exchange" would be politically acceptable because it is based on altruism, not the profit motive. (Gomez, "Summary")

4. *Check your draft summary against the source to make sure you have*
   - captured the author's ideas accurately and succinctly;
   - avoided inserting your own ideas or opinions;
   - put key terms (such as "altruism exchange" in Gomez's summary of Posner's article) in quotation marks;
   - avoided borrowing other words or sentence patterns.

An annotated bibliography for a writing project includes a summary of each source as well as a commentary, which consists of

- your thoughts on how you might use the source in your report, analysis, or other project;
- your ideas about the relationships among your sources (the beginning of your synthesis);
- an evaluation of each source's **credibility** (authority).

Use the following guidelines and sentence strategies as a jumping-off point for drafting the commentary for the sources you include in your annotated bibliography. You can make the sentences you generate your own later, as you revise.

WAYS IN

HOW DO I DRAFT A COMMENTARY FOR AN ANNOTATED BIBLIOGRAPHY?

1. *Explore how you could use the source in your project(s).*

   ▶ I plan to use ________ [title of article/book] to show ________, ________, and ________.

EXAMPLE I could use [Becker and Elías's] proposal as an example of a radical or extreme solution. (Gomez, "Annotated Bibliography")

I think I will use the NKF position statement as the voice of the status quo. (Gomez, "Annotated Bibliography")

2. *Make connections among your sources.*

   ▶ X is like/unlike Y in that ________.

EXAMPLE [Becker and Elias's] proposal . . . stands in sharp contrast to the NKF's opposition to financial compensation and Eric Posner's compromise. (Gomez, "Annotated Bibliography")

3. *Assess the credibility of your sources.*

   ▶ X is likely to carry authority with most people because ________.

EXAMPLE . . . Becker, a Nobel Prize–winning economist at the University of Chicago, and Elías, a professor of economics at a university in Argentina. Becker and Elías have the authority to carry off a proposal this bold. (Gomez, "Annotated Bibliography")

For citation models and detailed instructions on creating a citation for your annotated bibliography, see Chapter 16 (MLA style) or Chapter 17 (APA style).

Analyze your audience.

Once you have conducted research and added potential sources to your annotated bibliography, spend a few minutes thinking about your audience. Answering the following questions will help you decide on the best approach to take for your report or analysis.

WAYS IN

WHAT WILL MAKE THE REPORT OR ANALYSIS INTERESTING TO MY READERS?

Analyze your AUDIENCE *by brainstorming or freewriting answers to the following questions:*

- Who are your readers, and what are they likely to know about the topic? What opinions are they likely to hold? (Reconsider what you learned from the Test Your Choice activity earlier in this Guide to Writing.)
- How would you answer your readers' "So what?" question? Think of at least one aspect of the topic that will clarify its importance for your readers.

- What is your relationship with your readers? What **TONE** is most appropriate for addressing this audience? How do you want your readers to perceive you? (For an academic audience, a rational, dispassionate tone is usually most appropriate.)

Since you are reporting or analyzing a controversial topic rather than offering your own opinion, be sure to keep your tone impartial.

For more about brainstorming, freewriting, and other idea-generating strategies, see Chapter 9.

Brainstorm subtopics for a report.

If you have been asked to write a report, you will need to focus your attention on a few key subtopics that you can address thoroughly. A good way to come up with a list of subtopics is by reviewing what you already know:

- List the milestones in the history of your topic, noting laws, events, and publications that mark important turning points.
- Reread your annotated bibliography and other source notes, highlighting subtopics that are discussed in two or more sources.
- Make a list of the subtopics that seem most relevant.

Here's an example from Maya Gomez's report:

Topic: Solving the kidney-shortage problem

Possible Subtopics

- by preventing kidney disease (through education, diet, medication)
- by improving dialysis treatment
- by encouraging everyone to donate their kidneys after death (opt-out instead of the current opt-in system)
- by making kidney exchanges legal
- by removing the obstacles kidney donors face (paid time off)
- by compensating donors (money, health insurance, a kidney for themselves or for a loved one)
- by developing an artificial kidney to replace a non-functioning kidney

Gomez ended up focusing on the four topics that she knew she had enough information about from her sources to report on in depth.

Choose opposing argument essays to analyze.

If you have been asked to write a comparative analysis, you will need to select texts that

- take different positions on the same controversial topic;
- reflect different underlying basic values or worldviews.

It may also be helpful to choose opposing arguments that refer explicitly to one another or that at least address the same aspect of the topic from different perspectives.

While compiling your annotated bibliography or writing your report, you may have come across two (or three) essays that looked promising. If you have one promising text but need to find a good opposing one, consider doing additional research on LexisNexis Academic or other databases accessible through your college library using the key words or sources referred to in the essay you've already chosen. Visiting sites like procon.org or the Room for Debate pages on the *New York Times* Web site (nytimes.com) may also be helpful.

Synthesize sources for a report or an analysis.

One effective way to make sense of the information you have accumulated is to create a synthesis chart like the example that follows. Once you've devised a list of subtopics, go back to your annotated bibliography and source notes to synthesize the information and ideas you have accumulated.

Gomez selected four possible solutions to the kidney shortage to focus on in her report:

- Replace opt-in with opt-out
- Allow paired kidney exchanges
- Remove disincentives to donation
- Offer incentives to donation

She organized the information she found on those subtopics into a synthesis chart. Here is a portion of her chart on one of her subtopics:

Subtopics	Source	My Notes	Location
Offer Incentives	Becker & Elías	Only paying donors will "close the gap between the demand and supply of kidneys"	par. 8
	Delmonico open letter	Like NKF, opposed to pilot studies, $ incentives "would violate global standards and will not work." Favors paying costs for donors. Signed by over 300 national and international doctors, clergy, bioethicists, members of organ procurement organizations.	pars. 1–12
	Satel, "Case"	Satel had kidney transplant. "It is easy to condemn the black market and the patients who patronize it. But you can't fault people for trying to save their own lives."	par. 10; quote, par. 9
	Sullivan	1983 proposal by Dr. Barry Jacobs: People in US who need kidneys should be able to buy them from healthy third-world donors. Led to NOTA rules about compensation.	pars. 1–2, pars. 9–10
	US Transplant open letter	Calls on Congress/president for pilot study to find ways to motivate donors, to make more organs available. 300 signers; surgeons, bioethicists, clergy.	open-letter text tab, signer's tab

Notice that Gomez keeps track of where the information in her notes came from, so she can later check to make sure she has represented borrowed ideas fairly and cited her sources accurately.

Analyze and compare the opposing argument essays.

The following activities will help you analyze and compare the opposing argument essays. If you've composed a summary of one or both texts, you've begun your analysis already. You may have highlighted and outlined each essay to identify parts of the argument. Now probe more deeply, exploring the motivating factors—the values, concerns, and priorities—that help explain the fundamental disagreement underlying the opposing points of view. (Most writers will need to reread parts of the opposing argument essays more than once and may need to do some additional research in order to determine the factors motivating each author.) Completing the Comparative Analysis Chart on p. 170 can be very helpful in planning and drafting your analysis.

WAYS IN

HOW CAN I ANALYZE AND COMPARE THE OPPOSING ARGUMENTS?

Reread each essay, noting in the margin where you find indications of the following:

Position: The writer's main idea or **THESIS STATEMENT**, the writer's opinion about the topic

Arguments: How the writer supports the position and responds to alternative points of view

Motivating Factors:

- **Values:** Moral, ethical, or religious principles (for example, justice, equality, or "do unto others")
- **Worldviews and ideologies:** Political or religious belief systems (such as libertarianism, progressivism, conservatism, or orthodoxy)
- **Ideas and ideals** (for example, democratic ideals, including the right to vote and freedom of speech)
- **Concerns and fears** (for example, personal safety, abuse of power, or protecting the environment)
- **Goals and priorities** about what is most important or urgent (for example, whether obedience to authority is more important than independent thinking)

Fill in the Comparative Analysis Chart.

Enter your notes, useful quotations, and the page or paragraph numbers in which you found the borrowed information. Searching the text for evidence of underlying values and other motivating factors will deepen your analysis and help you go beyond summarizing what is said to explaining *why* each author holds her or his opinion. Creating this chart will also help you see points of comparison and contrast

(continued)

between the opposing arguments. (Remember that you may have to leave some sections of the chart blank because each essay may not contain examples of every feature.)

Chart for Analyzing Opposing Arguments		
TOPIC:		
Source		
Position		
Arguments		
Values		
Worldviews & Ideologies		
Ideas & Ideals		
Concerns & Fears		
Goals & Priorities		

TEST YOUR CHOICE

Evaluating Your Analysis

Get together with two or three other students to test the underlying value (or other motivating factor) you think plays an important role in the argument between the texts you're comparing:

Presenters. Briefly tell your listeners what the disagreement is about and what you think is an important motivating factor (such as a value, worldview, or special concern) driving the argument. Provide one or two examples to show where you see the factor you've identified in the opposing texts.

Listeners. Tell the presenter what the examples suggest to you about the motivating factor underlying the disagreement. Share any questions, comments, or insights with the presenter.

Draft a working thesis for your report or analysis.

The thesis statement announces the purpose and the focus or main idea in both a report and a comparative analysis.

REPORT
Purpose
Focus/Main idea
Forecast of subtopics

This report will survey an array of ideas that have been proposed to encourage people to donate their kidneys, including changing to an opt-out system of organ donation after death, facilitating paired kidney exchanges, reducing financial disincentives, and offering incentives. (Gomez, par. 3)

ANALYSIS
Purpose
Focus/Main idea
Forecast of subtopics

This essay compares the underlying values driving the arguments in the NKF position statement "Financial Incentives for Organ Donation" and Satel's article "When Altruism Isn't Moral." Their views are diametrically opposed. . . . The basis of their disagreement is the proper role of altruism. The NKF emphatically endorses the current "altruistic system" (par. 5). Satel, in contrast, argues that current policy is failing precisely because it is an "altruism-only system" (par. 13). (Gomez, par. 4)

Juxtaposing the thesis statements from Gomez's report and her analysis makes clear the different purposes of these two genres. They both focus on the issue of how to encourage more kidney donation, but whereas the report provides an overview, or survey, of different approaches to the problem, the analysis compares two conflicting documents to zero in on the factor (or factors) underlying the disagreement.

Create an outline to organize your report or analysis effectively for your readers.

Once you have drafted a working thesis, you may want to devise a tentative outline, drawing on your invention and research notes. An effective outline for a report typically divides the topic into subtopics. An effective outline for a comparative analysis typically offers a sequenced (or alternating) comparison centered on points of disagreement.

Following are simple outlines of Gomez's report and analysis, which you may use as a starting point:

Outline: Gomez's Report

I. **Introduction:** Provides a brief history of kidney transplantation and demonstrates the seriousness of the kidney shortage. Thesis statement identifies the topic (proposals to increase the number of kidneys available for transplantation) and forecasts subtopics. (pars. 1–3)

II. **Change from Opt-In to Opt-Out Donation (Subtopic 1):** Explains current opt-in system, surveys reasons for and against changing to opt-out, and concludes that this change is not enough to significantly increase the number of kidneys available. (pars. 4–5)

Outline: Gomez's Analysis

I. **Introduction:** Demonstrates the seriousness of the kidney shortage and provides background information; introduces the position of the National Kidney Foundation (NKF); introduces Satel, a key critic of the NKF, and her position. (pars. 1–3)

II. **Conflict:** Thesis identifies differing attitudes toward altruism as the basis of the conflict underlying Satel's and the NKF's positions on offering incentives to increase the supply of kidneys available for transplantation. (pars. 4–5)

(continued)

III. Facilitate Paired Kidney Exchanges (Subtopic 2): Provides history, explains current status, and concludes that paired kidney exchanges will not significantly increase the supply. (pars. 6–8)	**III. Satel's First Objection: Moral Absolutism:** Reviews Satel's argument that the NKF unfairly assumes that altruism is a shared value that trumps all others. (pars. 6–7)
IV. Remove Disincentives (Subtopic 3): Explores current efforts and proposed changes. (pars. 9–10)	**IV. Satel's Second Objection:** Reviews Satel's position that the NKF unfairly assumes that all agree that commodification of the human body is wrong. (par. 8)
V. Offer Incentives (Subtopic 4): Explores history, and positions for and against offering incentives. (pars. 11–13)	**V. Satel's Third Objection:** Criticizes the NKF's moral logic—claims it commits the false choice fallacy. (pars. 9–10)
VI. Conclusion: Reiterates the problem, and emphasizes its significance. (par. 13)	**VI. Conclusion:** Summarizes basic conflict: the NKF emphasizes purity of motive; Satel prioritizes importance of increasing the pool of organs available for donation. (par. 11)

Use your outline to guide your drafting, but do not feel tied to it. You may figure out a better way to organize your ideas as you draft.

Develop your report or analysis.

Once you have a working thesis statement and outline, review your notes, including the writing you may have done to analyze your audience (pp. 166–67), brainstorm possible subtopics (p. 167), synthesize information and ideas from your sources (pp. 168–69), and complete the Comparative Analysis Chart (p. 170) to determine how you can use the ideas and information you have to support your thesis.

The following Ways In activities provide some sentence strategies to help you analyze opposing arguments and develop supporting paragraphs using explanatory strategies like classification and comparison-contrast. Use the sentence strategies as a jumping-off point—you can always revise them later—or use your own language from the start.

WAYS IN

HOW CAN I PRESENT MY ANALYSIS OF THE OPPOSING ARGUMENTS?

Analyze a quotation. Compose a few sentences explaining why you think a particular quotation (or group of quotations) suggests a **BASIC VALUE** or another **MOTIVATING FACTOR** that plays an important role in the arguments you are analyzing.

- ▶ Use of the words/phrase "_______" shows that factor A is central to X's way of thinking about _______.

EXAMPLE Altruism, according to Satel, is "the guiding narrative of the transplant establishment," its underlying ideology or value system. (Gomez, "Analysis," par. 5)

SUMMARIZE *or* **PARAPHRASE** *the disagreement.*

- ▶ X, a member of group A, argues that _______ [describe approach] because _______. Y, a member of group B, disagrees, arguing that _______ [describe approach] because _______.

EXAMPLE One of the most vocal critics of NOTA's prohibition against compensating donors . . . is Sally Satel, M.D. . . . a lecturer in psychiatry at the Yale University Medical School and a resident scholar at the American Enterprise Institute, a conservative think tank "committed to expanding liberty, increasing individual opportunity and strengthening free enterprise." . . . And she is a kidney transplant recipient. . . . Whereas the NKF defends the status quo and urges retention of the valuable consideration clause, Satel deplores the "woeful inadequacy of our nation's transplant policy" and proposes "rewards" to "encourage more living and posthumous donation" (pars. 5, 6). The basis of their disagreement is the proper role of altruism. The NKF emphatically endorses the current "altruistic system" (par. 5). Satel, in contrast, argues that current policy is failing precisely because it is an "altruism-only system" (par. 13). (Gomez, "Analysis," pars. 3–4)

WAYS IN

WHAT EXPLANATORY STRATEGIES COULD I USE?

Consider which explanatory strategies would be most useful in reporting on a controversial topic or analyzing conflicting positions on that topic. Ask yourself questions like these:
How can I **classify** *aspects of the topic or different points of view?*

- ▶ Topic X can be broken down into such categories as _______, _______, and _______.
- ▶ Some of the reasons Professor X supports Y include _______, _______, and _______.

(continued)

EXAMPLE This report will survey an array of ideas that have been proposed to encourage people to donate their kidneys, including changing to an opt-out system of organ donation after death, facilitating paired kidney exchanges, reducing financial disincentives, and offering incentives. (Gomez, "Report," par. 3)

How can I use ANECDOTES *to tell a story and make the topic less abstract for my readers?*

- Consider the story of Ms. X, who did _______ in 2015.
- For example, in 2015, X and Y stated _______.

EXAMPLE The "first successful kidney transplant" took place in 1954 when Ronald Herrick donated one of his kidneys to his identical twin Richard, who was dying of kidney disease ("Milestones"). (Gomez, "Report," par. 1)

How could I use COMPARISON AND CONTRAST *to sharpen similarities and differences among the different points of view?*

- While/Whereas X believes/argues/claims _______, Y claims _______.
- X is like Y in these ways: _______, _______, and _______.

EXAMPLE Whereas the NKF defends the status quo and urges retention of the valuable consideration clause, Satel deplores the "woeful inadequacy of our nation's transplant policy" and proposes "rewards" to "encourage more living and posthumous donation" (pars. 5, 6). (Gomez, "Analysis," par. 4)

How do I DEFINE *terms or concepts that may be unfamiliar to my readers?*

- X means _______.
- X, a type of _______, is characterized by _______, _______, and _______.

EXAMPLE A paired kidney exchange essentially trades a biologically incompatible kidney, usually donated by a family member, for a compatible one donated by a stranger. (Gomez, "Report," par. 7)

What CAUSES or effects *are important to note?*

- The result of _______ is _______.
- Because of _______, we no longer do _______.

EXAMPLE Because of improvements in blood and tissue typing, . . . it is no longer necessary for an identical twin or even a relative to make the donation. (Gomez, "Report," par. 1)

Use visuals or multimedia illustrations to enhance your explanation.

Reports explaining a controversial topic may benefit from including visuals, such as timelines, graphs, or tables. Reports published online can include animated graphics and videos. Presentations can use presentation slides (such as PowerPoint or Prezi) with embedded graphics or videos.

When deciding whether to include illustrations, ask yourself questions like the following:

- Can you create your own graphics (for example, by using spreadsheet software to create bar graphs or pie charts)?
- Will you need to borrow materials that others have created (for example, by downloading materials from the Internet, taking screenshots from Web sites, or scanning visuals from books or magazines)? Remember that borrowed material must be cited, including the sources of data you use to create graphs and tables.
- Will your writing be published on a Web site that is available to readers beyond the classroom? If so, you may need to obtain permission to use borrowed media. (As an alternative, you may want to consider linking to the site rather than embedding the material in your presentation.)

Write the opening sentences.

Review what you have written to see if you have something you could use to start your report or analysis, or try one of these opening strategies:

Cite **statistics** *to impress on readers the importance of the topic:*

> According to the National Kidney Foundation (NKF), more than 120,000 people are on the U.S. transplant waiting list, with "nearly 3,000 new patients" joining the list every month and an estimated 12 patients dying every day while waiting for a kidney ("Organ Donation"). (Gomez, "Analysis," par. 1)

Begin with an **anecdote** *to humanize the topic:*

> The "first successful kidney transplant" took place in 1954 when Ronald Herrick donated one of his kidneys to his identical twin Richard, who was dying of kidney disease ("Milestones"). Richard and Ronald's successful tandem surgery was a historic event ushering in the era of kidney transplantation. (Gomez, "Report," par. 1)

At this point, you simply want an opening sentence to launch your draft. Later, you may discover a better way to capture your readers' attention.

Draft your report or analysis.

By this point, you have done a lot of writing to

- summarize sources accurately and concisely;
- comment on how sources relate to one another;
- create bibliographic citations for sources;
- synthesize an array of information on the topic;
- analyze opposing points of view;
- find an appropriate focus for your report or analysis;
- choose explanatory strategies;
- draft a working thesis;
- organize your ideas to make them clear, logical, and effective for readers.

Now stitch that material together to create a draft. The next two parts of the Guide to Writing will help you evaluate and improve your draft.

Evaluating the Draft: Using Peer Review

Your instructor may arrange a peer review session in class or online, where you can exchange drafts with your classmates and give one another a thoughtful critical reading, pointing out what works well and suggesting ways to improve the draft. A good critical reading does three things:

1. It lets the writer know how well the reader understands the point of the essay.
2. It praises what works best.
3. It indicates where the draft could be improved and makes suggestions on how to improve it.

One strategy for evaluating a draft is to use the basic features of the genre you are composing as a guide.

A PEER REVIEW GUIDE

An Informative Explanation

Is the report or analysis informative, interesting, and perceptive?

Summarize: Tell the writer why the topic is important and what makes the opposing points of view interesting.

Praise: Give an example of something in the draft that you think will especially interest the intended readers.

Critique: Tell the writer about any confusion or uncertainty you have about the topic's importance. Indicate if the focus of the report or analysis could be clearer, more interesting, or more appropriate for the intended readers.

A Clear, Logical Organization	Does the report or analysis explain the topic and opposing positions clearly, and is it easy to follow? **Summarize:** Look at the way the report or analysis is organized by making a scratch outline. **Praise:** Give an example of where the text succeeds in being readable—for instance, in its overall organization, forecast of topics, or use of transitions. **Critique:** Identify places where readability could be improved—for example, by adding a forecast, clarifying a topic sentence, or using headings.
Smooth Integration of Sources	Are sources incorporated into the report or analysis effectively? **Summarize:** Note each source mentioned in the text, and check to make sure it appears in the list of works cited, if there is one. Highlight signal phrases and other in-text citations. **Praise:** Give an example of the effective use of sources—for instance, a particularly well-integrated quotation, paraphrase, or summary that supports and illustrates the point. Note any especially descriptive verbs used to introduce information from sources. **Critique:** Point out where adding experts' credentials would make a source more credible. Indicate quotations, paraphrases, or summaries that could be more smoothly integrated or more fully interpreted or explained. Identify verbs in signal phrases that could more clearly signal the writer's moves.
Appropriate Explanatory Strategies	Are explanatory strategies (such as classification, definition, and comparison) used effectively to report on the topic and analyze the underlying values? Is research adequate? **Summarize:** Note which explanatory strategies the writer uses, such as classification, definition, comparison, or cause-effect. **Praise:** Point to an explanatory strategy that is especially effective, and highlight research that is particularly helpful. **Critique:** Point to any places where a definition is needed, where more (or better) examples might help, or where another explanatory strategy could be improved or added. Note where a visual (such as a flowchart or graph) would make the explanation clearer.

Before concluding your review, be sure to address any of the writer's concerns that have not already been addressed.

Improving the Draft: Revising, Editing, and Proofreading

Start improving your draft by reflecting on what you have written thus far:

- Review peer review comments from your classmates, as well as feedback from your instructor or writing center tutor: What basic problems do your readers identify?
- Look back at your invention writing: What else could you add? Is more research needed?
- Review your draft: What can you do to make your report or analysis more informative, interesting, perceptive, or clearly organized?

Revise your draft.

If your readers are having difficulty with your draft, or if you think there is room for improvement, try some of the strategies listed in the Troubleshooting Guide that follows. They can help you fine-tune your presentation of each genre's basic features.

A TROUBLESHOOTING GUIDE

An Informative Explanation

My readers are not clear about my topic or the opposing positions I'm exploring.

- State the topic explicitly, perhaps as a question, so the conflicting positions are clear.
- Clarify how your subtopics relate to your topic by forecasting them in your thesis statement.
- Sharpen the contrast between opposing positions by using transitions of contrast (such as *whereas* or *although*).

My readers are not interested or do not appreciate the issue's importance.

- Add information showing the impact of the issue or how it affects people's lives.
- Put the topic in context by providing historical, political, or cultural importance.
- Quote notable authorities to emphasize the issue's importance.
- Cite polls or research studies, or use graphics to demonstrate the widespread impact of the issue.

My readers do not understand my analysis.

- Determine whether you are trying to cover too many points.
- Explain in more detail the points that are harder for readers to grasp.
- Consider emphasizing the less obvious points of the disagreement.

An Informative Explanation	My report or analysis seems more like a summary. • Revisit your sources, brainstorm a list of subtopics some or all of them cover, and create a synthesis chart to help you understand the similarities and differences. • Consider how the writer's profession or biography could explain why a particular motivating factor (such as a value or priority) has so much persuasive power. • Think about the social and political situation in which each essay was written and how the writer was trying to appeal to readers.
A Clear, Logical Organization	My readers are confused by my report or analysis or find it difficult to read. • Outline your report or analysis. If necessary, move, add, or delete sections to strengthen coherence. • Consider adding a forecasting statement with key terms that are repeated in topic sentences throughout the report or analysis. • Consider adding headings to highlight subtopics; use key terms from the forecast in your headings. • Check for appropriate transitions between sentences, paragraphs, and major sections of your report or analysis. • Consider reorganizing your analysis to alternate between the sources you are comparing. • Review your opening and closing paragraphs. Be sure that your thesis is stated explicitly and that your closing paragraph revisits your thesis.
Smooth Integration of Sources	Quotations, summaries, and paraphrases don't flow smoothly with the rest of the text. • Reread all passages in which you quote outside sources. Ask yourself whether you provide enough context for the quotation or clearly establish the credentials of the source's author. • Use signal phrases to put sources in context. Choose descriptive verbs that clearly indicate what the source author is doing (making a claim, asserting a position, reporting on a study, and so forth). • Add a sentence explaining what the quotation, summary, or paraphrase means or why it is relevant.

(continued)

Smooth Integration of Sources	Readers are concerned that my list of sources is too limited or unbalanced. • Do additional research to balance your list, taking particular care that you have an adequate number of reliable sources from a variety of points of view. • Ask a librarian or your instructor for help finding sources on your topic. My readers wonder whether my sources are credible. • Clearly identify all sources and state the credentials of cited authorities. • Eliminate sources that are not relevant, credible, or otherwise appropriate.
Appropriate Explanatory Strategies	Readers don't understand my report or analysis. • Consider whether you have used the most appropriate writing strategies (defining, classifying, comparing and contrasting, narrating, illustrating, describing, or explaining causes and effects) for your topic. • Recheck your definitions for clarity. Be sure that you have explicitly defined any key terms your readers might not know. Readers want more information about certain aspects of the topic. • Expand or clarify definitions by adding examples. • Add examples or comparisons and contrasts to relate the topic to something readers already know. • Conduct additional research on your topic, and cite it in your report or analysis. Readers want visuals to help them understand certain aspects of the topic. • Check whether your sources use visuals (tables, graphs, drawings, photographs, and the like) that might be appropriate for your report or analysis. (If you are publishing your work online, consider video clips, audio files, and animated graphics as well.) • Consider drafting your own charts, tables, or graphs, or adding your own photographs or illustrations. Summaries lack *oomph*; paraphrases are too complicated; quotations are too long. • Revise the summaries to emphasize a single key idea. • Restate the paraphrases more succinctly, omitting irrelevant details. Consider quoting important words. • Use ellipsis dots to tighten the quotations to emphasize the memorable words.

Edit and proofread your draft.

Our research indicates that particular errors occur often in research reports and analyses of conflicting perspectives on a controversial topic: incorrect comma usage in sentences with interrupting phrases, and vague pronoun reference. The following guidelines will help you check your writing for these common errors.

Using Commas around Interrupting Phrases

What is an *interrupting phrase*? When writers are reporting on a controversial topic or analyzing opposing positions, they need to supply a great deal of information precisely and accurately. They add much of this information in phrases that interrupt the flow of a sentence, as in the following example:

▶ The National Kidney Foundation, one of the most conservative advocacy groups, had been adamantly opposed to financial compensation of any kind since 2002 (“Financial”). (Gomez, “Report,” par. 9)

Such interrupting phrases, as they are called, are typically set off with commas.

The Problem Forgetting to set off an interrupting phrase with commas can make sentences unclear or difficult to read.

How to Correct It Add a comma on either side of an interrupting phrase.

▶ A radical proposal^, aptly titled “Cash for Kidneys^,” was published in *The Wall Street Journal* by two respected economists^, Julio Elías and Nobel Laureate Gary Becker, who argue that the only way to “close the gap between the demand and supply of kidneys” is to pay people for their kidneys. (Gomez, “Report,” par. 11)

Correcting Vague Pronoun Reference

The Problem **Pronouns** replace and refer to nouns, making writing more efficient and cohesive. If the reference is vague, however, this advantage is lost. A common problem is vague use of *this, that, it,* or *which.*

How to Correct It Scan your writing for pronouns, taking special note of places where you use *this, that, it,* or *which.* Check to be sure that what *this, that, it, which,* or another pronoun refers to is crystal clear. If it is not, revise your sentence.

▶ Television evangelists seem to be perpetually raising money. ~~which~~ ^This habit makes some viewers question their motives.

▶ By the late 1960s, plate tectonics emerged as a new area of study. Tectonics was based on the notion of the earth’s crust as a collection of plates or land masses

startling new geological theory

above and below sea level, constantly in motion. This ^ took a while for most people to

accept. ~~because of its unexpected novelty.~~

▶ Inside the Summit Tunnel, the Chinese laborers were using as much as

Five hundred kegs a day of costly black powder to blast their way through the

The unexpected expense

solid rock. ^ ~~It~~ was straining the Central Pacific's budget.

Reflecting on What You Have Learned

You have learned a great deal by reading texts in four different genres on the same controversial topic and by composing all or part of a multistage project. To consolidate your learning, reflect not only on what you learned but also on how you learned it.

ANALYZE & WRITE

Write a blog post, a letter to your instructor or a classmate, or an e-mail message to a student who will take this course next term, using the writing prompt that seems most productive for you:

- Explain how your purpose and audience influenced *one* of your decisions as a writer, such as how much background information you provided, how you categorized the information in your report, or how you organized the comparison in your analysis.
- Discuss what you learned about yourself as a writer in the process of writing one or more of the genres in this chapter. For example, what part of the process did you find most challenging (such as deciding on categories for the report or understanding the factors motivating the conflict for the analysis)? Did you try anything new (such as going to the writing center or using a different research strategy)?
- If you got good advice from a critical reader, explain exactly how the person helped you—perhaps by helping you understand the kinds of evidence you needed to include or by deepening your analysis of the texts you compared.

6

Arguing a Position

Why should parents think twice before signing up their kids for Little League? Why might it *not* be a good idea for teens to get after-school jobs? Why should you care about online privacy if you haven't done anything wrong? These are some of the compelling issues argued about in this chapter. Because of the in-your-face kind of arguing in blogs and on talk shows, you may associate arguing with quarreling. Although this kind of "argument" lets people vent strong feelings, it seldom leads them to seriously consider other points of view or to think critically about their own reasons or underlying values. A more thoughtful, deliberative kind of argument—one that depends on a critical analysis of an issue, on giving logical reasons rather than raising voices—is more likely to convince others of the validity of your position. Reasoned argument is also more likely to be expected in college courses and in the workplace.

You might compose this thoughtful kind of argument for a variety of purposes and audiences and publish your efforts in a variety of media. For example, in a college course on law and society, a student might write a blog post supporting the position that the race of a murder *victim* is the crucial factor determining whether the death penalty is sought. A group of parents might publish an open letter in the local newspaper arguing that the school board should institute the Peacemakers program to help children in the district learn to negotiate conflicts rather than resort to their fists. In the workplace, a consultant may make a presentation, citing statistics and examples, to argue that sustainable business practices are good for business.

In this chapter, we ask you to compose a position argument on a controversial issue. Your argument should try to convince readers to adopt your point of view or at least to consider it seriously. From reading and analyzing the selections in the Guide to Reading that follows, you will learn how writers frame and support a position so readers will take it seriously. The Guide to Writing later in the chapter will support your composing by showing you how to choose and frame an arguable position, marshal compelling evidence to support it, respond to naysayers, and organize it in a way that presents your position as compellingly as possible.

PRACTICING THE GENRE

Debating a Position

To get a sense of what's involved in arguing a position, get together with a group of students (preferably four) to discuss an issue you have strong feelings about.

Part 1. Choose an issue you all know something about, or pick one of the following:

- Should college be paid for by taxes the way K–12 is?
- Should general education requirements be continued (or discontinued) at your college?
- Should drinking alcohol be banned on campuses?
- Should online courses replace large face-to-face lecture courses?

First, decide on your audience and purpose: Is your audience other students, faculty, administrators, or the general public? Is your purpose to persuade audience members to change their minds, confirm their opinions, move them to action, or something else? Then take five minutes to sketch out the arguments for and against your issue. Take turns presenting your arguments to each other.

Part 2. After your presentations, discuss what you learned:

- **What did you learn about the genre from listening to others' arguments?** Were you convinced by the arguments? Would the intended audience have been convinced? That is, was the position presented with the audience's values in mind?
- **What did you learn about the genre from presenting your group's position?** Discuss with your group what was easiest and hardest about presenting your position—for example, finding enough evidence that your audience would find convincing, anticipating opposing views, or appealing to the values of your audience.

Analyzing Position Arguments

As you read the selections in this chapter, you will see how different authors argue convincingly for their positions:

- Jessica Statsky argues that organized sports activities can be harmful for children aged six to twelve (pp. 190–96).
- Amitai Etzioni challenges the idea that after-school work is good for teenagers (pp. 196–99).
- Daniel J. Solove argues that protecting our privacy on the Internet is crucially important even if we feel we have "nothing to hide" (pp. 202–6).

Analyzing how these writers focus and frame their arguments to appeal to the hearts and minds of readers, anticipate and respond to opposing views, and select and present evidence that will convince readers and undermine objections will help you see how you can employ these techniques to make your own position argument clear and compelling for your readers.

Determine the writer's purpose and audience.

Although arguing a position helps writers decide where they really stand, writers typically compose arguments to influence their readers. As you read the position arguments that follow, ask yourself questions like these:

What seems to be the writer's main purpose in arguing for a position?

- To change readers' minds by convincing them to look at the issue in a new way?
- To confirm readers' opinions by providing them with authoritative arguments?
- To move readers to take action by stressing the urgency or seriousness of the issue?
- To remind readers what is at stake and establish common ground on which people might be able to agree?

What does the author assume about the audience?

- That readers are already knowledgeable about the issue and likely to be sympathetic to the writer's position?
- That they need to be inspired to care about the issue?
- That they have strong convictions and will likely have serious objections to the writer's position?

Basic Features

A Focused, Well-Presented Issue

A Well-Supported Position

An Effective Response to Opposing Views

A Clear, Logical Organization

Assess the genre's basic features.

As you read position arguments in this chapter, consider how different authors incorporate the basic features of the genre. The examples that follow are drawn from the reading selections that appear later in this Guide to Reading.

A FOCUSED, WELL-PRESENTED ISSUE

Read first to identify the issue. Look first at the title and the opening paragraphs. For current, hotly debated issues, the title may be enough to identify the issue for readers.

Topic Why Privacy Matters Even If You Have "Nothing to Hide" (Solove)
Position

Writers may use their opening paragraphs to remind readers about what is at stake or what the position is that they oppose, using a simple sentence pattern like this:

- When X happens, most people think ________, but I think ________ because ________.

For example, Solove uses this strategy in his opening paragraph:

> When the government gathers or analyzes personal information, many people say (par. 1)

His "but I think . . . because . . ." response to the common view takes up the bulk of the essay.

To present their positions effectively, writers must focus on a specific aspect of their issue, one they can address fully in the space allowed. An issue like youth employment, for example, is too complex to be tackled fully in a relatively brief essay, so writers must focus on one aspect of the issue, as Amitai Etzioni does (pp. 196–99) when he considers whether working at a fast-food restaurant, like McDonald's or Burger King, is a good idea for high school students.

Notice how the writer establishes the issue's significance. If readers are likely to be unfamiliar with an issue or consider it trivial, a writer will need to establish the issue's significance, as student Jessica Statsky does in her position essay:

> "Organized sports for young people have become an institution in North America," reports sports journalist Steve Silverman, attracting more than 44 million youngsters according to a recent survey by the National Council of Youth Sports. (par. 1)

To establish the significance of the issue, Statsky quotes a respected authority and also cites statistics.

Also consider how the writer frames the issue. **Framing** an issue is like cropping and resizing a photograph to focus the viewer's eye on one part of the picture (see Figure 6.1). Writers frame an issue to set the stage for their argument and promote their point of view. They may suggest that particular values are at stake or raise in readers' minds certain concerns having to do with the issue. As you read, notice how each writer frames the issue, asking yourself questions like these:

- Who, or what groups of people, does the writer associate with each position, and how does the writer characterize their views? For example, does one side appear thoughtful, moderate, and knowledgeable, and the other side extreme, unreasonable, or self-interested?
- What does the writer suggest is really at stake, and for whom? If you were unfamiliar with the issue, what did the writer lead you to think and feel about it? If you were already familiar with it, which of your preconceptions were reinforced and which were challenged by the writer's way of framing the issue?

FIGURE 6.1 Framing an Issue
By cropping this photograph of a protest march to focus on the little boy, the photographer softens the message; the broader issue of climate change is framed in terms of saving the planet for this child. © Patrick Ward/Alamy

A WELL-SUPPORTED POSITION

Identify the writer's position, and determine whether the position is appropriately qualified. To argue effectively, writers need to assert an arguable position (an opinion, not a fact that can be proved or disproved or a belief that must be taken on faith). They may also need to *qualify* that position (for example, by using words like *may* and by specifying conditions) to avoid making a claim that is too strong to be defended given the available evidence.

In a position argument, writers typically declare their positions in a thesis statement early on in the essay. Notice, for example, how Jessica Statsky states her thesis:

Qualifying terms

> When overzealous parents and coaches impose adult standards on children's sports, the result can be activities that are neither satisfying nor beneficial to children.
>
> I am concerned about all organized sports activities for children between the ages of six and twelve. (pars. 1–2)

She makes a claim that reasonable people could dispute, and she qualifies her claim by limiting its scope (not all children, just those between six and twelve, for example).

Examine the main reasons and the evidence the writer provides. Make sure that the reasons clearly support the writer's position and that the evidence (facts and statistics, examples and anecdotes, research studies, expert testimony) is credible.

Look for sentence strategies like these that introduce supporting reasons:

- What makes issue X problematic/praiseworthy is ________.
- Because of ________, I support/oppose X.

XAMPLE This statistic illustrates another reason I oppose competitive sports for children: because they are so highly selective, very few children get to participate. (Statsky, par. 7)

Credible evidence is both relevant and representative; that is, it must clearly support the reason (which must in turn support the topic sentence and thesis), and it must be typical. The following examples demonstrate some approaches to introducing supporting evidence:

Statistics
Reason

24 percent . . . worked . . . five to seven days. . . . There is just no way such amounts of work will not interfere with school work, especially homework. In an informal survey. . . , 58 percent of seniors acknowledged that their jobs interfere with their school work. (Etzioni, par. 13)

Also consider whether the evidence the writer provides appeals to readers' intellect, values, or emotions and avoids logical fallacies. Writers can draw on various types of evidence—from facts and statistics to examples and anecdotes to photographs and flowcharts—to support their positions, but position arguments are most convincing when writers are able to appeal to readers on three levels:

- **Logos:** Appeal to readers' intellect, presenting readers with logical reasoning and reliable evidence.
- **Ethos:** Appeal to readers' perception of the writer's credibility and fairness.
- **Pathos:** Appeal to readers' values and feelings.

Ask yourself how effectively the writers appeals to readers' intellect, sense of fairness, and emotions:

- Is the argument logical and reasonable (logos)?
- Does the writer appear credible and trustworthy (ethos)?
- Are the values and feelings sincere or manipulative (pathos)?

To learn more about evaluating sources, see Chapters 10 and 15; to learn more about avoiding logical fallacies, see Chapter 12.

AN EFFECTIVE RESPONSE TO OPPOSING VIEWS

Notice whether the author anticipates readers' objections and opposing arguments, and whether he or she refutes or concedes those objections and arguments. Writers **refute** (argue against) opposing views when they can show that the opposing view is weak or flawed. A typical refutation states the problem with the opposing view and then explains why the view is problematic, using sentence strategies like these:

- ▶ One problem with position A is that ________.
- ▶ Some claim ________, but in reality ________.

Writers often introduce the refutation with a **transition** that indicates contrast, such as *but, although, nevertheless,* or *however:*

Transition
Refutation

The deeper problem with the nothing-to-hide argument is that it myopically views privacy as a form of secrecy. In contrast, understanding privacy as a plurality of related issues demonstrates that the disclosure of bad things is just one among many difficulties caused by government security measures. (Solove, par. 10)

Writers may also **concede** (accept) valid objections, concerns, or reasons. A typical way of conceding is to use sentence strategies like these:

- I agree that ________.
- ________ is certainly an important factor.

Here is an example from Jessica Statsky's essay:

> Some children *want* to play competitive sports; they are not being forced to play. These children are eager to learn skills, to enjoy the camaraderie of the team, and earn self-respect by trying hard to benefit their team. I acknowledge that some children may benefit from playing competitive sports. (par. 12)

Concession

Conceding a strong opposing view reassures readers that the writer shares their values and builds a bridge of shared concerns.

Frequently, though, writers reach out to readers by making a concession but then go on to point out where they differ. We call this the **concession-refutation move**. Like writers refuting a point, writers making the concession-refutation move often follow their concession with a transition indicating contrast to show that an exception or refinement is coming. Here's an example:

Concession
Transition
Refutation

> True, you still have to have the gumption to get yourself over to the hamburger stand, but once you don the prescribed uniform, your task is spelled out in minute detail. (Etzioni, par. 7)

While reading position arguments, assess the effectiveness of the responses by asking yourself questions like these:

- Do they appeal to shared values (pathos) or seem trite or maudlin?
- Do they offer compelling reasons and credible evidence (logos) or simply make unsubstantiated assertions or criticisms?
- Do they draw on authorities whose expertise is established (ethos) or merely refer vaguely to "some" or "many" people with whom they agree? Do the responses to opposing views seem significant and genuine or trivial and insincere?
- Do they misrepresent the opposition (committing a *straw man fallacy*) or attack people personally (committing an *ad hominem fallacy*)?

To learn more about logical fallacies, see Chapter 12, p. 379.

A CLEAR, LOGICAL ORGANIZATION

Look for a thesis statement that asserts the writer's position and provides a forecast of the reasons the writer will offer as examples. For instance, Amitai Etzioni grabs readers' attention with an alarming sentence—"McDonald's is bad for your kids."—and then goes on to explain just how McDonald's is bad for kids in the next sentence:

> I do not mean the flat patties and the white-flour buns; I refer to the jobs teenagers undertake, mass-producing these choice items. (par. 1)

In addition to asserting the thesis, writers sometimes preview the reasons in the order they will bring them up later in the essay, as in this example of a *forecasting statement* by Jessica Statsky:

Transition / Reason 1 / Reason 2 / Reason 3

Highly organized competitive sports . . . are too often played to adult standards, which are developmentally inappropriate for children and can be both physically and psychologically harmful. Furthermore, . . . they are actually counterproductive for developing either future players or fans. Finally, . . . they . . . provide occasions for some parents and coaches to place their own fantasies and needs ahead of children's welfare. (par. 2)

Notice also where the writer uses *logical transitions* to indicate the following:

- supporting evidence (*because*)
- exceptions (*however*)
- concessions (*admittedly*)
- refutations (*on the other hand*)
- conclusions (*therefore*)
- reasons (*first, finally*)

Transitions may be useful in a forecasting statement, as in the preceding example, or in the *topic sentence* of a paragraph or group of paragraphs, as in the following example from Solove's position argument:

> One such harm, for example, . . . Another potential problem with . . . is . . . A related problem involves . . . Yet another problem . . . is . . . (pars. 11–14)

To learn more about using cues, see Chapter 11.

Readings

Jessica Statsky | *Children Need to Play, Not Compete*

THIS ESSAY by Jessica Statsky about children's competitive sports was written for a college composition course. When you were a child, you may have had experience playing competitive sports, in or out of school, for example in Peewee Football, Little League Baseball, American Youth Soccer, or some other organization. Or you may have had relatives or friends who were deeply involved in sports.

As you read, consider the following questions, as well as the notes in the margins:

- In your experience and observation, was winning unduly emphasized or was more value placed on having a good time, learning to get along with others, developing athletic skills, or something else altogether?
- The questions in the margin: Your instructor may ask you to post your answers to a class blog or discussion board or to bring them to class.

1 "Organized sports for young people have become an institution in North America," reports sports journalist Steve Silverman, attracting more than 44 million youngsters according to a recent survey by the National Council of Youth Sports. Though many adults regard Little League Baseball and Peewee Football as a basic part of childhood, the games are not always joyous ones. When overzealous parents and coaches impose adult standards on children's sports, the result can be activities that are neither satisfying nor beneficial to children.

2 I am concerned about all organized sports activities for children between the ages of six and twelve. The damage I see results from noncontact as well as contact sports, from sports organized locally as well as those organized nationally. Highly organized competitive sports such as Peewee Football and Little League Baseball are too often played to adult standards, which are developmentally inappropriate for children and can be both physically and psychologically harmful. Furthermore, because they eliminate many children from organized sports before they are ready to compete, they are actually counterproductive for developing either future players or fans. Finally, because they emphasize competition and winning, they unfortunately provide occasions for some parents and coaches to place their own fantasies and needs ahead of children's welfare.

3 One readily understandable danger of overly competitive sports is that they entice children into physical actions that are bad for growing bodies. "There is a growing epidemic of preventable youth sports injuries," according to the STOP Sports Injuries campaign ("Youth Sports" 2). "Among athletes ages 5 to 14, 28 percent of football players, 25 percent of baseball players, 22 percent of soccer players, 15 percent of basketball players, and 12 percent of softball players were injured while playing their respective sports." Although Little League Baseball and Softball acknowledges that children do risk injury playing baseball, it insists that "severe injuries . . . are infrequent," the risk "far less than the risk of riding a skateboard, a bicycle, or even the school bus" ("Little League Parent Responsibilities"). Nevertheless, Leonard Koppett in *Sports Illusion, Sports Reality* claims that a twelve-year-old trying to throw a curve ball, for example, may put abnormal strain on developing arm and shoulder muscles, sometimes resulting in lifelong injuries (294). Contact sports

Basic Features

A Focused, Well-Presented Issue

A Well-Supported Position

An Effective Response to Opposing Views

A Clear, Logical Organization

How does Statsky present the issue in a way that prepares readers for her argument?

How does Statsky qualify her position in par. 2?

What reasons does Statsky forecast here, and in which paragraphs does she discuss each reason? Do her reasons appeal primarily to readers' intellect (logos), to their sense of fairness and what's credible (ethos), or to their feelings (pathos)?

How does Statsky try to establish the credibility of her sources in pars. 3–5 (ethos)?

like football can be even more hazardous. Thomas Tutko, a psychology professor at San Jose State University and coauthor of the book *Winning Is Everything and Other American Myths*, writes:

> I am strongly opposed to young kids playing tackle football. It is not the right stage of development for them to be taught to crash into other kids. Kids under the age of fourteen are not by nature physical. Their main concern is self-preservation. They don't want to meet head on and slam into each other. But tackle football absolutely requires that they try to hit each other as hard as they can. And it is too traumatic for young kids. (qtd. in Tosches A1)

4 As Tutko indicates, even when children are not injured, fear of being hurt detracts from their enjoyment of the sport. The Little League ranks fear of injury as the seventh of seven reasons children quit ("Little League Parent Responsibilities"). One mother of an eight-year-old Peewee Football player explained, "The kids get so scared. They get hit once and they don't want anything to do with football anymore. They'll sit on the bench and pretend their leg hurts . . ." (qtd. in Tosches A1). Some children are driven to even more desperate measures. For example, in one Peewee Football game, a reporter watched the following scene as a player took himself out of the game:

Why do you think Statsky uses block quotations instead of integrating these quotes into her own sentences?

> "Coach, my tummy hurts. I can't play," he said. The coach told the player to get back onto the field. "There's nothing wrong with your stomach," he said. When the coach turned his head the seven-year-old stuck a finger down his throat and made himself vomit. When the coach turned back, the boy pointed to the ground and told him, "Yes there is, coach. See?" (Tosches A33)

5 Besides physical hazards and anxieties, competitive sports pose psychological dangers for children. Martin Rablovsky, a former sports editor for *The New York Times*, says that in all his years of watching young children play organized sports, he has noticed very few of them smiling. "I've seen children enjoying a spontaneous pre-practice scrimmage become somber and serious when the coach's whistle blows," Rablovsky says. "The spirit of play suddenly disappears, and sport becomes joblike" (qtd. in Coakley 94). The primary goal of a professional athlete—winning—is not appropriate for children. Their goals should be having fun, learning, and being

with friends. Although winning does add to the fun, too many adults lose sight of what matters and make winning the most important goal. Several studies have shown that when children are asked whether they would rather be warming the bench on a winning team or playing regularly on a losing team, about 90 percent choose the latter (Smith et al. 11).

6 Winning and losing may be an inevitable part of adult life, but they should not be part of childhood. Too much competition too early in life can affect a child's development. Children are easily influenced, and when they sense that their competence and worth are based on their ability to live up to their parents' and coaches' high expectations—and on their ability to win—they can become discouraged and depressed. Little League advises parents to "keep winning in perspective," noting that the most common reasons children give for quitting, aside from change in interest, are lack of playing time, failure and fear of failure, disapproval by significant others, and psychological stress ("Little League Parent Responsibilities"). According to Dr. Glyn C. Roberts, a professor of kinesiology at the Institute of Child Behavior and Development at the University of Illinois, 80 to 90 percent of children who play competitive sports at a young age drop out by sixteen (Kutner).

How does Statsky try to refute this objection?

7 This statistic illustrates another reason I oppose competitive sports for children: because they are so highly selective, very few children get to participate. Far too soon, a few children are singled out for their athletic promise, while many others, who may be on the verge of developing the necessary strength and ability, are screened out and discouraged from trying out again. Like adults, children fear failure, and so even those with good physical skills may stay away because they lack self-confidence. Consequently, teams lose many promising players who with some encouragement and experience might have become stars. The problem is that many parent-sponsored, out-of-school programs give more importance to having a winning team than to developing children's physical skills and self-esteem.

How effective do you think Statsky's argument in par. 7 is? Why?

8 Indeed, it is no secret that too often scorekeeping, league standings, and the drive to win bring out the worst in adults who are more absorbed in living out their own fantasies than in enhancing the quality of the experience for children (Smith et al. 9). Recent newspaper articles on

In criticizing some parents' behavior in pars. 8–9, Statsky risks alienating her readers. How effective is this part of her argument?

children's sports contain plenty of horror stories. *Los Angeles Times* reporter Rich Tosches, for example, tells the story of a brawl among seventy-five parents following a Peewee Football game (A33). As a result of the brawl, which began when a parent from one team confronted a player from the other team, the teams are now thinking of hiring security guards for future games. Another example is provided by a *Los Angeles Times* editorial about a Little League manager who intimidated the opposing team by setting fire to one of their team's jerseys on the pitcher's mound before the game began. As the editorial writer commented, the manager showed his young team that "intimidation could substitute for playing well" ("The Bad News Pyromaniacs?").

9 Although not all parents or coaches behave so inappropriately, the seriousness of the problem is illustrated by the fact that Adelphi University in Garden City, New York, offers a sports psychology workshop for Little League coaches, designed to balance their "animal instincts" with "educational theory" in hopes of reducing the "screaming and hollering," in the words of Harold Weisman, manager of sixteen Little Leagues in New York City (Schmitt). In a three-and-one-half-hour Sunday morning workshop, coaches learn how to make practices more fun, treat injuries, deal with irate parents, and be "more sensitive to their young players' fears, emotional frailties, and need for recognition." Little League is to be credited with recognizing the need for such workshops.

How effective is Statsky's use of concession and refutation here?

10 Some parents would no doubt argue that children cannot start too soon preparing to live in a competitive free-market economy. After all, secondary schools and colleges require students to compete for grades, and college admission is extremely competitive. And it is perfectly obvious how important competitive skills are in finding a job. Yet the ability to cooperate is also important for success in life. Before children are psychologically ready for competition, maybe we should emphasize cooperation and individual performance in team sports rather than winning.

11 Many people are ready for such an emphasis. In 1988, one New York Little League official who had attended the Adelphi workshop tried to ban scoring from six- to eight-year-olds' games—but parents wouldn't support him (Schmitt). An innovative children's sports program in New York City, City Sports for Kids, emphasizes fitness, self-esteem, and sportsmanship.

In this program's basketball games, every member on a team plays at least two of six eight-minute periods. The basket is seven feet from the floor, rather than ten feet, and a player can score a point just by hitting the rim (Bloch). I believe this kind of local program should replace overly competitive programs like Peewee Football and Little League Baseball. As one coach explains, significant improvements can result from a few simple rule changes, such as including every player in the batting order and giving every player, regardless of age or ability, the opportunity to play at least four innings a game (Frank).

12 Some children *want* to play competitive sports; they are not being forced to play. These children are eager to learn skills, enjoy the camaraderie of the team, and earn self-respect by trying hard to benefit their team. I acknowledge that some children may benefit from playing competitive sports. While some children do benefit from these programs, however, many more would benefit from programs that avoid the excesses and dangers of many competitive sports programs and instead emphasize fitness, cooperation, sportsmanship, and individual performance.

How effectively does Statsky conclude her argument?

Works Cited

"The Bad News Pyromaniacs? Fiery Anaheim Little League Manager Is, Rightly, Fired." *Los Angeles Times*, 16 June 1990, p. B6, articles.latimes .com/1990-06-16/local/me-31_1_team-manager.

Bloch, Gordon B. "Thrill of Victory Is Secondary to Fun." *The New York Times*, 2 Apr. 1990, p. C12.

Coakley, Jay J. *Sport in Society: Issues and Controversies*. Mosby, 1982.

Frank, L. "Contributions from Parents and Coaches." *CYB Message Board*, AOL, 8 July 1997, www.aol.com/.

Koppett, Leonard. *Sports Illusion, Sports Reality*. Houghton Mifflin, 1981.

Kutner, Lawrence. "Parent and Child." *The New York Times*, 23 Mar. 1989, www.nytimes.com/1989/03/23/garden/parent-child.html.

"Little League Parent Responsibilities." *Warwick National Little League 2007 Safety Plan*, Little League Baseball and Softball, 17 Apr. 2007, www .littleleague.org/Assets/forms_pubs/asap/Warwick_LL_safetyplan08.pdf.

Schmitt, Eric. "Psychologists Take Seat on Little League Bench." *The New York Times*, 14 Mar. 1988, p. B2. *LexisNexis Academic*, www.lexisnexis.com.

Silverman, Steve. "The History of Youth Sports." *Livestrong.com,* Demand Media, 26 May 2011, www.livestrong.com/article/353963-the-history-of-youth-sports/.

Smith, Nathan, et al. *Kidsports: A Survival Guide for Parents.* Addison-Wesley, 1983.

Tosches, Rich. "Game's Critics Are Not Amused—Peewee Football: Is It Time to Blow Whistle?" *Los Angeles Times,* 3 Dec. 1988, pp. A1+, articles.latimes.com/1988-12-03/news/mn-936_1_youth-football-games.

"Youth Sports Injuries Statistics." *STOP Sports Injuries: Community Outreach Toolkit,* American Orthopaedic Society for Sports Medicine, www.sportsmed.org/aossmimis/stop/downloads/CommunityOutreachToolkit.pdf. Accessed 14 May 2011.

Amitai Etzioni | *Working at McDonald's*

Poklekowski/ullstein bild via Getty Images

AMITAI ETZIONI is a sociologist who has taught at Columbia, Harvard, and George Washington University, where he currently directs the Institute for Communitarian Policy Studies. He has written numerous articles and more than two dozen books, including *The Spirit of Community: The Reinvention of American Society* (1983); *The Limits of Privacy* (2004); *Security First: For a Muscular, Moral Foreign Policy* (2007); and most recently, *The New Normal: Finding a Balance between Individual Rights and the Common Good* (2014). The following reading was originally published on the opinion page of the *Miami Herald* newspaper.

As you read, consider the following questions:

- What do you imagine Etzioni's teenage son Dari, who helped his father write the essay, contributed?
- What kinds of summer and school-year jobs, if any, have you and your friends held while in high school or college?

1 McDonald's is bad for your kids. I do not mean the flat patties and the white-flour buns; I refer to the jobs teen-agers undertake, mass-producing these choice items.

2 As many as two-thirds of America's high school juniors and seniors now hold down part-time paying jobs, according to studies. Many of these are in fast-food chains, of which McDonald's is the pioneer, trend-setter and symbol.

3 At first, such jobs may seem right out of the Founding Fathers' educational manual for how to bring up self-reliant, work-ethic-driven, productive youngsters. But in fact, these jobs undermine school attendance and involvement, impart few skills that will be useful in later life, and simultaneously skew the values of teen-agers — especially their ideas about the worth of a dollar.

4 It has been a long-standing American tradition that youngsters ought to get paying jobs. In folklore, few pursuits are more deeply revered than the newspaper route and the sidewalk lemonade stand. Here the youngsters are to learn how sweet are the fruits of labor and self-discipline (papers are delivered early in the morning, rain or shine), and the ways of trade (if you price your lemonade too high or too low . . .).

5 Roy Rogers, Baskin Robbins, Kentucky Fried Chicken, et al., may at first seem nothing but a vast extension of the lemonade stand. They provide very large numbers of teen jobs, provide regular employment, pay quite well compared to many other teen jobs and, in the modern equivalent of toiling over a hot stove, test one's stamina.

6 Closer examination, however, finds the McDonald's kind of job highly uneducational in several ways. Far from providing opportunities for entrepreneurship (the lemonade stand) or self-discipline, self-supervision and self-scheduling (the paper route), most teen jobs these days are highly structured—what social scientists call "highly routinized."

7 True, you still have to have the gumption to get yourself over to the hamburger stand, but once you don the prescribed uniform, your task is spelled out in minute detail. The franchise prescribes the shape of the coffee cups; the weight, size, shape and color of the patties; and the texture of the napkins (if any). Fresh coffee is to be made every eight minutes. And so on. There is no room for initiative, creativity, or even elementary rearrangements. These are breeding grounds for robots working for yesterday's assembly lines, not tomorrow's high-tech posts.

8 There are very few studies on the matter. One of the few is a 1984 study by Ivan Charper and Bryan Shore Fraser. The study relies mainly on what teen-agers write in response to questionnaires rather than actual observations of fast-food jobs. The authors argue that the employees develop many skills such as how to operate a food-preparation machine and a cash register. However, little attention is paid to how long it takes to acquire such a skill, or what its significance is.

9 What does it matter if you spend 20 minutes to learn to use a cash register, and then—"operate" it? What "skill" have you acquired? It is a long way from learning to work with a lathe or carpenter tools in the olden days or to program computers in the modern age.

10 A 1980 study by A. V. Harrell and P. W. Wirtz found that, among those students who worked at least 25 hours per week while in school, their unemployment rate four years later was half of that of seniors who did not work. This is an impressive statistic. It must be seen, though, together with the finding that many who begin as part-time employees in fast-food chains drop out of high school and are gobbled up in the world of low-skill jobs.

11 Some say that while these jobs are rather unsuited for college-bound, white,

middle-class youngsters, they are "ideal" for lower-class, "non-academic," minority youngsters. Indeed, minorities are "over-represented" in these jobs (21 percent of fast-food employees). While it is true that these places provide income, work and even some training to such youngsters, they also tend to perpetuate their disadvantaged status. They provide no career ladders, few marketable skills, and undermine school attendance and involvement.

12 The hours are often long. Among those 14 to 17, a third of fast-food employees (including some school dropouts) labor more than 30 hours per week, according to the Charper-Fraser study. Only 20 percent work 15 hours or less. The rest: between 15 and 30 hours.

13 Often the stores close late, and after closing one must clean up and tally up. In affluent Montgomery County, Md., where child labor would not seem to be a widespread economic necessity, 24 percent of the seniors at one high school in 1985 worked as much as five to seven days a week; 27 percent, three to five. There is just no way such amounts of work will not interfere with school work, especially homework. In an informal survey published in the most recent yearbook of the high school, 58 percent of seniors acknowledged that their jobs interfere with their school work.

14 The Charper-Fraser study sees merit in learning teamwork and working under supervision. The authors have a point here. However, it must be noted that such learning is not automatically educational or wholesome. For example, much of the supervision in fast-food places leans toward teaching one the wrong kinds of compliance: blind obedience, or shared alienation with the "boss."

15 Supervision is often both tight and woefully inappropriate. Today, fast-food chains and other such places of work (record shops, bowling alleys) keep costs down by having teens supervise teens with often no adult on the premises.

16 There is no father or mother figure with which to identify, to emulate, to provide a role model and guidance. The work-culture varies from one place to another: Sometimes it is a tightly run shop (must keep the cash registers ringing); sometimes a rather loose pot party interrupted by customers. However, only rarely is there a master to learn from, or much worth learning. Indeed, far from being places where solid adult work values are being transmitted, these are places where all too often delinquent teen values dominate. Typically, when my son Oren was dishing out ice cream for Baskin Robbins in upper Manhattan, his fellow teen-workers considered him a sucker for not helping himself to the till. Most youngsters felt they were entitled to $50 severance "pay" on their last day on the job.

17 The pay, oddly, is the part of the teen work-world that is most difficult to evaluate. The lemonade stand or paper route money was for your allowance. In the old days, apprentices learning a trade from a master contributed most, if not all, of their income to their parents' household. Today, the teen pay may be low by adult standards, but it is often, especially in the middle class, spent largely or wholly by the teens. That is, the youngsters live free at home ("after all, they are high school kids") and are left with very substantial sums of money.

18 Where this money goes is not quite clear. Some use it to support themselves, especially among the poor. More middle-class kids set some money aside to help pay for college, or save it for a major purchase — often a car. But large amounts seem to flow to pay for an early introduction into the most trite aspects of American consumerism: flimsy punk clothes, trinkets and whatever else is the last fast-moving teen craze.

19 One may say that this is only fair and square; they are being good American consumers and spend their money on what turns them on. At least, a cynic might add, these funds do not go into illicit drugs and booze. On the other hand, an educator might bemoan that these young, yet unformed individuals, so early in life driven to buy objects of no intrinsic educational, cultural or social merit, learn so quickly the dubious merit of keeping up with the Joneses in ever-changing fads, promoted by mass merchandising.

20 Many teens find the instant reward of money, and the youth status symbols it buys, much more alluring than credits in calculus courses, European history or foreign languages. No wonder quite a few would rather skip school—and certainly homework — and instead work longer at a Burger King. Thus, most teen work these days is not providing early lessons in the work ethic; it fosters escape from school and responsibilities, quick gratification and a short cut to the consumeristic aspects of adult life.

21 Thus, parents should look at teen employment not as automatically educational. It is an activity—like sports—that can be turned into an educational opportunity. But it can also easily be abused. Youngsters must learn to balance the quest for income with the needs to keep growing and pursue other endeavors that do not pay off instantly—above all education.

22 Go back to school.

[REFLECT] Make connections: Useful job skills.

Etzioni argues that fast-food jobs do not qualify as meaningful work experience because they do not teach young people the skills and habits they will need for fulfilling careers: "entrepreneurship . . . or self-discipline, self-supervision and self-scheduling" (par. 6).

To judge Etzioni's argument against your own experience and expectations, consider what you have learned and what you think others learn from summer and after-school jobs, either paid or volunteer. Your instructor may ask you to post your thoughts on a class discussion board or to discuss them with other students in class. Use these questions to get started:

- Which, if any, of the skills and habits Etzioni lists as important do you think young people learn at summer or after-school jobs?
- Why do you think these skills and habits are worth learning? If you think other skills and habits are as important or even more important, explain what they are and why you think so.

[ANALYZE] Use the basic features.

A FOCUSED, WELL-PRESENTED ISSUE: FRAMING AN ARGUMENT FOR A DIVERSE GROUP OF READERS

When Jessica Statsky wrote "Children Need to Play, Not Compete," she knew she would be addressing her classmates. But writers of position essays do not always have such a homogeneous audience. Often, they have to direct their argument to a diverse group of readers, many of whom do not share their concerns or values. From the first sentence, it is clear that Etzioni's primary audience is the parents of teenagers, but his concluding sentence is a direct address to the teenagers themselves: "Go back to school."

ANALYZE & WRITE

Write a paragraph analyzing and evaluating how Etzioni presents the issue to a diverse group of readers:

1. Reread paragraphs 1–7, highlighting the qualities—values and skills—associated with traditional jobs (the newspaper route and lemonade stand of yesteryear) and today's McDonald's-type jobs, at least according to Etzioni. How does Etzioni use this comparison to persuade parents to reconsider their assumption that McDonald's-type jobs are good for their kids?
2. Now skim the rest of the essay, looking for places where Etzioni appeals to teenagers themselves. (Notice, for example, how he represents teenagers' experience and values.) How effective do you think Etzioni's appeal would be to teenage readers? How effective do you think it is for you and your classmates?

A WELL-SUPPORTED POSITION: USING STATISTICS

Numbers can seem impressive—as, for example, when Jessica Statsky refers to the research finding that about 90 percent of children would choose to play regularly on a losing team rather than sit on the bench of a winning team (par. 5). However, without knowing the size of the sample (90 percent of 10 people, 100 people, or 10,000 people?), it is impossible to judge the significance of the statistic. Moreover, without knowing who the researchers are and how their research was funded and conducted, it is also difficult to judge the credibility of the statistic. That's why most critical readers want to know the source of **statistics** to see whether the research is **peer reviewed**—that is, whether it has been evaluated by other researchers knowledgeable about the subject and able to judge the reliability of the study's findings.

ANALYZE & WRITE

Write a paragraph analyzing and evaluating Etzioni's use of statistics:

1. Reread paragraphs 8–14, and highlight the statistics Etzioni uses. What is each statistic being used to illustrate or prove?
2. Identify what you would need to know about these research studies before you could accept their statistics as credible. Consider also what you would need to know about Etzioni himself before you could decide whether to rely on statistics he calls "impressive" (par. 10). How do your personal experience and observation influence your decision?

AN EFFECTIVE RESPONSE TO OPPOSING VIEWS: PRESENTING AND REINTERPRETING EVIDENCE TO UNDERMINE OBJECTIONS

At key points throughout his essay, Etzioni acknowledges readers' likely objections and then responds to them. One strategy Etzioni uses is to cite research that appears to undermine his claim and then offer a new interpretation of that evidence. For example, he cites a study by Harrell and Wirtz (par. 10) that links work as a student with greater likelihood of employment later on. He then reinterprets the data from this study to show that the high likelihood of future employment could be an indication that workers in fast-food restaurants are more likely to drop out of school, rather than an indication that workers are learning important employment skills. This strategy of presenting and reinterpreting evidence can be especially effective in academic writing, as Etzioni (a professor of sociology) knows well.

ANALYZE & WRITE

Write a paragraph or two analyzing and evaluating Etzioni's strategy of reinterpreting data elsewhere in his essay:

1. Reread paragraphs 8–9, in which Etzioni responds to the claim that employees in McDonald's-type jobs develop many useful skills.
2. Reread paragraphs 14–16, in which Etzioni discusses the benefits and shortcomings of various kinds of on-the-job supervision.
3. Identify the claim that appears in the research Etzioni cites. How does Etzioni reinterpret it? Do you find his reinterpretation persuasive? Why or why not?

A CLEAR, LOGICAL ORGANIZATION: PROVIDING CUES FOR READERS

Writers of position arguments generally try to make their writing logical and easy to follow. Providing **cues**, or road signs—for example, by forecasting their reasons in a thesis statement early in the argument, using topic sentences to announce each reason as it is supported, and employing transitions (such as *furthermore*, *in addition*, and *finally*) to guide readers from one point to another—can be helpful, especially for readers of print and online articles, who do not want to spend a lot of time deciphering arguments.

ANALYZE & WRITE

Write a paragraph analyzing and evaluating the cueing strategies Etzioni uses to help his readers follow his argument:

1. Find and highlight Etzioni's thesis statement, the cues forecasting his reasons, the transitions he provides, and any other cueing devices he uses.
2. Identify the paragraphs in which Etzioni develops each of his reasons.
3. How does Etzioni help readers track his reasons, and how effective are his cues?

[RESPOND] Consider possible topics: Issues facing students.

Etzioni focuses on a single kind of part-time work, takes a position on how worthwhile it is, and recommends against it. You could write a similar kind of essay. For example, you could take a position for or against students' participating in other kinds of part-time work or recreation during the high school or college academic year or over the summer—for example, playing on a sports team, volunteering, completing an internship, studying a musical instrument or a foreign language, or taking an elective class. If you work to support yourself and pay for college, you could focus on why the job either strengthens or weakens you as a person, given your life and career goals. Writing for other students, you would either recommend the job or activity to them or discourage them from pursuing it, giving reasons and support for your position.

Daniel J. Solove

Why Privacy Matters Even If You Have "Nothing to Hide"

© Dirk Anschütz

DANIEL J. SOLOVE is the John Marshall Harlan Research Professor of Law at the George Washington University Law School. In addition to writing numerous books and articles on issues of privacy and the Internet, Solove is the founder of a company that provides privacy and data security training to corporations and universities. Among his books are *The Future of Reputation: Gossip, Rumor, and Privacy on the Internet* (2007), which won Fordham University's McGannon Award for Social and Ethical Relevance in Communications Policy Research; *Nothing to Hide: The False Tradeoff between Privacy and Security* (2011); and *Privacy Law Fundamentals* (with Paul M. Schwartz, 2013).

An early version of this essay appearing in a law review journal included citations, which had to be eliminated for publication in the *Chronicle of Higher Education* in 2011; we have restored them here so that you can see how Solove uses a variety of sources to support his position.

As you read, consider the following questions:

- How do the sources cited in the opening paragraphs contribute to your understanding of why so many people think privacy is not something they should be concerned about?
- Do you use Internet privacy settings? How concerned are you about protecting your privacy on social networking and other Web sites?

1 When the government gathers or analyzes personal information, many people say they're not worried. "I've got nothing to hide," they declare. "Only if you're doing something wrong should you worry, and then you don't deserve to keep it private." The nothing-to-hide argument pervades discussions about privacy. The data-security expert Bruce Schneier calls it the "most common retort against privacy advocates." The legal scholar Geoffrey Stone refers to it as an "all-too-common refrain." In its most compelling form, it is an argument that the privacy interest is generally minimal, thus making the contest with security concerns a foreordained victory for security.

2 The nothing-to-hide argument is everywhere. In Britain, for example, the government has installed millions of public-surveillance cameras in cities and towns, which are watched by officials via closed-circuit television. In a campaign slogan for the program, the government declares: "If you've got nothing to hide, you've got nothing to fear" (Rosen 36). Variations of nothing-to-hide arguments frequently appear in blogs, letters to the

editor, television news interviews, and other forums. One blogger in the United States, in reference to profiling people for national-security purposes, declares: "I don't mind people wanting to find out things about me, I've got nothing to hide! Which is why I support [the government's] efforts to find terrorists by monitoring our phone calls!" (Oakey).

3 On the surface, it seems easy to dismiss the nothing-to-hide argument. Everybody probably has something to hide from somebody. As Aleksandr Solzhenitsyn declared, "Everyone is guilty of something or has something to conceal. All one has to do is look hard enough to find what it is" (192). . . . One can usually think of something that even the most open person would want to hide. As a commenter to my blog post noted, "If you have nothing to hide, then that quite literally means you are willing to let me photograph you naked? And I get full rights to that photograph—so I can show it to your neighbors?" (Andrew). . . .

4 But such responses attack the nothing-to-hide argument only in its most extreme form, which isn't particularly strong. In a less extreme form, the nothing-to-hide argument refers not to all personal information but only to the type of data the government is likely to collect. Retorts to the nothing-to-hide argument about exposing people's naked bodies or their deepest secrets are relevant only if the government is likely to gather this kind of information. In many instances, hardly anyone will see the information, and it won't be disclosed to the public. Thus, some might argue, the privacy interest is minimal, and the security interest in preventing terrorism is much more important. In this less extreme form, the nothing-to-hide argument is a formidable one. However, it stems from certain faulty assumptions about privacy and its value. . . .

5 Most attempts to understand privacy do so by attempting to locate its essence—its core characteristics or the common denominator that links together the various things we classify under the rubric of "privacy." Privacy, however, is too complex a concept to be reduced to a singular essence. It is a plurality of different things that do not share any one element but nevertheless bear a resemblance to one another. For example, privacy can be invaded by the disclosure of your deepest secrets. It might also be invaded if you're watched by a peeping Tom, even if no secrets are ever revealed. With the disclosure of secrets, the harm is that your concealed information is spread to others. With the peeping Tom, the harm is that you're being watched. You'd probably find that creepy regardless of whether the peeper finds out anything sensitive or discloses any information to others. There are many other forms of invasion of privacy, such as blackmail and the improper use of your personal data. Your privacy can also be invaded if the government compiles an extensive dossier about you. Privacy, in other words, involves so many things that it is impossible to reduce them all to one simple idea. And we need not do so. . . .

6 To describe the problems created by the collection and use of personal data, many commentators use a metaphor based on George Orwell's *Nineteen Eighty-Four*. Orwell depicted a harrowing totalitarian society ruled by a government called Big Brother that watches its citizens obsessively and demands strict discipline. The Orwell metaphor, which focuses on the harms of surveillance (such as inhibition and social control), might be apt to describe government monitoring of citizens. But much of the data gathered in computer databases, such as one's race, birth date, gender, address, or marital status, isn't particularly sensitive. Many people don't care about concealing the hotels they stay at, the cars they own, or the kind of beverages they drink. Frequently,

though not always, people wouldn't be inhibited or embarrassed if others knew this information.

7 Another metaphor better captures the problems: Franz Kafka's *The Trial*. Kafka's novel centers around a man who is arrested but not informed why. He desperately tries to find out what triggered his arrest and what's in store for him. He finds out that a mysterious court system has a dossier on him and is investigating him, but he's unable to learn much more. *The Trial* depicts a bureaucracy with inscrutable purposes that uses people's information to make important decisions about them, yet denies the people the ability to participate in how their information is used.

8 The problems portrayed by the Kafkaesque metaphor are of a different sort than the problems caused by surveillance. They often do not result in inhibition. Instead they are problems of information processing—the storage, use, or analysis of data—rather than of information collection. They affect the power relationships between people and the institutions of the modern state. They not only frustrate the individual by creating a sense of helplessness and powerlessness, but also affect social structure by altering the kind of relationships people have with the institutions that make important decisions about their lives.

9 Legal and policy solutions focus too much on the problems under the Orwellian metaphor—those of surveillance—and aren't adequately addressing the Kafkaesque problems—those of information processing. The difficulty is that commentators are trying to conceive of the problems caused by databases in terms of surveillance when, in fact, those problems are different. Commentators often attempt to refute the nothing-to-hide argument by pointing to things people want to hide. But the problem with the nothing-to-hide argument is the underlying assumption that privacy is about hiding bad things. By accepting this assumption, we concede far too much ground and invite an unproductive discussion about information that people would very likely want to hide. As the computer-security specialist Schneier aptly notes, the nothing-to-hide argument stems from a faulty "premise that privacy is about hiding a wrong." Surveillance, for example, can inhibit such lawful activities as free speech, free association, and other First Amendment rights essential for democracy.

10 The deeper problem with the nothing-to-hide argument is that it myopically views privacy as a form of secrecy. In contrast, understanding privacy as a plurality of related issues demonstrates that the disclosure of bad things is just one among many difficulties caused by government security measures. To return to my discussion of literary metaphors, the problems are not just Orwellian but Kafkaesque. Government information-gathering programs are problematic even if no information that people want to hide is uncovered. In *The Trial*, the problem is not inhibited behavior but rather a suffocating powerlessness and vulnerability created by the court system's use of personal data and its denial to the protagonist of any knowledge of or participation in the process. The harms are bureaucratic ones—indifference, error, abuse, frustration, and lack of transparency and accountability.

11 One such harm, for example, which I call aggregation, emerges from the fusion of small bits of seemingly innocuous data. When combined, the information becomes much more telling. By joining pieces of information we might not take pains to guard, the government can glean information about us that we might indeed wish to conceal. For example, suppose you bought a book about cancer. This purchase isn't very revealing on its own, for it indicates just an interest in the disease. Suppose you bought a wig. The purchase of a wig, by itself,

could be for a number of reasons. But combine those two pieces of information, and now the inference can be made that you have cancer and are undergoing chemotherapy. That might be a fact you wouldn't mind sharing, but you'd certainly want to have the choice.

12 Another potential problem with the government's harvest of personal data is one I call exclusion. Exclusion occurs when people are prevented from having knowledge about how information about them is being used, and when they are barred from accessing and correcting errors in that data. Many government national-security measures involve maintaining a huge database of information that individuals cannot access. Indeed, because they involve national security, the very existence of these programs is often kept secret. This kind of information processing, which blocks subjects' knowledge and involvement, is a kind of due-process problem. It is a structural problem, involving the way people are treated by government institutions and creating a power imbalance between people and the government. To what extent should government officials have such a significant power over citizens? This issue isn't about what information people want to hide but about the power and the structure of government.

13 A related problem involves secondary use. Secondary use is the exploitation of data obtained for one purpose for an unrelated purpose without the subject's consent. How long will personal data be stored? How will the information be used? What could it be used for in the future? The potential uses of any piece of personal information are vast. Without limits on or accountability for how that information is used, it is hard for people to assess the dangers of the data's being in the government's control.

14 Yet another problem with government gathering and use of personal data is distortion. Although personal information can reveal quite a lot about people's personalities and activities, it often fails to reflect the whole person. It can paint a distorted picture, especially since records are reductive—they often capture information in a standardized format with many details omitted. For example, suppose government officials learn that a person has bought a number of books on how to manufacture methamphetamine. That information makes them suspect that he's building a meth lab. What is missing from the records is the full story: The person is writing a novel about a character who makes meth. When he bought the books, he didn't consider how suspicious the purchase might appear to government officials, and his records didn't reveal the reason for the purchases. Should he have to worry about government scrutiny of all his purchases and actions? Should he have to be concerned that he'll wind up on a suspicious-persons list? Even if he isn't doing anything wrong, he may want to keep his records away from government officials who might make faulty inferences from them. He might not want to have to worry about how everything he does will be perceived by officials nervously monitoring for criminal activity. He might not want to have a computer flag him as suspicious because he has an unusual pattern of behavior. . . .

15 Privacy is rarely lost in one fell swoop. It is usually eroded over time, little bits dissolving almost imperceptibly until we finally begin to notice how much is gone. When the government starts monitoring the phone numbers people call, many may shrug their shoulders and say, "Ah, it's just numbers, that's all." Then the government might start monitoring some phone calls. "It's just a few phone calls, nothing more." The government might install more video cameras in public places. "So what? Some more cameras watching in a few more places. No big deal." The increase in cameras might lead to a more elaborate network of video surveillance.

Satellite surveillance might be added to help track people's movements. The government might start analyzing people's bank records. "It's just my deposits and some of the bills I pay—no problem." The government may then start combing through credit-card records, then expand to Internet-service providers' records, health records, employment records, and more. Each step may seem incremental, but after a while, the government will be watching and knowing everything about us.

16 "My life's an open book," people might say. "I've got nothing to hide." But now the government has large dossiers of everyone's activities, interests, reading habits, finances, and health. What if the government leaks the information to the public? What if the government mistakenly determines that based on your pattern of activities, you're likely to engage in a criminal act? What if it denies you the right to fly? What if the government thinks your financial transactions look odd—even if you've done nothing wrong—and freezes your accounts? What if the government doesn't protect your information with adequate security, and an identity thief obtains it and uses it to defraud you? Even if you have nothing to hide, the government can cause you a lot of harm.

Works Cited

Andrew. Comment on "Is There a Good Response to the 'Nothing to Hide' Argument?" by Daniel Solove. *Concurring Opinions,* 16 Oct. 2006, concurringopinions.com/archives/2006/05/is_there_a_good.html/comment-page-2.

Oakey, Carrie. "Look All You Want! I've Got Nothing to Hide!" *Reach for the Stars!,* 14 May 2006, greatcarrieoakey.blogspot.com/2006/05/look-all-you-want-ive-got-nothing-to.html.

Rosen, Jeffrey. *The Naked Crowd: Reclaiming Security and Freedom in an Anxious Age.* Random House, 2004.

Schneier, Bruce. "The Eternal Value of Privacy." *Wired,* Condé Nast, 18 May 2006, archive.wired.com/politics/security/commentary/securitymatters/2006/05/70886.

Solzhenitsyn, Aleksandr. *Cancer Ward.* Translated by Nicholas Bethell and David Burg. Farrar, Straus and Giroux, 1969.

Stone, Geoffrey R. "Freedom and Public Responsibility." *Chicago Tribune,* 21 May 2006, p. 11.

[REFLECT] Make connections: Privacy concerns on the Internet.

Whereas Solove's position argument focuses on concerns about government collection and use of personal information, many people today are concerned as well about corporate collection and use of personal information. For example, potential employers review blogs and social media Web sites to gather information about job candidates and to check their résumés. Corporations also use data mining to personalize advertising, sending diaper coupons, for example, to women in their thirties who have recently bought diaper bags or baby monitors online.

Think about the implications of corporate data mining, and reflect on how this could affect your own sense of online privacy. Your instructor may ask you to post your thoughts on a class discussion board or to discuss them with other students in class. Use these questions to get started:

- How, if at all, do you manage the privacy preferences or settings on sites you use? Do you ever defriend people or click the "do not track" tool when you have the opportunity to do so? Would you untag photos or delete comments on social networking sites like Facebook that you didn't want potential employers to see?
- What are the advantages and disadvantages of corporate data mining? Have targeted advertisements been a boon to you, or are you distressed about a corporation's knowing so much about you?

[ANALYZE] Use the basic features.

A FOCUSED, WELL-PRESENTED ISSUE: REFRAMING THROUGH CONTRAST

Writers sometimes have to remind their readers why an issue is controversial. Beginning with the title, Solove works to undermine the widely held assumption that the erosion of privacy should not be a concern. He does this primarily by contrasting two ways of thinking about threats to privacy, which he calls Orwellian and Kafkaesque, based on the novels *Nineteen Eighty-Four,* by George Orwell, and *The Trial,* by Franz Kafka. To present this contrast, Solove uses sentence patterns like these:

▶ Not ________, but ________.

▶ ________ focus on ________, which is characterized by ________, and they don't even notice ________, which is characterized by ________.

Here are a couple of examples from Solove's position argument:

> The problems are not just Orwellian but Kafkaesque. (par. 10)
>
> Legal and policy solutions focus too much on the problems under the Orwellian metaphor—those of surveillance—and aren't adequately addressing the Kafkaesque problems—those of information processing. (par. 9)

ANALYZE & WRITE

Write a paragraph analyzing and evaluating the effectiveness of Solove's use of contrast to reframe the issue for readers:

1. Reread paragraphs 6–7 to see how Solove explains the two contrasting metaphors.
2. Then skim paragraphs 8–10, highlighting any sentence patterns used to mark the contrast.
3. Has Solove's reframing of the discussion affected your understanding of privacy and your concerns about its loss? Why or why not?

A WELL-SUPPORTED POSITION: USING SOURCES

Writers of position arguments often quote, paraphrase, and summarize sources. Usually they use sources to support their positions, as Jessica Statsky does in her argument about children's sports. Sometimes, however, they use sources to highlight opposing positions to which they will respond, as Solove does on occasion in this essay.

In the following example, Solove signals his opinion through the words he chooses to characterize the source:

> As the computer-security specialist Schneier aptly notes, the nothing-to-hide argument stems from a faulty "premise that privacy is about hiding a wrong." (par. 9)

Elsewhere, readers have to work a little harder to determine how Solove is using the source.

Solove also uses what we might call **hypothetical quotations**—sentences that quote not what someone actually said but what they *might* have said:

Signal phrase

Hypothetical quotation

> Many people say they're not worried. "I've got nothing to hide," they declare. "Only if you're doing something wrong should you worry, and then you don't deserve to keep it private." (par. 1)
>
> "My life's an open book," people might say. "I've got nothing to hide." (par. 16)

You can tell from a signal phrase like "people might say" or "many people say" that no actual person made the statement, but Solove does not always supply such cues.

To learn more about using patterns of opposition to read critically, see Chapter 10, p. 346.

ANALYZE & WRITE

Write a paragraph analyzing and evaluating Solove's use of quotations:

1. Find and mark the quotations, noting which actually quote someone and which are hypothetical.
2. Identify the quotations—real or hypothetical—that Solove agrees with and those that represent an opposing view.
3. How effective did you find Solove's quoting strategy, given his purpose and audience? (Remember that this article appeared in the *Chronicle of Higher Education*, a weekly newspaper for college faculty and administrators.)

AN EFFECTIVE RESPONSE TO OPPOSING VIEWS: REFUTING BY DEMONSTRATING THE EFFECTS

As his title suggests, Solove refutes the claim that privacy does not matter "if you have 'nothing to hide.'" His primary way of refuting the nothing-to-hide argument is to argue that the collection and use of personal information (the cause) has negative effects, which he sometimes calls "problems" and sometimes calls "harms" (par. 6).

ANALYZE & WRITE

Write a paragraph or two analyzing and evaluating Solove's use of cause-and-effect reasoning to refute the claim that privacy only matters if you have something to hide:

1. Reread paragraphs 6–14, noting where Solove discusses potential problems or harms that could result from the collection of personal data.
2. Choose one of these harms, and examine Solove's argument more closely. How does he support this part of the argument—for example, what are his reasons, his evidence, the values and beliefs he uses to appeal to his audience?
3. How effective are Solove's reasons and evidence for you? How effective might they have been for his original audience?

A CLEAR, LOGICAL ORGANIZATION: USING CUEING DEVICES

Solove uses a number of cueing devices to help readers keep track of his argument. Perhaps the most obvious and helpful cues are the topic sentences that begin each paragraph and the logical transitions ("One such harm," "Another potential problem," "A related problem," "Yet another problem" [pars. 11–14]) that signal connections between and within paragraphs. In addition, Solove uses rhetorical questions, such as the series of "What if" questions in the final paragraph.

ANALYZE & WRITE

Write a paragraph or two analyzing and evaluating the effectiveness of Solove's use of cueing devices to help readers follow his argument:

1. Choose a couple of paragraphs that use topic sentences and logical transitions effectively. Look closely at the way Solove uses these cueing devices, and determine what makes them so effective.
2. Highlight the rhetorical questions posed in paragraphs 12–14 and 16. Why do you imagine Solove uses so many of them, especially in the final paragraph? Given his purpose and audience, how effective do you think these rhetorical questions were likely to have been? How effective do you find them?

[RESPOND] Consider possible topics: Issues concerning privacy.

Solove focuses on one concern about the erosion of privacy. You could write a similar type of essay, taking a position on issues such as state laws requiring women to have ultrasounds before terminating a pregnancy; airport security requiring passengers either to go through a full-body scanner or to submit to a "pat-down" before boarding a flight; cell phones making it possible for individuals to be located and tracked without their consent or knowledge; or houses, offices, and even people on the street being depicted on Google Maps without knowledge or consent.

The Writing Assignment

Compose a position argument on a controversial issue. Before you take a position, learn more about the issue and the debate surrounding it. Then frame the issue so readers can see why it merits their attention; consider and respond to views that differ from yours; and develop a well-supported, clearly organized argument that will confirm, challenge, or change your readers' views.

This Guide to Writing is designed to help you compose your own position argument and apply what you have learned from reading other position arguments. The Starting Points chart will help you find the guidance you need, when you need it.

STARTING POINTS: ARGUING A POSITION

A Focused, Well-Presented Issue

How do I come up with an issue to write about?

- Consider possible topics. (pp. 201, 209)
- Choose a controversial issue on which to take a position. (p. 212)
- Test Your Choice: Choosing an Issue (p. 213)

How can I effectively frame the issue for my readers?

- Assess the genre's basic features: A focused, well-presented issue. (pp. 185–87)
- A Focused, Well-Presented Issue: Framing an Argument for a Diverse Group of Readers (pp. 199–200)
- A Focused, Well-Presented Issue: Reframing through Contrast (p. 207)
- Frame the issue for your readers. (pp. 213–15)
- Test Your Choice: Frame Your Issue (pp. 214–15)
- A Troubleshooting Guide: A Focused, Well-Presented Issue (p. 224)

A Well-Supported Position

How do I come up with a plausible position?

- Assess the genre's basic features: A well-supported position. (pp. 187–88)
- Formulate a working thesis stating your position. (p. 215)
- Develop the reasons supporting your position. (pp. 215–16)
- Research your position. (p. 216)
- Use sources to reinforce your credibility. (p. 217)

A Well-Supported Position

How do I come up with reasons and evidence supporting my position?

- A Well-Supported Position: Using Statistics (p. 200)
- A Well-Supported Position: Using Sources (p. 208)
- Formulate a working thesis stating your position. (p. 215)
- Develop the reasons supporting your position. (pp. 215–16)
- Research your position. (p. 216)
- A Troubleshooting Guide: A Well-Supported Position (p. 224)

An Effective Response to Opposing Views

How do I respond to possible objections to my position?

- Assess the genre's basic features: An effective response to opposing views. (pp. 188–89)
- Identify and respond to your readers' likely reasons and objections. (pp. 218–19)
- Write the opening sentences. (p. 221)
- A Troubleshooting Guide: An Effective Response to Opposing Views. (p. 224)

How do I respond to possible alternative positions?

- Assess the genre's basic feature: An effective response to opposing views. (pp. 188–89)
- An Effective Response: Presenting and Reinterpreting Evidence to Undermine Objections (pp. 200–1)
- An Effective Response: Refuting by Demonstrating the Effects (pp. 208–9)
- Research your position. (p. 216)
- Identify and respond to your readers' likely reasons and objections. (pp. 218–19)

A Clear, Logical Organization

How can I help my readers follow my argument?

- Assess the genre's basic features: A clear, logical organization. (pp. 189–90)
- A Clear, Logical Organization: Providing Cues for Readers (p. 201)
- A Clear, Logical Organization: Using Cueing Devices (p. 209)
- Create an outline that will organize your argument effectively for your readers. (p. 220)
- A Troubleshooting Guide: A Clear, Logical Organization (p. 225)

Writing a Draft: Invention, Research, Planning, and Composing

The activities in this section will help you choose and research an issue as well as develop and organize an argument for your position. Your writing in response to many of these activities can be used in a rough draft, which you will be able to improve after receiving feedback from your classmates and instructor. Do the activities in any order that makes sense to you (and your instructor), and return to them as needed as you revise.

Choose a controversial issue on which to take a position.

When choosing an issue, keep in mind that the issue must be

- controversial—an issue that people disagree about;
- arguable—a matter of opinion on which there is no absolute proof or authority;
- one that you can research, as necessary, in the time you have;
- one that you care about.

Choosing an issue about which you have special interest or knowledge usually works best. If you are thinking of addressing an issue of national concern, focus on a local or very specific aspect of it. For example, instead of addressing censorship in general, write about a local lawmaker's recent effort to propose a law censoring the Internet, a city council's attempt to block access to Internet sites at the public library, or your school board's ban on certain textbooks.

You may already have an issue in mind. If you do, skip to Test Your Choice: Choosing an Issue (p. 213). If you do not, the topics that follow, in addition to those following the readings (pp. 190, 196, 202), may suggest an issue you can make your own:

- Should particular courses, community service, or an internship be a graduation requirement at your high school or college?
- Should students attending public colleges be required to pay higher tuition fees if they have been full-time students but have not graduated within four years?
- Should your large lecture or online courses have frequent (weekly or biweekly) exams instead of only a midterm and final?
- Should children raised in this country whose parents entered illegally be given an opportunity to become citizens upon finishing college or serving in the military?
- Should the football conference your school (or another school in the area) participates in be allowed to expand?
- Should you look primarily for a job that is well paid or for a job that is personally fulfilling or socially responsible?
- Should the racial, ethnic, or gender makeup of the police force resemble the makeup of the community it serves?
- Should public employees be allowed to unionize and to bargain collectively for improved working conditions, pay, or pensions?
- Should the state or federal government provide job training for those who are unemployed but able to work?

TEST YOUR CHOICE

Choosing an Issue

First, ask yourself the following questions:

- Does the issue matter to me? If not, could I argue convincingly that it ought to be of concern?
- Do I know enough about the issue to take a position that I can support effectively, or can I learn what I need to know in the time I have?
- Can I frame or reframe the issue in a way that might open readers to my point of view or help them reconsider what's at stake?

Then get together with two or three other students to take turns trying out your issues with potential readers. Ask group members questions like the following:

- What, if anything, do you already know about the issue?
- What about the issue (if anything) seems particularly intriguing or important to you?
- Do you already hold a position on this issue? If so, how strongly do you hold it? Would you be open to considering other points of view? If you don't care about the issue, what might convince you that it matters?

Consider these questions and their responses as you plan and draft your argument.

Frame the issue for your readers.

Once you have made a preliminary choice of an issue, consider how you can frame (or reframe) the issue so that readers who support opposing positions will listen to your argument. Consider how the issue has been debated in the past and what your readers are likely to think. Use the following questions and sentence strategies to help you put your ideas into writing.

WAYS IN

HOW CAN I EXPLORE THE ISSUE?

To explore the ISSUE, *ask yourself questions like these, using the sentence strategies as jumping-off points:*

What groups or notable individuals have shaped the debate on this issue? What positions have they taken?

- ▶ Although many people take Issue X for granted, groups A, B, and C oppose it on the grounds that ________.
- ▶ Whereas supporters of Issue X have argued that ________, opponents such as A, B, and C contend that ________.

WHAT DO MY READERS THINK?

To determine what your READERS *are likely to think, ask yourself questions like these, using the sentence strategies as jumping-off points:*

What values and concerns do my readers and I share regarding the issue?

- ▶ Concern about Issue X leads many of us to oppose ________. We worry about the consequences if ________ is implemented.
- ▶ X is a basic human right that needs to be protected. But what does it mean in everyday practice when ________?

(continued)

How has the issue, or people's opinions about the issue, changed? What makes the issue important now?

- Recent research/new reports have changed some people's minds on this issue. Instead of assuming ________, many people now think________.
- The debate over Issue X was initially focused on________ , but now the main concern seems to be ________.

What fundamental differences in worldview or experience might keep my readers from agreeing with me?

- Those who disagree about Issue X often see it as a choice between ________ and ________. But we don't have to choose between them.
- While others may view it as a matter of ________, for me what's at stake is ________.

HOW CAN I FRAME THE ISSUE EFFECTIVELY?

Once you have a good idea of how the issue has been debated and what your readers think, use these sentence strategies to FRAME *the issue for your readers:*

What is the issue, and why should my readers be concerned about it?

- Issue X is of concern to all members of group A because ________.

EXAMPLE I'm concerned about the high cost of tuition at state colleges like ours because students have to borrow more money to pay for their education than they will be able to earn once they graduate.

Why are popular approaches or attitudes inappropriate or inadequate?

- Although many in the community claim X, I think Y because ________.

EXAMPLE Some argue that college football players should be paid because of the money the school is earning off players' labor. I disagree. I think the current system should be maintained because without the money earned from football, less lucrative sports programs, like fencing and wrestling, would have to be cut.

TEST YOUR CHOICE

Framing Your Issue

Ask two or three other students to consider the way you have framed your issue.

Presenters. Briefly explain the values and concerns you think are at stake. (The sentence strategies in the Ways In section can help you articulate your position and approach.)

Listeners. Tell the presenter how you respond to this way of framing the issue, and why. You may use the language that follows as a model for structuring your response, or use language of your own.

- ▶ I'm also/not concerned about Issue X because ________.
- ▶ I agree/disagree with you about Issue X because ________.

Formulate a working thesis stating your position.

Try drafting a working thesis statement now. (If you prefer to conduct research or develop your argument before trying to formulate a thesis, skip this activity and return to it when you're ready.) As you develop your argument, rework your assertion to make it a compelling thesis statement by making the language clear and straightforward. You may also need to qualify it with words like *often, sometimes,* or *in part.* Be sure to forecast your reasons.

WAYS IN

HOW CAN I DEVISE AN ARGUABLE THESIS?

Begin by describing the **ISSUE**, *possibly indicating where others stand on it or what's at stake, and then stating your* **POSITION**. *These sentence strategies may help you get started:*

- ▶ At a recent meeting, many people argued ________. Although I sympathize with their point of view, this is ultimately a question of ________, not ________. Therefore, we must do ________.
- ▶ This issue is dividing our community. Some people argue X, others contend Y, and still others believe Z. However, it is in all of our interests to do ________ because ________.
- ▶ Conventional wisdom claims that ________. But I take a different view: I believe ________ because ________.

Develop the reasons supporting your position.

The following activities will help you find plausible reasons and evidence for your position. You can do some focused research later to fill in the details, or skip ahead to conduct research now.

For more idea-generating strategies, see Chapter 9.

WAYS IN

HOW CAN I COME UP WITH REASONS THAT SUPPORT MY POSITION?

Write nonstop for at least five minutes exploring your reasons. Ask yourself questions like these:

- How can I show readers that my reasons lead logically to my position (**LOGOS**)?
- How can I convince my readers that I am trustworthy (**ETHOS**)?
- How can I appeal to their feelings (**PATHOS**)?

At this point, don't worry about the exact language you will use in your final draft. Just write the reasons you hold your position and the evidence (as anecdotes, examples, statistics, expert testimony) that supports it. Keep your readers and their values in mind—what would they find most convincing, and why?

To brainstorm a list of reasons, try this:

- Start by writing your position at the top of the page.
- On the left half of the page, list as many potential reasons as you can think of to support your position. (Don't judge at this point.)
- On the right half of the page, make notes about the kinds of evidence you would need to provide to convince readers of each reason and to show how each supports your position.

Research your position.

Do some research to find out how others have argued in support of your position:

- Try entering keywords or phrases related to the issue or your position in the search box of an all-purpose database, such as *Academic OneFile* (InfoTrac) or *Academic Search Complete* (EBSCOhost), to find relevant articles in magazines and journals, or use the database *Lexis/Nexis* to find articles in newspapers. For example, Jessica Statsky could have tried a combination of keywords, such as *children's sports,* or variations on her terms (*youth sports*) to find relevant articles. A similar search of your library's catalog could also be conducted to locate books and other resources on your topic.
- If you think your issue has been dealt with by a government agency, explore the state, local, or tribal sections of USA.gov—the U.S. government's official Web portal—or visit the Library of Congress page on state government information and follow the links.
- Remember to bookmark promising sites and to record the URL and information you will need to cite and document any sources or visuals you use.

To learn more about searching a database or catalog, consult Chapter 14, pp. 407–8; about finding government documents, consult Chapter 14, p. 410; about documenting sources, consult Chapter 16 or Chapter 17.

Use sources to reinforce your credibility.

How you represent your sources can quickly establish your credibility (ethos)—or the reverse. For example, by briefly describing the author's credentials the first time you *summarize, paraphrase,* or *quote* from a source, you establish the source's authority and demonstrate that you have selected sources appropriately:

Signal phrase and author's credentials Source summary In-text citation follows quotation	Martin Rablovsky, a former sports editor for *The New York Times,* says that in all his years of watching young children play organized sports, he has noticed very few of them smiling. "I've seen children enjoying a spontaneous pre-practice scrimmage become somber and serious when the coach's whistle blows," Rablovsky says . . . (qtd. in Coakley 94).

Quotations can also reinforce the accuracy of your summary or paraphrase and establish your fairness to opposing points of view. In the following sentence, Jessica Statsky demonstrates her fairness by quoting from the Web site of the Little League, a well-known organization, and establishes her credibility by demonstrating that even those who disagree with her recognize that injuries occur:

Statsky's introduction: summarizes source In-text citation follows quotation	Although Little League Baseball and Softball acknowledges that children do risk injury playing baseball, it insists that "severe injuries . . . are infrequent," the risk "far less than the risk of riding a skateboard, a bicycle, or even the school bus" ("Little League Parent Responsibilities").

In both of these examples from "Children Need to Play, Not Compete" (pars. 5 and 3, respectively), Statsky introduces the source to her readers, explaining the relevance of the source material—including the author's credentials—to readers rather than leaving them to figure it out for themselves.

Whenever you borrow information from sources, be sure to double-check that you are summarizing, paraphrasing, and quoting accurately and fairly. Compare Statsky's sentence with its source passage. (The portions she uses are highlighted.) Notice that she has inserted ellipsis dots (. . .) to indicate that she has left out words from her source's second sentence.

Source

Injuries seem to be inevitable in any rigorous activity, especially if players are new to the sport and unfamiliar with its demands. But because of the safety precautions taken in Little League, severe injuries such as bone fractures are infrequent. Most injuries are sprains and strains, abrasions and cuts and bruises. The risk of serious injury in Little League Baseball is far less than the risk of riding a skateboard, a bicycle, or even the school bus.

In both of the preceding examples, Statsky uses quotation marks to indicate that she is borrowing the words of a source and provides an in-text citation so that readers can locate the sources in her list of works cited. Doing both is essential to avoid plagiarism; one or the other is not enough.

For more on integrating language from sources into your own sentences and avoiding plagiarism, see Chapter 15, pp. 419–21.

Identify and respond to your readers' likely reasons and objections.

The following activity will help you anticipate reasons your readers may use to support their argument or objections they may have. You may want to return to this activity as you do additional research and learn more about the issue and the arguments people make. Return to the section "Research your position" on p. 216, or consult Chapter 14, "Planning a Research Project and Selecting Sources."

WAYS IN

HOW CAN I FIGURE OUT WHAT MY READERS WILL BE CONCERNED ABOUT?

1. List the **REASONS** you expect your readers to have for their position and the **OBJECTIONS** (including those based on logical fallacies) you expect them to raise to your argument. How do your **VALUES**, **BELIEFS**, and **PRIORITIES** differ from those of your readers?
2. *Analyze your list of likely* **REASONS** *and* **OBJECTIONS**. Which can you refute, and how? Which may you need to concede?

For more on logical fallacies, see Chapter 12, p. 379.

HOW CAN I RESPOND TO READERS' REASONS AND OBJECTIONS?

Now, choose a **REASON** *or an* **OBJECTION**, *and try out a response:*

1. Summarize it accurately and fairly. (Do not commit the straw man fallacy of knocking down something that no one really takes seriously.)
2. Decide whether you can refute it, need to concede it, or can refute part and concede part.

Try sentence strategies like these to **REFUTE**, **CONCEDE**, *or* **CONCEDE** *and* **REFUTE** *reasons supporting readers' arguments or their objections to your argument:*

To Refute

Reason or Objection Lacks Credible Support

- My opponents cite research to support their reason/objection, but the credibility of that research is questionable because ________. In contrast, reliable research by Professor X shows ________.
- This reason/objection seems plausible on the surface, but evidence shows ________.

Readers' Values and Concerns Are Better Served by Your Position

- Some insist ________ without realizing that it would take away a basic right/make things even worse.
- X and Y think this issue is about ________. But what is really at stake here is ________.

Reasoning Is Flawed

- ▶ Proponents object to my argument on the grounds that ________. However, they are confusing results with causes. What I am arguing is ________.
- ▶ Polls show that most people favor ________, but an opinion's popularity does not make it true or right.
- ▶ While most would agree that ________, it does not necessarily follow that ________.

Times Have Changed

- ▶ One common complaint is ________. In recent years, however, ________.

To Concede

Accept an Objection Well Taken

- ▶ To be sure, ________ is true.
- ▶ Granted, ________ must be taken into consideration.

Qualify on Common Ground

- ▶ Some people argue that ________. I understand this reservation, and therefore, I think we should ________.

Refocus Your Argument

- ▶ A common concern about this issue is ________. That's why my argument focuses on [a different aspect of the issue].

To Concede and Refute

And Instead of *Or*

- ▶ I agree that ________ is important, and so is ________.

Yes, But

- ▶ I agree that ________ is important, but my opponents also need to consider ________.

On the One Hand . . . On the Other Hand

- ▶ On the one hand, I accept X's argument that ________, but on the other hand, I still think ________ is ultimately more important because ________.

Note: If a reason or an objection seems so damaging that you cannot refute it convincingly or concede it without undermining your own argument, discuss with your instructor how you could modify your position or whether you should choose a new issue to write about. If you do not know enough about readers' views to anticipate their reasons or likely objections to your argument, do more research.

Create an outline that will organize your argument effectively for your readers.

Whether you have rough notes or a complete draft, making an outline of what you have written can help you organize your essay effectively for your audience. Compare the possible outlines that follow to see how you might organize the essay depending on whether your readers primarily agree or disagree with you.

Readers Primarily Agree with You

Strengthen their convictions by organizing your argument around a series of reasons backed by supporting evidence or by refuting opposing arguments point by point:

I. **Present the issue.**

II. **Provide a thesis statement**—a direct statement of your position.

III. **Present your most plausible reasons and evidence.**

IV. **Concede or refute opposing reasons or objections to your argument.**

V. **Conclude:** Reaffirm your position.

Readers Primarily Disagree with You

Begin by emphasizing common ground, and make a concession to show that you have considered the opposing position carefully and with an open mind:

I. **Present the issue:** Reframe the issue in terms of common values.

II. **Concede:** Acknowledge the wisdom of an aspect of the opposing position.

III. **Provide a thesis statement**—a direct statement of your position, qualified as necessary.

IV. **Present your most plausible reasons and evidence.**

V. **Conclude:** Reiterate shared values.

Whatever organizational strategy you adopt, do not hesitate to change your outline as necessary while drafting and revising. For instance, you might find it more effective to hold back on presenting your own position until you have discussed unacceptable alternatives. Or you might find a more powerful way to order the reasons for supporting your position. The purpose of an outline is to identify the basic components of your argument and to help you organize them effectively, not to lock you into a particular structure.

For more on outlining, see Chapter 9, pp. 320–24.

Consider document design.

Think about whether visual or audio elements—photographs, graphics, snippets of interviews with experts—would strengthen your position argument. If you can recall position arguments you've read in newspapers (op-eds and editorials generally argue for positions), on Web pages, and on blogs, what visual or audio elements were used to establish the writer's credibility and to appeal to the reader logically, ethically, or emotionally? Position arguments do not require visual or audio examples to be effective, but these elements can be helpful.

Note: Be sure to cite the source of visual or audio elements you didn't create, and get permission from the source if your essay is going to be published on a Web site that will be accessible outside your class or college.

Consider also whether your readers might benefit from design features, such as headings, bulleted or numbered lists, or other typographic elements that can make your argument easier to follow.

Write the opening sentences.

Review what you have written to see if you have something that would help you frame or reframe the issue for your readers while also grabbing their attention, or try some of these opening strategies:

Begin with **statistics** *that would help readers grasp the importance of your topic:*

> "Organized sports for young people have become an institution in North America," reports sports journalist Steve Silverman, attracting more than 44 million youngsters according to a recent survey by the National Council of Youth Sports. (Statsky, par. 1)

Start with a **surprising statement** *to capture readers' attention:*

> McDonald's is bad for your kids. (Etzioni, par. 1)

Use a **hypothetical quotation** *to indicate how people typically think about the issue:*

> When the government gathers or analyzes personal information, many people say they're not worried. "I've got nothing to hide," they declare. (Solove, par. 1)

Draft your position argument.

By this point, you have done a lot of writing to

- devise a focused, well-presented issue and take a position on it;
- frame your issue so that readers will be open to your argument;
- support your position with reasons and evidence your readers will find persuasive;
- refute or concede alternative viewpoints on the issue;
- organize your ideas to make them clear, logical, and effective for readers.

Now stitch that material together to create a draft. The next two parts of this Guide to Writing will help you evaluate and improve your draft.

Evaluating the Draft: Using Peer Review

Your instructor may arrange a peer review session in class or online, where you can exchange drafts with your classmates and give one another a thoughtful critical reading, pointing out what works well and suggesting ways to improve the draft. A good critical reading does three things:

1. It lets the writer know how well the reader understands the point of the argument.
2. It praises what works best.
3. It indicates where the draft could be improved and makes suggestions on how to improve it.

One strategy for evaluating a draft is to use the basic features of a position argument as a guide.

A PEER REVIEW GUIDE

A Focused, Well-Presented Issue

How well does the writer present the issue?

Summarize: Tell the writer what you understand the issue to be. If you were already familiar with it and understand it differently, briefly explain.

Praise: Give an example from the essay where the issue and its significance come across effectively.

Critique: Tell the writer where more information about the issue is needed, where more might be done to establish its seriousness, or how the issue could be framed or reframed in a way that would better prepare readers for the argument.

A Well-Supported Position

How well does the writer argue in support of the position?

Summarize: Underline the thesis statement and the main reasons.

Praise: Give an example in the essay where the argument is especially effective; for example, indicate which reason is especially convincing or which supporting evidence is particularly compelling.

Critique: Tell the writer where the argument could be strengthened; for example, indicate how the thesis statement could be made clearer or more appropriately qualified, how the argument could be developed, or where additional support is needed.

An Effective Response to Opposing Views	How effectively has the writer responded to others' reasons and likely objections? **Summarize:** Identify where the writer responds to a reason others use to support their argument or an objection they have to the writer's argument. **Praise:** Give an example in the essay where a concession seems particularly well done or a refutation is convincing. **Critique:** Tell the writer how a concession or refutation could be made more effective, identify a reason or objection the writer should respond to, or note where common ground could be found.
A Clear, Logical Organization	How clearly and logically has the writer organized the argument? **Summarize:** Find the sentence(s) in which the writer states the thesis and forecasts supporting reasons, as well as transitions or repeated key words and phrases. **Praise:** Give an example of how or where the essay succeeds in being especially easy to read, perhaps in its overall organization, clear presentation of the thesis, clear transitions, or effective opening or closing. **Critique:** Tell the writer where the readability could be improved. Can you, for example, suggest better forecasting or clearer transitions? If the overall organization of the essay needs work, make suggestions for rearranging parts or strengthening connections.

Before concluding your review, be sure to address any of the writer's concerns that have not already been addressed.

Improving the Draft: Revising, Editing, and Proofreading

Start improving your draft by reflecting on what you have written thus far:

- Review critical reading comments from your classmates, instructor, or writing center tutor. What problems are your readers identifying?
- Consider your invention writing. What else should you consider?
- Review your draft. What else can you do to support your position more effectively?

Revise your draft.

If your readers are having difficulty with your draft, or if you think there is room for improvement, try some of the strategies listed in the Troubleshooting Guide. They can help you fine-tune your presentation of the genre's basic features.

A TROUBLESHOOTING GUIDE

A Focused, Well-Presented Issue

My readers don't get the point.

- Quote experts or add information—statistics, examples, anecdotes, and so on—to help readers understand what's at stake.
- Consider adding visuals, such as photos, graphs, tables, or charts, to present the issue more clearly.

My readers have a different perspective on the issue than I do.

- Show the limitations of how the issue has traditionally been understood.
- Reframe the issue by showing how it relates to values, concerns, needs, and priorities you share with readers.
- Give concrete examples or anecdotes, facts, and details that could help readers see the issue as you see it.

A Well-Supported Position

My readers do not find my argument clear or persuasive.

- Revisit your thesis statement to make sure your position is stated clearly and directly.
- Reconsider your reasons, or explain how they support your position.
- Add supporting evidence—statistics, examples, authorities, and so on.
- Consider adding visuals, graphs, tables, or charts to support your argument.
- Strengthen the logical, ethical, and emotional appeals of your argument.
- Try outlining your argument; if your organization is weak or illogical, or if your transitional strategies are not working, try reorganizing the material, adding transitional words and phrases, or repeating key words strategically.

An Effective Response to Opposing Views

My readers question my response to opposing arguments or objections to my argument.

- If your refutation is weak, strengthen it with additional or more compelling reasons and evidence.
- If your concession weakens your argument, qualify your position with words like *sometimes* or *often*.
- Consider adding a refutation to your concession.

A Clear, Logical Organization	My readers are confused by my essay or find it difficult to follow.
	• Outline your essay. If necessary, move, add, or delete sections to strengthen coherence. • Consider adding a forecasting statement with key terms that are repeated in topic sentences throughout the essay. • Check for appropriate transitions between sentences, paragraphs, and major sections of your essay. • Review your opening and closing paragraphs. Be sure that your thesis is clearly expressed and that you reaffirm your position in your closing.

Edit and proofread your draft.

Students frequently struggle to maintain a neutral tone when arguing a position they hold dearly. Our research also indicates that incorrect comma usage in sentences with *coordinating conjunctions* and punctuation errors in sentences that use *conjunctive adverbs* are common in position arguments. The following guidelines will help you check your essay for these common errors.

Editing for Tone

To demonstrate that you are treating alternative viewpoints fairly, use words with a positive or neutral connotation (emotional resonance) and avoid name-calling:

▶ Too often . . . the drive to win ~~turns~~ *encourages* parents ~~into monsters threatening~~ *to threaten* umpires.

As you edit your position argument, also watch out for language that is puffed up or pompous:

▶ A coach who had attended the Adelphi workshop tried to ~~operationalize~~ *put into practice* what he had learned there, but the players' ~~progenitors~~ *parents* would not support him.

Using Commas before Coordinating Conjunctions

In essays that argue a position, writers often use coordinating conjunctions (*and, but, for, or, nor, so,* and *yet*) to join related **independent clauses**—groups of words that can stand alone as complete sentences—to create *compound sentences*. Consider this example from Jessica Statsky's essay:

▶ [independent clause 1: Winning and losing may be an inevitable part of adult life][comma: ,] [coord. conj.: but] [independent clause 2: they should not be part of childhood.] (par. 6)

In this sentence, Statsky links two complete ideas of equal importance with the coordinating conjunction *but* to emphasize contrast.

The Problem Two common errors occur in sentences like these:

1. A comma may be left out when two independent clauses are linked by a coordinating conjunction.
2. A comma may be inserted before the coordinating conjunction when one of the sentence parts is not an independent clause.

The Correction Add a comma before coordinating conjunctions that join two independent clauses, as in the following example:

▶ The new immigration laws will bring in more skilled people, but their presence will take jobs away from other Americans.

Omit the comma when coordinating conjunctions join phrases that are not independent clauses:

▶ We need people with special talents/ and diverse skills to make the United States a stronger nation.

Avoiding Comma Splices When Using Conjunctive Adverbs to Link Independent Clauses

Conjunctive adverbs (such as *consequently, furthermore, however, moreover, therefore,* and *thus*) indicate the logical relationships among ideas. For example, words like *thus* and *therefore* are used to alert readers that a conclusion is coming, and words like *furthermore* and *moreover* are used to alert readers to expect additional ideas on the same topic. When writers take a position, they often use conjunctive adverbs to link independent clauses.

Consider this example:

conj. adv.

independent clause 1

▶ Children watching television recognize violence but not its intention; thus, they become desensitized to violence.

independent clause 2 — semicolon — comma

In this sentence, the writer uses the word *thus* to indicate that he is drawing a conclusion.

The Problem A *comma splice* is one error that often occurs when writers use a comma before a conjunctive adverb linking two independent clauses.

The Correction Use a semicolon before and a comma after a conjunctive adverb when it links two independent clauses:

▶ The recent vote on increasing student fees produced a disappointing turnout/; moreover, the presence of campaign literature on ballot tables violated voting procedures.

Make sure that both parts of the sentence are independent clauses before inserting a semicolon, a conjunctive adverb, and a comma to link them. If one or both parts cannot stand alone, add a subject, a verb, or both as needed to avoid a *sentence fragment:*

▸ Children watching television recognize violence; however, ~~not~~ *they do not recognize* its intention.

Alternatively, you may replace the semicolon, conjunctive adverb, and comma with a coordinating conjunction:

▸ Children watching television recognize violence~~; however,~~ *but* not its intention.

A Common Problem for Multilingual Writers: Subtle Differences in Meaning

Because the distinctions in meaning among some common conjunctive adverbs are subtle, nonnative speakers often have difficulty using them accurately. For example, the difference between *however* and *nevertheless* is small; each is used to introduce a contrasting statement. But *nevertheless* emphasizes the contrast, whereas *however* softens it. Check usage of such terms in an English dictionary rather than a bilingual one. *The American Heritage Dictionary of the English Language* has special usage notes to help distinguish frequently confused words.

Reflecting on What You Have Learned

You have learned a great deal about arguing for a position from reading several position arguments and from writing one of your own. To consolidate your learning, reflect not only on what you learned but also on how you learned it.

ANALYZE & WRITE

Write a blog post, a letter to your instructor or a classmate, or an e-mail message to a student who will take this course next term, using the writing prompt that seems most productive for you:

- Explain how your purpose and audience influenced one of your decisions as a writer, such as how you presented the issue, the strategies you used in arguing your position, or the ways in which you attempted to counter possible objections.
- Discuss what you learned about yourself as a writer in the process of writing this essay. For example, what part of the process did you find most challenging? Did you try anything new, like getting a critical reading of your draft or outlining your draft in order to revise it? If so, how well did it work?
- Which of the readings in this chapter influenced your essay? Be sure to cite specific examples from your essay and the reading.
- If you got good advice from a critical reader, explain exactly how the person helped you—perhaps by questioning the way you addressed your audience or the kinds of evidence you offered in support of your position.

7

Proposing a Solution

Can a student convince his professor that giving infrequent, high-stakes exams is a bad idea? Will placing a tax on sugary drinks help fight the country's "obesity epidemic"? Should we try out a law professor's idea to solve the shortage of kidneys for transplantation? These are some of the problems and solutions addressed by the proposals in this chapter. Proposals like these need to convince their audience, first, that the problem actually exists and is serious and, second, that the proposed solution not only will solve the problem but is the best available option.

People make proposals for various purposes and audiences and publish them in a variety of media. For example, students in a health sciences course might collaborate on a project to build a Web page that informs the community about a water quality problem, evaluates the feasibility of alternative solutions, and argues for their preferred solution. A blogger might post a proposal to solve the problem of the rising college loan default rate, arguing that truth in advertising laws should be used to crack down on for-profit colleges that use aggressive recruiting tactics to target low-income students.

In this chapter, we ask you to identify a problem you care about and write a proposal to solve it. By analyzing the selections in the Guide to Reading that follows, you will learn how to make a convincing case for the solution you propose. The Guide to Writing later in the chapter will show you ways to use the basic features of the genre to make your proposal inventive as well as practical.

PRACTICING THE GENRE

Arguing That a Solution Is Feasible

Proposals often succeed or fail on the strength of the argument that the proposed solution is feasible. To practice making a feasibility argument, get together with two or three other students and follow these guidelines:

Part 1. Begin by identifying a problem you face as a student in one of your college courses (this course or a different one). Next, discuss the problem in your group, and choose one of these solutions (or think of another solution): The instructor should drop one of the assigned books, offer special study sessions, or post study sheets on the readings.

Then discuss the following questions to determine how you could demonstrate to the instructor that your solution is feasible:

- Is it doable? List specific steps that the instructor would need to take.
- Is it worth doing? Identify what implementing the solution would cost the instructor (in terms of time, for example) compared to how much it would benefit students (in terms of learning, for example).
- Would it work? To prove that it would actually help solve the problem, you could show how it would eliminate a cause of the problem or how it has worked elsewhere, for example.

Part 2. As a group, discuss what you learned.

- **What did you learn about demonstrating that your proposed solution is feasible?** Typically, a proposal tries to convince the audience that the solution is doable, is worth the time and money, and would actually help solve the problem. Are all three elements of feasibility necessary? If not, which is most important? Why?
- **Think about how the rhetorical situation of your proposal—the purpose, audience, and medium—affects how you should argue for your solution's feasibility.** For example, how would you change your argument about the negative effects of relying on high-stakes exams if you were trying to convince a group of professors at a conference about undergraduate teaching versus an administrator who controls the budget or schedule? Would feasibility be equally important to both groups?

Analyzing Proposals

As you read the selections in this chapter, you will see how different writers argue for a solution:

- Patrick O'Malley argues for more low-stakes quizzes (pp. 235–41).
- Eric Posner argues for an "altruism exchange" to motivate kidney donors (pp. 241–44).
- Kelly D. Brownell and Thomas R. Frieden propose raising taxes on sugary soft drinks as a way to stem the "obesity epidemic" (pp. 248–52).

Analyzing how these writers define their problems, argue for their solutions, respond to opposing views, and organize their writing will help you see how you can use these techniques to make your own proposals clear and compelling for your readers.

Determine the writer's purpose and audience.

When reading the proposals that follow, ask yourself questions like these:

What seems to be the writer's purpose (or multiple purposes)?

- To convince readers that the problem truly exists and needs immediate action?
- To persuade readers that the writer's proposed solution is better than alternative solutions?
- To rekindle readers' interest in a long-standing problem?

What does the writer assume about the audience?

- That readers will be unaware of the problem?
- That they will recognize the existence of the problem but fail to take it seriously?
- That they will think the problem has already been solved?
- That they will prefer an alternative solution?

Assess the genre's basic features.

Basic Features

A Focused, Well-Defined Problem

A Well-Argued Solution

An Effective Response to Objections and Alternative Solutions

A Clear, Logical Organization

As you read the proposals in this chapter, consider how different authors incorporate the basic features of the genre. The examples that follow are drawn from the reading selections that appear later in this Guide to Reading.

A FOCUSED, WELL-DEFINED PROBLEM

Read first to see how the writer defines or frames the problem. Framing a problem is a way of preparing readers for the proposed solution by focusing on the aspect of the problem the proposal tries to solve. In "More Testing, More Learning," for example, student Patrick O'Malley frames the problem in terms of the detrimental effects of high-stakes exams on students' learning. If O'Malley were writing to students instead of their teachers, he might have framed the problem in terms of students' poor study habits or procrastination. By framing the problem as he does, he indicates that teachers, rather than students, have the ability to solve the problem and tries to convince readers that it is real and serious.

Determine, how (and how well) the writer frames the problem—for example,

- by recounting *anecdotes* or constructing *scenarios* to show how the problem affects people:

EXAMPLE It's late at night. The final's tomorrow. (O'Malley, par. 1)

- by giving *examples* to make the problem less abstract:

EXAMPLE For example, research by Karpicke and Blunt (2011) published in *Science* found that testing was more effective than other, more traditional methods of studying both for comprehension and for analysis. (O'Malley, par. 4)

- by listing the negative *effects* of the problem:

EXAMPLE Diet-related diseases also cost society in terms of decreased work productivity, increased absenteeism, poorer school performance, and reduced fitness on the part of military recruits, among other negative effects. (Brownell and Frieden, par. 5)

Cause
Effect

Consider also how the writer uses research studies and statistics to demonstrate the severity of the problem. Look for source material, and notice whether the writer emphasizes the credibility of the research by including the expert's name and credentials or by identifying the publication in which the study appeared at the beginning of the sentence in which the study is mentioned:

Emphasizes credibility

▶ Dr. X at University of Y has found that ________.

▶ A study published in *Journal X* shows that ________.

EXAMPLE A 2006 study reported in the journal *Psychological Science* concluded that "taking repeated tests . . . leads to better . . . retention . . . ," according to the study's coauthors, Henry L. Roediger and Jeffrey Karpicke (ScienceWatch.com, 2008). (O'Malley, par. 4)

Alternatively, the writer may emphasize the data by putting the results of the study or statistics up front and identifying the source later in the sentence or in the parenthetical citation, as in the following:

Emphasizes data

▶ ________ percent of group X believe/work/struggle ________.

EXAMPLE The estimated price—perhaps in the range of $100,000 per kidney—would be less than the cost of dialysis (more than $70,000 per patient per year [Costs]). (Posner, par. 2)

In contexts where sources are not normally cited (such as newspapers and certain Web sites) or where the information is widely available, the writer may cite statistics without indicating a specific source:

▶ Research findings show that ________ (source).

EXAMPLE More than 100,000 people languish on the waitlist for kidneys, thousands of them dying before they receive a transplant. In 2012, almost 35,000 people joined the waitlist, while only 17,000 received transplants. (Posner, par. 1)

In academic writing, the sources of such statistics must be cited.

A WELL-ARGUED SOLUTION

To argue convincingly for a solution to a problem, writers need to *make clear exactly what is being proposed and offer supporting reasons and evidence* showing that the proposed solution

- will help solve the problem;
- can be implemented;
- is worth the expense, time, and effort to do so.

Read first to find the proposed solution, usually declared in a *thesis statement* early in the essay. Typically, the thesis describes the proposed solution briefly and indicates how it would solve the problem, as in this example, which contrasts the problem's disadvantages with the solution's benefits:

Problem and its *disadvantages*

Thesis proposing solution and its benefits

So, not only do high-stakes exams *discourage frequent study and undermine students' performance, they also do long-term damage to students' cognitive development*. If professors gave brief exams at frequent intervals, students would be spurred to learn more and worry less. They would study more regularly, perform better on tests, and enhance their cognitive functioning. (O'Malley, par. 2)

Then check to see how the writer presents the supporting reasons *and* evidence, *and consider how compelling the argument is likely to be, given the writer's purpose and audience*. The following sentence strategies and accompanying examples suggest the kinds of reasons and evidence proposal writers often employ to present their argument, as well as the writing strategies they represent:

- The proposed solution would reduce or eliminate a major cause of the problem and would (or could) have beneficial effects:

Cause/effect

► As research shows, solution X would stop something harmful/change habits/reverse a decline, and would lead to/encourage ________.

EXAMPLE A review conducted by Yale University's Rudd Center for Food Policy and Obesity suggested that . . . a tax on sugared beverages would encourage consumers to switch to more healthful beverages, which would lead to reduced caloric intake and less weight gain. (Brownell and Frieden, par. 3)

- A similar solution has worked elsewhere:

Comparison

► Solution X has worked for problem Y, so it could work for this problem as well.

EXAMPLE Taxes on tobacco products have been highly effective in reducing consumption, and data indicate that higher prices also reduce soda consumption. (Brownell and Frieden, par. 3)

- The necessary steps to put the solution into practice can be taken without excessive cost or inconvenience:

Process analysis ▶ This solution is easy to implement: first do ________ and then do ________.

EXAMPLE Ideally, a professor would give an in-class test or quiz after each unit. . . . These exams should be given weekly or at least twice monthly. . . . Exams should take no more than 15 or 20 minutes. (O'Malley, par. 3)

- Stakeholders could come together behind the proposal:

▶ X and Y are working together on ________.

EXAMPLE Furthermore, professors could help students prepare for midterm and final exams by providing sets of questions from which the exam questions will be selected or announcing possible exam topics at the beginning of the course. (O'Malley, par. 13)

AN EFFECTIVE RESPONSE TO OBJECTIONS AND ALTERNATIVE SOLUTIONS

Read to see how the writer responds to readers' likely objections and to the alternative solutions readers may prefer—for example,

- by **conceding** (accepting) a valid objection and modifying the argument to accommodate it:

▶ To accommodate critic A's concern, instead of doing ________, you could do ________.

- by **refuting** (arguing against) criticism—for example, by demonstrating that an objection is without merit or arguing that an alternative solution would be more costly or less likely to solve the problem than the proposed solution:

▶ Some object that the proposed solution would cost too much/cause too much disruption. However, when you take into consideration the fact that inaction would cost even more/cause more disruption than implementing solution B, you have to conclude that ________.

▶ Although X and Y prefer approach A, solution B would be less expensive/easier to implement because ________.

Here are a few examples showing how the proposals in this chapter refute objections or alternative solutions. Notice that proposal writers often introduce the refutation with a transition that indicates contrast, such as *but, although, nevertheless,* or *however*:

EXAMPLES This system might run afoul of NOTA, but if so, Congress could easily change the law to make it legal, as it has done before. (Posner, par. 12)

Some believe that . . . From the student's perspective, however . . . (O'Malley, par. 9)

Contrasts alternative and proposed solutions

Some argue that . . . , but several considerations support . . . action. The first is . . . The second consideration is . . . A third consideration is . . . (Brownell and Frieden, par. 5)

- by **conceding** and then **refuting** (or the concession-refutation move):

▶ Yes, this solution might result in Problem X, but X can be overcome/avoided by ________.

EXAMPLE If weekly exams still seem too time-consuming to some professors, their frequency could be reduced to every other week or their length to 5 or 10 minutes. In courses where multiple-choice exams are appropriate, several questions could be designed to take only a few minutes to answer. (O'Malley, par. 9)

When reading a proposal, consider whether the writer presents others' views fairly and accurately and whether the writer's rebuttal is likely to be convincing to readers. Pay special attention to the writer's tone in responding to other views, noting any place the tone seems sarcastic or dismissive and considering whether such a tone would be effective given the writer's purpose and audience.

To learn more about constructing arguments, see Chapter 12.

A CLEAR, LOGICAL ORGANIZATION

Look for cues or signposts that help readers identify the parts of the proposal. Identify the topic and find the thesis, which in a proposal asserts the solution. Look also for topic sentences, particularly those that announce the parts of the proposal argument. Notice also any transitions and how they function. For example, all the transitions in the following topic sentences (*another, moreover, still,* and *furthermore*) indicate items in a list. Other transitions you can expect in proposals signal causes or effects (*because, as a result*), exceptions (*but*), concessions (*although*), refutations (*however*), emphasis (*more important*), conclusions (*then, therefore*), and enumerations (*first, second*). Here are the beginnings of several topic sentences from O'Malley's essay:

The main reason professors should give frequent exams is that . . . (par. 4)

Transitions

Another, closely related argument in favor of multiple exams is that . . . (par. 6)

Moreover, professors object to frequent exams because . . . (par. 10)

Still another solution might be to . . . (par. 12)

Furthermore, professors could . . . (par. 13)

For more about writing a thesis statement and topic sentences, see Chapter 11.

Finally, if headings or visuals (such as flowcharts, graphs, tables, photographs, or cartoons) are included, determine how they contribute. Notice whether visuals are referred to in the text and whether they have titles or captions.

Readings

Patrick O'Malley | *More Testing, More Learning*

FRUSTRATED BY what he calls "high-stakes exams," Patrick O'Malley wrote the following proposal while he was a first-year college student. To conduct research into opposing viewpoints, O'Malley interviewed two professors, talked with several students, and read published research on testing. He cited his sources using APA style, as his instructor requested.

As you read, consider the following:

- Think about your own feelings about high-stakes exams. How well does the opening scenario resonate for you?
- Given O'Malley's audience, how convincing do you think his use of sources is likely to be?
- The questions in the margin: Your instructor may ask you to post your answers to a class blog or discussion board or to bring them to class.

1 It's late at night. The final's tomorrow. You got a C on the midterm, so this one will make or break you. Will it be like the midterm? Did you study enough? Did you study the right things? It's too late to drop the course. So what happens if you fail? No time to worry about that now—you've got a ton of notes to go over.

2 Although this last-minute anxiety about midterm and final exams is only too familiar to most college students, many professors may not realize how such major, infrequent, high-stakes exams work against the best interests of students both psychologically and cognitively. They cause unnecessary amounts of stress, placing too much importance on one or two days in the students' entire term, judging ability on a single or dual performance. Reporting on recent research at Cornell University Medical School, Sian Beilock, a psychology professor at the University of Chicago, points out that "stressing about doing well on an important exam can backfire, leading students to 'choke under pressure' or to score less well than they might otherwise score if the stakes weren't so high." Moreover, Cornell's research using fMRI brain scans shows that "the pressures of a big test can reach beyond the exam itself—stunting the cognitive systems that support the attention and memory skills every day" (Beilock, 2010). So, not only do high-stakes exams discourage frequent study and undermine students' performance, they also do long-term damage to students' cognitive development. If professors gave brief exams at frequent

Basic Features

A Focused, Well-Defined Problem

A Well-Argued Solution

An Effective Response to Objections and Alternative Solutions

A Clear, Logical Organization

What is the function of the opening paragraph?

How does framing the problem this way set up the solution?

How does O'Malley use the key terms introduced here throughout the essay?

intervals, students would be spurred to learn more and worry less. They would study more regularly, perform better on tests, and enhance their cognitive functioning.

What does par. 3 contribute to the argument?

3 Ideally, a professor would give an in-class test or quiz after each unit, chapter, or focus of study, depending on the type of class and course material. A physics class might require a test on concepts after every chapter covered, while a history class could necessitate quizzes covering certain time periods or major events. These exams should be given weekly or at least twice monthly. Whenever possible, they should consist of two or three essay questions rather than many multiple-choice or short-answer questions. To preserve class time for lecture and discussion, exams should take no more than 15 or 20 minutes.

How does O'Malley introduce this reason? What kinds of support does he offer?

4 The main reason professors should give frequent exams is that when they do and when they provide feedback to students on how well they are doing, students learn more in the course and perform better on major exams, projects, and papers. It makes sense that in a challenging course containing a great deal of material, students will learn more of it and put it to better use if they have to apply or "practice" it frequently on exams, which also helps them find out how much they are learning and what they need to go over again. A 2006 study reported in the journal *Psychological Science* concluded that "taking repeated tests on material leads to better long-term retention than repeated studying," according to the study's coauthors, Henry L. Roediger and Jeffrey Karpicke (ScienceWatch.com, 2008). When asked what the impact of this breakthrough research would be, they responded: "We hope that this research may be picked up in educational circles as a way to improve educational practices, both for students in the classroom and as a study strategy outside of class." The new field of mind, brain, and education research advocates the use of "retrieval testing." For example, research by Karpicke and Blunt (2011) published in *Science* found that testing was more effective than other, more traditional methods of studying both for comprehension and for analysis. Why retrieval testing works is not known. UCLA psychologist Robert Bjork speculates that it may be effective because "when we use our memories by retrieving things, we change our access" to that information. "What we recall," therefore, "becomes more recallable in the future" (qtd. in Belluck, 2011).

How does O'Malley integrate and cite sources in pars. 4 and 5?

5 Many students already recognize the value of frequent testing, but their reason is that they need the professor's feedback. A Harvard study notes students' "strong preference for frequent evaluation in a course." Harvard students feel they learn least in courses that have "only a midterm and a final exam, with no other personal evaluation." Students believe they learn most in courses with "many opportunities to see how they are doing" (Light, 1990, p. 32). In a review of a number of studies of student learning, Frederiksen (1984) reports that students who take weekly quizzes achieve higher scores on final exams than students who take only a midterm exam and that testing increases retention of material tested.

6 Another, closely related argument in favor of multiple exams is that they encourage students to improve their study habits. Greater frequency in test taking means greater frequency in studying for tests. Students prone to cramming will be required—or at least strongly motivated—to open their textbooks and notebooks more often, making them less likely to resort to long, kamikaze nights of studying for major exams. Since there is so much to be learned in the typical course, it makes sense that frequent, careful study and review are highly beneficial. But students need motivation to study regularly, and nothing works like an exam. If students had frequent exams in all their courses, they would have to schedule study time each week and would gradually develop a habit of frequent study. It might be argued that students are adults who have to learn how to manage their own lives, but learning history or physics is more complicated than learning to drive a car or balance a checkbook. Students need coaching and practice in learning. The right way to learn new material needs to become a habit, and I believe that frequent exams are key to developing good habits of study and learning. The Harvard study concludes that "tying regular evaluation to good course organization enables students to plan their work more than a few days in advance. If quizzes and homework are scheduled on specific days, students plan their work to capitalize on them" (Light, 1990, p. 33).

How does O'Malley support this reason? Why does he include it?

How does O'Malley introduce and respond to this possible objection?

7 By encouraging regular study habits, frequent exams would also decrease anxiety by reducing the procrastination that produces anxiety. Students would benefit psychologically if they were not subjected to the emotional ups and downs caused by major exams, when after being virtually worry-free for weeks

How effectively does O'Malley use this source?

they are suddenly ready to check into the psychiatric ward. Researchers at the University of Vermont found a strong relationship among procrastination, anxiety, and achievement. Students who regularly put off studying for exams had continuing high anxiety and lower grades than students who procrastinated less. The researchers found that even "low" procrastinators did not study regularly and recommended that professors give frequent assignments and exams to reduce procrastination and increase achievement (Rothblum, Solomon, & Murakami, 1986, pp. 393–394).

8 Research supports my proposed solution to the problem I have described. Common sense as well as my experience and that of many of my friends support it. Why, then, do so few professors give frequent brief exams?

What is the purpose of this question?

9 Some believe that such exams take up too much of the limited class time available to cover the material in the course. Most courses meet 150 minutes a week—three times a week for 50 minutes each time. A 20-minute weekly exam might take 30 minutes to administer, and that is one-fifth of each week's class time. From the student's perspective, however, this time is well spent. Better learning and greater confidence about the course seem a good trade-off for another 30 minutes of lecture. Moreover, time lost to lecturing or discussion could easily be made up in students' learning on their own through careful regular study for the weekly exams. If weekly exams still seem too time-consuming to some professors, their frequency could be reduced to every other week or their length to 5 or 10 minutes. In courses where multiple-choice exams are appropriate, several questions could be designed to take only a few minutes to answer.

How does O'Malley argue against possible objections in pars. 9 and 10?

10 Moreover, professors object to frequent exams because they take too much time to read and grade. In a 20-minute essay exam, a well-prepared student can easily write two pages. A relatively small class of 30 students might then produce 60 pages, no small amount of material to read each week. A large class of 100 or more students would produce an insurmountable pile of material. There are a number of responses to this objection. Again, professors could give exams every other week or make them very short. Instead of reading them closely, they could skim them quickly to see whether students understand an idea or can apply it to an unfamiliar problem; and instead of numerical or letter grades, they could give a plus, check, or minus.

Exams could be collected and responded to only every third or fourth week. Professors who have readers or teaching assistants could rely on them to grade or check exams. And the Scantron machine is always available for instant grading of multiple-choice exams. Finally, frequent exams could be given *in place of* a midterm exam or out-of-class essay assignment.

11 Since frequent exams seem to some professors to create too many problems, however, it is reasonable to consider alternative ways to achieve the same goals. One alternative solution is to implement a program that would improve study skills. While such a program might teach students how to study for exams, it cannot prevent procrastination or reduce "large test anxiety" by a substantial amount. One research team studying anxiety and test performance found that study skills training was not effective in reducing anxiety or improving performance (Dendato & Diener, 1986, p. 134). This team, which also reviewed other research that reached the same conclusion, did find that a combination of "cognitive/relaxation therapy" and study skills training was effective. This possible solution seems complicated, however, not to mention time-consuming and expensive. It seems much easier and more effective to change the cause of the bad habit rather than treat the habit itself. That is, it would make more sense to solve the problem at its root: the method of learning and evaluation.

How effectively does O'Malley present alternative solutions in pars. 11 and 12?

How do the highlighted words and phrases make the argument easy to follow?

12 Still another solution might be to provide frequent study questions for students to answer. These would no doubt be helpful in focusing students' time studying, but students would probably not actually write out the answers unless they were required to. To get students to complete the questions in a timely way, professors would have to collect and check the answers. In that case, however, they might as well devote the time to grading an exam. Even if it asks the same questions, a scheduled exam is preferable to a set of study questions because it takes far less time to write in class, compared to the time students would devote to responding to questions at home. In-class exams also ensure that each student produces his or her own work.

13 Furthermore, professors could help students prepare for midterm and final exams by providing sets of questions from which the exam questions will be selected or announcing possible exam topics at the beginning of the course. This solution would have the advantage of reducing students' anxiety

about learning every fact in the textbook, and it would clarify the course goals, but it would not motivate students to study carefully each new unit, concept, or text chapter in the course. I see this as a way of complementing frequent exams, not as substituting for them.

How effective is this conclusion?

14 From the evidence and from my talks with professors and students, I see frequent, brief in-class exams as the only way to improve students' study habits and learning, reduce their anxiety and procrastination, and increase their satisfaction with college. These exams are not a panacea, but only more parking spaces and a winning football team would do as much to improve college life. Professors can't do much about parking or football, but they can give more frequent exams. Campus administrators should get behind this effort, and professors should get together to consider giving exams more frequently. It would make a difference.

References

Beilock, S. (2010, September 3). Stressing about a high-stakes exam carries consequences beyond the test [Blog post]. Retrieved from http://www.psychologytoday.com/blog/choke/201009/stressing-about-high-stakes-exam-carries-consequences-beyond-the-test

Belluck, P. (2011, January 20). To really learn, quit studying and take a test. *The New York Times*. Retrieved from http://www.nytimes.com/2011/01/21/science/21memory.html

Dendato, K. M., & Diener, D. (1986). Effectiveness of cognitive/relaxation therapy and study skills training in reducing self-reported anxiety and improving the academic performance of test-anxious students. *The Journal of Counseling Psychology, 33*, 131–135.

Frederiksen, N. (1984). The real test bias: Influences of testing on teaching and learning. *American Psychologist, 39*, 193–202.

Karpicke, J. D., & Blunt, J. R. (2011, February 11). Retrieval practice produces more learning than elaborative studying with concept mapping. *Science, 331*(6018), 772–775. doi:10.1126/science.1199327

Light, R. J. (1990). *Explorations with students and faculty about teaching, learning, and student life*. Cambridge, MA: Harvard University Graduate School of Education and Kennedy School of Government.

Rothblum, E. D., Solomon, L., & Murakami, J. (1986). Affective, cognitive, and behavioral differences between high and low procrastinators. *The Journal of Counseling Psychology, 33*, 387–394.

ScienceWatch.com (2008, February). Henry L. Roediger and Jeff Karpicke talk with ScienceWatch.com and answer a few questions about this month's fast breaking paper in the field of psychiatry/psychology [Interview]. Retrieved from http://sciencewatch.com/dr/fbp/2008/08febfbp/08febfbpRoedigerETAL

Eric Posner | *A Moral Market*

Lloyd DeGrane

ERIC POSNER is the Kirkland and Ellis Distinguished Service Professor at the University of Chicago Law School. A prolific author, Posner has over a dozen books and more than a hundred legal articles and book chapters to his credit. As a public intellectual, he also maintains a blog (www.ericposner.com) and an active Twitter feed and writes a regular column for *Slate,* where "A Moral Market" first appeared. Posner had first composed a well-researched academic study on "altruism exchanges" before writing this shorter, more accessible version for a general audience. (Posner's legal article "Altruism Exchanges and the Kidney Shortage," written in collaboration with law professors Stephen J. Choi and G. Mitu Gulati, is available online at chicagounbound.uchicago.edu.) We have converted Posner's links to in-text citations and provided a list of links at the end of the selection. You may have noticed that Chapter 5 of this book includes student writing on "A Moral Market." Your instructor may invite you to read Chapter 5, or you may choose to do so on your own. The activities following this selection, however, do not require familiarity with the material in Chapter 5.

As you read, consider the following questions:

- What might lead you to consider donating one of your kidneys, assuming you could do so without damaging your own health?
- It is currently against the law, as Posner points out, to buy and sell kidneys. Why do you imagine people object to a cash market for organs for transplantation?

1 Sunday is the thirtieth anniversary of the National Organ Transplant Act, but no one wants to celebrate. U.S. policy on organ transplants—especially as applied to kidneys—is a mess. More than 100,000 people languish on the waitlist for kidneys, thousands of them dying before they receive a transplant. In 2012, almost 35,000 people joined the waitlist, while only 17,000 received transplants.

2 Every year the waitlist lengthens. NOTA virtually guaranteed this shortage by shutting down an incipient market in kidneys. Some economists have argued that the best way to encourage people to donate kidneys is to allow people to sell them. Since almost everyone has one unneeded kidney, and most people could use some money, a market would form. The estimated price—perhaps in the range of $100,000 per kidney—would be less than the cost of dialysis (more than $70,000 per patient per year ["Costs"]), even taking into account transplant surgery, and so the donor fee would be paid by insurers, including Medicare and Medicaid.

3 The law reflected a popular, inchoate repugnance at the idea of kidney-selling. Ethicists have tried to supply a philosophical argument. They argue that, if a market for kidneys existed, poor people would be taken advantage of; moreover, we should not treat body parts as "commodities." Neither of these arguments is persuasive. A regulated market that required informed consent would eliminate the worst forms of exploitation and could ensure (as under current law) that kidneys were equally available to rich and poor. If poor people really can't be trusted to make good decisions on their own behalf, then a simple solution is to ban poor people from selling their kidneys while allowing everyone else to do so. Nor is it clear why it's more objectionable to sell a kidney than, say, one's hair, blood plasma, egg cells, or sperm (sale of which is legal in most places within the United States).

4 But political opposition to selling kidneys will not go away, and so the question is how to increase the supply of kidneys without creating a market. Most proposals, including a recent open letter (*Open Letter*) by transplant experts and bioethicists to top government officials, try to thread the needle by giving donors implicit or in-kind compensation, such as travel expenses to the hospital, a tax credit, or priority on the waitlist if they ever need a kidney themselves. The proposals amount to attempts to evade moral objections by allowing limited, implicit compensation rather than a price in dollars.

5 But it is possible to be more imaginative. It may help to sort out the source of moral objections to a market in kidneys. One possible view is that people should not *exchange* their body parts for other things of value. Another is that people shouldn't *profit* on the sale of their body parts. These ideas are different. To see why, imagine that Martha wants to donate her kidney to her daughter (this is legal, of course), but the daughter's body would reject her mother's kidney because the mother's and daughter's antigens are not matched ("Transplant Rejection"), or similar enough. Meanwhile, an unrelated person named Frank wants to donate his kidney to his son, but also cannot do so because of immunological incompatibility. But it happens that Martha matches with Frank's son and Frank matches with Martha's daughter. Could Martha donate her kidney to Frank's son in exchange for Frank donating his kidney to Martha's daughter? Under NOTA, the answer was (or was believed to be) no: An exchange of any kind was illegal. In a subsequent law, called the Charlie W. Norwood Living Organ Donation Act, Congress clarified that this type of exchange, called a "paired donation," is lawful. But only a few hundred transplants per year are arranged through paired donations because it is hard to find and arrange matches between strangers.

6 So while the Norwood Act did not solve the problem of undersupply of kidneys, it did reveal a key feature of public morality—that people don't object to exchanges of kidneys. That means the feature of markets they must object to is not exchange but profit. A donor like Martha

may give her kidney to a stranger like Frank, who wants it for his son, as long as what she gets in return is not money that she spends on herself, but something different—a benefit for another person, her daughter.

7 But if that's true, we can do better than paired donations, as I argue in a paper (Posner) written with law professors Stephen Choi and Mitu Gulati. Suppose that Martha needs a kidney for her daughter but Frank's son does not need a kidney. Martha proposes to Frank that if Frank donates his kidney to her daughter, Martha (or, actually, Martha's insurer, which, remember, wants to avoid the high cost of dialysis) will make a $100,000 contribution to Frank's favorite charity—say, Doctors Without Borders, which could use the money to combat Ebola in Liberia. Frank, of course, might say no; but there are likely other people who might be willing to take Martha up on the deal.

8 If you're skeptical, you should be aware that every year a few hundred people donate their kidneys to strangers in return for nothing at all. There must certainly be additional people who would stop short of donating a kidney to help merely a single stranger but would be willing to do so to help hundreds or thousands of desperate people—who need medical care, disaster relief, or basic infrastructure like irrigation systems. There are also probably thousands of people who can't help a friend or loved one who needs a kidney because of the lack of a match but who would be willing to donate their own kidney to a pool of organs if it would secure the matched kidney of someone else. And friends and relatives who can't donate a kidney would surely donate money if doing so enabled them to secure a kidney for a friend or loved one. Frank might donate his kidney to Martha's daughter for another reason. Suppose Frank's son does not yet have end-stage renal disease but he does suffer from a medical condition that will probably lead to kidney shutdown decades from now. Frank worries that by the time his son needs a kidney, Frank will be too old to participate in a paired donation. So Frank agrees to donate a kidney to Martha's daughter today in return for the right to have his son receive a kidney from someone else when the son needs it.

9 How would this work? Imagine that charities set up "altruism exchanges" that accept donations of various types—kidneys, money, whatever. The charities then do two things. First, they distribute kidneys and other resources to those who need them. Second, they give to donors "credits" that the donors can take back to the charity in the future. The credits can then be used to obtain kidneys for loved ones, cash distributions to causes that they care about, and other resources as long as they are allocated to people other than the donors themselves.

10 The charities would vastly strengthen people's incentives to donate a kidney. If you donate your kidney at age 20, you would be given a credit, which you could then use—immediately or later in life—to obtain a charitable benefit for someone you care about or a cause that matters to you. It could be a kidney for your own child, or it could be housing, food, and water for victims of natural disasters. It could be for malaria control in Africa or girls' education in Pakistan. The charity would also make it much easier to arrange kidney matches. Martha would no longer need to find someone who matched with her daughter. Instead, Martha would donate her kidney to a stranger via the altruism exchange, and then could use her credit when the first match for her daughter came along, which could be immediately or years later.

11 The system would increase the supply of kidneys by giving donors the power to help more than a single stranger. Everyone

would get to be a major philanthropist, and the more people who participated, the larger the benefits. At the same time, the profit motive would be avoided. All exchanges must be altruistically motivated. The system would not necessarily help everyone. People who don't have generous friends and relatives may still find themselves on the waitlist for transplants. But those people would still be better off than under the current system because the larger supply of kidneys—donated by people who exchanged their kidneys for other types of charitable benefits financed by people who donated money—would shorten the waitlist considerably.

12 This system might run afoul of NOTA, but if so, Congress could easily change the law to make it legal, as it has done before. Congress would simply need to provide that anyone may donate a kidney and receive in exchange the right to allocate future charitable benefits through a government-approved charity. The dollar value of those benefits could be based on the avoided costs of dialysis. Donors would be forbidden to receive cash or goods. So people couldn't donate kidneys to raise money to buy a Tesla Model D. They could donate kidneys only to help others.

Links

An Open Letter to President Barack Obama, Secretary of Health and Human Services Sylvia Mathews Burwell, Attorney General Eric Holder and Leaders of Congress. W. Kramer, 2014, www.ustransplantopenletter.org/openletter.html.

"Costs of End-Stage Renal Disease." *United States Renal Data Systems Annual Data Report: End-Stage Renal Disease (ESRD) in the United States,* vol. 2, National Institutes of Health / National Institute of Diabetes and Digestive and Kidney Diseases, 2014, www.usrds.org/2014/view/v2_09.aspx.

"Transplant Rejection." *Medline Plus,* US National Library of Medicine, National Institutes of Health / US Department of Health and Human Services, 2 Mar. 2013, www.nlm.nih.gov/medlineplus/ency/article/000815.htm.

Posner, Eric, et al. "Altruism Exchanges and the Kidney Shortage." *Chicago Unbound,* University of Chicago Law School, 2013, chicagounbound.uchicago.edu/cgi/viewcontent.cgi?article=1039&context=law_and_economics. Coase-Sandor Working Paper Series in Law and Economics.

[REFLECT] Make connections: Compromising on a solution.

Because he is determined to find a pragmatic solution—one that will garner widespread public support—Posner seems willing to forge a compromise. That is, although he appears to support the idea of a market in kidneys, he understands that "political opposition to selling kidneys will not go away, and so the question is how to increase the supply of kidneys without creating a market" (par. 4). Think about some conditions under which compromising is the right thing to do. Your instructor may ask you to post your thoughts to a class discussion board or blog, or to discuss them with other students in class. Use these questions to get started:

- What makes this problem so important? How does Posner try to inspire his audience to join with him in the search for a solution?
- How does Posner present his solution as a compromise? What is being compromised by those who support a kidney market and by those who oppose it?
- How does Posner try to convince his readers that this solution would not require them to compromise their moral values? How convincing do you think his argument is likely to be?

[ANALYZE] Use the basic features.

A FOCUSED, WELL-DEFINED PROBLEM: FRAMING THE PROBLEM

Every proposal begins with a problem. What writers say about the problem and how much space they devote to it depends on what they assume their audience already knows and thinks about it. Savvy proposal writers try to present even familiar problems in a way that reminds readers of the problem's seriousness and prepares them for the writer's preferred solution. They often *frame* the problem by focusing attention on *values* they share with their audience. For example, knowing that professors care about learning, Patrick O'Malley says he wants his audience of professors to "realize" that their current exam policy impairs learning and has a detrimental effect on "students' cognitive development" (par. 2).

ANALYZE & WRITE

Write a paragraph analyzing how Posner frames the problem:

1. Given his *Slate* audience, why do you think Posner opens his proposal by pointing out that it is the anniversary of the National Organ Transplant Act (NOTA)?
2. Skim paragraphs 1–3. What kinds of information does Posner include here, and how does this information help him frame the problem around shared values?
3. Consider how, in these paragraphs, Posner introduces the debate between economists and ethicists over what to do about the lack of organs for transplantation. How does setting up these opposing views help Posner frame the problem in a way that prepares his audience for the solution he proposes?

A WELL-ARGUED SOLUTION: MAKING A PERSUASIVE ARGUMENT

To be persuasive, a proposal must demonstrate to the audience that the proposed solution would work—that it would solve or at least lessen the problem—and that it could be implemented without too much effort, time, and cost. Proposals attempting to solve a highly controversial problem, like whether to pay people to donate their kidneys, must also meet a feasibility test. That is, the solution has to be seen as realistic. If your solution (or something like it) has never been implemented, then you might use sentence strategies like these to describe one or more hypothetical **scenarios** to show the audience the result of implementing your solution:

Cues indicating hypotheticals

- ▶ Suppose X does _______.
- ▶ If solution X were implemented, then _______ would result.

EXAMPLE

Ideally, a professor would give an in-class test. . . . A physics class might require a test on concepts . . . while a history class could necessitate quizzes. . . . Exams should be given weekly. (O'Malley, par. 3)

If students had frequent exams in all their courses, they would have to schedule study time each week and would gradually develop a habit of frequent study. (O'Malley, par. 6)

Note that sometimes these hypotheticals use an "if-then" construction, as in the second example. Scenarios work like examples by giving the audience a graphic image of what could happen. But, like an example or an anecdote, a scenario will not be effective unless the audience sees it as a credible, realistic possibility.

ANALYZE & WRITE

Write a paragraph or two analyzing Posner's argument for his proposed solution:

1. Skim paragraphs 9–11. How does Posner try to convince his audience that his proposed solution can be implemented and that it would indeed help solve the problem?
2. Now reread paragraphs 5–8 and 10. Notice the Martha-and-Frank scenarios and the sentence strategies Posner uses. How effective do you think these scenarios are likely to be in convincing Posner's *Slate* audience that his solution is workable?

AN EFFECTIVE RESPONSE TO OBJECTIONS AND ALTERNATIVE SOLUTIONS: FINDING A WAY TO BRIDGE DIFFERENCES

In addition to arguing for the proposed solution, proposal writers need to show that their solution is preferable to alternatives their readers might favor. Patrick O'Malley, for example, identifies several alternative solutions his intended audience (instructors) might bring up, including implementing programs to improve students' study skills, giving students study questions, and handing out possible exam topics to help students prepare. He concedes the benefits of some of these solutions, but he also points out their shortcomings, showing how his solution is better.

ANALYZE & WRITE

Write a paragraph or two analyzing how Posner attempts to show that his solution is the best option:

1. Skim paragraphs 2–5, in which Posner reviews three alternative solutions and the objections raised to each of them:
   - the economists' proposed solution (pars. 2–3);
   - the solution offered by "transplant experts and bioethicists" (par. 4);
   - the "paired donation" solution (par. 5).

   What, if anything, do the objections to all three proposed solutions have in common?
2. Choose one of these alternative solutions to examine closely, identifying the solution being proposed and the objections that have been raised to it.
3. Think about Posner's strategy to "sort out the source of moral objections to a market in kidneys" (par. 5) before proposing his own solution. How does Posner's "altruism exchange" (par. 9) emerge from his analysis of objections to the other solutions? How effective do you think his solution would be in avoiding the same objections?

A CLEAR, LOGICAL ORGANIZATION: CREATING COHERENCE

Writers use a variety of strategies to make a proposal clear and easy to follow. One common strategy is to use a rhetorical question (a question to which no answer is expected) to make a transition from one topic to the next. For example, O'Malley uses a rhetorical question at the end of paragraph 8—"Why, then, do so few professors give frequent brief exams?"—as a transition to the section dealing with likely objections. The two paragraphs following the rhetorical question both begin with an answer:

"Some believe that such exams . . ." (par. 9)

"Moreover, professors object to frequent exams because . . ." (par. 10)

Another strategy is to use transitions. O'Malley, for example, uses transitions such as *moreover* (par. 10), *still another* (12), and *furthermore* (13) in the opening sentence of a paragraph to connect it to the preceding one. Notice the different functions transitions have:

To add an idea	*moreover, also, in addition*
To indicate an opposing idea	*but, however, neither*
To cue a cause-effect relationship	*so, since, because*

ANALYZE & WRITE

Write a paragraph analyzing Posner's use of rhetorical questions and transitions:

1. Reread paragraphs 5 and 9, and highlight the rhetorical question in each. How do these rhetorical questions function as transitions?
2. Now skim the essay, highlighting some of the transitional words or phrases you find. How many appear at the beginning of a paragraph to link it to the preceding paragraph? What role does each play? For example, does the transition indicate that another related idea is coming or that the writer is going to offer an opposing idea?

See Chapter 11, pp. 362–65, for more about transitions.

[RESPOND] Consider possible topics: Moving the masses.

Although Posner proposes a change to law, he ultimately hopes to change the way large numbers of people behave. Think about problems that cannot be solved unless many people change what they are doing. Many such problems can be referred to collectively as the "tragedy of the commons": resources that no one owns—like air, water, and public spaces—are neglected, damaged, or recklessly depleted. For example, consider a proposal that would encourage dorm residents to change sloppy behavior in common areas, encourage those drinking communal coffee to help clean up or make the next pot, or discourage residents from dropping garbage in public parks or playgrounds. The challenge to solving such problems is, of course, that you're unlikely to change public behavior just by making a good argument. Like Posner, you may have to propose a policy change or come up with an incentive, a process that often starts with figuring out why people aren't already doing what you want them to do.

Kelly D. Brownell
Thomas R. Frieden

Ounces of Prevention—The Public Policy Case for Taxes on Sugared Beverages

Courtesy of Kelly Brownell

KELLY D. BROWNELL is a professor of psychology and neuroscience at Duke. An international expert who has published numerous books and articles, including *Food Fight: The Inside Story of the Food Industry, America's Obesity Crisis, and What We Can Do about It* (2003), Brownell received the 2012 American Psychological Association Award for Outstanding Lifetime Contributions to Psychology. He was also featured in the Academy Award–nominated film *Super Size Me*.

Centers for Disease Control and Prevention

THOMAS R. FRIEDEN, a physician specializing in public health, served as the director of the U.S. Centers for Disease Control and Prevention (CDC) under President Barack Obama and as the health commissioner for the city of New York.

Brownell and Frieden's proposal "Ounces of Prevention—The Public Policy Case for Taxes on Sugared Beverages" was originally published in 2009 in the highly respected *New England Journal of Medicine*, which calls itself "the most widely read, cited, and influential general medical periodical in the world." In fact, research published there is often referred to widely throughout the media.

As you read, consider the effect that Brownell and Frieden's use of graphs and formal citation of sources has on their credibility:

- How do the graphs help establish the seriousness of the problem? How do they also help demonstrate the feasibility of the solution the authors propose?
- How do the citations help persuade you to accept the authors' solution? What effect might they have had on their original readers? (Note that the authors use neither of the two citation styles covered in Part 3 of this text. Instead, they use one common to medical journals and publications of the U.S. National Library of Medicine.)

Sugar, rum, and tobacco are commodities which are nowhere necessaries of life, which are become objects of almost universal consumption, and which are therefore extremely proper subjects of taxation.

—Adam Smith, *The Wealth of Nations*, 1776

1 The obesity epidemic has inspired calls for public health measures to prevent diet-related diseases. One controversial idea is now the subject of public debate: food taxes. Forty states already have small taxes on sugared beverages and snack foods, but in the past year, Maine and New York have proposed large taxes on sugared beverages, and similar discussions have begun in other states. The size of the taxes, their potential for generating revenue and reducing consumption, and vigorous opposition by the

beverage industry have resulted in substantial controversy. Because excess consumption of unhealthful foods underlies many leading causes of death, food taxes at local, state, and national levels are likely to remain part of political and public health discourse.

2 Sugar-sweetened beverages (soda sweetened with sugar, corn syrup, or other caloric sweeteners and other carbonated and uncarbonated drinks, such as sports and energy drinks) may be the single largest driver of the obesity epidemic. A recent meta-analysis found that the intake of sugared beverages is associated with increased body weight, poor nutrition, and displacement of more healthful beverages; increasing consumption increases risk for obesity and diabetes; the strongest effects are seen in studies with the best methods (e.g., longitudinal and interventional vs. correlational studies);* and interventional studies show that reduced intake of soft drinks improves health.[1] Studies that do not support a relationship between consumption of sugared beverages and health outcomes tend to be conducted by authors supported by the beverage industry.[2] Sugared beverages are marketed extensively to children and adolescents, and in the mid-1990s, children's intake of sugared beverages surpassed that of milk. In the past decade, per capita intake of calories from sugar-sweetened beverages has increased by nearly 30 percent (see bar graph Daily Caloric Intake from Sugar-Sweetened Drinks in the United States);[3] beverages now account for 10 to 15 percent of the calories consumed by children and adolescents. For each extra can or glass of sugared beverage consumed per day, the likelihood of a child's becoming obese increases by 60 percent.[4]

3 Taxes on tobacco products have been highly effective in reducing consumption, and data indicate that higher prices also reduce soda consumption. A review conducted by Yale University's Rudd Center for Food Policy and Obesity suggested that for every 10 percent increase in price, consumption decreases by 7.8 percent. An industry trade publication reported even larger reductions: as prices of carbonated soft drinks increased by 6.8 percent, sales dropped by 7.8 percent, and as Coca-Cola prices increased by 12 percent, sales dropped by 14.6 percent.[5] Such studies—and the economic principles that support their findings—suggest that a tax on sugared beverages would encourage consumers to switch to more healthful beverages, which would lead to reduced caloric intake and less weight gain.

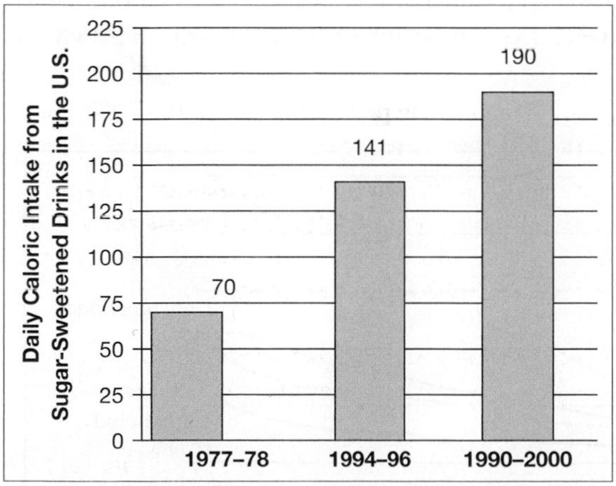

Daily Caloric Intake from Sugar-Sweetened Drinks in the United States.
Data are from Nielsen and Popkin.[3]

*In a *longitudinal* study, researchers observe changes taking place over a long period of time; in an *interventional* study, investigators give research subjects a measured amount of whatever is being studied and note its effects; and in a *correlational* study, researchers examine statistics to see if two or more variables have a mathematically significant similarity. [Editor's note]

4 The increasing affordability of soda—and the decreasing affordability of fresh fruits and vegetables (see line graph)—probably contributes to the rise in obesity in the United States. In 2008, a group of child and health care advocates in New York proposed a one-penny-per-ounce excise tax on sugared beverages, which would be expected to reduce consumption by 13 percent—about two servings per week per person. Even if one quarter of the calories consumed from sugared beverages are replaced by other food, the decrease in consumption would lead to an estimated reduction of 8,000 calories per person per year—slightly more than 2 pounds each year for the average person. Such a reduction in calorie consumption would be expected to substantially reduce the risk of obesity and diabetes and may also reduce the risk of heart disease and other conditions.

5 Some argue that government should not interfere in the market and that products and prices will change as consumers demand more healthful food, but several considerations support government action. The first is externality—costs to parties not directly involved in a transaction. The contribution of unhealthful diets to health care costs is already high and is increasing—an estimated $79 billion is spent annually for overweight and obesity alone—and approximately half of these costs are paid by Medicare and Medicaid, at taxpayers' expense. Diet-related diseases also cost society in terms of decreased work productivity, increased absenteeism, poorer school performance, and reduced fitness on the part of military recruits, among other negative effects. The second consideration is information asymmetry between the parties to a transaction. In the case of sugared beverages, marketers commonly make health claims (e.g., that such beverages provide energy or vitamins) and use techniques that exploit the cognitive vulnerabilities of young children, who often cannot distinguish a television program from an advertisement. A third consideration is revenue generation, which can further increase the societal benefits of

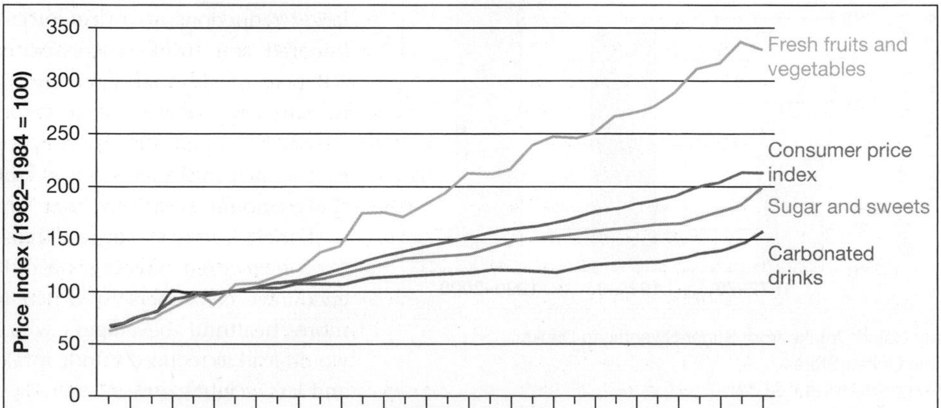

Relative Price Changes for Fresh Fruits and Vegetables, Sugar and Sweets, and Carbonated Drinks, 1978–2009.

Data are from the U.S. Bureau of Labor Statistics and represent the U.S. city averages for all urban consumers in January of each year.

a tax on soft drinks. A penny-per-ounce excise tax would raise an estimated $1.2 billion in New York State alone. In times of economic hardship, taxes that both generate this much revenue and promote health are better options than revenue initiatives that may have adverse effects.

6 Objections have certainly been raised: that such a tax would be regressive, that food taxes are not comparable to tobacco or alcohol taxes because people must eat to survive, that it is unfair to single out one type of food for taxation, and that the tax will not solve the obesity problem. But the poor are disproportionately affected by diet-related diseases and would derive the greatest benefit from reduced consumption; sugared beverages are not necessary for survival; Americans consume about 250 to 300 more calories daily today than they did several decades ago, and nearly half this increase is accounted for by consumption of sugared beverages; and though no single intervention will solve the obesity problem, that is hardly a reason to take no action.

7 The full impact of public policies becomes apparent only after they take effect. We can estimate changes in sugared-drink consumption that would be prompted by a tax, but accompanying changes in the consumption of other foods or beverages are more difficult to predict. One question is whether the proportions of calories consumed in liquid and solid foods would change. And shifts among beverages would have different effects depending on whether consumers substituted water, milk, diet drinks, or equivalent generic brands of sugared drinks.

8 Effects will also vary depending on whether the tax is designed to reduce consumption, generate revenue, or both; the size of the tax; whether the revenue is earmarked for programs related to nutrition and health; and where in the production and distribution chain the tax is applied. Given the heavy consumption of sugared beverages, even small taxes will generate substantial revenue, but only heftier taxes will significantly reduce consumption. Sales taxes are the most common form of food tax, but because they are levied as a percentage of the retail price, they encourage the purchase of less-expensive brands or larger containers. Excise taxes structured as a fixed cost per ounce provide an incentive to buy less and hence would be much more effective in reducing consumption and improving health. In addition, manufacturers generally pass the cost of an excise tax along to their customers, including it in the price consumers see when they are making their selection, whereas sales taxes are seen only at the cash register.

9 Although a tax on sugared beverages would have health benefits regardless of how the revenue was used, the popularity of such a proposal increases greatly if revenues are used for programs to prevent childhood obesity, such as media campaigns, facilities and programs for physical activity, and healthier food in schools. Poll results show that support of a tax on sugared beverages ranges from 37 to 72 percent; a poll of New York residents found that 52 percent supported a "soda tax," but the number rose to 72 percent when respondents were told that the revenue would be used for obesity prevention. Perhaps the most defensible approach is to use revenue to subsidize the purchase of healthful foods. The public would then see a relationship between tax and benefit, and any regressive effects would be counteracted by the reduced costs of healthful food.

10 A penny-per-ounce excise tax could reduce consumption of sugared beverages by more than 10 percent. It is difficult to imagine producing behavior change of this magnitude through education alone, even if government devoted massive resources to the task. In contrast, a sales tax on

sugared drinks would generate considerable revenue, and as with the tax on tobacco, it could become a key tool in efforts to improve health.

References

1. Vartanian LR, Schwartz MB, Brownell KD. Effects of soft drink consumption on nutrition and health: a systematic review and meta-analysis. Am J Public Health 2007;97:667–675.
2. Forshee RA, Anderson PA, Storey ML. Sugar-sweetened beverages and body mass index in children and adolescents: a meta-analysis. Am J Clin Nutr 2008;87:1662–1671.
3. Nielsen SJ, Popkin BM. Changes in beverage intake between 1977 and 2001. Am J Prev Med 2004; 27:205–210.
4. Ludwig DS, Peterson KE, Gortmaker SL. Relation between consumption of sugar-sweetened drinks and childhood obesity: a prospective, observational analysis. Lancet 2001;357:505–508.
5. Elasticity: big price increases cause Coke volume to plummet. Beverage Digest. November 21, 2008:3–4.

[REFLECT] Make connections: Government problem solving.

Brownell and Frieden explicitly argue in favor of federal or state government taking action to address public health problems, such as those related to obesity and smoking. Imposing taxes is one thing government can do. Another action is to require that foods be labeled with accurate nutritional information.

Write a few paragraphs considering the right and responsibility of government to solve public health problems. Your instructor may ask you to post your thoughts on a class discussion board or to discuss them with other students in class. Use these questions to get started:

- Consider what actions government *could* take to address public health problems and whether government *should* take such actions.
- Think about how you would respond to Brownell and Frieden's argument that "though no single intervention will solve the obesity problem, that is hardly a reason to take no action" (par. 6).

[ANALYZE] Use the basic features.

A FOCUSED, WELL-DEFINED PROBLEM: CITING RESEARCH STUDIES

Brownell and Frieden identify the problem for which they are proposing a solution in broad terms as the "obesity epidemic" (par. 1). However, they frame the issue by focusing on "sugar-sweetened beverages" (par. 2). To support a causal connection between consuming sugar-sweetened beverages and obesity, they cite research studies.

ANALYZE & WRITE

Write a paragraph or two analyzing more closely how Brownell and Frieden use research to establish a causal connection between sweetened drinks and obesity:

1. Skim paragraph 3 to identify the findings Brownell and Frieden summarize there. Note that these are the findings of a "meta-analysis," which compares different studies researching the same question.
2. Consider how effectively, if at all, these findings support Brownell and Frieden's argument about a cause-effect relationship between consuming sugar-sweetened beverages and obesity.
3. Think about what kinds of studies were done and consider how Brownell and Frieden rate these different kinds of studies. Why might it be helpful for Brownell and Frieden's readers from the *New England Journal of Medicine* to know the kinds of studies that have been used and which ones employ "the best methods" and get "the strongest effects" (par. 2)?

A WELL-ARGUED SOLUTION: USING COMPARISON-CONTRAST AND CLASSIFICATION

Like O'Malley, Brownell and Frieden use their title to announce the solution they are proposing: the imposition of a tax on certain beverages. They use writing strategies such as comparison-contrast and classification to support their claims. Even the epigraph quoting Adam Smith, the father of free market economics, is a kind of comparison in that it implicitly associates a figure linked to conservative politics with their proposal, which would generally be considered liberal.

ANALYZE & WRITE

Write a few paragraphs analyzing and evaluating how Brownell and Frieden use comparison and contrast as well as classification strategies to support their proposal:

1. Reread paragraphs 3–4. How do Brownell and Frieden use comparison and contrast to argue for a tax on sweetened beverages?
2. Reread paragraphs 8–9. How do they use classification?
3. Consider the strengths and weaknesses of using these two strategies to support the proposed solution. How are these two writing strategies effective ways of supporting the proposal? What other strategies might work better?

AN EFFECTIVE RESPONSE TO OBJECTIONS AND ALTERNATIVE SOLUTIONS: HANDLING OBJECTIONS

Proposal writers usually try to anticipate readers' objections and concede or refute them. How writers handle objections affects their credibility with readers, who usually expect writers to be respectful of other points of view and to take criticism seriously while still arguing assertively for their solution. Brownell and Frieden anticipate and respond to five objections they would expect their readers to raise.

ANALYZE & WRITE

Write a couple of paragraphs analyzing and evaluating how Brownell and Frieden respond to objections:

1. Reread paragraph 5. First, summarize the objection and their argument refuting it. Then evaluate their response: How effective is it likely to be with readers?
2. Reread paragraph 6, in which the authors respond to a number of objections. What cues do they provide to help you follow their argument?
3. Given their purpose and audience, why do you think Brownell and Frieden focus so much attention on the first objection and group the other objections together in a single paragraph?
4. How would you describe the tone of Brownell and Frieden's refutation? How is their credibility with readers likely to be affected by the way they respond to objections?

A CLEAR, LOGICAL ORGANIZATION: USING GRAPHS

Brownell and Frieden include two graphs in their proposal—a bar graph and a line graph. Bar graphs and line graphs can be used to display numerical and statistical information at different points in time and also to compare groups or data sets by using different color bars or lines.

ANALYZE & WRITE

Write a paragraph analyzing and evaluating how well Brownell and Frieden integrate these graphs:

1. Highlight the sentences in paragraphs 2 and 4 in which Brownell and Frieden introduce each graph. How else do they integrate the graphs into their argument?
2. Consider the sections in which these graphs appear. How might the graphs help demarcate sections and move readers from one section to the next?
3. Look closely at the graphs themselves to see how the information is presented. What do the graphs contribute? Given Brownell and Frieden's purpose and audience, why do you think they chose to include these graphs?

To learn more about using graphics and multimodal elements, see Chapter 13, pp. 390–96.

[RESPOND] Consider possible topics: Improving a group to which you belong.

Consider making a proposal to improve the operation of an organization, a business, or a club to which you belong. For example, you might propose that your college keep administrative offices open in the evenings or on weekends to accommodate working students, or that a child-care center be opened for students who are parents of young children. For a business, you might propose a system to handle customer complaints or a fairer way for employees to arrange their schedules. If you belong to a club that has a problem with the collection of dues, you might propose a new collection system or suggest alternative ways of raising money.

The Writing Assignment

Write an essay proposing a solution to a problem. Choose a problem faced by a community or group to which you belong, and address your proposal to one or more members of the group or to outsiders who might help solve the problem.

This Guide to Writing is designed to help you compose your own proposal and apply what you have learned from reading other essays in the same genre. This Starting Points chart will help you find answers to questions you might have about composing a proposal. The Starting Points chart will help you find the guidance you need, when you need it.

STARTING POINTS: PROPOSING A SOLUTION

A Focused, Well-Defined Problem

How do I come up with a problem to write about?

- Assess the genre's basic features: A focused, well-defined problem. (pp. 230–32)
- Consider possible topics. (pp. 247, 254)
- Choose a problem for which you can propose a solution. (p. 257)

How can I best define the problem for my readers?

- A Focused, Well-Defined Problem: Framing the Problem (p. 245)
- A Focused, Well-Defined Problem: Citing Research Studies (pp. 252–53)
- Frame the problem for your readers. (pp. 257–60)
- Test Your Choice: Defining the Problem (pp. 259–60)
- Assess how the problem has been framed, and reframe it for your readers. (pp. 260–61)
- A Troubleshooting Guide: A Focused, Well-Defined Problem (p. 268)

A Well-Argued Solution

How do I come up with a plausible solution?

- Assess the genre's basic features: A well-argued solution. (pp. 232–33)
- A Well-Argued Solution: Making a Persuasive Argument (pp. 245–46)
- A Well-Argued Solution: Using Comparison-Contrast and Classification (p. 253)
- Develop a possible solution. (pp. 261–62)
- Research your proposal. (pp. 262–63)

(continued)

A Well-Argued Solution	How do I construct an argument supporting my solution? • Assess the genre's basic features: A well-argued solution. (pp. 232–33) • Explain your solution. (p. 262) • Research your proposal. (pp. 262–63) • A Troubleshooting Guide: A Well-Argued Solution (p. 268)
An Effective Response to Objections and Alternative Solutions	How do I respond to possible objections and alternative solutions? • Assess the genre's basic features: An effective response to objections and alternative solutions. (pp. 233–34) • An Effective Response to Objections and Alternative Solutions: Finding a Way to Bridge Differences (p. 246) • An Effective Response to Objections and Alternative Solutions: Handling Objections (pp. 253–54) • Develop a response to objections or alternative solutions. (pp. 263–64) • A Troubleshooting Guide: An Effective Response to Objections and Alternative Solutions (p. 269)
A Clear, Logical Organization	How can I help my readers follow my argument? • Assess the genre's basic features: A clear, logical organization. (p. 234) • A Clear, Logical Organization: Creating Coherence (pp. 246–47) • A Clear, Logical Organization: Using Graphs (p. 254) • Create an outline that will organize your proposal effectively for your readers. (pp. 264–66) • A Troubleshooting Guide: A Clear, Logical Organization (p. 269)

Writing a Draft: Invention, Research, Planning, and Composing

The activities in this section will help you choose and research a problem as well as develop and organize an argument for your proposed solution. Your writing in response to many of these activities can be used in a rough draft, which you will be able to improve after receiving feedback from your classmates and instructor. Do the activities in any order that makes sense to you (and your instructor), and return to them as needed as you revise.

Choose a problem for which you can propose a solution.

When choosing a problem, keep in mind that it must be

- important to you and of concern to your readers;
- solvable, at least in part;
- one that you can research sufficiently in the time you have.

Choosing a problem affecting a group to which you belong (for example, as a classmate, teammate, participant in an online game site, or garage band member) or a place at which you have worked (a coffee shop, community pool, or radio station) gives you an advantage: You can write as an expert. You know the history of the problem, you know who to interview, and perhaps you have already thought about possible solutions. Moreover, you know who to address and how to persuade that audience to take action on your proposed solution.

If you already have a problem and possible solution(s) in mind, skip to Frame the Problem for Your Readers below. If you need to find a problem, consider the possible topics following the readings and suggestions here:

	Problems	Possible Solutions
School	Can't get into required courses	Make them large lecture courses.
		Make them online or hybrid courses.
		Give priority to majors.
Community	No safe place for children to play	Use school yards for after-school sports.
		Get high school students or senior citizens to tutor kids.
		Make pocket parks for neighborhood play.
		Offer programs for kids at branch libraries.
Work	Inadequate training for new staff	Make a training video or Web site.
		Assign experienced workers to mentor trainees (for bonus pay).

Frame the problem for your readers.

Once you have made a preliminary choice of a problem, consider what you know about it, what research will help you explore what others think about it, and how you can interest your readers in solving it. Then determine how you can frame or reframe it in a way that appeals to readers' values and concerns. Use the questions and sentence strategies that follow as a jumping-off point; you can make them your own as you revise later.

To learn more about conducting surveys and interviews, consult Chapter 14. For advice on listing, cubing, and freewriting, see Chapter 9.

WAYS IN

WHAT IS THE PROBLEM?

What do I already know about the problem?

BRAINSTORM *a list:* Spend 10 minutes listing everything you know about the problem. Write quickly, leaving judgment aside for the moment. After the 10 minutes are up, you can review your list and highlight or star the most promising information.

Use **CUBING**: Probe the problem from a variety of perspectives:

- Describe the problem.
- Compare the problem to other, similar problems, or contrast it with other, related problems.
- Connect the problem to other problems you have experienced.
- Analyze the problem to identify its parts, its causes, or its effects.
- Apply the problem to a real-life situation.

FREEWRITE (write without stopping) for 5 or 10 minutes about the problem. Don't stop to reflect or consider; if you hit a roadblock, just keep coming back to the problem. At the end of the specified time, review your writing, and highlight or underline promising ideas.

What do others think about the problem?

Conduct **SURVEYS**:

- Talk to a variety of students at your school (your friends and others).
- Discuss the problem with neighbors or survey shoppers at a local mall.
- Discuss the problem with coworkers or people who work at similar jobs.

WHY SHOULD READERS CARE?

How can I convince readers the problem is real and deserves attention?

Give an **EXAMPLE** *to make the problem specific:*

▸ Recently, ________ has been in the news/in movies/a political issue because of [name event].

EXAMPLE Sunday is the thirtieth anniversary of the National Organ Transplant Act, but no one wants to celebrate. U.S. policy on organ transplants—especially as applied to kidneys—is a mess. (Posner, par. 1)

Use a **SCENARIO** *or an* **ANECDOTE** *to dramatize the problem:*

EXAMPLE It's late at night. The final's tomorrow. You got a C on the midterm, so this one will make or break you. (O'Malley, par. 1)

Cite **STATISTICS** *to show the severity of the problem:*

▸ It has recently been reported that ________ percent of group A are [specify problem].

EXAMPLE More than 100,000 people languish on the waitlist for kidneys, thousands of them dying before they receive a transplant. In 2012, almost 35,000 people joined the waitlist, while only 17,000 received transplants.

Every year the waitlist lengthens. NOTA virtually guaranteed this shortage by shutting down an incipient market in kidneys. (Posner, pars. 1–2)

Conduct **INTERVIEWS**:

- Interview faculty experts.
- Discuss the issue with businesspeople in the community.
- Interview local officials (members of the city council, the fire chief, the local labor union representative).

What do most of my potential readers already think about the problem?

- ▶ Many complain about ________ but do nothing because solving it seems too hard/too costly.
- ▶ Some think ________ is someone else's responsibility/not that big of a problem.
- ▶ Others see ________ as a matter of fairness/human decency.

Who suffers from the problem?

- ▶ Studies have shown that ________ mostly affects groups A, B, and C.

Describe the problem's **NEGATIVE CONSEQUENCES**:

- ▶ According to Professor X, group A is suffering as a result of ________ [insert quote from expert].

EXAMPLE Sian Beilock, a psychology professor at the University of Chicago, points out that "stressing about doing well on an important exam can backfire, leading students to 'choke under pressure' or to score less well than they might otherwise score if the stakes weren't so high." (O'Malley, par. 2)

Why should readers care about solving the problem?

- ▶ We're all in this together. ________ is not a win-lose proposition. If group A loses, we all lose.
- ▶ If we don't try to solve ________, no one else will.
- ▶ Doing nothing will only make ________ worse.
- ▶ We have a moral responsibility to do something about ________.

TEST YOUR CHOICE

Defining the Problem

Ask two or three other students to help you develop your plan to frame the problem.

Presenters. Briefly explain how you are thinking of framing or reframing the problem for your audience. Use the following language as a model for presenting your problem, or use language of your own.

- ▶ I plan to define the problem not as ________ but as ________/in terms of ________ because I think my readers will share my concerns/values/priorities.

(continued)

Listeners. Tell the presenter what response this way of framing the problem elicits from you and why. You may also explain how you think other readers might respond. Use the following language as a model for structuring your response, or use your own words.

- I'm also/not concerned about X because of ______, ______, and ______.
- I agree/disagree that ______ because ______.

Assess how the problem has been framed, and reframe it for your readers.

Once you have a good idea of what you and your readers think about the problem, consider how others have framed the problem and how you might be able to reframe it for your readers.

WAYS IN

HOW HAS THE PROBLEM BEEN FRAMED?	HOW CAN I REFRAME THE PROBLEM?
Sink or Swim Argument EXAMPLE Providing tutoring for students who are failing a course is wrong because students should do what they need to do to pass the course or face the consequences. That's the way the system is supposed to work.	**Teaching Should Not Be Punitive Argument** EXAMPLE Providing tutoring for students who are failing a course assumes that the purpose of education is learning, not testing for its own sake or punishing those who have not done well.
Don't Reward Failure Argument EXAMPLE Providing tutoring for students who are failing a course is like a welfare system that makes underprepared students dependent and second-class citizens.	**Encourage Success Argument** EXAMPLE Providing tutoring for students who are failing a course encourages students to work hard and value doing well in school.
Reverse Discrimination Argument EXAMPLE Providing tutoring for students who are failing a course is unfair to the other students who don't need assistance.	**Level Playing Field Argument** EXAMPLE Providing tutoring for students who are failing a course is a way to make up for inadequacies in previous schooling.

Win-Lose Argument		Win-Win Argument	
EXAMPLE	Providing tutoring for students who are failing a course ignores the fact that grades should fall on a bell curve—that is, an equal proportion of students should get an *F* as get an *A*.	**EXAMPLE**	Providing tutoring for students who are failing a course assumes that it would be a good thing if every student earned an *A*. Providing tutoring enhances learning.

Develop a possible solution.

The following activities will help you devise a solution and develop an argument to support it. If you have already found a solution, you may want to skip this activity and go directly to the Explain Your Solution section (p. 262).

WAYS IN

HOW CAN I SOLVE THIS PROBLEM?

One way to generate ideas is to write steadily for at least five minutes, exploring some of the possible ways of solving the problem. Consider using the following approaches as a jumping-off point:

- Adapt a solution that has been tried or proposed for a similar problem.

  EXAMPLE Posner could have identified specific examples of "altruistic exchanges" by charities or nonprofits and adapted their efforts for his organ donation proposal.

- Focus on eliminating a cause or minimizing an effect of the problem.

  EXAMPLE O'Malley's solution to stressful high-stakes exams is to eliminate the cause of the stress by inducing instructors to give more frequent low-stakes exams.

- See the problem as part of a larger system, and explore solutions to the system.

  EXAMPLE Posner's solution to the problem of organ waiting lists is to reform the system for compensating donors.

- Focus on solving a small part of the problem.

  EXAMPLE Brownell and Frieden's solution to obesity is to reduce the consumption of sugared beverages through taxation.

(continued)

- Look at the problem from different points of view.

  EXAMPLE Consider what students, teachers, parents, or administrators might think could be done to help solve the problem.

- Think of a specific example of the problem, and consider how you could solve it.

  EXAMPLE O'Malley could have focused on solving the problem of high-stakes exams in his biology course.

For more idea-generating strategies, see Chapter 9.

Explain your solution.

You may not yet know for certain whether you will be able to construct a convincing argument to support your solution, but you should choose a solution that you feel motivated to pursue. Use the questions and sentence strategies that follow to help you put your ideas in writing. You will likely want to revise what you come up with later, but the questions and sentence strategies below may provide a convenient jumping-off point.

WAYS IN

HOW CAN I EXPLAIN HOW MY SOLUTION WOULD HELP SOLVE THE PROBLEM?	HOW CAN I EXPLAIN THAT MY SOLUTION IS FEASIBLE?
It would eliminate a cause of the problem. ▶ Research shows it would reduce ________.	**It could be implemented.** Describe the major stages or steps necessary to carry out your solution.
It has worked elsewhere. ▶ It works in ________, ________, and ________, as studies evaluating it show.	**We can afford it.** Explain what it would cost to put the solution into practice.
It would change people's behavior. ▶ ________ would discourage/encourage people to ________.	**It would not take too much time.** Create a rough schedule or timeline to show how long it would take to make the necessary arrangements.

Research your proposal.

You may have already begun researching the problem and familiarizing yourself with alternative solutions that have been offered, or you may have ideas about what you need to research. If you are proposing a solution to a problem about which others have written, use the following research strategies to help you find out what solutions others have proposed or tried. You may also use these strategies to find out how others have defined the problem and demonstrated its seriousness.

- Enter keywords or phrases related to your solution (or problem) into the search box of an all-purpose database, such as *Academic OneFile* (InfoTrac) or *Academic Search Complete* (EBSCOhost), to find relevant articles in magazines and journals; in the database *Lexis/Nexis* to find articles in newspapers; or in library catalogs to find books and other resources. (Database names may change, and what is available will differ from school to school. Some libraries may even combine all three into one search link on the library's home page. Ask a librarian if you need help.) Patrick O'Malley could have tried a combination of keywords, such as *learning* and *test anxiety,* or variations on his terms (*frequent testing, improve retention*) to find relevant articles.
- Bookmark or keep a record of the URLs of promising sites, and download or copy information you could use in your essay. When available, download PDF files rather than HTML files because these are likely to include visuals, such as graphs and charts. If you copy and paste relevant information into your notes, be careful to distinguish all material from sources from your own ideas.
- Remember to record source information and to cite and document any sources you use, including visuals and interviews.

For more about searching for information, consult Chapter 14. For more about avoiding plagiarism, see Chapter 15. For more about documenting sources, consult Chapter 16 (MLA style) or Chapter 17 (APA style).

Develop a response to objections or alternative solutions.

The topics you considered when developing an argument for your solution may be the same topics you need to consider when developing a response to likely criticisms of your proposal—answering possible objections to your solution or alternative solutions readers may prefer. The following sentence strategies may help you start drafting an effective response.

WAYS IN

HOW CAN I DRAFT A REFUTATION OR CONCESSION?

To draft a REFUTATION, *try beginning with sentence strategies like these:*

- Some people think we can't afford to do X, but it would cost only $ ________ to put my solution in place compared to $ ________, the cost of doing nothing/implementing an alternative solution.
- Although it might take X months/years to implement this solution, it would actually take longer to implement solution A.

(continued)

- ▶ There are critics who think that only a few people would benefit from solving this problem, but ________ would benefit because ________.
- ▶ Some may suggest that I favor this solution because I would benefit personally; however, the fact is we would all benefit because ________.
- ▶ Some may claim that this solution has been tried and hasn't worked. But research shows that [explain how proposed solution has worked] ***or*** my solution differs from past experiments in these important ways: ________, ________, and ________.

To draft a CONCESSION, *try beginning with sentence strategies like these:*

- ▶ I agree with those who claim X/object on X grounds; therefore, instead of ________, I think we should pursue ________.
- ▶ If ________ seems too time-consuming/expensive, let's try ________.
- ▶ Where ________ is a concern, I think ________ [name alternative] should be followed.
- ▶ Although ________ is the best way to deal with a problem like this, under ________ [describe special circumstances], I agree that ________ should be done.

Create an outline that will organize your proposal effectively for your readers.

Whether you have rough notes or a complete draft, making an outline of what you have written can help you organize your essay effectively for your audience. Compare the possible outlines that follow to see how you might organize the essay depending on whether your readers agree that a serious problem exists and are open to your solution—or not.

For more on outlining, see Chapter 9, pp. 320–24.

If you are writing primarily for readers who *acknowledge that the problem exists and are open to your solution:*

I. **Introduce the problem,** concluding with a thesis statement asserting your solution.

II. **Demonstrate the problem's seriousness:** Frame the problem in a way that prepares readers for the solution.

If you are writing primarily for readers who *do not recognize the problem or are likely to prefer alternative solutions:*

I. **Reframe the problem:** Identify common ground, and acknowledge alternative ways readers might see the problem.

II. **Concede strengths, but emphasize the weaknesses of alternative solution(s) that readers might prefer.**

III. **Describe the proposed solution:** Show what could be done to implement it.
IV. **Refute objections.**
V. **Conclude:** Urge action on your solution.

III. **Describe the proposed solution:** Give reasons and provide evidence to demonstrate that it is preferable to the alternative(s).
IV. **Refute objections.**
V. **Conclude:** Reiterate shared values.

Whatever organizational strategy you adopt, do not hesitate to change your outline as necessary while drafting and revising. For instance, you might find it more effective to hold back on presenting your solution until you have discussed unacceptable alternatives. The purpose of an outline is to identify the basic components of your proposal and to help you organize it effectively, not to lock you into a particular structure.

Write the opening sentences.

Review what you have written to see if you have something that would work to launch your proposal, or try out some of these opening strategies:

Begin with an **engaging scenario:**

> It's late at night. The final's tomorrow. You got a C on the midterm, so this one will make or break you. Will it be like the midterm? Did you study enough? Did you study the right things? It's too late to drop the course. So what happens if you fail? No time to worry about that now—you've got a ton of notes to go over. (O'Malley, par. 1)

Cite a **recent event** *demonstrating the seriousness of the problem:*

> Most proposals, including a recent open letter (*Open Letter*) by transplant experts and bioethicists to top government officials, try to thread the needle by giving donors implicit or in-kind compensation, such as travel expenses to the hospital, a tax credit, or priority on the waitlist if they ever need a kidney themselves. (Posner, par. 4)

Use **statistics** *to demonstrate the seriousness of the problem:*

> Sunday is the thirtieth anniversary of the National Organ Transplant Act, but no one wants to celebrate. U.S. policy on organ transplants—especially as applied to kidneys—is a mess. More than 100,000 people languish on the waitlist for kidneys, thousands of them dying before they receive a transplant. (Posner, par. 1)

Offer a **quotation** *that highlights support for your solution:*

> Sugar, rum, and tobacco are commodities which are nowhere necessaries of life, which are become objects of almost universal consumption, and which are therefore extremely proper subjects of taxation.
>
> —Adam Smith, *The Wealth of Nations*, 1776 (Brownwell and Frieden)

But don't agonize over the first sentences because you are likely to discover the best way to begin only after you have written a rough draft.

Draft your proposal.

By this point, you have done a lot of research and writing to

- focus and define a problem, and develop a solution to it;
- support your solution with reasons and evidence your readers will find persuasive;
- refute or concede objections and alternative solutions;
- organize your ideas to make them clear, logical, and effective for readers.

Now stitch that material together to create a draft. The next two parts of this Guide to Writing will help you evaluate and improve your draft.

Evaluating the Draft: Using Peer Review

Your instructor may arrange a peer review session in class or online, where you can exchange drafts with your classmates and give one another a thoughtful critical reading, pointing out what works well and suggesting ways to improve the draft. A good critical reading does three things:

1. It lets the writer know how well the reader understands the point of the draft.
2. It praises what works best.
3. It indicates where the draft could be improved and makes suggestions on how to improve it.

One strategy for evaluating a draft is to use the basic features of a proposal as a guide.

A PEER REVIEW GUIDE

A Focused, Well-Defined Problem

How well does the writer establish that the problem exists and is serious?

Summarize: Tell the writer what you understand the problem to be.

Praise: Give an example from the essay where the problem and its significance come across effectively, such as where an example dramatizes the problem or where statistics establish its significance.

Critique: Tell the writer where readers might need more information about the problem's causes and consequences, or where more might be done to establish its seriousness.

A Well-Argued Solution	Has the writer argued effectively for the solution? **Summarize:** Tell the writer what you understand the proposed solution to be. **Praise:** Give an example from the essay where support for the solution is presented especially effectively—for example, note particularly strong reasons, writing strategies that engage readers, or design or visual elements that make the solution clear and accessible. **Critique:** Tell the writer where the argument for the solution could be strengthened—for example, where steps for implementation could be laid out more clearly, where the practicality of the solution could be established more convincingly, or where additional support for reasons should be added.
An Effective Response to Objections and Alternative Solutions	Has the writer responded effectively to objections or alternative solutions? **Summarize:** Tell the writer what you understand to be the objections or alternative solutions that he or she is responding to. **Praise:** Give an example from the essay where the writer concedes or refutes a likely objection to the argument effectively, and where reasons showing the limitations of alternative solutions are most effectively presented. **Critique:** Tell the writer where concessions and refutations could be more convincing, where possible objections or reservations should be taken into account, or where alternative solutions should be discussed, where reasons for not accepting other solutions need to be strengthened, or where common ground should be sought with advocates of other positions.
A Clear, Logical Organization	Is the proposal clearly and logically organized? **Summarize:** Underline the sentence(s) in which the writer establishes the problem and proposes a solution. Also identify the places where the writer forecasts the argument, supplies topic sentences, and uses transitions or repeats key words and phrases. **Praise:** Give an example of how the essay succeeds in being readable—for example, in its overall organization, its use of forecasting statements or key terms introduced in the thesis and strategically repeated elsewhere, its use of topic sentences or transitions, or its inclusion of an especially effective opening or closing. **Critique:** Tell the writer where the readability could be improved. For example, point to places where adding key terms would help, where a topic sentence could be made clearer, or where transitions could be improved or added. Indicate whether the beginning or ending could be more effective.

Before concluding your review, be sure to address any of the writer's concerns that have not already been addressed.

Improving the Draft: Revising, Editing, and Proofreading

Start improving your draft by reflecting on what you have written thus far:

- Review the Test Your Choice responses and critical reading comments from your classmates, instructor, or writing center tutor: What are your readers getting at?
- Take another look at the notes from your earlier research and writing activities: What else should you consider?
- Review your draft: What else can you do to make your proposal more effective?

Revise your draft.

If your readers are having difficulty with your draft, or if you think there is room for improvement, try some of the strategies listed in the Troubleshooting Guide. They can help you fine-tune your presentation of the genre's basic features.

A TROUBLESHOOTING GUIDE

A Focused, Well-Defined Problem

My readers aren't convinced that my problem is serious or even exists.

- Change the way you present the problem to address readers' concerns more directly.
- Add information—statistics, examples, description, and so on—that members of your audience are likely to find persuasive or that they can relate to.
- Consider adding visuals, such as graphs, tables, or charts, if these would help clarify the problem for your audience.

A Well-Argued Solution

My readers aren't convinced that my solution is a good one.

- Try to make your solution more convincing by discussing similar solutions used successfully elsewhere or by demonstrating more clearly how it will solve the problem.
- Add evidence (such as facts, statistics, and examples) to support your reasons.
- Review the steps needed to enact your solution; if necessary, lay them out more clearly.

An Effective Response to Objections and Alternative Solutions

My readers have raised objections to my solution.

- Cite research studies, statistics, or examples to refute readers' objections.
- Concede valid points or modify your solution to accommodate the criticism.
- If you can neither refute nor accommodate objections, rethink your solution.

My readers have proposed alternative solutions that I don't discuss.

- If possible, establish shared values with those who propose alternative solutions, but show why their solutions will not work as well as yours.
- If you cannot demonstrate that your solution is preferable, consider arguing that both solutions deserve serious consideration.

A Clear, Logical Organization

My readers are confused by my proposal or find it hard to follow.

- Try outlining your proposal to be sure that the overall organization is strong; if it is not, try moving, adding, or deleting sections to strengthen coherence.
- Consider adding a forecasting statement and using key terms in your thesis and repeating them when you discuss your main points.
- Check to see that you use topic sentences to introduce your main points and that you provide appropriate transitions.

Edit and proofread your draft.

Several errors often occur in essays that propose solutions: ambiguous use of *this* and *that,* and sentences that lack an agent. The following guidelines will help you check your essay for these common errors.

Avoiding Ambiguous Use of *This* and *That*

The Problem Because you must frequently refer to the problem and the solution in a proposal, you will often use pronouns to avoid the monotony or wordiness of repeatedly referring to them by name. Using *this* and *that* vaguely to refer to other words or ideas, however, can confuse readers.

The Correction Add a specific noun after *this* or *that.* For example, in his essay in this chapter, Patrick O'Malley writes:

> Furthermore, professors could help students prepare for midterm and final exams by providing sets of questions from which the exam questions will be selected. . . . *This solution* would have the advantage of reducing students' anxiety about learning every fact in the textbook. (par. 13)

O'Malley avoids an ambiguous *this* in the second sentence by adding the noun *solution*. (He might just as well have used *preparation* or *action* or *approach*.) Here's another example:

increase
▶ Students would not resist a reasonable fee increase of $40 a year if that ^ would pay for needed dormitory remodeling.

Revising Sentences That Lack an Agent

The Problem A writer proposing a solution to a problem usually needs to indicate who should take action to solve it. Those who are in a position to take action are called "agents." Look, for example, at this sentence from Patrick O'Malley's proposal:

> To get students to complete the questions in a timely way, professors would have to collect and check the answers. (par. 12)

In this sentence, *professors* are the agents. They have the authority to assign and collect study questions, and they would need to take this action in order for this solution to be successfully implemented.

Had O'Malley instead written "the answers would have to be collected and checked," the sentence would lack an agent. Failing to name an agent would have made his argument less convincing because it would have left unclear one of the key parts of any proposal: who is going to take action.

The Correction When you revise your work, ask yourself *who* or *what* performed the action in any given sentence. If there's no clear answer, rewrite the sentence to give it an agent. Watch in particular for forms of the verb *to be* (the ball *was* dropped, exams should *be* given, etc.), which often signal agentless sentences.

Your staff should plan a survey
▶ ~~A survey could be planned~~ to find out more about students' problems in scheduling the ^ courses they need.

The registrar should extend
▶ ~~Extending~~ the deadline to mid-quarter. ~~would make sense.~~
^

Note: Sometimes, however, agentless sentences are appropriate, as when the agent is clear from the context, unknown, or less important than the person or thing acted upon.

Reflecting on What You Have Learned

In this chapter, you learned a great deal about this genre from reading several proposals and writing one of your own. To consolidate your learning, reflect not only on what you learned but also on how you learned it.

ANALYZE & WRITE

Write a blog post, a letter to your instructor or a classmate, or an e-mail message to a student who will take this course next term, using the writing prompt that seems most productive for you:

- Explain how your purpose and audience influenced *one* of your decisions as a writer, such as how you defined the problem, the strategies you used in presenting your solution, or the ways in which you attempted to counter possible objections.
- Discuss what you learned about yourself as a writer in the process of writing this essay. For example, what part of the process did you find most challenging? Did you try anything new, like getting a critical reading of your draft or outlining your draft in order to revise it? If so, how well did it work?
- If you were to give advice to a friend who was about to write an essay proposing a solution to a problem, what would you say?
- Which of the readings in this chapter influenced your essay? Explain the influence, citing specific examples from your essay and the reading.
- If you got good advice from a critical reader, explain exactly how the person helped you—perhaps by questioning the way you addressed your audience or the kinds of evidence you offered in support of your proposed solution.

8

Justifying an Evaluation

Does *Scott Pilgrim vs. the World* deserve its status as a cult film? Is binge-watching the HBO series *Game of Thrones* worthwhile? Does the popular *U.S. News* "Best Colleges" guide use a reliable system for ranking schools? These are some of the questions the evaluations in this chapter answer.

People make evaluations for various purposes and audiences and publish them in a variety of media. For example, students in a history course might be asked to write a review of a scholarly book and post it to the class blog, including a summary of the book's main assertions and an assessment of how well the author supports those claims with factual evidence and authoritative sources. A business executive might use Prezi slides to present an evaluation of how her company could benefit from investing in 3-D printer technology. A motorcycle enthusiast might review his tour of the Harley-Davidson factory in York, Pennsylvania, and publish it in a newsletter for motorcyle hobbyists.

In this chapter, we ask you to choose a subject for evaluation that you can examine closely. By analyzing the selections in the Guide to Reading that follows, you will learn how to use appropriate *criteria* to support your judgment. The Guide to Writing later in the chapter will show you ways to use the basic features of the genre to make your evaluation interesting and persuasive.

PRACTICING THE GENRE

Choosing Appropriate Criteria

The success of evaluation depends on whether readers agree that the criteria being applied are sound and based on widely accepted standards of judgment. To practice developing an evaluative argument based on appropriate criteria, get together with two or three other students and follow these guidelines:

Part 1. Choose a film everyone in the group has seen. Then take turns giving a quick review of the film:

1. Identify the type of film you think it was (romantic comedy, science fiction, action, and so on).
2. Say one thing you expect from films of this type.
3. Say whether this particular film surpassed, met, or fell short of your expectations for this type of film, and why.

For example, do you usually expect a film like this to have a surprising or predictable story; to present believable characters in realistic situations; to be all about special effects or exciting action sequences; to be funny, scary, or thought-provoking?

Part 2. As a group, discuss what you learned:

- **What did you learn about criteria, or standards, appropriate for evaluating the film you chose?** To think about criteria in evaluating a film, discuss the similarities and differences between what you expected and what others expected for the film. Our expectations represent the criteria we think are important when evaluating a subject. What is a *must have* (your main criterion) for judging a comedy? An action film? Were you surprised by how your classmates categorized the film or any of the criteria they applied? Why?
- **Think about how the context for your review—the purpose, audience, and medium—affects the criteria you use.** If you were going to post your evaluation on Facebook, turn it in for a grade, or submit it to an audience review Web site such as Rotten Tomatoes, would you use the same criteria you used in your group? What would you assume about your audience that would make them more or less likely to share your criteria? How could you justify the criteria you think are most important?

Analyzing Evaluations

As you read the selections in this chapter, you will see how different writers argue for an evaluation:

- William Akana argues that *Scott Pilgrim vs. the World* is "a hell of a ride" (pp. 278–83).
- Emily Nussbaum tries to persuade readers that *Game of Thrones* is an engrossing series well worth watching, despite its gruesome violence (pp. 283–86).
- Malcolm Gladwell argues that the *U.S. News* college ranking uses a flawed ranking system (pp. 289–93).

Analyzing how these writers present their subject, assert and justify their judgment, respond to alternative viewpoints, and organize their writing will help you see how you can use these techniques to make your own evaluations clear and compelling for your readers.

Determine the writer's purpose and audience.

Although writing a review usually helps writers better understand the criteria they use when making evaluations, most writers hope to influence people as well. As you read the evaluations that follow, ask yourself questions like these:

What seems to be the writer's main purpose?

- To influence readers' judgments and possibly their actions?
- To inspire readers to think critically about which criteria are appropriate for judging subjects of this kind?
- To get readers to look at the subject in a new way?

What does the writer assume about the audience?

- That readers will accept the writer's judgment?
- That they will use the review to make their own independent, informed judgment?
- That they already made up their minds and want to see what others think?
- That they will have serious objections to the writer's argument?

Assess the genre's basic features.

Basic Features

- A Well-Presented Subject
- A Well-Supported Judgment
- An Effective Response to Objections and Alternative Judgments
- A Clear, Logical Organization

As you read the evaluations in this chapter, consider how different authors make their evaluations helpful and convincing. The examples that follow are drawn from the reading selections that appear later in this Guide to Reading.

A WELL-PRESENTED SUBJECT

Read first to identify the subject of the review, which is often named in the title (for example, *"Scott Pilgrim vs. the World:* A Hell of a Ride") and described briefly in the opening paragraphs.

Look also to see how the writer classifies the subject in terms of its genre. Here's an example from the first reading selection in the chapter, by student William Akana:

subgenres genre	From start to finish, *Scott Pilgrim vs. the World* delivers intense action in a hilarious slacker movie that also somehow reimagines romantic comedy. (par. 1)

Even if readers don't recognize the title, Akana makes clear that the film he is reviewing combines elements of three different kinds of movies (or subgenres), so readers can determine whether he is using appropriate criteria, as you will see in the next section.

Knowing the genre is also important because readers need different kinds of information for different genres. For example, most readers of film reviews want to know what the story is about but do not want to know how it turns out. Film reviewers, therefore, try not to give too much plot detail, as you can see in this concise plot summary from Akana's essay:

> Pilgrim's life takes a dramatic turn when he falls in love with Ramona Flowers (Mary Elizabeth Winstead), who is, quite literally, the girl of his dreams. However, he soon discovers that Ramona's former lovers have formed a league of evil exes to destroy him, and he is forced to fight to the death to prove his love. (par. 2)

A WELL-SUPPORTED JUDGMENT

Identify the judgment the writer asserts, and determine whether he or she thinks the subject is good or bad, better or worse than other things in the same genre. Typically, writers announce their judgment in a *thesis statement* early in the evaluation. Below are a couple of sentence strategies typically used for thesis statements in evaluations, followed by examples from reviews in this chapter:

- ▶ What makes X a success/a failure is ________ and ________.
- ▶ X can be appreciated/criticized for ________, ________, and ________, but ultimately it is a success/failure because of ________.

EXAMPLES	Genre Subject *Judgment* Reasons	Although the film is especially targeted for old-school gamers, anime fans, and comic book fanatics, Scott Pilgrim vs. the World *can be appreciated and enjoyed* by all audiences because of its inventive special effects, clever dialogue, and artistic cinematography and editing. (Akana, par. 2)
		Game of Thrones is the latest entry in television's most esteemed category: the sophisticated cable drama about a patriarchal subculture. . . . These worlds are picturesque, elegantly filmed, and ruled by rigid etiquette—lit up, for viewers, by the thrill of seeing brutality enforced (or, in the case of *Downton Abbey*, a really nice house kept in the family). And yet the undergirding strength of each series is its insight into what it means to be excluded from power: to be a woman, or a bastard, or a "half man." (Nussbaum, par. 3)

Examine the thesis to see whether the writer asserts an overall judgment *and also note the features of the subject that are being praised or criticized and the* reasons *supporting the judgment. Finally, consider whether the reasons are based on criteria you would expect to be used for evaluating something of this kind.* For example, one of William Akana's reasons is that the film uses "special effects" that are "inventive." To support this reason, he devotes two paragraphs to detailing some of the film's special effects. He also gives examples of "video-game-like gimmicks" such as "gamertags," describing them and also providing a screenshot to show what they look like (pars. 3 and 4).

For advice on when to indent quotations rather than use quotation marks, see Chapter 15, pp. 425–26.

Consider the types of evidence provided, such as examples and visuals, and whether the writer cites sources by quoting, paraphrasing, *or* summarizing *source material.* Also notice whether the writer uses a *signal phrase* to identify the source and establish its credibility.

Signal phrase Paraphrase Quotation	[Director of Data Research Robert] Morse admitted that there was no formal reason for that position. It was just a feeling. "We're not saying that we're measuring educational outcomes," he explained. "We're not saying we're social scientists, or we're subjecting our rankings to some peer-review process. We're just saying we've made this judgment." (Gladwell, par. 9)

For more on citing sources, see Chapters 15, 16, and 17.

How writers treat sources depends on the rhetorical situation. Certain formal situations, such as college assignments or scholarly publications, require writers to cite sources in the text and document them in a bibliography (called a list of *works cited* in many humanities disciplines or a list of *references* in the sciences and social sciences), as we can see in Akana's essay. In writing for a general audience—blogs and newspaper articles, for example—readers do not expect references to appear in the article, but they do expect sources to be named and their credentials to be identified in a signal phrase.

Notice also whether the reviewer uses comparison and contrast. Malcolm Gladwell, for example, sets up his evaluation of the ranking system used by *U.S. News & World Report*'s annual "Best Colleges" guide by comparing it to the system used by *Car and Driver* magazine. Similarly, Emily Nussbaum compares and contrasts *Game of Thrones* with other programs to support her judgment:

Comparison cue	Like *Mad Men, Game of Thrones* is elementally concerned with the way that meaningful consent dissolves when female bodies are treated as currency. (par. 8)
Contrast cue	Artistically, *Game of Thrones* is in a different class from *House of Lies, Californication,* and *Entourage.* (par. 10)

AN EFFECTIVE RESPONSE TO OBJECTIONS AND ALTERNATIVE JUDGMENTS

Notice how the writer responds to objections to the argument or to alternative judgments readers might prefer. Writers may **concede** (accept) or **refute** (argue against) alternatives, providing a transition or other cues to alert readers.

The basic structure of a concession is:

Transition indicating concession

- ▶ Of course, ________ is an important factor.
- ▶ Granted, ________ must be taken into consideration.

CONCESSION Neil Genzlinger called it "vileness for voyeurism's sake," directed at "Dungeons & Dragons types."

It's true that *Game of Thrones* is unusually lurid, even within the arms race of pay cable. (Nussbaum. pars. 2–3)

The basic structure of a refutation is:

Transition indicating refutation

- ▶ Although________, I think ________.
- ▶ X says ________, but I think ________ because ________.

REFUTATION Some reviewers have criticized the film because they think that in the end it fails as a romantic comedy. . . . But I agree with *New York Times* reviewer A. O. Scott, who argues that "the movie comes home to the well-known territory of the coming-of-age story, with an account of lessons learned and conflicts resolved." (Akana, par. 9)

A CLEAR, LOGICAL ORGANIZATION

Read to see if the writer provides cues *to help readers follow the logic of the argument.* Notice, for example, if the reasons are *forecast* in the thesis or elsewhere in the opening and, if so, where they are brought up again later in the essay. Here are examples from William Akana's film review:

Thesis with topics forecast

Scott Pilgrim vs. the World can be appreciated and enjoyed by all audiences because of its inventive special effects, clever dialogue, and artistic cinematography and editing. (par. 2)

Topic sentences with reasons forecast

Scott Pilgrim vs. the World shines bright with superb special effects that serve to reinforce the ideas, themes, and style of the film. (par. 3)

Another strong point of *Scott Pilgrim vs. the World* is its clever and humorous dialogue. (par. 6)

The best attribute by far is the film's creative cinematography and editing. (par. 7)

Also notice how the writer uses logical transitions—such as *because* to introduce reasons and *another* to indicate the next reason in a list.

Finally, where visuals—such as film stills, cartoons, screenshots, and diagrams— are included, determine how they are integrated into the text. Akana, for example, uses the conventional phrase "see fig. 1" in parentheses following his written description and includes a descriptive caption with the visual. In contrast, writers publishing in newspapers and magazines may simply intersperse screenshots following their descriptions to illustrate their points.

To see how Akana integrated visuals into his essay, see p. 307.

Readings

William Akana | Scott Pilgrim vs. the World: *A Hell of a Ride*

THIS EVALUATION ESSAY was written by student William Akana for his composition course. The assignment prompt asked students to choose a film and write a review that includes a close analysis of the cinematic techniques used in at least one important scene. Akana's instructor illustrated various cinematic techniques, such as camera angles and movements, and demonstrated how to take screenshots, explaining that students can use visuals for a class project without asking permission, but to publish them they would have to get permission, as we did.

As you read, consider these questions, as well as those in the margin:

- How well do the screenshots illustrate Akana's analysis and support his evaluation?
- How would you describe Akana's tone in this essay? How is his tone affected by the fact that he uses the first-person pronoun "I" to refer to himself only in the opening and closing paragraphs?

Basic Features
A Well-Presented Subject
A Well-Supported Judgment
An Effective Response to Objections and Alternative Judgments
A Clear, Logical Organization

1 As I leaned back in the movie theater seat, accompanied by my friends on a typical Saturday night, I knew I was in for something special. I was reassured; not only had my friends and I reached a unanimous vote to watch *Scott Pilgrim vs. the World*, but two of my friends had already seen the film and were eager to see it again. As soon as the film began, with its presentation of the classic Universal Studios introduction in old-timer eight-bit music and pixilated format, I knew I was in for one hell of a ride. From start to finish, *Scott Pilgrim vs. the World* delivers intense action in a hilarious slacker movie that also somehow reimagines romantic comedy.

How appropriate is this narrative and informality for a film review? For a college paper?

Why do you think Akana gives readers this information?

2 *Scott Pilgrim vs. the World*, released in 2010 by Universal Studios, came into production as a comic book adaptation film under the direction of Edgar Wright (best known for the zombie movie masterpiece *Shaun of the Dead*). Scott Pilgrim (Michael Cera) is a twenty-two-year-old Canadian who plays bass for his indie band, Sex Bob-omb, located in Toronto, Canada. Pilgrim's life takes a dramatic turn when he falls in love with Ramona Flowers (Mary Elizabeth Winstead), who is, quite literally, the girl of his dreams. However, he soon discovers that Ramona's former lovers have formed a league of evil exes to destroy him, and he is forced to fight to the death to prove his love.

Although the film is especially targeted for old-school gamers, anime fans, and comic book fanatics, *Scott Pilgrim vs. the World* can be appreciated and enjoyed by all audiences because of its inventive special effects, clever dialogue, and artistic cinematography and editing.

How well does this thesis statement forecast Akana's argument? Skim the essay, noting where he discusses each of these reasons.

3 *Scott Pilgrim vs. the World* shines bright with superb special effects that serve to reinforce the ideas, themes, and style of the film. Special effects are plentiful throughout the entire film, ranging from superimposed annotations echoing classic gaming features to artful backgrounds and action sequences modeled on colorful comic book pages. For example, each of the main characters is described for the first time with "gamertags," short-timed boxes of information that include name, age, and rating (see fig. 1).

4 *Scott Pilgrim vs. the World* contains numerous amounts of other fun video-game-like gimmicks that were made possible through special effects. One humorous scene presents a pee bar that depletes as Pilgrim relieves himself. Another scene presents a bass battle between Pilgrim and one of the evil exes in the format of PlayStation's popular Guitar Hero (see fig. 2). It goes without saying that anyone who has ever dabbled in video games will greatly appreciate the gaming-culture inside jokes. As the reviewer for the Web site *Cinema Sight* wrote, this film is intended for "the video game generation" (Lovell).

How well do these details and the illustration he chose support Akana's claim that the special effects are "inventive" and "superb"?

5 Comic book references are also installed using special effects. In almost every battle between Pilgrim and his enemies, comic-book-like backgrounds, added through CGI, enhance the eye-popping fight sequences as characters

Fig. 1. Screen shot showing gamertags
Everett Collection, Inc.

Fig. 2. Guitar face-off
Everett Collection, Inc.

fly into the air to deliver devastating punches accompanied with traditional onomatopoeic "POWs" and "KAPOWs" (see fig. 3). However, comic book annotations are not reserved merely for fight scenes. Annotations range from even the simplest "RIIIINGs" of a telephone to trails of shouting "AAAAHs" of Pilgrim as he is thrown into the air in battle. To make the film even more visually appealing, *Scott Pilgrim vs. the World* portrays flashbacks using white and black comic strips similar to the original Scott Pilgrim comic books. Special effects play a truly vital part in enlivening the style of the film.

6 Another strong point of *Scott Pilgrim vs. the World* is its clever and humorous dialogue. One memorable scene in the film involves Knives Chau

Fig. 3. Comic-book-style annotations
Everett Collection, Inc.

(Ellen Wong) and Scott Pilgrim in an awkward situation where Knives states sheepishly: "I've never even kissed a guy." In a supposedly intimate gesture of affection, Pilgrim moves closer only to pause shortly before saying "Hey . . . me neither." Additionally, *Scott Pilgrim vs. the World* is rich in cultural satire that pokes fun at adolescent and young adult behaviors. One scene contains Pilgrim telling Ramona Flowers: "I feel like I'm on drugs when I'm with you, not that I do drugs, unless you do—in which case, I do drugs all the time." Dialogue like this gives the film a raw yet rich sense of humor that is one of the many inventive risks of the film that pay off.

7 The best attribute by far is the film's creative cinematography and editing, which can be illustrated in the ultimate fight scene of the movie. Pilgrim finally confronts his former band members, who are playing in an underground lair for Ramona's seventh evil ex, Gideon (Jason Schwartzman). As Pilgrim admits his faults and proceeds to apologize to the band for former wrongs, the shot assumes a point of view from Pilgrim's perspective looking up to the band on stage. Shortly before Pilgrim is finished, Gideon, sitting on his throne atop a miniature pyramid, interrupts him. The shot quickly cuts to a close-up of Gideon's eyes, emphasizing his anger at Pilgrim. From this point, soft focusing is utilized to blur the background as a tracking shot follows Pilgrim in a medium close-up as he marches to the base of the pyramid. Then, reverse shots are used between high- and low-angled frames to illustrate Pilgrim's challenge to Gideon for a final duel.

How do the highlighted transitions help readers follow Akana's analysis?

8 Gideon, in response to the challenge, asks Pilgrim if he is fighting for Ramona, which leads to a climactic epiphany for Pilgrim as he realizes his true motive, admitting in a tight close-up: "No. I want to fight you for me." As Pilgrim finishes this confession, a deep narrating voice announces that "Scott Pilgrim has earned the power of self-respect," and in turn, he is awarded a magical sword with which he can defeat Gideon. Subsequently, the camera pans from left to right in a subjective shot to illustrate Gideon's goons closing in on Pilgrim. Pilgrim, in a series of fast-paced jump cuts, quickly dispatches the bad guys before charging up the pyramid. After an extended battle, deep focusing is used with a long shot to establish that the hierarchy has changed between hero and villain: Pilgrim is seen standing atop the pyramid, looking down at the kneeling Gideon before Pilgrim kicks him to smithereens.

Fig. 4. Threshold of a new beginning?
Everett Collection, Inc.

For what purposes does Akana use these sources? How effective is his response to an opposing view?

9 This brilliantly executed scene illustrates the artful cinematography of *Scott Pilgrim vs. the World*. More importantly, it delivers the film's thematic message, which undercuts the cliché "love conquers all" and instead focuses on the fresh concept that, in the grand scheme of things, the only person you are fighting for is yourself. Some reviewers have criticized the film because they think that in the end it fails as a romantic comedy. For example, *Miami Herald* film reviewer Rene Rodriguez argues that the film ultimately fails because of the lack of "chemistry" or "emotional involvement" in the romance between Pilgrim and Ramona. But I agree with *New York Times* reviewer A. O. Scott, who argues that "the movie comes home to the well-known territory of the coming-of-age story, with an account of lessons learned and conflicts resolved." Fighting Ramona's exes forces Pilgrim to wake up out of his slacker stupor. Before he can begin a grown-up relationship with Ramona, he has to come to terms with his own failures, especially in relation to his own exes. The film ends, as director Edgar Wright explained in an interview, on the threshold of a new beginning: "Scott and Ramona might not make it past the end credits, or it might be the start of a beautiful relationship" (Cozzalio).

Works Cited

Cozzalio, Dennis. "*Scott Pilgrim*'s Dreamscape and the Glories of the Wright Stuff II: An Interview with Director Edgar Wright." *Sergio Leone and the Infield Fly Rule,* 15 Jan. 2011, sergioleoneifr.blogspot.com/2011/01/scott-pilgrims-dreamscape-and-glories.html.

Lovell, Wesley. Review of *Scott Pilgrim vs. The World,* directed by Edgar Wright. *Cinema Sight,* 13 Sept. 2010, www.cinemasight.com/review-scott-pilgrim-vs-the-world-2010/.

Rodriguez, Rene. Review of *Scott Pilgrim vs. the World,* directed by Edgar Wright. *Miami Herald,* 11 Aug. 2010, www.miami.com/scott-pilgrim-vs-world-pg-13-article.

Scott, A. O. "This Girl Has a Lot of Baggage, and He Must Shoulder the Load." Directed by Edgar Wright, *The New York Times,* 12 Aug. 2010, nyti.ms/1HWdSPX.

Emily Nussbaum — *The Aristocrats: The Graphic Arts of* Game of Thrones

Courtesy Emily Nussbaum

EMILY NUSSBAUM has written for numerous publications including the *New York Times, Slate,* and *New York* magazine, for which she worked as culture editor. Currently, she is the television critic for the *New Yorker,* in which this review originally appeared. Her initial fascination with analyzing and critiquing television programs sprang from an obsession with *Buffy the Vampire Slayer.* Her reviews and commentary have become influential particularly in discussions about the effects of technology and social media on television as a medium and on our viewing habits.

As you read, consider the following:

- Notice that Nussbaum begins with a little narrative about her job as a television reviewer. How does this story prepare you for what follows?
- How effectively does Nussbaum establish her credibility as a reviewer? What in her evaluation helps demonstrate her expertise?

1 For critics, sorting through television pilots is an act of triage. Last year, when *Game of Thrones* landed on my desk, I skimmed two episodes and made a quick call: we'd have to let this one go. The HBO series, based on the best-selling fantasy books by George R. R. Martin, looked as if it were another guts-and-corsets melodrama, like *The Borgias.* In the première, a ten-year-old boy was shoved out of a tower window. The episode climaxed with what might be described as an Orientalist gang rape/wedding dance. I figured I might catch up later, if the buzz was good.

2 It was the right decision, even if I made it for the wrong reason. *Game of Thrones* is an ideal show to binge-watch on DVD: with its cliffhangers and Grand Guignol[1] dazzle, it rewards a bloody, committed immersion in its foreign

[1] An over-the-top style of entertainment designed to shock and thrill viewers, originally of the kind produced at the Grand Guignol Theater in Paris. [Editor's note]

world—and by this I mean not only the medieval-ish landscape of Westeros (the show's mythical realm) but the genre from which it derives. Fantasy—like television itself, really—has long been burdened with audience condescension: the assumption that it's trash, or juvenile, something intrinsically icky and low. Several reviews of *Game of Thrones* have taken this stance, including two notable writeups in the *Times:* Ginia Bellafante sniffed that the show was "boy fiction" and Neil Genzlinger called it "vileness for voyeurism's sake," directed at "Dungeons & Dragons[2] types."

3 It's true that *Game of Thrones* is unusually lurid, even within the arms race of pay cable: the show is so graphic that it was parodied on *Saturday Night Live*, with a "behind-the-scenes" skit in which a horny thirteen-year-old boy acted as a consultant. To watch it, you must steel yourself for baby-stabbing, as well as rat torture and murder by molten gold. But, once I began sliding in disks in a stupor, it became clear that, despite the show's Maltese vistas and asymmetrical midriff tops, this was not really an exotic property. To the contrary, *Game of Thrones* is the latest entry in television's most esteemed category: the sophisticated cable drama about a patriarchal subculture. This phenomenon launched with *The Sopranos*, but it now includes shows such as *Deadwood, Mad Men, Downton Abbey,* and *Big Love*. Each of these acclaimed series is a sprawling, multi-character exploration of a closed, often violent hierarchical system. These worlds are picturesque, elegantly filmed, and ruled by rigid etiquette—lit up, for viewers, by the thrill of seeing brutality enforced (or, in the case of *Downton Abbey*, a really nice house kept in the family). And yet the undergirding strength of each series is its insight into what it means to be excluded from power: to be a woman, or a bastard, or a "half man."

4 The first season of *Game of Thrones* built up skillfully, sketching in ten episodes a conflict among the kingdoms of Westeros, each its own philosophical ecosystem. There were the Northern Starks, led by the gruffly ethical Ned Stark and his dignified wife, Catelyn, and their gruffly ethical and dignified children. There were the Southern Lannisters, a crowd of high-cheekboned beauties (and one lusty dwarf, played by the lust-worthy Peter Dinklage), who form a family constellation so twisted, charismatic, and cruel that it rivals *Flowers in the Attic*[3] for blond dysfunction. Across the sea, there were the Dothraki, a Hun-like race of horseman warriors, whose brutal ruler, Drogo, took the delicate, unspellable Daenerys as a bride. A teen girl traded like currency by her brother, Daenerys was initiated into marriage through rape; in time, she began to embrace both that marriage and her desert queenhood. (Although the cast is mostly white, the dusky-race aesthetics of the Dothraki sequences are head-clutchingly problematic.) By the finale, she was standing naked in the desert—widowed, traumatized, but triumphant, with three baby dragons crawling over her like vines. (This quick summary doesn't capture the complexity of the series' ensemble, which rivals a Bosch painting: there's also the whispery eunuch Spider; a scheming brothel owner named Littlefinger; and a ketchup-haired sorceress who gives birth to shadow babies.)

---

[2] A role-play war game in a fantasy setting. [Editor's note]

[3] A popular novel by V. C. Andrews in which a newly widowed (and indebted) mother moves her children into the attic of her estranged parents' home, while she tries to win back their affections so she will inherit their fortune. This novel has formed the basis of a number of movies and made-for-TV movies since it was published in 1979. [Editor's note]

5 In the season's penultimate episode, the show made a radical move: it killed off the protagonist. On a public stage, Ned Stark was beheaded, on the orders of the teen-age sadist King Joffrey, a sequence edited with unusual beauty and terror—birds fluttering in the air, a hushed soundtrack, and a truly poignant shot from Ned's point of view, as he looked out toward his two daughters. This primal act suggested the limits of ethical behavior in a brutalized universe, and also dramatized the show's vision of what aristocracy means: a succession of domestic traumas, as each new regent dispatches threats to his bloodline. (Or, as Joffrey's mother, Cersei, puts it, kinghood means "lying on a bed of weeds, ripping them out one by one, before they strangle you in your sleep.") It demonstrated, too, a willingness to risk alienating its audience. . . .

6 Still, the most compelling plots remain those of the subalterns, who are forced to wield power from below. These characters range from heroic figures like the tomboy Arya Stark to villains like Littlefinger, but even the worst turn out to have psychic wounds that complicate their actions. If the show has a hero, it's Tyrion (Dinklage), who is capable of cruelty but also possesses insight and empathy, concealed beneath a carapace of Wildean wit. So far, his strategic gifts have proved more effective than the torture-with-rats approach. Power is "a trick, a shadow on the wall," the eunuch tells Tyrion. "And a very small man can cast a very large shadow."

7 Then, of course, there are the whores. From the start, the show has featured copious helpings of pay-cable nudity, much of it in scenes that don't strictly require a woman to display her impressive butt dimples as the backdrop for a monologue about kings. (The most common fan idiom for these sequences is "sexposition," but I've also seen them referred to as "data humps.") These scenes are at once a turn-on and a turn-off. At times, I found myself marveling at the way that HBO has solved the riddle of its own economic existence, merging *Hookers at the Point*[4] with quasi-Shakespearean narrative. In the most egregious instance so far, Littlefinger tutored two prostitutes in how to moan in fake lesbianism for their customers, even as they moaned in fake lesbianism for us.

8 Viewed in another light, however, these sex scenes aren't always so gratuitous. Like *Mad Men*, *Game of Thrones* is elementally concerned with the way that meaningful consent dissolves when female bodies are treated as currency. War means raping the enemy's women; princesses go for a higher price, because their wombs are the coin of the realm, cementing strategic alliances. It helps that the narrative is equally fascinated by the ways in which women secure authority, and even pleasure, within these strictures, and that in the second season its bench of female characters has got even deeper—among them, a seafaring warrior princess, a butch knight, and Tyrion's prostitute girlfriend.

9 *Game of Thrones* is not coy about the way the engine of misogyny can grind the fingers of those who try to work it in their favor. An episode two weeks ago featured a sickening sequence in which King Joffrey ordered one prostitute—a character the audience had grown to care about—to rape another. The scenario . . . seemed designed not to turn viewers on but to confront them with the logical endgame of this pornographic system. . . . But while the scene may have been righteous in theory, in practice it was jarring, and slightly incoherent, particularly since it included the creamy nudity we've come to expect as visual dessert.

10 As with *True Blood*, the show's most graphic elements—the cruel ones, the fantasy

[4] A 2002 HBO documentary about prostitutes working the Hunts Point neighborhood in New York's South Bronx. [Editor's note]

ones, and the cruel-fantasy ones—speak to female as well as male viewers. (One of the nuttiest quotes I've ever read came from Alan Ball, *True Blood's* showrunner,[5] who said that a focus group had revealed that men watched his series for the sex and women for the romance. Please.) But there is something troubling about this sea of C.G.I.[6]-perfect flesh, shaved and scentless and not especially medieval. It's unsettling to recall that these are not merely pretty women; they are unknown actresses who must strip, front and back, then mimic graphic sex and sexual torture, a skill increasingly key to attaining employment on cable dramas. During the filming of the second season, an Irish actress walked off the set when her scene shifted to what she termed "soft porn." Of course, not everyone strips: there are no truly explicit scenes of gay male sex, fewer lingering shots of male bodies, and the leading actresses stay mostly buttoned up. Artistically, *Game of Thrones* is in a different class from *House of Lies*, *Californication*, and *Entourage*. But it's still part of another colorful patriarchal subculture, the one called Los Angeles.

[REFLECT] Make connections: Binge-watching.

Binge-watching is a marathon viewing of multiple episodes of the same television show in a single sitting. According to Nussbaum, "*Game of Thrones* is an ideal show to binge-watch" (par. 2). Her reason is that "with its cliffhangers and Grand Guignol dazzle, it rewards a bloody, committed immersion in its foreign world." But what Nussbaum seems to think makes *Game of Thrones* so good for sustained viewing is not primarily the horror or titillation it provides, but its immersive power to draw viewers into a complex imaginary world (par. 3). Think of your own experience. What, if anything, have you binge-watched or been tempted to binge-watch? What would make a program worth bingeing on? Your instructor may ask you to post your thoughts to a class discussion board or blog, or to discuss them with other students in class. Use these questions to get started:

- Is being immersed in an imagined world a—or even *the*—main attraction of binge-watching for you, or does something else matter more? If you think something else matters more, what is it, and why is it so important?
- Nussbaum suggests that the kinds of imagined worlds viewers gravitate toward (at least at the time she was writing) portray "a closed, often violent hierarchical system" that shows "what it means to be excluded from power" (par. 3). Why do you imagine viewers might be enticed by this theme?

[ANALYZE] Use the basic features.

A WELL-PRESENTED SUBJECT: PROVIDING INFORMATION

Reviews usually begin by providing basic information about the subject. For example, William Akana's title identifies his subject by name, "*Scott Pilgrim vs. the World*: A Hell of

[5] The producer responsible for day-to-day management of a television program. [Editor's note]
[6] Computer-generated imagery. [Editor's note]

a Ride." The second paragraph also provides the kinds of information readers expect to learn from film reviews, such as the name of the director (and his or her well-known films), the main actors and their roles, the setting, and a brief summary of the plot.

> *Scott Pilgrim vs. the World*, released in 2010 by Universal Studios, came into production as a comic book adaptation film under the direction of Edgar Wright (best known for the zombie movie masterpiece *Shaun of the Dead*). Scott Pilgrim (Michael Cera) is a twenty-two-year-old . . . in Toronto, Canada. Pilgrim's life takes a dramatic turn when he falls in love with Ramona Flowers (Mary Elizabeth Winstead), . . . and he is forced to fight to the death to prove his love. (Akana, par. 2)

Because Akana knows that his audience, particularly his instructor, might not have heard of *Scott Pilgrim vs. the World* (a cult classic but not a box-office hit), he opens the review with a brief anecdote. Recounting a personal experience in a review is an unusual move, but it allows Akana to take the same position vis-à-vis his readers that his friends had taken with him—sharing a favorite film with a friend—and, as a consequence, may contribute to his credibility with his audience.

ANALYZE & WRITE

Write a paragraph analyzing how Nussbaum identifies her subject:

1. Compare Nussbaum's way of presenting the subject with Akana's. For example, how does she use the series' name, and what kinds of information does she give her audience about it?
2. Why do you think Nussbaum, like Akana, begins with an anecdote? Notice that Akana uses the first-person pronoun "I" only in the opening paragraph, where he presents the anecdote. Skim Nussbaum's review, noting where she uses "I." Why do you think she uses the first person in those passages?

A WELL-SUPPORTED JUDGMENT: BASING A JUDGMENT ON CRITERIA

Reviewers assert an overall judgment of the subject in a thesis statement, which usually appears early in the review. Akana, for example, concludes his opening paragraph with this thesis statement:

Evaluation Genre	From start to finish, *Scott Pilgrim vs. the World* delivers intense action in a hilarious slacker movie that also somehow reimagines romantic comedy.

Notice that Akana praises the film here, making his overall judgment clear. (Of course, an evaluation doesn't have to be all positive or all negative; reviews are often mixed.) He also uses specific evaluative language: He doesn't claim simply that *Scott Pilgrim* is good. Instead, he points out what is good about the film based on the three genres it draws on (action, slacker, and romantic comedy) and the criteria usually used for evaluating those film genres. And he supports his judgment with evaluative analysis, explaining what is noteworthy about the climactic fight scene:

> This brilliantly executed scene illustrates the artful cinematography of *Scott Pilgrim vs. the World*. More importantly, it delivers the film's thematic message,

which undercuts the cliché "love conquers all" and instead focuses on the fresh concept that, in the grand scheme of things, the only person you are fighting for is yourself. (par. 9)

ANALYZE & WRITE

Write a paragraph or two analyzing how Nussbaum presents and supports her judgment of *Game of Thrones*:

1 Skim the essay to find the thesis statement in which Nussbaum asserts her overall judgment, and highlight the evaluative language she uses.

2 What genre or combination of genres does Nussbaum use to categorize *Game of Thrones?* Consider whether Nussbaum's evaluative language is typical of the criteria usually used when evaluating the genre (or genres) she identifies.

3 Now reread paragraph 4, 5, or 6, and analyze Nussbaum's use of examples to support her judgment. How does she present an example or examples and use evaluative language?

AN EFFECTIVE RESPONSE TO OBJECTIONS AND ALTERNATIVE JUDGMENTS: CONCEDING AND REFUTING ALTERNATIVE JUDGMENTS

Reviewers often acknowledge an alternative judgment and then either refute or concede it. To do so, they may use a sentence strategy like one of these:

- Programs in this genre have been dismissed as ________. But this misses the point because ________.
- Some reviewers criticize the film because it ________. However, I think ________ because ________.

EXAMPLE Some reviewers have criticized the film because they think that in the end it fails as a romantic comedy. . . . But I agree with *New York Times* reviewer A. O. Scott, who argues that "the movie comes home to the well-known territory of the coming-of-age story, with an account of lessons learned and conflicts resolved." (Akana, par. 9)

ANALYZE & WRITE

Write a paragraph or two considering the role of the initial negative evaluations of *Game of Thrones*:

1 Reread paragraphs 2–3, noting the negative evaluations and Nussbaum's response. Does she refute, concede, or make the refutation-concession move?

2 Now look at paragraphs 7–10, where Nussbaum returns to the criticism of sex in *Game of Thrones.* How does she respond to the criticism this time? What point is she making about "the logical endgame of this pornographic system" (par. 9)?

3 What's implied by the phrase "graphic arts" in the subtitle: "The Graphic Arts of *Game of Thrones*"?

A CLEAR, LOGICAL ORGANIZATION: CUEING READERS

Nussbaum's evaluation is complicated. She interweaves plot summary with analysis to support her claims about the merits (and demerits) of *Game of Thrones,* and she compares the series with other cable series, both good and bad. To keep her readers on track, she must use a variety of cueing strategies.

ANALYZE & WRITE

Write a paragraph analyzing how Nussbaum helps her audience follow her evaluation:

1. Skim the essay, noting Nussbaum's main topics and marking any key terms that she uses to orient readers.
2. Mark any transitions, considering how each transition helps readers follow the logical movement from topic to topic.
3. Consider how effective Nussbaum's strategies are. How difficult did you find it to follow the logic of the review? What would you suggest Nussbaum do, if anything, to make her evaluation easier to follow?

[RESPOND] Consider possible topics: Offering a mixed judgment.

Some of the most effective and interesting evaluations are neither wholly positive nor negative. Instead, they point out both strengths and weaknesses while developing a clear overall judgment. Try to think of a subject about which you have mixed feelings—such as a sports team, video game, film, musical performance, or course you've taken. What is your overall judgment? What would you praise about your subject, and what would you criticize? What are the criteria you think should be used in evaluating examples of this genre?

Malcolm Gladwell | *What College Rankings Really Tell Us*

Photo by Theo Wargo/WireImage for Bragman Nyman Cafarelli/Getty Images

MALCOLM GLADWELL is a staff writer for the *New Yorker* and has written a number of best-selling books, including *Outliers: The Story of Success* (2008) and *Blink: The Power of Thinking without Thinking* (2005). He received the American Sociological Association Award for Excellence in the Reporting of Social Issues and was named one of the hundred most influential people by *Time* magazine. As he explains on his Web site (gladwell.com), giving public readings, particularly to academic audiences, has helped him "re-shape and sharpen [his] arguments."

"What College Rankings Really Tell Us" (2011) evaluates the popular *U.S. News* annual "Best Colleges" guide. You may be familiar with this guide and may have even consulted it when selecting a college. Excerpted from a longer *New Yorker* article, Gladwell's evaluation focuses on the *U.S. News* ranking system. As you read Gladwell's review, consider these questions:

- Note the numbered list of "variables" *U.S. News* uses to rank colleges. For whom do you suppose *U.S. News*'s criteria are important? Why?
- If they are important for you, why? If they are not important for you, why not? What criteria for choosing a college are important for you?

1 *Car and Driver* conducted a comparison test of three sports cars, the Lotus Evora, the Chevrolet Corvette Grand Sport, and the Porsche Cayman S. . . . Yet when you inspect the magazine's tabulations it is hard to figure out why *Car and Driver* was so sure that the Cayman is better than the Corvette and the Evora. The trouble starts with the fact that the ranking methodology *Car and Driver* used was essentially the same one it uses for all the vehicles it tests—from S.U.V.s to economy sedans. It's not set up for sports cars. Exterior styling, for example, counts for four per cent of the total score. Has anyone buying a sports car ever placed so little value on how it looks? Similarly, the categories of "fun to drive" and "chassis"—which cover the subjective experience of driving the car—count for only eighty-five points out of the total of two hundred and thirty-five. That may make sense for S.U.V. buyers. But, for people interested in Porsches and Corvettes and Lotuses, the subjective experience of driving is surely what matters most. In other words, in trying to come up with a ranking that is heterogeneous—a methodology that is broad enough to cover all vehicles—*Car and Driver* ended up with a system that is absurdly ill-suited to some vehicles. . . .

2 A heterogeneous ranking system works if it focuses just on, say, how much fun a car is to drive, or how good-looking it is, or how beautifully it handles. The magazine's ambition to create a comprehensive ranking system—one that considered cars along twenty-one variables, each weighted according to a secret sauce cooked up by the editors—would also be fine, as long as the cars being compared were truly similar. It's only when one car is thirteen thousand dollars more than another that juggling twenty-one variables starts to break down, because you're faced with the impossible task of deciding how much a difference of that degree ought to matter. A ranking can be heterogeneous, in other words, as long as it doesn't try to be too comprehensive. And it can be comprehensive as long as it doesn't try to measure things that are heterogeneous. But it's an act of real audacity when a ranking system tries to be comprehensive and heterogeneous—which is the first thing to keep in mind in any consideration of *U.S. News & World Report's* annual "Best Colleges" guide.

3 The *U.S. News* rankings . . . relies on seven weighted variables:

1. Undergraduate academic reputation, 22.5 per cent
2. Graduation and freshman retention rates, 20 per cent
3. Faculty resources, 20 per cent
4. Student selectivity, 15 per cent
5. Financial resources, 10 per cent
6. Graduation rate performance, 7.5 per cent
7. Alumni giving, 5 per cent

From these variables, *U.S. News* generates a score for each institution on a scale of 1 to 100. . . . This ranking system looks a great deal like the *Car and Driver* methodology. It is heterogeneous. It doesn't just compare U.C. Irvine, the University of Washington, the University of Texas–Austin, the University of Wisconsin–Madison, Penn State, and the University of Illinois, Urbana–Champaign—all public institutions of roughly the same size. It aims to compare Penn State—a very large, public, land-grant university with a low tuition and an economically diverse student body, set in a rural valley in central Pennsylvania and famous for its football team—with Yeshiva University, a small, expensive, private Jewish university whose undergraduate program is set on two campuses in Manhattan (one in midtown, for the women, and one far uptown, for the men) and is definitely not famous for its football team.

4 The system is also comprehensive. It doesn't simply compare schools along one dimension—the test scores of incoming freshmen, say, or academic reputation. An algorithm takes a slate of statistics on each college and transforms them into a single score: it tells us that Penn State is a better school than Yeshiva by one point. It is easy to see why the *U.S. News* rankings are so popular. A single score allows us to judge between entities (like Yeshiva and Penn State) that otherwise would be impossible to compare. . . .

5 A comprehensive, heterogeneous ranking system was a stretch for *Car and Driver*—and all it did was rank inanimate objects operated by a single person. The Penn State campus at University Park is a complex institution with dozens of schools and departments, four thousand faculty members, and forty-five thousand students. How on earth does anyone propose to assign a number to something like that?

6 The first difficulty with rankings is that it can be surprisingly hard to measure the variable you want to rank—even in cases where that variable seems perfectly objective. . . . There's no direct way to measure the quality of an institution—how well a college manages to inform, inspire, and challenge its students. So the *U.S. News* algorithm relies instead on proxies for quality—and the proxies for educational quality turn out to be flimsy at best.

7 Take the category of "faculty resources," which counts for twenty per cent of an institution's score (number 3 on the list above). "Research shows that the more satisfied students are about their contact with professors," the College Guide's explanation of the category begins, "the more they will learn and the more likely it is they will graduate." That's true. According to educational researchers, arguably the most important variable in a successful college education is a vague but crucial concept called student "engagement"—that is, the extent to which students immerse themselves in the intellectual and social life of their college—and a major component of engagement is the quality of a student's contacts with faculty. . . . So what proxies does *U.S. News* use to measure this elusive dimension of engagement? The explanation goes on:

> We use six factors from the 2009–10 academic year to assess a school's commitment to instruction. Class size has two components, the proportion of classes with fewer than 20 students (30 percent of the faculty resources score) and the proportion with 50 or more students (10 percent of the score). Faculty salary (35 percent) is the average faculty pay, plus benefits, during the 2008–09 and 2009–10 academic years, adjusted for regional differences in the cost of living. . . . We also weigh the proportion of professors with the highest degree in their fields (15 percent), the student-faculty ratio (5 percent), and the proportion of faculty who are full time (5 percent).

8 This is a puzzling list. Do professors who get paid more money really take their teaching roles more seriously? And why does it matter whether a professor has the highest degree in his or her field? Salaries and degree attainment are known to be predictors of research productivity. But studies show that being oriented toward research has very little to do with being good at teaching. Almost none of the *U.S. News* variables, in fact, seem to be particularly

effective proxies for engagement. As the educational researchers Patrick Terenzini and Ernest Pascarella concluded after analyzing twenty-six hundred reports on the effects of college on students:

> After taking into account the characteristics, abilities, and backgrounds students bring with them to college, we found that how much students grow or change has only inconsistent and, perhaps in a practical sense, trivial relationships with such traditional measures of institutional "quality" as educational expenditures per student, student/faculty ratios, faculty salaries, percentage of faculty with the highest degree in their field, faculty research productivity, size of the library, [or] admissions selectivity. . . .

9 There's something missing from that list of variables, of course: it doesn't include price. That is one of the most distinctive features of the *U.S. News* methodology. Both its college rankings and its law-school rankings reward schools for devoting lots of financial resources to educating their students, but not for being affordable. Why? [Director of Data Research Robert] Morse admitted that there was no formal reason for that position. It was just a feeling. "We're not saying that we're measuring educational outcomes," he explained. "We're not saying we're social scientists, or we're subjecting our rankings to some peer-review process. We're just saying we've made this judgment. We're saying we've interviewed a lot of experts, we've developed these academic indicators, and we think these measures measure quality schools."

10 As answers go, that's up there with the parental "Because I said so." But Morse is simply being honest. If we don't understand what the right proxies for college quality are, let alone how to represent those proxies in a comprehensive, heterogeneous grading system, then our rankings are inherently arbitrary. . . . *U.S. News* thinks that schools that spend a lot of money on their students are nicer than those that don't, and that this niceness ought to be factored into the equation of desirability. Plenty of Americans agree: the campus of Vanderbilt University or Williams College is filled with students whose families are largely indifferent to the price their school charges but keenly interested in the flower beds and the spacious suites and the architecturally distinguished lecture halls those high prices make possible. Of course, given that the rising cost of college has become a significant social problem in the United States in recent years, you can make a strong case that a school ought to be rewarded for being affordable. . . .

11 The *U.S. News* rankings turn out to be full of these kinds of implicit ideological choices. One common statistic used to evaluate colleges, for example, is called "graduation rate performance," which compares a school's actual graduation rate with its predicted graduation rate given the socioeconomic status and the test scores of its incoming freshman class. It is a measure of the school's efficacy: it quantifies the impact of a school's culture and teachers and institutional support mechanisms. Tulane, given the qualifications of the students that it admits, ought to have a graduation rate of eighty-seven per cent; its actual 2009 graduation rate was seventy-three per cent. That shortfall suggests that something is amiss at Tulane. Another common statistic for measuring college quality is "student selectivity." This reflects variables such as how many of a college's freshmen were in the top ten per cent of their high-school class, how high their S.A.T. scores were, and what percentage of applicants a college admits. Selectivity quantifies how accomplished students are when they first arrive on campus.

12 Each of these statistics matters, but for very different reasons. As a society, we probably care more about efficacy: America's future depends on colleges that make sure the students they admit leave with an education and a degree. If you are a bright high-school senior and you're thinking about your own future, though, you may well care more about selectivity, because that relates to the prestige of your degree. . . .

13 There is no right answer to how much weight a ranking system should give to these two competing values. It's a matter of which educational model you value more—and here, once again, *U.S. News* makes its position clear. It gives twice as much weight to selectivity as it does to efficacy. . . .

14 Rankings are not benign. They enshrine very particular ideologies, and, at a time when American higher education is facing a crisis of accessibility and affordability, we have adopted a defacto standard of college quality that is uninterested in both of those factors. And why? Because a group of magazine analysts in an office building in Washington, D.C., decided twenty years ago to value selectivity over efficacy.

[REFLECT] Make connections: Ideology underlying judgments.

Gladwell asserts that "implicit ideological choices" underlie ranking systems (par. 11). The word *ideology* refers to the values and beliefs that influence people's thinking. An important sign of underlying ideology is the fact that the *U.S. News* rankings leave out how much it costs to go to each college. This omission is significant, especially at a time when there is "a crisis of accessibility and affordability" (par. 14).

To think about the role of ideology in your own choice of a college, reflect on your personal experience as well as your observations of others choosing a college. Your instructor may ask you to post your thoughts on a class discussion board or to discuss them with other students in class. Use these questions to get started:

- What colleges did you consider, and what criteria (cost, location, standing in the *U.S. News* college ranking, and so on) did you use?
- Choose one or two of your criteria, and consider what values and beliefs were behind your choice. For example, was it important to you to attend a college with a winning football team, with a particular religious orientation, with opportunities for undergraduates to do scientific research?
- How would comparing the criteria you used with the criteria your classmates used help you better understand the ideology—values and beliefs—behind your choices?

[ANALYZE] Use the basic features.

A WELL-PRESENTED SUBJECT: INTRODUCING A COMPLICATED SUBJECT

Every year, *U.S. News* publishes a special edition that ranks colleges and universities across the nation. In his essay, Gladwell does not simply evaluate one year's ratings; he evaluates the ranking system itself. But he begins by focusing on the ranking system of another magazine, *Car and Driver*.

ANALYZE & WRITE

Write a paragraph analyzing and evaluating how Gladwell introduces *U.S. News*'s ranking system:

1. Reread paragraph 1. Why do you think Gladwell begins his evaluation of *U.S. News*'s college ranking system by discussing the system used by another magazine to rank cars? How does Gladwell's evaluation of *Car and Driver*'s ranking system prepare readers for his evaluation of *U.S. News*'s ranking system?
2. Now reread paragraph 2. What cues does Gladwell provide to help readers follow his transition from the ranking system of *Car and Driver* to that of *U.S. News*?
3. What does Gladwell mean when he describes *U.S. News*'s ranking system as striving to be both comprehensive and heterogeneous?

A WELL-SUPPORTED JUDGMENT: DEFINING CRITERIA

In paragraph 3, Gladwell lists the "seven weighted variables" *U.S. News* uses to represent a school's quality. Then, in paragraph 6, he states his main reason for criticizing any system for ranking colleges: "There's no direct way to measure the quality of an institution. . . . So the *U.S. News* algorithm"—its formula or set of rules—"relies instead on proxies for quality—and the proxies for educational quality turn out to be flimsy at best."

ANALYZE & WRITE

Write a paragraph or two analyzing and evaluating how Gladwell supports his argument:

1. Reread paragraphs 7 and 8, in which Gladwell focuses on one criterion—"faculty resources"—from the list of variables *U.S. News* uses to measure a school's quality. Why does *U.S. News* focus on faculty resources, and what do the editors of the magazine use to measure this quality?
2. Now consider Gladwell's claim that faculty resources are an inappropriate criterion for evaluating student engagement. What reasons and evidence does Gladwell supply? Given your own experience as a student, how convincing is this part of his argument?
3. What single criterion would you consider most important in evaluating a school's quality? How would you measure that criterion?

AN EFFECTIVE RESPONSE TO OBJECTIONS AND ALTERNATIVE JUDGMENTS: SINGLING OUT A COMMENT FOR RESPONSE

Because it is a negative evaluation, one could say that Gladwell's entire essay is an implied refutation of those who think well of the *U.S. News* college rankings. However,

Gladwell also responds specifically to comments made by Robert Morse, the director of data research for *U.S. News & World Report.*

ANALYZE & WRITE

Write a paragraph analyzing Morse's response to Gladwell and Gladwell's response to Morse:

1 Reread paragraph 9. How would you describe Morse's response to Gladwell's criticism? Which of Gladwell's points does Morse concede or refute? Is Morse's response effective? Why or why not?

2 Now reread paragraphs 10–12. How does Gladwell respond to Morse? How does he concede or refute Morse's response? How would you describe the tone of Gladwell's response? Is he fair, mean, sarcastic, something else?

3 Given Gladwell's purpose and audience, how do you imagine readers would react to Morse's response to criticism as well as to Gladwell's handling of Morse's response? How did you respond?

A CLEAR, LOGICAL ORGANIZATION: USING COMPARISON AND CONTRAST

Lengthy evaluations can be difficult to follow, but writers have a number of strategies at their disposal to help guide readers. They may use transitional words and phrases or numbered lists, as Gladwell does. But they may also use more subtle strategies to help create cohesion. Gladwell, for example, uses comparison and contrast and strategic repetition to help readers follow his analysis.

ANALYZE & WRITE

Write a paragraph analyzing how Gladwell uses these two strategies:

1 Skim paragraphs 1–3, 5, and 10, noting where Gladwell mentions *Car and Driver* or compares *Car and Driver*'s ranking system with the ranking system used by *U.S. News*, and highlight Gladwell's repeated use of the word *heterogeneous* to describe these ranking systems. Consider the comparison Gladwell is making between *Car and Driver*'s and *U.S. News*'s ranking systems. How does this comparison help him structure his article logically?

2 Skim paragraphs 3, 8, and 11–14, underlining the words *selectivity* and *efficacy*. How does Gladwell use the contrast between selectivity and efficacy? How does this contrast help him guide readers and make his point?

3 Finally, evaluate Gladwell's use of these strategies. How effective are they in helping you follow Gladwell's logic? What, if anything, would you suggest Gladwell do to make his analysis easier to follow?

[RESPOND] Consider possible topics: Evaluating a text.

List several texts you would consider evaluating, such as an essay from one of the chapters in this book; a children's book that you read when you were young or that you now read to your own children; a magazine for people interested in a particular topic, like computers or cars; or a scholarly article you read for a research paper. If you choose an argument from Chapters 6–8, you could evaluate its logic, its use of emotional appeals, or its credibility. You need not limit yourself to texts written on paper. You might also evaluate a Web site or blog, a radio or television program or advertisement, or even a work of art. Choose one possibility from your list, and then come up with two or three criteria for evaluation.

The Writing Assignment

Write an essay evaluating a specific subject. Examine your subject closely, and make a judgment about it. Give reasons for your judgment that are based on widely recognized criteria or standards for evaluating a subject like yours. Support your reasons with examples and other details primarily from your subject.

This Guide to Writing is designed to help you compose your own evaluation and apply what you have learned from reading other essays in the same genre. This Starting Points chart will help you find answers to questions you might have about composing an essay evaluating a subject. The Starting Points chart will help you find the guidance you need, when you need it.

STARTING POINTS: JUSTIFYING AN EVALUATION

A Well-Presented Subject

How do I come up with a subject to write about?

- Consider possible topics. (pp. 289, 296)
- Choose a subject to evaluate. (pp. 299–300)
- Test Your Choice: Choosing a Subject (pp. 299–300)
- Assess your subject and consider how to present it to your readers. (pp. 300–1)

How can I present my subject clearly and convincingly?

- Determine the writer's purpose and audience. (p. 274)
- Assess the genre's basic features: A well-presented subject. (pp. 274–75)
- A Well-Presented Subject: Providing Information (pp. 286–87)
- A Well-Presented Subject: Introducing a Complicated Subject (pp. 293–94)
- Assess your subject, and consider how to present it to your readers. (pp. 300–1)
- A Troubleshooting Guide: A Well-Presented Subject (p. 311)

A Well-Supported Judgment

How do I come up with a thesis statement?

- Assess the genre's basic features: A well-supported judgment. (pp. 275–76)
- Formulate a working thesis stating your overall judgment. (pp. 301–2)

(continued)

A Well-Supported Judgment	How do I construct an argument supporting my judgment? • Assess the genre's basic features: A well-supported judgment. (pp. 275–76) • A Well-Supported Judgment: Basing a Judgment on Criteria (pp. 287–88) • A Well-Supported Judgment: Defining Criteria (p. 294) • Develop the reasons and evidence supporting your judgment. (pp. 302–3) • Research your evaluation. (p. 303) • A Troubleshooting Guide: A Well-Supported Judgment (pp. 311–12)
An Effective Response to Objections and Alternative Judgments	How do I respond to possible objections and alternative judgments? • Assess the genre's basic features: An effective response to objections and alternative judgments. (pp. 276–77) • An Effective Response to Objections and Alternative Judgments: Conceding and Refuting Alternative Judgments (p. 288) • An Effective Response to Objections and Alternative Judgments: Singling Out a Comment for Response (pp. 294–95) • Respond to a likely objection or alternative judgment. (pp. 304–5) • A Troubleshooting Guide: An Effective Response to Objections and Alternative Judgments (p. 312)
A Clear, Logical Organization	How can I help my readers follow my argument? • Assess the genre's basic features: A clear, logical organization. (p. 277) • A Clear, Logical Organization: Cueing Readers (p. 289) • A Clear, Logical Organization: Using Comparison and Contrast (p. 295) • Organize your draft to appeal to your readers. (pp. 305–6) • A Troubleshooting Guide: A Clear, Logical Organization (p. 312)

Writing a Draft: Invention, Research, Planning, and Composing

The activities in this section will help you choose and research a subject as well as develop and organize an evaluative argument. Your writing in response to many of these activities can be used in a rough draft, which you will be able to improve after receiving feedback from your classmates and instructor. Do the activities in any order that makes sense to you (and your instructor), and return to them as needed as you revise.

Choose a subject to evaluate.

When choosing a subject for evaluation, keep in mind that it must be one that

- has strengths or weaknesses you could write about;
- you can view and review (for example, a location you can visit, a printed text, or a Web site or digital recording from which you can capture stills or video clips to use as examples in a multimedia presentation);
- is typically evaluated according to criteria or standards of judgment that you understand and share with your readers.

You may already have a subject in mind. If you do, skip to Test Your Choice: Choosing a Subject below. If you do not, the following topics, in addition to those following the readings (pp. 278, 283, 289), may suggest one you can write about effectively.

Subjects Related to School

- Evaluate some aspect of your high school or college—for example, a particular program or major you are considering; a residence hall, library, or lab; sports facilities or teams; a campus research institute or center; or campus work-study or student support services.
- Evaluate an article, an essay, a textbook, or another book assigned in a course; a campus newspaper blog, editorial, or opinion piece; or a campus performance, exhibit, or film series.

Subjects Related to Your Community

- Evaluate how well one of the following meets the needs of residents of your town or city: public library, health clinic, neighborhood watch or block parent program, meals-on-wheels program, theater, or symphony.
- Evaluate a law or a proposed law, such as the DREAM Act, the balanced budget amendment, or the equal rights amendment to the Constitution.

Subjects Related to Work

- Evaluate a job you have had or currently have, or evaluate the job performance of someone you have observed closely, such as a coworker or supervisor.
- Evaluate a local job-training program, either one in which you have participated or one that will allow you to observe and interview trainees.

TEST YOUR CHOICE

Choosing a Subject

After you have made a provisional choice, ask yourself the following questions:

- Do I know enough about the subject, or can I learn enough in the time I have?
- Do I already have a judgment (either tentative or certain) about this subject?
- Do I know what criteria or standards my readers are likely to use for judging something of this kind? Would I use the same criteria?

To try out your choice of a subject and ideas about criteria, get together with two or three other students:

Presenters. Take turns describing your subject.

Listeners. Briefly tell the presenter what criteria or standards of judgment you would use to evaluate a subject of this kind.

As you plan and draft your evaluation, you may need to reconsider your choice of subject (for example, if you discover your criteria for evaluating are different from those your readers would use). If you have serious doubts about your choice, discuss them with your instructor before starting over with a new subject.

Assess your subject and consider how to present it to your readers.

Once you have made a preliminary choice of a subject, consider how you can frame or reframe it so that readers will be open to your evaluation. To do this, consider first how you regard the subject and what your readers are likely to think. Use the following questions and sentence strategies as a jumping-off point. You can make the sentences you generate your own later, as you revise.

WAYS IN

WHAT DO I THINK?

List those qualities of your **SUBJECT** that you like and dislike, or list its strengths and weaknesses or advantages and disadvantages.

- What makes X good/bad is ________, ________, and ________.
- Although X is stellar in ________ [ways], it falls short in ________ [other ways].

What **GENRE** or kind of subject is it?

- X is a ________ [name genre or category of subject, such as romantic comedy or horror movie].
- X is an innovative example of ________ [name category in which the subject belongs] that combines elements of ________ and ________.

WHAT DO MY READERS THINK?

Who are your **READERS**, and why will they be reading your review? Is the subject new or familiar to them?

- My readers are ________ and are probably reading my review to learn about the subject/to decide whether to see it, play it, or buy it.
- My readers will probably be familiar with the subject. They may be curious to know what I think because ________.

How might **DEMOGRAPHIC FACTORS** such as readers' age, gender, cultural background, or work experience affect their judgment of the subject?

- Older/Younger readers are less/more likely to ________.

- X is rather unconventional for a ________ [name category in which the subject belongs].

What **CRITERIA** or standards of judgment do you usually use to evaluate things of this kind?

- I expect X to be ________ or ________.
- I dislike it when X is ________.

How does your subject **COMPARE** to other examples of the genre?

- Compared to Y, X has the best/worst ________ [name trait].
- X is like Y in that both are/do/make ________, but X is more/less ________.
- Whereas Y can be faulted/praised for ________, X ________.

- People who work in ________ or who are familiar with ________ may be more/less critical, or apply different standards to a subject like this one.

What **CRITERIA** or standards of judgment do you expect your readers to use when evaluating subjects of this kind? What other **EXAMPLES** of the genre would they be familiar with?

- I expect readers to share my criteria.
- If they like/dislike Y, they are sure to like/dislike X.
- Judging X on the basis of ________ is likely to surprise readers because they are probably more familiar with ________ and ________.

Formulate a working thesis stating your overall judgment.

You may already have a good idea about how you want to assert your thesis: stating whether your subject is good or bad, or better or worse than something else in the same genre or category. Remember that evaluations can be mixed—you can concede shortcomings in a generally favorable review or concede admirable qualities in a mostly negative assessment. If you feel comfortable drafting a working thesis statement now, do so. You may use the following sentence strategies as a jumping-off point—you can always revise them later—or use language of your own. (Alternatively, if you prefer to develop your argument before trying to formulate a thesis, skip this activity now and return to it later.)

As you develop your argument, you may want to rework your thesis to make it more compelling by sharpening the language and perhaps also by forecasting your reasons. You may also need to qualify your judgment with words like *generally, may,* or *in part.*

WAYS IN

HOW CAN I ASSERT A TENTATIVE OVERALL JUDGMENT?

A good strategy is to begin by **NAMING** the subject and **IDENTIFYING** the kind of subject it is, and then using **VALUE TERMS** to state your judgment of the subject's strengths and weaknesses:

- X is a brilliant embodiment of ________ [genre/category], especially notable for its superb ________ and thorough ________.
- Because I admire ________ [another artist's other work], I expected X to be ________. But I was disappointed/surprised by ________.
- X has many good qualities, including ________ and ________; however, its pluses do not outweigh its one major drawback, namely that ________.

Develop the reasons and evidence supporting your judgment.

The following activities will help you find reasons and evidence to support your evaluation. Begin by writing down what you already know. You can do some focused research later to fill in the details.

For more idea-generating strategies, see Chapter 9.

WAYS IN

HOW CAN I COME UP WITH REASONS AND EVIDENCE TO SUPPORT MY JUDGMENT?

List the good and bad qualities of the subject. Begin by reviewing the **CRITERIA** and the **VALUE TERMS** you have already used to describe the good and bad qualities of the subject. These are the potential **REASONS** for your judgment. Try restating them using this basic sentence strategy, which is also illustrated by an example from student William Akana's film review:

- X is ________ [your overall judgment] *because* ________, ________, and ________.

Example:

> *Scott Pilgrim vs. the World* can be appreciated and enjoyed by all audiences because of its inventive special effects, clever dialogue, and artistic cinematography, and editing. (par. 2)

Write steadily for at least five minutes, developing your reasons. Ask yourself questions like these:

- Why are the characteristics I'm pointing out for praise or criticism so important in judging my subject?

Example:

Akana singles out special effects, dialogue, cinematography, and editing because of the particular kind of film *Scott Pilgrim vs. the World* is—"a hilarious slacker movie that also somehow reimagines romantic comedy" (par. 1).

▶ How can I prove to readers that the value terms I'm using to evaluate these characteristics are fair and accurate?

Example:

Akana analyzes the film's special effects and gives readers specific examples, including screenshots, to demonstrate that they are indeed "inventive."

Make notes of the **EVIDENCE** you will use to support your judgment. Evidence you might use to support each reason may include the following:

- Examples
- Quotations from authorities
- Textual evidence (quotations, paraphrases, or summaries)
- Images
- Statistics
- Comparisons or contrasts

You may already have some evidence you could use. If you lack evidence for any of your reasons, make a *Research To-Do* note for later.

Research your evaluation.

Consult your *Research To-Do* notes to determine what you need to find out. If you are evaluating a subject that others have written about, try searching for articles or books on your topic. Enter keywords or phrases related to the subject, genre, or category into the search box of

- an all-purpose database—such as *Academic OneFile* (InfoTrac) or *Academic Search Complete* (EBSCOhost)—to find relevant articles in magazines and journals;
- the database *Lexis/Nexis* to find newspaper reviews;
- a search engine like *Google* or *Yahoo!* (Akana used *Movie Review Query Engine* [mrqe.com] and *Rotten Tomatoes* to find film reviews of *Scott Pilgrim vs. the World*);
- your library's catalog to locate books on your topic.

Turn to databases and search engines for information on more recent items, like films and popular novels; use books, databases, and search engines to find information on classic topics. (Books are more likely to provide in-depth information, but articles in print or online are more likely to be current.)

To learn more about searching a database or catalog, see Chapter 14.

Respond to a likely objection or alternative judgment.

Start by identifying an objection or an alternative judgment you expect some readers to raise. To come up with likely objections or alternative judgments, you might try the following:

- *Brainstorm* a list on your own or with fellow students.
- *Freewrite* for ten minutes on this topic.
- Conduct research to learn what others have said about your subject.
- Conduct interviews with experts.
- Distribute a survey to a group of people similar to your intended readers.

Then figure out whether to concede or refute a likely objection or alternative judgment. You may be able simply to acknowledge an objection or alternative judgment. But if the criticism is serious, consider conceding the point and qualifying your judgment. You might also try to refute an objection or alternative judgment by arguing that the standards you are using are appropriate and important. Use the following strategies for generating ideas and sentences as a jumping-off point, then revise them later to make them your own.

For more on idea-generating strategies, see Chapter 9; for more on conducting research, see Chapter 14.

WAYS IN

HOW CAN I RESPOND EFFECTIVELY TO MY READERS?

1. Start by listing **OBJECTIONS** you expect readers to have as well as their preferred **ALTERNATIVE JUDGMENTS.** In the Ways In activity on p. 300, you considered your readers and the criteria they are likely to favor. If their criteria differ from yours, you may need to explain or defend your criteria.
2. Analyze your list of objections and alternative judgments to determine which are likely to be most powerful for your readers.
3. Draft **REFUTATIONS** and **CONCESSION** statements:

To Refute

- Reviewer A claims that ________. But I agree with Reviewer B, who argues that ________.
- Some people claim that subject X is ________ because of ________, ________, and ________. Although one can see why they might make this argument, the evidence does not back it up because ________.
- In contrast to popular opinion, a recent study of ________ showed that ________.

To Concede

- Indeed, the more hard-core enthusiasts, like A, B, and C, may carp that ______ is not sufficiently ______.
- The one justifiable criticism that could be made against X is ______.
- As some critics have pointed out, X follows the tried-and-true formula of ______.

To Concede and Refute

Frequently, writers concede a point only to come back with a refutation. To make the **CONCESSION-REFUTATION MOVE**, follow concessions with sentences that begin with a **TRANSITION**—like *but, however, yet,* or *nevertheless*—and then explain why you believe that your interpretation or position is more powerful or compelling.

- As some critics have pointed out, X follows the tried-and-true formula of ______. Still, the director/writer/artist is using the formula effectively to ______.

Research Note: You may want to return to this activity after conducting further research. (For example, when he researched published reviews of *Scott Pilgrim,* student William Akana found objections to his argument as well as alternative judgments he could quote and refute.)

For more on the concession-refutation move, see Chapter 6, p. 189.

Organize your draft to appeal to your readers.

Whether you have rough notes or a complete draft, making an *outline* of what you have written can help you organize the essay effectively for your audience. An evaluative essay contains as many as four basic parts:

1. Presentation of the subject
2. Judgment of the subject
3. Presentation of reasons and support
4. Consideration of readers' objections and alternative judgments

These parts can be organized in various ways; two options follow:

If you are writing primarily for readers who disagree with your judgment, you could start by showing them what you think they have overlooked or misjudged about the subject. Then you could anticipate and refute their likely objections before presenting your own reasons.

I. **Present the subject:** Reframe subject in terms that support your judgment.

II. **Provide a thesis statement—** a direct statement of your position.

III. **Refute alternative judgments**

IV. **Provide first reason/support with refutation of objection**

V. **Provide the second reason/ support**

VI. **Provide the third reason/ support (and so on)**

VII. **Conclude:** Reiterate why your judgment is preferable to the alternatives.

If you expect some readers to disagree with your judgment even though they share your standards, you could begin by restating these standards and then demonstrate how the subject fails to meet them. Then you could present your reasons and support before responding to alternative judgments.

I. **Presentation of the issue:** Reassert shared criteria.

II. **Provide a thesis statement—** a direct statement of your position.

III. **Provide first reason/support showing how subject falls short**

IV. **Provide second reason/ support**

V. **Provide third reason/support (and so on)**

VI. **Refute alternative judgment**

VII. **Conclude:** Reassert judgment based on shared criteria.

Never be a slave to an outline: As you draft, you may see ways to improve your original plan, and you should be ready to shift parts around or drop or add parts as needed. If you use the outlining function of your word processing program, changing your outline will be simple, and you may be able to write the essay simply by expanding that outline.

For more on outlining, see Chapter 9, pp.320–24.

Consider document design.

Because evaluations depend heavily on excerpts from the subject, they frequently include quotations, paraphrases, or summaries of the subject. When the subject of evaluation is in a visual medium (as with films, television shows, works of art, and Web sites), writers may use movie stills, photographs, or screenshots as evidence to support their claims. Consider how William Akana used film stills from *Scott Pilgrim vs. the World* as evidence to support his claim that this film "can be appreciated and enjoyed by all audiences because of its inventive special effects" (par. 2).

Scott Pilgrim vs. the World shines bright with superb special effects that serve to reinforce the ideas, themes, and style of the film. Special effects are plentiful throughout the entire film, ranging from superimposed annotations echoing classic gaming features to artful backgrounds and action sequences modeled on colorful comic book pages. For example, each of the main characters is described for the first time with "gamertags," short-timed boxes of information that include name, age, and rating (see fig. 1).

Uses a film still to support his claim that the film offers inventive special effects (film still shows "gamertags")

Connects text discussion to the illustration with a figure callout

Fig. 1. Screen shot showing gamertags
Everett Collection, Inc.

Uses a caption to highlight what the illustration shows

Write the opening sentences.

Review what you have written to see if you have something that would work to launch your concept explanation, or try out some of these opening strategies:

Offer an **anecdote**:

> As I leaned back in the movie theater seat, accompanied by my friends on a typical Saturday night, I knew I was in for something special. I was reassured; not only had my friends and I reached a unanimous vote to watch *Scott Pilgrim vs. the World*, but two of my friends had already seen the film and were eager to see it again. (Akana, par. 1)

Start with an **assumption** *or expectation that will be reversed, perhaps surprisingly:*

> For critics, sorting through television pilots is an act of triage. Last year, when *Game of Thrones* landed on my desk, I skimmed two episodes and made a quick call: we'd have to let this one go. (Nussbaum, par. 1)

Begin with a **comparison** *your readers are likely to be familiar with:*

> *Car and Driver* conducted a comparison test of three sports cars, the Lotus Evora, the Chevrolet Corvette Grand Sport, and the Porsche Cayman S. (Gladwell, par. 1)

But don't agonize over the first sentences because you are likely to discover the best way to begin only after you have written a rough draft.

Draft your evaluation.

By this point, you have done a lot of writing to

- devise a well-presented subject and make a judgment about it;
- support your judgment with reasons and evidence that your readers will find persuasive;
- refute or concede objections and alternative judgments;
- organize your ideas to make them clear, logical, and effective for readers.

Now stitch that material together to create a draft. The next two parts of this Guide to Writing will help you evaluate and improve your draft.

Evaluating the Draft: Using Peer Review

Your instructor may arrange a peer review session in class or online, where you can exchange drafts with your classmates to give one another a thoughtful critical reading, pointing out what works well and suggesting ways to improve the draft. A good critical reading does three things:

1. It lets the writer know how well the reader understands the point of the essay.
2. It praises what works best.
3. It indicates where the draft could be improved and makes suggestions on how to improve it.

One strategy for evaluating a draft is to use the basic features of evaluative essays as a guide.

A PEER REVIEW GUIDE

A Well-Presented Subject

Has the writer presented the subject effectively?

Summarize: Tell the writer what you understand the subject of the evaluation to be, and identify the kind of subject it is.

Praise: Point to a place where the subject is presented effectively — for example, where it is described vividly and accurately, where it is named, or where it is clearly placed in a recognizable genre or category.

Critique: Tell the writer where readers might need more information about the subject, and whether any information about it seems inaccurate or possibly only partly true. Suggest how the writer could clarify the kind of subject it is, either by naming the category or by giving examples of familiar subjects of the same type.

A Well-Presented Subject

Has the writer supported the judgment effectively?

Summarize: Tell the writer what you understand the overall judgment to be, and list the criteria on which it is based.

Praise: Identify a passage in the essay where support for the judgment is presented effectively—for example, note particularly strong supporting reasons, appeals to criteria readers are likely to share, or especially compelling evidence.

Critique: Let the writer know if you cannot find a thesis statement or think the thesis is vague or overstated. Tell the writer where the evaluation could be improved—for example, suggest another reason that could be added, propose a way to justify one of the criteria on which the evaluation is based, or recommend a source or an example that could be used to bolster support for the judgment.

An Effective Response to Objections and Alternative Judgments

Has the writer responded effectively to objections and alternative judgments?

Summarize: Choose an objection or alternative judgment about the subject, and explain it in your own words.

Praise: Identify a passage in the essay where the writer responds effectively to an objection or alternative judgment. An effective response may include making a concession—for example, agreeing that a subject the writer is primarily criticizing has some good points, or agreeing that the subject has weaknesses as well as strengths.

Critique: Tell the writer where a response is needed or could be made more effective—for example, suggest a likely objection or alternative judgment that should be taken into account, help the writer understand the criteria behind an alternative judgment, or offer an example that could be used to refute an objection.

A Clear, Logical Organization

Is the evaluation clearly and logically organized?

Summarize: Briefly describe the strategies used to make the essay clear and easy to follow.

Praise: Give an example of where the essay succeeds in being readable—in its overall organization, in its clear presentation of the thesis, in its effective opening or closing, or by other means.

Critique: Tell the writer where the readability could be improved. Can you, for example, suggest a better beginning or a more effective ending? If the overall organization of the essay needs work, make suggestions for rearranging parts or strengthening connections.

Before concluding your peer review, be sure to address any of the writer's concerns that have not already been addressed.

Improving the Draft: Revising, Editing, and Proofreading

Start improving your draft by reflecting on what you have written thus far:

- Review critical reading comments from your classmates, instructor, or writing center tutor: What are your readers getting at?
- Consider whether you can add any of the notes from your earlier writings: What else should you consider?
- Review your draft: What else can you do to present your position more compellingly?

Revise your draft.

If your readers are having difficulty with your draft, or if you think there is room for improvement, try some of the strategies listed in the Troubleshooting Guide. They can help you fine-tune your presentation of the genre's basic features.

A TROUBLESHOOTING GUIDE

A Well-Presented Subject

My readers find my subject vague or do not think it has been identified clearly.

- Identify the subject, name the author or director, and give the title.
- Describe the subject—summarize what it is about, cite statistics that establish its importance, or give examples to make it concrete.
- Consider adding visuals—photographs, tables, or charts—to help clarify the subject.

My readers aren't sure what kind of subject it is.

- Classify the subject by naming the genre or category it fits into.
- Refer to reviews or reviewers of subjects of this kind.
- Compare your subject to other, better-known subjects of the same kind.

A Well-Supported Judgment

My readers don't find my thesis or overall judgment clear.

- State your thesis early in the essay.
- Clarify the language in your thesis statement to indicate your overall judgment.
- Consider whether your judgment is arguable (not simply a matter of taste). If you cannot provide reasons and support for it, then your judgment probably isn't arguable; ask your instructor about modifying your judgment or writing about a different subject.

My readers aren't convinced that my evaluation is reasonable or persuasive.

- Clarify the criteria on which you base your judgment, and justify them by citing authorities or reviews of similar subjects, making comparisons, or explaining why your criteria are appropriate and perhaps even preferable to criteria readers may be more familiar with.
- Add support for your reasons by, for example, quoting respected experts or research studies; providing facts or statistics; giving specific examples; or quoting, summarizing, or paraphrasing the subject of your evaluation.

(continued)

A Well-Supported Judgment

My readers don't understand my evaluation.

- Review the way you present your evaluation to make sure that you have explained it clearly and that you state your supporting reasons clearly.
- Outline your argument to be sure that it is clearly organized; if it is not, try rearranging parts or strengthening connections.
- Make sure that you have cut out any irrelevant content, and revise to strengthen the connections among your ideas.

An Effective Response to Objections and Alternative Judgments

My readers raise objections I haven't considered or find fault with my response to alternative judgments.

- If readers raise only a minor concern, you may be able to ignore or dismiss it. (Not every objection requires a response.)
- If readers raise a serious objection, one that undermines your argument, try to refute it by showing that it's not based on widely held or appropriate criteria or that it's based on a misunderstanding of your argument or the subject.
- If readers raise a serious objection that you can't refute, acknowledge it but try to demonstrate that it doesn't invalidate your judgment.

My readers have proposed alternative judgments or have found fault with how I handle alternatives.

- Address the alternative judgments directly by conceding good or bad qualities of the subject that others focus on, but emphasize that you disagree about the overall value of the subject.
- Point out where you and your readers agree on criteria but disagree on how well the subject meets the criteria.
- Where you disagree with readers on criteria, try to justify the standards you are applying by citing authorities or establishing your own authority.

A Clear, Logical Organization

My readers find my essay confusing or hard to follow.

- Outline your essay to review its structure, and move, add, or delete sections as necessary to strengthen coherence.
- Consider adding a forecasting statement early in your essay.
- Repeat your key terms or use synonyms of key terms to keep readers oriented.
- Check to see that you introduce your reasons clearly in topic sentences.
- Check to be sure that you provide appropriate transitions between sentences, paragraphs, and sections of your essay, especially at points where your readers have trouble following your argument.
- Review your opening and closing paragraphs to be sure that your overall judgment is clear and appropriately qualified.

Edit and proofread your draft.

Our research indicates that particular errors occur often in essays that justify an evaluation: incomplete and illogical comparisons, and short, choppy sentences. The following guidelines will help you check your essay for these common errors.

Making Complete, Logical, and Grammatically Correct Comparisons

The Problem In essays that justify an evaluation, writers often engage in comparison—showing, for example, that one film is stronger than another, a new recording is inferior to an earlier one, or one restaurant is better than another. When comparisons are expressed incompletely, illogically, or incorrectly, however, the point of the comparison can be dulled or lost completely.

The Correction Reread your comparisons, checking for completeness, logic, and correctness.

A comparison is complete if two terms are introduced, and the relationship between them is clearly expressed:

▶ *Jazz* is as good, [^as] if not better than, Morrison's other novels.

▶ I liked the Lispector story because it's so different [^from anything else I've ever read.].

A comparison is logical if the terms compared are parallel (and therefore comparable):

▶ Will Smith's Muhammad Ali is more serious than any [^other] role he's played.

▶ Ohio State's offense played much better than ~~Michigan.~~ [^Michigan's did.]

Note that *different from* is correct; *different than,* though commonly used, is incorrect:

▶ Carrying herself with a confident and brisk stride, Katherine Parker seems different ~~than~~ [^from] the other women in the office.

▶ Films like *Drive,* which glorify violence for its own sake, are different ~~than~~ [^from] films like *Apocalypse Now,* which use violence to make a moral point.

Combining Sentences

The Problem When writers justify an evaluation, they generally present their subject in some detail—defining it, describing it, placing it in some context. Inexperienced writers often present such details one after another, in short, choppy sentences. These sentences can be difficult or irritating to read, and they provide the reader with no help in determining how the different details relate to one another.

The Correction Combine sentences to make your writing more readable and to clarify the relationships among ideas. Two common strategies for sentence combining involve converting full sentences into **appositive phrases** (a noun phrase that renames the noun or pronoun that immediately precedes it) or **verbal phrases** (phrases using words derived from verbs that function as adjectives, adverbs, or nouns). Consider the following example:

▶ In paragraph 5, the details provide a different impression/— ~~It is~~ a comic or perhaps even pathetic impression/— ~~The impression comes from~~ *based on* the boy's attempts to dress up like a real westerner.

From three separate sentences, this writer smoothly combines details about the "different impression" into a single sentence, using an appositive phrase ("a comic or perhaps even pathetic impression") and a verbal phrase ("based on the boy's attempts to dress up like a real westerner").

Here are two additional examples of the first strategy (conversion into an appositive phrase):

▶ *Something Pacific* was created by Nam June Paik/, ~~He is~~ a Korean artist who is considered a founder of video art.

▶ One of Dylan's songs *, "Talkin' John Birch Paranoid Blues,"* ridiculed the John Birch Society. ~~This song was called "Talkin' John Birch Paranoid Blues."~~

Finally, here are two additional examples of the second strategy (conversion into a verbal phrase):

▶ Spider-Man's lifesaving webbing sprung from his wristbands/, ~~They carried~~ *carrying* Mary Jane Watson and him out of peril.

▶ The coffee bar flanks the bookshelves/, ~~It entices~~ *enticing* readers to relax with a book.

Reflecting on What You Have Learned

You have learned a great deal about this genre from reading several essays that justify an evaluation and from writing an evaluation of your own. To consolidate your learning, reflect not only on what you learned but also on how you learned it.

ANALYZE & WRITE

Write a blog post, a letter to your instructor or a classmate, or an e-mail message to a student who will take this course next term, using the writing prompt that seems most productive for you:

- Explain how your purpose and audience influenced *one* of your decisions as a writer, such as how you presented the subject, the strategies you used in justifying your evaluation, or the ways in which you attempted to counter possible objections.

- Discuss what you learned about yourself as a writer in the process of writing this essay. For example, what part of the process did you find most challenging? Did you try anything new, like getting a critical reading of your draft or outlining your draft in order to revise it? If so, how well did it work?
- If you were to give advice to a friend who was about to write an essay justifying an evaluation, what would you say?
- Which of the readings in this chapter influenced your essay? Explain the influence, citing specific examples from your essay and the reading.
- If you got good advice from a critical reader, explain exactly how the person helped you—perhaps by questioning the way you addressed your audience or the kinds of support you offered in support of your position.

© Marek Uliasz/Alamy

PART 2
Critical Thinking and Writing Strategies

9

A Catalog of Invention and Inquiry Strategies

Writers are like scientists: They ask questions, systematically inquiring about how things work, what they are, where they occur, and how more information can be learned about them. Writers are also like artists in that they use what they know and learn to create something new and imaginative.

The invention and inquiry strategies described in this chapter are not mysterious or magical. They represent the ways that writers, engineers, scientists, composers—in fact, all of us—solve problems. Once you have mastered these strategies, you can use them to tackle many of the writing situations you will encounter in college, on the job, and in the community.

The strategies for invention and inquiry in this chapter are arranged alphabetically within two categories:

Mapping: A brief visual representation of your thinking or planning

Writing: The composition of phrases or sentences to discover information and ideas and to make connections among them

These invention and inquiry strategies will help you explore and research a topic fully before you begin drafting, and then help you creatively solve problems as you draft and revise.

Mapping

Mapping strategies, like clustering, listing, and outlining, involve making a visual record of invention and inquiry. In making maps, writers usually use key words and phrases to record material they want to remember, questions they need to answer, and new sources of information they want to check. The maps show the ideas, details, and facts as well as possible ways to connect and focus them. Mapping can be especially useful for working collaboratively, preparing presentations, and creating multimedia illustrations for written texts you will submit either on paper or electronically.

For more on multimodal texts, see Chapter 13.

Create a cluster diagram to reveal relationships among ideas.

Clustering is a strategy for revealing possible relationships among facts and ideas. Clustering works as follows:

1. In a word or phrase, write your topic in the center of a piece of paper. Circle it.
2. Also in words or phrases, write down the main parts or ideas of your topic. Circle these, and connect them with lines to the topic in the center.
3. Next, write down facts, details, and examples related to these main parts or ideas. Connect them with lines to the relevant main parts or ideas.

Clustering can be useful in the early stages of composing to narrow a topic, find subtopics, and organize information. You may try out and discard several clusters before finding one that is promising. Many writers also use clustering to plan brief sections of a writing project as they are drafting or revising. (A model of clustering is shown in Figure 9.1.)

Software vendors have created a variety of electronic tools to help people better visualize complex projects. These flowcharts, webs, and outlines can make it easier for you to see how to proceed at any stage of your project.

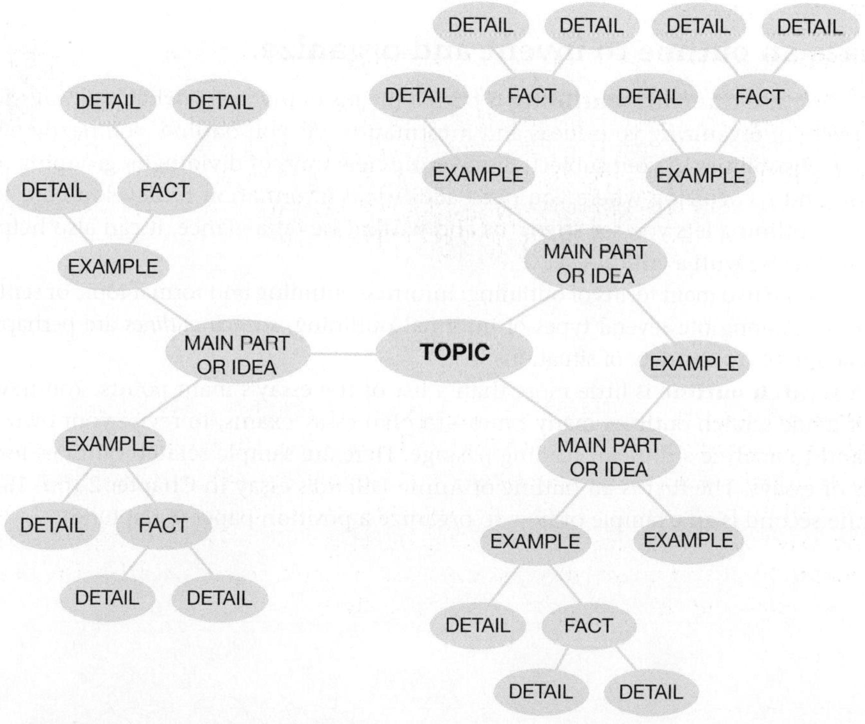

FIGURE 9.1 A Model of Clustering

Make a list to generate a plan quickly.

Listing is a familiar activity. You probably make shopping or to-do lists every day. But listing can also be a great help in planning a writing project. It enables you to recall what you already know about a topic and suggests what else you may need to find out. Listing is especially useful to those who have little time for planning—for example, reporters facing deadlines and college students taking essay exams—because it lets them order their ideas quickly. It can also serve as a first step in discovering possible writing topics.

Here is how listing works best for invention work:

1. Give your list a title that indicates your main idea or topic.
2. Write as fast as you can, relying on short phrases.
3. Include anything that seems at all useful. Try not to be judgmental at this point.
4. After you have finished or even as you write, reflect on and organize the list:
   - Put an asterisk next to the most promising items.
   - Number or reorder key items in order of importance.
   - Put items in related groups.
   - Cross out or delete items that do not seem promising.
   - Add new items.

Create an outline to invent and organize.

Like listing and clustering, **outlining** is both a means of inventing what you want to say and a way of organizing your ideas and information. As you outline, you nearly always see new possibilities in your subject, discovering new ways of dividing or grouping information and recognizing where you need additional information to develop your ideas. Because outlining lets you see strengths and weaknesses at a glance, it can also help you read and revise with a critical eye.

There are two main forms of outlining: informal outlining and formal topic or sentence outlining. Among the several types of informal outlining, *scratch outlines* are perhaps the most adaptable to a variety of situations.

A **scratch outline** is little more than a list of the essay's main points. You have no doubt made scratch outlines many times—to plan essay exams, to revise your own writing, and to analyze a difficult reading passage. Here are sample scratch outlines for two kinds of essays. The first is an outline of Annie Dillard's essay in Chapter 2 (pp. 18–20), and the second is an example of how to organize a position paper (Chapter 6):

Scratch Outline: Essay about a Remembered Event

¶1. explains what she learned from playing football
¶2. identifies other sports she learned from boys in the neighborhood
¶3. sets the scene by describing the time and place of the event
¶4. describes the boys who were playing with her
¶5. describes what typically happened: a car would come down the street, they would throw snowballs, and then they would wait for another car
¶6. describes the iceball-making project she had begun while waiting
¶7. describes the Buick's approach and how they followed the routine

Scratch Outline: Essay Arguing a Position

Presentation of the issue
Concession of some aspect of an opposing position
Thesis statement
First reason with support
Second reason with support
(etc.)
Conclusion

Remember that the items in a scratch outline do not necessarily coincide with paragraphs. Sometimes two or more items may be developed in the same paragraph, or one item may be covered in two or more paragraphs.

Chunking, a type of scratch outline commonly used by professional writers in business and industry and especially well suited to collaborative and multimodal composing, consists of a set of headings describing the major points to be covered in the final document. What makes chunking distinctive is that the blocks of text—or "chunks"—under each heading are intended to be roughly of the same length and scope. These headings can be discussed and passed around among several writers and editors before writing begins, and different chunks may be written by different authors, simply by typing notes into the space under each heading. The list of headings is subject to change during the writing, and new headings may be added or old ones subdivided or discarded as part of the drafting and revising processes.

The advantage of chunking in your own writing is that it breaks the large task of drafting into smaller tasks in a simple, evenly balanced way. Once the headings are determined, the writing becomes a matter of filling in the specifics that go in each chunk. Organization tends to improve as you get a sense of the weight of different parts of the document while filling in the blanks. Places where the writing project needs more information or where there is a problem with pacing tend to stand out because of the chunking structure, and the headings can be either taken out of the finished project or left in as devices to help guide readers. If they are left in, they should be edited into parallel grammatical form like the items in a formal topic or sentence outline.

For more on parallelism, see Chapter 11, p. 365.

Topic outlines and **sentence outlines** are considered more formal than scratch outlines because they follow a conventional format of numbered and lettered headings and subheadings:

Period follows numbers and letters

First word of each item is capitalized

```
I. Main topic
   A. Subtopic of I
   B.
      1. Subtopic of I.B
      2.
         a. Subtopic of I.B.2
         b.
            (1) Subtopic of I.B.2.b
            (2)
   C.
      1. Subtopic of I.C
      2.
```

The difference between a topic and a sentence outline is obvious: Topic outlines simply name the topics and subtopics, whereas sentence outlines use complete or abbreviated sentences. To illustrate, here are two partial formal outlines of an essay arguing a position, Jessica Statsky's "Children Need to Play, Not Compete," from Chapter 6 (pp. 190–96).

Formal Topic Outline

I. Organized sports harmful to children
  A. Harmful physically
    1. Curve ball (Koppett)
    2. Tackle football (Tutko)
  B. Harmful psychologically
    1. Fear of being hurt
      a. Little League
      b. Mother
      c. Reporter
    2. Competition
      a. Rablovsky
      b. Studies

Formal Sentence Outline

I. Highly organized competitive sports, such as Peewee Football and Little League Baseball, can be physically and psychologically harmful to children, as well as counterproductive for developing future players.
  A. Physically harmful because sports entice children into physical actions that are bad for growing bodies.
    1. Koppett claims throwing a curve ball may put abnormal strain on developing arm and shoulder muscles.
    2. Tutko argues that tackle football is too traumatic for young kids.
  B. Psychologically harmful to children for a number of reasons.
    1. Fear of being hurt detracts from their enjoyment of the sport.
      a. Little League ranks fear of injury seventh among top reasons children quit.
      b. One mother says, "Kids get so scared. . . . They'll sit on the bench and pretend their leg hurts."
      c. A reporter tells about a child who made himself vomit to get out of playing Peewee Football.
    2. Too much competition poses psychological dangers for children.
      a. Rablovsky reports: "The spirit of play suddenly disappears, and sport becomes joblike."
      b. Studies show that children prefer playing on a losing team to "warming the bench on a winning team."

Every level of a formal outline except the top level (identified by the roman numeral *I*) must include at least two items. Items at the same level of indentation in a topic outline should be grammatically parallel—all beginning with the same part of speech. For example, *I.A* and *I.B* are parallel when they both begin with an adverb (*Physically harmful* and *Psychologically harmful*) or with an adjective (*Harmful physically* and *Harmful psychologically*); they would not be parallel if one began with an adverb (*Physically harmful*) and the other with an adjective (*Harmful psychologically*).

Writing

Writing strategies—including cubing, dialoguing, dramatizing, freewriting, keeping a journal, looping, and questioning—invite you to produce complete sentences, so they provide considerable generative power. Because they are complete statements, they take you further than listing or clustering, enabling you to explore ideas and define relationships, bring ideas together or show how they differ, identify causes and effects, and develop a logical chain of thought.

Use cubing to explore a topic from six perspectives.

Cubing allows you to explore a writing topic from six perspectives (the number of sides in a cube):

Describing: What does your subject look like? What size is it? What is its color? Its shape? Its texture? Name its parts.

Comparing: What is your subject similar to? Different from?

Associating: What does your subject make you think of? What connections does it have to anything else in your experience?

Analyzing: What are the origins of your subject? What are the functions or significance of its parts? How are its parts related?

Applying: What can you do with your subject? What uses does it have?

Arguing: What arguments can you make for your subject? Against it?

These guidelines can help you use cubing productively:

1. **Select a topic, subject, or part of a subject.** This can be a person, a scene, an event, an object, a problem, an idea, or an issue. Hold it in focus.
2. **Limit your writing to three to five minutes for each perspective.** The whole activity should take no more than half an hour.
3. **Keep going until you have written about your subject from all six perspectives.** Remember that cubing offers the special advantage of enabling you to generate multiple perspectives quickly.
4. **As you write from each perspective, begin with what you know about your subject.** However, do not limit yourself to your present knowledge. Indicate what else you would like to know about your subject, and suggest where you might find that information.

5. **Reread what you have written.** Look for bright spots or surprises. Recall the part that was easiest for you to write. Recall the part where you felt a special momentum and pleasure in writing. Look for an angle or an unexpected insight. These special parts may suggest a focus or topic within a larger subject, or they may provide specific details to include in a draft.

Construct a dialogue to explore an experience or alternative view.

A *dialogue* is a conversation between two or more people. You can use **dialoguing** to search for topics, find a focus, explore ideas, or consider opposing viewpoints. When you write a dialogue as an invention strategy, you need to make up all parts of the conversation (unless, of course, you are writing collaboratively). Following these steps can help:

1. **Write a conversation between two speakers.** Label the participants *Speaker A* and *Speaker B,* or make up names for them.
2. **Write brief responses to keep the conversation moving fast.** Do not spend much time planning or rehearsing responses. Write what first occurs to you, just as in a real conversation, in which people take quick turns to prevent any awkward silences.
3. **If you get stuck, you might have one of the speakers ask the other a question.**

Dialogues can be especially useful in writing based on personal experience and persuasive essays because they help you remember conversations and anticipate objections.

Use dramatizing to analyze behavior.

Dramatizing is an invention activity developed by philosopher Kenneth Burke as a way of thinking about how people interact and as a way of analyzing stories and films. Thinking about human behavior in dramatic terms can be very productive for writers. Drama has action, actors, setting, motives, and methods. A five-pointed star can help you remember these five points of dramatizing (see Figure 9.2).

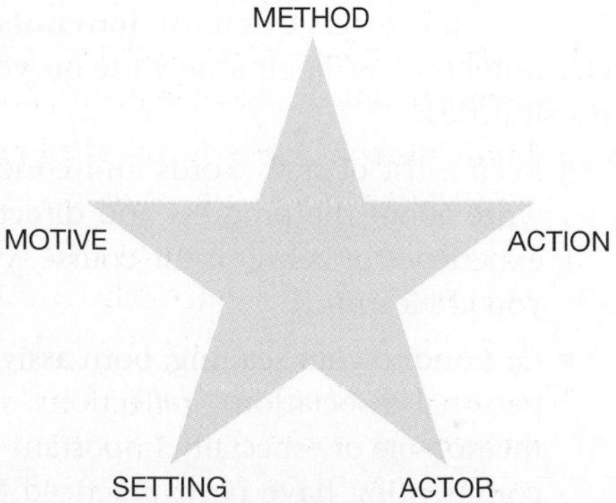

FIGURE 9.2 Dramatizing

Action *Action* answers the question "what?" An action is anything that happens, has happened, will happen, or could happen. Action includes events that are physical (running a marathon), mental (thinking about a book you have read), and emotional (falling in love).

Actor The *actor* answers the question "who?" The actor is either responsible for or affected by the action. The actor may be anything that causes an action. For example, if the action is a rise in the price of gasoline, the actor could be increased demand or short supply. Dramatizing may also include a number of actors working together or at odds.

Setting *Setting* answers the questions "when?" and "where?" We usually think of setting as the place and time of an event, but it may also be the historical background of an event or the childhood of a person.

Motive *Motive* answers the question "why?" The motive is the purpose or reason for an action—the actor's intention. Actions may have multiple, even conflicting, motives.

Method *Method* answers the question "how?" The method explains how an action occurs, including the techniques an actor uses. It refers to whatever makes things happen.

This list answers the questions reporters typically ask. But dramatizing goes further: It enables us to consider relations among these five elements. You can also use this invention strategy to analyze the readers you want to inform or convince.

Freewrite to generate ideas freely and creatively.

Freewriting is a technique that requires you to stop judging what you write and simply let your mind wander in order to generate ideas freely and creatively. To freewrite, set a certain amount of time, say ten to fifteen minutes, and then simply write, generating as much text as you can in the allotted time. While freewriting, try not to stop; if you cannot think of anything to say, simply write "don't know what to say" over and over until an idea comes to you. If you find it difficult to avoid editing yourself, try turning down the brightness on your monitor or lowering the screen on your laptop until you can no longer see what it says.

A variation on freewriting is **focused freewriting**. In focused freewriting, you begin from a specific topic, returning to the beginning topic whenever you find yourself getting off track.

Take notes in a journal.

Professional writers often use **journals** to keep notes. Starting one is easy. Buy a special notebook, or open a new file on your computer, and start writing. Here are some possibilities:

- Keep a list of new words and concepts you learn in your courses. You could also write about the progress and direction of your learning in particular courses—the experience of being in the course, your feelings about what is happening, and what you are learning.
- Respond to your reading, both assigned and personal. As you read, write about your personal associations, reflections, reactions, and evaluations. Summarize or copy memorable or especially important passages, and comment on them. (Copying and commenting have been practiced by students and writers for centuries in special journals called *commonplace books*.)

- Write to prepare for particular class meetings. Write about the main ideas you have learned from assigned readings and about the relationship of these new ideas to other ideas in the course. After class, write to summarize what you have learned. List questions you have about the ideas or information discussed in class. Journal writing of this kind involves reflecting, evaluating, interpreting, synthesizing, summarizing, and questioning.
- Write for ten or fifteen minutes every day about whatever is on your mind. Focus these meditations on your new experiences as you try to understand, interpret, and reflect on them, or write sketches of people who catch your attention, recording observations and overheard conversation.
- Organize your time. Write about your goals and priorities, or list specific things to accomplish and what you plan to do.
- Keep a log over several days or weeks about a particular event unfolding in the news—a sensational trial, an environmental disaster, a political campaign, a campus controversy, or the fortunes of a sports team.

Use looping to explore aspects of a topic.

Looping is especially useful for the first stages of exploring a topic. Like focused freewriting, **looping** involves writing quickly to explore some aspect of a topic. But it differs in that the focus is on looping back to your original starting point or to a new starting point to explore another aspect. Beginning with almost any starting point, looping enables you to find a center of interest and eventually a thesis for your essay. The steps are simple:

1. **Write down your area of interest.** You may know only that you have to write about another person or a movie or a cultural trend that has caught your attention. Or you may want to search for a topic in a broad historical period or for one related to a major political event. Although you may wander from this topic as you write, you will want to keep coming back to it. Your purpose is to find a focus for writing.
2. **Write nonstop for ten minutes.** Start with the first thing that comes to mind. Write rapidly, without looking back to reread or to correct anything. *Do not stop writing. Keep your pencil moving or keystrokes clacking.* Continuous writing is the key to looping. If you get stuck for a moment, rewrite the last sentence. Follow diversions and digressions, but keep returning to your topic.
3. **After ten minutes, pause to reread what you have written.** Decide what is most important—a single insight, a pattern of ideas, an emerging theme, a visual detail, anything at all that stands out. Some writers call this a "center of gravity" or a "hot spot." To complete the first loop, restate this center of gravity in a single sentence.
4. **Beginning with this sentence, write nonstop for another ten minutes.** Summarize in one sentence again to complete the second loop. Keep looping until one of your summary sentences produces a focus or thesis. You may need only two or three loops; you may need more.

Ask questions to explore a subject systematically.

Asking questions about a subject is a way to learn about it and decide what to write. When you first encounter a subject, however, your questions may be scattered. Also, you are not likely to think right away of all the important questions you ought to ask. The advantage of having a basic list of questions for invention, like the ones for cubing and for dramatizing discussed earlier in this chapter, is that it provides a systematic approach to exploring a subject.

The questions that follow are based on the work of linguist Kenneth Pike. Here are the steps in using questions for invention:

1. **In a sentence or two, identify your subject.** A subject could be any event, person, problem, project, idea, or issue—in other words, anything you might write about.
2. **Start by writing a response to the first question in the lists that follow, and move right through the lists.** Try to answer each question at least briefly with a word or a phrase. Some questions may invite several sentences or even a page or more of writing. You may draw a blank on a few questions. Skip them. Later, when you have more experience with questions for invention, you can start anywhere in the list.
3. **Write your responses quickly, without much planning.** Follow digressions or associations. Do not screen anything out. Be playful.

What Is Your Subject?

- What is your subject's name? What other names does it have or has it had?
- What aspects of the subject do these different names emphasize?
- Imagine a photograph or movie of your subject. What would it look like?
- What would you put into a time capsule to stand for your subject?
- What are its causes and effects?
- How would it look from different vantage points or perspectives?
- What experiences have you had with the subject? What have you learned?

What Parts or Features Does Your Subject Have, and How Are They Related?

- Name the parts or features of your subject.
- Describe each one, using the questions in the preceding subject list.
- How is each part or feature related to the others?

How Is Your Subject Similar to and Different from Other Subjects?

- What is your subject similar to? In what ways?
- What is your subject different from? In what ways?
- What seems to you most unlike your subject? In what ways? Now, just for fun, note how they are alike.

How Much Can Your Subject Change and Still Remain the Same?

- How has your subject changed from what it once was?
- How is it changing now—moment to moment, day to day, year to year?
- How does each change alter your way of thinking about your subject?
- What are some different forms your subject takes?
- What does it become when it is no longer itself?

Where Does Your Subject Fit in the World?

- When and where did your subject originate?
- What would happen if at some future time your subject ceased to exist?
- When and where do you usually experience your subject?
- What is your subject a part of, and what are the other parts?
- What do other people think of your subject?

10

A Catalog of Reading Strategies

This chapter presents strategies for reading critically that you can apply to the selections in this book as well as to your other college reading.

- ***Annotating:*** Recording your reactions to, interpretations of, and questions about a text as you read it
- ***Taking inventory:*** Listing and grouping your annotations and other notes to find meaningful patterns
- ***Outlining:*** Listing the text's main ideas to reveal how it is organized
- ***Paraphrasing:*** Restating what you have read to clarify or refer to it
- ***Summarizing:*** Distilling the main ideas or gist of a text
- ***Synthesizing:*** Integrating into your own writing ideas and information gleaned from different sources
- ***Contextualizing:*** Placing a text in its historical and cultural context
- ***Exploring the significance of figurative language:*** Examining how metaphors, similes, and symbols are used in a text to convey meaning and evoke feelings
- ***Looking for patterns of opposition:*** Inferring the values and assumptions embodied in the language of a text
- ***Reflecting on challenges to your beliefs and values:*** Examining the bases of your personal responses to a text
- ***Evaluating the logic of an argument:*** Determining whether an argument is well reasoned and adequately supported
- ***Recognizing emotional manipulation:*** Identifying texts that unfairly and inappropriately use emotional appeals based on false or exaggerated claims
- ***Judging the writer's credibility:*** Considering whether writers represent different points of view fairly and know what they are writing about

For more about annotating, see Chapter 5; for more about outlining, see Chapter 9; for more about paraphrasing, see Chapter 15; for more about summarizing and synthesizing, see Chapters 5 and 15; for more about logical fallacies, see Chapter 12.

Annotating

Annotations are the marks—underlines, highlights, and comments—you make directly on the page as you read. Annotating can be used to record immediate reactions and questions; outline and summarize main points; and evaluate and relate the reading to other ideas, readings, and points of view. Annotating can be done on paper with a pencil, pen, or highlighter, or on-screen by using your software's highlighting and commenting functions (or simply by typing annotations into the text using a different color or font).

Your annotations can take many forms, such as the following:

- Inserting comments, questions, or definitions in the margins
- Underlining or circling words, phrases, or sentences
- Connecting ideas with lines or arrows
- Numbering related points
- Bracketing sections of the text
- Noting anything that strikes you as interesting, important, or questionable

Most readers annotate in layers, adding further annotations on second and third readings. Annotations can be light or heavy, depending on your purpose and the difficulty of the material. Your purpose for reading also determines how you use your annotations.

The following selection, excerpted from Martin Luther King Jr.'s "Letter from Birmingham Jail," illustrates some of the ways you can annotate as you read. Add your own annotations, if you like.

Martin Luther King Jr. | *An Annotated Sample from "Letter from Birmingham Jail"*

Photo by Howard Sochurek/Time Life Pictures/Getty Images

MARTIN LUTHER KING JR. (1929–1968) first came to national notice in 1955, when he led a successful boycott against the policy of restricting African American passengers to rear seats on city buses in Montgomery, Alabama, where he was minister of a Baptist church. He subsequently formed the Southern Christian Leadership Conference, which brought people of all races from all over the country to the South to fight nonviolently for racial integration. In 1963, King led demonstrations in Birmingham, Alabama, that were met with violence; a bomb was detonated in a black church, killing four young girls. King was arrested for his role in organizing the protests, and while in prison, he wrote his "Letter from Birmingham Jail" to justify his strategy of civil disobedience, which he called "nonviolent direct action."

King begins his letter by discussing his disappointment with the lack of support he has received from white moderates, such as the group of clergy who published criticism of his organization in the local newspaper.

As you read, try to infer what the clergy's specific criticisms might have been, and notice the tone King uses. Would you characterize the writing as apologetic, conciliatory, accusatory, or something else?

¶1. White moderates block progress.

Contrasts: order vs. justice, negative vs. positive peace, ends vs. means

(treating others like children)

more contrasts

I must confess that over the past few years I have been gravely disappointed with the white moderate. I have almost reached the regrettable conclusion that the Negro's [great stumbling block in his stride toward freedom] is not the White Citizen's Counciler or the Ku Klux Klanner, but the white moderate, who is more devoted to "order" than to justice; who prefers a negative peace which is the absence of tension to a positive peace which is the presence of justice; who constantly says: "I agree with you in the goal you seek, but I cannot agree with your methods of direct action"; who paternalistically believes he can set the timetable for another man's freedom; who lives by a mythical concept of time and who constantly advises the Negro to wait for a "more convenient season." Shallow understanding from people of good will is more frustrating than absolute misunderstanding from people of ill will. [Lukewarm acceptance is much more bewildering than outright rejection.] 1

¶2. What the moderates don't understand

metaphor: law and order = dams (faulty?)

repeats contrast (negative/positive)

Tension already exists: We help dispel it. (True?)

simile: hidden tension is "like a boil"

I had hoped that the white moderate would understand that law and order exist for the purpose of establishing justice and that when they fail in this purpose they become the [dangerously structured dams that block the flow of social progress.] I had hoped that the white moderate would understand that the present tension in the South is a necessary phase of the transition from an [obnoxious negative peace,] in which the Negro passively accepted his unjust plight, to a [substantive and positive peace,] in which all men will respect the dignity and worth of human personality. Actually, we who engage in nonviolent direct action are not the creators of tension. We merely bring to the surface the hidden tension that is already alive. We bring it out in the open, where it can be seen and dealt with. [Like a boil that can never be cured so long as it is covered up but must be opened with all its ugliness to the natural medicines of air and light, injustice must be exposed, with all the tension its exposure creates, to the light of human conscience and the air of national opinion before it can be cured.] 2

¶13. Questions clergymen's logic: condemning his actions = condemning robbery victim, Socrates, Jesus

repetition ("Isn't this like . . .")

In your statement you assert that our actions, even 3
though peaceful, must be condemned because they precipitate violence. But is this a logical assertion? [Isn't this like condemning a robbed man because his possession of money precipitated the evil act of robbery? Isn't this like condemning Socrates because his unswerving commitment to truth and his philosophical inquiries precipitated the act by the misguided populace in which they made him drink hemlock? Isn't this like condemning Jesus because his unique God-consciousness and never-ceasing devotion to God's will precipitated the evil act of crucifixion?] We must come to see that, as the federal courts have consistently affirmed, it is wrong to urge an individual to cease his efforts to gain his basic constitutional rights because the question may precipitate violence. [Society must protect the robbed and punish the robber.]

(Yes!)

I had also hoped that the white moderate would reject 4
the myth concerning time in relation to the struggle for freedom. I have just received a letter from a white brother in Texas. He writes: "All Christians know that the colored people will receive equal rights eventually, but it is possible that you are in too great a religious hurry. It has taken Christianity almost two thousand years to accomplish what it has. The teachings of Christ take time to come to earth." Such an attitude stems from a tragic misconception of time, from the strangely irrational notion that there is something in the very flow of time that will inevitably cure all ills. Actually, time itself is neutral; it can be used either destructively or constructively. More and more I feel that the people of ill will have used time much more effectively than have the people of good will. We will have to repent in this generation not merely for the [hateful words and actions of the bad people] but for the [appalling silence of the good people.] Human progress never rolls in on [wheels of inevitability;] it comes through the tireless efforts of men willing to be co-workers with God, and without this hard work, time itself becomes an

example of a white moderate's view

¶14. Time must be used to do right.

Silence/passivity is as bad as hateful words and actions.

metaphor (mechanical?)

stop developing

metaphors (song, natural world)

ally of the forces of social stagnation. [We must use time creatively, in the knowledge that the time is always ripe to do right.] Now is the time to make real the promise of democracy and transform our pending [national elegy] into a creative [psalm of brotherhood.] Now is the time to lift our national policy from the [quicksand of racial injustice] to the [solid rock of human dignity.]

King accused of being an extremist

¶5. Puts self in middle of two extremes: complacency and bitterness

Malcolm X?

You speak of our activity in Birmingham as extreme. 5
At first I was rather disappointed that fellow clergymen would see my nonviolent efforts as those of an extremist. I began thinking about the fact that I stand in the middle of two opposing forces in the Negro community. One is a [force of complacency,] made up in part of Negroes who, as a result of long years of oppression, are so drained of self-respect and a sense of "somebodiness" that they have adjusted to segregation; and in part of a few middle-class Negroes, who because of a degree of academic and economic security and because in some ways they profit by segregation, have become insensitive to the problems of the masses. The other [force is one of bitterness and hatred,] and it comes perilously close to advocating violence. It is expressed in the various black nationalist [groups that are springing up] across the nation, the largest and best-known being Elijah Muhammad's Muslim movement. Nourished by the Negro's frustration over the continued existence of racial discrimination, this movement is made up of people who have lost faith in America, who have absolutely repudiated Christianity, and who have concluded that the white man is an incorrigible "devil."

¶6. Offers better choice: nonviolent protest

(How did nonviolence become part of King's movement?)

I have tried to stand between these two forces, saying 6
that we need emulate neither the "do-nothingism" of the complacent nor the hatred and despair of the black nationalist. For there is the more excellent way of love and nonviolent protest. I am grateful to God that, through the influence of the Negro church, the way of nonviolence became an integral part of our struggle.

If this philosophy had not emerged, by now many streets of the South would, I am convinced, be flowing with blood. And I am further convinced that if our white brothers dismiss as "rabble-rousers" and "outside agitators" those of us who employ nonviolent direct action, and if they refuse to support our nonviolent efforts, millions of Negroes will, out of frustration and despair, seek solace and security in black-nationalist ideologies—a development that would inevitably lead to a frightening racial nightmare. 7

¶7. Says movement prevents racial violence. (Threat?)

(comfort)

[Oppressed people cannot remain oppressed forever.] 8
The yearning for freedom eventually manifests itself, and that is what has happened to the American Negro. Something within has reminded him of his birthright of freedom, and something without has reminded him that it can be gained. Consciously or unconsciously, he has been caught up by the *Zeitgeist,* and with his black brothers of Africa and his brown and yellow brothers of Asia, South America and the Caribbean, the United States Negro is moving with a sense of great urgency toward the [promised land of racial justice.] If one recognizes this [vital urge that has engulfed the Negro community,] one should readily understand why public demonstrations are taking place. The Negro has many [pent-up resentments] and latent frustrations, and he must release them. So let him march; let him make prayer pilgrimages to the city hall; let him go on freedom rides—and try to understand why he must do so. If his repressed emotions are not released in nonviolent ways, they will seek expression through violence; this is not a threat but a fact of history. So I have not said to my people: "Get rid of your discontent." Rather, I have tried to say that this normal and healthy discontent can be [channeled into the creative outlet of nonviolent direct action.] And now this approach is being termed extremist.

(spirit of the times)

Not a threat, but a fact?

¶8. Discontent is normal, healthy, and historically inevitable, but it must be channeled.

But though I was initially disappointed at being categorized as an extremist, as I continued to think about the 9

¶9. Redefines "extremism"; embraces "extremist" label

matter I gradually gained a measure of satisfaction from the label. Was not Jesus an extremist for love: "Love your enemies, bless them that curse you, do good to them that hate you, and pray for them which despitefully use you, and persecute you." Was not Amos an extremist for justice: "Let justice roll down like waters and righteousness like an ever-flowing stream." Was not Paul an extremist for the Christian gospel: "I bear in my body the marks of the Lord Jesus." Was not Martin Luther an extremist: "Here I stand; I cannot do otherwise, so help me God." And John Bunyan: "I will stay in jail to the end of my days before I make a butchery of my conscience." And Abraham Lincoln: "This nation cannot survive half slave and half free." And Thomas Jefferson: "We hold these truths to be self-evident, that all men are created equal. . . ." [So the question is not whether we will be extremists, but what kind of extremists we will be.] Will we be extremists for hate or for love? Will we be extremists for the preservation of injustice or for the extension of justice? In that dramatic scene on Calvary's hill three men were crucified. We must never forget that all three were crucified for the same crime—the crime of extremism. Two were extremists for immorality, and thus fell below their environment. The other, Jesus Christ, was an extremist for love, truth and goodness, and thereby rose above his environment. Perhaps the South, the [nation and the world are in dire need of creative extremists.]

(Hebrew prophet)

(Christian apostle)

(founder of Protestantism)

(English preacher)

Compares self to great "extremists"— including Jesus

Disappointed in the white moderate

I had hoped that the white moderate would see this 10 need. Perhaps I was too optimistic; perhaps I expected too much. I suppose I should have realized that few members of the oppressor race can understand the deep groans and passionate yearnings of the oppressed race, and still fewer have the vision to see that [injustice must be rooted out] by strong, persistent and determined action. I am thankful, however, that some of our white brothers in the South have grasped the meaning of this social revolution

¶10. Praises whites who have supported movement

and committed themselves to it. They are still all too few in quantity, but they are big in quality. Some—such as Ralph McGill, Lillian Smith, Harry Golden, James McBride Dabbs, Ann Braden and Sarah Patton Boyle—have written about our struggle in eloquent and prophetic terms. Others have marched with us down nameless streets of the South. They have languished in filthy, roach-infested jails, suffering the abuse and brutality of policemen who view them as "dirty nigger-lovers." Unlike so many of their moderate brothers and sisters, they have recognized the urgency of the moment and sensed the need for [powerful "action" antidotes] to combat the [disease of segregation.]

(Who are they?)

(been left unaided)

Metaphor: segregation is a disease

ANALYZE & WRITE

1. Select a reading from Chapters 2 to 8 or from another text, and mark the text using annotations like these:
   - Circle words to be defined in the margin.
   - Underline key words and phrases.
   - Bracket important sentences and passages.
   - Use lines or arrows to connect ideas or words.
2. Write marginal comments like these:
   - Number and summarize each paragraph.
   - Define unfamiliar words.
   - Note responses and questions.
   - Identify interesting writing strategies.
   - Point out patterns.
3. Layer additional markings in the text and comments in the margins as you reread for different purposes.

Taking Inventory

Taking inventory helps you analyze your annotations for different purposes. When you take inventory, you make various kinds of lists to explore patterns of meaning you find in the text. For instance, in reading the annotated passage by Martin Luther King Jr., you might have noticed that certain similes and metaphors are used or that many famous people are named. By listing the names (Socrates, Jesus, Luther, Lincoln, and so on) and then grouping them into categories (people who died for their beliefs, leaders, teachers, and religious figures), you could better understand why the writer refers to these particular people. Taking inventory of your annotations can be helpful if you plan to write about a text you are reading.

ANALYZE & WRITE

1. Examine the annotations you made in the activity above for patterns or repetitions, such as recurring images, stylistic features, repeated words and phrases, repeated examples or illustrations, and reliance on particular writing strategies.
2. List the items that make up a pattern.
3. Decide what the pattern might reveal about the reading.

Outlining

Outlining is an especially helpful reading strategy for understanding the content and structure of a reading. **Outlining**, which identifies the text's main ideas, may be part of the annotating process, or it may be done separately. Writing an outline in the margins of the text as you read and annotate makes it easier to find information later. Writing an outline on a separate piece of paper or online gives you more space to work with, and therefore such an outline usually includes more detail.

The key to outlining is distinguishing between the main ideas and the supporting material, such as examples, quotations, comparisons, and reasons. The main ideas form the backbone that holds the various parts of the text together. Outlining the main ideas helps you uncover this structure.

Making an outline, however, is not simple. Readers must exercise judgment in deciding which are the most important ideas. The words used in an outline reflect the reader's interpretation and emphasis. Readers also must decide when to use the writer's words, their own words, or a combination of the two.

You may make either a formal, multileveled outline or an informal scratch outline. You might choose to make a formal outline of a reading about which you are writing an in-depth analysis or evaluation and a scratch outline to help you identify the main idea in each paragraph of a reading assignment. For example, here is a formal outline a student wrote for an essay evaluating the logic of the King excerpt:

Formal Outline of "Letter from Birmingham Jail"

I. "[T]he Negro's great stumbling block in his stride toward freedom is . . . the white moderate" (par. 1).
   A. White moderates are more devoted to "order" than to justice; however,
      1. law and order exist only to establish justice (par. 2)
      2. law and order *without* justice actually threaten social order ("dangerously structured dams" metaphor, par. 2)

B. White moderates prefer "negative peace" (absence of tension) to "positive peace" (justice); however,
   1. tension already exists; it is not created by movement (par. 2)
   2. tension is a necessary phase in progress to a just society (par. 2)
   3. tension must be allowed outlet if society is to be healthy ("boil" simile, par. 2)

C. White moderates disagree with methods of movement; however,
   1. nonviolent direct action can't be condemned for violent response to it (analogies: robbed man; Socrates; Jesus, par. 3)
   2. federal courts affirm that those who seek constitutional rights can't be held responsible for violent response (par. 3)

D. White moderates paternalistically counsel patience, saying time will bring change; however,
   1. time is "neutral"—we are obligated to use it *actively* to achieve justice (par. 4)
   2. the time for action is now (par. 4)

II. Contrary to white moderates' claims, the movement is not "extremist" in the usual sense (par. 5 ff.).
   A. It stands between extremes in black community: passivity, seen in the oppressed and the self-interested middle class; and violent radicalism, seen in Elijah Muhammad's followers (pars. 5–6).
   B. In its advocacy of love and nonviolent protest, the movement has forestalled bloodshed and kept more blacks from joining radicals (pars. 5–7).
   C. The movement helps blacks channel urge for freedom that's part of historical trend and the prevailing *Zeitgeist* (par. 8).

III. The movement can be defined as extremist if the term is redefined: "Creative extremism" is extremism in the service of love, truth, and goodness (examples of Amos, Paul, Luther, Bunyan, Lincoln, Jefferson, Jesus, par. 9).

IV. Some whites—"few in quantity, but . . . big in quality"—have recognized the truth of the arguments above and, unlike the white moderates, have committed themselves to the movement (par. 10).

The annotations include a summary of each paragraph's topic. Here is a scratch outline that lists the topics:

Scratch Outline of "Letter from Birmingham Jail"

¶1. White moderates block progress
¶2. What the moderates don't understand
¶3. Questions clergymen's logic: condemning his actions = condemning robbery victim, Socrates, Jesus
¶4. Time must be used to do right
¶5. Puts self in middle of two extremes: complacency and bitterness

¶6. Offers better choice: nonviolent protest
¶7. Says movement prevents racial violence
¶8. Discontent is normal, healthy, and historically inevitable, but it must be channeled
¶9. Redefines "extremism"; embraces "extremist" label
¶10. Praises whites who have supported movement

ANALYZE & WRITE

1 Reread each paragraph of the selection you have been working with in the previous activities in this chapter. Identify the topic and the comments made about the topic. Do not include examples, specific details, quotations, or other explanatory and supporting material.

2 List the author's main ideas in the margin, on a separate piece of paper, or in a new document.

For more about the conventions of formal and scratch outlines, see Chapter 9.

Paraphrasing

Paraphrasing is restating a text you have read by using mostly your own words. It can help you clarify the meaning of an obscure or ambiguous passage. It is one of the three ways of integrating other people's ideas and information into your own writing, along with **quoting** (reproducing exactly the language of the source text) and **summarizing** (distilling the main ideas or gist of the source text). You might choose to paraphrase rather than quote when the source's language is not especially arresting or memorable. You might paraphrase short passages but summarize longer ones.

Following are two passages. The first is from paragraph 2 of the excerpt from King's "Letter"; the second is a paraphrase of the first:

Original

I had hoped that the white moderate would understand that law and order exist for the purpose of establishing justice and that when they fail in this purpose they become the dangerously structured dams that block the flow of social progress. I had hoped that the white moderate would understand that the present tension in the South is a necessary phase of the transition from an obnoxious negative peace, in which the Negro passively accepted his unjust plight, to a substantive and positive peace, in which all men will respect the dignity and worth of human personality.

Paraphrase

> King writes that he had hoped for more understanding from white moderates—specifically that they would recognize that law and order are not ends in themselves but means to the greater end of establishing justice. When law and order do not serve this greater end, they stand in the way of progress. King expected the white moderate to recognize that the current tense situation in the South is part of a transition process that is necessary for progress. The current situation is bad because although there is peace, it is an "obnoxious" and "negative" kind of peace based on blacks passively accepting the injustice of the status quo. A better kind of peace—one that is "substantive," real and not imaginary, as well as "positive"—requires that all people, regardless of race, be valued.

When you compare the paraphrase to the original, you can see that the paraphrase contains all the important information and ideas of the original. Notice also that the paraphrase is somewhat longer than the original, refers to the writer by name, and encloses King's original words in quotation marks. The paraphrase tries to be *neutral,* to avoid inserting the reader's opinions or distorting the original writer's ideas.

ANALYZE & WRITE

1. Select an important passage from the selection you have been working with. (The passage need be only two or three sentences.) Then reread the passage, looking up unfamiliar words in a college dictionary.
2. Translate the passage into your own words, putting quotation marks around any words or phrases you quote from the original.
3. Revise to ensure coherence.

To learn more about paraphrasing, see Chapter 15.

Summarizing

Summarizing is important because it not only helps you understand and remember what is most significant in a reading but also creates a condensed version of the reading's ideas and information, which you can refer to later or insert into your own writing. Along with quoting and paraphrasing, summarizing enables you to integrate other writers' ideas into your own writing.

A **summary** is a relatively brief restatement, primarily in the reader's own words, of the reading's main ideas. Summaries vary in length, depending on the reader's purpose. Some summaries are very brief—a sentence or even a subordinate clause. For example, if you were referring to the excerpt from "Letter from Birmingham Jail" and simply needed to indicate how it relates to your other sources, your summary might look something like this: "There have always been advocates of extremism in politics. Martin Luther King Jr., in 'Letter from Birmingham Jail,' for instance, defends nonviolent civil disobedience as an extreme but necessary means of bringing about racial justice." If, however, you were surveying the important texts of the civil rights movement, you might write a longer, more detailed summary that not only identifies the reading's main ideas but also shows how the ideas relate to one another.

Many writers find it useful to outline the reading as a preliminary to writing a summary. A paragraph-by-paragraph scratch outline (like the one on pp. 339–40) lists the reading's main ideas in the sequence in which they appear in the original. But summarizing requires more than merely stringing together the entries in an outline; it must fill in the logical connections between the author's ideas. Notice how, in the following summary, the reader repeats selected words and phrases and refers to the author by name, indicating, with verbs like *expresses*, *acknowledges*, and *explains*, the writer's purpose and strategy at each point in the argument.

Summary

King expresses his disappointment with white moderates who, by opposing his program of nonviolent direct action, have become a barrier to progress toward racial justice. He acknowledges that his program has raised tension in the South, but he explains that tension is necessary to bring about change. Furthermore, he argues that tension already exists, but because it has been unexpressed, it is unhealthy and potentially dangerous.

He defends his actions against the clergy's criticisms, particularly their argument that he is in too much of a hurry. Responding to charges of extremism, King claims that he has actually prevented racial violence by channeling the natural frustrations of oppressed blacks into nonviolent protest. He asserts that extremism is precisely what is needed now—but it must be creative, rather than destructive, extremism. He concludes by again expressing disappointment with white moderates for not joining his effort as some other whites have.

A summary presents only ideas. Although it may use certain key terms from the source, it does not otherwise attempt to reflect the source's language, imagery, or tone; and it avoids even a hint of agreement or disagreement with the ideas it summarizes. Of course, a writer might summarize ideas in a source like "Letter from Birmingham Jail" to show readers that he or she has read it carefully and then proceed to use the summary to praise, question, or challenge King's argument. In doing so, the writer might quote specific language that reveals word choice, imagery, or tone.

ANALYZE & WRITE

1. Make a scratch outline of the reading you have been working with, or use the outline you created in the activity on p. 340.
2. Write a paragraph or more that presents the author's main ideas in your own words and sentence patterns, omitting supporting details and examples. Use the outline as a guide, but reread parts of the original text as necessary.
3. To make the summary coherent, fill in connections between the ideas you present.

To learn more about summarizing, see Chapter 5.

Synthesizing

Synthesizing involves presenting ideas and information gleaned from different sources. It can help you see how different sources relate to one another. For example, one reading may provide information that fills out the information in another reading, or a reading could present arguments that challenge arguments in another reading.

When you synthesize material from different sources, you construct a conversation among your sources, a conversation in which you also participate. Synthesizing contributes most when writers use sources not only to support their ideas but to challenge and extend them as well.

In the following example, the reader uses a variety of sources related to the King passage (pp. 331–37) and brings them together around a central idea. Notice how quotation, paraphrase, and summary are all used.

Synthesis

When King defends his campaign of nonviolent direct action against the clergymen's criticism that "our actions, even though peaceful, must be condemned because they precipitate violence" (King excerpt, par. 3), he is using what Vinit Haksar calls Mohandas Gandhi's "safety-valve argument" ("Civil Disobedience and Non-Cooperation" 117). According to Haksar, Gandhi gave a "non-threatening warning of worse things to come" if his demands were not met. King similarly makes clear that advocates of actions more extreme than those he advocates are waiting in the wings: "The other force is one of bitterness and hatred, and it comes perilously close to advocating violence" (King excerpt, par. 5). King identifies this force with Elijah Muhammad, and although he does not name him, King's contemporary readers would have known that he was referring also to his disciple Malcolm X, who, according to Herbert J. Storing, "urged that Negroes take seriously the idea of revolution" ("The Case against Civil Disobedience" 90). In fact, Malcolm X accused King of being a modern-day Uncle Tom, trying "to keep us under control, to keep us passive and peaceful and nonviolent" (*Malcolm X Speaks* 12).

ANALYZE & WRITE

1. Find and read two or three sources on the topic of the selection you have been working with, annotating the passages that give you ideas about the topic.
2. Look for patterns among your sources, possibly supporting or challenging your ideas or those of other sources.
3. Write a paragraph or more synthesizing your sources, using quotation, summary, and paraphrase to present what they say on the topic.

For more on synthesizing information and ideas from sources, see Chapters 5 and 15.

Contextualizing

All texts reflect historical and cultural assumptions, values, and attitudes that may differ from your own. To read thoughtfully, you need to become aware of these differences. **Contextualizing** is a critical reading strategy that enables you to make inferences about a reading's historical and cultural context and to examine the differences between its context and your own.

The excerpt from King's "Letter from Birmingham Jail" is a good example of a text that benefits from being read contextually. If you knew little about the history of slavery and segregation in the United States, it would be difficult to understand the passion expressed in this passage. To understand the historical and cultural context in which King wrote his "Letter from Birmingham Jail," you could do some library or Internet research. Comparing the situation at the time to situations with which you are familiar would help you understand some of your own attitudes toward King and the civil rights movement.

Here is what one reader wrote to contextualize King's writing:

> I have seen documentaries showing civil rights demonstrators being attacked by dogs, doused by fire hoses, beaten and dragged by helmeted police. Such images give me a sense of the violence, fear, and hatred that King was responding to. The creative tension King refers to comes across in his writing. He uses his anger and frustration to inspire his critics. He also threatens them, although he denies it. I saw a film on Malcolm X, so I could see that King was giving white people a choice between his own nonviolent way and Malcolm's more confrontational way.
>
> Things have certainly changed since the 1960s. For one: Barack Obama was elected president for two terms! When I read King's "Letter" today, I feel like I'm reading history. But then again, there have been a number of reports recently—often caught as cell-phone videos—of police brutality (like the death of Walter Scott, an unarmed black man who was shot in the back eight times by a cop in North Charleston, South Carolina). Some people have also suggested that in recent elections, there have been efforts to deprive African Americans and other minorities of the right to vote in some areas of the country.

ANALYZE & WRITE

1. Describe the historical and cultural situation as it is represented in the reading you have been working with and in other sources with which you are familiar. Your knowledge may come from other reading, television or film, school, or elsewhere. (If you know nothing about the historical and cultural context, you could do some library or Internet research.)
2. Compare the historical and cultural situation in which the text was written with your own historical and cultural situation. Consider how your understanding and judgment of the reading are affected by your own context.

Exploring the Significance of Figurative Language

Figurative language—*metaphor, simile,* and *symbolism*—enhances literal meaning by implying abstract ideas through vivid images and by evoking feelings and associations.

Metaphor implicitly compares two different things by identifying them with each other. For instance, when King calls the white moderate "the Negro's great stumbling block in his stride toward freedom" (par. 1), he does not mean that the white moderate literally trips the Negro who is attempting to walk toward freedom. The sentence makes sense only if understood figuratively: The white moderate trips up the Negro by frustrating every effort to achieve justice.

Simile, a more explicit form of comparison, uses the word *like* or *as* to signal the relationship of two seemingly unrelated things. King uses simile when he says that injustice is "like a boil that can never be cured so long as it is covered up" (par. 2). This simile makes several points of comparison between injustice and a boil. It suggests that injustice is a disease of society just as a boil is a disease of the skin, and that injustice, like a boil, must be exposed or it will fester and infect the entire body.

Symbolism compares two things by making one stand for the other. King uses the white moderate as a symbol for supposed liberals and would-be supporters of civil rights who are actually frustrating the cause.

How these figures of speech are used in a text reveals something of the writer's feelings about the subject. Exploring possible meanings in a text's figurative language involves (1) annotating and then listing the metaphors, similes, and symbols you find in a reading; (2) grouping and labeling the figures of speech that appear to express related feelings or attitudes; and (3) writing to explore the meaning of the patterns you have found. The following example shows the process of exploring figures of speech in the King excerpt.

Listing Figures of Speech

"stumbling block in his stride toward freedom" (par. 1)

"law and order . . . become the dangerously structured dams" (2)

"the flow of social progress" (2)

"Like a boil that can never be cured" (2)

"the light of human conscience and the air of national opinion" (2)

"the quicksand of racial injustice" (4)

Grouping and Labeling Figures of Speech

Sickness: "like a boil" (2); "the disease of segregation" (10)

Underground: "hidden tension" (2); "injustice must be exposed" (2); "injustice must be rooted out" (10)

Blockage: "dams that block the flow" (2); "Human progress never rolls in on wheels of inevitability" (4); "pent-up resentments" (8); "repressed emotions" (8)

Writing to Explore Meaning

The patterns labeled underground and blockage suggest a feeling of frustration. Inertia is a problem; movement forward toward progress or upward toward the promised land is stalled. The strong need to break through the resistance may represent King's feelings about both his attempt to lead purposeful, effective demonstrations and his effort to write a convincing argument.

The simile of injustice being "like a boil" links the two patterns of underground and sickness, suggesting that something bad, a disease, is inside the people or the society. The cure is to expose or to root out the blocked hatred and injustice as well as to release the tension or emotion that has long been repressed. This implies that repression itself is the evil, not simply what is repressed. Therefore, writing and speaking out through political action may have curative power for individuals and society alike.

ANALYZE & WRITE

1. Annotate all the figures of speech you find in the reading you have been working with (or another selection)—metaphors, similes, and symbols—and then list them.
2. Group the figures of speech that appear to express related feelings and attitudes, and label each group.
3. Write one or two paragraphs exploring the meaning of these patterns. What do they tell you about the text?

Looking for Patterns of Opposition

All texts carry within them voices of opposition. These voices may echo the views and values of readers the writer anticipates or predecessors to whom the writer is responding in some way; they may even reflect the writer's own conflicting values. Careful readers look closely for such a dialogue of opposing voices within the text.

When we think of oppositions, we ordinarily think of polarities: *yes* and *no, up* and *down, black* and *white, new* and *old*. Some oppositions, however, may be more subtle. The excerpt from King's "Letter from Birmingham Jail" is rich in such oppositions: *moderate* versus *extremist, order* versus *justice, direct action* versus *passive acceptance, expression* versus *repression*. These oppositions are not accidental; they form a significant pattern that gives a reader important information about the essay.

A careful reading will show that King always values one of the two terms in an opposition over the other. In the passage, for example, *extremist* is valued over *moderate* (par. 9). This preference for extremism is surprising. The reader should ask why, when white extremists like members of the Ku Klux Klan have committed so many outrages against African Americans, King would prefer extremism. If King is trying to convince his readers to accept his point of view, why would he represent himself as an extremist? Moreover, why would a clergyman advocate extremism rather than moderation?

Studying the **patterns of opposition** in the text enables you to answer these questions. You will see that King sets up this opposition to force his readers to examine their own values and realize that they are in fact misplaced. Instead of working toward justice, he says, those who support law and order maintain the unjust status quo. By getting his readers to think of white moderates as blocking rather than facilitating peaceful change, King brings readers to align themselves with him and perhaps even embrace his strategy of nonviolent resistance.

Looking for patterns of opposition involves annotating words or phrases in the reading that indicate oppositions, listing the opposing terms in pairs, deciding which term in each pair is preferred by the writer, and reflecting on the meaning of the patterns. Here is a partial list of oppositions from the King excerpt, with the preferred terms marked by an asterisk:

Listing Patterns of Opposition

moderate	*extremist
order	*justice
negative peace	*positive peace
absence of justice	*presence of justice
goals	*methods
*direct action	passive acceptance
*exposed tension	hidden tension
*expression	repression

ANALYZE & WRITE

1. Annotate the selection you have been working with (or another selection) for words or phrases indicating oppositions.
2. List the pairs of oppositions. (You may have to paraphrase or even supply the opposite word or phrase if it is not stated directly in the text.)
3. For each pair of oppositions, put an asterisk next to the term that the writer seems to value or prefer over the other.
4. Study the patterns of opposition. How do they contribute to your understanding of the text? What do they tell you about what the author wants you to believe?

Reflecting on Challenges to Your Beliefs and Values

To read thoughtfully, you need to scrutinize your own assumptions and attitudes as well as those expressed in the text you are reading. If you are like most readers, however, you will find that your assumptions and attitudes are so ingrained that you are not always fully aware of them. A good strategy for getting at these underlying beliefs and values is to identify and reflect on the ways the text challenges you and how it makes you feel—disturbed, threatened, ashamed, combative, pleased, exuberant, or some other way.

For example, here is what one student wrote about the King passage:

Reflections

In paragraph 1, Dr. King criticizes people who are "more devoted to 'order' than to justice." This criticism upsets me because today I think I would choose order over justice. When I reflect on my feelings and try to figure out where they come from, I realize that what I feel most is fear. I am terrified by the violence in society today. I'm afraid of sociopaths who don't respect the rule of law, much less the value of human life.

I know Dr. King was writing in a time when the law itself was unjust, when order was apparently used to keep people from protesting and changing the law. But things are different now. Today, justice seems to serve criminals more than it serves law-abiding citizens. That's why I'm for order over justice.

ANALYZE & WRITE

1 Using the text you have been working with (or another text), identify places where you feel your beliefs and values are being opposed, criticized, or unfairly characterized.

2 Write a few paragraphs reflecting on why you feel challenged. Do not defend your feelings; instead, search your memory to discover where they come from.

Evaluating the Logic of an Argument

An *argument* includes a thesis backed by reasons and support. The **thesis** asserts a position on a controversial issue or a solution to a problem that the writer wants readers to accept. The **reasons** tell readers why they should accept the thesis, and the **support** (such as examples, statistics, authorities, and textual evidence) gives readers grounds for accepting it. For an argument to be considered logically acceptable, it must meet the three conditions of what we call the ABC test:

The ABC Test

A. The reasons and support must be *appropriate* to the thesis.
B. The reasons and support must be *believable*.
C. The reasons and support must be *consistent* with one another as well as *complete*.

For more on argument, logical fallacies, and invoking authorities, see Chapter 12.

Test for appropriateness.

To evaluate the logic of an argument, first decide whether the argument's reasons and support are appropriate. To test for appropriateness, ask these questions:

- How does each reason or piece of support relate to the thesis?
- Is the connection between reasons and support and the thesis clear and compelling?

Readers most often question the appropriateness of reasons and support when the writer argues by analogy or by invoking authority. For example, in paragraph 2, King argues that when law and order fail to establish justice, "they become the dangerously structured dams that block the flow of social progress." The analogy asserts the following logical relationship: Law and order are to progress toward justice what a dam is to water. If you do not accept this analogy, the argument fails the test of appropriateness.

King uses both analogy and authority in paragraph 3: "Isn't this like condemning Socrates because his unswerving commitment to truth and his philosophical inquiries precipitated the act by the misguided populace in which they made him drink hemlock?" Not only must you judge the appropriateness of the analogy comparing the Greeks' condemnation of Socrates to the white moderates' condemnation of King, but you must also judge whether it is appropriate to accept Socrates as an authority. Since Socrates is generally respected for his teachings on justice, his words and actions are likely to be considered appropriate to King's situation in Birmingham.

Test for believability.

Believability is a measure of your willingness to accept as true the reasons and support the writer gives in defense of a thesis. To test for believability, ask these questions:

- On what basis am I being asked to believe this reason or support is true?
- If it cannot be proved true or false, how much weight does it carry?

In judging facts, examples and anecdotes, statistics, and authorities, consider the following points:

Facts are statements that can be proved objectively to be true. The believability of facts depends on the following:

- Their *accuracy* (they should not distort or misrepresent reality)
- Their *completeness* (they should not omit important details)
- The *trustworthiness* of their sources (sources should be qualified and unbiased)

King, for instance, asserts as fact that African Americans will not wait much longer for racial justice (par. 8). His critics might question the factuality of this assertion by asking: Is it true of all African Americans? How does King know what African Americans will and will not do?

Examples and anecdotes are particular instances that may or may not make you believe a general statement. The believability of examples depends on the following:

- Their *representativeness* (whether they are truly typical and thus generalizable)
- Their *specificity* (whether particular details make them seem true to life)

Even if a vivid example or gripping anecdote does not convince readers, it usually strengthens argumentative writing by clarifying the meaning and dramatizing the point. In paragraph 5 of the King excerpt, for example, King supports his generalization that some African American extremists are motivated by bitterness and hatred by citing the specific example of Elijah Muhammad's Black Muslim movement. Conversely, in paragraph 9, he refers to Jesus, Paul, Luther, and others as examples of extremists motivated by love and Christianity. These examples support his assertion that extremism is not in itself wrong and that any judgment of extremism must be based on its motivation and cause.

Statistics are numerical data. The believability of statistics depends on the following:

- The *comparability* of the data (the price of apples in 1985 cannot be compared with the price of apples in 2018 unless the figures are adjusted to account for inflation)
- The *precision* of the methods employed to gather and analyze data (representative samples should be used and variables accounted for)
- The *trustworthiness* of the sources

Authorities are people to whom the writer attributes expertise on a given subject. Not only must such authorities be appropriate, as mentioned earlier, but they must be credible as well—that is, the reader must accept them as experts on the topic at hand. King cites authorities repeatedly throughout his essay. He refers to religious leaders (Jesus and Luther) as well as to American political leaders (Lincoln and Jefferson). These figures are likely to have a high degree of credibility among King's readers.

Test for consistency and completeness.

In looking for consistency, you should be concerned that all the parts of the argument work together and that they are sufficient to convince readers to accept the thesis or at least take it seriously. To test for consistency and completeness, ask these questions:

- Are any of the reasons and support contradictory?
- Do the reasons and support provide sufficient grounds for accepting the thesis?
- Does the writer fail to acknowledge, concede, or refute any opposing arguments or important objections?

A thoughtful reader might regard as contradictory King's characterizing himself first as a moderate and later as an extremist opposed to the forces of violence. (King attempts to reconcile this apparent contradiction by explicitly redefining extremism in par. 9.) Similarly, the fact that King fails to examine and refute every legal recourse available to his cause might allow a critical reader to question the sufficiency of his argument.

For more on responding to objections and alternatives, see Chapter 12.

ANALYZE & WRITE

Use the ABC test on the selection you have been working with (or another selection):

A *Test for appropriateness* by checking that the reasons and support are clearly and directly related to the thesis.

B *Test for believability* by deciding whether you can accept the reasons and support as likely to be true.

C *Test for consistency and completeness* by deciding whether the argument has any contradictions and whether any important objections or opposing views have been ignored.

Recognizing Emotional Manipulation

Writers often try to arouse emotions in readers to excite their interest, make them care, or move them to take action. There is nothing wrong with appealing to readers' emotions. What is wrong is manipulating readers with false or exaggerated appeals. Therefore, you should be suspicious of writing that is overly sentimental, that cites alarming statistics and frightening anecdotes, that demonizes others and identifies itself with revered authorities, or that uses potent symbols (for example, the American flag) or emotionally loaded words (such as *racist*).

King, for example, uses the emotionally loaded word *paternalistically* to refer to the white moderate's belief that "he can set the timetable for another man's freedom" (par. 1). In the same paragraph, King uses symbolism to get an emotional reaction from readers when he compares the white moderate to the "Ku Klux Klanner." To get readers to accept his ideas, he also relies on authorities whose names evoke the greatest respect, such as Jesus and Lincoln. But some readers might object that comparing his own crusade to that of Jesus is pretentious and manipulative. A critical reader might also consider King's discussion of African American extremists in paragraph 7 to be a veiled threat designed to frighten readers into agreement.

ANALYZE & WRITE

1. Annotate places in the text you have been working with (or another text) where you sense that emotional appeals are being used.
2. Assess whether any of the emotional appeals are unfairly manipulative.

Judging the Writer's Credibility

Writers try to persuade readers by presenting an image of themselves in their writing that will gain their readers' confidence. This image must be created indirectly, through the arguments, language, and system of values and beliefs expressed or implied in the writing. Writers establish credibility in their writing in three ways:

- By showing their knowledge of the subject
- By building *common ground* with readers
- By responding fairly to objections and opposing arguments

Test for knowledge.

Writers demonstrate their knowledge through the facts and statistics they marshal, the sources they rely on for information, and the scope and depth of their understanding. You may not be sufficiently expert on the subject yourself to know whether the facts are accurate, the sources are reliable, and the understanding is sufficient. You may need to do some research to see what others say about the subject. You can also check credentials—the writer's educational and professional qualifications, the respectability of the publication in which the selection first appeared, and reviews of the writer's work—to determine whether the writer is a respected authority in the field. For example, King brings with him the authority that comes from being a member of the clergy and a respected leader of the Southern Christian Leadership Conference.

For more about evaluating sources, see Chapter 15.

Test for common ground.

One way writers can establish **common ground** with their readers is by basing their reasoning on shared values, beliefs, and attitudes. They use language that includes their readers (*we*) and qualify their assertions to keep them from being too extreme. Above all, they acknowledge differences of opinion. As you read, be sure to notice such appeals.

King creates common ground with readers by using the inclusive pronoun *we*, suggesting shared concerns between himself and his audience. Notice, however, his use of masculine pronouns and other references ("the Negro . . . he," "our brothers"). Although King addressed his letter to male clergy, he intended it to be published in the local newspaper, where it would be read by an audience of both men and women. By using language that excludes women—a common practice at the time the selection was written—King may have missed the opportunity to build common ground with more than half of his readers.

Test for fairness.

Writers reveal their character by how they handle opposing arguments and objections to their argument. As a critical reader, pay particular attention to how writers treat possible differences of opinion. Be suspicious of those who ignore differences and pretend that everyone agrees with their viewpoints. When objections or opposing views are represented, consider whether they have been distorted in any way; if they are refuted, be sure they are challenged fairly—with sound reasoning and solid support.

One way to gauge the author's credibility is to identify the tone of the argument, for it conveys the writer's attitude toward the subject and toward the reader. Is the text angry? Sarcastic? Evenhanded? Shrill? Condescending? Bullying? Do you feel as if the writer is treating the subject—and you, as a reader—with fairness? King's tone might be characterized in different passages as patient (he doesn't lose his temper), respectful (he refers to white moderates as "people of good will"), or pompous (comparing himself to Jesus and Socrates).

ANALYZE & WRITE

1. Using the selection you have been working with (or another selection), make annotations indicating the writer's knowledge of the subject, how well common ground is established, and whether the writer deals fairly with objections and opposing arguments.
2. Decide what in the essay you find credible and what you question.

11

Cueing the Reader

Readers need guidance. To guide readers through a piece of writing, a writer can provide five basic kinds of **cues**, or signals:

- Thesis and forecasting statements, to orient readers to ideas and organization
- Paragraphing, to group related ideas and details
- Cohesive devices, to connect ideas to one another and bring about clarity
- Transitions, to signal relationships or shifts in meaning
- Headings and subheadings, to group related paragraphs and help readers locate specific information quickly

This chapter illustrates how each of these cueing strategies works.

Orienting Statements

To help readers find their way, especially in difficult and lengthy texts, you can provide two kinds of **orienting statements**: a *thesis statement*, which declares the main point, and a *forecasting statement*, which previews subordinate points, showing the order in which they will be discussed in the essay.

Use thesis statements to announce the main idea.

To help readers understand what is being said about a subject, writers often provide a thesis statement early in the essay. The **thesis statement,** which can comprise one or more sentences, operates as a cue by letting readers know which is the most important general idea among the writer's many ideas and observations. In "Love: The Right Chemistry" in Chapter 4, Anastasia Toufexis expresses her thesis in the second paragraph:

> O.K., let's cut out all this nonsense about romantic love. Let's bring some scientific precision to the party. Let's put love under a microscope.
>
> When rigorous people with Ph.D.s after their names do that, what they see is not some silly, senseless thing. No, their probe reveals that love rests firmly on the foundations of evolution, biology and chemistry.

Readers naturally look for something that will tell them the point of an essay, a focus for the many diverse details and ideas they encounter as they read. They expect to find some information early on that will give them a context for reading the essay, particularly if they are reading about a new or difficult subject. Therefore, a thesis statement placed at the beginning of an essay, like Toufexis's, enables readers to anticipate the content of the essay and helps them understand the relationships among its various ideas and details.

Occasionally, however, particularly in fairly short, informal pieces, a writer may save a direct statement of the thesis until the conclusion. Ending with the thesis brings together the various strands of information or supporting details introduced over the course of the essay and makes clear the essay's main idea.

Some essays, particularly autobiographical essays, offer no direct thesis statement. Although this can make the point of the essay more difficult to determine, it can be appropriate when the essay is more expressive and personal than it is informative. In all cases, careful writers keep readers' needs and expectations in mind when deciding how—and whether—to state the thesis.

EXERCISE 11.1

In the essay by Jessica Statsky in Chapter 6, underline the thesis statement, the last sentence in paragraph 1. Notice the key terms: "overzealous parents and coaches," "impose adult standards," "children's sports," "activities . . . neither satisfying nor beneficial." Then skim the essay, stopping to read the sentence at the beginning of each paragraph. Also read the last paragraph.

Consider whether the idea in every paragraph's first sentence is anticipated by the thesis's key terms. Consider also the connection between the ideas in the last paragraph and the thesis's key terms. What can you conclude about how a thesis might assert the point of an essay, anticipate the ideas that follow, and help readers relate the ideas to one another?

Use forecasting statements to preview topics.

Some thesis statements include a **forecast**, which overviews the way a thesis will be developed, as in the following example:

> In the three years from 1348 through 1350 the pandemic of plague known as the Black Death, or, as the Germans called it, the Great Dying, killed at least a fourth of the population of Europe. It was undoubtedly the worst disaster that has ever befallen mankind. Today we can have no real conception of the terror under which people lived in the shadow of the plague. For more than two centuries plague has not been a serious threat to mankind in the large, although it is still a grisly presence in parts of the Far East and Africa. Scholars continue to study the Great Dying, however, as a historical example of human behavior under the stress of universal catastrophe. In these days when the threat of plague has been replaced by the threat of mass human extermination by even more rapid means, there has been a sharp renewal of interest in the history of the fourteenth-century calamity. With new perspective, students are investigating its manifold effects: demographic, economic, psychological, moral and religious.
>
> —William Langer, "The Black Death"

As a reader would expect, Langer divides his essay into explanations of the research into these five effects, addressing them in the order in which they appear in the forecasting statement.

EXERCISE 11.2

Turn to Patrick O'Malley's essay in Chapter 7, and underline the forecasting statement in paragraph 2. Then skim the essay. Notice whether O'Malley takes up every point he mentions in the forecasting statement and whether he sticks to the order he promises readers. How well does his forecasting statement help you follow his essay? What suggestions for improvement, if any, would you offer him?

Paragraphing

Paragraph cues as obvious as indentation keep readers on track. You can also arrange material in a paragraph to help readers see what is important or significant. For example, you can begin with a topic sentence, help readers see the relationship between the previous paragraph and the present one with an explicit transition, and place the most important information toward the end.

Paragraph indents signal related ideas.

One paragraph cue—the indentation that signals the beginning of a new paragraph—is a relatively modern printing convention. Old manuscripts show that paragraph divisions were not always marked. To make reading easier, scribes and printers began to use the symbol ¶ to mark paragraph breaks, and later, indenting became common practice. Indenting has been abandoned by most online and business writers, who now distinguish one paragraph from another by leaving a line of space between paragraphs.

Paragraphing helps readers by signaling when a sequence of related ideas begins and ends. Paragraphing also helps readers judge what is most important in what they are reading. Writers typically emphasize important information by placing it at the two points in the paragraph where readers are most attentive—the beginning and the end.

You can give special emphasis to information by placing it in its own paragraph.

EXERCISE 11.3

Turn again to Patrick O'Malley's essay in Chapter 7, and read paragraphs 4–7 with the following questions in mind: Does all the material in each paragraph seem to be related? Do you feel a sense of closure at the end of each paragraph? Does the last sentence offer the most significant or weighty information in the paragraph?

Topic sentences announce the paragraph's focus.

A **topic sentence** lets readers know the focus of a paragraph in simple and direct terms. It is a cueing strategy for the paragraph, much as a thesis or forecasting statement is for the whole essay. Because paragraphing usually signals a shift in focus, readers expect some kind of reorientation in the opening sentence, letting them know whether the new paragraph introduces another aspect of the topic or develops one already introduced.

Announcing the Topic Some topic sentences simply announce the topic. Here are some examples taken from Barry Lopez's book *Arctic Dreams:*

> A polar bear walks in a way all its own.
>
> What is so consistently striking about the way Eskimos used parts of an animal is the breadth of their understanding about what would work.
>
> The Mediterranean view of the Arctic, down to the time of the Elizabethan mariners, was shaped by two somewhat contradictory thoughts.

The following paragraph shows how one of Lopez's topic sentences (highlighted) is developed:

> What is so consistently striking about the way Eskimos used parts of an animal is the breadth of their understanding about what would work. Knowing that muskox horn is more flexible than caribou antler, they preferred it for making the side prongs of a fish spear. For a waterproof bag in which to carry sinews for clothing repair, they chose salmon skin. They selected the strong, translucent intestine of a bearded seal to make a window for a snowhouse—it would fold up for easy traveling and it would not frost over in cold weather. To make small snares for sea ducks, they needed a springy material that would not rot in salt water—baleen fibers. The down feather of a common eider, tethered at the end of a stick in the snow at an angle, would reveal the exhalation of a quietly surfacing seal. Polar bear bone was used anywhere a stout, sharp point was required, because it is the hardest bone.
>
> —BARRY LOPEZ, *Arctic Dreams*

EXERCISE 11.4

Turn to Jessica Statsky's essay in Chapter 6. Underline the topic sentence (the first sentence) in paragraphs 3 and 5. Consider how these sentences help you anticipate the paragraph's topic and method of development.

Making a Transition Not all topic sentences simply point to what will follow. Some also refer to earlier sentences. Such sentences work both as topic sentences, stating the main point of the paragraph, and as *transitions,* linking that paragraph to the previous one. Here are a few topic sentences from Elaine Hedges's "Quilts and Women's Culture," with transitions highlighted:

Transitions tie each topic sentence to a previous statement.

> Within its broad traditionalism and anonymity, however, variations and distinctions developed.
>
> Regionally, too, distinctions were introduced into quilt making through the interesting process of renaming.
>
> Finally, out of such regional and other variations come individual, signed achievements.
>
> Quilts, then, were an outlet for creative energy, a source and emblem of sisterhood and solidarity, and a graphic response to historical and political change.

Sometimes the first sentence of a paragraph serves as a transition, and a subsequent sentence states the topic, as in the following example:

> What a convenience, what a relief it will be, they say, never to worry about how to dress for a job interview, a romantic tryst, or a funeral!
>
> Transition sentences
>
> Convenient, perhaps, but not exactly a relief. Such a utopia would give most of us the same kind of chill we feel when a stadium full of Communist-bloc athletes in identical sports outfits, shouting slogans in unison, appears on TV. Most people do not want to be told what to wear any more than they want to be told what to say. In Belfast recently four hundred Irish Republican prisoners "refused to wear any clothes at all, draping themselves day and night in blankets," rather than put on prison uniforms. Even the offer of civilian-style dress did not satisfy them; they insisted on wearing their own clothes brought from home, or nothing. Fashion is free speech, and one of the privileges, if not always one of the pleasures, of a free world.
>
> —Alison Lurie, *The Language of Clothes*

Occasionally whole paragraphs serve as transitions, linking one sequence of paragraphs with those that follow, as in the following:

> Transition paragraph summarizes contrasts and sets up an analysis of the similarities.
>
> Yet it was not all contrast, after all. Different as they were—in background, in personality, in underlying aspiration—these two great soldiers had much in common. Under everything else, they were marvelous fighters. Furthermore, their fighting qualities were really very much alike.
>
> —Bruce Catton, "Grant and Lee: A Study in Contrasts"

EXERCISE 11.5

Turn to Jessica Statsky's essay in Chapter 6 and read paragraphs 3–7. As you read, underline the part of the first sentence in paragraphs 4, 5, and 7 that refers to the previous paragraph, creating a transition from one to the next. Notice the different ways Statsky creates these transitions, and consider whether they are all equally effective.

Positioning the Topic Sentence Although topic sentences may occur anywhere in a paragraph, stating the topic in the first sentence has the advantage of giving readers a sense of how the paragraph is likely to be developed. The beginning of the paragraph is therefore the most common position.

A topic sentence that does not open a paragraph is most likely to appear at the end. When a topic sentence concludes a paragraph, it usually summarizes or generalizes preceding information:

> Even black Americans sometimes need to be reminded about the deceptiveness of television. Blacks retain their fascination with black characters on TV: Many of us buy *Jet* magazine primarily to read its weekly television feature, which lists every black character (major or minor) to be seen on the screen that week. Yet our fixation with the presence of black characters

Topic is not stated until the last sentence.

on TV has blinded us to an important fact that *Cosby*, which began in 1984, and its offshoots over the years demonstrate convincingly: There is very little connection between the social status of black Americans and the fabricated images of black people that Americans consume each day. The representation of blacks on TV is a very poor index to our social advancement or political progress.

—Henry Louis Gates Jr., "TV's Black World Turns—but Stays Unreal"

When a topic sentence is used in a narrative, it often appears as the last sentence as a way to evaluate or reflect on events:

Topic sentence reflects on narrated events described earlier in paragraph.

A cold sun was sliding down a gray fall sky. Some older boys had been playing tackle football in the field we took charge of every weekend. In a few years, they'd be called to Southeast Asia, some of them. Their locations would be tracked with pushpins in red, white, and blue on maps on nearly every kitchen wall. But that afternoon, they were quick as young deer. They leapt and dodged, dove from each other and collided in midair. Bulletlike passes flew to connect them. Or the ball spiraled in a high arc across the frosty sky one to another. In short, they were mindlessly agile in a way that captured as audience every little kid within running distance of the yellow goalposts.

—Mary Karr, *Cherry*

It is possible for a single topic sentence to introduce two or more paragraphs. Subsequent paragraphs in such a sequence have no separate topic sentences of their own:

Topic sentence states topic of this paragraph and the next.

Anthropologists Daniel Maltz and Ruth Borker point out that boys and girls socialize differently. Little girls tend to play in small groups or, even more common, in pairs. Their social life usually centers around a best friend, and friendships are made, maintained, and broken by talk—especially "secrets." If a little girl tells her friend's secret to another little girl, she may find herself with a new best friend. The secrets themselves may or may not be important, but the fact of telling them is all-important. It's hard for newcomers to get into these tight groups, but anyone who is admitted is treated as an equal. Girls like to play cooperatively; if they can't cooperate, the group breaks up.

Little boys tend to play in larger groups, often outdoors, and they spend more time doing things than talking. It's easy for boys to get into the group, but not everyone is accepted as an equal. Once in the group, boys must jockey for their status in it. One of the most important ways they do this is through talk: verbal display such as telling stories and jokes, challenging and sidetracking the verbal displays of other boys, and withstanding other boys' challenges in order to maintain their own story—and status. Their talk is often competitive talk about who is best at what.

—Deborah Tannen, *That's Not What I Meant!*

EXERCISE 11.6

Consider the variety and effectiveness of the topic sentences in your most recent writing project. Begin by underlining the topic sentence in each paragraph after the first one. The topic sentence may not be the first sentence in a paragraph, though it often will be.

Then double-underline the part of the topic sentence that provides an explicit transition from one paragraph to the next. You may find a transition that is separate from the topic sentence. You may not always find a topic sentence.

Reflect on your topic sentences, and evaluate how well they serve to orient your readers to the sequence of topics or ideas in your essay.

Cohesive Devices

Cohesive devices guide readers, helping them follow your train of thought by connecting key words and phrases throughout a passage. Among such devices are pronoun reference, word repetition, synonyms, sentence structure repetition, and collocation.

Pronouns connect phrases or sentences.

One common cohesive device is *pronoun reference.* As noun substitutes, pronouns refer to nouns that either precede or follow them and thus serve to connect phrases or sentences. The nouns that come before pronouns are called **antecedents**.

Pronouns form a chain of connection with their antecedent.

In New York from dawn to dusk to dawn, day after day, you can hear the steady rumble of tires against the concrete span of the George Washington Bridge. The bridge is never completely still. It trembles with traffic. It moves in the wind. Its great veins of steel swell when hot and contract when cold; its span often is ten feet closer to the Hudson River in summer than in winter.

—Gay Talese, "New York"

This example has only one pronoun-antecedent chain, and the antecedent comes first, so all the pronouns refer to it. When there are multiple pronoun-antecedent chains with references forward as well as back, writers have to make sure that readers will not mistake one pronoun's antecedent for another's.

Word repetition aids cohesion.

To avoid confusion, writers often use *word repetition.* The device of repeating words and phrases is especially helpful if a pronoun might confuse readers:

Repeated words

Some odd optical property of our highly polarized and unequal society makes the poor almost invisible to their economic superiors. The poor can see the affluent easily enough—on television, for example, or on the covers of magazines. But the affluent rarely see the poor or, if they do catch sight of them in

> some public space, rarely know what they're seeing, since—thanks to consignment stores and, yes, Wal-Mart—the poor are usually able to disguise themselves as members of the more comfortable classes.
>
> —Barbara Ehrenreich, *Nickel and Dimed*

In the next example, several overlapping chains of word repetition prevent confusion and help the reader follow the ideas:

Repeated words with some variation of form

> Natural selection is the central concept of Darwinian theory—the fittest survive and spread their favored traits through populations. Natural selection is defined by Spencer's phrase "survival of the fittest," but what does this famous bit of jargon really mean? Who are the fittest? And how is "fitness" defined? We often read that fitness involves no more than "differential reproductive success"—the production of more surviving offspring than other competing members of the population. Whoa! cries Bethell, as many others have before him. This formulation defines fitness in terms of survival only. The crucial phrase of natural selection means no more than "the survival of those who survive"—a vacuous tautology. (A tautology is a phrase—like "my father is a man"—containing no information in the predicate ["a man"] not inherent in the subject ["my father"]. Tautologies are fine as definitions, but not as testable scientific statements—there can be nothing to test in a statement true by definition.)
>
> — Stephen Jay Gould, *Ever Since Darwin*

Synonyms connect ideas.

In addition to word repetition, you can use **synonyms**, words with identical or very similar meanings, to connect important ideas. In the following example, the author develops a careful chain of synonyms and word repetitions:

Synonym sequences:
region, particular landscape
local residents, native
stories, narratives
are remembered, does not become lost
intricate, . . . view, complex . . . "reality"

> Over time, small bits of knowledge about a region accumulate among local residents in the form of stories. These are remembered in the community; even what is unusual does not become lost and therefore irrelevant. These narratives comprise for a native an intricate, long-term view of a particular landscape. . . . Outside the region this complex but easily shared "reality" is hard to get across without reducing it to generalities, to misleading or imprecise abstraction.
>
> —Barry Lopez, *Arctic Dreams*

The result is a coherent paragraph that constantly reinforces the author's point.

Repetition of sentence structure emphasizes connections.

Writers occasionally use *sentence structure repetition* to emphasize the connections among their ideas, as in this example:

Repeats the if/then sentence structure

But the life forms are as much part of the structure of the Earth as any inanimate portion is. It is all an inseparable part of a whole. If any animal is isolated totally from other forms of life, then death by starvation will surely follow. If isolated from water, death by dehydration will follow even faster. If isolated from air, whether free or dissolved in water, death by asphyxiation will follow still faster. If isolated from the Sun, animals will survive for a time, but plants would die, and if all plants died, all animals would starve.

—Isaac Asimov, "The Case against Man"

Collocation creates networks of meaning.

Collocation—the positioning of words together in expected ways around a particular topic—occurs quite naturally to writers and usually forms recognizable networks of meaning for readers. For example, in a paragraph on a high school graduation, a reader might expect to encounter such words as *valedictorian, diploma, commencement, honors, cap and gown,* and *senior class*. The paragraph that follows uses five collocation chains:

Collocation chains:

housewife, cooking, neighbor, home

clocks, calculated, progression, precise

obstinacy, vagaries, problem

sun, clear days, cloudy ones, sundial, cast its light, angle, seasons, sun, weather

cooking, fire, matches, hot coals smoldering, ashes, go out, bed-warming pan

The seventeenth-century housewife not only had to make do without thermometers, she also had to make do without clocks, which were scarce and dear throughout the sixteen hundreds. She calculated cooking times by the progression of the sun; her cooking must have been more precise on clear days than on cloudy ones. Marks were sometimes painted on the floor, providing her with a rough sundial, but she still had to make allowance for the obstinacy of the sun in refusing to cast its light at the same angle as the seasons changed; but she was used to allowing for the vagaries of sun and weather. She also had a problem starting her fire in the morning; there were no matches. If she had allowed the hot coals smoldering under the ashes to go out, she had to borrow some from a neighbor, carrying them home with care, perhaps in a bed-warming pan.

—Waverly Root and Richard de Rouchement, *Eating in America*

EXERCISE 11.7

Now that you know more about pronoun reference, word repetition, synonyms, sentence structure repetition, and collocation, turn to Brian Cable's essay in Chapter 3 and identify the cohesive devices you find in paragraphs 1–5. Underline each cohesive device you can find; there will be many. You might also want to connect with lines the various pronoun, related-word, and synonym chains you find. You could also try listing the separate collocation chains. Consider how these cohesive devices help you read and make sense of the passage.

EXERCISE 11.8

Choose one of your recent writing projects, and select any three contiguous paragraphs. Underline every cohesive device you can find; there will be many. Try to connect with lines the various pronoun, related-word, and synonym chains you find. Also try listing the separate collocation chains.

You will be surprised and pleased at how extensively you rely on cohesive ties. Indeed, you could not produce readable text without cohesive ties. Consider these questions relevant to your development as a writer: Are all of your pronoun references clear? Are you straining for synonyms when repeated words would do? Do you ever repeat sentence structures to emphasize connections? Do you trust yourself to put collocation to work?

Transitions

A **transition** serves as a bridge to connect one paragraph, sentence, clause, or word with another. It also identifies the kind of connection by indicating to readers how the item preceding the transition relates to the one that follows it. Transitions help readers anticipate how the next paragraph or sentence will affect the meaning of what they have just read. There are three basic groups of transitions, based on the relationships they indicate: logical, temporal, and spatial.

Transitions emphasize logical relationships.

Transitions help readers follow the *logical relationships* within an argument. How such transitions work is illustrated in this tightly and passionately reasoned paragraph by James Baldwin:

Transitions reinforce the logic of the argument.

> The black man insists, by whatever means he finds at his disposal, that the white man cease to regard him as an exotic rarity and recognize him as a human being. This is a very charged and difficult moment, for there is a great deal of will power involved in the white man's naïveté. Most people are not naturally malicious, and the white man prefers to keep the black man at a certain human remove because it is easier for him thus to preserve his simplicity and to avoid being called to account for crimes committed by his forefathers, or his neighbors. He is inescapably aware, nevertheless, that he is in a better position in the world than black men are, nor can he quite put to death the suspicion that he is hated by black men therefore. He does not wish to be hated, neither does he wish to change places, and at this point in his uneasiness he can scarcely avoid having recourse to those legends which white men have created about black men, the most unusual effect of which is that the white man finds himself enmeshed, so to speak, in his own language which describes hell, as well as the attributes which lead one to hell, as being black as night.
>
> —James Baldwin, "Stranger in the Village"

Transitions Showing Logical Relationships

- ***To introduce another item in a series:*** first . . . , second; in the second place; for one thing . . . , for another; next; then; furthermore; moreover; in addition; finally; last; also; similarly; besides; and; as well as
- ***To introduce an illustration or some other specification:*** in particular; specifically; for instance; for example; that is; namely

- ***To introduce a result or a cause:*** consequently; as a result; hence; accordingly; thus; so; therefore; then; because; since; for
- ***To introduce a restatement:*** that is; in other words; in simpler terms; to put it differently
- ***To introduce a conclusion or summary:*** in conclusion; finally; all in all; evidently; clearly; actually; to sum up; altogether; of course
- ***To introduce an opposing point:*** but; however; yet; nevertheless; on the contrary; on the other hand; in contrast; still; neither; nor
- ***To introduce a concession to an opposing view:*** certainly; naturally; of course; it is true; to be sure; granted
- ***To resume the original line of reasoning after a concession:*** nonetheless; all the same; even though; still; nevertheless

Transitions can indicate a sequence in time.

In addition to showing logical connections, transitions may indicate **temporal relationships**—a sequence or progression in time—as this example illustrates:

Transitions to show relationships of time

> That night, we drank tea and then vodka with lemon peel steeped in it. The four of us talked in Russian and English about mutual friends and American railroads and the Rolling Stones. Seryozha loves the Stones, and his face grew wistful as we spoke about their recent album, *Some Girls*. He played a tape of "Let It Bleed" over and over, until we could translate some difficult phrases for him; after that, he came out with the phrases at intervals during the evening, in a pretty decent imitation of Jagger's Cockney snarl. He was an adroit and oddly formal host, inconspicuously filling our teacups and politely urging us to eat bread and cheese and chocolate. While he talked to us, he teased Anya, calling her "Piglet," and she shook back her bangs and glowered at him. It was clear that theirs was a fiery relationship. After a while, we talked about ourselves. Anya told us about painting and printmaking and about how hard it was to buy supplies in Moscow. There had been something angry in her dark face since the beginning of the evening; I thought at first that it meant she didn't like Americans; but now I realized that it was a constant, barely suppressed rage at her own situation.
>
> —Andrea Lee, *Russian Journal*

Transitions Showing Temporal Relationships

- ***To indicate frequency:*** frequently; hourly; often; occasionally; now and then; day after day; every so often; again and again; over and over
- ***To indicate duration:*** during; briefly; for a long time; minute by minute; while; until
- ***To indicate a particular time:*** now; then; at that time; in those days; last Sunday; next Christmas; in 2003; at the beginning of August; at six o'clock; first thing in the morning; two months ago; when

- ***To indicate the beginning:*** at first; in the beginning; since; before then
- ***To indicate the middle:*** in the meantime; meanwhile; as it was happening; at that moment; at the same time; simultaneously; next; then
- ***To indicate the end and beyond:*** eventually; finally; at last; in the end; subsequently; later; afterward

Transitions can indicate relationships in space.

Transitions showing **spatial relationships** orient readers to the objects in a scene, as illustrated in these paragraphs:

Transitions to show relationships in space

On Georgia 155, I crossed Troublesome Creek, then went through groves of pecan trees aligned one with the next like fenceposts. The pastures grew a green almost blue, and syrupy water the color of a dusty sunset filled the ponds. Around the farmhouses, from wires strung high above the ground, swayed gourds hollowed out for purple martins.

The land rose again on the other side of the Chattahoochee River, and Highway 34 went to the ridgetops where long views over the hills opened in all directions. Here was the tail of the Appalachian backbone, its gradual descent to the Gulf. Near the Alabama stateline stood a couple of LAST CHANCE! bars.

—William Least Heat Moon, *Blue Highways*

Transitions Showing Spatial Relationships

- ***To indicate closeness:*** close to; near; next to; alongside; adjacent to; facing; on
- ***To indicate distance:*** in the distance; far; beyond; away; there; here; through; around; over/under
- ***To indicate direction:*** up/down; sideways; along; across; to the right/left; in front of/behind; above/below; inside/outside; toward/away from

EXERCISE 11.9

Turn to William Akana's essay in Chapter 8. Relying on the lists of transitions just given, underline the transitions in paragraphs 4–6. Consider how the transitions connect the ideas from sentence to sentence. Suggest any further transitions that could be added to make the relationships even clearer.

EXERCISE 11.10

Select a recent writing project of your own. Choose at least three paragraphs, and underline the logical, temporal, and spatial transitions. Depending on the kind of writing you were doing, you may find few, if any, transitions in one category or another. For example, an essay speculating about causes might not include any spatial transitions; writing about a remembered event might not contain transitions showing logical relationships.

Consider how your transitions relate the ideas from sentence to sentence. Compare your transitions with those in the lists in this text. Do you find that you are making full use of the repertoire? Are there gaps between any of your sentences that a well-chosen transition would close?

Headings and Subheadings

Headings and **subheadings**—brief phrases set off from the text in various ways—can provide visible cues to readers about the content and organization of a text. Headings can be distinguished from the text in numerous ways, such as through the selective use of capital letters, bold and italic type, and different sizes of type. To be most helpful to readers, headings should be phrased similarly and follow a predictable system.

Headings indicate sections and levels.

In this chapter, the headings in the section "Paragraphing," beginning on p. 355, provide a good example of a system of headings that can be readily outlined:

> **Paragraphing**
> **Paragraph indents signal related ideas.**
> **Topic sentences announce the paragraph's focus.**
> **Announcing the Topic**
> **Making a Transition**
> **Positioning the Topic Sentence**

Notice that in this example, the heading system has three levels. The first-level heading sits on its own line and is set in a large, red font; this heading stands out most visibly among the others. (It is one of five such headings in this chapter.) The second-level heading also sits on its own line but is set in a smaller font (and uses black type). The first of these second-level headings has no subheadings beneath it, while the second has three. These third-level headings, in black, do not sit on their own lines but run into the paragraph they introduce, as you can see if you turn back to pp. 355–59.

All of these headings follow a parallel grammatical structure: nouns at the first level; complete sentences at the second level; and "-ing" nouns at the third level.

To learn more about distinguishing headings from surrounding text and designing your writing, see Chapter 13, pp. 393–96.

Headings are not common in all genres.

Headings may not be necessary in short essays; thesis statements, forecasting statements, well-positioned topic sentences, and transition sentences may be all the cues the reader needs. Headings are rare in some genres, such as essays about remembered events

(Chapter 2) and essays profiling people and places (Chapter 3). Headings appear more frequently in such genres as concept explanations, reports, position papers, public policy proposals, and evaluations (Chapters 4–8).

At least two headings are needed at each level.

Before dividing their essays into sections with headings and subheadings, writers need to make sure their discussion is detailed enough to support at least two headings at each level. The frequency and placement of headings depend entirely on the content and how it is divided and organized. Keep in mind that headings do not reduce the need for other cues to keep readers on track.

EXERCISE 11.11

Turn to Maya Gomez's "Report: Possible Solutions to the Kidney Shortage" in Chapter 5 (pp. 149–55) and survey its system of headings. If you have not read the report, read or skim it now. Consider how the headings help readers anticipate what is coming and how the argument is organized. Decide whether the headings substitute for or complement other cues for keeping readers on track. Consider whether the headings are grammatically parallel.

EXERCISE 11.12

Select one of your writing projects that might benefit from headings. Develop a system of headings, and insert them where appropriate. Be prepared to justify your headings in light of the discussion about headings in this section.

12

Arguing

This chapter presents the basic strategies for making *arguments* in writing. In it, we focus on asserting a thesis, backing it up with reasons and support, and anticipating readers' questions and objections. It concludes with some sentence strategies you might use when composing an argument.

Asserting a Thesis

Central to any argument is the **thesis**. In a sentence or two, a thesis asserts or states the main point of any argument you want to make. It can be assertive only if you make it clear and direct. The thesis statement usually appears at the beginning of an argument essay.

There are three kinds of argument essays in Part One of this book. Each of these essays requires a special kind of assertion and reasoning:

- ***Assertion of opinion:*** What is your position on a controversial issue? (Chapter 6, "Arguing a Position")

> When overzealous parents and coaches impose adult standards on children's sports, the result can be activities that are neither satisfying nor beneficial to children.
>
> —Jessica Statsky, "Children Need to Play, Not Compete"

- ***Assertion of policy:*** What is your understanding of a problem, and what do you think should be done to solve it? (Chapter 7, "Proposing a Solution")

> Although this last-minute anxiety about midterm and final exams is only too familiar to most college students, many professors may not realize how such major, infrequent, high-stakes exams work against the best interests of students both psychologically and cognitively. . . . If professors gave brief exams at frequent intervals, students would be spurred to learn more and worry less.
>
> —Patrick O'Malley, "More Testing, More Learning"

- ***Assertion of evaluation:*** What is your judgment of a subject? (Chapter 8, "Justifying an Evaluation")

> Although the film is especially targeted for old-school gamers, anime fans, and comic book fanatics, *Scott Pilgrim vs. the World* can be appreciated and enjoyed by all audiences because of its inventive special effects, clever dialogue, and artistic cinematography and editing.
>
> —William Akana, "*Scott Pilgrim vs. the World*: A Hell of a Ride"

Chapters 6–8 contain essays that argue for each of these kinds of assertions, along with guidelines for constructing an argument to support such an assertion.

As these thesis statements indicate, the kind of thesis you assert depends on the occasion for which you are writing and the question you are trying to answer for your readers. Whatever the writing situation, to be effective, every thesis must satisfy the same three standards: It must be *arguable, clear,* and *appropriately qualified.*

Make arguable assertions.

Reasoned argument is called for when informed people disagree over an issue or remain divided over how best to solve a problem, as is so often the case in social and political life. Hence, the thesis statements in reasoned arguments make **arguable assertions**—possibilities or probabilities, not certainties.

Therefore, a statement of fact could not be an arguable thesis statement because facts are easy to verify—whether by checking an authoritative reference book, asking an authority, or observing the fact with your own eyes. For example, these statements assert facts:

Jem has a Ph.D. in history.

I am less than five feet tall.

Eucalyptus trees were originally imported into California from Australia.

Each of these assertions can be easily verified. To find out Jem's academic degree, you can ask him, among other things. To determine a person's height, you can use a tape measure. To discover where California got its eucalyptus trees, you can search the library or Internet. There is no point in arguing such statements (though you might question the authority of a particular source or the accuracy of someone's measurement). If a writer asserts something as fact and attempts to support the assertion with *authorities* or *statistics,* the resulting essay is not an argument but a *report.*

Like facts, expressions of personal feelings are not arguable assertions. Whereas facts are unarguable because they can be definitively proved true or false, feelings are unarguable because they are purely subjective.

You can declare, for example, that you detest eight o'clock classes, but you cannot offer an argument to support this assertion. All you can do is explain why you feel as you do. If, however, you were to restate the assertion as "Eight o'clock classes are counterproductive," you could then construct an argument that does not depend solely on your subjective feelings, memories, or preferences. Your argument could be based on *reasons* and *support* that apply to others as well as to yourself. For example, you might argue that students' ability to learn is at an especially low ebb immediately after breakfast and provide scientific support for this assertion—in addition, perhaps, to personal experience and reports of interviews with your friends.

Use clear and precise wording.

The way a thesis is worded is as important as its arguability. The wording of a thesis, especially its key terms, must be *clear* and *precise.*

Consider the following assertion: "Democracy is a way of life." The meaning of this claim is uncertain, partly because the word *democracy* is abstract and partly because the phrase *way of life* is inexact. Abstract ideas like democracy, freedom, and patriotism are by their very nature hard to grasp, and they become even less clear with overuse. Too often, such words take on *connotations* that may obscure the meaning you want to emphasize. *Way of life* is fuzzy: What does it mean? Does it refer to daily life, to a general philosophy or attitude toward life, or to something else?

Thus, a thesis is vague if its meaning is unclear; it is ambiguous if it has more than one possible meaning. For example, the statement "My English instructor is mad" can be understood in two ways: The teacher is either angry or insane. Obviously, these are two very different assertions. You would not want readers to think you mean one when you actually mean the other.

Whenever you write an argument, you should pay special attention to the way you phrase your thesis and take care to avoid vague and ambiguous language.

Qualify the thesis appropriately.

In addition to being arguable and clear, the thesis of an argument must make **appropriate qualifications** that suit your writing situation. If you are confident that your case is so strong that readers will accept your argument without question, state your thesis emphatically and unconditionally. If, however, you expect readers to challenge your assumptions or conclusions, you must qualify your statement. Qualifying a thesis makes it more likely that readers will take it seriously. Expressions like *probably, very likely, apparently,* and *it seems* all serve to qualify a thesis.

EXERCISE 12.1

Write an assertion of opinion that states your position on one of the following controversial issues:

- Should English be the official language of the United States and the only language used in local, state, and federal governments' oral and written communications?
- Should teenagers be required to get their parents' permission to obtain birth control information and contraceptives?
- Should high schools or colleges require students to perform community service as a condition for graduation?
- Should parents be able to demand access to the social media accounts of their children under eighteen?

Constructing a persuasive argument on any of these issues would obviously require careful deliberation and research. For this exercise, however, all you need to do is construct an arguable, clear, and appropriately qualified thesis.

EXERCISE 12.2

Find the thesis in the student essays in one of the argument chapters (Chapters 6–8). Then decide whether the thesis is arguable, clear, and appropriately qualified.

EXERCISE 12.3

If you have written or are currently working on one of the argument assignments in Chapters 6–8, consider whether your thesis is arguable, clear, and appropriately qualified. If you believe it does not meet these requirements, revise it accordingly.

Giving Reasons and Support

Whether you are arguing a position, proposing a solution, or justifying an evaluation, you need to give reasons and support for your thesis.

Think of **reasons** as the main points supporting your thesis. Often they answer the question, *Why do you think so?* For example, if you assert among friends that you value a certain movie highly, one of your friends might ask, "Why do you like it so much?" And you might answer, "*Because* it has challenging ideas, unusual camera work, and memorable acting." Similarly, you might oppose restrictions on students' use of offensive language at your college *because* such restrictions would make students reluctant to enter into frank debates, *because* offensive speech is hard to define, and *because* restrictions violate the free-speech clause of the First Amendment. These *because* phrases are your reasons. You may have one or many reasons, depending on your subject and your writing situation.

For your argument to succeed with your readers, you must not only give reasons but also support your reasons. The main kinds of **support** writers use are examples, statistics, authorities, anecdotes, and textual evidence. Following is a discussion and illustration of each kind of support, along with standards for judging its reliability.

Use representative examples for support.

Examples may be used as support in all types of arguments. For examples to be believable and convincing, they must be representative (typical of all the relevant examples you might have chosen), consistent with the experience of your readers (familiar to them and not extreme), and adequate in number (numerous enough to be convincing and yet not likely to overwhelm readers).

The following illustration comes from a book on illiteracy in America by Jonathan Kozol, a prominent educator and writer:

Uses examples to support argument that human costs of illiteracy are high

> Illiterates cannot read the menu in a restaurant.
>
> They cannot read the cost of items on the menu in the window of the restaurant before they enter.
>
> Illiterates cannot read the letters that their children bring home from their teachers. They cannot study school department circulars that tell them of the courses that their children must be taking if they hope to pass the SAT exams. They cannot help with homework. They cannot write a letter to the teacher. They are afraid to visit in the classroom. They do not want to humiliate their child or themselves.
>
> Illiterates cannot read instructions on a bottle of prescription medicine. They cannot find out when a medicine is past the year of safe consumption; nor can they read of allergenic risks, warnings to diabetics, or the potential sedative effect of certain kinds of nonprescription pills. They cannot observe preventive health care admonitions. They cannot read about "the seven warning signs of cancer" or the indications of blood-sugar fluctuations or the risks of eating certain foods that aggravate the likelihood of cardiac arrest.
>
> —Jonathan Kozol, *Illiterate America*

Kozol collected these examples in his many interviews with people who could neither read nor write. Though all of his readers are literate and have presumably never experienced the frustrations of adult illiteracy, Kozol assumes they will accept that the experiences are a familiar part of lives of adults who cannot read. Most readers will believe the experiences to be neither atypical nor extreme.

EXERCISE 12.4

Identify the examples in paragraphs 8 and 11 in Jessica Statsky's essay "Children Need to Play, Not Compete" and paragraphs 16–18 in Amitai Etzioni's essay "Working at McDonald's" (both in Chapter 6). If you have not read the essays, pause to skim them so that you can evaluate these examples within the context of the entire essay. How well do the examples meet the standards of representativeness, consistency with experience of readers, and adequacy in number? You will not have all the information you need to evaluate the examples—you rarely do unless you are an expert on the subject—but make a judgment based on the information available to you in the headnotes and the essays.

Use up-to-date, relevant, and accurate statistics.

In many kinds of arguments about economic, educational, or social issues, *statistics* may be essential. When you use statistics in your own arguments, you will want to ensure that they are up-to-date, relevant, and accurate. In addition, take care to select statistics from reliable sources and to cite them from the sources in which they originally appeared if at all possible. For example, you would want to get medical statistics directly from a reputable and authoritative professional periodical like the *New England Journal of Medicine* rather than secondhand from a supermarket tabloid or an unaffiliated Web site, neither of which can be relied on for accuracy. If you are uncertain about the most authoritative sources, ask a reference librarian or a professor who knows your topic.

The following selection, written by a Harvard University professor, comes from an argument speculating about the decline of civic life in the United States. Civic life includes all the clubs, organizations, and communal activities in which people choose to participate:

Uses statistics to support claim that Americans devote less time to civic life because they are watching more television

> The culprit is television.
>
> First, the timing fits. The long civic generation was the last cohort of Americans to grow up without television, for television flashed into American society like lightning in the 1950s. In 1950 barely 10 percent of American homes had television sets, but by 1959, 90 percent did. . . . The reverberations from this lightning bolt continued for decades, as viewing hours grew by 17–20 percent during the 1960s and by an additional 7–8 percent during the 1970s. In the early years, TV watching was concentrated among the less educated sectors of the population, but during the 1970s the viewing time of the more educated sectors of the population began to converge upward. Television viewing increases with age, particularly upon retirement, but each generation since the introduction of television has begun its life cycle at a higher

> starting point. By 1995 viewing per TV household was more than 50 percent higher than it had been in the 1950s.
>
> Most studies estimate that the average American now watches roughly four hours per day (excluding periods in which television is merely playing in the background). Even a more conservative estimate of three hours means that television absorbs 40 percent of the average American's free time, an increase of about one-third since 1965. Moreover, multiple sets have proliferated: By the late 1980s three-quarters of all U.S. homes had more than one set, and these numbers too are rising steadily, allowing ever more private viewing. . . . This massive change in the way Americans spend their days and nights occurred precisely during the years of generational civic disengagement.
>
> —ROBERT D. PUTNAM, "The Strange Disappearance of Civic America"

These statistics come primarily from the U.S. Bureau of the Census, a nationwide count of the number of Americans and a survey, in part, of their buying habits, levels of education, and leisure activities. The Census reports are widely considered to be accurate and trustworthy. They qualify as original sources of statistics.

Chapter 14, p. 410, provides help finding statistical data.

EXERCISE 12.5

In Chapter 6, underline the statistics in paragraphs 5 and 6 of Jessica Statsky's essay "Children Need to Play, Not Compete." If you have not read the essay, pause to skim it so that you can evaluate the writer's use of statistics within the context of the whole essay. How well do the statistics meet the standards of up-to-dateness, relevance, accuracy, and reliance on the original source? Does the writer indicate where the statistics come from? What do the statistics contribute to the argument?

Cite reputable authorities on relevant topics.

To support an argument, writers often cite experts on the subject. *Quoting, paraphrasing,* or even just referring to a respected **authority** can add to a writer's *credibility.* Authorities must be selected as carefully as are facts and statistics, however. One qualification for authorities is suggested by the way we refer to them: They must be authoritative—that is, trustworthy and reputable. They must also be specially qualified to contribute to the subject you are writing about. For example, a well-known expert on the American presidency might be a perfect choice to support an argument about the achievements of a past president but a poor choice to support an argument on whether adolescents who commit serious crimes should be tried as adults. Finally, qualified authorities must have training at respected institutions or have unique real-world experiences, and they must have a record of research and publications recognized by other authorities.

The following example comes from a *New York Times* article about some parents' and experts' heightened concern over boys' behavior. The author believes that the concern is exaggerated and potentially dangerous. In the full argument, she is particularly concerned about the number of boys who are being given Ritalin, a popular drug for treating attention-deficit hyperactivity disorder (ADHD):

> Today, the world is no longer safe for boys. A boy being a shade too boyish risks finding himself under the scrutiny of parents, teachers, guidance counselors, child therapists—all of them on watch for the early glimmerings of a medical syndrome, a bona fide behavioral disorder. Does the boy disregard authority, make snide comments in class, push other kids around and play hooky? Maybe he has a conduct disorder. Is he fidgety, impulsive, disruptive, easily bored? Perhaps he is suffering from attention-deficit hyperactivity disorder, or ADHD, the disease of the hour and the most frequently diagnosed behavioral disorder of childhood. Does he prefer computer games and goofing off to homework? He might have dyslexia or another learning disorder.

Establishes Konner's professional qualifications by naming the university where he teaches and his areas of study

> "There is now an attempt to pathologize what was once considered the normal range of behavior of boys," said Melvin Konner of the departments of anthropology and psychiatry at Emory University in Atlanta. "Today, Tom Sawyer and Huckleberry Finn surely would have been diagnosed with both conduct disorder and ADHD." And both, perhaps, would have been put on Ritalin, the drug of choice for treating attention-deficit disorder.
>
> —Natalie Angier, "Intolerance of Boyish Behavior"

In this example, Angier relies on **informal citation** within her essay to introduce Melvin Konner, the authority she quotes, along with a reference to his professional qualifications. Such informal citation is common in newspapers, magazines, and some books intended for general audiences. In other scholarly books and articles, and in other academic contexts, writers use **formal citation**, providing a list of works cited at the end of their own writing.

For examples of two formal citation styles often used in college essays, see Chapters 16 and 17.

EXERCISE 12.6

Analyze how authorities are used in paragraphs 4 and 6 of Patrick O'Malley's essay "More Testing, More Learning" in Chapter 7. Begin by underlining the authorities' contributions to these paragraphs, whether through quotation, summary, or paraphrase. On the basis of the evidence you have available, decide to what extent each source is authoritative on the subject: qualified to contribute to the subject, trained appropriately, and recognized widely. How does O'Malley establish each authority's credentials? Then decide what each authority contributes to the argument as a whole. (If you have not read the essay, take time to read or skim it.)

Use vivid, relevant anecdotes.

Anecdotes are brief stories about events or experiences. If they are relevant to the argument, well told, and true to life, they can provide convincing support. To be relevant, an anecdote must strike readers as more than an entertaining diversion; it must seem to make an irreplaceable contribution to an argument. A well-told story is easy to follow, and the people and scenes are described memorably, even vividly. A true-to-life anecdote seems believable, even if the experience is foreign to readers' experiences.

The following anecdote appeared in an argument taking a position on gun control. The writer—an essayist, poet, and environmentalist who is also a rancher in South Dakota—always carries a pistol and believes that other people should have the right to do so as well:

Tells an engaging anecdote and explains its relevance

One day, while driving to the highway mailbox, I saw a vehicle parked about halfway to the house. Several men were standing in the ditch, relieving themselves. I have no objection to emergency urination; we always need moisture. But I noticed they'd also dumped several dozen beer cans, which can blow into pastures and slash a cow's legs or stomach.

As I drove slowly closer, the men zipped their trousers ostentatiously while walking toward me, and one of them demanded what the hell I wanted.

"This is private land. I'd like you to pick up the beer cans."

"What beer cans?" said the belligerent one, putting both hands on the car door and leaning in my window. His face was inches from mine, and the beer fumes were strong. The others laughed. One tried the passenger door, locked; another put his foot on the hood and rocked the car. They circled, lightly thumping the roof, discussing my good fortune in meeting them and the benefits they were likely to bestow upon me. I felt small and trapped; they knew it.

"The ones you just threw out," I said politely.

"I don't see no beer cans. Why don't you get out here and show them to me, honey?" said the belligerent one, reaching for the handle inside my door.

"Right over there," I said, still being polite, "—there and over there." I pointed with the pistol, which had been under my thigh. Within one minute the cans and the men were back in the car and headed down the road.

I believe this incident illustrates several important principles. The men were trespassing and knew it; their judgment may have been impaired by alcohol. Their response to the polite request of a woman alone was to use their size and numbers to inspire fear. The pistol was a response in the same language. Politeness didn't work; I couldn't intimidate them. Out of the car, I'd have been more vulnerable. The pistol just changed the balance of power.

—Linda M. Hasselstrom, "Why One Peaceful Woman Carries a Pistol"

Most readers would readily agree that this anecdote is well told: It has many concrete, memorable details; there is action, suspense, climax, resolution, and even dialogue. It is about a believable, possible experience. Finally, the anecdote is clearly relevant to the author's argument about gun control.

See Chapter 2, "Remembering an Event," for more information about narrating anecdotes.

EXERCISE 12.7

Evaluate the way an anecdote is used in paragraph 16 of Amitai Etzioni's essay "Working at McDonald's" in Chapter 6. Consider whether the story is well told and true to life. Decide whether it seems to be relevant to the whole argument. Does the writer make the relevance clear? Does the anecdote support Etzioni's argument?

Use relevant textual evidence.

When you analyze opposing arguments (Chapter 5) or argue claims of value (Chapter 8), **textual evidence** will be very important. In your college courses, if you are asked to evaluate a controversial article, you must quote, paraphrase, or summarize passages so that readers can understand why you think the author's argument is or is not credible.

For textual evidence to be considered effective support for an argument, it must be carefully selected to be relevant. You must help readers see the connection between each piece of evidence and the reason it supports. Textual evidence must also be highly selective—that is, chosen from among all the available evidence to provide the support needed without overwhelming the reader or weakening the argument with marginally relevant evidence. Textual evidence usually has more impact if it is balanced between quotation and paraphrase, and quotations must be smoothly *integrated* into the sentences of the argument.

The following example comes from a student essay in which the writer argues that the main character (referred to as "the boy") in the short story "Araby" by James Joyce is so self-absorbed that he learns nothing about himself or other people:

Cites textual evidence from "Araby" to convince readers to take her argument seriously

The story opens and closes with images of blindness—a framing device that shows the boy does not change but ends up with the same lack of understanding that he began with. The street is "blind" with an "uninhabited house . . . at the blind end" (par. 1). As he spies on Mangan's sister, from his own house, the boy intentionally limits what he is able to see by lowering the "blind" until it is only an inch from the window sash (par. 4). At the bazaar in the closing scene, the "light was out," and the upper part of the hall was "completely dark" (par. 36). The boy is left "gazing up into the darkness," seeing nothing but an inner torment that burns his eyes (par. 37).

> The boy's blindness appears to be caused by his obsession with Mangan's sister. When he tries to read at night, for example, the girl's "image [comes] between [him] and the page," in effect blinding him (par. 12). In fact, he seems blind to everything except this "image" of the "brown-clad figure cast by [his] imagination" (par. 16). The girl's "brown-clad figure" is also associated with the houses on "blind" North Richmond Street, with their "brown imperturbable faces" (par. 1). The houses stare back at the boy, unaffected by his presence and gaze.
>
> —Sally Crane, "Gazing into the Darkness"

Notice how the writer quotes selected words and phrases about blindness to support her reasoning that the boy learns nothing because he is blinded. There are twelve smoothly integrated quotations in these two paragraphs, along with a number of paraphrases, all of them relevant. The writer does not assume that the evidence speaks for itself; she comments and interprets throughout.

See Chapter 5 for more about summarizing; see Chapter 10 for more about paraphrasing; see Chapter 15 for more about quoting, paraphrasing, and summarizing, and integrating material from sources into your own writing.

EXERCISE 12.8

Analyze the use of evidence in paragraphs 3–7 of Maya Gomez's "Analysis: Satel vs. the National Kidney Foundation: Should Kidney Donors Be Compensated?" in Chapter 5. If you have not read this essay, read it now. Identify the quotes and paraphrases Gomez uses, and then try to identify the phrases or sentences that comment on or explain this evidence. Consider whether Gomez's evidence in these paragraphs seems relevant to her thesis and reasons, appropriately selective, well balanced between quotes and paraphrases, integrated smoothly into the sentences she creates, and explained helpfully.

Responding to Objections and Alternatives

Asserting a thesis and backing it with reasons and support are essential to a successful argument. Thoughtful writers go further, however, by anticipating and responding to their readers' objections or their alternative position or solutions to a problem.

To respond to objections and alternatives, writers rely on three basic strategies: acknowledging, conceding, and refuting. Writers show that they are aware of readers' objections and questions (*acknowledge*), modify their position to accept readers' concerns that they think are legitimate (*concede*), or explicitly argue that readers' objections may be invalid or that their concerns may be irrelevant (*refute*). Writers may use one or more of these strategies in the same essay. Readers find arguments more convincing when writers have anticipated their concerns in these ways.

For more about conceding and refuting, see Chapters 6–8.

Acknowledge readers' concerns.

When you **acknowledge** readers' questions or objections, you show that you are aware of their point of view and take it seriously even if you do not agree with it, as in the following example:

> The homeless, it seems, can be roughly divided into two groups: those who have had marginality and homelessness forced upon them and want nothing more than to escape them, and a smaller number who have at least in part chosen marginality, and now accept, or, in a few cases, embrace it.
>
> Acknowledges three doubts his readers may have
>
> I understand how dangerous it can be to introduce the idea of choice into a discussion of homelessness. It can all too easily be used for all the wrong reasons by all the wrong people to justify indifference or brutality toward the homeless, or to argue that they are getting only what they deserve.
>
> And I understand, too, how complicated the notion can become: Many of the veterans on the street, or battered women, or abused and runaway children, have chosen this life only as the lesser of evils, and because, in this society, there is often no place else to go.
>
> And finally, I understand how much that happens on the street can combine to create an apparent acceptance of homelessness that is nothing more than the absolute absence of hope.
>
> Nonetheless we must learn to accept that there may indeed be people on the street who have seen so much of our world, or have seen it so clearly, that to live in it becomes impossible.
>
> —Peter Marin, "Go Ask Alice"

You might think that acknowledging readers' objections in this way—addressing readers directly, listing their possible objections, and discussing each one—would weaken your argument. It might even seem reckless to suggest objections that not all readers would think of. On the contrary, however, most readers respond positively to this strategy because it makes the writer seem thoughtful and reasonable. By researching your subject and your readers, you will be able to use this strategy confidently in your own argumentative essays. And you will learn to look for it in arguments you read and use it to make judgments about the writer's credibility.

EXERCISE 12.9

Jessica Statsky acknowledges readers' concerns in paragraphs 10 and 12 of her essay "Children Need to Play, Not Compete" in Chapter 6. How, specifically, does Statsky attempt to acknowledge her readers' concerns? What do you find most and least successful in her acknowledgment? How does the acknowledgment affect your judgment of her credibility?

Concede readers' concerns.

To argue effectively, you must often take special care to acknowledge readers' objections; questions; and alternative positions, causes, or solutions. Occasionally, however, you may have to go even further. Instead of merely acknowledging your readers' concerns, you may decide to accept some of them and incorporate them into your argument. This strategy, called **concession**, can be very disarming to readers, for it recognizes that opposing views have merit. The following example comes from an essay enthusiastically endorsing e-mail:

Accommodates readers' likely reservations by conceding that e-mail poses certain problems

> To be sure, egalitarianism has its limits. The ease and economy of sending email, especially to multiple recipients, makes us all vulnerable to any bore, loony, or commercial or political salesman who can get our email address. It's still a lot less intrusive than the telephone, since you can read and answer or ignore email at your own convenience. . . .
>
> Another supposed disadvantage of email is that it discourages face-to-face communication. At Microsoft, where people routinely send email back and forth all day to the person in the next office, this is certainly true. Some people believe this tendency has more to do with the underdeveloped social skills of computer geeks than with Microsoft's role in developing the technology email relies on. I wouldn't presume to comment on that. Whether you think email replacing live conversation is a good or bad thing depends, I guess, on how much of a misanthrope you are. I like it.
>
> —Michael Kinsley, "Email Culture"

Notice that Kinsley's accommodation or concession is not grudging. He readily concedes that e-mail brings users a lot of unwanted messages and may discourage conversation in the workplace.

EXERCISE 12.10

How does Patrick O'Malley respond to readers' objections and alternatives in paragraphs 9 and 10 of his essay "More Testing, More Learning" in Chapter 7, which argues for more frequent exams? What seems successful or unsuccessful in his argument? How do his efforts to acknowledge readers' concerns or make concessions affect his argument and his credibility?

Refute readers' objections.

Your readers' possible objections and views cannot always be conceded. Sometimes they must be refuted. When you **refute readers' objections**, you assert that they are wrong and argue against them. Refutation does not have to be delivered arrogantly or dismissively, however. Because differences are inevitable, reasoned argument provides a peaceful and constructive way for informed, well-intentioned people who disagree strongly to air their differences.

In the following example, social sciences professor Todd Gitlin refutes one argument for giving college students the opportunity to purchase lecture notes prepared by someone else:

Concedes a possible objection

Now, it may well be argued that universities are already shortchanging their students by stuffing them into huge lecture halls where, unlike at rock concerts or basketball games, the lecturer can't even be seen on a giant screen in real time. If they're already shortchanged with impersonal instruction, what's the harm in offering canned lecture notes?

Refutes the objection

The amphitheater lecture is indeed, for all but the most engaging professors, a lesser form of instruction, and scarcely to be idealized. Still, Education by Download misses one of the keys to learning. Education is a meeting of minds, a process through which the student educes, draws from within, a response to what the teacher teaches.

The very act of taking notes—not reading someone else's notes, no matter how stellar—is a way of engaging the material, wrestling with it, struggling to comprehend or take issue, but in any case entering into the work. The point is to decide, while you are listening, what matters in the presentation. And while I don't believe that most of life consists of showing up, education does begin with that—with immersing yourself in the activity at hand, listening, thinking, judging, offering active responses. A download is a poor substitute.

—Todd Gitlin, "Disappearing Ink"

As this selection illustrates, writers cannot simply dismiss readers' possible concerns with a wave of their hand. Gitlin states a potential objection fully and fairly but then goes on to refute it by claiming that students need to take their own lecture notes to engage and comprehend the material that is being presented to them.

Effective refutation requires a restrained tone and careful argument. Although you may not accept this particular refutation, you can agree that it is well reasoned and supported. You need not feel attacked personally because the writer disagrees with you.

EXERCISE 12.11

Evaluate Kelly D. Brownell and Thomas R. Frieden's use of refutation in paragraphs 5 and 6 of "Ounces of Prevention—the Public Policy Case for Taxes on Sugared Beverages" (Chapter 7). How do Brownell and Frieden signal or announce the refutation? How do they support the refutation? What is the tone of the refutation, and how effective do you think the tone would be in convincing readers to take the writers' argument seriously?

Logical Fallacies

Fallacies are errors or flaws in reasoning. Although essentially unsound, fallacious arguments seem superficially plausible and often have great persuasive power. Fallacies are not necessarily deliberate efforts to deceive readers. Writers may introduce a fallacy accidentally by not examining their own reasons or underlying assumptions, by failing to establish solid support, or by using unclear or ambiguous words. Here is a summary of the most common logical fallacies (listed alphabetically):

- ***Begging the question:*** Arguing that a claim is true by repeating the claim in different words (also called *circular reasoning*) (Note: Writers are increasingly using *begging the question* to mean *raising the question*, but this is incorrect; asking questions is a legitimate strategy in reasoned argument.)
- ***Confusing chronology with causality:*** Assuming that because one thing preceded another, the former caused the latter (also called *post hoc, ergo propter hoc*—Latin for "after this, therefore because of this")
- ***Either-or reasoning:*** Assuming that there are only two sides to a question and representing yours as the only correct one
- ***Equivocating:*** Misleading or hedging with ambiguous word choices
- ***False analogy:*** Assuming that because one thing resembles another, conclusions drawn from one also apply to the other
- ***Hasty generalization:*** Offering only weak or limited evidence to support a conclusion
- ***Overreliance on authority:*** Assuming that something is true simply because an expert says so and ignoring evidence to the contrary
- ***Oversimplifying:*** Giving easy answers to complicated questions, often by appealing to emotions rather than logic
- ***Personal attack:*** Demeaning the proponents of a claim instead of refuting their argument (also called *ad hominem*—Latin for "against the man"—*attack*)
- ***Red herring:*** Attempting to misdirect the discussion by raising an essentially unrelated point
- ***Slanting:*** Selecting or emphasizing the evidence that supports your claim and suppressing or playing down other evidence
- ***Slippery slope:*** Pretending that one thing inevitably leads to another
- ***Sob story:*** Manipulating readers' emotions to lead them to draw unjustified conclusions
- ***Straw man:*** Directing the argument against a claim that nobody actually makes or that everyone agrees is very weak

Sentence Strategies for Argument

Writers frequently argue to persuade others, whether they are arguing for an intepretation of a story in a literature class or for an interpretation of sales data to a supervisor. You, too, are likely to assert and support positions, respond to alternatives, and concede or refute objections. Sentence strategies like these may provide a jumping-off point for articulating your thoughts:

To Assert a Position

▸ When issue/event X happens, most people think ________, but I think ________ because ________.

- People focus on X, which is characterized by ________, and they don't even notice Y, which is characterized by ________.
- Although many people take X for granted, groups A, B, and C oppose it on the grounds that ________.
- Whereas supporters of X have argued that ________, opponents such as A, B, and C contend that ________.
- Though others may view it as a matter of ________, for me, the issue hinges on ________.
- According to A, what's at stake in this issue is ________. For me, however, what is most important is ________.
- On this issue, A and B say ________. Although I understand and to some degree sympathize with their point of view, this is ultimately a question of ________. What's at stake is not ________ but ________. Therefore, we must ________.
- This issue is dividing our community. Some people argue ________. Others contend ________. And still others believe ________. It is in all our interests to ________, however, because ________.
- Conventional wisdom is that ________. But I take a different view: ________.
- X has many good qualities, including ________ and ________; however, the pluses do not outweigh its one major drawback, namely that ________.
- X is a brilliant embodiment of ________ [name genre or category], especially notable for its superb ________ and thorough ________.
- Because I admire A's other work, I expected X to be ________. But I was disappointed/surprised by it because ________.
- Many complain about problem X but do nothing because solving it seems too hard/too costly. I think we need to tackle problem X because ________.

To Support a Position

- What makes X problematic/praiseworthy is ________.
- Because ________, I support/oppose X.
- Studies such as ________ have shown that X mostly affects groups A, B, and C because ________.
- Studies by Professors A and B at University C show that X has worked in cases such as ________, ________, and ________.
- The reasons for X may surprise you, such as ________, ________, and ________.
- The cause(s) of X may be surprising/alarming/disturbing/amazing, but they are clear: ________ [state cause(s) and provide evidence].
- X plays a surprising/alarming/disturbing/amazing role in our lives/our families/our communities/our workplaces: It does/is/provides ________ [describe role].

- For many years, group A has believed that ________. Now there is research supporting this claim, but not for the reasons you may think. It's not ________ that has been causing this phenomenon but ________.
- Researchers studying X have shown a causal connection between ________ [my causes] and ________ [my subject]. They claim ________ [quote/paraphrase/summarize information from source] (cite source).
- A large number of people have been polled on this question, and it appears that X was an important factor in their decision to ________.
- Reliable research by Professor A shows ________.

To Refute an Opposing Position

- One problem with position Y is that ________.
- Some claim position Y, but in reality, ________.
- My opponents cite research to support position Y, but the credibility of that research is questionable because ________.
- This argument seems plausible because it is consistent with our preconceptions. Nevertheless, evidence shows ________.
- Activists insist ________. Still, in spite of their good intentions, doing ________ would take away a basic right/make things even worse.
- A and B think this issue is about ________. But what is really at stake here is ________.
- Proponents object to my argument on the grounds that ________. However, they are confusing results with causes. What I am arguing is X.
- Polls show that most people favor Y, but an opinion's popularity does not make it true or right.
- Though most would agree that Y is true, it does not necessarily follow that ________.
- One common complaint is ________. In recent years, however, ________.
- Some people think we can't afford to implement solution X, but it would only cost $ ________ to put my solution in place compared to $ ________, the cost of doing nothing/implementing an alternative solution.
- Although it might take ________ months/years to implement my solution, it would actually take longer to implement solution Y.
- Some may suggest that I favor this solution because I would benefit personally; however, the fact is we would all benefit because ________.
- Some may claim that this solution has been tried and hasn't worked. But research shows that my solution differs from past experiments in several important ways: ________, ________, and ________ [list differences].

- X, reviewer for newspaper A, claims that ________. But I agree with Y, reviewer for newspaper B, who argues that ________.
- Some people think Y occurs because of ________, ________, and ________. Although it is easy to see why they might make this argument, the evidence does not back it up: ________ [explanation].
- Reviewers have remarked that X is a pale imitation of Y. I disagree. Whereas Y is ________, X is ________.
- X has generated criticism for its supposed ________. But X is not ________. Instead, it is ________.
- A recent study of X showed that ________.

To Concede an Objection

- I agree that ________.
- ________ is certainly an important factor.
- To be sure, ________ is true.
- Granted, ________ must be taken into consideration.
- Some people argue that ________. I understand this reservation, and therefore, I think we should ________.
- A common concern about this issue is ________. That's why my argument focuses on ________ [name a different aspect] of the issue.
- I agree with those who claim X/object on X grounds; therefore, instead of implementing option A, I think we should pursue option B.
- If ________ seems too time-consuming/expensive, let's try ________.
- Where ________ is a concern, I think X should be considered because ________.
- The one justifiable criticism that could be made against X is ________.
- As some critics have pointed out, X does follow the tried-and-true formula of ________.

To Concede and Refute an Objection

- Indeed, hard-core enthusiasts like A, B, and C may carp that X is not sufficiently ________ [list shortcomings]. However, ________.
- ________ may be true for Y but not for X.
- Although ________, I think ________.
- A and B insist that ________. Nevertheless, in spite of their good intentions, ________.
- I agree that ________ is important, but so is ________.

- I agree that _______ is important, but my opponents need to consider _______.
- On the one hand, I accept A's argument that _______, but on the other hand, I still think X is ultimately more important because _______.
- As some critics have pointed out, X does follow the tried-and-true formula of _______. Still, the director/writer/artist is using the formula effectively to _______.
- The objection that X can be caused by things other than cause Y may be true. But there is strong evidence showing that cause Y played a central role in making X happen by _______.
- Those who disagree about X often see it as a choice between _______ and _______. But both are important. We don't have to choose between them because _______.

13

Analyzing and Composing Multimodal Texts

As readers, we are often confronted by multimodal texts—such as advertisements, videos, or podcasts—that involve more than just words on a page. Whether their purpose is to sell us an idea or a car, spur us to action, or inspire us to dream, these texts require careful analysis of both their key components and their *rhetorical context*. As we "read" a multimodal text, we should ask ourselves a series of questions: Who created it? Where was it published? What *audience* is it addressing? What is it trying to get this audience to think and feel about the subject? How does it attempt to achieve this *purpose*?

As writers, too, we must consider not only what we want to say but also how best we can deliver that message. This means determining who will consume the message (your audience); what you are trying to get your audience to think, feel, or do about the subject; and how you can best achieve your purpose, given the goals, preferences, experiences, and knowledge of your readers. Often we can achieve our purpose with text presented in sentences and organized into paragraphs. But there are other times when words alone cannot convey the exact meaning that we have in mind.

Understanding Multimodality

Increasingly, we consume and create texts in different media (print, digital, or face-to-face) using multiple modes of communication. This gives us the term **multimodal**.

Modes of Communication

- Linguistic (words, written or spoken)
- Visual (photos, drawings, videos)
- Aural (speech, music)
- Spatial (layout, white space, paragraph indents)
- Gestural (facial expressions, hand or body movements)

Forms of communication that once used only the written word (thank-you notes, books, term papers) or the spoken word (telephone conversations, lectures) are today multimodal: They are enhanced with visual or audio components (such as calls on FaceTime or Skype) or even gestural elements (think of the various ways information enters or leaves in Prezi or PowerPoint presentations) for greater impact.

In a sense, all texts are multimodal. Even an essay written in words and printed on paper uses more than just the linguistic mode and the print medium. The fact that a printed text has margins, paragraph indents, headings, or a title centered on the page means that it also uses the spatial mode. If that essay were also illustrated or used color, it would include the visual mode. However, we typically talk about texts as multimodal when they are composed in a mode that is not primarily linguistic or printed on paper, such as video or images.

Analyzing Multimodal Texts

The primary purpose of this chapter is to help you analyze multimodal texts and give you strategies for composing your own multimodal projects. In your college courses, you may be asked to write entire papers analyzing one or more multimodal texts (paintings or films, for example). You may also find yourself writing papers in which analysis of one or more multimodal texts is included within the context of the larger paper (for example, by analyzing the brochures, television ads, and social media posts authorized by a political candidate in an argument about his or her campaign). Understanding what modes can do for a text can help you make rhetorical choices that will allow you to convey your message to your audience most effectively.

The chart "Criteria for Analyzing Multimodal Texts" (pp. 388–89) outlines key criteria for analyzing multimodal texts, including questions that will help you think critically about them.

With the Criteria for Analyzing Multimodal Texts in mind, consider the World Wildlife Fund public service announcement (PSA) shown in Figure 13.1. This PSA is primarily visual; its central image is a photo of attractive, smiling young newlyweds. The photo-mounting corners make the image seem as if it is a photo from a wedding album, rather than an ad agency's creation (which would be easier to ignore). The body language of the couple (angled toward each

FIGURE 13.1 "Wedding," from the WWF's "Beautiful Day U.S." Series

other), posture, and facial expressions (gestural mode) as well as their position in the center of the frame (spatial mode) reveal a seemingly conventional photo. But something is wrong: A hurricane rages in the background, and the gale blows the couple's hair forcefully to one side (gestural mode), showers the bride's white gown with mud, and threatens to rip the bouquet from her hand.

The text below the image (linguistic mode) is needed to make sense of the disruption of the conventional wedding photo. It reads: "Ignoring global warming won't make it go away." The disjunction between the couple's blissful expression and the storm raging around them turns out to be the point of the PSA: Like the young couple in the image, we are blithely ignoring the impending disaster that global warming represents. The reputable nonprofit's logo and URL, which constitute its "signature," are meant to be an assurance that this threat is real, and not just an idea of a profit-seeking ad agency dreamed up to manipulate us. (It is also a hint as to where we can send our contributions.)

Not everyone will be convinced by the PSA to support the work of the WWF, and some viewers may feel manipulated by the visual image. Nevertheless, most people would agree that with a single cleverly constructed image, a single line of text, and a logo, the PSA delivers its message clearly and forcefully. Scientific papers on global warming and the dire effects it will have on our planet abound, and while such papers are an effective means of communicating with an audience of scientists, this PSA is intended to speak to a general audience and to elicit contributions; thus, it uses multiple modes—visual, linguistic, and spatial—to communicate its message.

EXERCISE 13.1

Analyze one of the ads that follow by using the Criteria for Analyzing Multimodal Texts on pp. 388–89. Be sure to consider the role that writing plays in the ad's overall meaning. Write an essay with a thesis that discusses the ad's central meaning and significance.

The Advertising Archives

MINI Cooper magazine ad

The Advertising Archives

Coca-Cola TV ad

CRITERIA FOR ANALYZING MULTIMODAL TEXTS

OVERALL COMPOSITION

- What modes are used in the text: linguistic, visual, aural, spatial, or gestural? What modes are emphasized? Why were these modes chosen over others? What might be lost if other modes were emphasized?
- What tone or mood does the text convey? Is it lighthearted, somber, frightening, shocking, joyful?
- What elements in the text (color, sound, composition, words, people, setting) convey this tone or contribute to the mood?

Linguistic Mode

- What do the words say? Are they recognizable—a well-known slogan, a famous quotation, song lyrics?
- What role do the words play: explanation, identification, or something else?
- Is the tone of the language used humorous? Elegiac? Ironic?
- How are the words incorporated into the text? Are they written or spoken? Are they spoken by someone on- or off-screen or page? How do they relate to the rest of the text?

Visual Mode

- If the text is primarily visual, what is depicted? What is the focal point—that is, the place your eyes are drawn to?
- From what perspective do you view the focal point? Are you looking straight ahead at it, down at it, or up at it? If the visual is a photograph, what angle was the image shot from—straight ahead or looking down or up?
- What colors are used? Do these colors have cultural significance? How do they function with other colors (contrast for emphasis, soothing tones for mood, or something else)?
- Are there obvious special effects employed? Are there additional graphic elements? If so, what do these elements contribute to your reading of the text?
- Who or what is represented?
- If people are depicted, how would you describe their age, gender, subculture, ethnicity, profession, level of attractiveness, and socioeconomic class? How do these factors relate to other elements in the text and to the intended audience?
- Who is looking at whom? Do the people represented seem conscious of the viewer's gaze?
- If a recognizable scene is depicted, what is its setting? What is in the background and the foreground?

Aural Mode

- How might the voices heard, songs played, or sound effects used affect the listener's reception of the audio and other elements of the text?
- How does the sound (timbre, cadence, volume, pitch) of the speaker's voice contribute to his or her credibility (authority, trustworthiness, or expertise)?
- If there are multiple voices (such as in interviews or podcast roundtables), what is their relationship?
- Are sound clips recognizable (a popular song, famous speech, sound effect)? What cultural significance

do these sound bites have, and how does that affect the message or achieve the author's purpose?

- What tone or mood does the audio create?
- If the audio is a piece of music, does it belong to a recognizable genre (pop, hip-hop, classical)? What is the significance of the genre?

Spatial Mode

- What is the layout of the text? How are the elements arranged on the page or screen?
- How is information grouped together (paragraphs, a montage, layers)? How does the organization help the audience read through the text?
- How close do elements appear? Is there a lot of white space, and how does the white space affect the way the audience reads the text?

Gestural Mode

- What do facial expressions and body language tell you about attitudes (self-confident, vulnerable, anxious, subservient, angry, aggressive, sad) and relationships between the people featured (equal, subordinate, in charge)?
- Do facial expressions and body language complement or contradict spoken or written language? Is this intentional? What does the relationship reveal?
- How does the text control the way in which you interpret it? If the text is a presentation, are there arrows or special effects that guide your attention? If it is an infographic, a comic strip, or a film, what elements inform you of the order in which you're supposed to read?

RHETORICAL SITUATION

- What is the text's main purpose? Are we being asked to buy a product? Form an opinion or judgment about something? Support a political party's candidate? Take some other kind of action?
- Who is the text's target audience? Is it the instructor? Children? Men? Women? Some sub- or super-set of these groups (African American men, tweens, seniors)?
- Who is the author? Who sponsored its publication? What background/associations do the author and the sponsoring publication have? What other works have they produced?
- How do the words and media elements relate to each other? Do they convey the same message, or are they at odds in any way? Are the media elements essential or merely decorative?
- Where and in what form was it published? Does it appear online? On television? In print? In a commercial publication (a sales brochure, billboard, ad) or an informational one (newspaper, magazine)?
- What is the immediate social and cultural context within which the text is operating? What other social/cultural/historical knowledge does the text assume its audience already has? How do references to prior knowledge relate to the text's audience and purpose?
- How does the text connect, relate to, or contrast with any other significant texts (in any mode) that you are aware of? How do such considerations inform your ideas about this particular text?

EXERCISE 13.2

Find a video ad or public service announcement on television or online, or a short documentary with a strong purpose aimed at spurring the audience to action. Analyze your chosen multimodal text by using the Criteria for Analyzing Multimodal Texts on pp. 388–89. Be sure to consider the role that the modes (linguistic, visual, aural, spatial, and gestural) play in the text and how each contributes to the text's overall meaning and purpose. Write an essay with a thesis that discusses the text's central meaning and significance.

Composing Multimodal Texts

When composing a project for a college course, your instructor may define many of the characteristics of the project in the assignment itself. Traditional assignments, such as a research project or essay exam, are primarily linguistic. For an art history course, you may choose to include a photograph of the visual you are analyzing, but the focus of the composition will be a verbal analysis of the image. In many college classrooms, however, what constitutes an acceptable course paper or project is in transition. Many instructors now allow—and in some cases require—the creation of multimodal and multimedia projects in place of traditional papers. These projects can include blogs, collages, timelines, videos, Prezi or PowerPoint presentations, and even playlists.

When the mode(s) and medium (print, oral, digital) are not specified, how do you decide which will be most effective? Start by analyzing the **rhetorical situation.** Recall that a rhetorical situation is essentially any situation in which you create or consume a text of any kind (essay, photograph, advertisement, Web site, blog post, podcast, film, and so on). You analyze the rhetorical situation by considering the text's *purpose, audience, context, genre* (or type), and *medium.*

To learn more about the rhetorical situation, see Chapter 1, p. 2.

Reimagine your writing in a new genre or medium.

Sometimes a change in one or more aspects of the rhetorical situation requires writers to adapt their message to a new genre or medium. Consider, for example, study results published by a team of research scientists in a scholarly journal. The scientists format the article in the journal's style, using text and simple charts to report their findings, and using language appropriate for members of the scientific community, who will read their report (the audience). Now, imagine if the audience and context change, and the results of the study are being published online for a general audience. This happens often with online magazines and newspapers, when a reporter translates the findings of an article and embeds hyperlinks to cite the original study, or when a designer creates an infographic to depict the data.

Your instructor may ask you to reimagine one of your essays in a new genre or medium. This type of assignment is often called a *remix.* A remix challenges you to rethink your earlier decisions about purpose, audience, context, genre, and medium

FIGURE 13.2 Jean Brandt's graphic memoir

to deepen your understanding of the rhetorical situation. For example, Jean Brandt's story about shoplifting in Chapter 2 (pp. 14–18) could be remixed as an example in a proposal to curb juvenile delinquency or as a coming-of-age movie. After writing her essay, Brandt decided to remix her story as a graphic memoir for her college newspaper (see Figure 13.2). She thought her chosen genre would appeal to a wide audience of college students, who would be immediately drawn to the graphic form. She also felt that the visuals would allow her to depict her feelings more powerfully and directly than she could in words.

Student Maya Gomez remixed information as a timeline that she had gathered while conducting research for her report on the shortage of kidneys for donation. With the timeline, interested readers could get an overview of the history of kidney transplantation at a glance (Figure 13.3).

Design a multimodal text.

In our increasingly multimodal world, design plays a prominent role in gaining readers' interest and in communicating the ideas of a text clearly. By designing a text, you are making rhetorical choices about how to use different modes. At a minimum, the design should make texts easy for the audience to navigate and understand. But design can also have a more profound effect. Consider this familiar phrase, rendered in four different ways:

I l o v e y o u

I love you

The words in each rendering are the same, but the different uses of fonts, colors, and white space encourage us to read them very differently. The first message is vaguely unsettling (Is that a ransom note? A message from a stalker?); the second seems conventionally sweet; the third carries no emotional or context clues, but the spacing makes it

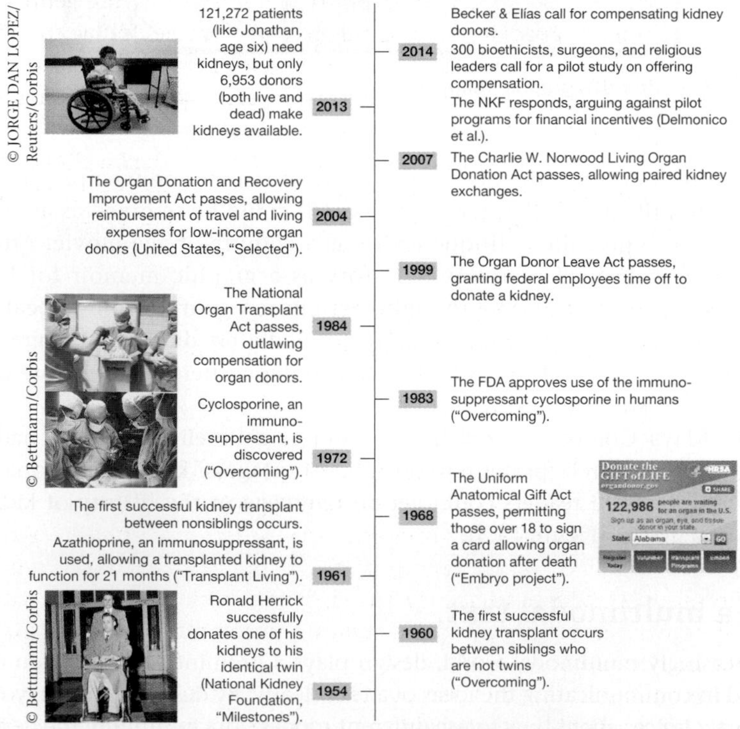

FIGURE 13.3 Maya Gomez's Timeline of Kidney Transplantation

irritatingly difficult to read; and the fourth offers no tone or context clues whatsoever (though this in itself might strike us as odd, given the meaning of the words). Thus, design does far more than add visual interest: It actually directs how we read and, to a certain extent, determines the meaning we derive.

The freedom you have in terms of using design elements in the college projects you compose will vary quite a bit, depending on your instructor's preference, the nature of the assignment, and the media you choose. For instance, if you are designing a poster representing your research, your text will likely contain more text and fewer images than a flyer advertising a campus music festival. If you are creating a video, your design choices must take into account the abilities or limits of the software tools at your disposal.

If you are writing an essay for a college course, you can expect that your instructor will read it carefully. Your design decisions should therefore make sustained reading as easy as possible; fonts that are too small to read easily or margins that are too narrow to comment in will make the reader's job unnecessarily difficult. In most college courses, guidelines on design have traditionally followed a "less is more" rule, with written assignments printed on white $8^1/_2'' \times 11''$ paper, and the use of extravagant fonts, decorative visuals, and the like discouraged. The growing number of multimodal assignments has obviously required some adjustments to traditional notions of acceptable design for college writing. In principle, however, "less is more" still applies. Good design gives priority to clarity.

Frequently, too, your design decisions will be determined by the genre (or type) of text you are preparing. Business letters and e-mails, for example, follow specific formats; movie trailers and TED talks have a familiar pacing and appearance. Because your readers will bring certain expectations to these kinds of texts, altering an established format can cause confusion and should therefore be considered carefully.

It is impossible to cover effective design in all modes and media. Since the majority of your college writing will primarily be in the linguistic mode, it is important to consider how to design written texts. A few key design elements are central:

- Use readable fonts
- Select legible colors with adequate contrast
- Use white space to chunk content and make it easy to read

Choosing a Font

Typography is a design term for the letters and symbols that make up the print on a page or a screen. You are already using important aspects of typography when you use capital letters, italics, boldface, or different sizes of type to signal a new sentence, identify the title of a book or presentation, or distinguish a heading from body text. Perhaps the most important advice for working with typography is to choose fonts that are easy to read. Lengthy passages in italics, a decorative font, or too small a font, for example, can detract from readability.

Considering the audience and purpose of the text will help you decide what style of font is most appropriate for a specific writing situation. For most academic and business writing, you will probably want to choose a traditional font style that is easy to read, such as Arial or Times New Roman. Texts that will be read on paper may be easier to read if composed in a serif font, such as Georgia, Times Roman, or Century. (A serif is the little line projecting from the ends of a letter.) Texts that will be read on-screen may be easier to read if composed in a sans serif font, like Univers, Helvetica, or Verdana. Sentences and paragraphs printed in fonts that imitate calligraphy (typically called *script fonts*) or those that mimic *handwriting* are not only difficult to read but also too informal for most academic and business purposes.

To ensure that your text can be easily read, you also need to choose an appropriate font size (traditionally measured in units called *points*). For most types of academic writing, a 12-point font is standard for the main (body) text. For Web pages, however, you should consider using a slightly larger font to compensate for the difficulty of reading from a computer monitor. For presentations, you should use an even larger font size (such as 32-point, and typically no smaller than 18-point) to ensure that the text can be read from a distance.

Although technology now makes hundreds of font styles and sizes available to writers, you should avoid confusing readers with too many fonts in one composition. Limit the number of fonts to one or two that complement each other well. A common practice, for instance, is to choose one font for all titles and headings (such as 14-point Arial boldface for printed text) and another for the body text (such as 12-point Times New Roman for printed texts). For texts delivered and read online, you might reverse the fonts, using 12-point Arial for the body text and 14-point Times New Roman boldface for headings.

Using Colors

Color printers, photocopiers, and online technology facilitate the use of color, but color does not necessarily make text easier to read. In most academic documents, the only color you should use is black. Though color is typically used more freely in academic writing delivered on Web pages or in multimodal presentations, it should still be used in moderation and always with the aim of increasing your readers' understanding of what you have to say. Always consider, too, whether your readers might have low vision or be color-blind and whether they will have access to a full-color version of the document.

Although the slide design in Figure 13.4 is visually interesting and the heading is readable, the bulleted text is very hard to read because there is too little contrast between the text color and the background color.

Also consider the meanings associated with different colors. For example, in the United States and other Western cultures, white is typically associated with goodness and purity; in China, however, white represents grief and mourning. Although your use of color in a report, blog, or multimodal presentation might not carry such deep meaning, bear in mind that most people have emotional or psychological responses to colors and color combinations. Without considering who is likely to read a text and what social or cultural factors are associated with that group, you may invite unintended interpretations, which can affect the specific meaning that a reader develops from a text.

Most people with color blindness have difficulty distinguishing between reds and greens of the same density. If designing in color, make sure that you do not convey important information in confusing colors or that you include a secondary means of distinguishing, such as by including a label or an explanation in the text.

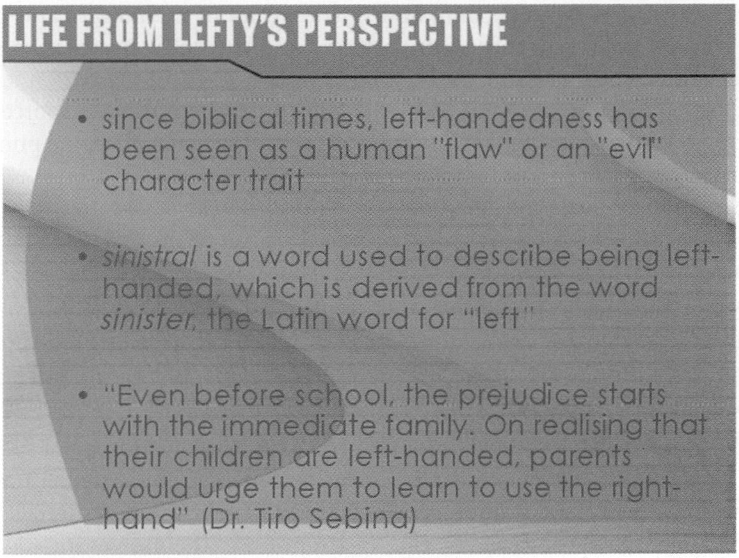

FIGURE 13.4 Document with Too Little Color Contrast

Using White Space

Another basic element of design is white space, the open (or blank) space on a page. White space is usually used between a heading and the text that follows it and in the area surrounding visuals to emphasize an image or create a clean, modern look. In documents, you also use white space when you set the margins on a page and when you indent or leave a space between paragraphs. In all these cases, the white space makes your text easier to read. When used generously, white space facilitates reading by helping the eye find and follow the words or images.

Chunking, the breaking up of text or visuals into smaller units, also facilitates reading. In comics, individual frames or panels group images and text into a scene or moment. In documents, paragraphing is a form of chunking that divides text into units of closely related information. In most academic essays and reports, text is double-spaced, and paragraphs are distinguished by indenting the first line one-half inch. In single-spaced text or text that will be read on-screen, adding extra space between paragraphs serves to chunk the content. This format, referred to as block style, is often used in business letters, e-mails, and other electronic documents. When creating electronic documents—especially Web pages—you might consider chunking your material into separate pages or screens, with links connecting the chunks.

Embed visuals and media in texts.

Tables, graphs, charts, diagrams, photographs, maps, and screenshots, as well as embedded video and audio files, add interest and are often more effective in conveying information than prose alone.

When integrating a visual or media file into your text, introduce and discuss it before revealing it. In an academic composition, include a figure number both in your text and in the caption accompanying the visual or media file, and make clear in your text the kind of information it contains and the point it makes or supports.

If your composition is going to be posted online on a site that is not password-protected and you borrow a visual or media file from a copyrighted source, you may need to request written permission from the copyright holder (such as the photographer, publisher, or site sponsor).

Caution: Though media can enhance your writing, it's easy to create visuals, videos, or sound clips that distract readers and work against the goals of the text. Keep the following advice in mind when creating visuals:

- **Make the decisions that your computer cannot make for you.** A computer can automatically turn spreadsheet data into a chart or graph, but only you can decide which visual—or what use of color, if any—is appropriate given your purpose.
- **Avoid "chart junk."** Many computer programs provide an array of special effects that can be used to alter visuals, including three-dimensional renderings, textured backgrounds, and shadowed text. Such special effects often detract from the intended message of the visual by calling attention to themselves instead. Use them sparingly, and only when they emphasize key information.
- **Use visual or audio files purposefully.** Consider your audience, context, and genre when incorporating visuals or other inserts. Academic audiences typically want visuals included only if they serve a specific purpose. Including items for merely decorative purposes is frowned on.

The following chart, Criteria for Analyzing Document Design, includes questions that will help you think about how to design your multimodal compositions.

CRITERIA FOR ANALYZING DOCUMENT DESIGN

- Does the design follow the conventions of the genre, or type of text, you are creating?
- Does the design enhance the content of the text or distract from the message in any way?

VISUAL MODE

- What do the colors in the design signify? Is there effective contrast between elements? Is the typography (font type, size, and treatment) appropriate?
- How do images, charts, graphs, or graphics convey information? What is their relationship to the words in the text? What is their relationship to other visuals?

SPATIAL MODE

- What is placed where? Why? What elements come first in the text? Next? Last?
- How is white space used throughout the text? What does it help to emphasize? Minimize?
- How are words and other elements grouped in the text? Do these "chunks" effectively divide related information for the audience?

Creating a Multimodal Presentation

This chapter has discussed at length the characteristics of a multimodal text. Now let's apply these considerations to one of the most common types of multimodal texts—the presentation.

Presentations make use of multiple modes and sometimes multiple media: Speakers use linguistic and gestural modes as they speak, move about, and advance the presentation deck for the audience. Presentation slides will also demonstrate the spatial mode in bulleted and numbered lists and other textual elements. If speakers incorporate images, videos, or sound files in their presentation slides, then they expand to use all five modes of communication.

Assess your rhetorical situation.

As with any text, to make an effective presentation you must assess your rhetorical situation. Even for an impromptu presentation, take a few moments to think about why, to whom, and where you are speaking.

Define your purpose by completing the following statement:

▶ In this presentation, I want to ________.

For instance, you may want to speculate on the causes of companies' hiring part-time rather than full-time workers, or you may want to argue your position on the ethics of this new hiring policy.

To assess your audience, ask questions like these: Why are the members of my audience here? What do they already know about my subject? How do they feel about my topic? What objections might they have to my argument? What media will help me convey my points most effectively, given my audience and what kind of media (including presentation slides, like PowerPoint or Prezi) they will expect?

Consider the context within which you will be presenting and how that will affect your content and delivery. The amount and type of media you use will differ depending on whether you are speaking at the front of your classroom, in a large auditorium, or online via Skype or Google Hangouts.

Determine how much information you can present in the allotted time.

Your presentation should be exactly as long as the time allotted. Using substantially less time will make your presentation seem incomplete or superficial; using substantially more time may alienate your audience. Plan your presentation to allocate sufficient time for an introduction, concluding remarks, and follow-up questions (if a question-and-answer session is to be part of the presentation). If you are giving a scripted presentation, each double-spaced page of text will probably take two minutes to deliver. To get a realistic sense of how long your presentation will take, rehearse several times, using any multimedia aids you plan to use. Then time yourself.

Use cues to orient audience members.

Listening is one of the most difficult ways to comprehend information, in part because listeners cannot look back at previous information or scan forward, as readers can. To help your audience follow your presentation, use the same kinds of cues that you would use for readers, but use them more frequently and overtly. Here are four basic cues that are especially helpful for listeners:

- **Thesis and forecasting statements.** Begin by announcing to the audience what you intend to communicate (your thesis) and the order in which you will present your materials (your forecast).
- **Transitions.** Provide transitions when you move from point to point. For example, when you finish discussing your first reason, state explicitly that you are now turning to your second reason.
- **Summaries.** End your presentation with a summary of your main points, and look for opportunities to include summaries at the end of each section. A brief summary that indicates the point you are making and its relation to your overall thesis can help listeners understand how the parts of your argument fit together to support your thesis.
- **Presentation slides.** An outline of your presentation, including your thesis and main topics (in a bulleted or numbered list), can be shown on an introductory slide. Slides indicating each main point and key supporting evidence can be displayed as you arrive at each point.

Design your presentation effectively.

As mentioned previously, presentation software, such as PowerPoint or Prezi, allows you to list the major points of your presentation, which helps your listeners understand and remember what you say. Presentation slides also allow you to incorporate images—like photographs and pie charts, videos and audio files—which can be used to illustrate your points and provide supporting evidence. Simple presentation slides, such as the one shown in Figure 13.5, can be created and displayed with relative ease.

Presentation software has the advantage of allowing the use of animation, video, and audio. Online sites and apps such as Prezi allow you to create more visual and gestural presentations that zoom in and out, engaging your audience and freeing your narrative from the linear movement of slides. After writing his essay proposing a solution to the problem of "high-stakes exams" (see Chapter 7, pp. 235–41), student writer Patrick O'Malley thought his target audience (professors) would be more likely to replace a few high-stakes exams with a greater number of lower-stakes quizzes and tests if he remixed his essay as a presentation that laid out the evidence clearly. (See a snapshot of his Prezi presentation in Figure 13.6.)

As you prepare presentations:

- Use a large, easy-to-read font; allow generous amounts of space around text; and maintain sharp contrast. Make sure fonts are large enough that your slides can be read by audience members at the back of the room.

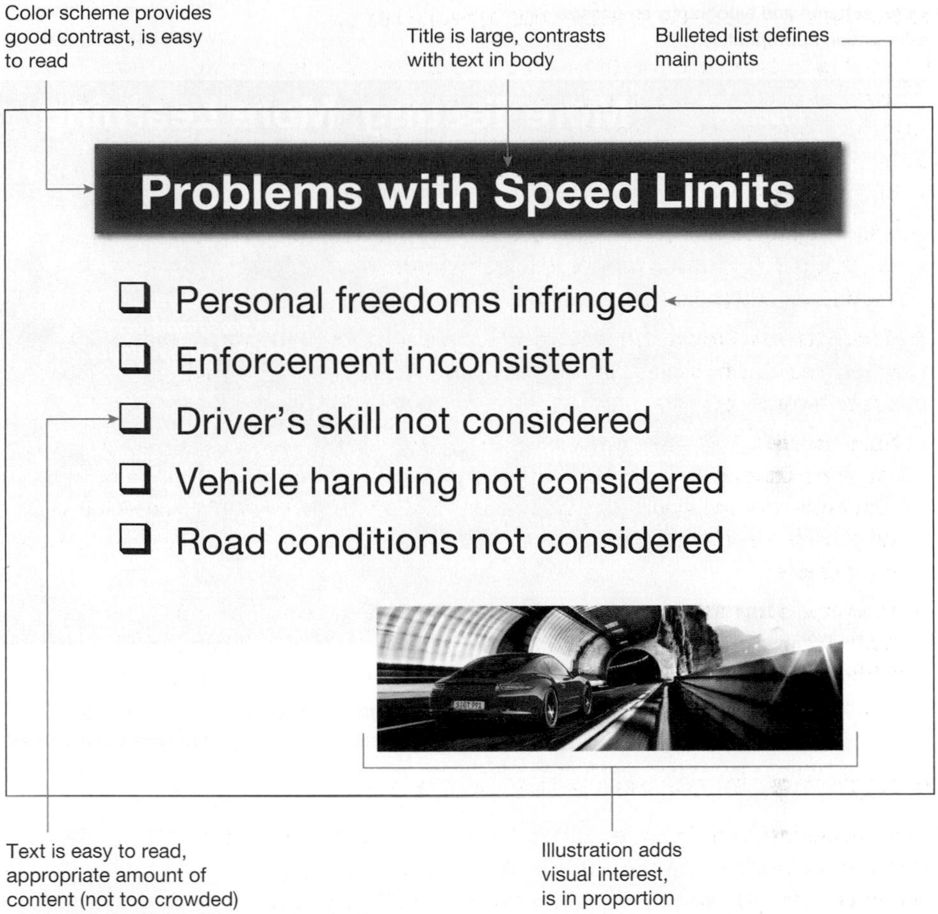

FIGURE 13.5 Sample PowerPoint Slide
The Advertising Archives

- The text you include should be concise, easy to read, and uncluttered. Remember that audience members will have only a few moments to examine each slide, so avoid filling them with text.
- If using sound or video files, make sure the volume is consistent and clearly audible but not deafening.
- If using software or apps with more capabilities in animation, video, or sound, make sure the bells and whistles don't drown you out or distract your audience from your message.

Finally, keep in mind that the point of a presentation is to convey information to the audience, not present lengthy presentation slides. Slides should support your presentation, not dominate it.

Color scheme and typography emphasize information appropriately

Title is large, contrasts with supporting text

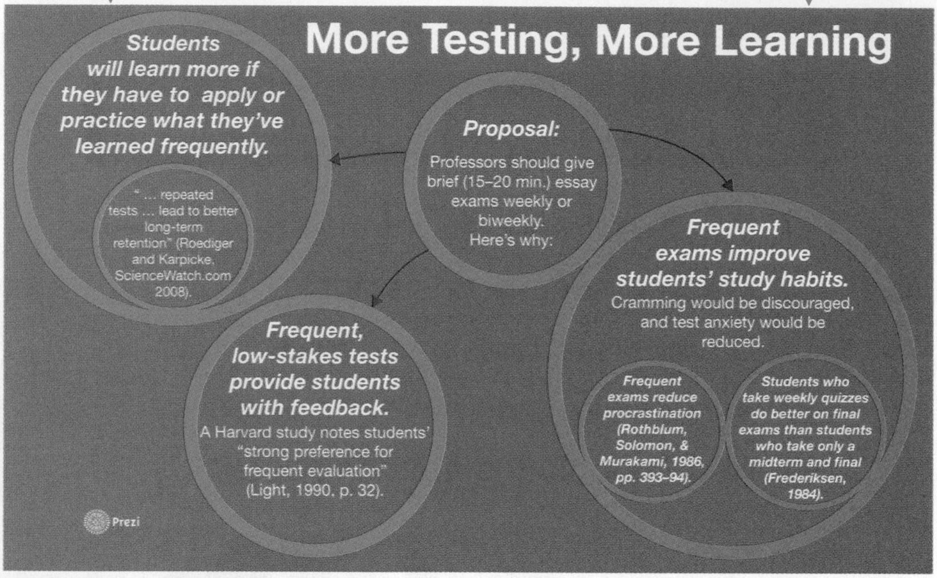

FIGURE 13.6 Sample Prezi

Text chunking, spatial arrangement, and arrows show relationships between information and provide visual interest

© Greg Gard/Alamy

PART 3

Research Strategies

14

Planning a Research Project and Selecting Sources

To research a topic effectively at the college level requires a plan. A clear sense of your rhetorical situation, as well as the practical needs of your research task (such as the due date and the level of detail required), will help you

- develop an appropriate, focused topic;
- identify source types your readers will recognize as varied and appropriate;
- find an appropriate number of the right kinds of sources you will need to write an effective research project.

Analyzing Your Rhetorical Situation and Setting a Schedule

Making your research project manageable begins with defining the scope and goals of your project. Begin by analyzing your *rhetorical situation:*

- What is your *purpose*? Is it to explain a concept, report on or argue for a position, or analyze the causes of an event or a behavior?
- Who is your *audience,* and what will your readers' interests, attitudes, and expectations for the project be? How many and what kinds of resources does your audience expect you to consult? (For college research projects, your audience will likely be your instructor.)
- What *genre* (or *type*) is the research project, and how will that affect the kinds of sources you use? An observational report in the social sciences may demand mainly *primary research,* whereas an argument essay for a history course may require a variety of *secondary* and primary sources.
- What medium will you use to present your research project? A research project presented in print will allow you to incorporate visuals and use parenthetical citations and a works-cited or reference list to acknowledge your sources; a project presented in person, using PowerPoint or Prezi slides, may allow you to incorporate video and sound but require you to name your sources during the presentation.

Also be sure to consider the following practical issues before you begin your research project:

- How long should the research project be?
- When is it due?
- Are any interim assignments required (such as an outline or an annotated bibliography)?

If you're not sure of the answers to these questions, ask your instructor to clarify the assignment or to define any confusing terms so that you can work most efficiently.

Finally, set a schedule. Be sure to take into consideration the projects you have due for other classes as well as other responsibilities (to work or family, for example) or activities.

To learn more about primary and secondary research, see pp. 406–7.

Choosing a Topic and Getting an Overview

Often students will be assigned a topic for a research project. If you are free to choose your own topic, consult course materials, such as textbooks and handouts, to get ideas, and consult your instructor to make sure your topic is appropriate. Sometimes conducting an Internet search may give you an idea for a topic. Once you've chosen an appropriate topic, an overview can help you determine the kinds of issues you should consider.

Wikipedia offers a wealth of information, and it is often the first stop for students who are accustomed to consulting the Internet first for information. Be aware, though, that *Wikipedia* is user generated rather than traditionally published, and for this reason, the quality of information found there can be inconsistent. Many instructors do not consider *Wikipedia* a reliable source, so you should ask your teacher for advice on consulting it at this stage.

Your library will likely subscribe to databases, such as *Gale Virtual Reference Library* or *Oxford Reference Online*, that you can search to find information from general encyclopedias and dictionaries as well as from specialized, or subject-specific, encyclopedias and dictionaries.

General encyclopedias, like *Britannica Online*, provide basic information about many topics. **Specialized encyclopedias**, like *Encyclopedia of Addictions* or *Grove Art Online*, provide a comprehensive introduction to your topic, including the key terms you will need to find relevant material in catalogs and databases, and they present subtopics, enabling you to see many possibilities for focusing your research.

Frequently, libraries prepare **research guides**—lists of reliable sources on popular topics. A guide can offer very useful resources for research, so check your library to find out if such a guide is available. You may also find resources that provide good overviews of topics, such as *CQ Researcher.* A reference librarian can help point you in the right direction.

Focusing Your Topic and Drafting Research Questions

After you have gotten a sense of the kinds of sources available on your topic, you may be ready to narrow it. Focus on a topic that you can explore thoroughly in the number of pages assigned and the length of time available. Finding your own take on a subject can help you narrow it as well. The invention strategies in Chapter 9 can help you focus in on one aspect of your topic.

You may also want to write questions about your topic and then focus on one or two that can be answered through research. These will become the research questions that will guide your search for information. You may need to add or revise questions as you conduct your search. The answers you come up with can form the basis for your thesis statement.

Developing a List of Keywords

Finding useful sources depends on determining the right **keywords**—words or phrases that describe your topic—to use while searching catalogs, databases, and the Internet. Start your list of keywords by noting the main words from your research questions or thesis statement. Look for useful terms in your search results, and use these to expand your list. Then add synonyms (or words with a similar meaning) to expand your list. Keep in mind that different subjects or disciplines may use different terminology, and these differences may be reflected in the terms databases use.

For example, student Cristina Dinh might have started with a term like *home schooling*. She might have added *home education* or *home study*. After reading an article in an encyclopedia about her subject, she might have added *student-paced education* or *autonomous learning* to expand her scope. After consulting the thesaurus in *ERIC*, a database focusing on education, she might have added *parents as teachers;* after consulting the thesaurus in the database *PsycARTICLES*, she might have added *nontraditional education*.

Creating a Working Bibliography

A **working bibliography** is an ongoing record of the sources you discover while researching your subject. In your final project, you will probably not cite every source you list in your working bibliography, but recording the information you will need to cite a source—*as you identify it*—will save you time later. (Just be sure to double-check that your entries are accurate!) Your working bibliography should include the following for each source:

- **Author's (or authors') name(s)**
- **Title and subtitle**

- **Publication information:** For books: version or an edition number (for example, *revised edition, 3rd ed.*), the name of the publisher, the copyright year, and the page numbers of the section(s) you consulted; for periodicals, the periodical's name, volume and issue number and date or season, and the article's page numbers
- **Location information:** The call number of a book (for your reference); the name of the database through which you accessed the source; the **DOI** (digital object identifier—a permanent identifying code that won't change over time or from database to database) for an article or, if one is unavailable, the full URL (ideally a permalink, if the site provides one); the date you last accessed the source (for a Web page, though you will rarely need to include an access date in your paper's works-cited entry; see Chapter 16 for more information)

Note: If you store your working bibliography in specialized citation management software (such as RefWorks, Zotero, or EndNote), it will format your citations in the citation style (such as MLA or APA) you specify. These software programs are not perfect, however; you still need to double-check your citations against the models in the style manual you are using or in Chapter 16 or 17 of this text.

Chapters 16 and 17 present two common documentation styles—one created by the Modern Language Association (MLA) and widely used in the humanities, and the other advocated by the American Psychological Association (APA) and used in the social sciences. Other disciplines have their own preferred styles of documentation. Confirm with your instructor which documentation style is required for your assignment so that you can follow that style for all the sources you put into your working bibliography.

Annotating Your Working Bibliography

An **annotated bibliography** provides an overview of sources that you have considered for your research project. Researchers frequently create annotated bibliographies to keep a record of sources and their thoughts about them. Researchers sometimes also publish annotated bibliographies to provide others with a useful tool for beginning a research project of their own.

What an annotated bibliography includes depends on the researcher's rhetorical situation. But most entries answer these questions:

- What kind of source is this?
- What is the main point of the source?
- How might I use the source?
- How might my sources be related?
- What information will I need to cite the source?

Some also include an introduction that explains the purpose and scope of the annotated bibliography and may describe how and why the researcher selected the sources. The annotated bibliography in Chapter 5 by Maya Gomez, written for her composition instructor, might have included an introduction like this:

My annotated bibliography is intended to provide me with the sources I need to write a report on compensating organ donors. It includes sources that provide background on evolving government policy and that offer arguments for and against compensating donors. These sources represent a number of perspectives, including economic, political, moral, and personal; they have been written by well-respected scholars (for example, Nobel Prize–winning economist Gary S. Becker) and organizations (the National Kidney Foundation).

For more about annotating a bibliography, see Chapter 5.

Taking Notes on Your Sources

The summaries that you include in a working bibliography or the annotations that you make on a printed or digital copy of a source are useful reminders, but you should also make notes that analyze the text, synthesize what you are learning with your own ideas or ideas you have gleaned elsewhere, and evaluate the quality of the source.

You will mine your notes for language to use in your draft, so be careful to

- summarize accurately, using your own words and sentence structures;
- paraphrase without borrowing the language or sentence structure of the source;
- quote accurately and place all language from the source in quotation marks.

You can take notes on a photocopy of a printed text or use comments or highlighting to annotate a digital text. Whenever possible, download, print, photocopy, or scan useful sources, so that you can not only read and make notes at your leisure but also double-check each of your summaries, paraphrases, and quotations against the original. These strategies, along with those discussed in Chapter 15, "Evaluating and Using Sources," will keep you from plagiarizing inadvertently.

For more on synthesizing, see Chapters 5 and 10; for more on annotating sources, see Chapter 10; for more on avoiding plagiarism see Chapter 15.

Finding Sources

Students are surrounded by a wealth of information—in print, online, in videos and podcasts, even face to face! Much of this information is excellent, but some is of dubious quality. This can make finding the information you need to support your ideas exciting, but it also means you will have to develop a research strategy and sift through possible sources carefully. What you are writing about, who will read your writing project, and the type of writing you are doing (a story for your college newspaper, a proposal for your employer, a research project for your U.S. history course) will help you decide which types of sources are most appropriate. Does your writing project require you to depend mainly on **secondary sources**—like books and articles that analyze and summarize a subject—or develop **primary sources,** such as interviews with experts, surveys, or observational studies you conduct yourself, and laboratory reports, historical documents, diaries, letters, or works of literature written by others? Whatever sources you decide will best help you support your claims, the following sections will help you find or develop the resources you need.

To learn how to evaluate sources, see Chapter 15.

Search library catalogs and databases.

For most college research projects, finding appropriate sources begins with your library's home page, where you can

- find (and sometimes access) books, reference sources (such as general and subject-specific encyclopedias and dictionaries), reports, documents, multimedia resources (such as films and audio recordings), and much more;
- use your library's database to find (and sometimes access) articles in newspapers, magazines, and scholarly journals, as well as in reference sources;
- find **research guides**, or lists of reliable sources on topics frequently studied by students.

Many libraries offer unified search, which allows patrons to search for books and articles in magazines, newspapers, and scholarly journals simultaneously, from the home page. If you aren't sure whether you will need to search for books and articles using separate catalogs and databases, consult a librarian.

Your library's home page is also the place to find information about the brick-and-mortar library—its floor plan, its hours of operation, and the journals it has available in print. You might even be able to find links to what you need in other libraries or get online help from a librarian.

Using Appropriate Search Terms

Just as with a search engine like *Google,* you can search a library catalog or database by typing your search terms—an author's name, the title of a work, a subject term or keyword, even a call number—into the search box. To search successfully, put yourself in the position of the people writing about your topic to figure out what words they might have used. If your topic is ecology, for example, you may find information under the keywords *ecosystem, environment, pollution,* and *endangered species,* as well as a number of other related keywords, depending on the focus of your research and your area of study.

Broadening or Narrowing Your Results

When conducting a search, you may get too few hits and have to broaden your topic. To broaden your search, try the following:

Replace a specific term with a more general term	Replace *sister* or *brother* with *sibling*
Substitute a synonym for one of your keywords	Replace *home study* with *home schooling* or *student-paced education*

Combine terms with or to get results with either or both terms	Search *home study or home schooling* to get results that include both *home study* and *home schooling*
Add a wildcard character, usually an asterisk (*) or question mark (?) (Check the search tips to find out which wildcard character is in use.)	Search *home school** or *home school?* to retrieve results for *home school, home schooling,* and *home schooled*

Most often, you'll get too many hits and need to narrow your search. To narrow a search, try the following:

Add a specific term	Instead of just *home schooling,* search *home schooling statistics*
Combine search terms into phrases or word strings	Search *home schooling and California* or *"California home schooling"*

In many cases, using phrases or word strings will limit your results to items that include *all* the words you have specified. You may need to insert quotation marks around the terms or insert the word *and* between them to create a search phrase or word string. Check the search tips for the database, catalog, or search engine you are using.

Find books (and other sources).

Books housed in academic library collections offer two distinct advantages to the student researcher:

1. They provide in-depth coverage of topics.
2. They are likely to be published by reputable presses that strive for accuracy and reliability.

You can generally search for books and other library resources, like reference works and multimedia resources, by author name, title, keyword, or subject heading, and narrow your search by using advanced search options.

Some libraries also allow you to search by call number, which makes it easy to find other items on the same or a similar topic. (You might think of a call-number search as the electronic equivalent of looking at books shelved nearby.) For example, typing *LC40* (the first part of the call number) into the search box calls up the records of other items on the subject of home schooling:

Title	Call number
Well-Trained Mind: A Guide to Classical Education at Home	**LC40**.B39 2004
Love in a Time of Homeschooling: A Mother and Daughter's Uncommon Year	**LC40**.B76 2010
Homeschool: An American History	**LC40**.G34 2008
Family Matters: Why Homeschooling Makes Sense	**LC40**.G88 1992
Home Schooling: Parents as Educators	**LC40**.H65 1995
How Children Learn at Home	**LC40**.T48 2007

If your search for books in your college library turns up little that is useful to you, do not give up. You may be able to request an item from another library via your library's interlibrary loan service. Inquire at your library for services available to you that can connect you to resources in other libraries.

Find articles in periodicals.

Much of the information you will use to write your research project will come from articles in **periodicals**, publications such as newspapers, magazines, or scholarly journals that are published at regular intervals. To locate relevant articles on your topic, start your search with your library's unified search bar or one of your library's databases. Why not just start with a *Google* search? There are two very good reasons:

1. *Google* will pull up articles from any publication it indexes, from personal Web sites to scholarly journals. Results rise to the top of the list based on a number of factors but not necessarily the reliability of the source. A *Google* search will turn up helpful sources, but you will need to spend a good deal of time sifting through the numerous hits you get to find sources that are both relevant and reliable. (*Google Scholar* may help you locate more reliable sources than those you might find through a typical *Google* search.)
2. Sources you find through *Google* may ask you to pay for access to articles, or they may require a subscription. Your library may already subscribe to these sources on your behalf. Also, adding databases to your search strategy will diversify your search and provide you with access to resources not available through a search engine such as *Google*.

Most college libraries subscribe to **general databases** and **subject-specific databases** as well as databases that index newspapers. General databases (such as *Academic OneFile, Academic Search Premier* or *Elite* or *Complete,*[1] and *ProQuest Central*) index articles from both scholarly journals and popular magazines. Subject-specific databases (such as *ERIC, MLA International Bibliography, PsycINFO,* and *General Science Full Text*) index articles only in their discipline. Newspaper databases (such as *Alt-Press Watch, LexisNexis Academic, National Newspaper Index,* and *ProQuest Newspapers*) index newspaper articles. For college-level research projects, you may use all three types of databases to find appropriate articles. (Note that many libraries also offer ways to search multiple databases at once.) For the research project on home schooling that appears in Chapter 16, "Citing and Documenting Sources in MLA Style," Cristina Dinh might have consulted both a general database and a subject-specific database like *ERIC*.

Increasingly, databases provide access to full-text articles, either in HTML or in PDF format. When you have the option, choose the PDF format, as this will provide you with photographs, graphs, and charts in context, and you will be able to include the page numbers in your citation. If you find a citation to an article that is not accessible through a database, however, do not ignore it. Check with a librarian to find out how you can get a copy of the article.

---

[1] The names of databases change over time and vary from library to library, so ask your instructor or a reference librarian if you need help.

Find government documents and statistical information.

Federal, state, and local governments make many of their documents available directly through the Web. For example, you can access statistical data about the United States through the U.S. Census Bureau's Web site, and you can learn a great deal about other countries through the Web sites of the U.S. State Department and the CIA.

The Library of Congress provides a useful portal for finding government documents (federal, state, local, and international) through its Web site, and the U.S. Government Printing Office provides free electronic access to documents produced by the federal government through its FDsys Web page.

Some libraries have collections of government publications and provide access to government documents through databases or catalogs. Your library may also offer statistical resources and data sets. See if your library has a guide to these resources, or ask a librarian for advice. You can also find government documents online using an advanced *Google* search and specifying *.gov* as the type of site, or *domain*.

To learn more about the domains of Web sites, see Chapter 15.

Find Web sites and interactive sources.

Undoubtedly, you are quite familiar with searching the Web. This section introduces you to some tools and strategies for using it more efficiently. But first, a few cautions:

- ***Your research project will be only as credible as the sources you use.*** Because search engines index Web sources without evaluating them, not all the results a search engine like *Google* generates will be reliable and relevant to your purposes.
- ***Web sources may not be stable.*** A Web site that existed last week may no longer be available today, or its content may have changed. Be sure to record the information you need to cite a source when you first find it.
- ***Web sources must be documented.*** No matter what your source—a library book, a scholarly article, or a Web site or Web page—you will need to cite and document your source in your list of works cited or references. If you are publishing your report online, check to determine whether you will need permission to reproduce an image or any other elements.

For guidelines on how to cite Web sources, see Chapter 16, "Citing and Documenting Sources in MLA Style," or Chapter 17, "Citing and Documenting Sources in APA Style"; for more on evaluating sources, especially Web sources, see Chapter 15.

Using *Google Scholar* and *Google Book Search*

Although you may use search engines like *Google* with great rapidity and out of habit, as a college researcher you are likely to find it worthwhile to familiarize yourself with other parts of the *Google* search site. Of particular interest to the academic writer are *Google Scholar* and *Google Book Search*. *Google Scholar* retrieves articles from a number of scholarly databases and a wide range of general-interest and scholarly books. *Google Book Search* searches both popular and scholarly books. Both *Google Scholar* and *Google Book Search* offer overviews and, in some cases, the full text of a source.

Note: Whatever search engine you use, always click on the link called Help, Hints, or Tips on the search tool's home page to find out more about the commands and advanced-search techniques it offers. Most search engines allow searches using the techniques discussed earlier in the chapter (pp. 407–8). Many also provide advanced-search options that allow you to limit results to those created between specific dates, in specific languages, and so on.

Using Interactive Sources

Interactive sources, including blogs, wikis, social networking sites (like *Facebook* and *Twitter*), and discussion lists, can also be useful sources of information, especially if your research project focuses on a current event or late-breaking news.

- **Blogs** are Web sites that are updated regularly, often many times a day. They are usually organized chronologically, with the newest posts at the top, and though they may contain links or news stories, they generally focus on the opinions of the blog host and visitors. Blogs by experts in the field are likely to be more informative than blogs by amateurs or fans.
- **Wikis**—of which *Wikipedia* is the best known example—offer content contributed and modified collaboratively by a community of users. Wikis can be very useful for gleaning background information, but because (in most cases) anyone can write or revise wiki entries, many instructors will not accept them as reliable sources for college-level research projects. Use wikis cautiously.
- **Social networking sites**, like *Facebook* and *Twitter,* allow users to create groups or pages on topics of interest or to follow the thoughts and activities of newsmakers.
- **Discussion lists** are electronic mailing lists that allow members to post comments and get feedback from others interested in the same topic. The most reliable discussion lists are moderated and attract experts on the topic. Many online communities provide some kind of indexing or search mechanism so that you can look for "threads" (conversations) related to your topic.

Although you need to evaluate the information you find in all sources carefully, you must be especially careful with information from social networking sites and discussion lists. However, such sources can provide up-to-the-minute information. Also be aware that whereas most online communities welcome guests and newcomers, others may perceive your questions as intrusive or naive. It may be useful to "lurk" (that is, just read posts) before making a contribution.

Conducting Field Research

In universities, government agencies, and the business world, field research can be as important as library research. In some majors, like education or sociology, as well as in service-learning courses, primary research projects are common. Even in the writing projects covered in Chapters 2–8, observations, interviews, and surveys may be useful or even necessary. As you consider how you might use field research in your writing projects, ask your instructor whether your institution requires you to obtain approval, and check Chapter 16, "Citing and Documenting Sources in MLA Style," or 17, "Citing and Documenting Sources in APA Style," for information about citing interviews you conduct yourself.

Conduct observational studies.

Observational studies, such as you would conduct when profiling a place (see Chapter 3), are common in college. To conduct an observational study effectively, follow these guidelines:

- **Arrange access if necessary.** Visits to a private location (such as a school or business) require special permission, so be sure to arrange your visit in advance, and have a fallback plan in case your request is refused or the business or institution places constraints on you that hamper your research.
- **Develop a hypothesis.** In advance, write down a tentative assumption about what you expect to learn from your study—your **hypothesis**. This will guide your observations and notes, and you can adjust your expectations in response to what you observe if necessary. Consider, too, how your presence will affect those whom you are observing, so you can minimize your impact or take the effect of your presence into consideration.
- **Take notes when making observations, using description, narration, analysis, and classification.** Describe in detail the setting and the people you are observing. Record as many details as possible, draw diagrams or sketches if helpful, and take photographs or videos if allowed (and if those you are observing do not object). Try initially to be an innocent observer: Pretend that you have never seen anything like this activity or place before, and explain what you are seeing step by step, even if what you are writing seems obvious. Break the scene down into its component parts, identify common threads and organize the details into categories. Take careful notes during your visit if you can do so unobtrusively or immediately afterward if you can't. You can use a notebook and pencil, a laptop or tablet, or even a smartphone to record your notes. Choose whatever note-taking tools will be least disruptive to those around you.
- **Write up your observations.** After your visit, fill in any gaps in your notes, then review them to look for meaningful patterns. Ask yourself questions like these: How did what I observed fit or undermine any of my own or my readers' likely preconceptions of the place or activity? What most interested me (or would most interest my readers) about the activity or place? What are my readers likely to find interesting about it? What did I learn?

Your purpose in writing about your visit is to share your insights into the meaning and significance of your observations. Assume that your readers have never been to the place, and provide enough detail for it to come alive for them. Decide on the perspective you want to convey, and choose the details necessary to convey your insights.

Conduct interviews.

A successful interview involves careful planning before the interview, but it also requires keen listening skills and the ability to ask appropriate follow-up questions while conducting the interview. Courtesy and consideration for your subject are crucial at all stages of the process. Follow these guidelines when planning and conducting interviews:

- **Choose an interview subject, and arrange the interview.** Prepare a list of interview candidates, as busy people might turn you down. Keep in mind that the person you want to interview will be donating valuable time to you, so call ahead to arrange the interview, allow your subject to specify the amount of time she or he can spare, and come prepared.
- **Consider your objectives.** Do you want details or a general orientation (the "big picture")? Do you want mainly facts or opinions? Do you need to clarify something you have observed or read?
- **Do some background reading beforehand.** Find out as much as you can about the organization or company (size, location, purpose, etc.), as well as the key people.
- **Write some questions in advance.** You will likely want to ask a few **closed questions** ("How do you do ________?" "What does ________ mean?") and a number of **open questions** ("What do you think about ________?" "Tell me about a time you were ________."). The best questions encourage the subject to talk freely but stick to the point. If you are unsure about a subject's answer, follow up by rephrasing the answer, prefacing it by saying something like "Let me see if I have this right." Avoid *forced-choice questions* ("Which do you think is the better approach: ________ or ________?") and *leading questions* ("How well do you think ________ is doing?").
- **Be flexible.** Ask the questions you have prepared, but also be ready to shift gears to take full advantage of what your subject can offer.
- **Take notes but also listen carefully.** Take notes during the interview, even if you are recording your discussion. Remember that how something is said is as important as what is said. Look for material that will give texture to your writing—gesture, verbal inflection, facial expression, body language, physical appearance (dress, hair), or anything that makes the person an individual. Avoid interrupting your subject or talking about yourself; rather, listen carefully and guide the discussion by asking follow-up questions and probing politely for more information.
- **Be considerate.** Do not stay longer than the time you were allotted unless your subject agrees to continue the discussion; show your appreciation for the time you have been given by thanking your subject and offering her or him a copy of your finished project. After the interview, reflect on what you've learned and review and amplify your notes. Make a list of any questions that arise. You may want to follow up with your subject for more information, but limit yourself to one e-mail or phone call to avoid becoming a bother.

Conduct surveys.

Surveys let you gauge the opinions and knowledge of large numbers of people. You might conduct a survey to gauge opinion in a political science course or to assess familiarity with a television show for a media studies course. Use the following guidelines to design an effective survey, administer the survey, and report on your results:

- **Conduct background research, focus your study, and identify the population you are trying to reach.** Before starting out, decide what you expect to learn (your *hypothesis*). Make sure to limit your focus to only one or two important issues so that you can craft a questionnaire that respondents can complete quickly and easily, as well as organize and report on your results more easily. If necessary, conduct background research to draft your hypothesis or narrow your focus. Even for an informal study, you should try to get a reasonably representative group. Determine the demographic makeup of your school, and arrange to reach out to a representative sample.
- **Write questions.** Plan to use a number of *closed questions* (questions that request specific information), such as yes/no questions, multiple-choice questions, ranking scale questions, and checklist questions. You will also likely want to include a few open questions (questions that give respondents the opportunity to write their answers in their own words). Whatever questions you develop, be sure that they are clear and unambiguous.
- **Design and test the questionnaire.** Begin your questionnaire with a brief introduction clearly stating the purpose of your survey and explaining how you intend to use the results. Give advice on answering the questions, estimate the amount of time needed to complete the questionnaire, and give a due date. Organize your questions logically (say, by topic or from least to most complicated), and format your questionnaire so that it is easy to read. Once you have a draft you are happy with, ask at least three readers to complete your questionnaire before you distribute it. Time them as they respond, and discuss with them any confusion or problems they experienced. Then revise your questionnaire accordingly.
- **Administer the survey.** You can conduct the survey in person, use an online service such as *SurveyMonkey* (surveymonkey.com) or *Zoomerang* (zoomerang.com), or use a social media site such as *Facebook*. Though fewer than half the surveys you solicit using survey software are likely to be completed, online software will tabulate survey responses automatically.
- **Write the report.** When writing your report, include a summary of the results, as well as an interpretation of what they mean. Research reports in the social sciences use a standard format, with headings introducing the following categories of information: *Abstract* (a brief summary), *Introduction* (context, background, and limitations of the research program), *Methods* (a copy of the questionnaire and a description of administration methods), *Results* (survey data with limited interpretation), and *Discussion* (interpretation of results and conclusions drawn).

15

Evaluating and Using Sources

As soon as you start your search for sources, you should begin evaluating what you find both to determine how *credible,* or reliable, they are and to decide how you could use them to support your ideas.

Choosing Sources

Determining which sources are likely to be *relevant* and *reliable*—and which sources *your readers* will perceive as being relevant and reliable—is a crucial part of the research process. Academic audiences are likely to find works relevant that provide evidence not only to support your claims but also to support alternative viewpoints or interpretations.

Reliability is often in the eye of the beholder. When selecting sources, ask yourself not only which sources you think are most reliable but also which sources your readers will find most convincing. And remember that sources that are appropriate in one rhetorical situation might not be the best choice in another. Certain aspects of reliability that academic readers will likely expect you to consider are discussed in the following sections.

Who wrote it?

Consider, first, whether the author is an *expert* in the field. The fact that someone has a PhD in astrophysics is no indication that he or she will be an expert in military history, for example, so be careful that the area of expertise is directly relevant to the topic.

To determine the author's area of expertise, look for the author's professional affiliation (where he or she works or teaches). This may be indicated at the bottom of the first page of an article (often labeled "Author Affiliations") or in an "About the Author" section in a book or on a Web site. Frequently, Googling the author will reveal the author's affiliation, but double-check to make sure the affiliation is current and that you have located the right person. You might also consult a biographical reference source, available through a reference database at your library. Looking to see what other works the author has published, and with whom, can also help you ascertain his or her area of expertise.

Contributors to blogs, wikis, and online discussion forums may or may not be experts in the field. Determine whether the site screens contributors, and double-check any information taken from sites for which you cannot determine the credentials of contributors.

Also consider the author's *perspective*. Most writing is not neutral or objective and does not claim to be. Knowledge of the author's perspective enables you to assess *bias* and determine whether the author's perspective affects the presentation of his or her argument. To determine the author's perspective, look for the main point while asking yourself questions like these:

- What evidence does the author provide to support this point? Is it from authoritative sources? Is it persuasive?
- Does the author make concessions to or refute opposing arguments?
- Does the author avoid fallacies, confrontational phrasing, and loaded words?

For more details on these argumentative strategies, see Chapter 12.

How recently was it published?

In general, especially when you are writing about science or technology, current events, or emerging trends, you should consult the most up-to-date sources available on your subject. You may also need older, "classic" sources that establish the principles, theories, and data on which later work is based; classics may also provide a useful perspective for evaluating other works. To determine which sources are classics, note the ones that are cited most often in encyclopedia articles, lists of works cited or references, and recent works on the subject. You may also want to consult your instructor or a librarian to help you determine which works are classics in your field.

For more help locating publication information, see the documentation maps in Chapter 16.

Is the source scholarly or popular?

Scholarly sources (whether books or articles) are written by and for experts in a field of study, frequently professors or academic researchers. (See Table 15.1.) **Popular sources** are written to entertain and educate the general public. They report on and summarize original research and are written for interested, nonspecialist readers. Of course, popular sources range widely along the reliability spectrum. Highly respected newspapers and magazines, such as the *New York Times* and *Harper's Magazine,* publish original research on news and culture. Magazines that focus on celebrity gossip, such as *People* and *Us Weekly,* are unlikely to be considered appropriate sources for a college-level research project.

Who published it?

Determining who published or sponsored a source you are considering can help you gauge its reliability and ascertain the publication's slant (or point of view). Look to see whether the source was published by a commercial publisher (such as St. Martin's or Random House); a university press (such as the University of Nebraska Press); a corporation, an

TABLE 15.1 Scholarly Journals versus Popular Magazines

Scholarly Journals	***Popular Magazines***
Journals are usually published 4 to 6 times per year.	Magazines are usually published weekly or monthly.
Articles are usually written by scholars (with *PhD* or academic affiliations after their names).	Authors of articles are journalists but may quote experts.
Many articles have more than one author.	Most articles have a single author.
In print journals, the title page often appears on the cover, and the covers frequently lack artwork.	Photographs, usually in color, appear on the covers of most print magazines and their Web sites.
Articles may include charts, tables, figures, and quotations from other scholarly sources.	Articles frequently include color pictures and sidebars.
An abstract (summary) of the article may appear on the first page.	A headline or engaging description may precede the article.
Most articles are fairly long—5 to 20 pages.	Most articles are fairly short—1 to 5 pages.
Articles cite sources and provide a bibliography (works-cited or reference list).	Articles rarely include a list of works cited or references but may mention or quote experts.

organization, or an interest group (such as the World Wildlife Fund or the National Restaurant Association); a government agency (such as the U.S. Census Bureau); or the author on his or her own. Determining the publisher or sponsor is particularly important for material published on the Web.

If your source is a Web page, look at the URL (uniform resource locator) to find its top-level domain, which is indicated by a suffix. Some of the most useful ones are listed here:

.com	businesses and commercial enterprises
.gov	U.S. federal government and some state or local government institutions
.org	nonprofit organizations
.edu	educational institutions
.net	usually businesses or organizations associated with online networks
.mil	the U.S. military

For the most part, *.gov* and *.edu* are the most likely to offer reliable sources of information for a college research project. However, sources with any of these domains may vary in reliability. For example, a file with a *.com* suffix may offer a highly reliable history of a corporation and be an appropriate source for someone writing a history of corporate America, whereas a file with a *.edu* suffix may have been posted by a student or by a faculty member outside his or her area of expertise.

It is essential to look at Web sites carefully. Determine who sponsors the site: Is it a business, a professional group, a private organization, an educational institution, a government agency, or an individual? Look for a link, usually at the top or the bottom of the home page, called something like "Who We Are" or "About Us." If you cannot determine who sponsors a site, carefully double-check any information you find there.

Consider, too, checking how often the Web site has been linked to and the types of links provided by the Web site. That a site has been linked to repeatedly does not guarantee reliability, but that information may be helpful in conjunction with other recommendations in this chapter. To determine the number of times a Web page has been linked to, type *link:* plus the URL into a *Google* search box. To check the links provided, click on them and apply the criteria in this chapter.

If the source was published by a commercial publisher, check out the publisher's Web site, and ask yourself questions like these:

- Does the publisher offer works from a single perspective or from multiple perspectives?
- Do the works it publishes cover a wide variety of topics or focus on a particular array?
- Does the publisher's Web site host links to a particular type of site?

The Web sites of book publishers may offer a link to a catalog. If so, look at the works the catalog lists. Does the publisher seem to focus on a particular topic or take a particular point of view? Does the publisher generally offer popular, academic, or professional works?

If your source is a periodical (a magazine, newspaper, newsletter, or scholarly journal), consider whether it focuses on a particular topic or offers a single point of view. In addition to looking at the article you are considering and back issues of the periodical, visit the publisher's Web site, which may help you determine topic and point of view.

How is the source written?

Most works that are published professionally (including popular newspapers and magazines, as well as scholarly journals and trade magazines) will have been edited carefully. These sources will generally avoid errors of grammar, punctuation, and spelling, and will be fact-checked carefully, as will Web sites sponsored by professional organizations. Personal Web sites, however, are unlikely to have been professionally edited and fact-checked. If a Web site is riddled with errors, be very careful to double-check any information you take from that site.

What does the source say?

Finally, and perhaps most important, consider the source itself. Answering the following questions can help you determine whether the source is worth consideration:

- What is the intended audience of the source? Does the source address an audience of experts or a general audience?
- What is the purpose of the source? Does it review a number of different positions, or does it argue for a position of its own? If it makes its own argument, analyze the argument closely.
- What is the tone of the source? Is the tone reasonable? Does the source respond to alternative viewpoints, and are those responses logical and reasonable?
- What evidence is offered to support the argument? Is the evidence relevant and reliable? What kinds of citations or links does the source supply?

To learn more about analyzing an argument, see Chapter 10.

Acknowledging Sources and Avoiding Plagiarism

In your college writing, you will be expected to use and acknowledge **secondary sources**—books, articles, published or recorded interviews, Web sites, lectures, and other print and nonprint materials—in addition to your own ideas, insights, and field research. The following information will help you decide what does and does not need to be acknowledged and what will enable you to avoid *plagiarizing* inadvertently.

What does and does not need to be acknowledged?

For the most part, any ideas, information, or language you borrow from a source—whether the source is in print or online—must be acknowledged by including an in-text citation and an entry in your list of works cited (MLA style) or reference list (APA style). The only types of information that do not require acknowledgment are common knowledge (John F. Kennedy was assassinated in Dallas), facts widely available in many sources (U.S. presidents used to be inaugurated on March 4 rather than January 20), well-known quotations ("To be or not to be / That is the question"), and material you created or gathered yourself (photographs that you took, data from surveys that you conducted, and so on).

Remember that you need to acknowledge the source of any visual (photograph, table, chart, graph, diagram, drawing, map, screenshot) that you did not create yourself as well as the source of any information that you used to create your own visual. (You should also request permission from the source of a visual if your essay is going to be posted online without password protection.) When in doubt about whether you need to acknowledge a source, do so.

The documentation guidelines in the next two chapters present two styles for citing sources: MLA and APA. Whichever style you use, the most important thing is that your readers be able to tell where words or ideas that are not your own begin and end. You can accomplish this most readily by placing parenthetical source citations correctly and by separating your words from those of the source with **signal phrases,** such as "According to Smith," "Peters claims," and "As Olmos asserts." (When you cite a source for the first time in a signal phrase, use the author's full name; after that, use just the last name.)

For more on citing sources in MLA and APA style, see Chapters 16 and 17.

Avoid plagiarism by acknowledging sources and quoting, paraphrasing, and summarizing carefully.

When you use material from another source, you need to acknowledge the source, usually by citing the author and page or publication date in your text and including a list of works cited or reference list at the end of your essay. Failure to acknowledge sources—even by accident—constitutes plagiarism, a serious transgression. By citing sources correctly, you give appropriate credit to the originator of the words and ideas you are using, offer your readers the information they need to consult those sources directly, and build your own credibility.

Writers—students and professionals alike—occasionally fail to acknowledge sources properly. Students sometimes mistakenly assume that plagiarizing occurs only when another writer's exact words are used without acknowledgment. In fact, plagiarism can also apply to paraphrases as well as to such diverse forms of expression as musical compositions, visual images, ideas, and statistics. Therefore, keep in mind that you must indicate the source of any borrowed information, idea, language, or visual or audio material you use in your essay, whether you have *paraphrased, summarized,* or *quoted* directly from the source or have reproduced it or referred to it in some other way.

Remember especially the need to document electronic sources fully and accurately. Perhaps because it is so easy to access and distribute text and visuals online and to copy material from one electronic document and paste it into another, some students do not realize, or may forget, that information, ideas, and images from electronic sources require acknowledgment just as those from print sources do. At the same time, the improper (unacknowledged) use of online sources is often very easy for readers to detect.

Some people plagiarize simply because they do not know the conventions for using and acknowledging sources. Others plagiarize because they keep sloppy notes and thus fail to distinguish between their own and their sources' ideas. If you maintain a working bibliography and take careful notes, you will not make this serious mistake. If you are unfamiliar with the conventions for documentation, this and the next two chapters will clarify how you can incorporate sources into your writing and properly acknowledge your use of those sources.

Another reason some people plagiarize is that they feel intimidated by the writing task or the deadline. If you experience this anxiety about your work, speak to your instructor. Do not run the risk of failing a course or being expelled from your college because of plagiarism.

If you are confused about what is and what is not plagiarism, be sure to ask your instructor, or consult your school's plagiarism policy.

Using Sources to Support Your Ideas

Once you have identified, analyzed, and taken notes on a number of relevant and reliable sources, you are ready to start drafting your research project. Begin by synthesizing information from sources to support, extend, and challenge your own ideas. Then integrate relevant ideas and information to support your own claims. This process will help you do what all scholars aspire to: contribute something new to the conversation on your topic.

Synthesize information from sources with your own ideas.

Synthesizing means making connections among information and ideas from texts and from your own experience. Once you have analyzed a number of sources on your topic, consider questions like these to help you connect the dots:

- Do any of your sources use similar approaches or come to similar conclusions? What common themes do they explore? Do any of them use the same evidence (facts, statistics, research studies, examples) to support their claims?
- What differentiates their various positions? Where do the writers disagree, and why? Does one writer seem to be responding to or challenging one or more of the others?
- Do you agree with some sources and disagree with others? What makes some more convincing than others? Do any of the sources you have read offer support for your claims? Do any of them challenge your conclusions? If so, can you *refute* the challenge, or do you need to *concede* a point?

Sentence strategies like the following can help you clarify where you differ from or agree with the sources you have read:

- ▶ A study by X supports my position by demonstrating that ________.
- ▶ X and Y think this issue is about ________. But what is really at stake here is ________.
- ▶ X claims that ________. But I agree with Y, who argues that ________.
- ▶ On this issue, X and Y say ________. Although I understand and to some degree sympathize with their point of view, I agree with Z that this is ultimately a question of ________.

The report by Maya Gomez (pp. 149–55) and the synthesis chart she created (p. 168) show how ideas and information from sources can be synthesized.

To learn more about synthesis, see Chapters 5 and 10.

Use information from sources to support your claims.

When writing a research project, remember that the goal is to use the ideas and information you find in sources *to support your own ideas*. Make sure that each of your supporting paragraphs does three things:

1. States a claim that supports your thesis
2. Provides evidence that supports your claim
3. Explains to readers how the evidence supports your claim

Consider this paragraph from Patrick O'Malley's proposal in Chapter 7, "More Testing, More Learning"[1] (pp. 235–41):

States claim

Explains how evidence supports claim

Provides evidence

The main reason professors should give frequent exams is that when they do and when they provide feedback to students on how well they are doing, students learn more in the course and perform better on major exams, projects, and papers. It makes sense that in a challenging course containing a great deal of material, students will learn more of it and put it to better use if they have to apply or "practice" it frequently on exams, which also helps them find out how much they are learning and what they need to go over again. A 2006 study reported in the journal *Psychological Science* concluded that "taking repeated tests on material leads to better long-term retention than repeated studying," according to the study's coauthors, Henry L. Roediger and Jeffrey Karpicke (ScienceWatch.com, 2008). When asked what the impact of this breakthrough research would be, they responded: "We hope that this research may be picked up in educational circles as a way to improve educational practices, both for students in the classroom and as a study strategy outside of class." The new field of mind, brain, and education research advocates the use of "retrieval testing." For example, research by Karpicke and Blunt (2011) published in *Science* found that testing was more effective than other, more traditional methods of studying both for comprehension and for analysis. Why retrieval testing works is not known. UCLA psychologist Robert Bjork speculates that it may be effective because "when we use our memories by retrieving things, we change our access" to that information. "What we recall," therefore, "becomes more recallable in the future" (qtd. in Belluck, 2011).

O'Malley connects this body paragraph to his thesis by beginning with the transition *The main reason* and by repeating the phrase *perform better* from his forecasting statement. He synthesizes information from a variety of sources but doesn't merely stitch quotations

[1] Note that O'Malley uses APA style, as his instructor requested. All the other examples in this chapter use MLA style.

and summary together; rather, he explains how the evidence supports his claim by stating that it "makes sense" that students "apply or 'practice'" what they learn on frequent exams.

Decide whether to quote, paraphrase, or summarize.

As illustrated in O'Malley's paragraph (p. 422), writers integrate supporting evidence by quoting, paraphrasing, or summarizing information or ideas from sources. As a rule, quote only in these situations:

- When the wording of the source is particularly memorable or vivid or expresses a technical point you can't rephrase clearly
- When the words of reliable and respected authorities would lend support to your position
- When you wish to cite an author whose opinions challenge or vary greatly from those of other experts
- When you are going to discuss the source's choice of words

Paraphrase passages whose details you wish to use but whose language is not particularly striking. Summarize any long passages whose main points you wish to record as support for a point you are making.

Copy quotations exactly, or use italics, ellipses, and brackets to indicate changes.

Quotations should duplicate the source exactly, even if they contain spelling errors. Add the notation *sic* (Latin for "thus") in brackets immediately after any such error to indicate that it is not your error but your source's. As long as you signal them appropriately, you may make changes to

- emphasize particular words;
- omit irrelevant information;
- insert information necessary for clarity;
- make the quotation conform grammatically to your sentence.

Using Italics for Emphasis You may italicize any words in the quotation that you want to emphasize; add a semicolon and the words *emphasis added* (in regular type, not italicized or underlined) to the parenthetical citation:

> In her 2001 exposé of the struggles of the working class, Ehrenreich writes, "The wages Winn-Dixie is offering—*$6 and a couple of dimes to start with*—are not enough, I decide, to compensate for this indignity" (14; emphasis added).

Using Ellipsis Marks for Omissions You may decide to omit words from a quotation because they are not relevant to the point you are making. When you omit words from within a quotation, use **ellipsis marks**—three spaced periods (. . .)—in place of the missing words. When the omission occurs within a sentence, include a space before the first ellipsis mark and after the last mark:

> Hermione Roddice is described in Lawrence's *Women in Love* as a "woman of the new school, full of intellectuality and . . . nerve-worn with consciousness" (17).

When the omission falls at the end of a sentence, place a period *directly after* the final word of the sentence, followed by a space and three spaced ellipsis marks:

> But Grimaldi's commentary contends that for Aristotle rhetoric, like dialectic, had "no limited and unique subject matter upon which it must be exercised. . . . Instead, rhetoric as an art transcends all specific disciplines and may be brought into play in them" (6).

When you quote only single words or phrases, you do not need to use ellipsis marks because it will be obvious that you have left out some of the original. For the same reason, you need not use ellipsis marks if you omit the beginning of a quoted sentence unless the rest of the sentence begins with a capitalized word and appears to be a complete sentence.

Using Brackets for Insertions or Changes Use brackets around an insertion or a change needed to make a quotation conform grammatically to your sentence, such as a change in the form of a verb or pronoun or in the capitalization of the first word of the quotation:

> In the dark, cold streets during the "short days of winter," the boys must generate their own heat by "play[ing] till [their] bodies glowed." Music is "[shaken] from the buckled harness" as if it were unnatural, and the singers in the market chant nasally of "the troubles in our native land" (30).

You may also use brackets to add or substitute explanatory material in a quotation:

> Guterson notes that among Native Americans in Florida, "education was in the home; learning by doing was reinforced by the myths and legends which repeated the basic value system of their [the Seminoles'] way of life" (159).

Some changes that make a quotation conform grammatically to another sentence may be made without any signal to readers:

- A period at the end of a quotation may be changed to a comma if you are using the quotation within your own sentence.
- Double quotation marks enclosing a quotation may be changed to single quotation marks when the quotation is enclosed within a longer quotation.

Adjusting the Punctuation within Quotations Although punctuation within a quotation should reproduce the original, some adaptations may be necessary. Use single quotation marks for quotations within the quotation:

Guterson claims that E. D. Hirsch "also recognizes the connection between family and learning, suggesting in his discussion of family background and academic achievement 'that the significant part of our children's education has been going on outside rather than inside the schools'" (16–17).

If the quotation ends with a question mark or an exclamation point, retain the original punctuation:

"Did you think I loved you?" Edith later asks Dombey (566).

If a quotation ending with a question mark or an exclamation point concludes your sentence, retain the question mark or exclamation point, and put the parenthetical reference and sentence period outside the closing quotation mark:

Edith later asks Dombey, "Did you think I loved you?" (566).

Use in-text or block quotations.

In MLA style, incorporate brief quotations (three or fewer typed lines of prose or poetry) into your text, and use the block form for prose quotations of four or more typed lines. (In APA style, indent quotations of forty or more words as a block.)

In-Text Quotations You may place an in-text quotation virtually anywhere in your sentence:

"To live a life is not to cross a field," Sutherland, quoting Pasternak, writes at the beginning of her narrative (11).

Woolf begins and ends by speaking of the need of the woman writer to have "money and a room of her own" (4)—an idea that certainly spoke to Plath's condition.

In *The Second Sex*, Simone de Beauvoir describes such an experience as one in which the girl "becomes an object, and she sees herself as object" (378).

"Science usually prefers the literal to the nonliteral term," Kinneavy writes, "—that is, figures of speech are often out of place in science" (177).

When you quote poetry within your text, use a slash (/) with spaces before and after to signal the end of each line of verse:

Alluding to St. Augustine's distinction between the City of God and the Earthly City, Lowell writes that "much against my will / I left the City of God where [faith] belongs" (4–5).

Block Quotations Indent the quotation half an inch from the left margin, as shown in the following example:

In "A Literary Legacy from Dunbar to Baraka," Margaret Walker says of Paul Lawrence Dunbar's dialect poems:

> He realized that the white world in the United States tolerated his literary genius only because of his "jingles in a broken tongue," and they found the old "darky"

> tales and speech amusing and within the vein of folklore into which they wished to classify all Negro life. This troubled Dunbar because he realized that white America was denigrating him as a writer and as a man. (70)

In a block quotation, double-space between lines just as you do in your text. *Do not* enclose the passage within quotation marks. Use a colon to introduce a block quotation unless the context calls for another punctuation mark or none at all. Note that in MLA style, the parenthetical page reference follows the period in block quotations.

Use punctuation to integrate quotations into your writing.

Statements that introduce in-text quotations take a range of punctuation marks and lead-in words. A *colon* usually follows an independent clause placed before the quotation:

> As George Williams notes, protection of white privilege is critical to patterns of discrimination: "Whenever a number of persons within a society have enjoyed for a considerable period of time certain opportunities for getting wealth, for exercising power and authority, and for successfully claiming prestige and social deference, there is a strong tendency for these people to feel that these benefits are theirs 'by right'" (727).

A *comma* usually follows an introduction that incorporates the quotation in its sentence structure:

> Similarly, Duncan Turner asserts, "As matters now stand, it is unwise to talk about communication without some understanding of Burke" (259).

No punctuation is generally needed with *that*, and no capital letter is used to begin the quotation:

> Noting this failure, Alice Miller asserts that "the reason for her despair was not her suffering but the impossibility of communicating her suffering to another person" (255).

Paraphrase sources carefully.

In a **paraphrase**, the writer restates in his or her own words all the relevant information from a passage, without any additional comments or any suggestion of agreement or disagreement with the source's ideas. A paraphrase is useful for recording details of a passage when the source's wording is not important. Because all the details of the passage are included, a paraphrase is often about the same length as the original passage. It is better to paraphrase than to quote ordinary material in which the author's way of expressing things is not worth special attention.

Here is a passage from a book on home schooling and an example of an acceptable paraphrase of it:

Original Source

Bruner and the discovery theorists have also illuminated conditions that apparently pave the way for learning. It is significant that these conditions are unique to each learner, so unique, in fact, that in many cases classrooms can't provide them. Bruner also contends that the more one discovers information in a great variety of circumstances, the more likely one is to develop the inner categories required to organize that information. Yet life at school, which is for the most part generic and predictable, daily keeps many children from the great variety of circumstances they need to learn well.

—David Guterson, *Family Matters: Why Homeschooling Makes Sense,* p. 172

Acceptable Paraphrase

According to Guterson, the "discovery theorists," particularly Bruner, have found that there seem to be certain conditions that help learning take place. Because individuals require different conditions, many children are not able to learn in the classroom. According to Bruner, when people can explore information in many different situations, they learn to classify and order what they discover. The general routine of the school day, however, does not provide children with the diverse activities and situations that would allow them to learn these skills (172).

The highlighting shows that some words in the paraphrase were taken from the source. Indeed, it would be nearly impossible for paraphrasers to avoid using any key terms from the source, and it would be counterproductive to try to do so because the original and the paraphrase necessarily share the same information and concepts. Notice, though, that of the total of eighty-four words in the paraphrase, the paraphraser uses only a name (*Bruner*) and a few other key nouns and verbs for which it would be awkward to substitute other words or phrases. If the paraphraser had wanted to use other, more distinctive language from the source—for example, the description of life at school as "generic and predictable"—these adjectives would need to be enclosed in quotation marks. In fact, the paraphraser puts quotation marks around only one of the terms from the source: "discovery theorists"—a technical term likely to be unfamiliar to readers.

Paraphrasers must, however, avoid borrowing too many words and repeating the sentence structures from a source. Here is an unacceptable paraphrase of the first sentence in the Guterson passage:

Unacceptable Paraphrase: Too Many Borrowed Words and Phrases

Repeated phrase Repeated words	Apparently, some conditions, which have been illuminated by Bruner and other discovery theorists, pave the way for people to learn.

Here, the paraphrase borrows almost all of its key language from the source sentence, including the entire phrase *pave the way for*. Even if you cite the source, this heavy borrowing would be considered plagiarism.

Here is another unacceptable paraphrase of the same sentence:

Unacceptable Paraphrase: Sentence Structure Repeated Too Closely

Repeated words
Synonyms
Repeated sentence structure

Bruner and other *researchers* have also *identified circumstances* that *seem to ease the path* to learning.

If you compare the source's first sentence and this paraphrase of it, you will see that the paraphraser has borrowed the phrases and clauses of the source and arranged them in an almost identical sequence, simply substituting synonyms for most of the key terms. This paraphrase would also be considered plagiarism.

Write summaries that present the source's main ideas in a balanced and readable way.

Unlike a paraphrase, a **summary** presents only the main ideas of a source, leaving out examples and details.

Here is one student's summary of five pages from Guterson's book *Family Matters*. You can see at a glance how drastically summaries can condense information—in this case, from five pages to five sentences. Depending on a summarizer's purpose, five pages could be summarized in one sentence, in five sentences (as shown here), or in two or three dozen sentences.

> In looking at different theories of learning that discuss individual-based programs (such as home schooling) versus the public school system, Guterson describes the disagreements among "cognitivist" theorists. One group, the "discovery theorists," believes that individual children learn by creating their own ways of sorting the information they take in from their experiences. Schools should help students develop better ways of organizing new material, not just present them with material that is already categorized, as traditional schools do. "Assimilationist theorists," by contrast, believe that children learn by linking what they don't know to information they already know. These theorists claim that traditional schools help students learn when they present information in ways that allow children to fit the new material into categories they have already developed (171–75).

A summary like this one is more than a dry list of main ideas from a source; rather, it is a coherent, readable new text composed of the source's main ideas. Summaries provide balanced coverage of a source, following the same sequence of ideas and avoiding any hint of agreement or disagreement with them.

For more about how to summarize, see Chapter 5.

16

Citing and Documenting Sources in MLA Style

When using the MLA system of documentation, include both an in-text citation and a list of works cited. **In-text citations** tell your readers where the ideas or words you have borrowed come from, and the entries in the **works-cited list** allow readers to locate your sources so that they can read more about your topic.

Citing Sources in the Text

In most cases, include the author's last name and the page number on which the borrowed material appears in the text of your research project. You can incorporate this information in two ways:

SIGNAL PHRASE By naming the author in the text of your research project with a signal phrase (*Simon described*) and including the page reference (in parentheses) at the end of the borrowed passage:

Author's last name — *Appropriate verb*

Simon, a well-known figure in New York literary society, described the impression Dr. James made on her as a child in the Bronx: He was a "not-too-skeletal Ichabod Crane" (68).

Page number

PARENTHETICAL CITATION By including the author's name and the page number together in parentheses at the end of the borrowed passage:

Author's last name + page number

Dr. James is described as a "not-too-skeletal Ichabod Crane" (Simon 68).

WORKS-CITED ENTRY Simon, Kate. "Birthing." *Bronx Primitive: Portraits in a Childhood*. Viking Books, 1982, pp. 68–77.

In most cases, you will want to use a *signal phrase* because doing so lets you put your source in context. The signal-phrase-plus-page-reference combination also allows you to make crystal clear where the source information begins and ends. Use a parenthetical citation alone when you have already identified the author or when you are citing the source of an uncontroversial fact.

The in-text citation should include as much information as is needed to lead readers to the source in your list of works cited and allow them to find the passage you are citing in that source. In most cases, that means the author's last name and the page number on which the borrowed material appears. In some cases, you may need to include other information in your in-text citation (such as a brief version of the title if the author is unnamed or if you cite more than one work by this author). In a few cases, you may not be able to include a page reference, as when you cite a Web site or film. In such cases, you may include other identifying information, such as a paragraph number, section heading, or time stamp (if provided by the source).

The most common types of in-text citations follow. For other, less common citation types, consult the *MLA Handbook*, Eighth Edition. Most libraries will own a copy or offer an online subscription to www.mla.org. If the MLA does not provide a model citation, use the information here to create a citation that will lead your readers to the source. (Citation managers like *EndNote* and *RefWorks* will format your citations in MLA style, but check them carefully, as the software sometimes makes errors and may not be up to date.)

Directory to In-Text-Citation Models

One author When citing most works with a single author, include the author's name (usually the last name is enough)* and the page number on which the cited material appears.

Author's last name + appropriate verb *Page number*

SIGNAL PHRASE Simon describes Dr. James as a "not-too-skeletal Ichabod Crane" (68).

Author's last name + page number

PARENTHETICAL CITATION Dr. James is described as a "not-too-skeletal Ichabod Crane" (Simon 68).

Author's name

BLOCK QUOTATION In Kate Simon's story "Birthing," the description of Dr. James captures both his physical appearance and his role in the community:

> He looked so much like a story character—the gentled Scrooge of a *St. Nicholas Magazine* Christmas issue, a not-too-skeletal Ichabod Crane. . . . Dr. James was, even when I knew him as a child, quite an old man, re-tired from a prestigious and lucrative practice in Boston. . . . His was a

* But see entries for "Two or more works by the same author," "Two or more authors with the same last name," and "Work without page numbers or a one-page work" on pp. 431 and 433.

> prosperous intellectual family, the famous New England Jameses that produced William and Henry, but to the older Bronx doctors, *the* James was the magnificent old driven scarecrow. (68)
>
> *Page number*

(A works-cited entry for "Birthing" appears on p. 429.)

More than one author To cite a source by two authors, include both authors' last names. To cite a source with three or more authors, provide just the first author's last name followed by *et al.* ("and others" in Latin, not italicized).

SIGNAL PHRASE Bernays and Painter maintain that a writer can begin a story without knowing how it will end (7).

Dyal et al. identify several types of students, including the "Authority-Rebel" (4).

PARENTHETICAL CITATION A writer should "resist the temptation to give the reader too lengthy an explanation" (Bernays and Painter 7).

The Authority-Rebel "tends to see himself as superior to other students in the class" (Dyal et al. 4).

Unknown author If the author's name is unknown, use a shortened version of the title, beginning with the word by which the title is alphabetized in the works-cited list. Use the first noun and any modifiers. (In this example, the full title is "Plastic Is Found in the Sargasso Sea; Pieces of Apparent Refuse Cover Wide Atlantic Region.")

> An international pollution treaty still to be ratified would prohibit ships from dumping plastic at sea ("Plastic" 68).

Two or more works by the same author If you cite more than one work by the same author, include a shortened version of the title.

> When old paint becomes transparent, it sometimes shows the artist's original plans: "a tree will show through a woman's dress" (Hellman, *Pentimento* 1).

Two or more authors with the same last name When citing works by authors with the same last name, include each author's first name in the signal phrase or first initial in the parenthetical citation.

> Chaplin's *Modern Times* uses montage to make an editorial statement (E. Roberts 246).

Corporation, organization, or government agency as author In a signal phrase, use the full name of the corporation, organization, or government agency. In a parenthetical citation, use the full name if it is brief or a shortened version if it is long.

SIGNAL PHRASE The Washington State Board for Community and Technical Colleges will raise tuition to offset budget deficits from Initiative 601 (4).

PARENTHETICAL CITATION A tuition increase has been proposed for community and technical colleges to offset budget deficits from Initiative 601 (Washington State Board 4).

Literary work (novel, play, poem) Provide information that will help readers find the passage you are citing no matter what edition of the novel, play, or poem they are using. In a signal phrase, spell out titles; in a parenthetical citation, abbreviate famous works. For a novel or other prose work, provide the part or chapter number as well as the page numbers from the edition you used.

NOVEL OR OTHER PROSE WORK	In *Hard Times,* Tom reveals his utter narcissism by blaming Louisa for his own failure: "'You have regularly given me up. You never cared for me'" (Dickens 262; bk. 3, ch. 9).

For a play in verse, use act, scene, and line numbers instead of page numbers.

PLAY (IN VERSE)	At the beginning, Regan's fawning rhetoric hides her true attitude toward Lear: "I profess / myself an enemy to all other joys . . . / And find that I am alone felicitate / In your dear highness' love" (*Lr.* 1.1.74–75, 77–78).

For a poem, indicate the line numbers and stanzas or sections (if they are numbered) instead of page numbers.

POEM	In "Song of Myself," Whitman finds poetic details in busy urban settings, as when he describes "the blab of the pave, tires of carts . . . the driver with his interrogating thumb" (8.153–54).

If the source gives only line numbers, use the term *lines* in your first citation and use only the numbers in subsequent citations.

> In "Before you thought of spring," Dickinson at first identifies the spirit of spring with a bird, possibly a robin—"A fellow in the skies / Inspiriting habiliments / Of indigo and brown" (lines 4, 7–8)—but by the end of the poem, she has linked it with poetry and perhaps even the poet herself, as the bird, like Dickinson, "shouts for joy to nobody / But his seraphic self!" (15–16).

Work in an anthology Use the name of the author of the work, not the editor of the anthology, in your in-text citation.

SIGNAL PHRASE	In "Six Days: Some Rememberings," Grace Paley recalls that when she was in jail for protesting the Vietnam War, her pen and paper were taken away and she felt "a terrible pain in the area of my heart—a nausea" (191).
PARENTHETICAL CITATION	Writers may have a visceral reaction—"a nausea" (Paley 191)— to being deprived of access to writing implements.

Religious work In your first citation, include the element that begins your entry in the works-cited list, such as the edition name of the religious work you are citing (see p. 439), and include the book or section name (using standard abbreviations in parenthetical citations) and any chapter or verse numbers.

> She ignored the admonition "Pride goes before destruction, and a haughty spirit before a fall" (*New Oxford Annotated Bible,* Prov. 16.18).

Multivolume work (one volume, more than one volume) If you cite only one volume of a multivolume work, treat the in-text citation as you would any other work, but include the volume number in the works-cited entry (see p. 439).

ONE VOLUME Forster argued that modernist writers valued experimentation and gradually sought to blur the line between poetry and prose (150).

When you use two or more volumes of a multivolume work, include the volume number and the page number(s) in your in-text citation.

MORE THAN ONE VOLUME Modernist writers valued experimentation and gradually sought to blur the line between poetry and prose (Forster 3: 150).

Indirect citation (quotation from a secondary source) If possible, locate the original source and cite that. If not possible, name the original source but also include the secondary source in which you found the material you are citing, plus the abbreviation *qtd. in*. Include the secondary source in your list of works cited.

> E. M. Forster says, "The collapse of all civilization, so realistic for us, sounded in Matthew Arnold's ears like a distant and harmonious cataract" (qtd. in Trilling 11).

Entire work Include the reference in the text without any page numbers or parentheses.

> In *The Structure of Scientific Revolutions,* Thomas Kuhn discusses how scientists change their thinking.

Work without page numbers or a one-page work (with/without other section numbers) If a work (such as a Web page) has no page numbers or is only one page long, omit the page number. If it uses screen numbers or paragraph numbers, insert a comma after the author's name, an identifying term (such as *screen*) or abbreviation (*par.* or *pars.*), and the number.

WITHOUT PAGE OR OTHER NUMBERS The average speed on Montana's interstate highways, for example, has risen by only 2 miles per hour since the repeal of the federal speed limit, with most drivers topping out at 75 (Schmid).

WITH OTHER SECTION NUMBERS Whitman considered African American speech "a source of a native grand opera" (Ellison, par. 13).

Work in a time-based medium To cite a specific portion of a video or an audio recording, include a time or range of times, as provided by your media player. Cite hours, minutes, and seconds, placing colons between them.

> President Obama joked that he and Dick Cheney agreed on one thing—*Hamilton* is phenomenal ("*Hamilton* Cast" 00:02:34–38).

Two or more works cited in the same parentheses If you cite two or more sources for a piece of information, include them in alphabetical order in the same parentheses, separated by semicolons.

> A few studies have considered differences between oral and written discourse production (Gould; Scardamalia et al.).

Creating a List of Works Cited

In your MLA-style research project, every source you cite must have a corresponding entry in the list of works cited, regardless of its medium of publication (printed book, online newspaper, Tweet, text message), and every entry in your list of works cited must correspond to at least one citation in your research project.

The MLA Handbook, Eighth Edition, offers these general principles for citing sources:

- **Author or authors.** Start with the author's name (or authors' names). The first author is listed last name first: *Smith, Jane. Follow the author's name with a period.*
- **Title of source.** Include the title of the source. Italicize the title if the work is self-contained (books, television series, and Web sites titles fall into this category); put the title in quotation marks if the work is contained within a larger work (titles of magazines, newspapers, journal articles, and episodes of television series fall into this category). *Follow the title of the source with a period.*
- **Title of container, or larger work in which the source appears, if any.** A newspaper, magazine, or journal contains the articles that appear in it; a Web site contains the Web pages that compose it; and a blog contains the blog posts and comments that appear in it. Container titles are typically italicized; the information that relates to the container is not. (Common types of container-related information appear in the following list.) *Follow the container title and every item that relates to the container with a comma—except for the last, which should be followed by a period.*
  - **Other contributors.** Translators, editors, producers, narrators, and illustrators are examples of other contributors.
  - **Version.** Edition names or numbers (*revised edition, eighth edition*) and *director's cut* are examples of versions.
  - **Number.** The volume number of a multivolume work, the volume and issue number of a journal, and the disk number of a set of DVDs fall into this category.
  - **Publication information.** The name of the publisher, government and agency, and site sponsor fall into this category.
  - **Publication date.** The date might be a day, month, and year for weekly magazines, daily or weekly television episodes, and daily newspapers; a month and year for journals and monthly magazines; or just a year for books and movies.
  - **Source locator.** The source locator might be the page number(s) of the section you used from a printed text, the DOI (digital object identifier, a permanent code) or URL of an online source, or the time stamp of a Tweet or a video.
- **Additional information.** Include additional information if your readers are likely to need it to identify your source. For an undated online source, you might include the date on which you accessed the source. A source might require a label if the type of source you are citing (such as an editorial or a lecture) is unclear from the citation. *Follow any additional information you provide with a period.*

To cite a source without a model, use a similar model, or devise your own using the general principles.

Nowadays, many print sources are also available in an electronic format, either online or through a database your school's library subscribes to. For most online versions of a source, follow the form of the corresponding print version. Then add the information about the online source.

For example, if you are citing an article from a journal that appears in print but that you accessed through a database, start with the citation for the print journal. Then add the information about the online source (a second container). Separate each piece of information within this second container by commas, and end the section with a period.

Author · *Title of article* · *Container 1: journal title*

Coles, Kimberly Anne. "The Matter of Belief in John Donne's Holy Sonnets." *Renaissance Quarterly*, vol. 68, no. 3, Fall 2015, pp. 899–931. *JSTOR*, doi:10.1086/683855.

Number · *Publication date* · *Source locator* · *Container 2: database name* · *Source locator (DOI)*

For sources accessed through a database, include the following:

- Title of the database (in italics), *followed by a comma*
- Location where you accessed the source, *followed by a period.* Ideally this is a DOI, or digital object identifier (a permanent code), but when one is not available, provide a URL (if available, use a permalink).

For other online sources, include the following:

- Title of the Web site (in italics), *followed by a comma*
- Version or edition used (if any), *followed by a comma*
- Publisher of the site, but only if distinct from the title of the publication, *followed by a comma*
- Date of publication or last update, *followed by a comma.* If no date of publication or update is available, provide the date you last accessed the source at the end of the entry.
- DOI, if one is available. If not, a URL (ideally a permalink), *followed by a period.*

You may not always find the exact model you need to cite your sources, but MLA style is flexible. Using these general principles, you can adapt another model or devise your own.

Format your list of works cited.

Follow these rules when formatting your list of works cited in MLA style:

- On a new page, type "Works Cited" (centered), and double-space the whole works-cited list, from the heading on.

- Alphabetize entries by the first word in the citation, usually the first author's last name or the title if the author is unknown. (Ignore *A, An,* or *The.*)
- Use a hanging indent for all entries: Do not indent the first line, but indent second and subsequent lines of the entry by half an inch. (Your word processor can be set to create a hanging indent automatically.)
- Abbreviate the names of university presses, shortening the words *University* and *Press* to *U* and *P*. Spell out other publishers' names in full, including words like *Press* or *Books*. Omit only initial articles like *The* and corporate-sounding words or abbreviations (*Limited, Co.*). If a work has more than one publisher, separate them with a slash: *University of Texas / International Digital Media Arts.*

Directory to Works-Cited-List Models

Author Listings

One author List the author last name first (followed by a comma), and insert a period at the end of the name.

Isaacson, Walter.

Two authors List the first author last name first (followed by a comma). List the second author in the usual first-name/last-name order. Insert the word *and* before the second author's name, and follow it with a period.

Bernays, Anne, and Pamela Painter.

Three or more authors List the first author last name first (followed by a comma). Then insert *et al.* (which means *and others* in Latin) in regular type (not italics).

Hunt, Lynn, et al.

Unknown author Begin the entry with the title.

Primary Colors: A Novel of Politics.

"Out of Sight."

Corporation, organization, or government agency as author Use the name of the corporation, organization, or government agency as the author.

RAND Corporation.

United States, National Commission on Terrorist Attacks.

Two or more works by the same author Replace the author's name in subsequent entries with three hyphens, and alphabetize the works by the first important word in the title:

Eugenides, Jeffrey. *The Marriage Plot.*

---. *Middlesex.*

---. "Walkabout."

Books (Print, Electronic, Database)

Basic format

Author, last name first | *Title (and subtitle, if any), italicized* | *Publisher* | *Publication date (year)*

PRINT Eugenides, Jeffrey. *The Marriage Plot.* Farrar, Straus and Giroux, 2011.

Version (edition) | *Publisher* | *Publication date*

E-BOOK Eugenides, Jeffrey. *The Marriage Plot.* Kindle ed., Farrar, Straus and Giroux, 2011.

Original publication date | *Database name, italicized*

DATABASE Whitman, Walt. *Leaves of Grass.* 1900. *Bartleby.com,* 1999, www.bartleby.com/142/.

Online publication date | *Location (URL)*

Figure 16.1 shows you where to find the source information you will need to create a works-cited entry for a book.

Anthology or edited collection If you are referring to the anthology as a whole, put the editor's name first.

Masri, Heather, editor. *Science Fiction: Stories and Contexts*. Bedford/St. Martin's, 2009.

Work in an anthology or edited collection If you're referring to a selection in an anthology, begin the entry with the name of the selection's author. Include specific page references, preceding the page number(s) with *p.* or *pp.*

Hopkinson, Nalo. "Something to Hitch Meat To." *Science Fiction: Stories and Contexts*, edited by Heather Masri, Bedford/St. Martin's, 2009, pp. 838–50.

THE BOOK OF

JONAH

a novel

JOSHUA MAX FELDMAN

HENRY HOLT AND COMPANY NEW YORK

Henry Holt and Company, LLC
Publishers since 1866
175 Fifth Avenue
New York, New York 10010
www.henryholt.com

Henry Holt® and ® are registered trademarks of Henry Holt and Company, LLC.

Copyright © 2014 Joshua Max Feldman
All rights reserved.

"To Live and Die in L.A," words and music by Quincy Jones III, Val Young and Tupac Shakur; Copyright © 1996 by DEEP TECHNOLOGY MUSIC, MUSIC OF WINDSWEPT, UNIVERSAL MUSIC CORP., SONGS OF UNIVERSAL, INC. and VAL YOUNG PUBLISHING; All Rights for DEEP TECHNOLOGY MUSIC and MUSIC OF WINDSWEPT administered by BUG MUSIC INC., A BMG CHRYSALIS COMPANY; all rights reserved. Used by permission. Reprinted by permission of Hal Leonard Corporation.

"There's a certain slant of light" reprinted by permission of the publishers and the Trustees of Amherst College from THE POEMS OF EMILY DICKINSON: VARIORUM EDITION, edited by Ralph W. Franklin, Cambridge, Mass.; The Belknap Press of Harvard University Press, Copyright © 1998 by the President and Fellows of Harvard College. Copyright © 1951, 1955, 1979, 1983 by the President and Fellows of Harvard College.

Library of Congress Cataloging-in-Publication Data
Feldman, Joshua Max.
The book of Jonah : a novel / Joshua Max Feldman.—First edition.
pages cm
ISBN 978-0-8050-9776-4 (hardcover)—ISBN 978-0-8050-9777-1 (electronic book)
1. Jewish lawyers—Fiction. 2. Life change events—Fiction. 3. New York (N.Y.)—Fiction. 4. Psychological fiction. I. Title.
PS3606.E3865B66 2014
813'.6—dc23 2013014308

Henry Holt books are available for special promotions and premiums. For details contact: Director, Special Markets.

First Edition 2014

Designed by Kelly S. Too

Printed in the United States of America
10 9 8 7 6 5 4 3 2 1

FIGURE 16.1 Documentation Map for a Book
Look for the author, title, and publisher on the title page (at the front of the book) and the year of publication (or copyright date) on the copyright page (usually on the back of the title page in print books). The title page and copyright page may appear in a different location or look a little different in an e-book or a book accessed through a database.

If you cite more than one selection from an anthology or collection, you may create an entry for the collection as a whole (see the model above) and then cross-reference individual selections to that entry.

Selection author | *Selection title* | *Anthology editor*

Hopkinson, Nalo. "Something to Hitch Meat To." Masri, pp. 838–50.

Selection pages in anthology

Introduction, preface, foreword, or afterword

Murfin, Ross C. Introduction. *Heart of Darkness*, by Joseph Conrad, 3rd ed., Bedford/St. Martin's, 2011, pp. 3–16.

Translation

Tolstoy, Leo. *War and Peace*. Translated by Richard Pevear and Larissa Volokhonsky, Vintage Books, 2009.

Graphic narrative If the graphic narrative was a collaboration between a writer and an illustrator, begin your entry with the name of the person on whose work your research project focuses. If the author also created the illustrations, then follow the basic model for a book with one author (p. 437).

Pekar, Harvey, and Joyce Brabner. *Our Cancer Year*. Illustrated by Frank Stack, Four Walls Eight Windows, 1994.

Religious work Include an entry in the list of works cited only if you cite a specific edition of a sacred text.

The Qu'ran: English Translation and Parallel Arabic Text. Translated by M. A. S. Abdel Haleem, Oxford UP, 2010.

Multivolume work If you use only one volume from a multivolume work, indicate the volume number after the title, using the abbreviation *vol.* If you use more than one volume, indicate the total number of volumes at the end of the entry.

One volume cited

Sandburg, Carl. *Abraham Lincoln*. Vol. 2, Charles Scribner's Sons, 1939.

More than one volume cited

Sandburg, Carl. *Abraham Lincoln*. Charles Scribner's Sons, 1939. 6 vols.

Later edition of a book Include the edition name (such as *Revised*) or number following the title.

Rottenberg, Annette T., and Donna Haisty Winchell. *The Structure of Argument*. 6th ed., Bedford/St. Martin's, 2009.

Republished book Provide the original year of publication (followed by a period) after the title of the book, followed by publication information for the edition you are using.

Original publication date

Alcott, Louisa May. *An Old-Fashioned Girl*. 1870. Puffin Books, 1995.

Republication information

More than one publisher named If the book was published by two or more publishers, separate the publishers with a slash, and include a space before and after the slash.

Hornby, Nick. *About a Boy*. Riverhead / Penguin Putnam, 1998.

Title within a title When a title that is normally italicized appears within a book title, do not italicize it. If the title within the title would normally be enclosed in quotation marks, include the quotation marks and also set the title in italics.

Hertenstein, Mike. *The Double Vision of* Star Trek: *Half-Humans, Evil Twins, and Science Fiction*. Cornerstone Press, 1998.

Miller, Edwin Haviland. *Walt Whitman's "Song of Myself": A Mosaic of Interpretation.* U of Iowa P, 1989.

Book in a series Include the series title (without italics) and number (if any) at the end of the entry, after a period (never a comma). (This information will appear on the title page or on the page facing the title page.)

Zigova, Tanya, et al. *Neural Stem Cells: Methods and Protocols.* Humana Press, 2002. Methods in Molecular Biology 198.

Dictionary entry or article in another reference book If no author is listed, begin with the entry's title. (But check for initials following the entry or article and a list of authors in the front of the book.) For familiar reference works, the publication information is probably not necessary.

PRINT "Homeopathy." *Webster's New World College Dictionary,* 4th ed., 1999.

PRINT Trenear-Harvey, Glenmore S. "Farm Hall." *Historical Dictionary of Atomic Espionage,* Scarecrow Press, 2011.

Web site (same name as publisher) *Most recent update*

ONLINE "Homeopathy." *Merriam-Webster,* 2011, www.merriam-webster.com/dictionary/homeopathy.

DATABASE Powell, Jason L. "Power Elite." *Blackwell Encyclopedia of Sociology,* edited by George Ritzer, Wiley, 2007. *Blackwell Reference Online,* doi:10.1111/b.9781405124331.2007.x.

Database (italics)

Location (DOI)

Government document If no author is named, begin with the government and agency that issued the document. If the work does have an author, begin with this information and place the government information after the source's title. In the United States, the publication information for most official government documents is *Government Printing Office,* both in print and online.

Authors

PRINT Newes-Adeyi, Gabriella, et al. *Trends in Underage Drinking in the United States, 1991-2007.* United States, Department of Health and Human Services, Government Printing Office, 2009.

Issuing government *Issuing department*

ONLINE United States, Department of Health and Human Services, Centers for Disease Control. "Youth Risk Behavior Surveillance—United States, 2009." *Morbidity and Mortality Weekly Report,* vol. 59, no. SS5, 4 June 2010, www.cdc.gov/mmwr/pdf/ss/ss5905.pdf.

Publication date

Published proceedings of a conference If the name of the conference is part of the title of the publication, it need not be repeated. If it isn't part of the title, insert the name of the conference following the title. Use the format for a work in an anthology (p. 438) to cite an individual presentation. Include the location (city) where the conference took place after its date. Separate conference information from publication information with a period.

Conference name included in title

Duffett, John, editor. *Against the Crime of Silence: Proceedings of the International War Crimes Tribunal.* Nov. 1967, Stockholm. Simon and Schuster, 1970.

Pamphlet or brochure

Hypothermia and Cold Water Survival. U.S. Foundation for Boating Safety and Clean Water, 2001.

Doctoral dissertation Cite a published dissertation as you would a book, but add pertinent dissertation information before the publication data. Enclose the title of an unpublished dissertation in quotation marks.

Title in italics

PUBLISHED Jones, Anna Maria. *Problem Novels/Perverse Readers: Late-Victorian Fiction and the Perilous Pleasures of Identification.* Dissertation, U of Notre Dame, 2001.

Dissertation information

Title in quotation marks

UNPUBLISHED Bullock, Barbara. "Basic Needs Fulfillment among Less Developed Countries: Social Progress over Two Decades of Growth." Dissertation, Vanderbilt U, 1986.

Dissertation information

Articles (Print, Online, Database)

Articles appear in periodicals—works that are issued at regular intervals, such as scholarly journals, newspapers, and magazines. Most periodicals today are available both in print and in electronic form (online or through an electronic database); some are available only in electronic format. If you are using the online version of an article, use the models provided here. If no model matches your source exactly, choose the closest match, and add any other information your reader will need to track down the source.

From a scholarly journal Scholarly journals are typically identified using their volume and issue numbers, separated by a period. If a journal does not use volume numbers, provide the issue number only. Online journals may not include page numbers; if paragraph or other section numbers are provided, use them instead. If an article in a printed journal is not on a continuous sequence of pages, give the first page number followed by a plus sign. (See entry for a print version of a newspaper for an example.)

For help distinguishing between scholarly journals and magazines, see Chapter 15.

Figure 16.2 shows where to find the source information you will need to create a works-cited entry for three of the journal articles cited here.

Author, last name first / *Article in quotation marks*

PRINT Haas, Heather A. "The Wisdom of Wizards--and Muggles and Squibs: Proverb Use in the World of *Harry Potter*." *Journal of American Folklore*, vol. 124, no. 492, Spring 2011, pp. 29–54.

Date of publication / *Page numbers*

Garas-York, Keli. "Overlapping Student Environments: An Examination of the Homeschool Connection and Its Impact on Achievement." *The Journal of College Admission*, vol. 42, no. 4, May 2010, pp. 430–39.

ONLINE Markel, J. D. "Religious Allegory and Cultural Discomfort in Mike Leigh's *Happy-Go-Lucky*: And Why *Larry Crowne* Is One of the Best Films of 2011." *Bright Lights Film Journal*, no. 74, 2011, brightlightsfilm.com/religious-allegory-and-cultural-discomfort-in-mike-leighs-happy-go-luckyand-why-larry-crowne-is-one-of-the-best-films-of-2011/.

URL

Saho, Bala S. K. "The Appropriation of Islam in a Gambian Village: Life and Times of Shaykh Mass Kay, 1827–1936." *African Studies Quarterly*, vol. 12, no. 4, 2011, asq.africa.ufl.edu/files/Saho-Vol12Is4.pdf.

DATABASE Coles, Kimberly Anne. "The Matter of Belief in John Donne's Holy Sonnets." *Renaissance Quarterly*, vol. 68, no. 3, Fall 2015, pp. 899–931. *JSTOR*, doi:10.1086/683855.

Database (italics) / *DOI*

From a newspaper Newspapers are identified by date, not by volume and issue numbers, with the names of months longer than four letters abbreviated. If articles are not on a continuous series of pages, give only the first page number followed by a plus sign. If an article is unsigned, start with the title (in quotation marks); ignore articles (*A, An, The*) when alphabetizing. (See *Editorial or letter to the editor*, p. 444, for an example.)

PRINT Weisman, Jonathan, and Jennifer Steinhauer. "Patriot Act Faces Revisions Backed by Both Parties." *The New York Times*, 1 May 2015, pp. A1+.

Noncontinuous pages

ONLINE Weisman, Jonathan, and Jennifer Steinhauer. "Patriot Act Faces Revisions Backed by Both Parties." *The New York Times*, 30 Apr. 2015, nyti.ms/1OKw1YN.

Web site (italics) / *Publication date* / *URL*

DATABASE Weisman, Jonathan, and Jennifer Steinhauer. "Patriot Act Faces Revisions Backed by Both Parties." *The New York Times*, 1 May 2015, pp. A1+. *LexisNexis Academic*, www.lexisnexis.com.

Database (italics) / *URL*

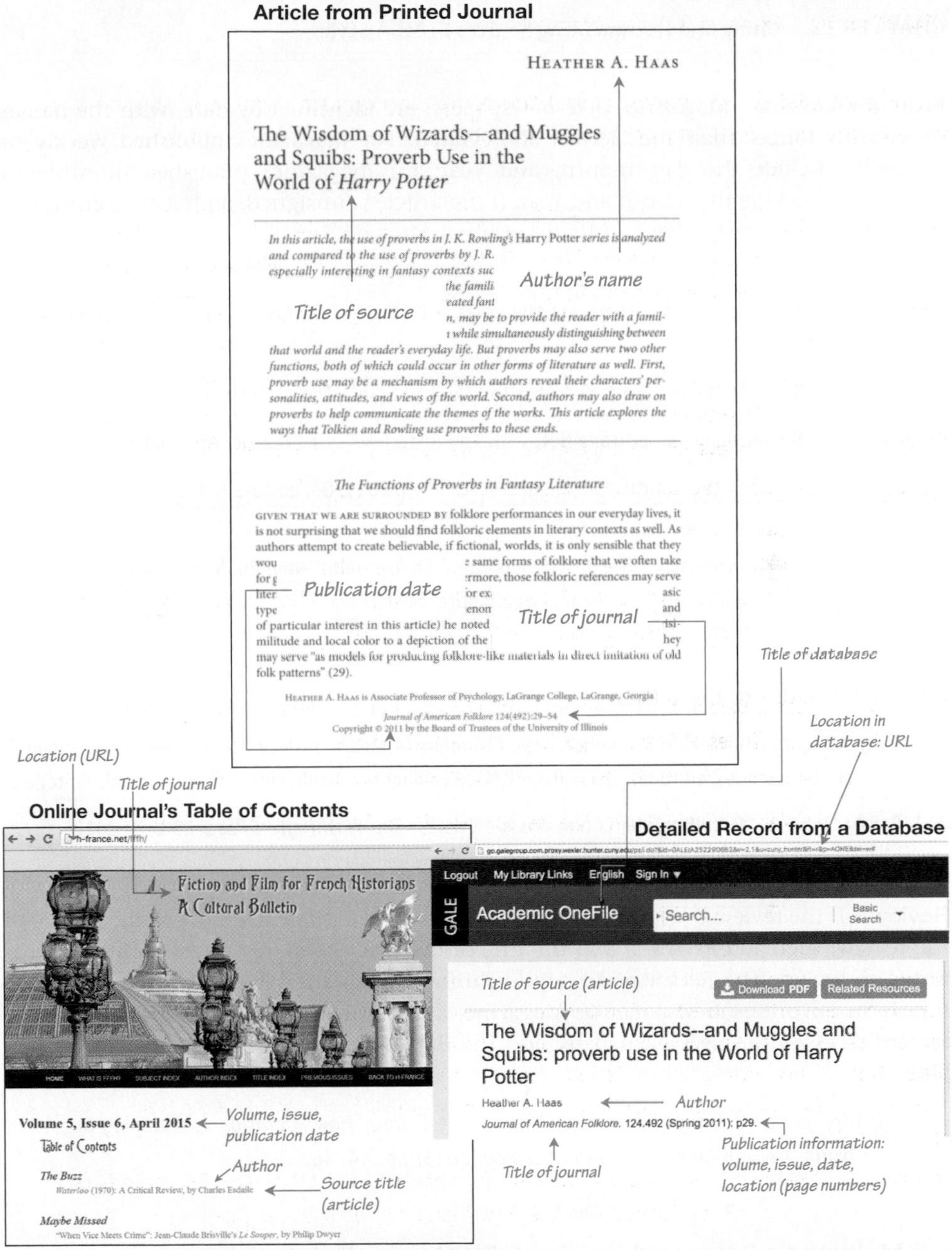

FIGURE 16.2 Documentation Map for a Journal Article For a print journal, look for the title of the journal on the front cover or in the table of contents. The author and article title will also be listed there; they will, of course, appear on the first page of the article (shown here) as well. The information you will need to cite an article you access through a database will appear in the list of results, the detailed record of the article, and the PDF (or HTML) version of the article itself. For an article published in an electronic journal, look for the information you need to create the works-cited entry on the journal's home page, table of contents, or the page on which the article appears. Sometimes the URL that appears in your browser's address bar is not the best way to cite your source. Some databases provide shorter, more stable permalinks for journal articles, often as part of a sharing feature or detailed record. If your source has a DOI, use this instead of the URL. DOIs may be listed near the beginning of an article, on the top or bottom of all pages in a PDF, or in the detailed record for the source in a database. You can look up the DOI for any source that has one at www.crossref.org.

From a magazine Magazines (like newspapers) are identified by date, with the names of months longer than four letters abbreviated. For magazines published weekly or biweekly, include the day, month, and year; for magazines published monthly or bimonthly, include the month and year. If the article is unsigned, alphabetize entries by the first important word in the title (ignoring *A, An,* and *The*).

Publication date (weekly)

PRINT Stillman, Sarah. "Where Are the Children?" *The New Yorker,* 27 Apr. 2015, pp. 40–41.

Publication date (monthly)

Bennet, James. "Editor's Note: To Stay or to Go." *The Atlantic,* Apr. 2015, p. 8.

ONLINE Bennet, James. "Editor's Note: To Stay or to Go." *The Atlantic,* Apr. 2015, www.theatlantic.com/magazine/archive/2015/04/editors-note/386285/.

URL

DATABASE Sharp, Kathleen. "The Rescue Mission." *Smithsonian,* Nov. 2015, pp. 40–49. *OmniFile Full Text Select,* web.b.ebscohost.com.

Database (italics) *URL (shortened)*

Editorial or letter to the editor

"City's Blight Fight Making Difference." *The Columbus Dispatch,* 17 Nov. 2015, www.dispatch.com/content/stories/editorials/2015/11/17/1-citys-blight-fight-making-difference.html. Editorial.

Fahey, John A. "Recalling the Cuban Missile Crisis." *The Washington Post,* 28 Oct. 2012, p. A16. Letter. *LexisNexis Library Express,* www.lexisnexis.com.

Review If the review does not include an author's name, start the entry with the title of the review; then add *Review of* and the title of the work being reviewed. If the review is untitled, include the *Review of* description immediately after the author's name. For a review in an online newspaper or magazine, add the URL, ideally a permalink. For a review accessed through a database, add the database title (in italics) and the DOI or URL.

Deparle, Jason. "Immigration Nation." Review of *Exodus: How Migration Is Changing Our World,* by Paul Collier, *The Atlantic,* Nov. 2013, pp. 44–46.

Multimedia Sources (Live, Print, Electronic, Database)

Lecture or public address

Title of lecture

Stephenson, Brittany. "Wading Out of Web Stew: Reader-Centric Course Design." Conference on College Composition and Communication, 20 Mar. 2015, Marriott Waterside, Tampa.

Date of lecture *Location of conference*

Letter If the letter has been published, treat it like a work in an anthology (p. 438), but add the recipient, the date, and any identifying number after the author's name. If the letter is unpublished, note the sender, recipient, and date.

Sender *Recipient* *Date*

DuHamel, Grace. Letter to the author. 22 Mar. 2008.

Map or chart

PRINT *Map of Afghanistan and Surrounding Territory*. GiziMap, 2001.

ONLINE "Vote on Secession, 1861." *Perry-Castañeda Library Map Collection*, U of Texas at Austin, 1976, www.lib.utexas.edu/maps/atlas_texas/texas_vote_secession_1861.jpg.

Cartoon or comic strip Provide the title (if given) in quotation marks directly following the artist's name.

Wheeler, Shannon. Cartoon. *The New Yorker*, 11 May 2015, p. 50.

Advertisement

PRINT Hospital for Special Surgery. *The New York Times*, 13 Apr. 2009, p. A7. Advertisement.

BROADCAST Norwegian Cruise Line. *WNET*, PBS, 29 Apr. 2012. Advertisement.

ONLINE Volkswagen Passat. *Slate*, www.slate.com/. Accessed 1 Dec. 2011. Advertisement.

Access date (no pub date available)

Work of art Include the year the work was created, and provide the museum or collection and its location. If you accessed the work online, include the Web site name and the URL.

Location

MUSEUM Palmer Payne, Elsie. *Sheep Dipping Time*. c. 1930s, Nevada Museum of Art, Reno.

PRINT Chihuly, Dale. *Carmine and White Flower Set*. 1987, Tacoma Art Museum. *Dale Chihuly: A Celebration*, Abrams Press, 2011, p. 109.

Print publication information

Web site

ONLINE Sekaer, Peter. *A Sign Business Shop, New York*. 1935, *International Center of Photography*, www.icp.org/exhibitions/signs-of-life-photographs-by-peter-sekaer.

Location (URL)

Musical composition

Beethoven, Ludwig van. Violin Concerto in D Major, op. 61. 1809. IMSLP Music Library, imslp.org/wiki/Violin_Concerto_in_D_major,_Op.61_(Beethoven,_Ludwig_van).

Gershwin, George. *Porgy and Bess*. 1935. Alfred A. Knopf, 1999.

Performance

The Draft. Directed by Diego Arciniegas, 10 Sept. 2015, Hibernian Hall, Boston.

Beethoven, Ludwig van. Piano Concerto no. 3. Conducted by Andris Nelsons, performances by Paul Lewis and Boston Symphony Orchestra, 9 Oct. 2015, Symphony Hall, Boston.

Television show, radio program, or podcast Include the network and broadcast date. If you streamed the program, treat it like an article you accessed through a database: at the end of your entry, include information about the streaming service (its name and a URL). Separate program information from database information with a period. If you streamed or downloaded the program through an app like an iPhone's *Podcasts*, list the app as you would a streaming service or database (see *Downloaded* entry). Treat a podcast that you listened to or watched online as you would an online television or radio program (see *Streamed* entry).

Episode — *Program* — *Key contributors*

BROADCAST "Being Mortal." *Frontline,* written by Atul Gawande and Tom Jennings, directed by Tom Jennings and Nisha Pahuja, PBS, 22 Nov. 2011.

Network — *Broadcast date*

STREAMED "The Choice." *The Borgias,* directed by Kari Skogland, season 2, episode 5, Showtime, 6 May 2012. *Netflix,* www.netflix.com/watch/70261634.

DOWNLOADED (OR VIA APP) "Patient Zero." *Radio Lab,* hosted by Jad Abumrad and Robert Krulwich, season 10, episode 4, National Public Radio, 14 Nov. 2011. *Podcasts,* iTunes.

Film

THEATER *Space Station*. Produced and directed by Toni Myers, narrated by Tom Cruise, IMAX, 2002.

DVD *Casablanca*. Directed by Michael Curtiz, performances by Humphrey Bogart, Ingrid Bergman, and Paul Henreid, 1942. Warner Home Video, 2003.

Online video

Film School. "Sunny Day." *YouTube,* 12 June 2010, www.youtube.com/watch?v=8oTJFUCbsfI.

Music recording

Beethoven, Ludwig van. Violin Concerto in D Major, Op. 61. Performances by David Oistrakh and the U.S.S.R. State Orchestra, conducted by Alexander Gauk, Allegro Music, 1980.

Maroon 5. "Moves Like Jagger." *Hands All Over,* A&M Octone Records, 2011.

Interview

PRINT Ashrawi, Hanan. "Tanks vs. Olive Branches." Interview by Rose Marie Berger. *Sojourners,* Feb. 2005, pp. 22–26.

BROADCAST Dobbs, Bill. "Occupy Wall Street." Interview by Brooke Gladstone. *On the Media,* National Public Radio, 7 Oct. 2011, www.wnyc.org/story/163283-occupy-wall-street/.

PERSONAL Ellis, Trey. Personal interview. 3 Sept. 2015.

Other Electronic Sources

Online sources have proliferated in the last ten years. With that proliferation has come access to more information than ever before. But not all of that information is of equal value. Before including a source found on *Google* in your research project, be sure that it is appropriate for a college-level writing project, and evaluate its reliability carefully.

If you are using the online version of a source for which there is no model shown here, choose the model that best matches your source and add any other information that readers will need to find the source themselves. If an online source does not include a publication date or information about its latest update, provide the date you accessed it at the end of your entry. Separate access information from source information with a period.

For help evaluating online sources, see Chapter 15.

Web page or other document on a Web site

Document title (in quotation marks) — *Title of site (italicized)*

"Introduction to the Final Installment of the Rossetti Archive." *The Complete Writings and Pictures of Dante Gabriel Rossetti: A Hypermedia Archive,* edited by Jerome J. McGann,

Editor (no author)

Publisher — *Publication date/last update*

Institute for Advanced Technology in the Humanities, U of Virginia, 2008, www.rossettiarchive.org/about/index.html.

Figure 16.3 shows where to find the source information you will need to create a works-cited entry for the Web page cited here.

Entire Web site or online scholarly project If the author's name is not given, begin the citation with the title.

Gardner, James Alan. *A Seminar on Writing Prose.* 2001, www.thinkage.ca/~jim/prose/prose.htm.

The Complete Writings and Pictures of Dante Gabriel Rossetti: A Hypermedia Archive. Edited by Jerome J. McGann, Institute for Advanced Technology in the Humanities, U of Virginia, 2008, www.rossettiarchive.org/index.html.

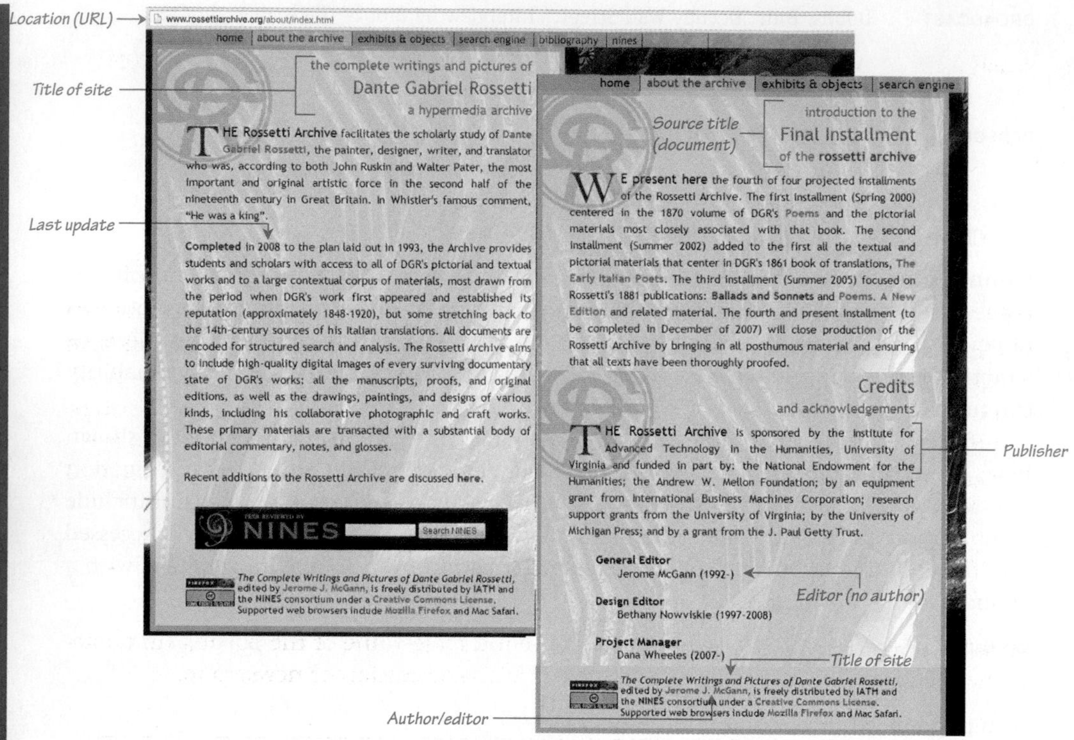

FIGURE 16.3 Documentation Map for a Web Page
Look for the author or editor and title of the Web page on the Web page itself. The title of the Web site may appear on the Web page, on the site's home page, or both. The publisher (sponsor) may be listed at the bottom of the Web page, on the home page, or somewhere else. (Look for an "About Us," "Who We Are," or "Contact Us" page.) If no publication or copyright date or "last update" appears on the Web page, the home page, or elsewhere on the site, include a date of access at the end of your works-cited entry. Otherwise, conclude with a permalink or the URL provided in your browser's address bar.

Book or a short work in an online scholarly project Treat a book or a short work in an online scholarly project as you would a Web page or another document on a Web site, but set the title in italics if the work is a book and in quotation marks if it is an article, an essay, a poem, or some other short work, and include the print publication information (if relevant to your particular use) following the title.

Heims, Marjorie. "The Strange Case of Sarah Jones." *The Free Expression Policy Project*, 2 Nov. 2011, www.fepproject.org/commentaries/sarahjones.html.

Original publication date

Corelli, Marie. *The Treasure of Heaven*. 1906. *Victorian Women Writers Project*, edited by Percy Willett, Indiana U, 10 July 1999, webapp1.dlib.indiana.edu/vwwp/view?docId=VAB7176.

Blog Cite an entire blog as you would an entire Web site (see p. 447). If the author of the blog or blog post uses a pseudonym (or *handle*), use it in place of the author's real name. If you know the author's real name, include it in parentheses following the pseudonym.

Blog title

ENTIRE BLOG Marshall, Josh. *Talking Points Memo*. talkingpointsmemo.com/. Accessed 1 Dec. 2011.

Pseudonym

Negative Camber. *Formula1Blog*, 2014, www.formula1blog.com/.

Post author *Post title*

BLOG POST Marshall, Josh. "Coke and Grass at Amish Raid." *Talking Points Memo*, 1 Dec. 2011, talkingpointsmemo.com/edblog/coke-grass-at-amish-raid.

Wiki article Since wikis are written and edited collectively, start your entry with the title of the article you are citing. But check with your instructor before using information from a wiki in your research project; because content is written and edited collectively, it is difficult to assess its reliability and impossible to determine the expertise of the contributors. Some wikis, such as *Wikipedia*, offer unique permalinks for each updated version of every article (click on "Permanent link" under "Tools" in the menu). If you cannot locate a unique permalink for the version you're citing, include your access date.

"John Lydon." *Wikipedia*, 19 Mar. 2016, 3:17 a.m., en.wikipedia.org/w/index.php ?title=John_Lydon&oldid=710801155.

Discussion group or newsgroup posting Use the subject line of the posting (in quotation marks) as the title, and include the name of the discussion or newsgroup.

Post author *Subject line* *Group name* *Post date*

Yen, Jessica. "Quotations within Parentheses (Study Measures)." *Copyediting-L*, 18 Mar. 2016, list.indiana.edu/sympa/arc/copyediting-l/2016-03/msg00492.html.

E-mail message

Sender *Subject line* *Recipient* *Date sent*

Olson, Kate. "Update on State Legislative Grants." Received by Alissa Brown, 5 Nov. 2015.

Student Research Project in MLA Style

Student Cristina Dinh uses MLA documentation style in her research project on home schooling, which follows. As you work on college writing projects in the humanities, use the formatting instructions in this paper (pp. 450–59) as a guide, but be sure to check with your instructor before preparing a final draft. Some instructors may prefer that you use APA or another style.

1/2''

1''

Dinh 1

1''

1''

Double-spaced

Cristina Dinh

Professor Cooper

English 100

15 May 2015

Double-spaced

Title centered; no underlining, quotes, or italics

Educating Kids at Home

Every morning, Mary Jane, who is nine, doesn't have to worry about gulping down her cereal so she can be on time for school. School for Mary Jane is literally right at her doorstep.

Paragraphs indented one-half inch

In this era of serious concern about the quality of public education, increasing numbers of parents across the United States are choosing to educate their children at home. These parents believe they can do a better job teaching their children than their local schools can. *Home schooling*, as this practice is known, has become a national trend over the past thirty years, and according to education specialist Brian D. Ray, the home-schooled population is growing at a rate between 5% and 12% per year. A 2008 report by the U.S. Department of Education's Institute of Education Sciences estimated that, nationwide, the number of home-schooled children rose from 850,000 in 1999 to approximately 1.5 million in 2007 (*Issue Brief* 1). Some home-schooling advocates believe that even these numbers may be low because not all states require formal notification when parents decide to teach their children at home.

Author named in text; no parenthetical page reference because source is not paginated

What is home schooling, and who are the parents choosing to be home-schoolers? David Guterson, a pioneer in the home-schooling movement, defines home schooling as "the attempt to gain an education outside of institutions" (5). Home-schooled children spend the majority of the conventional school day learning in or near their homes rather than in traditional schools; parents or guardians are the prime educators. Former teacher and home-schooler Rebecca Rupp notes that home-schooling

Author named in text; parenthetical page reference falls at end of sentence

1''

parents vary considerably in what they teach and how they teach, ranging from those who follow a highly traditional curriculum within a structure that parallels the typical classroom to those who essentially allow their children to pursue whatever interests them at their own pace (3). Home-schoolers commonly combine formal instruction with life skills instruction, learning fractions, for example, in terms of monetary units or cooking measurements (Saba and Gattis 89). According to the U.S. Department of Education's 2008 report, while home-schoolers are also a diverse group politically and philosophically--libertarians, conservatives, Christian fundamentalists--most say they home school for one of three reasons: they are concerned about the quality of academic instruction, the general school environment, or the lack of religious or moral instruction (Stevens 2).

Work by two authors cited

The first group generally believes that children need individual attention and the opportunity to learn at their own pace to learn well. This group says that one teacher in a classroom of twenty to thirty children (the size of typical public-school classes) cannot give this kind of attention. These parents believe they can give their children greater enrichment and more specialized instruction than public schools can provide. At home, parents can work one-on-one with each child and be flexible about time, allowing their children to pursue their interests at earlier ages. Many of these parents, like home-schooler Peter Bergson, believe that

> home schooling provides more of an opportunity to continue the natural learning process that's in evidence in all children.
> [In school,] you change the learning process from self-directed to other-directed, from the child

Quotation of more than four lines typed as a block and indented a half inch

Brackets indicate alteration of quotation

Dinh 3

> asking questions to the teacher asking questions. You shut down areas of potential interest. (qtd. in Kohn 22)

Parenthetical citation of secondary source falls after period when quotation is indented as a block

This trend can be traced back to the 1960s, when many people began criticizing traditional schools. Various types of "alternative" schools were created, and some parents began teaching their children at home (Friedlander 150). Parents like this mention several reasons for their disappointment with public schools and for their decision to home school. A lack of funding, for example, leaves children without new textbooks. In a 2002 survey, 31% of teachers said that their students are using textbooks that are more than ten years old, and 29% said that they do not have enough textbooks for all of their students (National Education Association). Many schools also cannot afford to buy laboratory equipment and other teaching materials. At my own high school, the chemistry teacher told me that most of the lab equipment we used came from a research firm he worked for. In a 2006 Gallup poll, lack of proper financial support ranked first on the list of the problems in public schools (Rose and Gallup 45).

Corporate author's name cited

Parents also cite overcrowding as a reason for taking their kids out of school. The more students in a classroom, the less learning that goes on, as Cafi Cohen discovered before choosing to home school; after spending several days observing what went on in her child's classroom, she found that administrative duties, including disciplining, took up to 80% of a teacher's time, with only 20% of the day devoted to learning (6). Moreover, faced with a large group of children, a teacher ends up gearing lessons to the students in the middle level, so children at both ends miss out. Gifted children and those with learning disabilities particularly suffer in this situation. At home, parents of these children say they can tailor the material and the pace for each child. Studies show that home-schooling methods seem to work well in preparing children academically. Lawrence Rudner, director of the ERIC Clearinghouse on Assessment and Evaluation at the University of Maryland and a researcher on home schooling, found that testing of home-schooled students showed them to be between one and three years ahead of public school students their age (xi). Home-schooled children have also made particularly strong showings in academic competitions; since the late 1990s, 10% of National Spelling Bee participants have been home schooled, as have two National Spelling Bee and two National Geographic Bee winners (Lyman). More and more selective colleges are admitting, and even recruiting, home-schooled applicants (Basham et al. 15).

Work by three or more authors cited

Parents in the second group--those concerned with the general school environment--claim that their children are more well-rounded than those in school. Because they don't have to sit in classrooms all day, home-schooled kids can pursue their own projects, often combining crafts or technical skills with academic subjects. Home-schoolers participate in outside activities, such as 4-H competitions, field trips with peers in home-school support groups, science fairs, musical and dramatic productions, church activities, and Boy Scouts or Girl Scouts (Saba and Gattis 59-62). In fact, they may even be able to participate to some extent in actual school activities. A 1999 survey conducted by the United States Department of Education's Institute of Education Sciences found that 28% of public schools allowed home-schooled students to participate in extracurricular activities alongside enrolled students, and 20% allowed home-schooled students to attend some classes (Princiotta and Bielick 12).

Many home-schooling parents believe that these activities provide the social opportunities kids need without exposing their children to the peer pressure they would have to deal with as regular school students. For example, many kids think that drinking and using drugs are cool. When I was in high school, my friends would tell me a few drinks wouldn't hurt or affect driving. If I had listened to them, perhaps I wouldn't be alive today. Four of my friends were killed under the influence of alcohol. Between 1992 and 2008, the number of high school seniors surveyed who had used any illicit drug in the last year climbed from 27.1% to 36.6% (Johnston et al. 59).

Work by three or more authors cited

Another reason many parents decide to home school their kids is that they are concerned for their children's safety. Samuel L. Blumenfeld notes that "physical risk" is an important reason many parents remove their children from public schools as "[m]ore and more children are assaulted, robbed, and murdered in school" and a "culture of violence, abetted by rap music, drug trafficking, . . . and racial tension, has engulfed teenagers" (4). Beginning in the mid-1990s, a string of school shootings--including the 1999 massacres in Littleton, Colorado, and Conyers, Georgia, and the 2001 massacre in Santee, California--has led to increasing fears that young people are simply not safe at school.

While all of the reasons mentioned so far are important, perhaps the single most significant cause of the growing home-schooling trend is Christian fundamentalist dissatisfaction with "godless" public schools. Sociologist Mitchell L. Stevens, author of one of the first comprehensive studies of home schooling, cites a mailing sent out by Basic Christian Education, a company that markets home-schooling materials, titled "What Really Happens in Public Schools." This publication sums up the fears of fundamentalist home-schoolers about public schools: that they encourage high levels of teenage sexual activity and pregnancies "out of wedlock"; expose children to "violence, crime, lack of discipline, and, of course, drugs of every kind"; present positive portrayals of communism and socialism and negative portrayals of capitalism; and undermine children's Christian beliefs by promoting "New Age philosophies, Yoga, Transcendental Meditation, witchcraft demonstrations, and Eastern religions" (51).

As early as 1988, Luanne Shackelford and Susan White, two Christian home-schooling mothers, were claiming that because schools expose children to "[p]eer pressure, perverts, secular textbooks, values clarification, TV, pornography, rock music, bad movies [,]. . . [h]ome schooling seems to be the best plan to achieve our goal [to raise good Christians]" (160). As another mother more recently put it:

> I don't like the way schools are going. . . . What's wrong with Christianity all of a sudden? You know? This country was founded on Christian, on religious principles. [People] came over here for religious freedom, and now all of a sudden all religious references seem to be stricken out of the public school, and I don't like that at all. (qtd. in Stevens 67)

Although many nonfundamentalist home-schoolers make some of these same criticisms, those who cite the lack of "Christian values" in public schools have particular concerns

Brackets used to indicate changes in capitalization and addition to quotation for clarification

Ellipsis marks used to indicate words left out of quotations

Quotation cited in a secondary source

Single quotation marks indicate a quotation within a quotation

Citation placed close to quotation, before comma but after closing quotation mark

Internet source cited by a shortened form of the title; author name and page numbers unavailable

Source cited by title

of their own. For example, home-schooling leader Raymond Moore talks of parents who are "'sick and tired of the teaching of evolution in the schools as a cut-and-dried fact,' along with other evidence of so-called secular humanism" (Kohn 21), such as textbooks that contain material contradicting Christian beliefs. Moreover, parents worry that schools undermine their children's moral values. In particular, some Christian fundamentalist parents object to sex education in schools, saying that it encourages children to become sexually active early, challenging values taught at home. They see the family as the core and believe that the best place to instill family values is within the family. These Christian home-schooling parents want to provide their children not only with academic knowledge but also with a moral grounding consistent with their religious beliefs.

Still other home-schooling parents object to a perceived government-mandated value system that they believe attempts to override the values, not necessarily religious in nature, of individual families. For these parents, home schooling is a way of resisting what they see as unwarranted intrusion by the federal government into personal concerns ("Is").

Armed with their convictions, parents such as those who belong to the Christian Home School Legal Defense Association have fought in court and lobbied for legislation that allows them the option of home schooling. In the 1970s, most states had compulsory attendance laws that made it difficult, if not illegal, to keep school-age children home from school. Today, home schooling is permitted in every state, with strict regulation required by only a few ("State Action Map"). As a result, Mary Jane is one of hundreds of thousands of American children who can start their school day without leaving the house.

1/2"
1"
1"

Dinh 8

Works Cited

Basham, Patrick, et al. *Home Schooling: From the Extreme to the Mainstream*. 2nd ed., Fraser Institute, Oct. 2007, www.fraserinstitute.org/sites/default/files/Homeschooling2007.pdf. Studies in Education Policy.

Blumenfeld, Samuel L. *Homeschooling: A Parent's Guide to Teaching Children*. Replica Publishing, 1999.

Cohen, Cafi. *And What about College? How Home-Schooling Leads to Admissions to the Best Colleges and Universities*. 2nd ed., Henry Holt, 2000.

Friedlander, Tom. "A Decade of Home Schooling." *The Home School Reader,* edited by Mark Hegener and Helen Hegener, Home Education Press, 1988, pp. 147–56.

Guterson, David. *Family Matters: Why Homeschooling Makes Sense*. Harcourt, 1992.

Issue Brief: 1.5 Million Homeschooled Students in the United States in 2007. United States, Department of Education, National Center for Education Statistics, Dec. 2008, nces.ed.gov/pubs2009/2009030.pdf.

"Is There a Problem?" *Alliance for the Separation of School and State,* 29 Jan. 2008, www.schoolandstate.org/parentrights.htm.

Johnston, Lloyd D., et al. *Monitoring the Future: National Results on Adolescent Drug Use, Overview of Key Findings, 2008*. United States, Department of Health and Human Services, National Institutes of Health, National Institute on Drug Abuse, 2009, monitoringthefuture.org/pubs/monographs/overview2008.pdf.

Works-cited entries begin on a new page; entries are in alphabetical order.

Title centered

Double-spaced

Entries begin flush with left margin; subsequent lines indent half an inch.

Dinh 9

Kohn, Alfie. "Home Schooling." *The Atlantic,* Apr. 1988, pp. 20–25.

Lyman, Isabel. "Generation Two." *American Enterprise,* Oct.-Nov. 2002, pp. 48–49. *Business Insights: Essentials,* bi.galegroup.com.

National Education Association. *2002 Instructional Materials Survey*. Association of American Publishers, www.publishers.org/search/node/instructional%20 materials%20survey%202002. Accessed 7 May 2015.

Princiotta, Daniel, and Stacey Bielick. *Homeschooling in the United States: 2003*. United States, Department of Education, Institute of Education Sciences, National Center for Education Statistics, 2006, nces.ed.gov/ pubs2006/2006042.pdf.

Ray, Brian D. "Research Facts on Home Schooling." *National Home Education Research Institute,* 23 Mar. 2015, www.nheri.org/research/research -facts-on-homeschooling.html.

Rose, Lowell C., and Alec M. Gallup. "The 38th Annual Phi Delta Kappa/Gallup Poll of the Public's Attitudes toward the Public Schools." *Phi Delta Kappan,* vol. 88, no. 1, Sept. 2006, pp. 41–56. *Larry Cuban on School Reform and Classroom Practice,* larrycuban.files .wordpress.com/2012/10/k0609pol.pdf.

Untitled section labeled

Rudner, Lawrence. Foreword. *The McGraw-Hill Home-Schooling Companion,* by Laura Saba and Julie Gattis, McGraw-Hill, 2002, pp. xi–xiii.

Rupp, Rebecca. *The Complete Home Learning Source Book.* Three Rivers Press, 1998.

Saba, Laura, and Julie Gattis. *The McGraw-Hill Home-Schooling Companion*. McGraw-Hill, 2002.

Dinh 10

Shackelford, Luanne, and Susan White. *A Survivor's Guide to Home Schooling*. Crossway, 1988.

"State Action Map." *Home School Legal Defense Association*, 2011, www.hslda.org/hs/state/.

Stevens, Mitchell L. *Kingdom of Children: Culture and Controversy in the Homeschooling Movement*. Princeton UP, 2001.

17

Citing and Documenting Sources in APA Style

When using the APA system of documentation, include both an in-text citation and a list of references at the end of the research project. **In-text citations** tell your readers where the ideas or words you have borrowed come from, and the entries in the **list of references** provide readers with the information they need to locate your sources so that they can read more about your topic.

The most common types of in-text citations and reference-list models follow. For other, less common citation types, consult the *Publication Manual of the American Psychological Association,* Sixth Edition. Most libraries will own a copy.

Citing Sources in the Text

When citing ideas, information, or words borrowed from a source, include the author's last name and the date of publication in the text of your research project. In most cases, you will want to use a *signal phrase* to introduce the works you are citing, since doing so gives you the opportunity to put the work and its author in context. A signal phrase includes the author's last name, the date of publication, and a verb that describes the author's attitude or stance:

> Smith (2015) complained that . . .
>
> Jones (2015) defended her position by . . .

Use a parenthetical citation—*(Jones, 2015)*—when you have already introduced the author or the work or when citing the source of an uncontroversial fact. When quoting from a source, also include the page number: *Smith (2015) complained that he "never got a break" (p. 123).* When you are paraphrasing or summarizing, you may omit the page reference, although including it is not wrong.

Directory to In-Text-Citation Models

One author

SIGNAL PHRASE Upton Sinclair (2005), a crusading journalist, wrote that workers sometimes "fell into the vats; and when they were fished out, there was never enough of them left to be worth exhibiting" (p. 134).

PARENTHETICAL CITATION *The Jungle,* a naturalistic novel inspired by the French writer Zola, described in lurid detail the working conditions of the time, including what became of unlucky workers who fell into the vats while making sausage (Sinclair, 2005, p. 134).

Author's last name + Date + Page

REFERENCE-LIST ENTRY Sinclair, U. (2005). The jungle. New York, NY: Oxford University Press. (Original work published 1906)

More than one author In a signal phrase, use the word *and* between the authors' names; in a parenthetical citation, use an ampersand (&). When citing a work by three to five authors, list all the authors in your first reference; in subsequent references, just cite the first and use *et al.* (Latin for *and others*).

SIGNAL PHRASE As Jamison and Tyree (2001) have found, racial bias does not diminish merely through exposure to individuals of other races.

PARENTHETICAL CITATION Racial bias does not diminish through exposure (Jamison & Tyree, 2001).

FIRST CITATION Rosenzweig, Breedlove, and Watson (2005) wrote that biological psychology is an interdisciplinary field that includes scientists from "quite different backgrounds" (p. 3).

LATER CITATIONS Biological psychology is "the field that relates behavior to bodily processes, especially the workings of the brain" (Rosenzweig et al., 2005, p. 3).

For works with more than five authors, cite the first author and use *et al.* for the first and subsequent references.

Unknown author To cite a work when the author is unknown, the APA suggests using a shortened version of the title. (The full title of the article cited below is "Plastic Is Found in the Sargasso Sea; Pieces of Apparent Refuse Cover Wide Atlantic Region.")

> An international pollution treaty still to be ratified would prohibit all plastic garbage from being dumped at sea ("Plastic Is Found," 1972).

Two or more works by the same author in the same year When your list of references includes two works by the same author, the year of publication is usually enough to distinguish them. Occasionally, though, you may have two works by the same author in the same year. If this happens, alphabetize the works by title in your list of references, and add a lowercase letter after the date (2005a, 2005b).

> Middle-class unemployed are better off than their lower-class counterparts, because they "are likely to have some assets to invest in their job search" (Ehrenreich, 2005b, p. 16).

Two or more authors with the same last name Include the author's initials.

F. Johnson (2010) conducted an intriguing study on teen smoking.

Corporation, organization, or government agency as author Spell out the name of the organization the first time you use it, but abbreviate it in subsequent citations if readers will know what the abbreviation refers to.

(National Institutes of Health, 2015)

(NIH, 2015)

Indirect citation (quotation from a secondary source) To quote material taken not from the original source but from a secondary source that quotes the original, give the secondary source in the reference list, and acknowledge the original but cite the secondary source in your essay.

E. M. Forster said "the collapse of all civilization, so realistic for us, sounded in Matthew Arnold's ears like a distant and harmonious cataract" (as cited in Trilling, 1955, p. 11).

Two or more works cited in the same parentheses List sources in alphabetical order, separated by semicolons.

(Johnson, 2014; NIH, 2015)

Creating a List of References

Directory to Reference-List Models

Author Listings

When the list of references includes several works by the same author, the APA provides the following rules for arranging these entries in the list:

- Same-name single-author entries precede multiple-author entries:

  Zettelmeyer, F. (2000).

  Zettelmeyer, F., Morton, F. S., & Silva-Risso, J. (2006).

- Entries with the same first author and a different second author are alphabetized under the first author according to the second author's last name:

  Dhar, R., & Nowlis, S. M. (2004).

  Dhar, R., & Simonson, I. (2003).

- Entries by the same authors are arranged by year of publication, in chronological order:

  Golder, P. N., & Tellis, G. J. (2003).

  Golder, P. N., & Tellis, G. J. (2004).

- Entries by the same authors with the same publication year should be arranged alphabetically by title (according to the first word after *A, An,* or *The*), and lowercase letters (*a, b, c,* and so on) should be appended to the year in parentheses:

  Aaron, P. (1990a). Basic . . .

  Aaron, P. (1990b). Elements . . .

One author

Schneier, B. (2015). *Data and Goliath: The hidden battles to collect your data and control your world*. New York, NY: Norton.

More than one author

Robinson, K., & Aronica, L. (2015). *Creative schools: The grassroots revolution that's transforming education*. New York, NY: Viking.

Hunt, L., Po-Chia Hsia, R., Martin, T. R., Rosenwein, B. H., Rosenwein, H., & Smith, B. G. (2001). *The making of the West: Peoples and cultures*. Boston, MA: Bedford.

If there are more than seven authors, list only the first six, insert ellipsis marks (. . .), and add the last author's name.

Unknown author Begin the entry with the title.

Communities blowing whistle on street basketball. (2003, June 2). *USA Today*, p. 20A.

If an author is designated as "Anonymous," include the word *Anonymous* in place of the author, and alphabetize it as "Anonymous" in the reference list.

Anonymous. (2006). *Primary colors*. New York, NY: Random House.

Corporation, organization, or government agency as author

American Medical Association. (2004). *Family medical guide.* Hoboken, NJ: Wiley.

Two or more works by the same author

When you cite two or more works by the same author, arrange them in chronological (time) order.

Pinker, S. (2005). So how does the mind work? *Mind and Language, 20*(1), 1–24. doi:10.1111/j.0268-1064.2005.00274.x

Pinker, S. (2011). *The better angels of our nature: Why violence has declined.* New York, NY: Viking.

When you cite two works by the same author in the same year, alphabetize entries by title and then add a lowercase letter following each year.

Pinker, S. (2005a). *Hotheads.* New York, NY: Pocket Penguins.

Pinker, S. (2005b). So how does the mind work? *Mind and Language, 20*(1), 1–24. doi:10.1111/j.0268-1064.2005.00274.x

Books (Print, Electronic)

When citing a book, capitalize only the first word of the title and subtitle and any proper nouns (*Dallas, Darwin*). Book titles are italicized.

Basic format for a book

Author — *Year* — *Title*

PRINT Pinker, S. (2011). *The better angels of our nature: Why violence has declined.* New York, NY: Viking.

City, State (abbr) — *Publisher*

E-BOOK Pinker, S. (2011). *The better angels of our nature: Why violence has declined* [Nook version]. Retrieved from www.barnesandnoble.com

E-publication information

DATABASE Darwin, C. (2001). *The origin of species.* Retrieved from http://bartleby.com (Original work published 1909–14)

Database information

If an e-book has been assigned a **digital object identifier** (or *doi*)—a combination of numbers and letters assigned by the publisher to identify the work—add that information at the end of the citation.

Author and editor

Arnold, M. (1994). *Culture and anarchy* (S. Lipman, Ed.). New Haven, CT: Yale University Press. (Original work published 1869)

Edited collection

Waldman, D., & Walker, J. (Eds.). (1999). *Feminism and documentary.* Minneapolis: University of Minnesota Press.

Work in an anthology or edited collection

Fairbairn-Dunlop, P. (1993). Women and agriculture in western Samoa. In J. H. Momsen & V. Kinnaird (Eds.), *Different places, different voices* (pp. 211–226). London, England: Routledge.

Translation

Tolstoy, L. (2002). *War and peace* (C. Garnett, Trans.). New York, NY: Modern Library. (Original work published 1869)

Dictionary entry or article in another reference book

Rowland, R. P. (2001). Myasthenia gravis. In *Encyclopedia Americana* (Vol. 19, p. 683). Danbury, CT: Grolier.

Introduction, preface, foreword, or afterword

Graff, G., & Phelan, J. (2004). Preface. In M. Twain, *Adventures of Huckleberry Finn* (pp. iii–vii). Boston, MA: Bedford.

Later edition of a book

Axelrod, R., & Cooper, C. (2016). *The St. Martin's guide to writing* (11th ed.). Boston, MA: Bedford.

Government document

U.S. Department of Health and Human Services. (2009). *Trends in underage drinking in the United States, 1991–2007*. Washington, DC: Government Printing Office.

Note: When the author and publisher are the same, use the word *Author* (not italicized) as the name of the publisher.

Unpublished doctoral dissertation

Bullock, B. (1986). *Basic needs fulfillment among less developed countries: Social progress over two decades of growth* (Unpublished doctoral dissertation). Vanderbilt University, Nashville, TN.

Articles (Print, Electronic)

For articles, capitalize only the first word of the title, proper nouns (*Barclay, Berlin*), and the first word following a colon (if any). Omit quotation marks around the titles of articles, but capitalize all the important words of journal, newspaper, and magazine titles, and set them in italics. If you are accessing an article through a database, follow the model for a comparable source.

From a scholarly journal

Author | *Year* | *Article title*

PRINT Kardefelt-Winther, D. (2015). A critical account of DSM-5 criteria for Internet gaming disorder. *Addiction Research and Theory, 23*(2), 93–98.

Journal title | *Volume (issue)* | *Pages*

Goodboy, A. K., & Martin, M. M. (2015). The personality profile of a cyberbully: Examining the dark triad. *Computers in Human Behavior, 49,* 1–4.

Volume only Pages

Include the digital object identifier (or *doi*) when available. When a doi has not been assigned, include the journal's URL.

ELECTRONIC Goodboy, A. K., & Martin, M. M. (2015). The personality profile of a cyberbully: Examining the dark triad. *Computers in Human Behavior, 49,* 1–4. doi:10.1016/j.chb.2015.02.052

DOI

Houston, R. G., & Toma, F. (2003). Home schooling: An alternative school choice. *Southern Economic Journal, 69*(4), 920–936. Retrieved from http://www.southerneconomic.org/

URL

From a newspaper

Year Month Day

PRINT Peterson, A. (2003, May 20). Finding a cure for old age. *The Wall Street Journal*, pp. D1, D5.

ELECTRONIC Zimmer, C. (2015, May 6). Under the sea, a missing link in the evolution of complex cells. *The New York Times*. Retrieved from http://www.nytimes.com/

From a magazine If a magazine is published weekly or biweekly (every other week), include the full date following the author's name. If it is published monthly or bimonthly, include just the year and month (or months).

Weekly or biweekly

PRINT Gladwell, M. (9 September 2013). Man and superman. *The New Yorker, 89*(27), 76–80.

Monthly or bimonthly

Freeland, C. (2015, May). Globalization bites back. *Atlantic, 315*(4), 82–86.

ELECTRONIC Freeland, C. (2015, May). Globalization bites back. *Atlantic*. Retrieved from http://theatlantic.com/

Editorial or letter to the editor

Kosinski, T. (2012, May 15). Who cares what she thinks? [Letter to the editor]. *The Chicago Sun-Times*. Retrieved from http:// www.suntimes.com/opinions/letters/12522890-474/who-cares-what-she-thinks.html

Review

"Review of" + item type + title of item reviewed

Nussbaum, E. (2015, January 26). House of chords [Review of the television series *Empire* and *Mozart in the Jungle*]. *The New Yorker, 90*(45), 70–72.

If the review is untitled, use the bracketed information as the title, retaining the brackets.

Multimedia Sources (Print Electronic)

Television program

Label

O'Connell, C. (Writer and director). (2015, Jan. 6). Ripley: Believe it or not [Television series episode]. In H. Hampton and S. Fitzmeyer (Creators), *American experience*. Boston, MA: WGBH.

Film, video, or DVD

Label

Nolan, C. (Writer and director). (2010). *Inception* [Motion picture]. Los Angeles, CA: Warner Bros.

Sound recording

PODCAST Dubner, S. (2012, May 17). Retirement kills [Audio podcast]. *Freakonomics radio*. Retrieved from http://www.freakonomics.com/

Label

RECORDING Maroon 5. (2010). Moves like Jagger. On *Hands all over* [CD]. New York, NY: A&M/Octone Records.

Interview Do not list personal interviews in your reference list. Instead, cite the interviewee in your text (last name and initials), and in parentheses give the notation *personal communication* (in regular type, not italicized) followed by a comma and the date of the interview. For published interviews, use the appropriate format for an article.

Other Electronic Sources

A rule of thumb for citing electronic sources not covered in one of the preceding sections is to include enough information to allow readers to access and retrieve the source. For most online sources, provide as much of the following as you can:

- Name of author
- Date of publication or most recent update (in parentheses; if unavailable, use the abbreviation *n.d.*)
- Title of document (such as a Web page)
- Title of Web site
- Any special retrieval information, such as a URL; include the date you last accessed the source only when the content is likely to change or be updated (as on a wiki, for example)

Web site The APA does not require an entry in the list of references for entire Web sites. Instead, give the name of the site in your text with its Web address in parentheses.

Web page or document on a Web site

American Cancer Society. (2011, Oct. 10). *Child and teen tobacco use*. Retrieved from http://www.cancer.org/Cancer/CancerCauses/TobaccoCancer/ChildandTeenTobaccoUse/child-and-teen-tobacco-use-what-to-do

Heins, M. (2014, September 4). Untangling the Steven Salaita case. In *The free expression policy project*. Retrieved from http://www.fepproject.org/commentaries/Salaita.html/

Discussion list and newsgroup postings Include online postings in your list of references only if you can provide data that would allow others to retrieve the source.

Label

Paikeday, T. (2005, October 10). "Esquivalience" is out [Electronic mailing list message]. Retrieved from http://listserv.linguistlist.org/cgi-bin/wa?A1=ind0510b&L=ads-1#1

Label

Ditmire, S. (2005, February 10). NJ tea party [Newsgroup message]. Retrieved from http://groups.google.com/group/TeaParty

Blog post

Label

Mestel, R. (2012, May 17). Fructose makes rats dumber [Blog post]. Retrieved from http://www.latimes.com/health/boostershots/la-fructose-makes-rats-stupid-brain-20120517,0,2305241.story?track=rss

Wiki entry Start with the article title and include the post date (or *n.d.,* if there is no date), since wikis may be updated frequently, as well as the retrieval date.

Sleep. (2011, November 26). Retrieved May 21, 2011, from Wiki of Science: http://wikiofscience.wikidot.com/science:sleep

E-mail message Personal correspondence, including e-mail, should not be included in your reference list. Instead, cite the person's name in your text, and in parentheses give the notation *personal communication* (in regular type, not italicized) and the date.

Computer software If an individual has proprietary rights to the software, cite that person's name as you would for a print text. Otherwise, cite as you would for an anonymous print text.

Label

How Computers Work [Software]. (1998). Available from Que: http://www.howcomputerswork.net/

For more information on finding sources, see Chapter 15.

A Sample Reference List in APA Style

To see the complete text of this student research project in APA style, see Patrick O'Malley's proposal, "More Testing, More Learning" in Chapter 7, pp. 235–41.

References

Beilock, S. (2010, September 3). Stressing about a high-stakes exam carries consequences beyond the test [Blog post]. Retrieved from http://www.psychologytoday.com/blog/choke/201009/stressing-about-high-stakes-exam-carries-consequences-beyond-the-test

Belluck, P. (2011, January 20). To really learn, quit studying and take a test. *The New York Times*. Retrieved from http://www.nytimes.com/2011/01/21/science/21memory.html

Dendato, K. M., & Diener, D. (1986). Effectiveness of cognitive/relaxation therapy and study skills training in reducing self-reported anxiety and improving the academic performance of test-anxious students. *The Journal of Counseling Psychology, 33,* 131–135.

Frederiksen, N. (1984). The real test bias: Influences of testing on teaching and learning. *American Psychologist, 39,* 193–202.

Karpicke, J. D., & Blunt, J. R. (2011, February 11). Retrieval practice produces more learning than elaborative studying with concept mapping. *Science, 331*(6018), 772–775. doi:10.1126/science.1199327

Light, R. J. (1990). *Explorations with students and faculty about teaching, learning, and student life*. Cambridge, MA: Harvard University Graduate School of Education and Kennedy School of Government.

Rothblum, E. D., Solomon, L., & Murakami, J. (1986). Affective, cognitive, and behavioral differences between high and low procrastinators. *The Journal of Counseling Psychology, 33,* 387–394.

ScienceWatch.com (2008, February). Henry L. Roediger and Jeff Karpicke talk with ScienceWatch.com and answer a few questions about this month's fast breaking paper in the field of psychiatry/psychology [Interview]. Retrieved from http://sciencewatch.com/dr/fbp/2008/08febfbp/08febfbpRoedigerETAL

Acknowledgments

Text Credits

Lynda Barry. Excerpt from "Lost and Found." From *One! Hundred! Demons!* Copyright Lynda Barry, used with permission by Drawn & Quarterly.

Kelly D. Brownell and Thomas R. Frieden. "Ounces of Prevention—the Public Policy Case for Taxes on Sugared Beverages." From *The New England Journal of Medicine* 360 (April 30, 2009): 1805–8. Copyright © 2009 Massachusetts Medical Society. Reprinted by permission of the Massachusetts Medical Society.

Amanda Coyne. "The Long Good-Bye: Mother's Day in Federal Prison." Copyright © 1997 by *Harper's Magazine*. All rights reserved. Reproduced from the May issue by special permission.

Jenée Desmond-Harris. "Tupac and My Non-Thug Life." From *The Root*, September 13, 2011. Reprinted by permission of the author.

Annie Dillard. Excerpt from *An American Childhood* (pp. 45–49). Copyright © 1987 by Annie Dillard. Reprinted by permission of HarperCollins Publishers and Russell & Volkening as agents for the author.

Amitai Etzioni. "Working at McDonald's." Originally published in *The Miami Herald*, August 24, 1986. Copyright © 1986 by Amitai Etzioni (author of *The Spirit of Community*; director, George Washington University Center for Communication Policy Studies). Reprinted by permission of the author.

William Gibson. Excerpt from "The Art of Fiction No. 211," an interview by David Wallace-Wells. Originally published in *The Paris Review* 197 (Summer 2011). Copyright © 2011 by The Paris Review. Used by permission of the Wylie Agency LLC.

Malcolm Gladwell. "The Order of Things: What College Rankings Really Tell Us." Originally published in *The New Yorker*. Copyright © 2005 by Malcolm Gladwell. Reprinted by permission of the author.

Emily Nussbaum. "The Aristocrats: The Graphic Arts of *Game of Thrones*." *The New Yorker*, May 7, 2012. © 2012 Conde Nast. Reprinted by permission.

Eric Posner. "A Moral Market." *Slate*, October 17, 2014. Reprinted by permission.

Daniel J. Solove. "Why Privacy Matters Even If You Have 'Nothing to Hide.'" From *The Chronicle Review*, May 15, 2011. Copyright © 2011 by Daniel J. Solove. Reprinted by permission of the author.

Amy Tan. Excerpt from "Mother Tongue." Copyright © 1989 by Amy Tan. Originally appeared in *The Threepenny Review*. Reprinted by permission of the author and the Sandra Dijkstra Literary Agency.

Gabriel Thompson. "A Gringo in the Lettuce Fields." From *Working in the Shadows: A Year of Doing the Jobs That (Most) Americans Won't Do*. Copyright © 2010 by Gabriel Thompson. Reprinted by permission of Nation Books, a member of the Perseus Books Group.

John Tierney. "Do You Suffer from Decision Fatigue?" Originally published as "To Choose Is to Lose," *New York Times Magazine*, August 21, 2011. All rights reserved. Used by permission and protected by the copyright laws of the United States. The printing, copying, redistribution, or retransmission of this content without express written permission is prohibited. www.nytimes.com.

Anastasia Toufexis. "Love: The Right Chemistry." From *TIME*, June 24, 2001. Originally published February 15, 1993. Reported by Hannah Bloch and Sally B. Donnelly. Copyright © by Time Inc. TIME is a registered trademark of Time Inc. All rights reserved. Reprinted by permission.

Acknowledgments

Text Credits

Index

Ohio
HWZ 8529
64
Blue Durango